NORTH DAKOTA BLUE BOOK
2019-2021

November 2019

Compiled by
DEDICATED VOLUNTEERS

Published by
SECRETARY OF STATE
ALVIN A. JAEGER

Editorial Notes and Acknowledgments

The *2019-2021 North Dakota Blue Book* traces its lineage back to 1887. This 33rd edition continues the tradition by presenting a review of the state's social, economic, environmental, cultural, and political status.

Published under the authority of the territorial legislature, the 1887 and 1889 books, produced by Mandan attorney, Theodore K. Long, reflect their purpose in the title – *Long's Legislative Handbook and Rules of the Legislative Assembly of the Territory of Dakota*. These early books were intended primarily to provide information to legislators.

Following statehood, a series of North Dakota books under the name *Legislative Manual* appeared biennially from 1889 through 1919, with the exception of 1915 and 1917. The earliest contained contents similar to Long's handbooks. Beginning with the 1897 edition, the books, bound in hard blue covers, offered historical, statistical, and political information. See the "North Dakota Blue Books" chart in these introductory pages for a history of publication dates.

The first volume carrying the title *North Dakota Blue Book* appeared in 1942. Until release of the 1995 edition, specific legislative authorization and appropriation was used to publish the Blue Books. In 1995, Secretary of State Alvin A. Jaeger began publishing the Blue Book using funds appropriated to his office and has continued to do so. The book was printed with spiral comb binding to make photocopying easier and changed to a book style perfect binding in 2003. This book and the 11 immediate past editions are important companions to each other in presenting a complete story of the state's history. Copies of recent editions are available through the State Historical Society of North Dakota Museum Store at the North Dakota Heritage Center at 701-328-2822. Digital versions are available on the Digital Horizons website at http://digitalhorizonsonline.org. A digital version of this edition is also available at https://sos.nd.gov.

The Secretary of State thanks the many state employees and private citizens from across the state who spent untold volunteer hours writing documents, compiling information, completing data entry, providing photographs, proofreading, and editing. Without the assistance of these dedicated individuals, the production of the *North Dakota Blue Book* would not be possible. The list of contributors to the 2019-2021 edition follows these acknowledgments.

The 1995 and 1999-2001 Blue Books have been recognized with "Notable Document" Awards from the North Dakota Library Association. The 2007-2009 edition received national recognition from the National Conference of State Legislatures in the category of Citizen's Guide.

While every effort by authors and editors of the *2019-2021 North Dakota Blue Book* has been made to provide accurate information, errors and oversights naturally occur. Please provide comments regarding discrepancies or errors to:

    Secretary of State
    600 East Boulevard Avenue, Dept. 108
    Bismarck, ND 58505-0500

    Call: 701-328-3664
    Fax: 701-328-2992
    Email: sos@nd.gov

Copies of the *2019-2021 North Dakota Blue Book* may be purchased at:
    State Historical Society of North Dakota Museum Store
    North Dakota Heritage Center
    612 East Boulevard Avenue
    Bismarck, ND 58505

    Call: 701-328-2822

Alternate formats of this publication are available upon request.
Call 701-328-2900 or the North Dakota Relay System at 800-366-6888.

Cataloging in Publication
North Dakota blue book. — 1942- .—
[Bismarck, N.D. :s.n.]
v. :ill. ; 23-24 cm.
Frequency varies.
Issue for 2019-2021 has title: North Dakota Blue Book
Issued by the North Dakota Secretary of State
ISSN 0191-0612 = North Dakota blue book

1. North Dakota—Registers. 2. North Dakota—Politics and government—Periodicals.
I. North Dakota Department of State. II. Title: North Dakota Blue Book.

JK6430.N6   353.9'784'002   56-129

ISBN 978-0-9742898-7-8

The material in this book is in the public domain. No permission is required to reprint material if the following credit is included: *2019-2021 North Dakota Blue Book***, published by the North Dakota Secretary of State, 600 East Boulevard Avenue, Dept. 108, Bismarck, ND 58505-0500.**

North Dakota Blue Books

Legislative Manual	Printer	Secretary of State
1889-1890	*Bismarck Daily Tribune* State Printers & Binders	
1897	*Bismarck Tribune* State Printers & Binders	
1899*	*Bismarck Tribune* State Printers & Binders	
1901*	*Bismarck Tribune* State Printers & Binders	
1903	*Bismarck Tribune* State Printers & Binders	
1905*	*Bismarck Tribune* State Printers & Binders	
1907*	*Bismarck Tribune* State Printers & Binders	Alfred Blaisdell**
1909*	*Bismarck Tribune* State Printers & Binders	Alfred Blaisdell**
1911*	*Bismarck Tribune* State Printers & Binders	Patrick D. Norton**
1913*	*Bismarck Tribune* State Printers & Binders	Thomas Hall
1919*	*Bismarck Tribune* State Printers & Binders	Thomas Hall

* Outside book cover reads North Dakota Blue Book, inside title is Legislative Manual

** Secretary of State's name does not appear on the books until 1907

Manual for the State of North Dakota	Editor	Printer	Secretary of State
1926	Charles Liessman (Deputy Secretary of State)	Allied Printing, Fargo	Robert Byrne
1930	Charles Liessman	Knight Printing, Fargo	Robert Byrne
1932	Charles Liessman	Bismarck Tribune	Robert Byrne

North Dakota Blue Book	Editor	Printer	Secretary of State
1942	G.A. Gilbertson (Deputy Secretary of State)	Bismarck Printing Co.	Herman Thorson
1954		*Bismarck Tribune*	Thomas Hall
1961		*Bismarck Tribune*	Ben Meier
1973	Jay Bryant		Ben Meier
1981	Jay Bryant	Kaye's Printing, Fargo	Ben Meier
1889-1989 North Dakota Centennial Blue Book	Curtis Eriksmoen	Kaye's Printing, Fargo	Ben Meier
1995-1997	Volunteer Editorial Board	Quality Printing, Bismarck	Alvin A. Jaeger
1997-1999	Volunteer Editorial Board	United Printing, Bismarck	Alvin A. Jaeger
1999-2001	Volunteer Editorial Board	The Printers, Bismarck	Alvin A. Jaeger
2001-2003	Volunteer Editorial Board	Quality Printing, Bismarck	Alvin A. Jaeger
2003-2005	Volunteer Editorial Board	Quality Printing, Bismarck	Alvin A. Jaeger
2005-2007	Volunteer Editorial Board	Richtman's Printing, Bismarck	Alvin A. Jaeger
2007-2009	Volunteer Editorial Board	Richtman's Printing, Bismarck	Alvin A. Jaeger
2009-2011	Volunteer Editorial Board	Image Printing, Bismarck	Alvin A. Jaeger
2011-2013	Volunteer Editorial Board	Image Printing, Bismarck	Alvin A. Jaeger
2013-2015	Volunteer Editorial Board	Image Printing, Bismarck	Alvin A. Jaeger
2015-2017	Volunteer Editorial Board	Image Printing, Bismarck	Alvin A. Jaeger
2017-2019	Volunteer Editorial Board	Image Printing, Bismarck	Alvin A. Jaeger
2019-2021	Volunteer Editorial Board	Forum Communications, Fargo	Alvin A. Jaeger

 | Governor Doug Burgum

Greetings from the Office of the Governor!

North Dakota has a fascinating history and a compelling story to tell. From the Native American tribes who first flourished on these lands to the homesteaders who sought adventure and opportunity on the abundant prairie, to the entrepreneurs who continue to stride into the new frontiers of the 21st century economy, North Dakotans eagerly answer the call to Be Legendary.

North Dakota is a state characterized by boundless opportunity, unparalleled experience and incomparable people. Our vibrant communities, our thriving economy and our growing population provide opportunity for generations of North Dakotans and new citizens alike. We seek adventure in the excitement of our urban centers, the wild expanse of our outdoors and in the promise of new ideas. We take pride in the rich cultural heritage passed down from our ancestors and aspire to make a difference in the lives of those around us. Ours is a history filled with the pioneering spirit – a spirit we carry forward with respect for the past, gratitude for the present and inspiration for the future.

The Blue Book is a treasure trove of information about all things North Dakota, offering a wealth of facts on state government, politics, history, culture and the unique qualities and attractions that make our state a special place to live and visit. This edition of the Blue Book highlights the impact of the aviation industry in North Dakota. Throughout a long history in our state, aviation has sparked curiosity and innovation in many North Dakotans. Today, the aviation industry plays a significant role in our economy and transportation needs and the future is bright with North Dakota positioned as a leader in Unmanned Aircraft Systems research and application.

For all those seeking to learn more about our wonderful and unique state, the North Dakota Blue Book is a tremendous resource. This delightful book is made possible through the hard work and dedication of the authors, editors and other volunteers who contributed countless hours to its production. Thank you for your incredible efforts and great love of North Dakota.

Curiosity is the key to unlocking our potential. Let the North Dakota Blue Book ignite yours, and enjoy the journey!

Regards,

Doug Burgum
Doug Burgum

ALVIN A. JAEGER
SECRETARY OF STATE

HOME PAGE www.nd.gov/sos

SECRETARY OF STATE
STATE OF NORTH DAKOTA
600 EAST BOULEVARD AVENUE DEPT 108
BISMARCK ND 58505-0500

PHONE (701) 328-2900
FAX (701) 328-2992

E-MAIL sos@nd.gov

Dear Reader,

The publication of the *North Dakota Blue Book 2019-2021* represents the thirteenth consecutive biennial edition published by the Secretary of State's office. The sequence began with the 1995 edition, which covered the six year information gap between it and the Centennial edition published in 1989 when North Dakota celebrated its 100th birthday. In comparison, only twenty editions were published in the 106 years between statehood in 1889 and 1995.

As with the other twelve editions, this publication was created with the help of faithful volunteers. Over fifty individuals contributed their research and writing skills to this edition. The group included librarians, historians, agency personnel, and others who are committed and passionate about the preservation of valuable North Dakota history.

A highlight of this edition is the story of aviation in North Dakota, from the state's first recorded aeronautical flight in 1910 to today's unmanned aircraft systems. The feature chapter explores the importance of aviation to many of the state's industries and its economy. In addition, along with information about energy, education, agriculture, elections, state officials, legislators, tribal entities, etc., this edition includes a chapter dedicated to the 50th anniversary of United Tribes Technical College and recognizes the 100th anniversaries of the Bank of North Dakota and Workforce Safety & Insurance.

I believe this book is unique because it covers information about North Dakota not readily available in any other single resource. It is an indispensable source for research and for gaining general knowledge of the state. In addition, each of the individual biennial editions beginning in 1995 contains selected information not published in any of the others.

Because of that, I am pleased that (beginning with 1919) the editions of the *Blue* Book are digitally available online through the Secretary of State's website at sos.nd.gov. A valuable feature is the ability to search each book individually or all books collectively. Bound copies also continue to be available for viewing and research at the North Dakota State Library in Bismarck, the State Archives, all state university libraries, and several municipal libraries throughout the state.

I am grateful for everyone who made this publication a reality. Especially, I thank Kim Shaw and Jill Schwab, my executive assistants, the staff of Clearwater Communications, and the members of the editorial board – Marietta Kemmet, Michelle Mielke, Marlene Anderson, Shari Mosser, Sarah Walker, Dana Schaar Jahner, Kim Shaw and Jill Schwab. Their editing skills, insight, dedication, and understanding of the significance of the *Blue Book,* and its role in preserving the history of North Dakota, is what makes this publication a reality.

As with the previous editions, I am confident the state's fascinating history and its exciting future will prompt your interest to learn more about this wonderful state that we call home – North Dakota.

Sincerely,

Al Jaeger
Secretary of State

A Brief Word About the Origin of the Term 'Blue Book'

The *Merriam-Webster Online Dictionary* offers four contemporary definitions of "blue book:"

1. a register especially of socially prominent persons
2. a book of specialized information often published under government auspices
3. a blue-covered booklet used for writing examinations
4. a periodically issued price list (as of used cars)

With respect to the *North Dakota Blue Book*, the term "blue book" refers to a compendium of information about the state's political, economic, social, cultural, and environmental history and current status. Most states regularly produce a "blue book."

To determine where the term "blue book" originated, look to our English ancestors. In the 1800s, the British government printed reams of reports from Parliamentary committees and royal commissions. These documents became commonly known as "blue books" because of their blue paper covers. These "blue books" were generally loaded with testimonies, figures, and facts. Their purpose was to provide the public with government information, legal, political, or commercial, and to assist policymakers with decision making. The term "blue book" later came to mean any report published and distributed by the British Parliament.

On the Covers

The cover of the *2019-2021 North Dakota Blue Book* highlights the state's diverse aviation industry and the role it plays in the success of one of North Dakota's top industries, agriculture. Pictured is an aerial applicator, or "crop duster," flying low in the summer blue sky over a field of golden yellow sunflowers. In the early 1950s, aerial application was introduced to the agriculture community and, although billed as one of the most challenging aviation operations today, it continues to serve an important role in the agricultural success of the state.

The back cover photo captures a time when the aviation industry was emerging in North Dakota. Photographed is Jack Watts flying a Bellanca airplane in the 1940s over Bismarck, with the North Dakota State Capitol and Liberty Memorial Building visible in the background. In the mid-1940s, World War II veterans were returning home. Aviation had advanced greatly during the war and now provided many opportunities for returning pilots to grow the industry in North Dakota. In 1947, the North Dakota Aeronautics Commission was created by the state legislature to represent North Dakota in aviation matters and provide oversight of the state's aviation programs and regulations, a role the agency continues today.

Chapter Title Photographs

The chapter title photos pay homage to this edition's feature chapter, "Aviation in North Dakota." With photos ranging from the 1930s to present day, the images represent snapshots of the state's aviation industry's timeline that started with a single aviation event in the early 1900s and today has emerged on the leading edge of the research and development of unmanned aircraft systems (UAS).

Photographs from the early days of aviation in North Dakota show the juxtaposition of available transportation in the state with a covered wagon and passenger plane parked together at an airport. Another photo captures an airplane using a rural dirt road as a runway. Selected photos also highlight an important presidential visit for the dedication of the Garrison Dam in 1953 and the role a specially painted military aircraft played in the state's centennial celebration in 1989.

An aerial photo of one of North Dakota's many rural airports captures the importance of aviation as a mode of transportation, commerce, and communication in a vastly rural state. Photos from the present day highlight the growing role of UAS in North Dakota, from the use of drones for research in the Badlands to the use of drones in capturing commercial images of the state's landmarks.

Blue Book Contributors and Photography

Foreword: Doug Burgum, Governor; Alvin A. Jaeger, Secretary of State

2019-2021 Blue Book Committee Members: Marlene Anderson, Director of Library Services, Bismarck State College; Kylah Aull, Library and Records Manager, North Dakota Legislative Council; Annie Bennett, Communication Specialist, Clearwater Communications; Kylie Blanchard, Communication Specialist, Clearwater Communications; Jesse Bradley, Communications Manager, North Dakota Department of Commerce; Jim Davis, Head of Reference (retired), State Historical Society of North Dakota; Marietta Kemmet, Executive Assistant to the Commissioner, North Dakota Indian Affairs Commission; Ned Kruger, Geologist, North Dakota Geological Survey; Michelle Mielke, Public Information Specialist, North Dakota Department of Agriculture; Shari Mosser, Librarian, North Dakota State Library; Catherine Palsgraaf, Acting Law Librarian, North Dakota Supreme Court Library; Robin Pursley, Graphic Designer, Clearwater Communications; Dana Schaar Jahner, Vice President, Clearwater Communications; Jill Schwab, Executive Assistant, North Dakota Secretary of State; Kim Shaw, Executive Assistant (retired), North Dakota Secretary of State; Jessie Wald, Public Information Officer, North Dakota State Water Commission; Sarah Walker, Head of Reference Specialist, State Historical Society of North Dakota; Dale Wetzel, Public Information Specialist, North Dakota Department of Instruction

2019-2021 Blue Book Editorial Committee Members: Marlene Anderson, Director of Library Services, Bismarck State College; Kylie Blanchard, Communication Specialist, Clearwater Communications; Marietta Kemmet, Executive Assistant to the Commissioner, North Dakota Indian Affairs Commission; Michelle Mielke, Public Information Specialist, North Dakota Department of Agriculture; Shari Mosser, Librarian, North Dakota State Library; Dana Schaar Jahner, Vice President, Clearwater Communications; Jill Schwab, Executive Assistant, North Dakota Secretary of State; Sarah Walker, Head of Reference Specialist, State Historical Society of North Dakota

Chapter 1 – Aviation in North Dakota: Elizabeth Bjerke, Associate Dean, University of North Dakota School of Aerospace Sciences; Jesse Bradley, Communications Manager, North Dakota Department of Commerce; Jeremiah R. Colbert, Public Affairs Officer, 119th Wing, North Dakota Air National Guard; David Dodds, Director of Communications, *UND Today*, University of North Dakota; Nicholas Flom, Executive Director, North Plains UAS Test Site; Eric Jensen, Deputy Public Information Officer, West North Dakota National Guard; Emily A. Kenney, Chief, Command Information 21st Space Wing Public Affairs, United States Air Force; Don Larson, Board President, Dakota Territory Air Museum; Paul Lucy, Aerospace/UAS Business Development Manager, North Dakota Department of Commerce; Mike McHugh, Aviation Education Coordinator, North Dakota Aeronautics Commission; Gary Ness, Executive Director (retired), North Dakota Aeronautics Commission; John Nowatzki, Extension Ag Machine System Specialist, North Dakota State University; Jason Patrick, 319th ABW Historian, Grand Forks Air Force Base; Michelle Saari, Board Secretary, Dakota Territory Air Museum;

Sarah Swartz, Education Coordinator, Fargo Air Museum; Kyle Wanner, Executive Director, North Dakota Aeronautics Commission; Jackie Williams, Executive Director, Fargo Air Museum; Kylie Blanchard, Communications Specialist, Clearwater Communications

Photo Credits: page 1, North Dakota Air National Guard; page 2, State Historical Society of North Dakota (SHSND) 00100-00204; page 5, North Dakota Air National Guard; page 8, SHSND 10958-0012-024-00009; pages 11-17, North Dakota Aeronautics Commission; page 18, U.S. Air Force photo by Mike Dey; pages 19-23, U.S. Air Force courtesy photos; page 25, U.S. Army National Guard photo by Staff Sgt. Ashley Johlfs, Joint Force Headquarters; page 26, U.S. Army National Guard photo by Bill Prokopyk, North Dakota National Guard Public Affairs; page 28, North Dakota Air National Guard photo by Senior Mast. Sgt. David H. Lipp; page 30, Paul Snyder; page 31, Sarah Swartz; page 32, Aaron Allmon; pages 33-34, University of North Dakota; page 38, North Dakota State University; page 42, University of North Dakota

Chapter 2 – North Dakota Almanac: Mark Armstrong, Communications Liaison, North Dakota Workforce Safety and Insurance; John Boyle, Director of Facility Management Division, North Dakota Office of Management and Budget; Kristin Byram, Public Information Officer, North Dakota Parks and Recreation Department; Beth Campbell, Visitor Services Coordinator, State Historical Society of North Dakota; Melissa Casteel, Research Analyst, FARS Supervisor-Safety Division, North Dakota Department of Transportation; Tim Chapman, CEO, International Peace Garden; Eric Jensen, Deputy Public Information Officer, West North Dakota National Guard; Darcie Handt, Executive Director, North Dakota Cares Coalition; Kevin Kirkey, Site Manager, CIG, Lewis & Clark Interpretive Center and Fort Mandan; Shari Mosser, Librarian, North Dakota State Library; Mike Nowatzki, Communications Director, North Dakota Office of the Governor; Karen Olsen, Program Director, North Dakota KIDS COUNT; Nicole Peske, Chief Information Officer, North Dakota Department of Health; Kim Schmidt, Public Relations and Digital Communications Manager, North Dakota Department of Commerce-Tourism Division; Janel Schmitz, Communications and Marketing Manager, Bank of North Dakota; Stephanie Schoenrock, Director of Development and Communications, North Dakota State Fair; Laura Thomas, Visual Information Specialist, Theodore Roosevelt National Park; Sarah Walker, Head of Reference Specialist, State Historical Society of North Dakota; Annie Bennett, Communications Specialist, Clearwater Communications

Photo Credits: page 43, SHSND A1120-00001; page 44, SHSND 978-02 J66j; page 45, Shutter Stock 64051492; pages 47-51, North Dakota Secretary of State; page 52, North Dakota Parks and Recreation Department; page 53, North Dakota Game and Fish Department; page 54, (top) North Dakota Forest Service and (bottom) North Dakota Secretary of State; pages 55-57, North Dakota Secretary of State; page 58, North Dakota Museum of Art; pages 59-63, North Dakota Secretary of State; page 64, Lewis and Clark Fort Mandan Foundation; page 66, Castle McLaughlin, Peabody Museum of Archaeology and Ethnology, Harvard University;

page 67, North Dakota Tourism; page 73, Mark Staples, North Dakota Office of the Governor; page 81, Clearwater Communications; pages 83-127, North Dakota Office of the Governor; page 130, Staff Sgt. Brett Miller, North Dakota National Guard; page 132, Tessie Jones Photography; page 133, Matt Boyd Photography; page 134, Phyne Photography; page 138, North Dakota Tourism; page 139, Jesse Veeder; page 140, State Historical Society of North Dakota; page 141, North Dakota Parks and Recreation Department; page 142, North Dakota Tourism; page 143, International Peace Garden; page 146, Institute for Regional Studies, North Dakota State University (2023.P-170); page 147, SHSND C1188; page 148, Bank of North Dakota

Chapter 3 – Federal-State Relationships: Shari Mosser, Librarian, North Dakota State Library; Catherine Palsgraaf, Acting Law Librarian, North Dakota Supreme Court Library; Sarah Walker, Head of Reference Specialist, State Historical Society of North Dakota
Photo Credits: page 149, SHSND 2014-P-038-00074; page 155, North Dakota Department of Transportation; page 159, *Minot Daily News*; pages 173-178, North Dakota Federal Courts

Chapter 4 – Judicial Branch: Catherine Palsgraaf, Acting Law Librarian, North Dakota Supreme Court Library
Photo Credits: page 179, North Dakota Aeronautics Commission; pages 183-187, North Dakota Supreme Court; page 192, North Dakota Supreme Court

Chapter 5 – Executive Branch: Jill Schwab, Executive Assistant, North Dakota Secretary of State; Kim Shaw, Executive Assistant (retired), North Dakota Secretary of State; Annie Bennett, Communications Specialist, Clearwater Communications
Photo Credits: page 213, North Dakota State Water Commission

Chapter 6 – Legislative Branch: Dustin Assel, Counsel; Kylah E. Aull, Library and Records Services Manager; Briana Beaner, Legislative Library Intern; John Bjornson, Director; Justin J. Blasy, Legislative Services Specialist II; Jennifer S. N. Clark, Counsel; Andrea Cooper, Lead Legislative Services Specialist; Harry Farnsworth, Legislative Services Specialist I; Kyle W. Forster, Information Technology Manager; Jill Grossman, Counsel; Christopher S. Joseph, Counsel; Donavan D. Klein, Administrative Unit Supervisor; Allen H. Knudson, Legislative Budget Analyst and Auditor; Samantha E. Kramer, Counsel; Brad Metz, Legislative Services Specialist II; Claire Ness, Counsel; Vonette J. Richter, Legal Division Director; Robert Tallman, Legislative Services Specialist I; Emily L. Thompson, Code Revisor; Lori Ziegler, Legislative Administrative Officer, North Dakota Legislative Council; Mike Gerhart, Executive Vice President, North Dakota Motor Carriers Association; Susan Wefald, Author and former Public Service Commissioner
Photo Credits: page 331, SHSND 2003-P-002-00005-1; pages 338-384, Don Anderson Photography; page 385, North Dakota Secretary of State; page 402, SHSND C0278-00001

Chapter 7 – Tribal-State Relationships: Scott Davis, Executive Director, North Dakota Indian Affairs Commission; Brad Hawk, Indian Health Systems Administrator, North Dakota Indian Affairs Commission; Marietta Kemmet, Executive Assistant to the Commissioner, North Dakota Indian Affairs Commission
Photo Credits: page 419, U.S. Army National Guard, Bill Prokopyk, North Dakota National Guard Public Affairs; pages 422-428, State Historical Society of North Dakota; page 429, North Dakota Indian Affairs Commission; page 430, David Swenson; page 431-432, North Dakota Indian Affairs Commission; page 433, Mike Glatt; pages 434-435, North Dakota Indian Affairs Commission; page 436, Tanya Anderson; page 437, Arnie Grady; page 438, Marilyn Hudson; page 439, Kade Ferris; page 440, Mike Glatt; page 441, Marilyn Hudson; page 443, Dennis J. Neumann; page 444, Mike Glatt; page 445, *Turtle Mountain Times Newspaper;* page 446, North Dakota Indian Affairs Commission; page 458, United Tribes Technical College

Chapter 8 – Elections: John Arnold, State Election Director, North Dakota Secretary of State; Jill Schwab, Executive Assistant, North Dakota Secretary of State; Kim Shaw, Executive Assistant (retired), North Dakota Secretary of State
Photo Credits: page 459, D&N Cinematics; page 470, North Dakota Association of Counties

Chapter 9 – Education: Marlene Anderson, Director of Library Services, Bismarck State College; Dale Wetzel, Public Information Specialist, North Dakota Department of Instruction
Photo Credits: page 471, Aaron Allmon; page 474, North Dakota Department of Public Instruction; page 478, courtesy of the Elwyn B. Robinson Department of Special Collections, Chester Fritz Library, University of North Dakota; page 486, North Dakota University System

Chapter 10 – Agriculture: Michelle Mielke, Public Information Specialist, North Dakota Department of Agriculture
Photo Credits: page 513, North Dakota Aeronautics Commission; page 514, Lindsay and Mike Ostlie, Ostlie's Sunnyside Acres; page 515, Tyler Tjelde, Williston Research Extension Center; page 516, Lindsay Ostlie, Ostlie's Sunnyside Acres; page 517 (left), Lindsay and Mike Ostlie, Ostlie's Sunnyside Acres; (right), Kyla Splichal, Williston Research Extension Center; pages 518-520, Two Track Malting Company; page 521, Laughing Sun Brewing Company; page 530, Samantha Brunner

Chapter 11 – Natural Resources: Craig Bihrle, Communications Supervisor, North Dakota Game and Fish Department; Patrick Fridgen, Planning & Education Division Director, North Dakota Water Commission; Jessie Wald, Natural Resource Economist, North Dakota State Water Commission
Photo Credits: page 531, Tanner Overland, North Dakota Aeronautics Commission

Chapter 12 – Energy: Jesse Bradley, Communications Manager, North Dakota Department of Commerce; Ned Kruger, Geologist, North Dakota Geological Survey; Retha Mattern, Director, Great Plains Energy Corridor, National Energy Center of Excellence, Bismarck State College; Shari Mosser, Librarian, North Dakota State Library
Photo Credits: page 543, North Dakota Geological Survey; page 545, Minnkota Power Cooperative; page 546, Great Plains Energy Corridor, National Energy Center of Excellence, Bismarck State College; page 551, Great Plains Energy Corridor, National Energy Center of Excellence, Bismarck State College

Chapter 13 – United Tribes Technical College: The *United Tribes Technical College Winter Count* was compiled by Phil Baird and reviewed in 2009 by members of the United Tribes 40th Anniversary History Subcommittee: Kathy Aller; Phil Baird; Ann Kraft; Anne Kuyper; Glenna Mueller; Dennis J. Neumann; Charlene Weis, Chair. It was updated in 2019 by Dennis J. Neumann and reviewed by the United Tribes 50th Anniversary Subcommittee: Lisa Azure; Jolene DeCoteau; Kathy Dye-Chapin, Chair; Amanda Hairy Shirt; Dan Henry; Brent Kleinjan; Leander R. McDonald, UTTC President; Lydell Merrick; Melvin Miner; Dennis J. Neumann; LuAnn Poitra
Photo Credits: page 555, Dennis J. Neumann; page 556, Rusty Gillette; pages 557-560, United Tribes Technical College; page 565, Dennis J. Neumann; page 566, Shaun Holz; pages 568-569, Dennis J. Neumann; page 570, Frank White Bill

Coordination and Formatting: Jill Schwab, Executive Assistant, North Dakota Secretary of State; Kim Shaw, Executive Assistant (retired), North Dakota Secretary of State; Robin Pursley, Graphic Designer, Clearwater Communications; Dana Schaar Jahner, Vice President, Clearwater Communications

Indexing: Robin Pursley, Graphic Designer, Clearwater Communications; Dana Schaar Jahner, Vice President, Clearwater Communications

Editing, Proofreading, and Marketing: Jill Schwab, Executive Assistant, North Dakota Secretary of State; Annie Bennett, Communication Specialist, Clearwater Communications; Kylie Blanchard, Communication Specialist, Clearwater Communications; Dana Schaar Jahner, Vice President, Clearwater Communications

Table of Contents

Chapter One: *Aviation in North Dakota* 1
    History of Aviation 2
    Airports 8
    Air Service 12
    Economic Impact of Aviation 15
    Military Aviation Components 17
    Aviation Education 29
    Unmanned Aircraft Systems 33
    Aviation Hall of Fame 40

Chapter Two: *North Dakota Almanac* 43
    State Origin 44
    State Symbols 46
    Official State Designations 52
    North Dakota State Capitol and Grounds 67
    Statues, Monuments, and Markers 79
    North Dakota Peace Officers Memorial 80
    Theodore Roosevelt Rough Rider Award 82
    North Dakota Statistical Information 128
    North Dakota Rankings and Vital Statistics 129
    Military Preparedness in North Dakota 130
    Veterans in North Dakota 131
    Miss North Dakota 132
    Miss America 2018 133
    Miss Rodeo North Dakota 134
    North Dakota's Authors and Poets 135
    Holidays in North Dakota 137
    North Dakota Tourism 138
    North Dakota State Historical Sites Map 140
    North Dakota State Parks and Recreation Areas Map 141
    Visitation at North Dakota Sites 142
    International Peace Garden 143
    North Dakota Theatre 145
    100 Years of Caring for North Dakota Injured Workers 146
    Bank of North Dakota Celebrates Its First 100 Years 147

Chapter Three: *Federal-State Relationships* 149
    Presidential Visits to North Dakota 150
    North Dakota's International Border Crossings 154
    Medal of Honor Memorial 159
    Representation at the Federal Level 160
    Profile of Present Congressional Delegation 161
    Chronology of United States Senators from North Dakota 166
    Chronology of United States House Members from North Dakota 167
    Justices of the United States Supreme Court 171

Judges of the Eighth Circuit Court of Appeals 171
United States District Court for the District of North Dakota Judges 172
United States Magistrate Judges for the District of North Dakota 175

Chapter Four: *Judicial Branch* **179**
Profile of the North Dakota Judicial System 181
North Dakota Supreme Court Justices 183
North Dakota Supreme Court 188
North Dakota Court of Appeals 189
District Courts 191
Judicial Districts Map 192
Municipal Courts 203
North Dakota Judicial System Committees, Commissions, and Boards 203
Chronology of Justices of the North Dakota Supreme Court 208

Chapter Five: *Executive Branch* **213**
Elected State Officials 215
Chronology of Elective State Officers Since Statehood 232
State Officials Appointed by the Governor to Head State Agencies 250
Executive Commissions and Boards 265
Agencies Headed by Gubernational Appointees... 273
Administrative Departments under Boards and Commissions 309
North Dakota Boards and Commissions 328

Chapter Six: *Legislative Branch* **331**
Legislative Branch.. 332
Members of the 66th Legislative Assembly 334
How a Bill Becomes a Law 386
North Dakota's Revenue Forecasting and Budgeting Process 388
Legislative Documents and Resources 393
Citizen Involvement.. 395
Legislative Management 396
Legislative Compensation 398
The Role of the Legislature in Achieving Women's Right to Vote 401
The 66th Legislative Assembly.. 404

Chapter Seven: *Tribal-State Relationships* **419**
Native American Hall of Honor 420
North Dakota Tribal Nations 446
North Dakota Tribal Colleges 452
North Dakota Tourism Partners with Native American Tourism 455
North Dakota Native Tourism Alliance 455
First Nations Day... 456
Indian Youth Leadership Academy 457
Native American Youth Leadership Summit 457
Woodrow Keeble Award 457

Chapter Eight: *Elections* **459**
    Vote of the People 460
    Amending the Constitution 460
    1971-1972 Constitutional Convention 461
    Initiating and Referring Laws 462
    Special Elections 464
    Summary of Initiative and Referendum Activity 466
    North Dakota Measures before the Voters 2018 to Present 467
    2018 General Election Report of Vote Totals 468
    2020 North Dakota Election Calendar 469

Chapter Nine: *Education* **471**
    North Dakota State Teacher of the Year 473
    North Dakota School Data 474
    Computer Science and Cybersecurity Instruction 475
    Seal of Biliteracy 476
    Milken Awards 476
    School Safety 477
    Higher Education in North Dakota 478
    Governance of Public Institutions of Higher Education 483
    North Dakota University System 484
    North Dakota Colleges and Universities 487
    National Athletic Championships 500

Chapter Ten: *Agriculture* **513**
    Barley, Hops, and Craft Breweries 514
    North Dakota's Agriculture Profile 524
    North Dakota's Rank Among the States 526
    North Dakota's Top Agricultural Exports 527
    North Dakota's Cash Receipts 528
    North Dakota's Leading Commodities 529
    North Dakota's Dairy Ambassadors 530

Chapter Eleven: *Natural Resources* **531**
    Climate 532
    Weather Facts 535
    Water Facts 535
    Water Resources 536
    Water Use 538
    Sovereign Lands 539
    Aquatic Nuisance Species 539
    Threatened or Endangered Species 540
    Fishing and Hunting Licenses 541

Chapter Twelve: *Energy* 543
    Project Tundra: Energy Industry Looks to Reduce Carbon Footprint............. 544
    North Dakota's Total Energy Production... 546
    Biofuel.. 547
    Biomass 548
    Energy Efficiency 548
    Ethanol 549
    Lignite.. 549
    Natural Gas 550
    Oil 550
    Petroleum Marketing 551
    Refining 552
    Solar, Geothermal, Hydrogen, and Hydro Power 552
    Transmission 553
    Wind.. 553
    Getting a Charge Out of North Dakota 554

Chapter Thirteen: *United Tribes Technical College* 555
    50-Year Winter Count 556

Chapter One
Aviation in North Dakota

To celebrate the North Dakota Centennial in 1989, the North Dakota Air National Guard painted one of its F-4 Phantoms a "Centennial Special," which visited many small and large celebrations with fly-bys.

History of Aviation..2
Airports 8
Air Service..12
Economic Impact of Aviation 15
Military Aviation Components 17
Aviation Education 29
Unmanned Aircraft Systems 33
Aviation Hall of Fame...40

History of Aviation

The First 50 Years

Soon after the Wright Brother's first flight on December 17, 1903, as the dawn of powered flight began to take shape, the state of North Dakota began writing its own aviation history. North Dakota's first recorded aeronautical event was the flight of a Wright Model B on July 19, 1910, flown by Wright Exhibition Team member Archibald Hoxsey at the Grand Forks Air Meet. The first successful airplane flight in Fargo took place in 1911 at the old fairgrounds. In July 1916, the city of Bismarck experienced its first-ever aircraft landing.

Like the rest of the country, North Dakota saw increased aviation activity during World War I, with aircraft playing a major role in the conflict from 1914 to 1918.

The Air Commerce Act of 1926 provided for federal rules regarding aircraft, airmen, and navigational facilities and established air traffic regulations, empowering the U.S. government to modernize air travel. Important conditions in this act included requirements for the government to establish a system for air commerce, issue regulations for air traffic rules, enforce procedure requirements for pilot licensing, develop a procedure for certifying the airworthiness of aircraft, and standardize airways to bring order to the open skies.

Shortly after Charles Lindberg's 1927 transcontinental flight, North Dakota's own Carl Ben Eielson demonstrated how to fly over the top of the world when he departed Point Barrow, Alaska, for Spitzbergen, an island located off the coast of Norway.

Pioneer aviator Carl Ben Eielson was born and raised in Hatton, North Dakota.

In 1928, the North Dakota State School of Science (NDSSS) in Wahpeton started one of the first established aviation programs in the nation, chaired by Art Sampson. In 1931, the aviation department was one of the first schools to be approved by the U.S. Department of Commerce for the repair of licensed aircraft. The NDSSS aviation program was approved for participation in the civil aeronautics pilot training program and conducted both the pilot training program and the ground school program for the new government flight program, which was open to young men between the ages of 18 and 24 and conducted by the Civil Aeronautics Authority in 1939.

During the 1929 North Dakota Legislative Session, the Board of Railroad Commissioners was authorized to license aircraft, airmen, and non-government owned aircraft and to regulate air traffic rules. Aviation terms were also defined during this session. An aircraft meant "any contrivance now known or invented, used, or designed for navigation of, or flight in, the air." The term airman meant "any individual including a person in command or any pilot, mechanic, or member of the crew who engaged in the navigation of an aircraft while underway, anyone charged with inspection, overhauling, or repairing of aircraft." Legislation spelled out the requirements of licensing for both airmen and aircraft.

By 1931, the legislature encouraged government bodies such as cities, towns, villages, and townships to acquire land and maintain airports or landing fields so airports could be constructed across the state.

By 1945, the state legislature created a Division of Aeronautics within the Public Service Commission (PSC), formerly the Board of Railroad Commissioners, to promote and develop aviation, air commerce, and a state system of airways and airports and to represent the state in aeronautical matters before federal and state agencies. The PSC also assisted in the enforcement of state laws relating to aeronautics.

A director of aeronautics was hired, and the governor chose five committee members to guide the division and serve six-year terms. The first director of aeronautics was Erling Nasset. The first committee was comprised of members Wesley Keller, Minot; Harry Potter, Bismarck; Dalton LeMausoer, Grand Forks; James Flannery, Jamestown; and M.C. McDonald, Bismarck.

In 1947, the North Dakota Aeronautics Commission (NDAC) was created by the legislature to provide representation of the state in aviation matters and to provide responsibility for the state's aviation programs and regulatory framework. Governing the policies and direction of the commission is a five-member board appointed by the governor for five-year terms. Division committee members in place when the NDAC was created continued their service on the board.

After 18 months as director, Nasset resigned in October 1947. Harold Vavra, airport engineer, was appointed acting director. In early 1948, the NDAC appointed Vavra as director.

The first years were the "high-water mark" of North Dakota aviation history. World War II veterans returned from across the world, and veteran pilots invented ways to make aviation a business. The Federal GI Bill invested in the education of veterans and provided funding for pilot training, as well as college degrees. The evolution of aviation, which had advanced greatly during the war, provided many opportunities for returning pilots. This expansion of aviation was recognized by its growth across the state.

Business Expansion and Airport Development

In the early 1950s, a new aviation enterprise called aerial application "duster" was introduced to the agricultural community. The NDAC was charged with licensing all aerial applicator operations and providing direction in the industry's safety. Aerial applicator businesses grew throughout the state and reached a peak of 230 businesses in 1984. As larger and more efficient turbine aircraft became available, the number of aerial applicator businesses decreased.

In 1959, Chapter 2-06 of the North Dakota Century Code, the "Airport Authority Act," allowed local airport authorities, established by cities, counties, or townships, to concentrate on airport development. This led to many entities backing airports for economic development in their communities.

Where no public agencies were available, the NDAC owned and operated airports and supported areas close to border crossings, parks, and other recreation areas. The International Peace Garden (S28), Garrison Dam Recreational Airpark at Riverdale (37N), and a border airport near Noonan were developed by the NDAC. Noonan was closed in the late 1980s because of air strip safety concerns. The Peace Garden airport is still in operation as an International Customs Border Crossing and access to the Peace Garden. Garrison Dam Airpark is also still in use.

In 1978, the Airline Deregulation Act removed federal government control from areas such as fares, routes, and market entry of new airlines and introduced a free market in the commercial airline industry. This led to a great increase in the number of flights, a decrease in fares, and an increase in the number of passengers in North Dakota and around the United States.

Vavra and NDAC members steered the legislation for the commission to represent the state in all aeronautical matters before state and federal agencies. He was the original author of Federal Regulation Part 137, which is the authority the Federal Aviation Administration (FAA) uses to write the regulations on aerial application.

The North Dakota National Guard's F-4 Phantom "Centennial Special" was created to commemorate the state's centennial in 1989.

Vavra retired from the NDAC in 1986. During his 39 years of service, aviation grew from 59 public airports and 121 private grass strips to 102 public airports and 485 private grass strips. Airport infrastructure continued to evolve and consolidate as the industry changed.

In September 1986, the NDAC hired Gary R. Ness as director. His aviation background and private business experience followed the vision and mission of the agency. He served until December 2008.

In 1987, three new sections were added to North Dakota Century Code regarding registration fees and definitions of classic and antique aircraft. In 1991, legislation established a special aeronautics fund to be used for statewide airport construction or improvement projects as approved by the NDAC. Funding came from aircraft registration fees, aviation fuel taxes, and aircraft excise taxes. Airport infrastructure throughout the state continued to grow to accommodate an increased number of passengers and a change of fleet mix to jet-fueled, turbine-powered aircraft.

The aviation community joined the 1989 North Dakota centennial celebration by developing a connection between the state's 100 public-use airports with a "mail run." Each stop had 100 envelopes, stamped USPS, flown from its airport to the neighboring airport by Stearman aircraft. The Stearman, flown by owner Vince Buraas and Helen Walkinshaw, daughter of owner Warren Walkinshaw, shared a north and south route touching the whole state. The program was sponsored by the Dakota Territory Air Museum in Minot and Don Larson, president. Diane Herr of Turtle Lake organized the postmasters in the state, who were the glue that held the endeavor together.

To celebrate the state's centennial, the North Dakota Air National Guard painted one of its F-4 Phantoms a "Centennial Special," which visited many small and large city celebrations with fly-bys. The "Party on the Capitol Grounds" on July 4, 1989, included a special fly-by for the large crowd on hand.

The North Dakota Aviation Council was founded in 1983 by six aviation organizations interested in promoting aviation in the state and presenting their concerns before government and the general public. The Aviation Council seeks to serve aviation professionals by providing a forum for the exchange of information, ideas, and experiences among their peers-pilots, agricultural operators, airport managers, fixed-base operators, aviation mechanics, educators, and aviation museums in Fargo and Minot. Advancing the goals of the member organization is an important function of the annual Upper Midwest Aviation Symposium, the state's annual aviation conference.

9/11 Impacts

Following the use of hijacked airplanes in an attack against the World Trade Center towers and the Pentagon on September 11, 2001, and in response to a request by the White House through the FAA and newly formed Transportation Security Administration (TSA), a statewide security plan was formulated. The first step was the inventory of all aircraft on public use general aviation airports, with an emphasis on all aerial applicator aircraft on public use or private airstrips.

Next, a closure plan for all general aviation airports and private strips was formulated. The NDAC, with the cooperation of the Airport Association of North Dakota, developed the communication for the closure requirements. The Civil Air Patrol accepted responsibility to deactivate those airports still in operation when or if required. Closure procedures were developed, and a plan was published with the approval of the governor on October 19, 2001.

In follow up to the security plan, the NDAC developed a General Aviation Airport Crisis Communication Program in 2002. This planning effort was developed to help the state's 81 general aviation airports better understand the facilities' vulnerabilities and how to handle communications related to a crisis event. A vulnerability report for all airports summarized data collected from both airports and local emergency responders, and an individualized communication plan gave each airport a snapshot of its vulnerabilities. The plans also provided airport management teams a template for disseminating information if an emergency event happened at the airport.

Since 1986, all the commercial service airports at the eight regional centers have constructed new terminal facilities, along with the critical infrastructure of the airport property. The events of 9/11 changed the air service airport dramatically across the state and the nation. Most of the new facilities were driven by passenger and airline safety and security. All TSA requirements have been met, and airports continue to adjust to the ever-changing world of security.

In 2008, the state expanded its statewide automated weather observation system network at multiple public use airports to provide better weather reporting for both pilots and North Dakota citizens.

Effects of the Bakken Oil Boom

From 2009 to 2015, North Dakota's airline passenger counts grew by an astounding average annual growth rate of 18 percent. In 2015, a record 1.24 million people boarded a commercial flight in the state. This growth prompted the state to work with communities to identify a plan to accommodate larger aircraft and expanded operations.

The NDAC hired Larry Taborsky in May 2009 as director. Under his tenure, North Dakota realized a large airport infrastructure funding gap that grew tremendously with the state's rapid population growth due to activity in the Bakken oil fields. Taborsky served through 2013 when the NDAC appointed the agency's airport planner, Kyle Wanner, as its director.

In 2014, the NDAC completed a new statewide aviation system plan, which identified current and future system needs. The Upper Great Plains Transportation Institute also produced a study identifying the statewide needs of airports.

The state and federal government worked together during this timeframe to provide a historical funding effort to help local communities complete multiple large-scale infrastructure projects. A new general aviation airport opened in Bowman in 2015, and a new commercial service airport opened in Williston in 2019.

Aviation Today

The NDAC continues its essential role to support aviation activities in North Dakota through communication with state, local, and FAA officials; congressional offices; and national aviation groups. The commission is responsible for administering North Dakota's laws regarding the registration of aircraft, aircraft dealers, and aerial applicators and the collection of aircraft excise tax. The NDAC provides grant funding for airport infrastructure projects and manages aviation education initiatives and programs throughout the state. The office also provides airport planning services, helps maintain the state's automated weather observation systems, and provides airport inspections for the general aviation airports.

The NDAC works to maintain and update publicized planning documents to help maintain and grow North Dakota's aviation transportation system. The executive director also serves as an ex-officio member of the Northern Plains UAS Test Site

Authority, Upper Great Plains Transportation Institute Advisory Board, Atmospheric Resource Board, and North Dakota Aviation Council. The 32 members who have served on the NDAC Board are listed at https://aero.nd.gov/about-us/agency-history/.

Over the years, the North Dakota Aviation Council has become an influential voice for the flying public and aviation services in the state. The Aviation Council has published *North Dakota Aviation Quarterly* for 30 years, providing information to all of North Dakota aviation. This publication received a national award of excellence from the National Association of State Aviation Officials in 2017. More information is available at https://ndacaero.com.

Due to recent economic growth and airport improvements, North Dakota has witnessed a resurgence in the numbers of pilots and aircraft based in the state. In 2019, 3,614 pilots and 2,030 aircraft were licensed in North Dakota.

Airports

The development of North Dakota's airports is connected to the historical development of railroads across the state. When the Great Northern and Northern Pacific railroads developed regional population hubs approximately 100 miles apart, east to west and north to south, it provided one of the nation's best networks of airport facilities to service the citizens of the state. Essentially, North Dakotans are not more than 60 miles away from a commercial service airport that provides all weather instrument landing capabilities and scheduled airline service.

The first of the state's eight commercial airports were established in the 1920s.

Williston's first airport was located near Little Muddy Creek.

Bismarck Municipal Airport (BIS)
http://www.bismarckairport.com
 In the 1920s, the city of Bismarck built its first airport on South Washington Street. Known as Straus Field, it consisted of approximately 80 acres. Several years later, the city relocated the airport from Washington Street to its present-day location on University Drive (Highway 1804). In the late 1960s, a crosswind runway (Runway 17-35) and other supporting infrastructure were constructed. In 1976, a new air traffic control tower was built on the south side of the airport, and it is still used today by the FAA. As passenger numbers continued to grow over the next two decades, the airport constructed a new state-of-the-art terminal, which was completed in May 2005.

Devils Lake Regional Airport (DVL)
https://www.devilslakeairport.com
 The Devils Lake Regional Airport is located west of Devils Lake. It is owned by the Devils Lake Airport Authority and was formerly known as Devils Lake Municipal Airport. The airport is primarily used for general aviation, but is also served by one commercial airline, with flights three times daily. Scheduled passenger service is subsidized by the Essential Air Service program.

Dickinson Theodore Roosevelt Regional Airport (DIK)
http://dickinsonairport.com/
 The Dickinson airport opened in 1938 and is named for Theodore Roosevelt, the 26th president of the United States. Located south of Dickinson, it is owned by the Dickinson Airport Authority and was formerly known as the Dickinson Municipal Airport. The airport serves western North Dakota and Medora, home to Theodore Roosevelt National Park; eastern Montana; and northwest South Dakota. The airport is served by one airline.

Fargo Hector International Airport (FAR)
https://fargoairport.com
 On September 9, 1927, Martin Hector leased a quarter-section of land at the northwest corner of Fargo to the city for five years at $1 per year. On April 9, 1931, Hector paved the way for Fargo's airport with his outright gift of the land, which is part of the present airport property, along with acreage purchased from many adjacent landowners. Northwest Airlines began scheduled weekly flights into Fargo on February 1, 1928. On February 3, 1931, the new Fargo airport inaugurated air service from Minneapolis, Minnesota, to Grand Forks, and then on to Winnipeg, Manitoba. In 1953, a terminal and administration building were built. In 1982, Hector Field became Hector International Airport, and U. S. Customs opened an office on the field. When the city built a new terminal in 1986, the original building became an aviation office complex.

Grand Forks International Airport (GFK)
https://gfkairport.com

Grand Forks' first airport and municipal landing field was started in 1928 just south of Highway 2, where I-29 is today. The concrete runways and a terminal were built in 1942 and 1943. Eventually, commercial aircraft became too large to use the runways. In January 1961, city council members voted to construct a new airport five miles west of the city in its current location. The airport project cost almost $3 million, including the terminal, two runways, and taxiways. In May 1987, a joint resolution of Grand Forks County and the city authorized what is now the Grand Forks Regional Airport Authority. The Grand Forks airport grew into one of the busiest airports in the region. Two new runways were developed, and a new $22 million, 50,000-square-foot terminal was built.

Jamestown Regional Airport (JMS)
www.flyjamestown.net/

The Jamestown Regional Airport opened in 1938 and is located northeast of Jamestown. It is owned by the Jamestown Regional Airport Authority and was formerly known as Jamestown Municipal Airport. It is mostly used for general aviation, but is also served by one commercial airline, with flights twice each weekday and once on Saturdays and Sundays. Scheduled passenger service is subsidized by the Essential Air Service program.

Minot International Airport (MOT)
https://www.motairport.com/

Minot's first airstrip was developed in the late 1920s on a 20-acre tract in the southern portion of the present-day airport property. The dedication of the "Port of Minot" was held on July 23, 1928. The original runway had an east-west orientation. Improvements (i.e., grading, apron area, and lighting) were provided by the Works Progress Administration prior to World War II, and additional improvements were provided in 1942 through the Defense Landing Area Program. These improvements included land acquisition and the construction and paving of three runways. The airport was administered by the City Park Board until June 13, 1947, and is now under the direction of a full-time airport director and the Minot City Council. The city, in response to oil boom air traffic, opened a state-of-the-art airline terminal in 2016.

Williston Basin International Airport (XWA)
http://www.xwaproject.com/

The first airport to serve Willison was east of the city near Little Muddy Creek. The environment was unsuitable, and operations shifted to a new airport in 1936, but the 23-acre site became too small. Sloulin Field International Airport was built in 1947, covering 740 acres. It was two miles north of downtown and owned and operated by the city. The 2004 master plan noted limited room for expansion because of the surrounding terrain and buildings. In light of the issues and increased air service to Williston amid the North Dakota oil boom, city officials decided to relocate the airport and build the new Williston Basin International Airport, which opened in 2019.

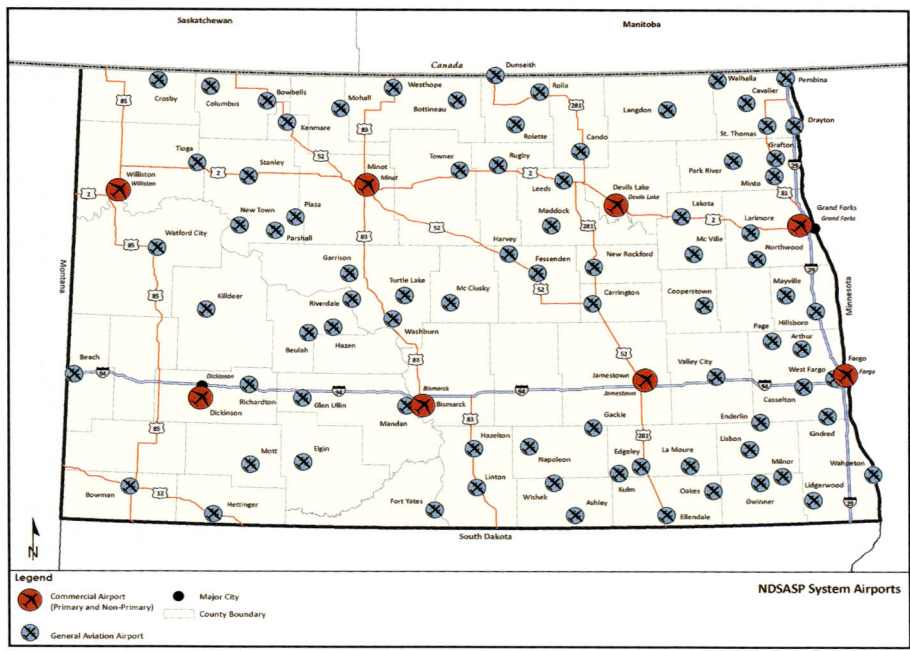

Eighty-nine airports are part of the North Dakota State Aviation System Plan.

In addition to the state's eight commercial service airports, there are 81 general aviation airports. Due to the vast size of the state and limited rural transit options, aviation continues to be a critical method of transportation in North Dakota. Many industries rely on air transportation and airport infrastructure to move employees and materials for businesses, transport patients and medical supplies for life-saving operations, spray crops to yield larger harvests, provide weather research and modification, and protect the northern U.S. border.

At the national level, the Federal Aviation Administration (FAA) is responsible for overseeing the development of the aviation system in the United States. The National Plan of Integrated Airport Systems (NPIAS) is the program through which the FAA conducts national planning efforts and produces an annual plan for more than 3,300 airports included in the system. This plan is derived from a compilation of local, regional, and state system planning studies and provides an evaluation of the national aviation system as a whole.

To be included in the NPIAS, an airport must meet certain criteria. Only those airports included in the NPIAS are eligible for federal funding through a program called the Airport Improvement Program. Of the 89 public-use airports in North Dakota, 54 are included in the NPIAS. The 35 remaining airports are part of North Dakota's aviation system and are often municipally-owned and receive support from their local community and the NDAC.

There are also 167 private-use airports across North Dakota that vary in size and type of use. These facilities do not receive funding assistance from the FAA or the state, with maintenance and operation solely the responsibility of the owner.

The North Dakota Aeronautics Commission has a statewide aviation system plan that provides more details, available at https://aero.nd.gov.

Air Service

Public Air Services

North Dakota's air service history started in the 1920s. Airmail activity in the United States started commercial passenger and cargo aviation. Building of airport runways and terminals in North Dakota lagged because communities lacked legislative authority to spend public funds on airports.

Due to limited airfield facilities, North Dakota's first commercial airline service was a customs stop at Pembina on a Winnipeg, Manitoba, to Minneapolis, Minnesota, flight in February 1928. The hangar built by Northwest Airways for this stop was used until the 1997 flood destroyed it.

By 1932, air mail and passenger service were established at Fargo, Grand Forks, Pembina, Valley City, Jamestown, Bismarck, and Dickinson through Northwest Airways. During these growth years, aviation became the engine that helped run the

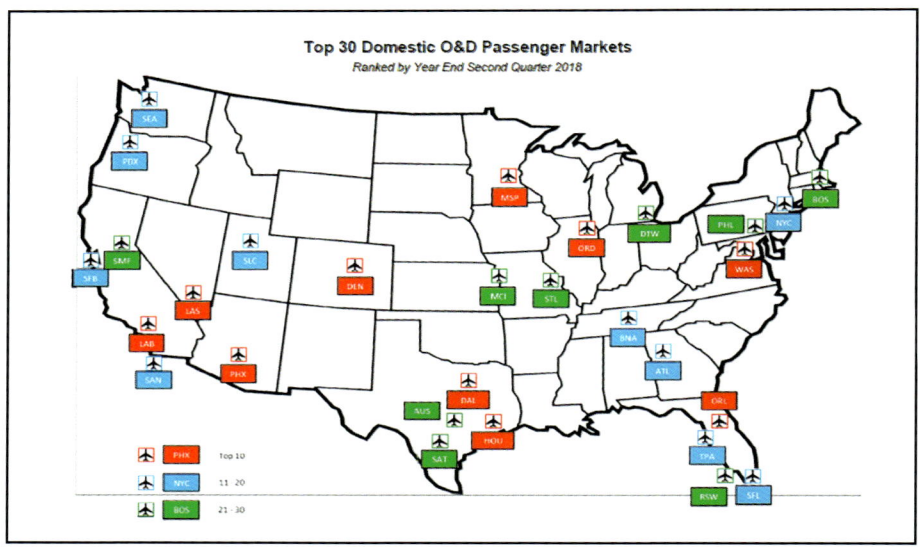

This map shows the most popular destinations of North Dakota airline passengers (2018).

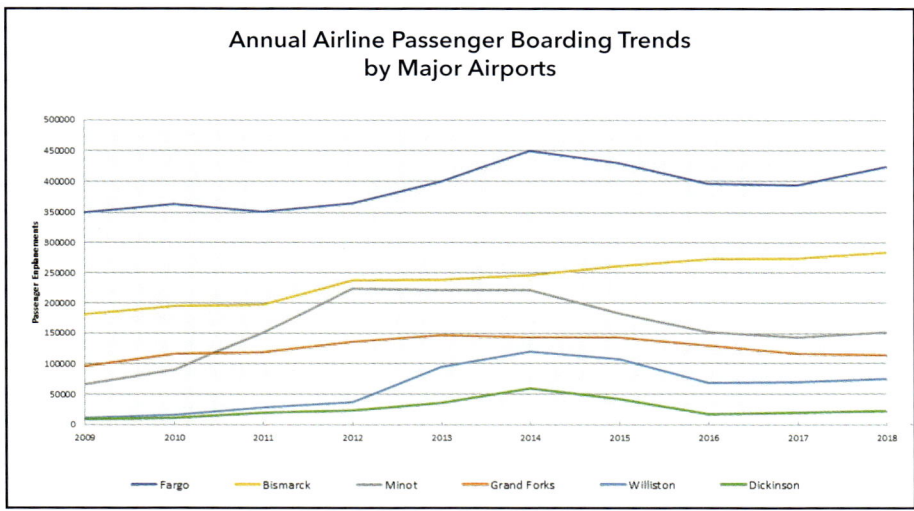

country. After World War II, the Civil Aeronautics Board gave airlines permanent route certificates, and U.S. Air Mail contracts brought stability to the airline business.

North Dakota was served for most of this time by Northwest Airlines, Frontier Airlines, and North Central Airlines. Since deregulation in 1978, a variety of airlines have served the state.

Today, more than two million passengers fly to or from North Dakota's commercial service airports on an annual basis. These airports currently provide jet service to nine non-stop destinations, of which two are seasonal. The state averages approximately 60 airline flight departures per day, with an estimated 4,000 available daily seats. The top destination airline passenger markets in 2018 for North Dakota travelers were:
1. Phoenix/Mesa, Arizona
2. Las Vegas, Nevada
3. Denver, Colorado
4. Orlando/Sanford, Florida
5. Minneapolis/St. Paul, Minnesota

North Dakota has been seeing steady growth in airline passenger boardings in the last 10 years. These numbers and trends are tracked by the North Dakota Aeronautics Commission.

Private Air Services

Charter and on-demand air carriers utilize the airport system to transport passengers to destinations throughout the world, and these services connect North Dakota communities and businesses globally. North Dakota communities rely on general aviation travel to shorten the duration of a trip or to fly directly to a destination not served by scheduled commercial airlines.

Medical Air Services

Air ambulance service is critical in a rural state like North Dakota. Air medical providers utilize both fixed-wing and rotor-wing aircraft to safely and efficiently transport patients to medical facilities both within the state and nationally. These operators utilize the state's airport infrastructure on a regular basis.

In addition to patient transport, medical doctors utilize the airport network to provide critical medical services in rural communities. Through the utilization of aircraft, rural communities have access to many of the same medical professionals as larger communities.

Aerial Applicators

The airport system helps support the state's aerial applicators, or crop dusters, which help increase crop yields for those engaged in agriculture, North Dakota's number one industry. In 2018, 99 commercial aerial applicators were licensed in North Dakota flying 196 aircraft. These operators applied more than three million acres with insecticide, fungicide, herbicide, or fertilizer.

Crop dusters support North Dakota agriculture.

Aviation Manufacturing

Strong market growth, both domestically and internationally, have contributed to a healthy manufacturing economy in North Dakota. Several manufacturing companies based in the state build aircraft parts and components.

Manned and unmanned aviation manufacturing companies in North Dakota that manufacture equipment and components include:
- AegisFlow – Fargo
- Appareo Systems – Fargo
- Botlink – Fargo (UAS)
- Cirrus Aircraft – Grand Forks
- Comdel Innovations – Wahpeton
- Field of View – Fargo (UAS)
- Ideal Aerosmith – Grand Forks
- Killdeer Mountain Manufacturing – Killdeer and Dickinson
- Moog – Fargo
- Northrop Grumman Systems Corporation – New Town
- Sioux Manufacturing – Fort Totten
- Spectrum Aeromed – Fargo
- Tri-State Aviation, Inc. – Wahpeton
- UTC Aerospace – Jamestown

Economic Impact of Aviation

In 2016, the North Dakota Aeronautics Commission (NDAC) completed a research project, funded in part by a FAA grant, to estimate the annual economic impacts of all facets of aviation on North Dakota's economy.

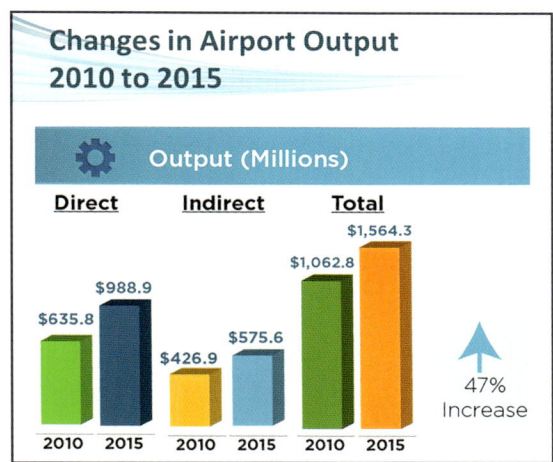

The study of North Dakota's public-use airport system measured jobs, annual payroll, and annual output. Output represents the purchase of goods and services within North Dakota. These economic impacts were measured for activities associated with airport management, on-airport aviation related businesses, capital investment, and spending by visitors to North Dakota who utilize the airports.

Economic Impacts from Airports, Aviation, and Aerospace in North Dakota

	TOTAL EMPLOYMENT	TOTAL PAYROLL	TOTAL OUTPUT
Grand Forks AFB	2,565	$105.2 million	$203.7 million
Minot AFB	7,283	$321 million	$513.5 million
Off-Airport Aerial Applicators	156	$5.6 million	$15.6 million
Off-Airport Aviation /Aerospace Businesses	4,479	$227.1 million	$497 million
Aviation Supported Jobs	5,513	$271.8 million	$882.7 million
Sub-Total	19,996	$930.7 million	$2.1 billion
Total for 89 Study Airports	12,217	$505.2 million	$1.56 billion
Total for All Airport / Aviation/Aerospace Impacts	32,213	$1.44 billion	$3.66 billion

Since statewide economic impacts were last measured in 2010:

- Annual economic benefits from public-use airports in North Dakota and the activities they support increased 47 percent.
- Jobs supported by North Dakota airports grew from 8,872 to 12,217, an increase of 3,345 jobs.
- Annual state and local sales tax revenues for airports and airport-supported activities increased from $31.1 million to more than $60 million.
- Visitors coming to North Dakota each year on general aviation aircraft or commercial airline flights grew from 545,300 to 915,290.

The NDAC's research also considered the economic impacts of other facets of aviation in North Dakota, including the annual economic impacts associated with the U.S. Air Force bases in Minot and Grand Forks; North Dakota businesses engaged in producing aviation and aerospace products; and benefits employers throughout the state gain from using commercial airline, general aviation, or air cargo services. These other aviation and aerospace-related activities provide an additional $2.1 billion in annual economic output and support approximately 20,000 additional jobs that have an annual payroll estimated at $931 million.

The almost $1.6 billion in annual output from the public-use airports combined with the output from other aviation and aerospace-related activities results in a total estimated annual economic output of $3.66 billion, approximately eight percent of North Dakota's Real Gross State Product. Airports and aviation are major drivers and contributors to North Dakota's economy.

North Dakota airports connect the state to business centers throughout the United States. The map shows recorded instrument flight rule arrivals to and departures from North Dakota over a 12-month period in 2018. Most of these flights were on general aviation aircraft. According to FAA data, nonstop flights

North Dakota's Connections to U.S. Business Centers

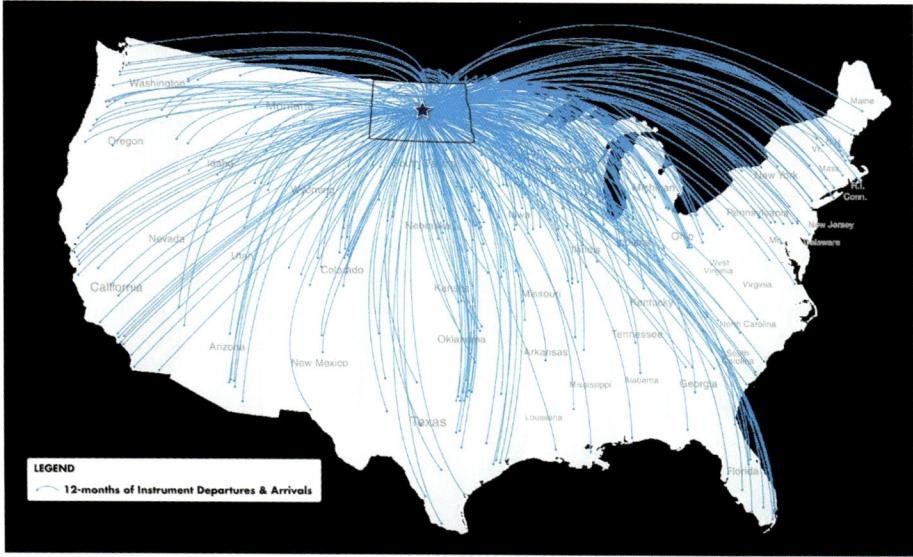

represent only three percent of all aircraft arrivals and departures to North Dakota airports. The map clearly shows the important role airports play in providing the transportation infrastructure that has supported the state's recent economic growth.

More information on the study is available at www.aero.nd.gov.

Military Aviation Components

Minot Air Force Base

The Minot Air Force Base (AFB) opened in February 1957, filling the need for a fighter interceptor base responsible for protecting the northern U.S. border from Soviet bombers. The 5th Fighter Interceptor Squadron under Air Defense Command operated F-106 and F-15 aircraft until 1988, when the air defense mission was eliminated. In 1961, B-52Hs were stationed at Minot and have operated continuously under the 5th Bomb Wing since it relocated from Travis AFB, California, in July 1968. The 5th Bomb Wing, which dates to 1919, saw combat during World War II, the Vietnam War, and in Operations Desert Fox, Allied Forces, Enduring Freedom, and Iraqi Freedom. It has supported Continuous Bomber Presence in the Pacific Area of Responsibility since 2003.

The 91st Missile Wing began as the 91st Strategic Reconnaissance Wing in November 1948, flying RB 29s. In 1963, they flew B-52Cs and Ds, deploying twice during the Vietnam War. In 1968, the 91st Missile Wing transitioned from B-52s at Glasgow AFB, Montana, to Minot AFB and the Minuteman I intercontinental ballistic missile (ICBM). In 1971, they became the first wing to operate the Minuteman III. They have been on continuous alert operation every day since June 1968.

Minot AFB is the only dual-wing nuclear-capable base in the Air Force, hosting two legs of the Strategic Triad. The 5th Bomb Wing operates 26 B-52 aircraft, and the 91st Missile Wing operates 150 ICBM sites.

5th Bomb Wing
The 5th Bomb Wing is a B-52H Stratofortress wing at Minot AFB. Known by its nickname, the Warbirds, the 5th Bomb Wing is the host wing at Minot AFB and part of Air Force Global Strike Command (AFGSC). The bomb wing and its fleet of B-52H Stratofortress bombers serve as part of the Air Force's strategic and conventional combat force.

The B-52H is a long-range nuclear and conventional heavy bomber than can perform a variety of missions. The bomber can fly at high subsonic speeds at altitudes reaching 50,000 feet. It has an unrefueled combat range in excess of 8,800 miles. The B-52H can carry precision guided ordnance with worldwide precision navigation.

The B-52A first flew in 1954, and the B model entered service in 1955. A total of 744 B-52s were built with the last, a B-52H, delivered in October 1963. Only the H model is still in the Air Force inventory and is assigned to AFGSC and the Air Force Reserves. The first of 102 B-52Hs was delivered to Strategic Air Command in May 1961.

A B-52 Stratofortress is prepared for takeoff on the runway at Hickam Air Force Base, Hawaii. The B-52s are deployed from Minot AFB.

For more than 40 years, B-52 Stratofortresses have been the backbone of the manned strategic bomber force for the United States. The B-52 can drop or launch the widest array of weapons in the U.S. inventory. Current engineering analyses shows the B-52's lifespan extends beyond the year 2040.

91st Missile Wing

The 91st Missile Wing (MW) is an ICBM wing at Minot AFB. The 91 MW is one of the Air Force's three ICBM wings. The missile wing is responsible for defending the United States by operating, maintaining, and securing a fleet of Minuteman III missiles located in underground launch facilities scattered across the northwest part of the state. The wing's missile complex stretches more than 8,500 square miles, approximately 12 percent of North Dakota. The wing's major organizations include three groups and special staff functions: 91st Operations Group, 91st Maintenance Group, and 91st Security Forces Group.

Approximately 400 Minuteman III missiles provide a critical component of America's on-alert strategic forces. As the nation's "silent sentinels," ICBMs, and the people who operate them, have remained on continuous, around-the-clock alert since 1959.

AFGSC is the Air Force's lead command for and largest operator of UH-1N Iroquois helicopters. The UH-1N supports ICBM operations in missile fields controlled by Minot AFB.

The UH-1N "Huey" helicopter supports a variety of missions and agencies.

CHAPTER ONE - AVIATION IN NORTH DAKOTA

The UH-1N is a light-lift utility helicopter used to support AFGSC missile wings and groups, Air Force District of Columbia, Air Force Survival School training, Air Advisory Operations, test and evaluation at Elgin AFB, Florida, and U.S. Pacific Command, as well as other agencies. The UH-1N entered the Air Force inventory in 1970 to provide search and rescue capabilities. The missions expanded to include missile, distinguished visitor, survival school support, test support, and air advisor operations.

The 91st Operations Group (OG) is the operational backbone of the 91st Missile Wing. During World War II, the group, known then as the 91st Bombardment Group, flew the most famous plane of that era, the Memphis Belle. Today, the group remains a key facet of the nation's deterrent force. Through its four squadrons and one helicopter flight, the 91 OG continues to keep Minot's missiles safe, secure, and ready to operate.

The "Pathfinders" of the 91st Operations Support Squadron provide training to 224 missile combat crew members, 56 facility managers, 60 missile field chefs, and 75 maintainers and prepare ICBM targeting materials and code components.

The LGM-30G Minuteman ICBM is an element of the nation's strategic deterrent forces under the control of the AFGSC. The Minuteman is a strategic weapon system using a ballistic missile of intercontinental range. Missiles are dispersed in hardened silos to protect against attack and connected to an underground launch control center through a system of hardened cables. Launch crews, consisting of two officers, perform around-the-clock alert in the launch control center. The Minuteman weapon system was conceived in the late 1950s, and Minuteman I was deployed in the early 1960s. Minuteman was a revolutionary concept and an extraordinary technical achievement. Today's Minuteman weapon system is the product of almost 40 years of continuous enhancement.

The three missile operations squadrons of the 91st Operations Group – the 740th, 741st, and 742nd Missile Squadrons – include missile crewmembers, alert facility chefs, and facility managers. These squadrons vigilantly maintain the missile force at all times. Each squadron controls 50 launch facilities and five missile alert facilities. Missile squadrons are divided into missile operations flights and an operation support flight.

Grand Forks Air Force Base

The Grand Forks AFB opened on February 8, 1957, with Air Defense Command's activation of the 478th Fighter Group. This unit served as the host unit for a fighter-interceptor squadron, an air defense sector operation, and Strategic Air Command units. In December 1957, the U.S. Air Force activated the Grand Forks Air Defense Sector of the North American Air Defense Command (NORAD). This sector became operational with the semi-automatic ground environment system on

December 15, 1959, enabling the Grand Forks Air Defense Sector to cover the air space of three U.S. states and one Canadian province.

Through the 1960s, Grand Forks AFB became home to the 905th Air Refueling Squadron (ARFES-Heavy) flying KC-135 Stratotankers, the 478th Fighter Wing flying the F-101 Voodoo, the 319th Bombardment Wing (Heavy) operating the B-52 Stratofortress, and the 321st Strategic Missile Wing with its complement of Minutemen III missiles. In the 1980s, the B-52s were replaced at Grand Forks AFB by the more capable B-1B Lancer.

The 1990s saw major organizational changes made by Strategic Air Command at Grand Forks AFB. The 319th Bomb Wing was redesignated as the 319th Air Refueling Wing and reassigned to Air Mobility Command. By May 1994, the last B-1B Lancer departed Grand Forks AFB. In 1995, the Air Force began the removal of the 150 Minuteman III missiles from Grand Forks AFB, and in 1998, the 321st Missile Wing inactivated. The base continued to be home to one of three supertanker wings in the U.S. Air Force until 2010 when the last KC-135 departed Grand Forks AFB. At that time, the base began the mission of supporting the 69th Reconnaissance Group's operations as an Air Base Wing, until redesignation in 2019.

319th Reconnaissance Wing
The 319th Wing's mission is to provide a decisional advantage to U.S. warfighters and national leaders through support of the nation's Global Hawk High-Altitude ISR mission, ensure strategic command and control through operation of the nation's High Frequency Global Communication System, afford Combatant Commanders mission-ready airmen anytime anywhere, and provide airmen and families of the Grand Forks AFB team, including geographically-separated units, with responsive, tailored, and mission-focused support.

319th Medical Group
The 319th Medical Group's mission at Grand Forks AFB is to promote healthy lifestyles and optimize mission performance through quality care for all Warriors of the North with a commitment to operational readiness, outstanding customer service, and always delivering world-class health care.

319th Mission Support Group
In May 2005, the Department of Defense's 2005 Base Realignment and Closure recommended the Grand Forks AFB for realignment. The closure was prevented, but its KC-135 tanker mission was lost, with a significant reduction of personnel. On December 4, 2010, the last KC-135 departed Grand Forks AFB for its new home at McConnell AFB Kansas, marking the end of the 50-year-long refueling mission at Grand Forks.

The unmanned RQ-4 Global Hawk was assigned to Grand Forks, and on March 1, 2011, and the wing was redesignated as the 319th Air Base Wing (319

An RQ-4 Global Hawk soars through the sky to record intelligence, surveillance, and reconnaissance data.

ABW). The first RQ-4 arrived in Grand Forks in May 2011, operated by the 69th Reconnaissance Group of ACC. Starting in 2012, the base received several new Block 40 Global Hawks.

The RQ-4 Global Hawk is a high-altitude, long-endurance, remotely piloted aircraft with an integrated sensor suite that provides global, all-weather, day or night intelligence, surveillance, and reconnaissance (ISR) capability. Global Hawk's mission is to provide a broad spectrum of ISR collection capabilities to support joint combatant forces in worldwide peacetime, contingency, and wartime operations.

Global Hawk is flown by a Launch and Recovery Element and a Mission Control Element. The system offers a wide variety of employment options. The unmatched range and 30-plus hour endurance allows tremendous flexibility in meeting mission requirements. In 2014, an RQ-4 Block 40 flew a 34.3 hour flight, setting the endurance record for the longest unrefueled flight by a U.S. Air Force aircraft.

Global Hawk began as an Advance Concept Technology Demonstration in 1995. The system was determined to have military utility and provided warfighters with an evolutionary high-altitude, long-endurance ISR capability. The Global Hawk has been deployed operationally to support overseas contingency operations since November 2001.

319th Operations Group

On June 28, 2019, the 319th Operations Group (OG) was reactivated as the flying component of the 319th Reconnaissance Wing. It serves as the operations group for the RQ-4 Global Hawk mission at Grand Forks AFB. It was originally activated as the 319th Bombardment group (Light) on June 26, 1942, flying the B-26 Marauder and B-25 Mitchell in northwest Africa and the Mediterranean and then moving to the Pacific Theater of Operations in 1945 flying A-26 Invaders. Following the war and initial inactivation, they were reactivated in the reserves in December 1946 and inactivated in March 1951. The group was redesignated as the 319th Fighter-Bomber Group in April 1955, activated in May 1955, and inactivated in November 1957. In July 1985, the 319th was redesignated as the 319th Bombardment Group (Heavy) but remained on an inactive status until it was redesignated as the 319th OG in August 1991, then again inactivated on December 31, 2010.

Cavalier Air Force Station

The 10th Space Warning Squadron (SWS) at Cavalier Air Force Station (AFS) is located 15 miles south of the Canadian and U.S. border. The squadron is a geographically separated unit of the 21st Space Wing, Peterson Air Force Base, Colorado.

Mission
The mission of the Cavalier AFS is to provide flawless missile warning and space surveillance to ensure space superiority and to defend our nation and allies.

The squadron operates and maintains the world's most capable phased-array radar system. The Perimeter Acquisition Radar Attack Characterization System (PARCS) continuously provides critical missile warning and space surveillance data to NORAD, U.S. Strategic Command, and regional combatant commanders. PARCS monitors and tracks more than half of all earth-orbiting objects to enable space

The PARCS radar is the most prominent building on the Cavalier AFS, standing 121 feet high.

situational awareness and space control. Additionally, the 10th SWS provides attack characterization data to the secretary of defense and the president for real-time war plan execution decisions.

History

The unit was originally the acquisition radar portion of the only U.S. operational antiballistic missile system, known as SAFEGUARD. Due to the 1972 Anti-Ballistic Missile Treaty (SALT II), components of the SAFEGUARD complex, with the exception of the PARCS radar at Cavalier AFS, were deactivated in February 1975.

The forerunner of the present-day 10th SWS began passing tactical warning and attack assessment data to Cheyenne Mountain Air Station, Colorado, in January 1977. In October 1977, the NORAD Early Warning Mission was transferred to the Air Force and two months later the spacetrack capability was added. In December 1979, the unit was transferred from Aerospace Defense Command to Strategic Air Command.

The unit, as it exists today, joined Air Force Space Command in 1983 as Detachment 5, 1st Space Wing. On August 1, 1986, the unit was redesignated as the 10th Missile Warning Squadron, 1st Space Wing. It was renamed the 10th Space Warning Squadron on May 15, 1992, when the 1st Space Wing and 3rd Space Support Wing were inactivated and the 21st Space Wing was activated. In September 2007, the installation, along with PARCS, was transferred to the Air Force.

Equipment and Facilities

The PARCS radar is easily the most prominent building on Cavalier AFS. It is a concrete structure that stands 121 feet high. Additional facilities at 10th SWS include the industrial building, which houses the unit motor pool and supply areas, and a fire station and gymnasium in separate buildings. There is also a 12-unit bachelor crew quarters and 14-unit bachelor enlisted quarters. The Community Activity Center houses a heritage hall, hobby and activities area, shoppette, lounge area, library, and bowling lanes.

A mixture of military and civil service people are permanently assigned to 10th SWS. Most of the military members are assigned to the operations directorate, which is responsible for the Missile Warning Operations Center where missile warning and spacetrack missions are performed. The remainder of the assigned military and civilian workers provide support functions and the quality assurance evaluation functions for various contracted activities on Cavalier AFS. There are also contract workers at the unit who provide such services as fire protection, law enforcement, custodial care, operations, maintenance, and supply. Security forces personnel from Grand Forks AFB provide both internal and external security for the radar.

North Dakota Army National Guard

Army Aviation Support Facilities

The North Dakota Army National Guard uses the Army Aviation Support Facilities (AASF) in Bismarck and Fargo to provide support for Army aviation units assigned to the state. The AASFs provide helicopter flight support, conduct flight training for pilots and non-rated crewmembers to maintain individual proficiency, and satisfy the Army's regulatory flying hour and readiness requirements. Personnel at the facilities are responsible for performing all required maintenance and inspections on the assigned UH-72A Lakota and UH-60 Black Hawk helicopters, as well as a fixed wing aircraft, the C-12 Huron.

A UH-60 Black Hawk helicopter, operated by the N.D. Army National Guard's Company C, 2nd Battalion, 285th Aviation Regiment (Assault), uses a 640-gallon Bambi bucket to suppress a wildfire south of Bismarck.

The Bismarck AASF is located at the south end of the Bismarck Airport and hangars up to 14 aircraft on a daily basis. The Fargo facility is operated out of leased space on the east side of Hector International Airport and houses three aircraft during normal operations.

These two facilities allow the North Dakota Army National Guard to recruit, train, and support aviation personnel and perform flight operations in both the east and west regions of North Dakota and provide emergency response to their supported communities.

Forty-six full-time federal technicians are employed between the two facilities. Their positions include responsibilities as instructor pilots, mechanics, fuelers, and other operational support personnel required for the aviation mission. In addition to their daily duties, the guardsmen are often the initial response force for state emergencies requiring aviation assets. Federal technicians also serve as traditional guardsmen in a military capacity as members within the state's aviation units.

North Dakota Lt. Gov. Brent Sanford, left, offers remarks during the Bismarck-based Detachment 7, Company C, 2nd Battalion, 245th Aviation Regiment, Operational Airlift Support open house on August 17, 2018. The event celebrated the unit's upcoming nine-month mobilization to Djibouti, Africa. From left to right are Maj. Gen. Al Dohrmann, North Dakota adjutant general, and unit members Sgt. Cassandra Mosbrucker, Warrant Officer 1 Christian Thorson, Capt. Stoelting, and Chief Warrant Officer 3 Robert Smette.

1st Battalion, 112th Aviation Regiment (Security and Support)

The 1st Battalion, 112th Aviation Regiment (1-112th) operates and maintains UH-60 Black Hawk and UH-72A Lakota helicopters. Four units fall within the Battalion, located in Bismarck: Company A of the 1-112th; Company H of the 1-112th; Company C, 2nd Battalion, 285th Aviation Regiment (Assault) (2-285th); and Company D, 1-112th Aviation Battalion MEDEVAC, which is stationed in Fargo. The units operate Black Hawks primarily for troop movement and internal/external transport. The Lakota is ideally suited for logistics and missions in support of homeland security, emergency response, and medical evacuations.

Detachment 7, Company C, 2nd Battalion, 245th Aviation Regiment, Operational Support Airlift

Detachment 7, Company C, 2nd Battalion, 245th Aviation Regiment, Operational Support Airlift conducts personnel and cargo movement using fixed-wing aircraft throughout the contiguous United States and, when required, deploys to perform similar missions in regions throughout the world.

UAS Testing and Training

In July 2012, restricted airspace was designated over the Army National Guard's land at Camp Grafton South. This is an area where unmanned aircraft pilots are allowed to practice with lasers used in battle to designate targets for laser-guided bombs and missiles. During training exercises, restricted to certain times, commercial and private aircraft are prohibited from flying through this airspace.

On March 1, 2018, the North Dakota National Guard and the Northern Plains Unmanned Aircraft Systems Test Site announced an agreement that allows UAS to conduct flights over portions of the Guard's Camp Grafton Training Center near Devils Lake. The test site is permitted to overfly the Center's 12,000 acres and use camp facilities.

North Dakota Air National Guard

In 2005, the Base Realignment and Closure Commission recommended that the mission of the North Dakota Air National Guard be realigned. The 119th Fighter Wing's F-16As (15 aircraft) were reaching the end of their operational life and would retire. In January 2007, the 119th ended its F-16 mission after almost 60 years of air defense interceptor missions.

The squadron began to receive the C-21A Learjet and was redesignated the 178th Airlift Squadron. Later in 2007, it was announced that C-21 operations would be transferred to the newly activated 177th Airlift Squadron, and the 179th would convert to operating the unmanned MQ-1 Predator and be redesignated the 178th Reconnaissance Squadron. In 2008, it received its first Predator.

The MQ-1 Predator is an American remotely piloted aircraft (RPA) built by General Atomics that was used primarily by the U.S. Air Force and Central Intelligence Agency. Initially conceived in the early 1990s for aerial reconnaissance and forward observation roles, the Predator carries cameras and other sensors. The Air Force describes the Predator as a "Tier II" MALE UAS (medium-altitude, long-endurance unmanned aircraft system). The UAS consists of four aircraft or "air vehicles" with sensors, a ground control station, and a primary satellite link communication suite. Powered by a Rotax engine and driven by a propeller, the air vehicle can fly up to 400 nautical miles (460 miles) to a target, loiter overhead for 14 hours, then return to its base.

During fall 2016, the North Dakota Air National Guard's 119th Wing was transitioning to a new, remotely piloted aircraft. The change-over took about a year to complete. The current model, the MQ-1 Predator, was being retired and replaced by the MQ-9 Reaper. Designated MQ-9 Reaper by its U.S. Air Force and Royal Air Force customers, the turboprop-powered, multi-mission Predator B RPA was developed with GA-ASI funding and provides significantly greater capabilities than Predator. First flown in 2001, Predator B is a highly sophisticated development built on the experience gained with the company's battle-proven Predator RPA and is a major evolutionary leap forward in overall performance and reliability.

Featuring unmatched operational flexibility, Predator B has an endurance of more than 27 hours, speeds of 240 KTAS, can operate up to 50,000 feet, and has a 3,850-pound payload capacity that includes 3,000 pounds of external stores. Twice as fast as Predator, the aircraft carries 500 percent more payload and has nine times the horsepower. It provides a long-endurance, persistent surveillance/strike capability for the war fighter.

The primary mission of the MQ-1 Predator and MQ-9 Reaper is to provide intelligence, surveillance, reconnaissance, and strike capability to joint force commanders engaged in the area of operations.

119th Operations Support Squadron

The 119th Operations Support Squadron (OSS) consists of 86 personnel and fills manning requirements for the aviation resource management, airfield management, weather, special security staff, and RPA communications element.

Between July 1, 2017, and September 30, 2018, the OSS supported two combat lines for the mission control element and 44 sorties flown by the launch and recovery element (LRE). LRE sorties are critical in establishing a continuation training program that is desperately needed throughout the MQ-9 Reaper enterprise.

The OSS is also leading the way in distributed mission operations for the RPA community. In collaboration with the Air Force Research Laboratory, the OSS recently installed two MQ-9 Block 30 Ground Control Stations and a PRINCE (Predator Reaper Integrated Combat Environment) station. This is the first of its kind outside Wright-Patterson AFB and allows the Hooligans to train and test emerging threat training protocols used by the entire RPA enterprise.

178 Attack Squadron

The 178th Attack Squadron (ATKS) consists of 92 pilots, sensor operators, intelligence professionals, and other personnel involved in 24/7 combat operations supporting numerous named operations throughout the world. The ATKS continues to be the "go-to" unit requested by name for MQ-9 Reaper missions across the enterprise.

119th Aircraft Maintenance Squadron

The 119th Aircraft Maintenance Squadron (AMXS) was officially activated on June 1, 2018, after previously being deactivated on October 9, 2014. The AMXS consists of 114 personnel and fills manning requirements for flight-line, avionics, weapons, munitions, cyber support, aircraft ground equipment, metals, structural, and non-destructive inspection shops.

The first taxi of a North Dakota Air National Guard MQ-9 in 2017.

The Operations Group and AMXS are fully disassociated from Grand Forks Air Force Base and now operate out of Hector IAP, Fargo, with two MQ-9 aircraft. Initial operating capability for the AMXS was declared effective March 29, 2018, as the first flight to the Devils Lake restricted area was successfully accomplished. The AMXS is awaiting arrival of two additional MQ-9 aircraft, with estimated delivery of summer 2020.

The first successful MQ-9 mission out of Hector IAP took place in Fargo on August 8, 2017. This first flight was historic in two ways. This was the first time a Happy Hooligan tail had flown over the skies of Fargo since 2013, and the 119th Wing was the first unit in the continental United States to fly a MQ-9 block 5 aircraft from a joint-use airfield, pioneering national airspace integration.

Aviation Education
University of North Dakota

The University of North Dakota's (UND) aviation education program began in 1968 with two donated planes, 12 students, and the formation of a Department of Aviation. UND alumnus John Odegard, who once scrimped together enough money to pay his college tuition from money earned crop dusting North Dakota fields, was the department's founder and first chairman.

Odegard would eventually propel UND Aerospace, as it's known, to international prominence with precedent-setting programs in aviation, atmospheric sciences, earth system sciences and policy, and space studies. The college was officially renamed the John D. Odegard School of Aerospace Sciences in 1997.

Today, more than 50 years after its founding, it is the second largest of UND's degree-granting colleges and operates one of the largest fleets of civilian flight training aircraft in North America.

Paul Lindseth, current dean of the school, oversees more than 2,000 students from around the world, more than 500 experienced faculty and staff, and a well-equipped Grand Forks-based headquarters on UND's main campus. UND flies nearly 120,000 flight hours annually out of the Grand Forks International Airport (GFK), making GFK the 22nd busiest airport in the country in 2018.

UND Aerospace, supported by the UND Aerospace Foundation, also has satellite flight training centers at nearby University of Minnesota-Crookston and in Arizona.

UND Aerospace is a go-to source for student-pilots by the commercial airlines and civil agencies. The school has signed career pathway agreements with numerous industry partners, including United, Delta, and Sun Country Airlines, as well as

UND's ScanEagle instructor crew gathers for a photo during a May 2017 flight. Left to right: Erin Roesler, Trey Langaas, Paul Snyder, James Moe, and Alex Volberding.

the U.S. Customs and Border Protection, all providing UND pilots with clear paths to succeed. UND Aerospace has relaunched a successful relationship with the U.S. Army to provide rotary, fixed-wing, and unmanned aircraft training to its future aviation officers.

Flying has always been at the heart of UND Aerospace. The students of UND's Flying Teams have become national juggernauts, finishing first or second overall in 29 of the past 35 years of competitions. Recently, other UND aviation teams have been making national waves, such as the UND Aerobatics Team, with its 10th national collegiate title, and the all-female Air Race Classic Teams, which zig-zag thousands of miles cross-country each year in search of fair weather, good tailwinds, and top times.

For decades, UND has been educating future air traffic controllers. UND graduates can be found in all major air traffic control facilities in North Dakota and around the country. The program uses state-of-the-art simulation to expose students to realistic scenarios and operations.

UND Aerospace has also provided training to aspiring pilots and air traffic controllers from around the world, including students from China, Japan, Saudi Arabia, and Norway.

UND Aerospace was first to offer an unmanned aircraft systems operations degree in 2009 and soon after became the first to be fully accredited. It is the birthplace for many innovations involving sense-and-avoid and beyond-visual-line-of-sight technologies, which are driving advances for commercial unmanned systems.

Another first for the aviation program at UND is in aviation safety. In 2016, UND became the first, and currently only, FAA "Part 141" flight school with an FAA-approved Safety Management System. The school also leads in using flight data in general aviation aircraft and analyzing aircraft fleet trends as a proactive safety approach.

North Dakota State University

The State Board of Higher Education authorized North Dakota State University (NDSU) to initiate an aviation program in 1972. The Department of Mechanical Engineering was assigned the administrative responsibility for the operation and coordination of this program. Michael Jesse Paulson, chief flight instructor of Fargo Jet Center, Inc., at Fargo Hector International Airport, has been the instructor for this program since 1989. The program courses include introduction to aviation, introduction to flight, commercial instrument ground school, and introduction to instrument flight.

Dakota Territory Air Museum

The Dakota Territory Air Museum was founded in 1986. Its mission is to be a vital historical aviation resource honoring the men, women, and machines that have impacted the rich history of aviation through displays and events that educate, inspire, and entertain people of all ages.

The Dakota Territory Air Museum provides educational programs and tours to expand aerospace opportunities for the state's youth.

Located on the north end of the Minot International Airport, the museum provides a virtual and physical window into the history of North Dakota's role in military, general, and commercial aviation.

The objective of the Dakota Territory Air Museum's educational program is to expand aerospace education opportunities for North Dakota youth. Tours are available during the museum's open season from May through October.

The Aviation Camp Experience (ACE) program is designed for third and fourth grade students. Camps are held at the museum on Saturdays from January through March. The ACE program introduces kids to overall aviation concepts involving hands-on fun and activities.

The Passport Aviation Camp Experience (PACE) program, designed for fifth- and sixth-grade students, introduces kids to a more in-depth aviation education involving hands-on experiments while focusing on one aviation topic per session. For each education session a child attends and completes, their passport is stamped by the museum. Attending the required five PACE sessions throughout the year earns a child enough stamps for a ride in an aircraft on a designated fly date.

The museum also hosts two guest speakers during the year to make aviation presentations to students, educators, and museum membership.

Fargo Air Museum

Started in 2001, the Fargo Air Museum is a nonprofit organization that promotes interest in aviation through education, preservation, and restoration. In addition to its display of aircraft, military memorabilia, and exhibits, the Fargo Air Museum houses one of the Midwest's largest aviation libraries. The museum engages the community by hosting seminars, events for military veterans, school partnerships, guided tours, and more.

The Fargo Air Museum hosts youth aviation education camps monthly for K-12 students. Experts in related careers join the museum instructors, who present STEM-based activities.

With funding from the North Dakota Aeronautics Commission, the museum welcomes classrooms for complimentary guided tours. Every other year, the museum hosts a Vietnam Memorial week that several area high school classes attend. The Fargo Air Museum houses historical aircraft, which coincides with curriculum, making it a valuable field trip destination. The museum hosts aviation-themed box office movie viewings, as well as the Veteran's Coffee Hour social connection event.

The primary mission of the Fargo Air Museum is to inspire new generations of aviators. The museum's education program provides opportunities designed to motivate future pilots, aircraft mechanics, air traffic controllers, and more. Aviation camps and school partnerships offer a variety of hands-on learning for school-age flight enthusiasts. The museum also offers group tours and activities for young children.

The Fargo Air Museum hosts monthly aviation education camps. Junior campers receive an introduction to each topic through active engagement, literature, guest presenters, and a variety of visual learning stimulation. Senior campers delve deeper into the same topics. The museum's educational programming addresses the need for pilots and technicians who service aircraft and drones. Students travel from Grand Forks, Wahpeton, Valley City, and surrounding cities for the museum's specialized aviation camps.

Unmanned Aircraft Systems

North Dakota is among the leaders in today's growing UAS industry.

The state of North Dakota not only has a deep history with unmanned aircraft systems (UAS), commonly referred to as drones, but also a wide breadth of operations across many entities. As the UAS industry has expanded for both military and civilian uses, North Dakota has been among those leading the charge. The range of UAS operations in North Dakota encompasses academia and research to military use to commercial operations. Through strong leadership at the highest levels of government, North Dakota has been able to position itself as a leader in UAS.

University of North Dakota

In 2006, the University of North Dakota (UND) was named a Department of Defense Center of Excellence for UAV Education, now called the Center for UAS Research, Education, and Training. UND researchers teaming in the Center represent the John D. Odegard School of Aerospace Sciences, School of Engineering and Mines, Northern Plains Center for Behavioral Research, and Center for Innovation.

The Center for UAS Research, Education, and Training designation provided a vehicle for convenient collaboration with the Grand Forks Air Force Base (AFB) and the Fargo Air National Guard, also designated UAS bases. UND was also invited to collaborate in UAS research and development with several private sector partners, including Lockheed Martin, Frasca International, Inc., and Alion Science and Technology. In addition, UND Aerospace was already collaborating with the FAA Center of Excellence for General Aviation Research on integrating UAS into the national airspace system and with Mayo Clinic for a Flight Medicine Residency incorporating UAS training.

The researchers involved in these cross-campus collaborations have a history of working together for more than 15 years in federally-supported projects,

A Hermes UAS in flight from UND.

including Department of Defense-funded human factors research, National Institutes of Health-funded human factors research, and NASA-funded airborne sensor development and flight training. These campus investigators, along with the Center for Innovation, work together to foster economic development in UAS and simulation applications.

The UND Research Institute for Autonomous Systems (RIAS), established in 2017, is built on the core UND values of community, lifelong learning, and discovery. The RIAS' mission is to create new autonomous systems through multidisciplinary research and lead development of world-changing autonomous policies, with the goal of driving a vibrant, diverse, and sustainable economy consistent with ethical and legal standards.

U.S. Customs and Border Protection

Grand Forks provides a strategic, central location for UAS operations in support of law enforcement personnel throughout the region. U.S. Customs and Border Protection (CBP) opened the Grand Forks Air Branch, the fourth of five branches on the northern border, in 2007. CBP's first Predator B UAS arrived on the northern border on December 6, 2008.

CBP Air and Marine's UAS reduces the number of personnel required to gain operational control of the border and can assist other law enforcement agencies upon request. Built by General Atomics Aeronautical Systems in San Diego, California, CBP Air and Marine's MQ-9 Predator B aircraft are capable of flying at speeds of up to 260 miles per hour for more than 18 hours at altitudes up to 50,000 feet. The aircraft is equipped with the state-of-the-art Raytheon electro-optical sensors. This advanced aircraft is also equipped with Synthetic Aperture Radar, helpful in documenting changes such as monitoring water levels due to flooding. The aircraft and crews support the CBP priority mission of anti-terrorism, as well as homeland security and disaster relief efforts. The virtually-piloted Predator B allows CBP Air and Marine personnel to safely conduct missions in areas that are difficult to access by CBP personnel on the ground.

National Air Security Operations-Grand Forks (NASOC-GF) operates fixed- and rotary-wing aircraft and UAS from Grand Forks AFB. NASOC-GF conducts initial and recurrent UAS training and enforcement operations with manned and unmanned aircraft. Additionally, NASOC-GF aids in disaster relief and emergency response efforts of its federal, state, local, and tribal partners.

CBP UAS completed more than 30 hours of flight time mapping the flood water in and around the Red River Valley flood areas in 2009. The three UAS mission flights were conducted in support of North Dakota and Minnesota emergency managers and the Federal Emergency Management Agency at the request of the state of North Dakota.

Northern Plains UAS Test Site

The U.S. FAA Modernization and Reform Act of 2012 was a pivotal bill for the UAS industry. Section 332 included guidance from Congress to the FAA to select six test sites around the country to help with the integration of UAS into the National Airspace System. On February 14, 2013, the FAA issued the Screening Information Request (SIR), or a Request for Proposal.

The North Dakota Airspace Integration Team was established to help support the response to the SIR. The purpose of the team was to bring private industry, university, and other North Dakota stakeholders together to provide "one voice" for North Dakota on UAS.

On May 28, 2013, Governor Jack Dalrymple signed Executive Order 2014-02, which established the Northern Plains Unmanned Systems Authority (Authority). As stated in the executive order, "The mission of the Authority is to oversee operation of a UAS test site for the integration of unmanned systems into the national airspace in a manner that is consistent with public safety and privacy and that is organized to allow full participation by private enterprise, public and private research organizations, and educational institutions."

The Authority consists of seven voting members:
1. The Lieutenant Governor, who serves as chairman;
2. The University of North Dakota Vice President of Research and Economic Development;
3. The North Dakota State University Vice President of Research and Creative Activity;
4. The Director of the North Dakota Aeronautics Commission;
5. The Commissioner of Commerce or the Commissioner's designee;
6. The Adjutant General or the Adjutant General's designee; and
7. An individual appointed by the Governor from a list of at least three names provided by the Aviation Council, who shall serve at the pleasure of the Governor for three-year terms of service.

In July 2013, Robert Becklund was hired as the first executive director of the Northern Plains UAS Test Site. On December 30, 2013, the Northern Plains UAS Test Site was selected along with representation from Alaska, Nevada, New York, Texas, and Virginia.

In April 2014, FAA Administrator Mike Huerta visited Grand Forks to declare the Northern Plains UAS Test Site had met the requirements to execute flight operations and to declare the first operational test site. In May 2014, the first UAS flight, using a Draganflyer X4-ES, was conducted under the provisions of the FAA Test Site Program in partnership with NDSU's Carrington Research Extension Center to support UAS agricultural applications.

UAS activity has continued to grow in the state, and the Northern Plains UAS Test Site has drawn national attention for its efforts in getting approval to fly beyond visual line of sight of the pilot and many other incremental approvals along the way. This national recognition has led many companies to not only use North Dakota as their proving grounds for advanced operations but also to establish a UAS business presence within the state.

The Northern Plains UAS Test Site has worked with many private entities to research everything from precision agriculture to the inspection of transmission lines for the utility industry. It has also partnered with NASA and the FAA to support federal initiatives.

Commercial UAS Use

It was not until September 2014 that the first commercial operations of UAS were authorized in the United States. Under the FAA Modernization and Reform Act of 2012, Section 333 allowed for applicants to request a petition of exemption from certain regulations that were prohibiting the use of commercial UAS in the National Airspace System. As a part of the process to receive the exemptions, the applicants had to show their UAS operations would not adversely affect safety or would provide at least an equal level of safety to the rules from which they sought the exemptions. More than 5,500 exemptions were accepted by the FAA, with North Dakota companies receiving 22 exemptions to fly UAS commercially.

On August 29, 2016, the operational rules for routine non-hobbyist use of small UAS were issued by the FAA. The provisions of this rule, formally known as Part 107, are designed to minimize risks to other aircraft and people and property on the ground. Part 107 of the regulation has many restrictions for operators to fly under. The UAS must weigh less than 55 pounds and must remain within visual line of sight of the remote pilot in command and the person manipulating the flight controls of the small UAS. This new regulation has allowed many operators across the state of North Dakota to use UAS as a part of their businesses.

As of November 2018, almost 1.3 million drones were registered in the United States, with almost 3,500 registered in North Dakota.

Grand Sky Business Park

An underutilized space at Grand Force AFB was turned into something special for North Dakota. Plans were developed for the county of Grand Forks to enter into a long-term lease with the U.S. Air Force to develop an unmanned aircraft business park. The county entered into an agreement for an outside, private company to run this business park. On February 18, 2015, Grand Sky, America's first UAS business and aviation park, opened and accepted applications for build-to-suit site tenancy. On that day, the U.S. Air Force, Grand Forks County, and Grand Sky Development Company commemorated the execution of an Enhanced Use Lease during a ceremony at Grand Forks AFB, officially marking the commencement of the park's development.

Northrop Grumman, a Global Security company, was the first tenant to sign a lease at Grand Sky and broke ground for its facility on October 15, 2015. The company is a major provider of systems and technology to the U.S. Air Force, including the RQ-4 Global Hawk, a large autonomous aircraft system which is used at the nearby Grand Forks AFB.

Northrop Grumman intended to use its Grand Sky facility primarily for research and development, aircrew and maintenance training, operations and mission analysis, and aircraft maintenance. The facility was positioned in an anchor space along the alert pad at Grand Sky, which allows quick access to the Grand Forks AFB runway for launch and recovery operations. Just four months after officially opening its facility at Grand Sky, Northrop Grumman announced plans to double its physical footprint at the park.

On March 30, 2016, officials of the U.S. Air Force and Grand Forks County signed a Joint Use Agreement (JUA) that allows tenants at Grand Sky to launch and recover both manned and unmanned aircraft from the military's 12,351-foot runway at Grand Forks AFB. The JUA is unique in that it allows manned, unmanned, and optionally manned commercial aircraft to utilize the runway.

On August 22, 2017, General Atomics Aeronautical Systems, Inc., (GA-ASI) held a grand opening event for its new hangar at the Grand Sky Business Park. The event included a ribbon-cutting ceremony to commemorate the completion of GA-ASI's new Flight Test and Training Center hangar, which houses GA-ASI operational hardware, including Remotely Piloted Aircraft and Ground Control Stations, as well as offices and conference rooms.

North Dakota State University

UAS provide a significant opportunity for many areas of research at North Dakota State University (NDSU). Opportunities exist for technology-based research in such areas as airframe design, flight controls, propulsion systems, power management, and sensor payloads. Other types of research are focused on the countless potential applications for the technology, including agriculture production, transportation infrastructure monitoring, public utility inspections, land surveying, construction, and plant and wildlife surveys.

Flying the DJI S100 at the NDSU Agronomy Seed Farm.

Personnel in several departments at NDSU are using UAS in teaching, research, and Extension. The Agricultural and Biosystems Engineering Department (ABEN) has been collaborating with UND, Northern Plains UAS Test Site, private companies, state government agencies, and farmers since 2014 to demonstrate ways to use UAS in agriculture.

The ABEN faculty are leading UAS applications to improve crop management, including conducting plant stand counts; quantifying crop health; and identifying crop diseases, nutrient deficiencies, and insect damage. The department has an inventory of small unmanned aerial vehicle (UAV) equipment, including fixed-wing and rotocopter vehicles. These small UAVs operate autonomously for up to an hour with single power supplies. The department's equipment inventory includes a variety of cameras and sensors developed specifically for small UAVs, including color, multispectral, hyperspectral, and thermal cameras.

A significant objective of NDSU's UAS work is identifying individual weeds in crop fields, quantifying areas of weed infestations, and identifying herbicide-resistant weeds. Researchers are using thermal imagery on UAVs to identify herbicide-resistant weeds after applying an initial herbicide application.

The NDSU ABEN Department recently acquired an autonomous UAS sprayer. The UAS sprayer is a small, electric-powered rotocopter that weighs approximately 30 pounds and operates for 30 minutes on one battery. The ABEN personnel are evaluating the sprayer capabilities and intend to demonstrate the use of it to spray individual herbicide-resistant weeds and small weed patches.

ABEN personnel are also collaborating with others at NDSU on additional UAS imagery applications, including identifying types and areas of flowers visited by natural bee pollinators. Another project is using UAS imagery to identify sharp-tailed grouse leks and count the number of grouse at each lek, which is the area where the grouse gather in the springtime for mating.

The NDSU ABEN Department is collaborating with Elbit Systems of America to demonstrate the potential uses of UAS capable of collecting imagery of thousands of acres per hour. The large UAS project was conducted in Cass, Traill, Steele, and Grand Forks counties.

The small UAS projects are being conducted at each of the seven NDSU Research Extension Centers across North Dakota. In addition to ABEN personnel using UAS, the Research Extension Centers at Carrington and Williston have purchased UAVs and cameras and are incorporating UAS imagery into their ongoing crop research.

The NDSU ABEN Department began a new precision agriculture major and minor in 2019. The department offers five courses directly related to data management, mapping, electronics, and robotics for precision agriculture. Each precision agriculture student acquires a UAS Part 107 license from the FAA as a part of their major.

Finally, NDSU is developing a Center for Digital Agriculture and Big Data. A primary objective of the center will be to promote the UAS applications and include the image analyses data in big data applications for crop and livestock production.

UAS Integration Pilot Program

First announced in October 2017, the UAS Integration Pilot Program was a White House initiative that partnered the FAA with local, state, and tribal governments, which then can partner with private sector participants to safely explore the further integration of drone operations. The UAS Integration Pilot Program helps tackle the most significant challenges to integrating drones into the national airspace and reduces risks to public safety and security. The program is a coordinated effort to provide certainty and stability to communities, drone owners, and the rapidly evolving drone industry. In less than a decade, the potential economic benefit of integrating UAS in the nation's airspace is estimated at $82 billion and could create 100,000 jobs.

The U.S. Department of Transportation (USDOT) and the FAA carefully evaluated each of the 149 proposals received according to the requirements outlined in the program's SIR. The 10 finalists then worked with the FAA to refine their operational concepts through Memorandums of Agreement.

Over a two-and-a-half-year period, the selectees collected drone data involving night operations, flights over people and beyond the pilot's line of sight, package delivery, detect-and-avoid technologies, and the reliability and security of data links between pilot and aircraft. The data collected from these operations help the

USDOT and the FAA craft new enabling rules that allow more complex low-altitude operations, as well as identify ways to balance local and national interests related to UAS integration, improve communications with local, state, and tribal jurisdictions, address security and privacy risks, and accelerate the approval of operations that currently require special authorizations.

On May 9, 2018, the North Dakota Department of Transportation (NDDOT) was selected as one of 10 participants in the UAS Integration Pilot Program. The program enables agencies to work on policies that can safely advance UAS operations, including beyond visual line of sight, flights over people, and night operations. As the lead applicant and program manager in North Dakota, the NDDOT works with partners and stakeholders from across the state, including the Northern Plains UAS Test Site in Grand Forks and city, state, and tribal agencies.

Aviation Hall of Fame

The North Dakota Aviation Hall of Fame was established in 1997 to honor those who have made major achievements in aviation in North Dakota. Inductees must have the following attributes:

- Major achievements in aviation in North Dakota.
- Significant contributions to the development of others in aviation in North Dakota.
- Special service to the state of North Dakota in aviation activities.
- Activities that bring credit to North Dakota aviation, either nationally or internationally.
- Significant contributions to the local community or the state of North Dakota that are not related to aviation (i.e., service clubs, church related, political activities, etc.).

The Aviation Hall of Fame committee is led by the executive director of the North Dakota Aeronautics Commission and meets annually to select new inductees.

The North Dakota Aviation Hall of Fame is located in the terminal building at the Bismarck Municipal Airport. Kiosks containing information regarding each inductee also exist at the Fargo Air Museum, Minot Air Museum, and the Bismarck Heritage Center.

Video introductions of recent Hall of Fame inductees are available at https://aero.nd.gov.

North Dakota Aviation Hall of Fame Inductees

Name	Year Inducted
Carl Ben Eielson	1997
Leland Brand	1997
Jack Daniels	1997
Charles Klessig	1997
Duane "Pappy" Larson	1997
Oscar Ness	1997
Thomas Nord	1997
Alfred C. Piestch	1997
Art Sampson	1997
Harold Vavra	1997
Wilbur E. Brewer	1998
Daniel Wakefield	1998
John D. Odegard	1999
Warren Walkinshaw	1999
Vincent S. Buraas	2000
Ernest "Hod" Hutson	2000
Alfred Dahl	2001
Gordon W. Person	2001
Jack and Bob Watts	2001
Thomas Clifford	2002
Palmer "PT" Foss	2002
Vernon Baltzer	2003
Richard Halldorson	2004
Clifford Beeks	2005
Phillip Miller	2005
Edward A. Skroch, Sr.	2006
Robert "Bob" Milller	2007
Kenneth Koehn	2007
Gerald "Gerry" Beck	2008
Roger L. Pffeifer	2009
Darrol G. Schroeder	2009
Ronald P. Deck	2010
Alexander Macdonald	2010
Robert "Bob" Odegaard	2011
Jay B. Lindquist	2012
Geneva Schow Oleson	2013
Martin Schow	2014
Robert H. Simmers	2015
Fred Adams	2016
Gary Ness	2016
Don Larson	2017
Rod Brekken	2018
Brian Rau	2019

The range of UAS operations in North Dakota encompasses academia and research to military use to commercial operations, positioning the state as a leader in the country's UAS industry.

Chapter Two
North Dakota Almanac

A team of oxen hitched to a covered wagon stands near a passenger plane at the Bismarck Airport in the 1930s.

State Origin, Symbols, and Official Designations 44
North Dakota State Capitol and Grounds 67
Theodore Roosevelt Rough Rider Award 82
North Dakota Statistical Information 128
North Dakota Tourism 138
North Dakota Theatre 145
100 Years of Caring for North Dakota Injured Workers 146
Bank of North Dakota Celebrates Its First 100 Years 147

North Dakota
Origin of the Name

On March 2, 1861, President James Buchanan signed the bill creating the Dakota Territory, which originally included the area covered today by both Dakotas as well as much of Montana and Wyoming. The name was taken from that of the Dakota or Sioux Indian Tribe. Beginning about 1877, efforts were made to bring Dakota into the Union as both a single state and as two states. The latter was successful, and on November 2, 1889, both North and South Dakota were admitted.

Since President Benjamin Harrison went to great lengths to obscure the order in which the statehood proclamations were signed, the exact order in which the two states entered is unknown. However, because of alphabetical position, North Dakota is often considered as the 39th state.

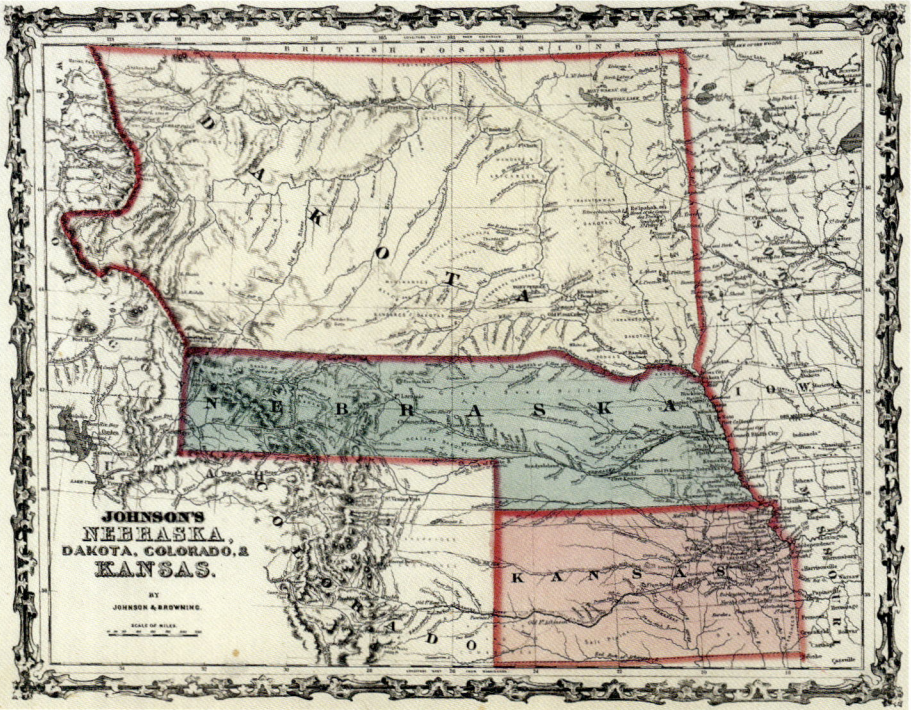

This 1862 Dakota Territory map by Johnson and Browning includes part of the present states of Montana and Wyoming. It shows numerous Indian tribes and their homelands, but the new territorial capital at Yankton is not located on the map. The eastern boundary of Dakota Territory is in the general area, but not quite tied to the Red River of the North.

Nicknames

Peace Garden State – The International Peace Garden straddles the international boundary between North Dakota and the Canadian province of Manitoba. In 1956, the North Dakota Motor Vehicle Department, on its own initiative, placed the words "Peace Garden State" on license plates. The name proved so popular that it was formally adopted by the 1957 Legislature (North Dakota Century Code [NDCC], Section 39-04-12).

Flickertail State – Flickertail refers to the Richardson ground squirrel, which is abundant in North Dakota. The animal flicks or jerks its tail in a characteristic manner while running or just before entering its burrow. On December 15, 1889, during the first session of the North Dakota Legislature, Representative Frank Thompson from Cass County introduced the following resolution in the House:

A flickertail peering out of his home.

Whereas, The Spirmophilus Richardsoni, or flicker-tail gopher, is a creature endemic to this land of the Dakotas; therefore be it Resolved, That we, the house of representatives of the state of North Dakota, do by this resolution christen every child born or who may hereafter be born within the boundaries of this state with the name "Flickertail," which christened name shall be applied in the same manner as the word "Sucker" is applied to children born in Illinois, "Wolverine" to those born in Michigan, "Badger" to those born in Wisconsin, etc.

The resolution was adopted and, for 10 minutes, North Dakota stood dubbed "the Flickertail state." It was then reconsidered and all mention of it was expunged from the House Journal. In 1953, the Legislative Assembly defeated Senate Bill (S.B.) 134 that would have adopted the Flickertail facsimile as the official emblem of the state.

Roughrider State – This name originated in a state-supported tourism promotion of the 1960s and 1970s. It refers to the First U.S. Volunteer Cavalry, which Theodore Roosevelt organized to fight in the Spanish-American War. In fact, the "Roughriders," which included several North Dakota cowboys, fought dismounted in Cuba due to logistical problems. In both 1971 (H.B. 1383) and 1973 (H.B. 1443), the Legislative Assembly defeated bills intended to change the words "Peace Garden State" on state license plates to "Roughrider Country."

Dakota – An attempt to drop the word "North" from the state name was defeated by the 1947 Legislative Assembly (House Concurrent Resolution [H.C.R.] J). Again in 1989, the Legislature rejected two resolutions (Senate Concurrent Resolutions [S.C.R.] 4031 and 4032) intended to rename the state "Dakota."

Great Seal of North Dakota

From the time of its ratification in 1889, North Dakota's Constitution has always contained the same detailed description of the state's Great Seal. Now found in Section Two of Article XI (titled General Provisions), the description of the Great Seal was initially located in Section Two of Article XVII (titled Miscellaneous) in the 1889 version of the Constitution. Some of the wording contained in the Constitution's description is the same as that used for the territorial seal approved on January 3, 1863, by the Legislative Assembly of the Territory of Dakota.

The description reads as follows: A tree in the open field, the trunk of which is surrounded by three bundles of wheat; on the right a plow, anvil and sledge; on the left, a bow crossed with three arrows, and an Indian on horseback pursuing a buffalo toward the setting sun; the foliage of the tree arched by a half circle of 42 stars, surrounded by the motto "Liberty and Union Now and Forever, One and Inseparable;" the words "Great Seal" at the top; the words "State of North Dakota" at the bottom; "October 1st" on the left and "1889" on the right.

Research has failed to reveal the reasons the selected symbols were chosen. As a result, various theories have been advanced over the years. For example, the tree has been identified as an American Elm. However, the American Elm was not adopted as the state's official tree until 1947. The three bundles of wheat could represent the three branches of government – executive, legislative, and judicial. The plow, anvil, and sledge may make reference to the agricultural background of the state and to its strong work ethic. The bow and arrows, buffalo, Indian on horseback, and setting sun could be reminders of an integral segment in the history of the northern plains. The motto is a quote by Daniel Webster.

Although North Dakota became the 39th state, the seal has 42 stars across the top. Since it was not known at statehood as to which "number" North Dakota would be, it is assumed that the stars represent the 42 states that would comprise the Union by the end of 1889.

While the content has generally been true to the description, the design of the Great Seal itself has varied through the years. The first known design is found in the *1887 Blue Book*. There were designs with slight variations from its predecessor in at least 1899, 1907, 1909, 1911, 1913, 1919, 1926, 1929, 1973, and 1987. In the spring of 1987, then-Secretary of State Ben Meier commissioned Dickinson artist Lili Stewart to create a new design. That design was approved on September 17, 1987, and is still used today.

Since statehood, the Secretary of State has been charged with the custody of the Great Seal. The first legislation related to the Great Seal was passed by the First Legislative Assembly in 1890 (S.B. 23). Nevertheless, relatively few changes in the law were made through the years. A major change was made in 1975 which

North Dakota's seal is shown here in three presentations.

prohibited the use of the Great Seal in advertising and for commercial purposes. An exception was passed in 1985 (effective until June 30, 1991) allowing the use of the Great Seal for approved commercial purposes as a part of North Dakota's Centennial Celebration. Otherwise, for many years the use of the Great Seal was largely dependent on numerous opinions issued by the Attorney General.

To more clearly define the acceptable uses of the Great Seal and to end the dependency on the opinions, S.B. 2448 was passed by the 1995 Legislative Assembly. The bill gave the Secretary of State greater flexibility and authority in carrying out the custodial responsibilities related to the Great Seal. In addition, it specifically prohibited the use of the Great Seal for political purposes. The existing law was also amended to allow the Great Seal to be reproduced, with the concurrence of the Secretary of State, on items offered for sale as gifts and souvenirs by the State Historical Society and the Parks and Recreation Department.

The bronze likeness of the Great Seal in the Capitol's Memorial Hall was dedicated in a ceremony held on February 22, 2006. It measures six feet across and weighs 440 pounds. The Capitol Grounds Planning Commission undertook the project to coincide with the 117th anniversary of the Enabling Act, which allowed North Dakota, South Dakota, Montana, and Washington to join the Union as individual states. The seal and its commemorative 570-pound plaque were made by Metal Arts Company, a Mandan foundry. The seal, plaque, and installation cost approximately $48,000.

State Motto

"Liberty and Union Now and Forever, One and Inseparable" is the state motto (North Dakota Constitution Article XI, Section 2).

The motto of Dakota Territory was "Liberty and Union, One and Inseparable, Now and Forever." This language was suggested by Dr. Joseph Ward of Yankton, South Dakota, who was quoting from Daniel Webster's *Reply to Hayne*. However, the motto used for the Territory had two of the phrases reversed; when North Dakota became a state, that error was corrected.

State Latin Motto

A state Latin motto was adopted by the 62nd Legislative Assembly in 2011, creating a new section to Chapter 54-02 of the North Dakota Century Code.

"Serit ut alteri saeclo prosit." "One sows for the benefit of another age."

A State Creed
(Never Officially Adopted)

We believe in North Dakota, in the beauty of her skies, and in the glory of her prairies.

We believe in the People of North Dakota, in their strength of Body and Mind, in their High Sense of Right, and in their Desire to establish a Great Commonwealth wherein the things that count for Human Welfare shall be first.

We believe that by Thought and Act we can magnify our State and the Life of our People, bind the East and the West, the North and the South by Roadways, Communication and Good Will, and give our Sons and Daughters the Opportunity to Work at Useful Tasks within our borders.

We pledge to those seeking new homes the Hand of Hospitality and extend to them a Welcome to our Commonwealth where they may find Peace and Happiness.

We pledge that the freedom our Fathers won here and elsewhere shall continue as the Heritage of our Children.

We, as a People, because of growing Intelligence and a Nobler Outlook, seek Unity of Purpose; we desire to lead a Richer Common Life, and hope to render a Larger Service to the State and the Nation.

(This state creed, written by Frank L. McVey, former president of the University of North Dakota, is first found in the *1926 Manual for the State of North Dakota*.)

The State Flag

On January 21, 1911, Representative Colonel John H. Fraine introduced H.B. 152 designating an official flag for the state of North Dakota (1911 S.L., ch. 283). The legislation specifically required that the flag conform to the color, form, and size of the regimental flag carried by the North Dakota Infantry in the Spanish-American War in 1898 and Philippine Island Insurrection in 1899; the only exception was the name "North Dakota" placed on the scroll below the eagle. On March 3, 1911, the Legislative Assembly adopted the North Dakota state flag. North Dakota Century Code Section 54-02-02 describes the state flag in detail.

In 1951, S.B. 156 established the North Dakota State Flag Commission to consider changes to the flag (1951 S.L., ch. 303). The commission concluded the flag "too closely resembled the coat of arms of the United States and that the flag was not symbolic of North Dakota." The commission's conclusions were widely challenged and its suggested changes rejected. S.B. 265 was introduced during the 1953 session and contained the recommendations of the flag commission. That legislation was defeated.

In 2011, H.B. 1097 established design and color codes for the flag. The State Historical Society is required to provide to the public a description in writing of the flag, and any flags purchased by a state entity or a political subdivision must substantially meet the requirements of this section.

Although there are requests for information regarding a 39-star flag for North Dakota, such a flag never existed. North Dakota was the 39th state to be admitted to the Union. It entered at the same time as three other states, and a separate flag was never made for North Dakota.

State Coat of Arms and the Governor's Flag

In 1957, the Legislative Assembly passed H.B. 822, sponsored by Representatives Clifford Lindberg and Gillman Olson, to create the North Dakota coat of arms (1957 S.L., ch. 330). When the Governor is using the coat of arms as a flag, there must be a white star placed in each of the four corners (North Dakota Century Code Section 54-41-04). The North Dakota coat of arms was displayed for the first time by the National Guard at Camp Grafton on June 16, 1957.

54-41-02 Significant elements of coat of arms – The colors of yellow, gold, and green are indicative of the great agricultural state of North Dakota and has particular reference to ripening grain and the abundant grazing areas. The Indian arrowhead forms the shield of the coat of arms and symbolizes the "Sioux State." The three stars denote the trinity of government: legislative, executive, and judicial. Each star in the bend is given the heraldic value of thirteen, which signifies the thirteen original colonies of the United States, and the cumulative numerical value of the three stars indicates that North Dakota was the thirty-ninth state admitted to the Union. The stars also allude to the history of the territory under three foreign flags. Three stars are borne upon the coat of arms of Meriwether Lewis of the Lewis and Clark expedition and also on the coat of arms of Lord Selkirk, head of the first permanent settlement in this state. The fleur-de-lis alludes to LaVerendrye, a French explorer who was the first known white man to visit the territory of this state. The blue and gold wreath in the crest reflects the history of the territory as part of the Louisiana Purchase. The crest, which shall constitute the military crest of the state of North Dakota, is a motif taken from the state seal, and to the Sioux Indian tribes, signifies mighty warriors.

State Coat of Arms

54-41-03 Authorized use – The coat of arms of this state may be used in a manner consistent with the respect and dignity due a state coat of arms and its symbolic values by the following persons, organizations, and agencies:

1. The governor of North Dakota.

2. The North Dakota national guard.

3. Departments and agencies of the state of North Dakota.

4. North Dakota veterans organizations.

5. Officially recognized North Dakota educational institutions, systems, or divisions thereof.

6. Recognized North Dakota patriotic organizations.

Constitution of North Dakota

The Constitution of North Dakota was adopted on October 1, 1889, with a vote of 27,441 to 8,107. As of July 2019, the North Dakota Constitution has 21,357 words.

State Flower
(North Dakota Century Code Section 54-02-03)

Wild Prairie Rose (Rosa Blanda or Arkansana) – The flower has been identified as Rosa Pratincula in species.

Created by: 1907 S.L., ch. 231, S.B. 134
Sponsored by: Senator Louis B. Hanna

The flower sports five bright pink petals with a tight cluster of yellow stamens in the center. The wild prairie rose grows along roadsides, in pastures, and in native meadows.

State Bird
(North Dakota Century Code Section 54-02-06)

Western Meadowlark (Sturnella Neglecta)

Created by: 1947 S.L., ch. 329, H.B. 270
Sponsored by: Representatives John Halcrow, Alexandar Dalzell, Freeman M. Einarson, Palmer Levin, Leo E. Callahan, Daniel Power, Arthur W. Benno, Winfield M. Smart, Walter Bubel

Approximately the size of a robin, the meadowlark sports a yellow breast with a black bib over its mottled brown body. These song birds are found from Wisconsin to Texas and westward to the Pacific.

State Tree
(North Dakota Century Code Section 54-02-05)

**American Elm
(Ulmus Americana)**

Created by: 1947 S.L., ch. 329, H.B. 270
Sponsored by: Representatives John Halcrow, Alexandar Dalzell, Freeman M. Einarson, Palmer Levin, Leo E. Callahan, Daniel Power, Arthur W. Benno, Winfield M. Smart, Walter Bubel

Common across the state, the American Elm can reach 120 feet or taller. The tallest American Elm in the state has been recorded by the North Dakota Forest Service at 87 feet.

State Insect
(North Dakota Century Code Section 54-02)

**Convergent Lady Beetle
(Hippodamia Convergens)**

Created by: 2011 S.L., ch. 54-02, H.B. 1219
Sponsored by: Representatives Glen Froseth, Patrick Hatlestad, Gary Kreidt; Senator Karen Krebsbach

The convergent lady beetle is commonly known as a ladybug. A group of second graders from Kenmare lobbied for this legislation.

State Fruit
(North Dakota Century Code Section 54-02-17)

Chokecherry (Prunus Virginiana)

Created by: 2007 S.L. ch. 452, S.B. 2145
Sponsored by: Senators Stanley Lyson, Nicholas Hacker; Representatives Patrick Hatlestad, Gary Sukut

Mentioned by Lewis and Clark in their journals and long a staple of the Native Americans on the Northern Plains, the chokecherry is a thicket forming shrub or small tree and is a valuable habitat for birds and small game animals. The fruit, which is deep red and relatively small in size, is somewhat bitter tasting when taken from the plant but is prized for making jams, wines, and syrups.

The designation was spearheaded by the sixth grade class at Rickard Elementary School in Williston, which lobbied for a state fruit beginning in February 2006.

State Song
(North Dakota Century Code Section 54-02-04)

North Dakota Hymn with words by James W. Foley and music by Dr. C. S. Putnam

Created by: 1947 S.L., ch. 327, H.B. 130
Sponsored by: Representatives Kenneth Fitch, Charles Yirchott, Clair Brickner, John Brady, Arthur Johnson

In 1926, Minnie J. Nielson, North Dakota Superintendent of Public Instruction, asked Poet Laureate James Foley of Bismarck to write the lyrics for a song about North Dakota. Foley created a poem that could be sung to the tune, *The Austrian Hymn*. Dr. C. S. Putnam, conductor of the North Dakota Agricultural College Band in Fargo, arranged music for Foley's work. The first public presentation of the *North Dakota Hymn* was in the Bismarck City Auditorium in 1927.

The *North Dakota Hymn* is found on the following pages.

State Art Museum
(North Dakota Century Code Section 54-02-11)

Established in 1972 at the University of North Dakota in Grand Forks, the state's first professional art gallery researches, records, collects, and exhibits North Dakota's visual art history. Gallery leadership in the development of cultural life through art was recognized by the Legislative Assembly. In the fall of 1996, the State Board of Higher Education transferred ownership of the gallery to a private, nonprofit organization – the Friends of the Museum of Art.

The University of North Dakota Art Galleries were known as the State Art Gallery until the 2003 Legislative Assembly changed the name to North Dakota Art Museum.

Created by: 1981 S.L., ch. 519, S.B. 2359
Sponsored by: Senator Evan Lips; Representatives Jim Gerl, Michael Unhjem

Amended by: 2003 S.L., ch. 456, S.B. 2318
Sponsored by: Senators Duaine C. Espegard, Linda Christiansen, Ray Holmberg; Representative Eliot Glassheim

State Fossil
(North Dakota Century Code Section 54-02-08)

Teredo-bored Petrified Wood

Created by: 1967 S.L., ch. 378, H.B. 933
Sponsored by: Representative Wayne Sanstead

The Teredo was a worm-shaped mollusk related to clams, mussels, and oysters. It burrowed its way through sequoias and other trees growing near warm-water swamps in North Dakota 60 to 80 million years ago. As the trees in the mineral rich water petrified, some of the wood was replaced by silica and quartz, thereby preserving evidence of the Teredo. North Dakota was not represented in the Smithsonian Institution's mineral collection. Naming of the Teredo-bored petrified wood as the state fossil remedied that situation and promoted the fossil to tourists, geologists, and rockhounds.

State Fish

Northern Pike (Esox Lucius)

Created by: 1969 S.L., p. 1385, S.C.R. 21
Sponsored by: Senators Frank Wenstrom, Robert Chesrown, John Decker, Guy Larson

North Dakota waters have yielded mammoth size Northern Pike, resulting in a national sports fishing reputation for the state.

Official Academy of Science

North Dakota Academy of Science (originally at the University of North Dakota, moved to North Dakota State University in 1989)

Created by: 1959 S.L., p. 920, H.C.R. "X"
Sponsored by: Senators George Longmire, George Saumur

The purpose of the academy is to promote and conduct scientific research and disseminate scientific knowledge. Toward that end, the North Dakota Science Research Foundation raises funds and distributes grants on behalf of the academy.

State March
(North Dakota Century Code Section 54-02-09)

Flickertail March

Created by: 1989 S.L., ch. 628, H.B. 1671
Sponsored by: Representative Harold Trautman

In 1975, the Legislative Assembly passed H.B. 1160, which designated James D. Ployhar's *Spirit of the Land* as the official state march (1975 S.L., ch. 462). Ployhar had been commissioned by the North Dakota Band Directors Association to compose a march appropriate for official state functions. *Spirit of the Land* was played in the Capitol's Memorial Hall by the Jamestown High School Band on the day the bill passed the House of Representatives in February 1975. Once designated as the state march, *Spirit of the Land* was sent to a publisher. The title happened to be nearly identical to that of another march. As a result, the publisher requested a new title be selected. Ployhar agreed to *Flickertail March*. In 1989, the Legislative Assembly approved the change.

Official Salmon Derby

Trophy Takers Salmon Club's Blackjaw Fever Salmon Derby

Created by: 1989 S.L., ch. 892, S.C.R. 4038
Sponsored by: Senator Joe Keller; Representatives Bob O'Shea, Lyle Hanson, Clarence Martin

The Blackjaw Fever Salmon Derby annually brings in contestants from many states and North Dakota communities to Lake Sakakawea. To recognize the economic impact of the derby and its role in promoting tourism through sport fishing, the Legislative Assembly made this designation.

Sports Hall of Fame

Created by: 1993 S.L., ch. 737, S.C.R. 4030
Sponsored by: Senators David E. Nething, Dale Marks; Representatives Lyle L. Hanson, John M. Howard, Joe Kroeber, Terry M. Wanzek

To honor persons who worked to promote and develop athletics in North Dakota, the Legislative Assembly established the Sports Hall of Fame in Jamestown.

Official High School Hockey Flag

Created by: 1977 S.L., p. 1438, H.C.R. 3035
Sponsored by: Representative Earl Strinden

The 1976 Bicentennial state high school hockey tournament displayed an official flag that became the North Dakota state high school hockey flag. It recognized the growing popularity of the sport.

State Beverage
(North Dakota Century Code Section 54-02-12)

Milk

Created by: 1983 S.L., ch. 548, H.B. 1301
Sponsored by: Representatives Leslie Gullickson, Brynhild Haugland, Charles Mertens; Senators Francis Barth, Pete Naaden

By official designation, the Legislative Assembly recognized the importance of North Dakota's dairy industry.

Agricultural Hall of Fame

Created by: 1997 S.L., ch. 70, H.B. 1362
Sponsored by: Representatives Gereld F. Gerntholz, Robert Huether, Leland Sabby; Senators Larry J. Robinson, Terry M. Wanzek

Established to recognize individuals who have made outstanding contributions to the state's agricultural industry, the Agricultural Hall of Fame is officially located at the North Dakota Winter Show in Valley City.

State Grass
(North Dakota Century Code Section 54-02-10)

Western Wheatgrass (Agropyron Smithii)

Created by: 1977 S.L., ch. 475, S.B. 2444
Sponsored by: Senators Kenneth Morgan, Robert Albers, Francis Barth

Western Wheatgrass, a tough native prairie grass, once covered nearly all of the state. The North Dakota Chapter of the Society for Range Management called for adopting an official state grass. Western Wheatgrass was selected for its adaptability to soil conditions, its performance record for hay and pasture, and its role in range management as a species found in all the state's counties.

State Dance
(North Dakota Century Code Section 54-02-16)

Square Dance

Created by: 1995 S.L., ch. 492, H.B. 1412
Sponsored by: Representatives Ben Tollefson, Bob Martinson, Clara Sue Price, RaeAnn Kelsch; Senators Terry M. Wanzek, Corliss Mushik

The 1995 Legislative Assembly designated the square dance as the official American folk dance of North Dakota.

Fort Mandan and Lewis and Clark Interpretive Center

Created by: 1995 S.L., ch. 493, S.C.R. 4029
Sponsored: by: Senator Layton W. Freborg; Representatives Jeff W. Delzer, Albert "Mick" Grosz

The 1995 Legislative Assembly designated Fort Mandan and the Lewis and Clark Interpretive Center as the official Lewis and Clark Bicentennial Project for North Dakota.

State Language
(North Dakota Century Code Section 54-02-13)

English

Created by: 1987 S.L., ch. 619, S.B. 2096
Sponsored by: Senators Harvey Tallackson, Pete Naaden, Earl Kelly; Representatives Rosemarie Myrdal, Orville Schindler

North Dakota joined other states in a nationwide movement to make English the official language. Opposition came from organizations and persons fearing loss of foreign and native language or diminished access to diversity of other cultures. Supporters acknowledged the measure and legalized what was already in practice. The designation made official the common bond that allows for communication and conduct of business.

State Railroad Museum
(North Dakota Century Code Section 54-02-14)

Mandan Railroad Museum

Created by: 1989 S.L., ch. 629, S.B. 2496
Sponsored by: Senators Corliss Mushik, Walter Meyer; Representatives Dan Ulmer, Jim Gerl, Dick Tokach

Selection of the Mandan Railroad Museum, established in 1972, reflects the importance of Mandan as a railroad town. Since 1989 was the state's centennial year, legislators also recognized the influence of railroads in North Dakota history.

First Nations Day
(North Dakota Century Code Section 01-03-13)

Created by: 2003 S.L., S.B. 2410
Sponsored by: Senators Dennis Bercier, April Fairfield, Ronald Nichols, David O'Connell, Harvey D. Tallackson; Representative Merle Boucher

To recognize the indigenous peoples of the State of North Dakota and their contributions to the state and to the United States, the governor shall issue a proclamation each year designating the Friday before the second Monday in October as First Nations Day.

Honorary Equine

(North Dakota Century Code Section 54-02-15)

Nokota Horse

Created by: 1993 S.L., ch. 504, S.B. 2498
Sponsored by: Senator Pete Naaden

The Nokota breed may well be those distinct horses descended from Sioux Chief Sitting Bull's war ponies. Some still run wild in Theodore Roosevelt National Park.

North Dakota Governors

✔ Biographies and photos of North Dakota governors can be found in the *2001-2003 North Dakota Blue Book*.

Aerial shot of the North Dakota state capitol grounds.

North Dakota State Capitol and Grounds

State Capitol

North Dakota's present capitol is, like many of the state's residents, a child of the Great Depression of the 1930s. It was designed and built after fire destroyed the original capitol on December 28, 1930. Hard-pressed for cash, the 1931 Legislative Assembly scraped together funds from a number of sources: insurance, income from the sale and rental of land assigned to capitol development since statehood, and a decades-old capitol building fund. Then legislators placed a $2 million limit on expenditures for the new building.

The three-member Board of State Capitol Commissioners charged with overseeing construction sorted through a series of proposals offered by architects from throughout the country before selecting Chicago architects John A. Holabird and John W. Root to design the building. To fulfill a statutory requirement that North Dakota architects participate in the design process, William F. Kurke of Fargo and Joseph Bell DeRemer of Grand Forks were designated as associates to the Chicago firm.

The selection of Holabird & Root probably related to the firm's long experience with tall, office-style structures, a building style which found favor with the commissioners after visits to Lincoln, Nebraska, and Baton Rouge, Louisiana, where skyscraper capitol projects were nearing completion. The final design combined a 19-story tower, intended to house the executive and judicial branches of government, with a legislative wing, fronted by a columned memorial hall. The tower, in both massing and details, closely resembled another Holabird & Root project, the Ramsey County Courthouse-St. Paul City Hall, then being built in St. Paul, Minnesota.

Historically, capitols have offered an opportunity for states to show off their culture and development through the lavish use of art in the form of paintings and sculpture. The spending limit imposed by the legislative assembly made this almost impossible for the Bismarck building. The architect's selection of Moderne architecture and its companion decorative form, Art Deco, both focused largely on geometric shapes, offering opportunities for inexpensive decoration. To save money, this style was limited to the legislative wing and the lower two floors of the tower. More than half of the tower's interior was left unfinished in 1934. Later the area was decorated by Depression-era federal agencies which utilized the space as the 1930s progressed.

Ironically, the first state capitol, originally that of the Dakota Territory, built in 1883-1884 with additions in 1893-1894 and again in 1903-1904, was similarly bereft of decorative features and for the same reasons: legislatively-imposed spending limits. To stretch their decorating budget, the architects chose to make extensive use of bronze and brass, as well as various examples of exotic stone and woods. These materials were available to builders at considerably reduced costs during the 1930s because of the economic depression then afflicting the nation. Even so, a number of decorative features, including a 30-foot statue centered on the capitol steps, had to be eliminated.

The construction contract was awarded to the Lundoff-Bicknell Company of Cleveland, Ohio, in June 1932, and construction began soon after. State agencies began moving into the structure in the latter half of 1934. Although the building has had two separate cornerstones, both laid with appropriate ceremonies, there is no record of its ever having been formally dedicated. The second cornerstone was installed in 1933 by newly elected Governor William Langer, who insisted that the original had been damaged by souvenir hunters. That 1933 cornerstone, hewn from rock near St. Anthony, North Dakota, can be found at the east side of the foyer.

The capitol reaches 242 feet – or 19 stories – into the North Dakota sky. The outside dimensions of the tower measure 95 feet by 95 feet. West of the tower are the three stories of the legislative wing. The tower and the legislative wing are joined together by the Memorial Hall, the central feature found in the building and the most beautiful interior setting in North Dakota.

The exterior walls were covered with Bedford white limestone, a material commonly used on both skyscrapers and public buildings; Rosetta black granite from Wisconsin was used around the foundations and on the tower, while Minnesota granite covered the front steps and foyer. A controversy arose in 1932 when the capitol commissioners, intent upon using North Dakota building materials to the greatest extent possible, considered facing the structure with locally manufactured brick. When an investigation determined that state brickmakers could not produce the material in sufficient volume to keep construction on schedule, the commissioners chose limestone to cover the building. This matched the Liberty Memorial Building, the only other structure then standing on the capitol grounds.

There are two revolving bronze doors in the foyer. Above these doors, inside and outside, are bronze figures representing farming and mining. Between the two revolving doors are six bronze columns that have weathered to a black finish. Between the columns and on the bronze canopies atop the glass panels are five raised sculptured bronze figurines representing a blacksmith, a farmer and his family, a woman with three children, a hunter and his family, and a Native American. (Bronze is a metal consisting of copper and tin with traces of other minerals.) The main entrance doors located at ground level are made of bronze and are accessible for all persons. The walls of the ground floor lobby are covered with Yellowstone Travertine, cream-colored marble from Gardiner, Montana. (Yellowstone Travertine marble is found on the north edge of the Yellowstone National Park and is formed by lime and calcium deposits carried in solutions of hot water springs and geysers.) The floor is covered by very dense Tennessee gray marble intermixed with dark cedar Tennessee marble.

On the first floor, the hallway extends 342 feet from the west end of the building to the east side of the Memorial Hall. It is 25 feet wide and 42 feet high, but the effects of the glass windows make it seem much larger. Travertine marble is found throughout the Memorial Hall. This is the first large building in the United States in which Travertine marble was extensively used. The hall is the site of official state functions and hosts the state Christmas tree during the holiday season.

When the Judicial Wing was added in 1981, the corridor was extended another 164 feet east. The corridor plus the length of the Legislative Assembly Hall and Memorial Hall measures 505 feet from the west end to the front door of the Supreme Court office. The corridor went through part of the Secretary of State's office when the new wing was built.

On either side and at the ends of the Memorial Hall are 16 bronze pillars reaching to the ceiling. The pillars are 40 feet tall. Five bronze chandeliers visually portraying a head of wheat hang from the ceiling. They are 12 feet long and 30 inches in diameter. One hundred and nine light bulbs in each fixture light the hallway, making it beautiful by night and by day.

On the north wall, opposite the main entrance, a stairway leads to the ground floor. Black Belgium marble, polished to such a brightness that one gets the impression of dark looking glass, panels the stairwell and accentuates other features in the hall. Bronze railings contribute to the richness of the hall. Again, black marble accentuates the bronze pillars and many other features throughout the hall. All staircases between the first floor and the ground floor are finished with Travertine marble and bronze metal.

Legislative Wing of the Capitol

On the west end of the Memorial Hall is situated the Legislative Assembly Hall. It is 20 feet wide. The walls are covered with dark East Indian rosewood panels offset with lighter curly maple. (Curly maple wood comes from the eastern United States.) Ten canopies of curly maple wood and rosewood cover alcoves found in this area of the Legislative Assembly Hall. The canopies have the Greek Key Meander classical design built into the wood.

The chamber of the House of Representatives feature walls covered with American chestnut wood. The rostrum and furniture are made of American walnut. (Chestnut wood comes from the Appalachia area of the United States, and the black walnut found in this room came from the Missouri Ozarks.) The ceiling could represent the moon and the evening rays radiating outward. Bronze railings and columns encircle the chamber where the 94 representatives sit among 116 desks found on the chamber's floor. The House balcony can accommodate 248 persons sitting behind the bronze railing.

The walls in the Senate chamber are covered with English oak. The rostrum and furniture are made of American oak. The ceiling could represent the rising rays of the sun at sunrise. Bronze railings and columns encircle the chamber where 47 state senators sit among 52 seats on the floor. The Senate balcony can accommodate seating for 184 persons behind the bronze railing. Several small offices are situated at the back of the Senate chamber. These offices, which include a conference room, are covered with American walnut.

There are 17 legislative meeting rooms of various sizes situated throughout the capitol. The Prairie Room is located in the former Supreme Court chambers on the second floor of the tower, and the Coteau and Sheyenne River rooms are located on the second floor of the judicial wing. The remaining rooms are located on the ground floor: the Fort Union, Fort Totten, Peace Garden, Roosevelt, and Medora rooms on the north side of the legislative wing; the Fort Lincoln, Lewis and Clark, Missouri River, and Brynhild Haugland rooms on the south side of the legislative wing; the Sakakawea, Red River, Roughrider, and Harvest rooms in the center of the building; and the Pioneer Room in the judicial wing.

Each committee room features pictures of its namesake North Dakota point of interest, as well as one or more digital signs displaying the committee hearing schedule. Master committee hearing schedules are also available, along with daily House and Senate calendar information, on large digital signs distributed between the legislative wing's ground floor hallway and first floor Information Kiosk.

Administrative Offices and Tower

The architects of the original building added several features to the three main offices located on the east end of the first floor.

The walls of the Governor's reception office are covered with laurel wood, which comes from either East India or the East Indies. The Governor's private office walls are covered with Honduras mahogany. The Lieutenant Governor's private office walls and ceiling are covered with teak wood from Burma. The corridor leading into the Governor's office is covered with prima vera wood. (Prima vera wood may be a species of mahogany from South America.)

The walls of the Secretary of State's office are also covered with prima vera wood. The private entrance to the Secretary of State's office, sometimes referred to as the "Monkey Room," is covered with California walnut. This is very rare and has wavy, highly figured grains known as "wild figure."

The Attorney General's private office walls are covered by English brown oak. (English brown oak is known for its beauty and rich brown color, which comes from the aging process after the tree has been harvested.)

The doors to the elevators on the first floor are finished with sculptured bronze metal. Figurines on those doors represent different eras in North Dakota's pioneer history: American Indians, buffalo hunters, the frontier army, railroads and wagons, pioneer farm families, miners and construction workers, and various kinds of grain grown in the state. All offices located on the first floor have doors and casings made from American walnut.

On the east side of the Memorial Hall is the mezzanine to the second floor. Once the Supreme Court chambers and offices, the floor now houses the Legislative Council. The former Supreme Court chamber, now known as the Prairie Room, has walls covered with rosewood. The walls to the mezzanine and entryway to the Prairie Room are covered with American walnut trimmed with black Belgium marble. The walls in the former Chief Justice's office are covered by Honduras mahogany. This wood comes from Central America and is generally darker in color, finer in texture, and has more pleasing features than other mahoganies.

The upper floors of the capitol contain offices for elected officials, departments, agencies, and their staffs. The top floor of the capitol, now accessible for handicapped persons, is an observation tower allowing visitors to look to the south and west. A southern panoramic view of bluffs of the Missouri River and small buttes can be seen in the distance on clear days.

The legislative assembly approved $3,155,000 in 2005 for a capitol fire suppression system, which included sprinklers, ceiling replacement, and lighting modification. The system was installed on a floor-by-floor basis over a 10-month period. During the project, employees on the affected floors were moved either off-site or into another part of the capitol.

1981 Addition

Facing a need to provide additional office space for state government during the 1960s and 1970s, the legislative assembly formulated a number of plans to solve the problem. Through a combination of political maneuvering and referral elections, several projects to construct state office buildings on the capitol grounds went down to defeat. Finally during the late 1970s, a financing plan was developed based on funds loaned by the Board of University and School Lands, thus avoiding the need for a legislative appropriation.

With the funds finally available, a new building provided office space in the form of an east wing attached to the old capitol. The design, while not completely sympathetic with the architecture of the original structure, placed the bulk of the addition north of and behind the capitol tower. This judicial wing, which houses a number of state agencies, was completed and occupied in 1981. In what has now almost become a North Dakota tradition, outside of the metal and stone utilized in the east-side entry and atrium, very little money was spent on decorative features.

Judicial Wing's Physical Features

The atrium located on the east side of the judicial wing measures 35 feet wide and 64 feet in length, with the ceiling reaching 62 feet. The walls of the foyer are covered with white Indiana limestone. The fig trees located in the foyer were imported from Israel and planted when the building was finished. Mezzanines accentuate each of the upper three floors. Aluminum, terazzo, vinyl, and natural plants add to the beauty of the east entrance. The railings are stainless steel accentuated with bronze.

The Supreme Court chambers, located on the first floor, are covered with Travertine marble behind the justices' chairs with dyed black wool on the remaining walls. The wool is a North Dakota product. The justices' offices are finished with oak woodwork and vinyl. The foyer in front of the Supreme Court reaches to the ceiling. It is also finished with oak and glass. An assortment of plants add a touch of freshness. Terazzo floor tiles and segmented glass panels add to the geometric design of the entrance to the court.

State Office Building

In 1959, the legislative assembly purchased a building on the corner of Highway 83 and Boulevard that had been constructed originally with a local mill levy for Bismarck Junior College (1959 S.L., ch. 369). Currently, the State Office Building houses the State Water Commission, and for approximately six months of each year, staff from the State Tax Department. During the 1991-1993 biennium, the building was totally remodeled and re-faced with an exterior to blend with other capitol complex buildings. The State Office Building contains 28,838 square feet and is the smallest facility housing state agencies on the capitol grounds.

Governor's Residence

Located on the southwest corner of the capitol grounds, the new Governor's Residence, authorized in 2015 by Senate Bill 2304 for $4 million with an additional $1 million in private funding, contains 13,700 square feet. Construction began in 2016, and the first family relocated into the home in March 2018. The project was completed for $4,888,000.

The new home occupies a site just north of the second Governor's Residence, which was completed in 1960 and replaced an aging Fourth Street mansion of 1884 vintage. The third Governor's Residence dwarfs the now demolished 10,000-square-foot residence built for $250,000.

The Governor's Residence sits at the southwest corner of the capitol grounds.

The interior of the third Governor's Residence.

Department of Transportation Building

Prior to 1968 when the State Highway Department first occupied its present home, the agency had been located in various buildings, such as both the original and current capitol buildings, the old Bismarck Junior College building, and rented quarters. The structure became the Department of Transportation Building after the 1989 Legislative Assembly created that agency to assume the functions of the Highway Department, its commissioner, and its chief engineer, as well as those of the Motor Vehicle Department and its registrar. In addition to these, today it houses the Highway Patrol's permit section. The building has 125,000 square feet on five floors and was built with a limestone exterior, which harmonized visually with other capitol grounds structures.

A three-phase project from 2010 until 2014 removed asbestos from the building, updated original air handlers from 1967, and reconfigured the first floor to handle all public services, including the Driver's License and Motor Vehicle Divisions, Mapping Services, Administrative Hearings, and the Highway Patrol Permit and Routing section. In addition, the east parking lot belonging to the department was expanded with an additional 66 parking spots to accommodate the influx of citizens using the east entrance. A customer flow management and wait time management system was added to eliminate standing in line and to handle multiple requests, such as driver permitting and exams.

Liberty Memorial Building

In 1919, the legislative assembly authorized construction of the Liberty Memorial Building to honor the 30,000 North Dakotans who served in the military during World War I. As completed in 1924, it housed the State Historical Society, Adjutant General, Library Commission, and Supreme Court. A proposal to erect a similar building opposite the Liberty Memorial Building on the west side of the capitol mall, to house the Supreme Court, was never funded. Present-day occupants include the State Library and the Tax Department. It is the oldest building on the capitol grounds and was completely renovated in 1982.

The State Library [NDCC 54-24] was established in 1890 and was placed within the Department of Public Instruction in 1989 for administration purposes. The library is administered by the state librarian, who is appointed by the superintendent. The State Library's mission is to provide access to information, which it does through direct service to North Dakota libraries, state agencies, and underserved or unserved citizens. It maintains a collection of more than 365,000 titles, most of which are available for loan; offers technical assistance to public, academic, school, and special libraries; creates continuing educational opportunities for librarians and public library board members; provides library service for persons who are unable to read or use standard printed materials; explores and recommends use of technology to increase library effectiveness; collects both paper and electronic state documents and maintains the State Document Depository Program; provides consultative services in the development and coordination of North Dakota libraries; coordinates the purchase of online resources, including magazine and newspaper databases, that are available statewide; administers state aid to public libraries; and administers the Federal Library Services and Technology Act and state-funded grants. The library's catalog is part of the Online Dakota Information Network (ODIN), an online catalog with participation of more than 70 other libraries in the state.

Capitol Grounds Arboretum Trail

This trail, which winds around various parts of the capitol grounds, was completed in 1985 and allows pedestrians to view and identify about 75 species of trees and shrubs found in North Dakota. It also guides people through the Centennial Grove. Also visible from the trail are many of the statues and memorials located on the capitol grounds.

Capitol Grounds Prairie Trail

Similar to the Arboretum Trail, this trail runs north of the capitol's judicial wing and leads pedestrians into an area filled with grasses and wild flowers typical of North Dakota's native prairie. It was placed on the Natural Areas Registry in 1987.

Centennial Grove

The Centennial Grove is located west of the capitol mall along Fourth Street and north of the Governor's Residence. During his North Dakota Centennial visit in 1989, President George Bush dedicated the Centennial Grove. This project was sponsored by the North Dakota Forest Service, the North Dakota Centennial Commission, and the Centennial Decade Trees Committee.

North Dakota Heritage Center

The North Dakota Heritage Center, which began as a 1976 U.S. Bicentennial project for the state, opened its doors in 1981. The original building was designed to be expanded in a 20-year plan. Under the recommendation of Governors Guy, Link, Olson, Sinner, and Schafer, expansion planning began in 2002 with Governor Hoeven's State Historical Society of North Dakota Commission. The Commission was chaired by Lt. Governor Dalrymple. Since 2001, as a result of the Commission Report, $21 million was invested across the state in heritage tourism infrastructure; the last remaining piece was the expansion of the North Dakota Heritage Center. Phase I, the expansion of the State Archives, was completed in 2007. This 25-year plan added 30,000 square feet of collections storage at a cost of $5.7 million, doubling archives collections space.

The second phase of expansion doubled the existing exhibit, visitor services, public and educational programming, collections storage, labs, and office space by adding 97,000 square feet. The 2005 and 2007 Legislative Assemblies allocated planning dollars, and the 2009 Assembly authorized $40 million toward this $52 million project. The remaining $12 million was raised by the State Historical Society of North Dakota Foundation from private sources, corporations, foundations, and other groups.

Collections

The State Historical Society has several different collection responsibilities. Because of trained staff, an environmentally controlled facility, and extensive security, the Heritage Center is the federal repository for the state in all collection areas. The State Archives, by law, is the official repository of state and local government records of enduring value.

The State Archives manages a collection of more than 115,000 books and periodicals; 10,000 maps; 2.5 million photographs; 2,659 manuscript collections; 4,244 archival records series; 1,400 titles of newspapers; 3,000 oral histories; and 132 moving image collections.

Archaeology and historic preservation collections include millions of artifacts representing more than 13,000 years of human activity recovered from across the state. There are also thousands of resource files critical to oil, coal, wind, road, and bridge contractors and developers across the state. Also considered collections, a statewide network of 57 state historic sites is administered from the Heritage Center. Ten of these sites have interpretive centers or museums.

The museum consists of three-dimensional objects, including items such as natural history specimens, textiles, vehicles, agricultural equipment, art, toys, weapons, and furniture. There are more than 75,000 objects, ranging in age from a 10,000-year-old mastodon skeleton to disposable items used yesterday and in scale from tiny glass beads to a locomotive.

Paleontology collections are housed at the Heritage Center through an agreement with the Department of Mineral Resources, North Dakota Geological Survey. The center also houses the Johnsrud Paleontology Laboratory. Representing more than 500 million years of fossil history and geology of North Dakota, specimens in the paleontology lab include a gem, mineral, and rock collection and the state fossil collection containing millions of specimens ranging in scale from microscopic shells of marine animals to huge dinosaur bones.

Public Level

The building areas reference nature's elements of earth, air, fire, and water and correspond to the geography of the state from east to west: Pembina River Plaza, Red, Sheyenne, and Mouse River Halls, James River Café, Missouri River Special Events Center, and Badlands Plaza. Several improvements were made to the Russell Reid Auditorium, and the Museum Store doubled in size. The café features North Dakota-grown and ethnic specialties. All these areas focus on enhancing the visitor's North Dakota experience.

Hub of History

A tourist information center, the Hub of History, directs visitors to all corners of the state to experience the people, landscape, and history where it happened. The expanded Heritage Center is a destination, part of a string of pearls of heritage tourism opportunities across the northern border. The opportunities include North Dakota events, places to visit, and Main Street tourism venues. The hub is a statewide network of partnerships offering the best of the state to those who live near and those visiting from afar.

Exhibit Galleries

The Heritage Center exhibition space encompasses more than 47,000 square feet. Galleries, each with a learning lab, include:

- The Adaptation Gallery: Geological Time presents 500 million years of the geologic history of life in North Dakota from the earliest life forms up to the last glaciation, about 10,000 years ago. These exhibits, which include the dinosaurs and many more fossils, set the stage for the fossil fuel stories of North Dakota's oil and coal industries and explain landscape and soil development that will shape the state's agricultural future.

- The Innovation Gallery: Early Peoples covers more than 12,000 years of the earliest human history in what is now North Dakota to the present day. When the Giza pyramids in Egypt or pre-Columbian civilizations of South America flourished, so did American Indian civilizations in North Dakota. The gallery features archaeological artifacts from prehistoric cultures, the international story of the fur trade, oral histories, and stunning collections representing prehistoric, historic, and contemporary tribal life.

- The Inspiration Gallery: Yesterday & Today features the last 150 years of the state's history, with room for the future. It investigates agriculture, industry and energy, newcomers and settlement, conflicts, communities, and cultural expressions through captivating stories that illustrate North Dakota's unique character and its creative thinkers.

- The Governor's Gallery hosts temporary and traveling exhibits, creating regional and world-class blockbuster events. This gallery provides an opportunity to bring the world to North Dakota and share the state with other museums across the country and world.

- The Treehouse provides young children with their very own museum space. This hands-on, fun experience is located on the mezzanine above the Missouri River Event Center.

The Grand Opening of the North Dakota Heritage Center expansion was a centerpiece of the statewide celebration of North Dakota's 125th anniversary of statehood on November 2, 2014.

For more information about the North Dakota Heritage Center, visit the State Historical Society of North Dakota's website at www.history.nd.gov.

✔ More information about the State Historical Society is in the *2015-2017 North Dakota Blue Book*.

References:

North Dakota's State Capitol, by Simons, Kenneth W., 1934

North Dakota State Capitol, Self Guided Walking Tour, State Historical Society of North Dakota, 1991

North Dakota State Capitol, information brochure by Facilities Management, Office of Management and Budget

North Dakota State Capitol, Bidders Specifications Manual, June 10, 1932

Remele, Larry, editor, *The North Dakota State Capitol: Architecture and History*, (Bismarck: State Historical Society of North Dakota, 1989)

Statues, Monuments, and Markers on the Capitol Grounds

Identified As	Title or Description	Artist	Year Dedicated	Sponsor or Donor
Statue	Sakakawea	Leonard Crunelle	1910	ND Federation of Women's Clubs
Marker	Tree planted in memory of President Franklin D. Roosevelt		1945	American War Mothers
Statue	Pioneer Family	Avard Fairbanks	1946	H.F. McLean
Boxcar	French Gratitude Boxcar		1949	French Government
Statue	John Burke	Avard Fairbanks	1963	National Statuary Hall Commission & Legislative Assembly
Statue	American Buffalo	Bennett Brien	1986	Dayton-Hudson, Inc.
Marker	Capitol Grounds Prairie Trail		1987	ND Parks & Recreation Dept.
Marker	Centennial Grove		1989	ND Forest Service, ND Centennial Commission & Centennial Decade Trees Committee
Marker	Flower Bed (Heritage Center Square)		1989	Bismarck/Mandan Junior Service League
Statue	Pioneers of the Future (children holding hands)	Jeff Barber	1989	ND Federation of Women's Clubs
Monument	All Veterans Centennial Memorial	Warren Tvenge (architect)	1989	ND All Veterans Memorial Centenntial Memorial Assn.
Monument	U.S.S. North Dakota Battleship Bowplate	U.S. Navy	1989	State Historical Society of ND
Marker	Petrified Meta-sequoia Tree Stumps and Log		1988, 1991	Central Dakota Gem & Mineral Society
Monument	ND Peace Officers Memorial	Warren Tvenge (architect)	1994	ND Peace Officers Association
Statue	"Cortes" - Arabian Horse	Bennett Brien	1994	ND Heritage Foundation & eight power companies
Marker	Capitol overlook - three plaques showing Capitol complex design, describing native prairie remnant on the Capitol grounds and providing brief history of the Capitol building	Metal Arts Company Mandan foundry	2005	N.D. Dept. of Transportation
Monument	Purple Heart Memorial	DeIasi Enterprises, Jersey City, NJ	2005	Military Order of the Purple Heart and Arnold Maier
Monument	Bronze likeness of the Great Seal in Memorial Hall	Metal Arts Company Mandan foundry	2006	Capitol Grounds Planning Commission

North Dakota Peace Officers Memorial
Police Officers Killed in the Line of Duty

Name	Location of Duty	Date
Fred D. Alderman	Fargo PD	1882
Evan Paulson	Mayville PD	1890
James Rauland	Northern Pacific RR	1899
H. M. Personius	Valley City PD	1906
George E. Moody	Richland County SO	1911
Carl G. Nelson	Carrington PD	1915
Seymour H. Douglas	McKenzie County SO	1917
Evan M. Jones	Richland SO	1917
George Dixon	Wilton PD	1917
Patrick J. Devaney	Minot PD	1918
Kersey E. Gowin	Attorney General's Office	1918
Earnest W. Thompson	Ward County SO	1920
Lee S. Fahler	Minot PD	1921
Julius A. Nielson	Kenmare PD	1921
Christian A. Madison	Stanley PD	1922
Carl Peterson	Westhope PD	1922
Charles R. Sneesby	Devils Lake PD	1924
E. M. "Ned" Morris	New Rockford PD	1926
Nels H. Romer	Mandan PD	1926
Hans C. Jess	Mandan PD	1929
Martin G. Johnson	Ray PD	1930
George Peipkorn	Burleigh County SO	1930
Leo Dagner	Willow City PD	1933
David L. Stewart	Hope PD	1933
Aslak "Oscar" Thorsen	Bottineau County SO	1936
Fred A. Patrickus	Billings County SO	1940
Joesph Runions	Mercer County SO	1941
Arthus M. Sem	Stanley PD	1942
Charles M. Allmaras	Eddy County SO	1942
Jacob M. Hoerner	New Leipzig PD	1942
John Oles	North Dakota Penitentiary	1946
Rudolph F. Howell	Ramsey County SO	1950
William W. Hansen	Velva PD	1950
Henry S. Halvorson	Grand Forks County SO	1952
Edward E. Mumby	New Salem PD	1953
Beryl E. McLane	North Dakota Highway Patrol	1954
John Holcolmb	North Dakota Penitentiary	1954
Ralph L. Burdick	Benson County SO	1954
Lee E. Morrow	Federal Bureau of Investigation	1960
Max L. Taylor	Bowman County SO	1960

Name	Location of Duty	Date
Nathan N. Bear	Bureau of Indian Affairs	1960
Ralph J. Hansen	Ransom County SO	1962
Frank A. Peterson	Rugby PD	1963
Burdette M. Miller	Ray PD	1966
Theodore C. Wanner	Dickinson PD	1966
Robert D. Martin	Grand Forks PD	1966
Raymond A. Wietstock	State Industrial School	1966
Ronald E. Trautman	Jamestown PD	1966
Frank C. Schultz Burlington	Northern RR	1970
P.A. "Tex" Goyne	New Salem PD	1971
Herbert A. Parmeter	Sargent County SO	1974
Kenneth A. Lenerville	Reeder PD	1975
Kenneth B. Muir	United States Marshal	1983
Robert S. Cheshire Jr.	United States Marshal	1983
Timothy L. Wells	Williams County SO	1989
Valence L. Pascal	Benson County SO	1993
Charles V. Pulver	North Dakota Game & Fish	1995
Keith A. Braddock	Watford City PD	1996
Roger C. Sorensen	Youth Correctional Center	1996
Steven R. Kenner	Bismarck PD	2011
Bryan K. Sleeper	Burleigh County SO	2011
Jason Moszer	Fargo PD	2016
Colt Eugene Allery	Rolette County SO	2017

(**Note**: PD means Police Department; SO means Sheriff's Office)

Police Officers Memorial, North Dakota State Capitol Grounds.

Theodore Roosevelt Rough Rider Award
North Dakota Hall of Fame

On August 29, 1961, Governor William L. Guy announced the establishment of an honorary commission of colonel in the North Dakota Theodore Roosevelt Rough Riders. The first commission was given in a surprise presentation to Lawrence Welk at a Minot Diamond Jubilee Celebration the day before the announcement.

In 1963, the 38th Legislative Assembly authorized the Theodore Roosevelt Rough Rider Award as the highest recognition the state of North Dakota can bestow upon present or former North Dakotans. The award was to go to those "who have been influenced by this state in achieving national recognition in their fields of endeavor thereby reflecting credit upon this state and its citizens."

The initial meeting of the committee was held on August 29, 1963, close to the second anniversary date of the first award. At this first meeting, the committee affirmed three previous awards made to Lawrence Welk, Dorothy Stickney, and Ivan Dmitri. Three new members, Roger Maris, Peggy Lee, and Eric Sevareid, were also selected.

The award has continued to the present day. Recipients of the award are chosen by the Governor, with the concurrence of the Secretary of State and the Director of the State Historical Society of North Dakota.

Forty-four North Dakotans have received the award. Their portraits are on display on the ground floor of the North Dakota State Capitol Building.

Theodore Roosevelt

Theodore Roosevelt was the 26th president of the United States. As a young man, Roosevelt spent several years in the North Dakota Badlands. Of that time, Roosevelt said, "If it had not been for what I learned during the years I spent in North Dakota, I never in the world would have been President of the United States."

Roosevelt vigorously championed the conservation of America's scenic, natural, and historical resources. In recognition of his valuable contributions toward conservation, Theodore Roosevelt National Park was established in 1947, in the North Dakota Badlands that Roosevelt loved.

Portrait artist: Vern Skaug

(Note: Recipients are listed in order of the year the award was presented.)

Lawrence Welk
(1903-1992)

Award Presented:
August 28, 1961, Minot
Governor William Guy

Portrait Artist: Emmett Morgan

North Dakota's most famous "favorite son," Lawrence Welk became one of the greatest entertainers in the world through his weekly television show featuring his distinctive "champagne music."

Welk was one of eight children born on a farm near Strasburg, North Dakota. Welk displayed a musical interest at an early age. After leaving school in his elementary years because of a prolonged illness, he spent more time practicing his talent.

Welk played for local farm dances to pay for a new professional accordion he had purchased. He later added a saxophone player, a drummer, and a piano player, and then Welk had his first band. The band gained recognition for its program on WNAX, Yankton, South Dakota, in 1935. In the years to follow, the band went on to play at hotels and resorts, eventually playing in the top ballrooms in the nation. From 1950-1955, the Lawrence Welk Orchestra appeared on KTLA-TV in Los Angeles, California, and so began the many years of televised performances of Welk and the Champagne Music Makers.

Welk authored several books including *Wunnerful, Wunnerful*; *Ah One, Ah Two*; and *My America, Your America*.

Dorothy Stickney
(1896-1998)

Award Presented:
November 2, 1961, Bismarck
Governor William Guy

Portrait Artist:
Emmett Morgan

A Broadway actress who received stage immortality in the long-running "*Life With Father*," co-starring with her husband, Howard Lindsay, Dorothy Hayes Stickney was one of the great leading ladies of the legitimate theater.

Stickney was born in Dickinson, North Dakota, June 21, 1896. She attended school in St. Paul and Minneapolis, Minnesota, and Auburndale, Massachusetts. Stickney played in stock companies and vaudeville for several years. Her New York performances include *The Way of the World*, *On Borrowed Time*, and *Life with Father*. Stickney received the Barter Award for best performance of the year for her role as Mother in *Life with Father*. The award was given in 1940 by Eleanor Roosevelt.

Stickney is also the author of a number of poems, including *You're Not the Type* and *My Dressing Room*.

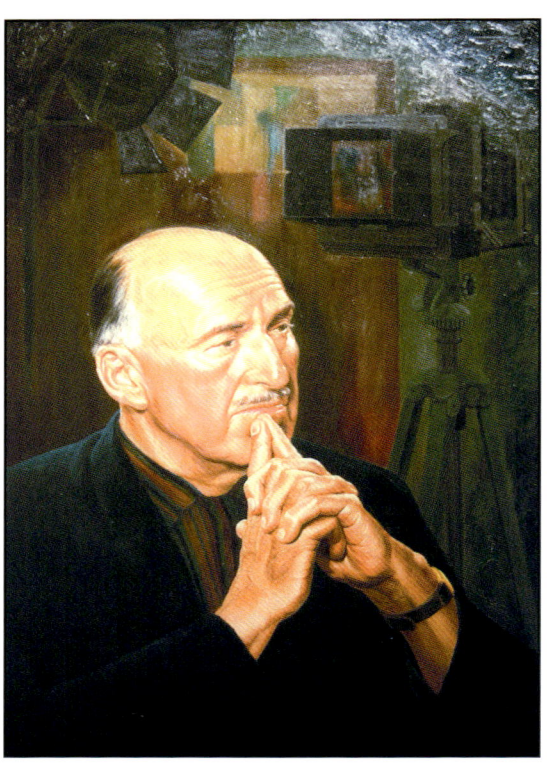

Ivan Dmitri
(1900-1968)

Award Presented:
April 13, 1962, Dickinson
Governor William Guy

Portrait Artist: Emmett Morgan

Gaining international fame for his sensitive portrayals in color photography, etchings, and water colors, Ivan Dmitri's work has been exhibited in nearly every major art museum in the western world.

Born Levon West, he moved throughout North Dakota during his youth, as his father was a Congregational preacher. He graduated valedictorian of his high school class at Harvey, North Dakota, taught school for a year, and enlisted in the United States Navy. After WWI, he received a scholarship to the University of Minnesota where, despite his interest in art, he studied business administration at his father's insistence.

His first break as an artist came with the publication of his etching of *The Spirit of St. Louis* upon Charles Lindbergh's arrival in Paris. The etchings of Levon West soon were in great demand.

His interest in photography brought recognition in the new medium and in order to separate his two artistic fields and protect those that had purchased his etchings, West took the name of Ivan Dmitri for his photographic work.

In 1959, Dmitri, in an effort to gain acceptance of photography as an art medium, founded Photography in the Fine Arts.

Roger Maris
(1934-1985)

Selected:
September 4, 1963

Award Presented:
January 4, 1964, Fargo
Governor William Guy

Portrait Artist:
Emmett Morgan

Baseball's Single-Season Home Run King, Roger Maris, hit 61 home runs during the 1961 season, while he was a member of the New York Yankees. This record stood for 37 years until Mark McGwire hit 70 home runs in 1998. Barry Bonds went on to break McGwire's record with 73 home runs in 2001. Maris also played for the Cleveland Indians, Kansas City Athletics, and St. Louis Cardinals.

Raised in Fargo, North Dakota, Maris was a football and basketball star at Shanley High School. After trying out with the Chicago Cubs, he played in the American League until the end of his career when he played for the St. Louis Cardinals. Maris began playing for the Cleveland Indians in 1959 and hit 14 home runs. In 1958 and 1959, he hit 28 and 16 homers respectively, while playing for Kansas City. Maris was traded to the Yankees in 1960, and his legend began. He was voted most valuable player in the American League that year, after hitting 39 home runs with 112 RBIs. The year 1961 saw Maris hit 61 home runs, one more than Babe Ruth hit in a season, and again Maris earned the most valuable player award.

Peggy Lee
(1920-2002)

Selected:
September 4, 1963

Award Presented:
May 23, 1975, Fargo
Governor Art Link and former Governor William Guy

Portrait Artist:
Emmett Morgan

A motion picture actress and singer, a distinctive "rhythm and blues" style, and beautiful voice quickly established Peggy Lee as one of the most brilliant performers in the field of popular music.

Born Norma Delores Egstrom at Jamestown, North Dakota, on May 26, 1920, Peggy Lee was one of eight children. She received much encouragement and recognition for her singing in school and church choirs. In 1938, after graduating from high school, she went to Hollywood, California, but later returned to Fargo and worked for WDAY radio. She moved to Minneapolis, where she met and began touring with the Will Osborne Band and later with Benny Goodman.

Lee wrote music and lyrics, both for herself and the movie industry. She published a book of verse entitled *Softly With Feeling*.

Lee starred in several films with Bing Crosby and Danny Thomas and was nominated for an Academy Award.

Eric Sevareid
(1912-1992)

Selected:
September 4, 1963

Awarded:
April 17, 1964, Minot
Governor William Guy

Portrait Artist:
Emmett Morgan

Nationally known television commentator, news analyst, and author, Eric Sevareid is particularly noted for his perceptive essays on public events and personalities.

Sevareid grew up in Velva, North Dakota, and knew from his youth that he wanted to be a journalist, which accounted for his fascination with the local newspaper. At the age of 18, Sevareid began working as a copy boy. He later became a reporter for *The Minneapolis Journal* while attending the University of Minnesota.

Upon receiving his B.A. degree, Sevareid traveled to London and Paris to continue his studies. He joined the Paris edition of the *New York Herald* and became a radio correspondent for CBS in 1939, covering the war in Europe. In later years, Sevareid was known for his coverage of presidential elections and meetings of the United Nations Assembly in Paris. Sevareid retired as a CBS television news commentator on November 30, 1977.

Sevareid was the author of *Not So Wild a Dream*.

General Harold K. Johnson
(1912-1983)

Award Presented:
April 23, 1965, Fargo
Governor William Guy

Portrait Artist:
Emmett Morgan

A professional soldier who became Chief of Staff of the United States Army in 1965, General Harold Johnson was the youngest man to hold the position since General Douglas MacArthur.

Johnson was born in Bowesmont, North Dakota, in 1912. He graduated from Grafton High School in 1929 and West Point Military Academy in 1933.

Captain Johnson was operations officer for the 57th Infantry in Manila, prior to the Pearl Harbor attack by the Japanese. The 57th was ordered to Bataan where the Japanese were engaged. Johnson was promoted to major and then lieutenant colonel and given command of the battalion. After a surrender to the superior Japanese force, Johnson and the 57th were forced on the Bataan Death March, which claimed 8,150 prisoners.

Johnson saw combat again in Korea, emerging from the conflict as a Full Colonel. In 1956, he was made a Brigadier General. In 1957, Johnson was named Chief of Staff of the U.S. Seventh Army in Germany. General Johnson was chosen Chief of Staff to NATO's Central Army Group in West Germany in 1959. In 1964, General Johnson was named Chief of Staff of the U.S. Army and was awarded his fourth star.

Dr. Anne H. Carlsen
(1915-2002)

Selected:
May 13, 1966

Award Presented:
September 9, 1966, Fargo
Governor William Guy

Portrait Artist: Vern Skaug

Former long-time superintendent of the Crippled Children's School at Jamestown, North Dakota, Dr. Anne Carlsen was born without hands or feet. Nevertheless, her great courage and keen intellect enabled her to earn a Doctor of Philosophy degree and international honors.

Carlsen, born in Gratsburg, Wisconsin, was one of six children. As a child, she received much assistance from her sister, four brothers, and childhood playmates, making it possible for her to participate in their games. She attended and completed elementary school in Gratsburg and high school in St. Paul, Minnesota. She graduated from the University of Minnesota, cum laude in 1936, and set about to realize her dream of self-support, hopefully by teaching.

After some teaching experience, Carlsen accepted a teaching position at the Good Samaritan School in Fargo, North Dakota, a Lutheran school for crippled children. She continued her education, earning a M.A. from Northern University of Colorado in 1946 and a Ph.D. from the University of Minnesota in 1949. The following year she was named superintendent of the Crippled Children's School in Jamestown, which is now named the Anne Carlsen School. Under her guidance, the school, established in 1940, gained national recognition.

Edward K. Thompson
(1907-1996)

Selected:
January 2, 1968

Award Presented:
April 19, 1968, Bismarck
Governor William Guy

Portrait Artist:
Emmett Morgan

A former editor of *Life* magazine, Edward Thompson received his early journalism experience with the *Foster County Independent* in the city of Carrington and later the *Fargo Forum*.

Raised in St. Thomas, North Dakota, Thompson began his journalism career as editor of the *Foster County Independent* in 1927. Two months later, he was the night city editor of the *Fargo Forum*. In another two months, he was a reporter for the *Milwaukee Journal* in Wisconsin. Thompson later became picture editor and assistant news editor at Milwaukee, and in 1937, he joined *Life* magazine.

In 1942, Thompson joined the Army, where he edited a magazine for Air Force intelligence. By 1944, he was in charge of intelligence concerning the German air force.

In 1945, Thompson returned to *Life* magazine and became assistant managing editor. In 1949, he was named managing editor. After his retirement from *Life* in 1968, Thompson served as special assistant to the Secretary of State for Far Eastern Affairs.

Dr. Robert Henry Bahmer
(1904-1990)

Award Presented:
July 28, 1970, Minot
Governor William Guy

Portrait Artist: Vern Skaug

Dr. Robert Bahmer was the fourth Archivist of the United States (1966-1969) in the nation's history. He headed the National Archives and Records Service and directed the offices of the Hoover, Roosevelt, Truman, and Eisenhower Presidential Libraries.

Bahmer was born near Gardena, North Dakota, on September 27, 1904. He attended high school at Omemee and spent a year at the University of North Dakota. He later transferred to Valley City State Teachers College where he received a B.A. degree in 1928.

From 1925 to 1927, Dr. Bahmer was principal at Bentley school in Hettinger County. In 1938, he received his M.A. degree from the University of Colorado and a Ph.D. from the University of Minnesota in 1941.

Bahmer joined the National Archives staff in 1936 and served as a specialist in records management in several governmental agencies, including the Navy Department and the War Department. In 1948, he was appointed Assistant Archivist of the United States, serving until 1966, when he was appointed Archivist of the United States.

Louis L'Amour
(1908-1988)

Selected:
February 15, 1972

Award Presented:
May 26, 1972, Jamestown
Governor William Guy

Portrait Artist: Vern Skaug

An award winning western author and screen writer, Louis L'Amour published more than 400 short stories and more than 100 novels. He wrote 65 TV scripts and sold more than 30 stories to the motion picture industry, including *Hondo*, starring John Wayne.

L'Amour was born in Jamestown, North Dakota, March 22, 1908. At 15, he joined a circus and later worked in mining and lumber camps. He was a prize fighter and traveled throughout the world. During World War II, he was an officer in the Army Tank Corps. He was a self-educated man, whose hobbies included archaeology and the study of wildlife.

L'Amour's books have been translated into 27 languages. He produced the movie *Catlow*, in addition to writing for the film screen. In addition to his prose, he wrote a volume of poetry entitled *Smoke From the Altar*.

Bertin C. Gamble
(1898-1986)

Selected:
September 13, 1972

Award Presented:
October 20, 1972, Grand Forks
Governor William Guy

Portrait Artist: Vern Skaug

With partner Phil Skogmo, Bertin Gamble developed nearly 4,200 merchandising outlets in 38 states and Canada, since the first store was established in 1925, making Gamble-Skogmo one of the largest retailers in the nation.

Born in Chicago, Illinois, in 1898, Gamble claims North Dakota as home, since he was raised and attended school here. He lived with his family in Hunter, North Dakota, and later in nearby Arthur. It was there, at the age of seven, that he met Phil Skogmo, who would be his future partner.

After finishing high school, Gamble went to Minneapolis, Minnesota, where he worked and attended business school. He and Skogmo purchased an auto dealership in Fergus Falls, Minnesota, and prospered.

In 1925, the first Gamble-Skogmo store opened in St. Cloud, Minnesota. The second and third stores opened in Fargo and Grand Forks, North Dakota, respectively. Their business survived many financial crises, including the depression of the 1930s. Gamble was company president at Gamble-Skogmo from 1925-1945 and was board chairman until his retirement in 1977. The company was acquired in 1980 by the California-based Wickes Corporation.

Casper Oimoen
(1906-1995)

Selected:
January 24, 1973

Award Presented:
February 12, 1973, Minot
Governor Art Link

Portrait Artist: Vern Skaug

Captain of the Olympic ski team in 1936, Casper Oimoen won more than 400 medals and trophies during his skiing career. He was inducted into the U.S. Skiing Hall of Fame in 1963.

Born May 6, 1906, in Norway, Casper Oimoen came to Minot, North Dakota, in 1923. He had learned to ski while a boy in Norway and began to compete in ski jumping after coming to North Dakota. He did not compete in the 1928 Olympics because he was not an American citizen, but continued to compete regionally and entered the Olympics as captain of the U.S. team in 1936.

His winning record was unmatched. He won the Northwestern Ski Jumping Championship nine times in nine entries, the Montana State Jumping Championship six times in six entries, the Central United States Championship 10 times, six of them in consecutive years (1925-1931), and the United States National Ski Jumping Championship three times. In 1930, he won the Eastern, Central, and National Championships, plus eight other firsts, a feat which has never been equaled.

Casper Oimoen was also a brick layer, a trade he learned from his uncle when he lived in Minot. During the 1930s, he worked on the construction crew that built the North Dakota State Capitol.

Harold Schafer
(1912-2001)

Selected:
November 18, 1974

Award Presented:
July 4, 1975, Medora
Governor Art Link

Portrait Artist: Vern Skaug

Creator and Chairman of the Board of Gold Seal Company, Harold Schafer was the founder of North Dakota's largest home-owned business. Schafer was the youngest-ever recipient of the Horatio Alger Award, a national award that annually recognizes individuals who have faced and overcome significant personal adversity through hard work, integrity, determination, and have a strong dedication to helping others. He was also responsible for restoration and development of Medora, one of North Dakota's leading tourist attractions.

Schafer was born in Stanton and attended public schools at Stanton, Hazen, Killdeer, Glen Ullin, and Jamestown and graduated from Bismarck High School in 1929. He attended North Dakota State University in Fargo.

Schafer traveled western North Dakota while working for several Bismarck firms before founding the Gold Seal Company on May 1, 1942. At that time, the company was regional, but the products of the Gold Seal Company, among them Glass Wax, Mr. Bubble, and Snowy Bleach, were known worldwide. The Gold Seal Company was also noted for its Medora restoration project and the Medora Musical, which entertains nearly 100,000 visitors each season.

Era Bell Thompson
(1905-1986)

Selected:
April 12, 1976

Award Presented:
August 14, 1976, Bismarck
Governor Art Link

Portrait Artist: Vern Skaug

International editor of *Ebony* magazine, Era Bell Thompson grew up in North Dakota. This noted journalist and author wrote several books, including *American Daughter*, which tells the story of her youth in North Dakota.

Thompson was born in Des Moines, Iowa, and in 1914, moved with her family to the Driscoll area where she attended school. Later she studied at the University of North Dakota, where she established five state women's track records and tied two national intercollegiate women's track records. She graduated from Morningside College in Sioux City, Iowa.

Thompson served as associate editor of *Ebony* for four years, co-managing editor from 1951-1964, and was international editor of Johnson Publishing Company.

Thompson also wrote *Africa, Land of My Father*, and *White on Black*.

Dr. Leon Orris Jacobson
(1911-1992)

Selected:
April 12, 1976

Award Presented:
October 1, 1976, Jamestown
Governor Art Link

Portrait Artist: Vern Skaug

Dr. Leon Jacobson held clinical, teaching, and research positions in the field of medical science with the University of Chicago and served as director of the Franklin McLean Memorial Research Institute. Much of his research dealt with modern cancer chemotherapy.

Jacobson was born in Sims, North Dakota, a small town in Morton County that no longer exists. At age 16, he began college in Fargo, North Dakota, but was forced to drop out for financial reasons. He then taught all eight grades in a two-room schoolhouse. In 1935, he received his bachelor of science degree at North Dakota State University and earned his medical degree from the University of Chicago in 1939.

He was a founder of the Argonne Cancer Research Hospital, now known as the Franklin McLean Memorial Research Institute.

Elizabeth Bodine
(1898-1986)

Selected:
May 2, 1979

Award Presented:
July 27, 1979, Bismarck
Governor Art Link

Portrait Artist: Vern Skaug

Named to the Rough Rider Award Hall of Fame during the International Year of the Child, Mrs. Frank Bodine served as the 1968 North Dakota Mother of the Year.

Education played an important role in Bodine's life. All 18 of the Bodine children received post-high school education. Her 10 sons received college degrees. Six of her daughters attended college, and the other two daughters received business training. For 26 years, including 10 summer sessions, one or more of her family was enrolled at Minot State College.

Bodine was active in church, civic, and community projects for many years. Assisting the Indian people in the Belcourt area, contributing clothing and food to her relatives in Poland during World War II, and sending boxes of clothing to Vietnam are but a few of the many projects to which she contributed.

Cliff Purpur
(1912-2001)

Selected:
September 15, 1980

Award Presented:
May 16, 1981, Grand Forks
Governor Allen Olson

Portrait Artist: Vern Skaug

Cliff "Fido" Purpur was the first North Dakota native to become a National Hockey League player. He achieved this at a time when there were only six NHL teams and an American player playing on any of these teams was an oddity. After his active hockey days were over, Purpur returned to his native state to live and work in Grand Forks. He gained further success as a coach at Grand Forks Central High School and the University of North Dakota.

Purpur was enshrined in the Sports Hall of Fame and also the United States Hockey Hall of Fame. As the first native North Dakotan to play in the National Hockey League, he was as much responsible as anyone for North Dakota's reputation as one of the nation's hockey hotbeds.

Serving as an example to a countless number of young men, Purpur showed the true spirit of North Dakota pioneers. His personal honesty and integrity, plus his determination, enabled him to achieve what few men even dare to dream.

Phyllis Frelich
(1944-2014)

Selected:
January 23, 1981

Award Presented:
April 27, 1981, Bismarck
Governor Allen Olson

Portrait Artist: Vern Skaug

Tony Award winner for the most outstanding performance by an actress for her role in the play *Children of a Lesser God*, Phyllis Frelich is an exceptional woman.

Deaf all her life, Frelich dreamed of becoming an actress. After graduating from the School for the Deaf in her hometown of Devils Lake, North Dakota, she went to Gallaudet College in Washington, D.C., a liberal arts college for the deaf. Few theater courses were offered there, but Frelich devoured the limited number available.

Frelich was one of the founding members of the National Theater of the Deaf (NTD). Through her involvement with the NTD, Frelich met the playwright Mark Medoff. Intrigued by the difficulties of a deaf actress in finding suitable roles, he wrote a play which portrayed the problems of deaf people in a hearing world on one level and the difficulty of all human communication on another level.

Although the play, *Children of a Lesser God*, was written for her and the similarities between the lead character and Frelich are numerous, it is not her life story, but rather illustrates the life of one deaf person in a hearing world.

General David C. Jones
(1921-2013)

Selected:
January 20, 1982

Award Presented:
May 21, 1982, Bismarck
Governor Allen Olson

Portrait Artist: Vern Skaug

    Appointed Chairman of the Joint Chiefs of Staff in 1978, General David C. Jones was re-appointed to a second two-year term in 1980. In this capacity, he served as the senior military advisor to the President, the National Security Council, and the Secretary of Defense. He was also responsible for executing the decisions of the National Command Authorities regarding world-wide readiness and employment of combat forces of the United States Army, Navy, Air Force, and Marine Corps. Prior to his appointment, General Jones served four years as Chief of Staff to the United States Air Force.

    Jones served as inspector, operator, planner, and Commander in Chief of the United States Air Forces in Europe. He also served as Commander of the Fourth Allied Tactical Air Force and led the way toward establishing the integrated air headquarters in North Atlantic Treaty Organization's Central Region, Allied Air Forces, Central Europe.

    Raised in Minot, North Dakota, and a graduate of Minot High School, Jones attended the University of North Dakota and Minot State College until the outbreak of World War II. He entered the Army Air Corps and began aviation training in 1942, receiving his commission and pilot wings in February 1943. He is also a graduate of the National War College in Washington, D.C.

Ronald N. Davies
(1904-1996)

Selected:
May 1987

Award Presented:
June 11, 1987, Bismarck
Governor George Sinner

Portrait Artist: Vern Skaug

Ronald Davies is the federal jurist who ordered the integration of Little Rock, Arkansas, Central High School in September 1957. *The New York Times* called Judge Davies' ruling the "landmark decision on racial integration in our nation."

Davies attended high school in Grand Forks and went on to graduate from the University of North Dakota in 1927. He earned his law degree at Georgetown University and then returned to Grand Forks to practice law. He was a municipal judge from 1931-1940. Davies served in the U.S. Army during World War II, rising from Lieutenant to Lieutenant Colonel before his discharge in 1946.

Davies resumed his practice in Grand Forks after the war, and in 1955, he was appointed U.S. District Judge in Fargo. In Davies' most famous case, while filling a temporary vacancy, he faced down Governor Orval Faubas and the Arkansas National Guard with the simple principle that "integration must begin forthwith."

Davies was named a Senior U.S. District Judge in 1971.

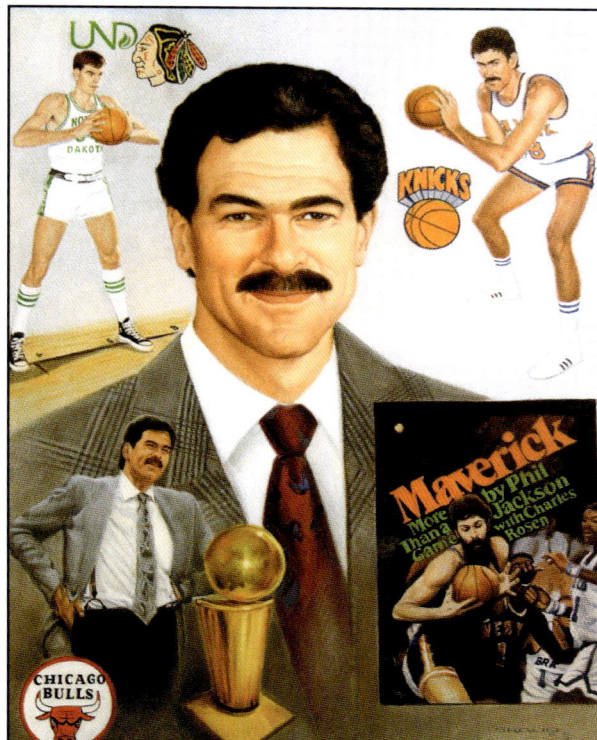

Phil Jackson
(1945-)

Selected:
June 1992

Award Presented:
July 30, 1992, Williston
Governor George Sinner

Portrait Artist:
Vern Skaug

Phil Jackson grew up in Williston, North Dakota, where he was a standout basketball player at Williston High School. While attending the University of North Dakota, he earned consecutive All-American honors for his star performances and was drafted by the New York Knicks in 1967. Jackson was instrumental in leading the Knicks to a National Basketball Association championship in 1973.

Jackson took his brilliant knowledge of the courts to a successful coaching career. He became the head coach of the Chicago Bulls in 1989 and led the Bulls to six national championships in nine years. After nine years as head coach of the Bulls, Jackson resigned and took a one-year sabbatical. In June 1999, he became head coach of the Los Angeles Lakers. He led the team to the 2000 NBA championship title in his first season as head coach and subsequent championships in 2001, 2002, 2009 and 2010. Jackson left the Lakers at the end of the 2004 season and returned as head coach in June 2005.

Self-possessed, focused and confident, Jackson will go down in NBA history not only for his dynamic leadership, but as the only person to both play and coach teams to titles for the NBA and Continental Basketball Association.

Larry Woiwode
(1941-)

Selected:
June 1992

Award Presented:
October 23, 1992, Bismarck
Governor George Sinner

Portrait Artist:
Vern Skaug

Larry Woiwode was born in 1941 in Carrington, near his hometown of Sykeston, North Dakota. In 1950, his family moved to Illinois. This award-winning novelist's writing career began in New York City and by 1966 he was publishing stories and poetry in *The New Yorker*. He has since published two dozen stories in that publication and has also appeared in the *Atlantic, Esquire, Harper's*, and *The Paris Review*.

Woiwode is the author of five novels, *What I'm Going To Do, I Think* (1969), *Beyond the Bedroom Wall* (1975), *Poppa John* (1981), *Born Brothers* (1988), and *Indian Affairs* (1992,) besides books of short stories, poetry, and non-fiction. He has been a Guggenheim Fellow, a John Dos Passos Prize winner, a recipient of the William Faulkner Foundation Award, and the Medal of Merit from the American Academy of Arts and Letters. He has been a finalist for both the Book Critics Circle and the National Book Awards and appears in four volumes of *Best American Short Stories*.

In his success, Woiwode has not forgotten his native state of North Dakota. Many of his books contain references to the state, and two novels are set in North Dakota. Woiwode returned to North Dakota in 1978. He continues his writing on a 160-acre farm near Mott, where he and his wife raised four children.

Angie Dickinson
(1931-)

Selected:
June 1992

Award Presented:
December 2, 1992, Bismarck
Governor George Sinner

Portrait Artist: Vern Skaug

Angie Dickinson was born Angeline Brown in the small farming community of Kulm, North Dakota. She was one of three daughters of Leo and Frederica Brown and grew up around the sights and sounds of her family's weekly newspaper offices in the 1930s. Her family owned and operated the *Kulm Messenger* and later, the *Edgeley Mail*.

Dickinson's family moved to California when she was 10 years old, but her time in North Dakota gave her the grounding she needed to take a shot at stardom. She took her prairie work ethic to the aircraft industry and worked in a parts plant to finance acting lessons. A talent scout spotted her in a beauty contest and so began the career of Dickinson. Her first big break came when Howard Hawks cast her opposite John Wayne in *Rio Bravo*.

Dickinson has appeared on the big screen with such Hollywood notables as Gregory Peck, Richard Burton, Marlon Brando, Roger Moore, Burt Reynolds, Peter Finch, and Ronald Reagan. She has appeared in more than 50 major movies and television productions, most known for her roles in *Police Woman* and *Dressed to Kill*. Among her many accolades, she has a star on Hollywood's Walk of Fame and her work in *Police Woman* earned her a Golden Globe for Best Actress in a Dramatic Series.

Rev. Richard C. Halverson
(1916-1995)

Selected:
December 1993

Award Presented:
March 26, 1994, Bismarck
Governor Ed Schafer

Portrait Artist:
Ann Linton Hodge

Reverend Halverson was born in Pingree, North Dakota. He was the United States Senate Chaplain from February 2, 1981, until his retirement on December 31, 1994.

Before becoming Senate Chaplain, Halverson was a minister at the Fourth Presbyterian Church in Bethesda, Maryland, for 23 years. Since 1956, he was active in the International Prayer Breakfast movement. He was chairman of the Board of World Vision-U.S., from 1966 to 1983. He also wrote several inspirational books.

Halverson was recognized for moving his job beyond that of giving the Senate daily opening prayer to include ministering to those on Capitol Hill. Former President George H. W. Bush wrote that Halverson is "one of God's very special messengers. He is one of the most thoughtful individuals I have ever met...He cared deeply, and his caring was so evident to me and to the members of Congress whose paths crossed his."

Brynhild Haugland
(1905-1998)

Selected:
October 1994

Award Presented:
March 20, 1995, Bismarck
Governor Ed Schafer

Portrait Artist:
Ann Linton Hodge

At her retirement in 1990, Brynhild Haugland was the longest serving incumbent state legislator in the nation, with 52 years in the North Dakota House of Representatives. Former First Lady Eleanor Roosevelt in 1954 wrote in the book *Ladies of Courage*, "Go down the list of laws passed by the North Dakota Legislature in the last 15 years to help meet the farmer's problems and improve his living conditions, and you will find that Brynhild Haugland had a hand in every one of them." Haugland was also instrumental in developing legislation in the 1940s that created a medical care program that other states have modeled. She cast an estimated 22,000 votes during her state service.

Haugland was born in Ward County near Minot, North Dakota, the daughter of Norwegian immigrant parents. She taught in Ward County schools from 1923-1925, before leaving to help run her parents' farm. In 1928, she received a teaching certificate from Minot State Normal School, now Minot State University. In 1988, she was recognized as one of two top award winners in the Public Service category of the Council of Advancement and Support of Education (CASE). Haugland had served on the Board of Directors of the International Peace Garden.

Admiral William A. Owens
(1940-)

Selected:
December 1995

Award Presented:
January 29, 1996, Bismarck
Governor Ed Schafer

Portrait Artist:
Ann Linton Hodge

Admiral William A. Owens was born and raised in Bismarck, North Dakota, and graduated from Bismarck High School in 1958. At the encouragement of his father, who had been in the Navy, he decided to apply to the U.S. Naval Academy in Annapolis. Owens was accepted and graduated in 1962 with a bachelor's degree in mathematics.

In the 1980s, his leadership and management skills brought him to Washington, where he served in several different capacities in the Office of the Chief of Naval Operations. Owens directed the Office of Program Appraisal under the Secretary of the Navy and was the first director of the Navy's Strategic Think Tank.

From November 1990 to July 1992, Owens commanded the U.S. Sixth Fleet, from which the first attacks of Desert Storm were launched, and NATO's Naval Striking and Support Forces Southern Europe. On March 1, 1994, Owens was appointed by President Clinton to serve as Vice Chairman of the Joint Chiefs of Staff. While serving in these demanding military duties, Owens also obtained bachelor's and master's degrees in politics, philosophy, and economics at Oxford University and a MBA from George Washington University.

In addition to numerous medals and awards, Owens has received Defense Distinguished Service and Superior Service Medals, a Legion of Merit with three Gold Stars, a Navy Commendation Medal with one Gold Star, and a Vietnam Service Medal with two Bronze Stars. He has also been awarded high-level foreign awards from France, Sweden, and Indonesia.

Carl Ben Eielson
(1897-1929)

Selected:
July 1997

Award Presented:
August 26, 1997, Hatton
Governor Ed Schafer

Portrait Artist:
Ann Linton Hodge

Pioneer aviator Carl Ben Eielson was born and raised in Hatton, North Dakota. After studying at the University of North Dakota, he enlisted in the Army Air Service in 1917 and completed pilot training.

Following his father's advice in 1921, Eielson enrolled in law school at Georgetown University, abandoning his passion for flying. During his time in Washington, he became friends with an Alaskan representative in Congress, and through him was offered a job at a high school in Fairbanks, Alaska. He quickly realized the value aviation could have for the remote land. He ordered a plane and began flying passengers and supplies throughout the northern territory.

Known as the "Father of Aviation" in Alaska, Eielson piloted the first airmail route in 1924. Eielson was later introduced to Captain George Hubert Wilkins, another outstanding pilot, and the two together earned international acclaim for their non-stop, 2,200 mile flight over the North Pole on April 15, 1928. In September of the same year, Wilkins and Eielson completed a 1,200 mile flight in the Antarctic, where they discovered six new islands.

In 1929, U.S. President Herbert Hoover granted Eielson the Harmon Trophy, an award presented annually to the outstanding aviator of the year. Eielson returned to Alaska and established Alaskan Airways, Inc. In 1929, he was killed while attempting to rescue passengers and cargo from an ice-bound ship in the Bering Strait. Eielson is the first individual to receive the Rough Rider Award posthumously.

Warren Christopher
(1925-2011)

Selected:
December 1997

Award Presented:
June 20, 1998, Scranton
Governor Ed Schafer

Portrait Artist:
Ann Linton Hodge

Warren Christopher was born in Scranton, North Dakota, on October 27, 1925. He graduated magna cum laude from the University of Southern California in 1945 and earned a law degree from Stanford University in 1949.

After law school, Christopher clerked for U.S. Supreme Court Justice William O. Douglas for one year. He joined the O'Melveny & Myers law firm of Los Angeles in 1950. He became a partner in 1958 and has worked with O'Melveny & Myers for 37 years in between several prestigious federal executive branch appointments.

Christopher served as Deputy Secretary of State in the Carter Administration. In that position, he led negotiations for the release of 52 American hostages in Iran, spearheaded the normalization of relations with China, helped to win ratification of the Panama Canal treaties, and headed the first interagency group on human rights. President Carter awarded him the Medal of Freedom on January 16, 1981.

In 1993, Christopher was sworn in by President Bill Clinton as the 63rd Secretary of State. During his four years of service, he logged 780,000 miles representing the United States abroad, more miles than any Secretary of State in a comparable period. At a ceremony honoring his retirement from public service President Clinton said, "The cause of peace and freedom and decency have never had a more tireless or tenacious advocate…." He retired from public service on November 7, 1996.

Bobby Vee
(1943-2016)

Selected:
February 3, 1999

Award Presented:
June 20, 1999, Bismarck
Governor Ed Schafer

Portrait Artist:
Ann Linton Hodge

Bobby Vee's rise to national prominence in the "rock and roll" industry began as the result of tragedy. The 15-year-old Bobby and his band, the "Shadows," were replacements for Buddy Holly, Richie Valens, and the Big Bopper the evening after they were killed in a plane crash on February 3, 1959. Ten days later, Bobby and his band had their first paying gig and later that fall they signed with Liberty Records.

His first regional hit was *Susie Baby*, his first national hit was *Devil or Angel*. Since then Bobby Vee has had 38 songs on *Billboard's* Top 100 chart, six gold singles, 14 top 40 hits, and two gold albums. He produced six gold records: *Devil or Angel*, *Rubber Ball*, *Take Good Care of My Baby*, *Run to Him*, *The Night Has a Thousand Eyes*, and *Come Back When You Grow Up*. He has seven top 10 hits in England and top 10 hits in Australia, Chile, Hong Kong, New Zealand, Israel, and the Philippines. *Billboard* magazine has called Bobby Vee, "One of the top ten most consistent chart makers ever."

Bobby Vee, born Robert Thomas Velline, was born April 30, 1943, in Fargo, North Dakota. In 1963, he married his high school sweetheart, Karen Ann Bergen, and they make their home in St. Cloud, Minnesota. They have four children, Jeff, Tom, Rob, and Jennifer. The boys now form part of his back-up band. Bobby Vee's popularity has remained constant; between Europe and America, Bobby and his band perform about 100 dates a year.

Chester "Chet" Reiten
(1923-2013)

Selected:
February 26, 2002

Award Presented:
October 8, 2002, Minot
Governor John Hoeven

Portrait Artist:
Ann Linton Hodge

Chester "Chet" Reiten was born in Hastings, North Dakota, in 1923 and served in the U.S. Navy during World War II. He graduated from North Dakota State University in Fargo with a degree in agriculture and worked as a county agent until entering the radio and television field in 1951. His company, Reiten Broadcasting Co., eventually owned four television and three radio stations in North Dakota.

In 1978, Chester Reiten and some of his Norwegian friends sat down to discuss a way in which they could celebrate their ancestry. Their discussion led to the birth of Norsk Høstfest, with Reiten as the founding father. Twenty-five years later, Norsk Høstfest has become an international phenomenon, steering the course of a Nordic festival that is both an ethnic celebration and a great source of entertainment. The event draws some 60,000 people from throughout North America and abroad. Over the years, royalty, ambassadors, national war and sports heroes, members of Congress, a former vice president of the United States, and many of North Dakota's governors have attended the festival.

Reiten has a long history of public service to his community and state, as a state senator, mayor of Minot, and community leader. As a result of the success of Norsk Høstfest, His Majesty King Olav V of Norway awarded Reiten the St. Olav Medal, one of the highest honors bestowed by the Norwegian government, outside of Norway.

Thomas J. Clifford
(1921-2009)

Selected:
February 26, 2002

Award Presented:
November 23, 2002, Grand Forks
Governor John Hoeven

Portrait Artist:
Ann Linton Hodge

Thomas J. Clifford, a native of Langdon, North Dakota, is recognized as one of the most effective university presidents in the nation. He became the eighth president of the University of North Dakota (UND) in 1971. Clifford's history with UND spans more than 50 years, as a UND student, faculty member, and administrator. Clifford received his Bachelor of Science in Commerce and Juris Doctorate from the University of North Dakota and a Master of Business Administration from Stanford University. He served in the U.S. Marine Corps during World War II, rising from the rank of Private First Class to Major and earning the Purple Heart, Bronze Star, and Silver Star in the Pacific Campaign.

Under Clifford's leadership, UND evolved into the largest and most comprehensive university in a five-state region: North Dakota, South Dakota, Montana, Wyoming, and Idaho. During his presidency, a four-year medical school, energy and environmental research center, and aviation and aerospace science programs were developed and became world-class, multi-million dollar enterprises. He played a key role in facilitating one of the nation's largest gifts to a public university, resulting in the finest college hockey facility in the world.

Clifford was named to the North Dakota Aviation Hall of Fame in 2002. He was regarded with high esteem for his entrepreneurial spirit, leadership in economic development, and service to his community, state, and nation.

Sister Thomas Welder
(1940-)

Award Presented:
May 1, 2004, Bismarck
Governor John Hoeven

Portrait Artist: Vern Skaug

Sister Thomas Welder, a native of Bismarck, North Dakota, served the University of Mary, formerly Mary College, since 1963 and was named college president in 1978. She attended the College of St. Benedict, graduated from the College of St. Scholastica, Duluth, and earned a master's degree in music from Northwestern University in Evanston, Illinois. She is a member of the Benedictine Sisters of Annunciation Monastery and has led an extraordinary life committed to God and her community.

Under the leadership of Sister Thomas, Mary College expanded to university status in 1986 and added undergraduate and graduate degree programs at locations throughout the state and region, including Fargo, Minot, Grand Forks, New Town, Belcourt, Montana, and Wyoming. During her presidency, enrollment grew from 925 students to nearly 3,000 in 2009. She retired on June 30, 2009, after 40 years of service to the University.

Sister Thomas is recognized as a woman who lives, serves, and leads by example. She has served on numerous boards and has been actively involved in professional organizations and religious affiliations on both a state and national level. Her personal achievements, character, and leadership have been an inspiration to countless individuals, students, entrepreneurs, and business and state leaders.

Envisioning the University of Mary as the nation's premier institution for the preparation of servant leaders, Sister Thomas promotes competence in communication, commitment to values, and service to community. Her strong belief in the ability of an individual to grow into leadership through service is an example for North Dakota and the nation.

Harry J. Pearce
(1942-)

Award Presented:
August 11, 2004, Bismarck
Governor John Hoeven

Portrait Artist: Vern Skaug

Harry J. Pearce is recognized statewide and nationally as an inspirational business leader and philanthropist. A native of Bismarck, North Dakota, he received a bachelor's degree in engineering sciences from the U.S. Air Force Academy and his juris doctor degree from Northwestern University School of Law.

Pearce was a senior partner in the law firm of Pearce & Durick in Bismarck from 1970-1985. He helped rewrite the North Dakota Criminal Code and Rules of Criminal Procedure while serving on several volunteer judicial and legislative committees. He served as a police commissioner, a municipal judge, and a U.S. magistrate. He joined General Motors (GM) in 1985 as Associate General Counsel and two years later was promoted to GM's General Counsel. He was promoted to Executive Vice President in 1992 and was responsible for GM's non-automotive operations, including electronic data systems and Hughes Electronics. In 1996, he was appointed Vice Chairman and served as a Director of the GM Corporation Board of Directors until his retirement from GM in 2001. He was then elected Chairman of the Hughes Electronics Corporation Board of Directors, a subsidiary of GM, and retired in 2003.

With an unbounded commitment to service, Pearce has received numerous state and national awards. He has turned his personal battle with leukemia into a public mission, serving on the boards of six different foundations supporting leukemia and bone marrow research. Pearce is a board member of MDU Resources Group, Inc., and is an active supporter of North Dakota's education system, the Bismarck-Mandan Symphony, the Nature Conservancy, and numerous other state organizations. He has served on the Theodore Roosevelt Medora Foundation Board of Directors and the Bismarck Hospital Board of Trustees and Executive Committee.

Pearce attributes his life of professional achievement and personal compassion to his North Dakota roots and the values he says make this state an extraordinary place to live and work – honesty and integrity, respect and responsibility, diversity and community, and faith in ourselves and our ability to succeed.

William C. Marcil
(1936-)

Award Presented:
May 18, 2006

Portrait Artist: Vern Skaug

William C. Marcil is a visionary state and national leader who has defined his career and business success with a steadfast commitment to respect, integrity, and responsibility. Getting his start as a young retail advertising salesman, Marcil quickly became a prominent leader in the state's newspaper industry as publisher of *The Forum*, and later, as president and chief executive officer of Forum Communications Company, a multi-media company based in Fargo.

A native of Rolette, Marcil graduated from the University of North Dakota in 1958 and then served in the U.S. Army and Reserves. In 1960, he married Jane Black, daughter of Norman D. Black, Jr., who was publisher of *The Forum* at the time. He began his newspaper career at *The Forum* in 1961 in retail advertising, and over the next eight years, worked his way up through the company, eventually becoming its president and publisher in 1969. Marcil placed a strong emphasis on public trust and consistently demonstrated a deep passion for publishing the best possible newspaper for the consumer.

Under Marcil's leadership, Forum Communications Company has retained its identity as an independent, family-owned publishing business, with deep roots in its community, while growing and diversifying into a multi-state, multi-media company. Forum Communications now includes more than 30 daily and community newspapers, as well as broadcasting, interactive media, and commercial printing in North Dakota, South Dakota, Minnesota, and Wisconsin.

Throughout his career, Marcil has had an impact on a national level, as well. He was the first North Dakotan to be elected chair of the American Newspaper Publishers Association, now known as the Newspaper Association of America. He has also been a strong advocate for business growth in general and served as chairman of the U.S. Chamber of Commerce.

Master Sgt. Woodrow W. Keeble
(1917-1982)

Award Presented: July 23, 2008

Portrait Artist: Vern Skaug

Master Sergeant Woodrow "Woody" Wilson Keeble is one of North Dakota's most highly decorated soldiers. A veteran of World War II and the Korean War, Keeble was presented with the Medal of Honor posthumously on March 3, 2008, at the White House. He is the first full-blooded Sioux Indian to receive the nation's highest military honor. He was inducted into the Pentagon Hall of Heroes on March 4, 2008.

Born on the Sisseton-Wahpeton Sioux Reservation in Waubay, South Dakota, he lived much of his life in Wahpeton, North Dakota. He joined the North Dakota National Guard in 1942 and was a member of Company I, 3rd Battalion, 164th Infantry Regiment (Rifle). His unit became the first U.S. Army unit to engage in offensive operations in WWII. They reinforced the 1st Marine Division at Guadalcanal and significantly contributed to decisive victory in the battle. Keeble received his first Bronze Star Medal, his first of four Purple Hearts, and the Combat Infantryman Badge for his actions at Guadalcanal.

Keeble reenlisted with the 164th Infantry Regiment at the beginning of the Korean War and later volunteered for a combat assignment with an active duty Army unit. He served with Company G, 19th Infantry of the 24th Infantry Division in Korea, where his actions would eventually earn him the nation's highest military honor. On October 20, 1951, when all of the officers of his company were killed or wounded, Keeble took charge of the support platoon attempting to complete the company's mission of taking control of a steep, rocky, and heavily fortified hill.

Keeble was treated for over 80 shrapnel wounds one day, but he returned to duty the next to earn the Medal of Honor. Armed with grenades and his rifle, he successfully conducted multiple, single-handed assaults against three well-fortified enemy positions, saving the lives of his fellow soldiers and inspiring his company to achieve its important objective. Keeble's famous comments exemplify his military service. "There were terrible moments that encompassed a lifetime, an endlessness when terror was so strong in me that I could feel idiocy replace reason. Yet I have never left my position, nor have I shirked hazardous duty. Fear did not make a coward out of me."

Doug Burgum
(1956-)

Award Presented:
November 20, 2009, Fargo

Portrait Artist: Vern Skaug

Recognized globally for his visionary business leadership, entrepreneur and philanthropist Doug Burgum credits his success to the values and ethics instilled in his early years by his family and community. Others cite his deep commitment to improving both the personal and business lives of people worldwide as the distinguishing attribute of his leadership.

A native of Arthur, North Dakota, Burgum earned a Bachelor of University Studies degree from North Dakota State University, then went on to achieve a MBA from the Stanford Graduate School of Business. After building national experience as a consultant at McKinsey & Company, he returned to North Dakota in 1983 and joined Great Plains Software – then a very small startup company in the fledgling computer software industry. Driven by a firm belief in the region's people and a powerful dream, he led the company's growth as chairman and CEO to a very successful initial public offering in 1997. He then steered Great Plains through its strategic acquisition by Microsoft Corporation in 2001 for $1.1 billion – at the time the largest acquisition Microsoft had ever made. He remained at Microsoft as senior vice president through 2007, helping the company capture a leading position in the business applications software industry.

As a testimony to his people-centric philosophy, Great Plains was named to *FORTUNE* magazine's list of "100 Best Companies to Work for in America" four times, a distinction also held by Microsoft Corporation during Burgum's tenure there.

In 2006, Burgum reaffirmed his passion for the region by founding Kilbourne Group, a company committed to the redevelopment of downtown Fargo through the restoration of historic buildings and the creation of new buildings that honor the past and inspire the future.

In 2008, Burgum co-founded Arthur Ventures, a regional venture capital fund that seeks to identify and invest in businesses with potential for strong growth. He has also served as a member of the advisory council for the Stanford Graduate School of Business, the board of directors of SuccessFactors, and other companies.

Ronald Offutt
(1942-   )

Award Presented: September 15, 2011

Portrait Artist: Vern Skaug

Ron Offutt is one of North Dakota's and the nation's premiere agribusiness leaders and philanthropists. As the nation's largest producer of potatoes and as owner of the largest network of John Deere construction and agricultural equipment dealerships in the U.S., Ron has brought jobs, revenue, and opportunities to North Dakota, especially within the state's agriculture industry.

Ron is the founder and chairman of the R. D. Offutt Company and RDO Equipment Company. With its corporate headquarters in Fargo, North Dakota, the company is comprised of a variety of businesses covering the agriculture, food processing, and retail equipment industries.

His companies and partnerships have resulted in several equipment and truck center locations across the state, the creation of more than 500 North Dakota jobs, an average annual payroll of more than $25 million, and three farm partnerships that grow nearly 12,000 acres of potatoes annually. The company's cornerstone is a 12-state, 190,000-acre farming operation for the production of potatoes.

In addition to his economic contributions, Ron is highly regarded for his philanthropy and civic involvement, serving on multiple boards and dedicating his time to several organizations and charities.

Ron attended Concordia College in Moorhead, Minnesota, where he majored in economics and starred in football and wrestling. After graduating from Concordia in 1964, he became a business partner in his father's farming operation and became the fourth generation to work in his family's potato business. In 1968, he purchased the John Deere store in Casselton, North Dakota, and began laying the foundation for the companies he founded and still owns and operates today.

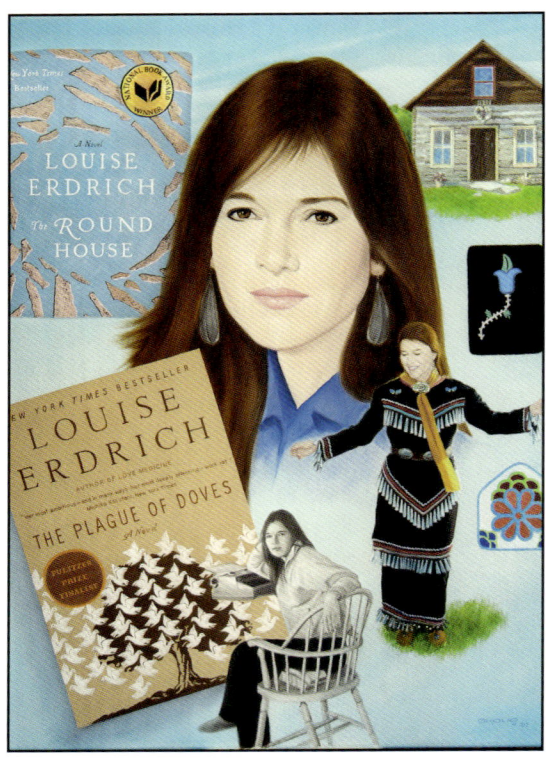

Louise Erdrich
(1954-)

Award Presented: April 19, 2013

Portrait Artist: Vern Skaug

Louise Erdrich is an internationally-acclaimed author and prominent literary figure who has numerous professional achievements and philanthropic contributions to her credit. The oldest in a family of seven children, Karen Louise Erdrich was born in Little Falls, Minnesota, in 1954, and grew up in Wahpeton, North Dakota, where her parents worked for the Bureau of Indian Affairs School. She is a member of the Turtle Mountain Band of Chippewa.

Louise graduated from Dartmouth College and received a master of fine arts degree from Johns Hopkins University. She is the author of 14 novels, as well as volumes of poetry, children's books, and a memoir of early motherhood. Her novel *Love Medicine* (1984) won the National Book Critics Circle Award. The *Last Report on the Miracles at Little No Horse* was a finalist for the National Book Award. *The Plague of Doves* (2008) won the Anisfield-Wolf Book Award and was a finalist for the Pulitzer Prize in 2009. In November 2012, Louise won the National Book Award for her novel, *The Round House*.

Louise lives in Minnesota and is the owner of Birchbark Books, a small independent bookstore in St. Paul. In an interview with Bill Moyers, Louise credited her achievements to the support of a widely extended loving family, to her parents, and to "a small, incremental, persistent, insect-like devotion to putting one word next to the next word. It's a very dogged process." In one of her poems, "Advice to Myself," Louise wrote, "Pursue the authentic. Decide first what is authentic, then go after it with all your heart."

Herman Stern
(1887-1980)

Award Presented: March 13, 2014

Portrait Artist: Vern Skaug

Businessman and visionary leader Herman Stern was born in Oberbrechen, Germany, in 1887. He came to America at the age of 16 to work at the Straus Clothing Store in Casselton, a clothing store established by his cousin, Morris Straus. In 1910, Herman became manager of the company's second store located in Valley City, where he remained for the next 70 years. In addition to Casselton and Valley City, the company operated stores in LaMoure, Carrington, Grand Forks, Jamestown, and Devils Lake. Today, after more than 130 years of operation, Straus Clothing has a store in Fargo with a third generation of Stern family members running the business.

In addition to his business contributions, Herman was also very active in community and statewide organizations and initiatives, establishing many programs that were pivotal in North Dakota's progress and remain so today. In 1924, he founded the Greater North Dakota Association, known today as the Greater North Dakota Chamber, and served as the organization's first president.

In 1937, under Herman's vision and direction, the North Dakota Winter Show made its debut in Valley City, and today, is the oldest and longest running agriculture show in the state, drawing visitors and exhibitors from across the country and Canada. He was active with Boy Scouts of America and was instrumental in establishing councils in Fargo, Valley City, Wahpeton, and Grand Forks, and raising money to build Camp Wilderness, a 2,400-acre camp in Minnesota that focuses on character building, citizenship training, and physical and mental fitness.

With family and friends in Germany during the rise of Adolf Hitler and the Nazi Party, Herman became worried about their welfare and embarked on a mission to bring them to America. With assistance from state and federal leaders, he made it possible for between 175 and 200 German Jews to escape the Holocaust and come to America.

Herman was also active in Rotary and the Masonic Order and was instrumental in establishing a program called the Community Chest. That program later became the United Way of Barnes County, another of his visions that is still impacting people today.

Herman passed away in 1980 at the age of 92.

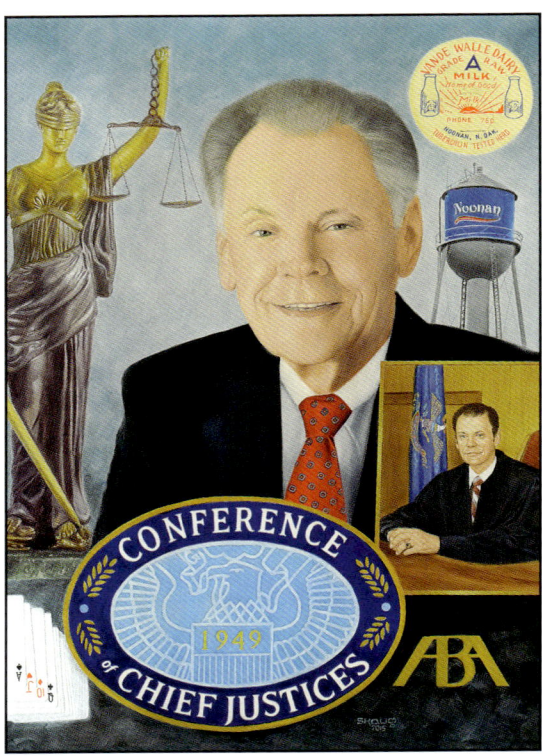

Gerald W. VandeWalle
(1933-)

Award Presented:
January 7, 2015

Portrait Artist: Vern Skaug

Chief Justice Gerald W. VandeWalle has served on the North Dakota Supreme Court for more than 36 years and was recently re-elected to his fourth 10-year term. He has served as the court's Chief Justice for the past 21 years, making him the longest-serving Chief Justice in North Dakota history and the longest-serving of all sitting Chief Justices in the nation.

Throughout his career, Chief Justice VandeWalle has made important contributions to the North Dakota Supreme Court and the state court system. He played an integral role in the unification of the court system, establishing a unified, statewide approach to court proceedings and the administration of justice. He was instrumental in redefining North Dakota's judicial districts and increasing the number of judges to accommodate growth in the state's economy and population. He also promoted the establishment of a mediation program for family law cases and created a trial court administration system to place administrators within the judicial districts to oversee court procedures.

A native of Noonan, North Dakota, Chief Justice VandeWalle attended the University of North Dakota, and in 1955, received a bachelor of science degree in commerce from the School of Business. In 1958, he received a juris doctor degree magna cum laude from the University of North Dakota School of Law.

He was admitted to the State Bar of North Dakota in 1958 and spent the next 20 years working in the Attorney General's Office. In August 1978, VandeWalle was appointed to the North Dakota Supreme Court. That November, he was elected to serve an unexpired term and was re-elected to 10-year terms in 1984, 1994, 2004, and 2014. In 1993, he was elected Chief Justice of the North Dakota Supreme Court and has been re-elected to that post for five consecutive terms.

Chief Justice VandeWalle has served as chair of several prestigious national organizations and has received numerous national awards and recognitions for his outstanding contributions to the justice system and the practice of law.

John D. Odegard
(1941–1998)

Award Presented:
October 15, 2015

Portrait Artist: Vern Skaug

John D. Odegard is the founder and former dean of the John D. Odegard School of Aerospace Sciences at the University of North Dakota (UND) in Grand Forks. In 1968, John pioneered UND's aviation program, which has grown to become one of UND's largest degree-granting colleges, one of the nation's most widely-respected aerospace education programs, and a leader in atmospheric research.

Throughout his 32-year career as an aerospace educator, John's reputation for leadership earned him industry acclaim and numerous recognitions. In 1982, he directed the development of the Federal Aviation Administration's (FAA) four-year degree. He helped initiate a joint effort between UND Aerospace and the FAA to broadcast aviation classes via satellite to college campuses across the country, and in 1986, led the development of the SPECTRUM airline pilot training program, an industry standard for commercial pilot training around the globe.

Under John's leadership, UND Aerospace moved to the forefront of research aimed at modernizing the nation's aging weather radar surveillance system. In 1987, UND Aerospace established the nation's first multi-disciplinary space studies program to provide a comprehensive understanding of the impact of humankind's move into space.

John was honored with the FAA's Excellence in Aviation Award and Distinguished Service Award for his many achievements in aerospace education and aviation safety. He was honored by the National Air Transportation Association with its Excellence in Pilot Training Award and received the prestigious Frank G. Brewer Trophy from the National Aeronautics Association for his distinguished and inspiring leadership in creating new educational opportunities. He was named North Dakota Business Innovator of the Year and was inducted into the North Dakota Entrepreneur Hall of Fame, the North Dakota Aviation Hall of Fame, and the Norsk Hostfest Scandinavian-American Hall of Fame.

John passed away in 1998 at the age of 57.

Eugene Dahl
(1924-2008)

Award Presented: October 27, 2016

Portrait Artist: Vern Skaug

Eugene Dahl, an entrepreneur and business leader who led the successful growth of several equipment manufacturing businesses in North Dakota, including Bobcat and Steiger, was responsible for creating thousands of manufacturing jobs in the state.

A native of Gwinner, Dahl graduated from Gwinner High School and attended North Dakota State University (NDSU) and Michigan State University before serving in World War II with the 75th Infantry at the Battle of the Bulge as a cryptographer. After the war, he finished his education at the University of North Dakota (UND), earning a degree in math and chemistry.

In 1947, Dahl taught school for one year in Cavalier before returning to his hometown of Gwinner where he became a partner in the Melroe Company. Dahl and his four brothers-in-law built the Melroe Manufacturing Company, now known as Bobcat, before selling it in 1970 to Clark Equipment.

Dahl served in numerous leadership roles in his church and the community, including two terms in the North Dakota House of Representatives.

In 1971, Dahl assumed the role of CEO of Steiger Tractor, and his family moved to Fargo. Under his leadership, the company grew from $2 million to $105 million in sales in six years and became a world leader in the manufacturing of four-wheel drive tractors. While at Steiger, Dahl formed one of the first employee stock ownership plans in the nation. Steiger was sold to JI Case in 1986.

He helped his sons establish Concord, Inc., which became the leading manufacturer in the United States of air seeders. He served as board chairman from 1977 until the company's sale to Case Corporation in 1996. He was also pivotal in the creation of Amity Technology, an industry-leading firm specializing in the manufacturing of agriculture machinery.

Dahl co-founded First Dakota Capital, North Dakota's first venture capital firm, and served as the first chairman of the Center for Innovation at UND. He served on numerous boards and received many honors, including an honorary doctorate from UND, induction into the North Dakota Entrepreneurial Hall of Fame, and the 2008 NDSU Harvest Bowl Agribusiness Award.

Clint Hill
(1932-)

Award Presented: November 19, 2018

Portrait Artist: Vern Skaug

Clint Hill will be remembered as the Secret Service agent who leapt onto the limousine during the assassination of President John F. Kennedy in Dallas, Texas, on November 22, 1963. Hill's primary responsibility was protection of First Lady Jacqueline Kennedy. At the first shot, Hill jumped from his position on the follow-up car, racing to shield the president and first lady with his body. Three shots were fired within six seconds, but Hill's actions saved Mrs. Kennedy's life.

Clinton J. Hill was born on January 4, 1932, in Larimore, North Dakota. He was adopted as an infant by Chris and Jennie Hill. He attended Washburn Public Schools and participated in every school activity available, including football, baseball, basketball, and band. Upon graduation in 1950, Hill attended Concordia College in Moorhead, Minnesota, but returned to work every summer in the Washburn area.

After college, Hill intended to teach history and coach athletics but was required to fulfill his military obligation. He served three years in the U.S. Army and trained to be a Counter Intelligence Agent. In 1958, Hill joined the U.S. Secret Service in Denver. One year later, he was assigned to the White House Detail protecting President Dwight D. Eisenhower. When President Kennedy was elected, Hill was one of two agents assigned to protect the first lady. He became the special agent in charge of the Presidential Protective Division during Lyndon B. Johnson's administration. In 1971, during the Richard M. Nixon administration, he was promoted to assistant director, responsible for all Secret Service protective forces. In 1975, Hill retired at age 43.

In 2012, Hill collaborated with journalist Lisa McCubbin to write *Mrs. Kennedy and Me*. Two more books followed: *Five Days in November* and *Five Presidents: My Extraordinary Journey with Eisenhower, Kennedy, Johnson, Nixon, and Ford*.

Hill has traveled the world representing North Dakota and the United States. His many awards and commendations include an Honorary Doctorate Degree from Niagara University, the American Valor Award from the American Veterans Conference, and the U.S. Treasury Department's highest award for valor.

North Dakota Statistical Information

Highest geographical point: White Butte, Slope County, 3,506 feet
Highest elevation for a city: Rhame, Slope County, 3,194 feet
Mean elevation: 1,900 feet
Lowest elevation: Pembina County, where the Red River enters Canada, 750 feet
Geographic center: McClusky

Square miles in land area 68,976
State ranking in land area 18th
Total acres occupied by farmland and ranches .... 39.1 million

Geographic Description of Location
Border to the north: Saskatchewan and Manitoba, on 49th Parallel
Border to the south: South Dakota, on 45 degrees 55 minutes North
Border to the east: Minnesota, Red River of the North divides the two states
Border to the west: Montana, on 104 degrees 2 minutes West
North Dakota is 310 miles wide at the Canadian border, 360 miles wide at the South Dakota border, and 210 miles from north to south.

The Geographic Center of the North American continent: located precisely six miles west of Balta or 15 miles southwest of Rugby. (National Oceanic & Atmospheric Administration)

The Continental Divide dissects North Dakota, roughly dividing the state from the southeastern part of the state diagonally northwest across the state to the northwest corner of the state. This is a north-south drainage divide. Waters north of this divide drain into the Hudson Bay. Waters south of this divide drain into the Missouri River and the Gulf of Mexico.

Soil: North Dakota has more black humus soil (Chernozem) in the eastern part of the state than any other state in the nation.

North America's tallest structure: 2,063-foot television transmission tower near Blanchard (KVLY television tower).

Tallest buildings in North Dakota:
- The Antelope Valley power plant near Beulah has two buildings that stand 361 feet tall.
- The Coal Creek Station power plant near Underwood has two buildings that measure 290 feet tall.
- The Garrison Dam water intake structure for power generators located on Lake Sakakawea near Riverdale is 249 feet tall.
- The North Dakota State Capitol in Bismarck is 242 feet tall. It is the third tallest capitol building in the country, following Nebraska and Louisiana at 450 feet tall.

North Dakota KIDS COUNT

The KIDS COUNT Data Book annually ranks child health and the well-being of children in the country. Indicators reflect the educational, social, economic, and physical well-being of children. It is produced by the Annie E. Casey Foundation.

Here are some rankings released in 2019 of North Dakota children compared to children in other states:

Ranking	Measure
1	Lowest percentage of children in households that spend more than 30 percent of their income on housing
1	Lowest percentage of teens ages 16-19 not attending school and not working
2	Lowest percentage of children living in poverty
3	Lowest percentage of children in single-parent families
4	Lowest percentage of low-birthweight babies

More data is available at www.ndkidscount.org and www.aecf.org.

North Dakota Vital Statistics

	2017	2018
Number of Marriages	4,352	4,319
Number of Divorces	1,878	2,804
Number of Births	10,738	10,630
Number of Deaths	6,311	6,343

Leading Causes of Death by Rank in North Dakota in 2018

1. Diseases of the Heart
2. All Cancers
3. Alzheimer's Disease
4. Chronic Lung Diseases
5. Accidental Deaths and Strokes

North Dakota Traffic Fatalities

Year	2017	2018
Fatal Crashes	106	95
Traffic Fatalities	116	105

Military Preparedness in North Dakota

ND National Guard Strength: 4,020 assigned/4,294 authorized (94%)
ND Army National Guard Strength: 2,920 assigned/3,100 authorized (94%)
ND Air National Guard Strength: 1,100 assigned/1,197 authorized (92%)

The North Dakota National Guard is a trained and highly motivated force of about 4,000 Citizen-Soldiers and Citizen-Airmen. It is prepared to provide ready units, individuals, and equipment in support of their communities, state, and nation. Always ready, always there.

✔ More information on the North Dakota National Guard can be found in the *1999-2001 North Dakota Blue Book: The Citizen-Soldiers: An Abbreviated History of the North Dakota National Guard.*

North Dakota National Guard Soldiers rappel down a tower at Camp Grafton Training Center August 19, 2016, during the annual Best Warrior Competition.

Veterans in North Dakota

There are **51,677 VETERANS** in North Dakota

— WHICH IS —

9% of the state's adult population

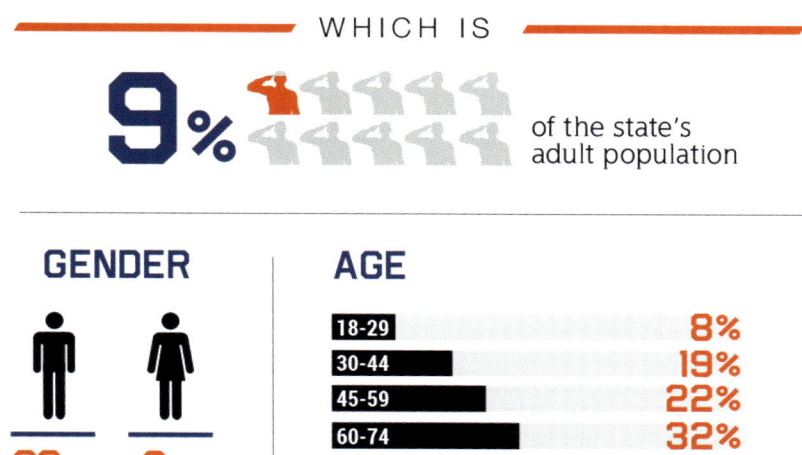

GENDER
- Male: **90.4%**
- Female: **9.6%**

AGE
- 18-29: **8%**
- 30-44: **19%**
- 45-59: **22%**
- 60-74: **32%**
- 75+: **19%**

PERIOD OF SERVICE
of North Dakota Veterans

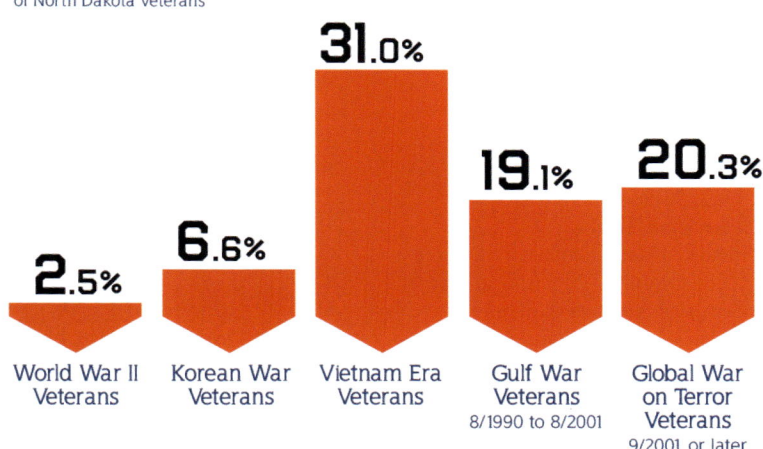

- World War II Veterans: **2.5%**
- Korean War Veterans: **6.6%**
- Vietnam Era Veterans: **31.0%**
- Gulf War Veterans 8/1990 to 8/2001: **19.1%**
- Global War on Terror Veterans 9/2001 or later: **20.3%**

NOTE: 20.5% of ND Veterans are from periods of service other than depicted above.

Sources:
North Dakota Veterans: U.S. Census Bureau, 2012-2016 American Community Survey 5-Year Estimates
https://www.va.gov/vetdata/Veteran_Population.asp

Miss North Dakota

Miss North Dakota 2019
Haley Wolfe, Carrington

1949	Kitty Gates Page, Fargo
1950	Joan Teets, Minot
1951	Marilyn Walker, Minot
1952	Margaret Winnifred Aandahl, Bismarck
1953	Marilyn Joy Wentz, Napoleon
1954	Dolores Ann Paulsen, Bismarck
1955	Mary Ann Gibbs, Crosby
1956	Janet Elizabeth Smith, Steele
1957	Helen Jane Winje, Minot
1958	Helen Estelle Korfhage, Grand Forks
1959	Claudia Jean Gullickson, Grand Forks
1960	Carol Ruth Olson, Fargo
1961	Diane Leda Ulvedal, Grand Forks
1962	Claudia Ellen Revland, Fargo
1963	Jo Ann Syvrud, Mandan
1964	Karen Victoria Kopseng, Bismarck
1965	Onalee Louise Olson, Fargo
1966	Denise Lee Fledderman, Inkster
1967	Wanda Lou Lowry, New Town
1968	Virginia Lee Hanson, Killdeer
1969	Charlene Hope Seifert, Gascoyne
1970	Nancy Jean Tangen, Aneta
1971	Lana Jean Herreid, Williston
1972	Georgia Ann Becker, Napoleon
1973	Linda Joyce Cole, Lisbon
1974	Susan Kaye Myhr, Bottineau
1975	Cathy Marie Woell, Minot
1976	Donna Grotberg, Valley City
1977	Kathryn L. Power, Beulah
1978	Sheila Jean Lindeman, Linton
1979	Daureen Podenski, Edgeley
1980	Karen Moe, Minot
1981	Stacie Anfinson, Hettinger
1982	Jeana Wolf, Rugby
1983	Phyllis Jeanette Hankey, Park River
1984	Callie Lynn Northagen, Grand Forks
1985	Elizabeth Ann Jaeger, Fargo
1986	Barbara Ann Kerzman, Garrison
1987	Susan Campbell, Grand Forks
1988	Tina Curran, Grand Forks
1989	Susan Jacobson, Grand Forks
1990	Lezlie Lund, Tolna
1991	VanNessa Straub, Fargo
1992	Stephanie Jean Fisher, Larimore
1993	Suzanne Spilde, Casselton
1994	Nicci Elkins, Grand Forks
1995	Kimberly Ann Cooley, Grand Forks
1996	Stephanie Hamilton, Williston
1997	Roxana Saberi, Fargo
1998	Sonja Marie Gedde, Fargo
1999-00	Kay Picconatto, Minot
2001	Carrie Haverstroh, Lisbon
2002	Jillayne Mertens, Wahpeton
2003	Stacey Thomas, Bismarck
2004	Sara Schelkoph, Grand Forks
2005	Ashley Ford, Cavalier
2006	Jacqueline Marie Johnson, Fargo
2007	Annette Olson, Baldwin
2008	Ashley Young, Grand Forks
2009	Tessie Jones, West Fargo
2010	Kate Ralston, Carrington
2011	Beth Dennison, Grand Forks
2012	Arianna Walker, Bismarck
2013	Laura Harmon, Grand Forks
2014	Jacky Arness, Fargo
2015	Delanie Wiedrich, Hazen
2016	Macy Christianson, Minot
2017	Cara Mund, Bismarck
2017	Lizzie Jensen, West Fargo*
2018	Katie Olson, Williston
2019	Haley Wolfe, Carrington

*Jensen was named Miss North Dakota 2017 after Cara Mund was crowned Miss America 2018.

Miss North Dakota Scholarship Organization, PO Box 607, Williston, ND 58802, www.missnorthdakota.org.

Miss America 2018

On September 10, 2017, Cara Mund, daughter of Doug Mund and DeLora Kautzmann Mund of Bismarck, North Dakota, made history by becoming the first woman from the state of North Dakota to be awarded the title of Miss America.

In 2007, at the age of 14, Mund founded North Dakota's Annual Make-A-Wish Fashion Show in honor of her two middle school classmates. She independently raised more than $80,000 for Make-A-Wish North Dakota and became a certified wish granter.

Cara Mund

Mund graduated valedictorian from Century High School in 2012. In high school, she was National Honor Society president and a national dance champion. She also trained with the Radio City Rockettes. Mund's high school classmates voted her "Most Likely to Become Miss America."

In 2016, Mund graduated with honors in business, entrepreneurship, and organizations from Brown University. Excelling inside and outside of the classroom, she was a teaching assistant, research assistant, director of a dance company, president of her sorority, cheerleader, and tour guide. She also served on Brown's Peer Community Standards Board.

Mund was crowned Miss North Dakota 2017 and represented North Dakota at the next level where she was crowned Miss America 2018. In her role as Miss America, she embarked on a national speaking tour where she traveled an average of 20,000 miles a month and changed location nearly every 48 hours. She advocated the importance of empowering women, education, and community service. She served as the National Goodwill Ambassador for Children's Miracle Network Hospitals, as well as promoted her own personal platform, the Make-A-Wish Foundation. As a former intern for U.S. Senator John Hoeven, Mund was invited to be his guest at the 2018 State of the Union. To date, she is the only Miss America to have ever attended.

Miss Rodeo North Dakota

1955	Vonnie Young
1956	Pat Shipley
1957	Kay VanDyke
1958	Jamie Childs
1959	Barbara Kennedy
1960	Ellen Trotter
1961	Sharon Burkhardt
1962	Joan Hecker
1963	Virginia Eck
1964	Bonita Bohnsack
1965	Janice Brettin
1966	Terrilyn Todd
1967	Kathy Sandberg
1968	Celeste Hill
1969	Janet Mutchler
1970	Cathy Moon
1971	Bonnie Kuntz
1972	Patty Backhaus
1973	Pat Carlson
1974	Katie Osborn
1975	Karen Paulson
1976	Vicki Solheim
1977	Judi Fischer
1978	Deb Sterns
1979	Nancy Jo Rustad
1980	Sue Vuylsteke
1981	Lynn Brokaw
1982	Brenda Lee Bonogofsky

**Miss Rodeo America 1983

1983	Tammy Schaubert
1984	Shauna Rangen
1985	Tracy Pearce
1986	Janet Voight
1987	Melissa Berger
1988	Jessica Severson
1989	Tammy Peterson
1990	Ellen Thomas
1991	Leah Mecklenberg
1992	Tanya Jo Zahn
1993	Ashlee Ehr
1994	Larri Pfliiger
1995	Nacole Needham
1996	Korrey Tweed

Miss Rodeo North Dakota 2019
Kara Bernston

1997	Sonya Dee Froelich
1998	Jamie Erhardt
1999	Shanda Doan
2000	Robyn Nelson
2001	Shannon Rustad
2002	Kami Fladeland (disqualified)
2003	Melanie Marquart
2004	Amanda Schaff
2005	Cara Ness
2006	Ashley Andrews

**Miss Rodeo America 2007

2007	Reba Bucholtz (resigned)
2008	Lindy Ellis
2009	Jessinta Hammer
2010	Tiffany Kuntz
2011	Sam Stanke
2012	Sadie Wardner
2013	Krystal Carlascio
2014	Codi Miller
2015	Dani Taylor
2016	Megan Haag
2017	Cassidy Rasmusson
2018	Hope Ebel
2019	Kara Bernston

Pictures and list are also available at www.missrodeond.org.

North Dakota's Published Authors

Below are North Dakota authors published in 2017 and 2018:

2017
- Kari L. Barchenger, *Hens and Chicks: The Vitko Collection*
- Margaret M. Barnhart, *Home for Supper: Memories and Recipes*
- Renita Brannan and Monica Hannan, *Nice and F.A.T.*
- Louise Erdrich, *Future Home of the Living God*
- Mark Kennedy, *Shapeholders: Business Success in the Age of Activism*
- Chuck Klosterman, *X: A Highly Specific, Defiantly Incomplete History of the Early 21st Century*
- Denise K. Lajimodiere, *Thunderbird*
- Timothy Murphy, *Devotions*
- Julie Neidlinger, *Blue Like a River: Burning the Bridge between Red and White at Standing Rock*
- Gayle Larson Schuck, *Secrets of the Dark Closet*
- Jessie Veeder, *Coming Home*
- Paula (Pfeiffer) Winskye, *Rewriting History: A Randy McKay Mystery*

2018
- Francie M. Berg, *Buffalo Heartbeats Across the Plains: The Last Great Hunts and Saving the Buffalo*
- Heid E. Erdrich, editor, *New Poets of Native Nations*
- Thomas D. Isern, *Pacing Dakota*
- Barbara Handy Marchello and Fern E. Swenson, *Traces: Early Peoples of North Dakota*
- Patrick J. McCloskey, *Open Secrets of Success: The Gary Tharaldson Story*
- Rodney Nelson, *Minded Places: Poems*
- Bonnie Larson Staiger, *Destiny Manifested*

North Dakota's Official Poets

The following people have received recognition as official poets in North Dakota. Formal recognition of an individual as poet laureate has been made by resolution of the Legislative Assembly. Such recognition is honorary and carries no duties or stipend.

Larry Woiwode, a native North Dakotan, is the state's fourth poet laureate. He assumed the position in 1995 under Senate Concurrent Resolution 4039. The nominee for state poet laureate requires a joint resolution of the state legislature and confirmation by the governor. According to former Governor George Sinner, Woiwode's work "shows the beauty of the truth prism of life here on the prairie and the broad beauty of the promise of humanity itself."

Woiwode is the author of the poetry collection *Even Tide* (Farrar, Straus, Giroux; New York, 1977) and a chapbook, *Land of Sunlit Ice* (North Dakota State University Press; Fargo, N.D., 2016). His poetry has appeared in several publications, including *The Atlantic, GQ, Harpers, The New Yorker*, and *Transatlantic Review*, and is reprinted in a dozen anthologies. His novels include *Beyond the Bedroom Wall*, which was a finalist for the National Book Award and the Book Critics Circle Award. Six of his books have been selected as "notable books of the year" by the *New York Times Book Review*. His stories appear in four volumes of *Best American Short Stories*. Woiwode has published two memoirs, two collections of essays, the biography of Harold Schafer, and a children's book, among others.

Woiwode is currently a writer in residence at the University of Jamestown where he teaches creative writing, world literature, contemporary American fiction, and Native American literature and religion.

Woiwode has won the William Faulkner Foundation Award and the Medal of Merit from the American Academy of Arts and Letters. He was also a fellow with the John Simon Guggenheim Foundation. Woiwode is also a recipient of the Theodore Roosevelt Rough Rider Award, the highest honor bestowed up a citizen of North Dakota. To read more about Woiwode and his accomplishments, see page 106.

David Solheim, English professor from Dickinson State University, was selected by the North Dakota Centennial Commission as the North Dakota Centennial poet.

Lydia O. Jackson became poet laureate by action of the 1983 Legislative Assembly as Henry R. Martinson died in November 1981. (Senate Concurrent Resolution No. 4055, 1983 S.L., ch. 853) (Lydia Jackson died in April 1984.)

Lydia O. Jackson and **Henry R. Martinson** were given the title of poets laureate by the 1979 Legislative Assembly as Corbin A. Waldron died in April 1978. (Senate Concurrent Resolution No. 4017, 1979 S.L., p. 1871)

Corbin A. Waldron was named North Dakota poet laureate by the 1957 Legislative Assembly. (Senate Concurrent Resolution E, 1957 S.L., p. 843)

James W. Foley, while considered to be North Dakota's first poet laureate, never officially received that designation.

✔ For complete biographies, photos, and poetry by these poets, see the feature of the *2003-2005 North Dakota Blue Book*.

✔ See the *2017-2019 North Dakota Blue Book* for details about the Pulitzer Prize in North Dakota.

Holidays in North Dakota

North Dakota Century Code Section 1-03-01

The Revised Codes of Dakota 1877 list Sunday, January 1, February 22 (Washington's birthday), July 4, December 25, and territorial election days as specific holidays (Civil Code, Part V, Section 2115).

1885	Added May 30, Decoration Day.
1897	Added February 12, Lincoln's birthday, and changed Decoration Day to Memorial Day.
1909	Added Labor Day as the first Monday in September.
1919	Added October 12, Discovery Day.
1921	Added November 11, Armistice Day.
1927	Expanded Discovery Day by adding "to commemorate the discovery of America by Leif Erikson about the year A.D. 1000; and by Christopher Columbus in the year A.D. 1492." Additional language in 1927 provided that legislative meetings held on or decisions made on any of the holidays other than Sunday were legal.
1937	Added Good Friday, which falls two days before Easter.
1945	Added Thanksgiving Day as the last Thursday in November.
1949	Changed Thanksgiving Day to the fourth Thursday in November.
1955	Changed the name of Armistice Day to Veterans Day (leaving it on November 11).
1969	Changed February 22, Washington's birthday, to the third Monday in February; Memorial Day from May 30 to the last Monday in May; Discovery Day from October 12 to the second Monday in October.
1973	Changed Veterans Day to November 11.
1987	Established third Monday of January as Martin Luther King, Jr., Day.

North Dakota Tourism

Tourism continues to play a major role in the economic well-being of North Dakota. The industry ranks third in the state behind agriculture and oil and gas in terms of economic impact and unlike the top two – which are prone to spikes in the market – it has shown a steady and sustained increase over the years.

North Dakota Tourism promotes events whose reach extends beyond the state's borders. It launched Travel Matters, a Tourism Division video series highlighting the people who help visitors "Be Legendary" in North Dakota.

North Dakota Tourism's advertising campaign continued with Minot native and actor Josh Duhamel and expanded to capitalize on several high-profile national sporting events. Tourism wrapped a Minneapolis Light Rail Train for eight weeks leading up to and after Super Bowl LII, sponsored the U.S. Hockey Hall of Fame hockey game between the University of North Dakota and Minnesota in Las Vegas with a regional reach of 23,442 households, and partnered with Fox Sports North to

Ice fishing at Devils Lake.

reach 2 million homes during Minnesota Twins games. Meanwhile, North Dakota State University won a seventh national championship in eight seasons to remain the talk of the Football Championship Subdivision.

In 2018, total web visits to www.NDtourism.com were 1,238,092, while total social media impressions surpassed 19 million. Media visits resulted from hosted writers and bloggers led to features in the *Chicago Tribune*, *Today Show*, *NY Times*, *USA Today* and *CNN Travel*.

Travelers continue to be fascinated by the North Dakota ways to "Be Legendary," including hunting and fishing, outdoor recreation, historic sites, state and national parks, and museums. The state's eclectic downtowns feature unique dining and nightlife.

Overseas visitors are also taking notice thanks to the cooperative efforts of the Great American West, a marketing collective made up of North Dakota, South Dakota, Montana, Wyoming, and Idaho. The number of overseas tour operators offering North Dakota products increased to 101 in 2018.

North Dakota is attractive to travelers for its beautiful sunsets, clear blue skies, and welcoming communities. Its exciting outdoor activities are unmatched and appreciated by visitors and residents alike.

The official tourism website (www.NDtourism.com) helps connect hundreds of thousands of people to opportunities, adventures, travel accommodations, festivals, and entertainment throughout North Dakota.

Kayaking on Lake Sakakawea.

North Dakota State Historical Sites

1. Big Mound Battlefield
2. Bismarck-Deadwood Stage Trail
3. Brenner Crossing
4. Buffalo Creek
5. Camp Arnold
6. Camp Atchison
7. Camp Buell
8. Camp Coming
9. Camp Grant
10. Camp Hancock
11. Camp Kimball
12. Camp Sheardown
13. Camp Weiser
14. Camp Whitney
15. Cannonball Stage Station
16. Crowley Flint Quarry
17. David Thompson
18. DeMores
19. Double Ditch Indian Village
20. Former Governors' Mansion
21. Fort Abercrombie
22. Fort Buford & MYCIC
23. Fort Clark Trading Post
24. Fort Dilts
25. Fort Mandan Overlook
26. Fort Ransom
27. Fort Rice
28. Fort Totten
29. Gingras Trading Post
30. Hudson Townsite
31. Huff Indian Village
32. Killdeer Mountain Battlefield
33. Lake Jessie
34. Lake Johnson
35. Maple Creek Crossing
36. McPhail's Butte
37. Medicine Rock
38. Menoken Indian Village
39. Molander Indian Village
40. Oak Lawn
41. Palmer's Spring
42. Pembina State Museum
43. Pulver Mounds
44. Ronald Reagan Minuteman Missile
45. St. Claude
46. Standing Rock
47. Steamboat Warehouse
48. Stutsman County Courthouse
49. Sully's Heart River Corral
50. Sweden
51. Turtle Effigy
52. Walhalla
53. Welk Homestead
54. Whitestone Hill
55. Writing Rock

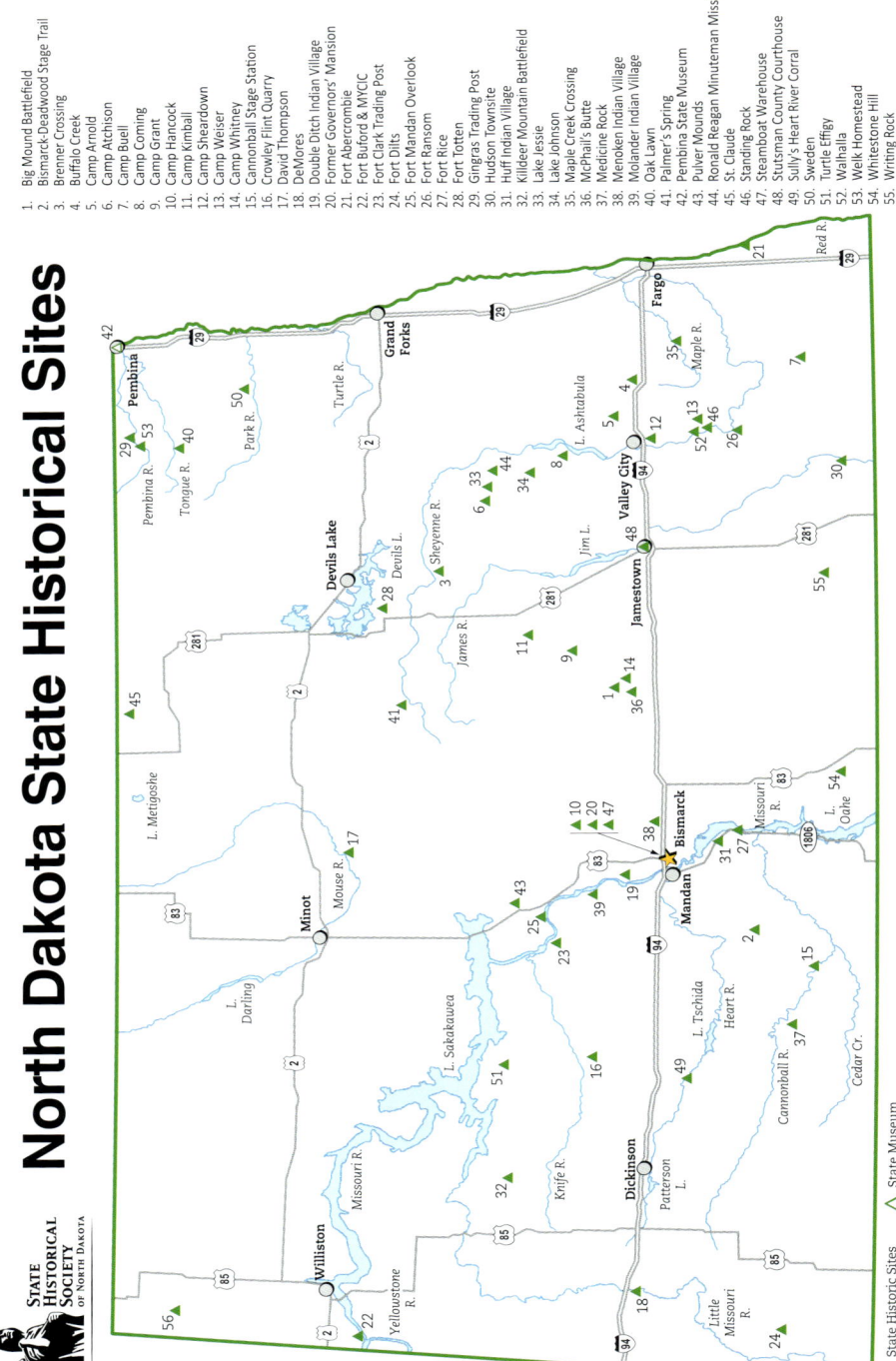

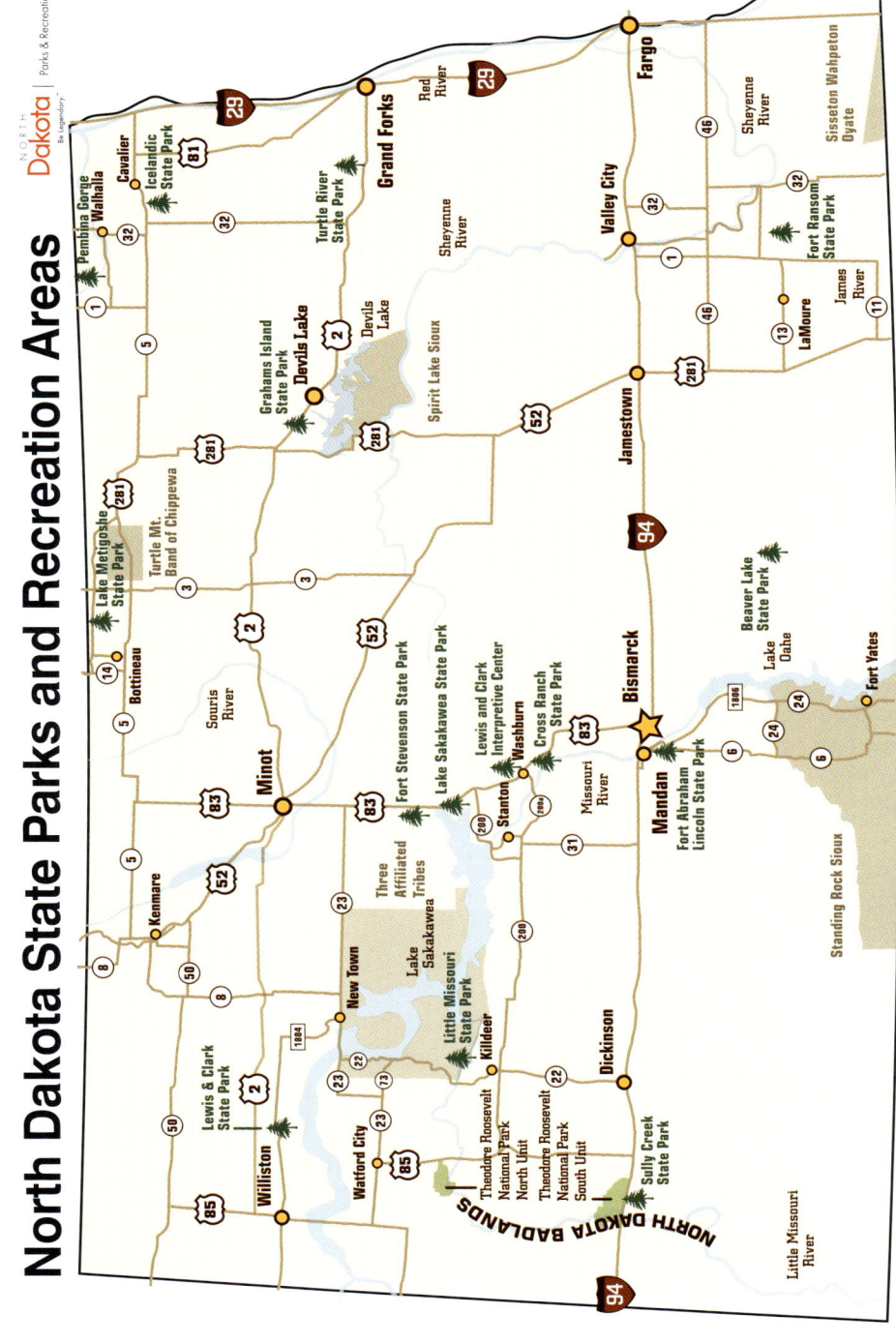

Visitation at North Dakota Sites

	2015	2016	2017	2018
North Dakota State Parks	1,109,460	1,147,183	1,081,064	1,109,797
Theodore Roosevelt National Park	580,033	753,880	708,003	749,389
Fort Union Trading Post National Historic Site	13,605	17,502	13,329	13,551
Knife River Indian Villages National Historic Site	11,377	13,328	11,644	11,682
North Dakota State Fair	305,093	293,123	299,077	318,248
Lewis and Clark Interpretive Center/Fort Mandan	52,119	48,532	70,726	104,809
North Dakota Heritage Center	305,265	238,313	228,347	209,014
North Dakota Historic Sites	82,409	84,674	81,074	113,520

    North Dakota State Parks that collect visitor data include: Fort Abraham Lincoln State Park, Cross Ranch State Park, Fort Stevenson State Park, Lake Metigoshe State Park, Lake Sakakawea State Park, Lewis and Clark State Park, Little Missouri State Park, Turtle River State Park, Icelandic State Park, Fort Ransom State Park, Sully Creek State Park, and Grahams Island State Park.

    Theodore Roosevelt National Park, Fort Union Trading Post National Historic Site, and Knife River Indian Villages National Historic Site are all owned and operated by the U.S. government.

✔ More information on state parks is in the *1997-1999 North Dakota Blue Book*.

Horseback riders.

International Peace Garden

A visitor enjoys the cacti and succulents collection at the International Peace Garden.

The International Peace Garden is located in the heart of the Turtle Mountains, along the Manitoba and North Dakota border, and provides a serene setting to contemplate and advocate for peace everywhere. It is registered as a charitable nonprofit organization in Canada and the United States.

In 1928, Henry J. Moore and other horticulturists in the United States and Canada met to discuss recognizing the peaceful coexistence between the two countries. On July 14, 1932, a simple stone cairn was placed at the entrance of the project, set centrally along the 49th Parallel between the two coasts. The cairn reads: "To God in His Glory. We two nations dedicate this Garden and pledge ourselves that as long as man shall live; we will not take up arms against one another."

Nestled among lakes and woodlands is the one-of-a-kind garden. More than 75,000 flowers are planted each year, in addition to flowering shrubs and perennials. The most photographed feature is the working floral clock. The only displays that remain the same each year are the two floral flag displays.

The world-class cacti and succulents collection resides in a 10,000-square-foot Conservatory, which is open year-round. The Garden's Interpretive Center shares a foundation with the Conservatory and features a café, retail store, library, and conference room. The Conservatory holds the Don Vitko Collection, a breathtaking display of more than 6,000 plants with more than 4,000 unique species and cultivars. Vitko collected the xeric plants for nearly five decades in Minot, North Dakota. The plants are native to North America, South America, and Africa.

The Sunken Garden is located directly across from the Interpretive Center. The garden's focal point is an octagon-shaped pond with a water feature in the center. The plantings of trees, shrubs, flowers, and walkways surround the pond in repeated octagonal rows.

Visitors may stand with a foot in each country as they see a panoramic view from the Formal Garden area's top terrace. Below is a water feature where garden weddings take place. At the far end of the Formal Garden is the Peace Chapel. It is the only building in the International Peace Garden straddling the international border, and one of three buildings on the entire U.S.-Canadian border. Etched in limestone tablets embossed with marine fossils are inspiring quotes of people of peace.

Also along the Formal Garden border walk is the Carillion Bell Tower; the beautiful tones ring on the hour and half hour. Across from the Bell Tower is the 9/11 Memorial Site with steel girders from the World Trade Center. The site is sponsored by the Rotary International Clubs of Brandon, Manitoba, and Minot, North Dakota.

The International Peace Garden is also home to the International Music Camp and Royal Canadian Legion Athletic Camp, providing arts appreciation and athletic training to thousands of young people each year.

The more than 2,300-acre International Peace Garden has many buildings to accommodate bus tours, conventions, wedding receptions, reunions, and conferences, as well as private campsites and hiking and biking trails.

✔ A list of North Dakota Olympians can be found in the *2003-2005 North Dakota Blue Book*.

✔ See *2013-2015 North Dakota Blue Book* for information about the North Dakota Cowboy Hall of Fame.

✔ See *2013-2015 North Dakota Blue Book* for information about the North Dakota Country Woman of the Year.

✔ See *2013-2015 North Dakota Blue Book* for information about the North Dakota Champion Tree Program and answers to common tree questions.

✔ See *2015-2017 North Dakota Blue Book* for information about North Dakota license plates.

✔ North Dakota record fish caught while recreational fishing can be found in the *2015-2017 North Dakota Blue Book*.

✔ See *2015-2017 North Dakota Blue Book* for information on the sister states of North Dakota and Taiwan.

✔ See *2017-2019 North Dakota Blue Book* for a history of the North Dakota Council on the Arts.

✔ North Dakota zoos are listed in the *2017-2019 North Dakota Blue Book*.

North Dakota Theatre

North Dakota has a rich theatre tradition. In addition to the community, college, and university theatres listed here, many high schools in the state provide theatre arts programs for their students. The Communication, Speech, and Theatre Association of North Dakota (http://cstand.org/) supports and enriches speech and theatre arts programs, both as academic disciplines and as performing arts, at all levels throughout the state, including high school, college, university, and community.

City	Theatre
Bismarck	Bismarck State College
Bismarck	Capitol Shakespeare
Bismarck	Dakota Stage Ltd. / Shade Tree Players
Bismarck	Sleepy Hollow Summer Theatre & Arts Park
Bismarck	TruNorth Theatre Company
Bismarck	University of Mary
Bottineau	Dakota College at Bottineau LumberActs Drama Club
Devils Lake	Fort Totten Little Theatre
Devils Lake	Lake Region State College Theatre Arts
Dickinson	Dickinson State University Theatre Program
Fargo	Fargo Moorhead Community Theatre
Fargo	Trollwood Performing Arts School
Fargo	Theatre B
Fargo	North Dakota State University Department of Theatre Arts
Grand Forks	Empire Theatre Company
Grand Forks	Greater Grand Forks Community Theatre (Fire Hall Theatre)
Grand Forks	Summer Performing Arts Company
Grand Forks	University of North Dakota Department of Theatre Arts
Grand Forks	University of North Dakota Chester Fritz Auditorium
Jamestown	University of Jamestown Theatre
Jamestown	The 2nd ACT
LaMoure	LaMoure County Summer Musical Theatre
Lisbon	Lisbon Opera House
Mayville	Mayville State University Theater
Medora	Medora Musical
Minot	Minot State University Summer Theatre
Minot	Minot State University Theatre Arts
Minot	Mouse River Players
New Rockford	Dakota Prairie Regional Center for the Arts
Valley City	Valley City State University Theatre
Walhalla	Frost Fire Summer Theatre
Wahpeton	North Dakota State College of Science Performing Arts Department
Williston	Entertainment Inc!

100 Years of Caring for North Dakota Injured Workers

1919 was a watershed year in North Dakota politics. World War I, the Great War in Europe, had ended the year before, bringing mechanization and change back to the country. North Dakota soldiers returning home were ready to go back to work and continue the Industrial Revolution.

That revolution had brought changes to the workforce. Workers were beginning to leave the farms and were working in sometimes dangerous factory conditions. If they got hurt, maimed, or killed on the job, there was no government program to help them pay for their medical bills or provide a wage replacement to them or their family and dependents.

Beginning in the early 20th century, states began to adopt workers' compensation laws, designed to provide a safety net for workmen hurt on the job. The idea came from Germany. In 1884, Otto Von Bismarck, chancellor of the German Empire, introduced the programs to assist workers in the event of accidental injury or illness. This initial workers' compensation system was financed by workers and employers.

Not surprisingly, German immigrants brought the idea to America in the early 20th century. Wisconsin passed the first comprehensive workers' compensation law in 1911, while Mississippi was the last state to jump onboard in 1948.

In 1919, the Nonpartisan League was the majority party in the North Dakota Legislature. They brought forward a radical legislative agenda of social change for the

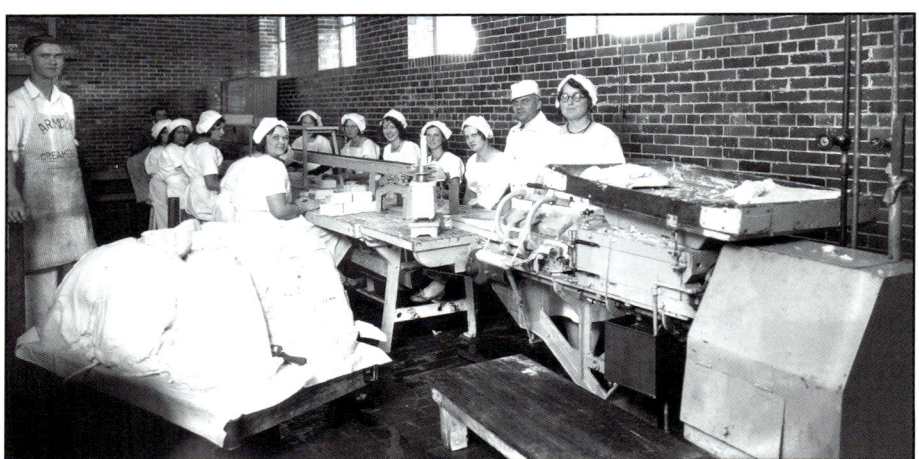

Creamery workers in the 1920s in North Dakota.

state. The League created three institutions that year that still resonate strongly in the state 100 years later: Bank of North Dakota, State Mill and Elevator, and Workmen's Compensation Bureau, now known as Workforce Safety & Insurance (WSI).

Over the last 100 years, despite several changes in the management structure, WSI still regulates an exclusive employer-financed, no-fault workers' compensation insurance system. North Dakota is just one of four states to have this exclusive arrangement with its citizens.

WSI is funded solely by employer premiums and receives no general fund dollars. WSI charges employers insurance premiums based on the risk of a job. In return, WSI provides North Dakota workers coverage for their work-related injuries. WSI sets, maintains, and manages its financial reserves to ensure adequate funding to pay the medical and wage-replacement claims for injured workers.

For 100 years, despite economic, political, and management changes, WSI remains prepared to care for injured workers.

Bank of North Dakota Celebrates Its First 100 Years

As the Bank of North Dakota entered its 100th year, it reported capital reserves of $825 million and total assets of $7 billion. It's highly unlikely our forefathers could have imagined the impact legislation signed into law February 25, 1919, would have on the state.

Life was challenging for North Dakota farmers in the early 1900s. Many felt they were being unfairly treated by eastern bankers charging high interest rates, the railway imposing excessive transportation fees, and elevators downgrading the grain quality. This dissatisfaction fueled the Nonpartisan League to select candidates that supported a platform that ultimately included the Industrial Commission, Bank of North Dakota (BND), and State Mill and Elevator.

Employees were hired, and policies established. The Bank opened its doors on the corner of 7th Street and Main Avenue in Bismarck, North Dakota, July 28, 1919. It remained in that location for 90 years.

The original Bank of North Dakota location in downtown Bismarck.

The founding principles of the Bank stated:

Therefore, the policy of Bank of North Dakota is to be established essentially along the following lines:

- To promote agriculture, commerce, and industry
- To be helpful to and assist in the development of …. financial institutions and public corporations within the state and not, in any manner, to destroy or to be harmful to existing financial institutions
- To redeposit in the state, so far as is consistent with the operation of the Bank, such public funds
- To stabilize interest rates

In 2019, the Bank still adheres to these founding principles by serving as the depository for state funds, providing interest rate buydown programs, and partnering with financial institutions across the state to grow local economies.

Only student loans and two agriculture loans are made directly to residents. All other loans are made in participation with local lenders, allowing them to utilize BND's capacity to better serve their customers and grow their local economies.

BND's profits are reinvested to generate capital and can be designated by the North Dakota Legislature to balance the general fund and support special needs, such as a disaster relief effort or infrastructure building. Since inception, the Bank has returned more than $1 billion to the state.

A team of 46 employees opened the Bank, and today there are 180 employees. After 90 years at its original location, the Bank was moved to its current location, which houses a museum commemorating its first 100 years.

The Bank of North Dakota at its current location.

Chapter Three
Federal-State Relationships

This aerial view of the Bismarck Airport includes President Dwight D. Eisenhower's planes after arrival on June 11, 1953, for the dedication of the Garrison Dam.

Presidential Visits to North Dakota 150
North Dakota's International Border Crossings 154
Medal of Honor Memorial.. 159
Representation at the Federal Level 160
Profile of Present Congressional Delegation 161
Chronology of United States Senators from North Dakota................................... 166
Chronology of United States House Members from North Dakota...................... 167
Justices of the United States Supreme Court 171
Judges of the Eighth Circuit Court of Appeals 171
United States District Court for the District of North Dakota Judges 172
United States Magistrate Judges for the District of North Dakota 175

Presidential Visits to North Dakota

Even before North Dakota existed as a state in the United States of America, presidential visits were marked as an immense event. From the first presidential visit in 1878 through 2018, 16 incumbent presidents have visited while in office. Past presidents, candidates stumping for their right to serve, vice presidents, and presidents' wives all would also find their way into the state.

The following list denotes confirmed years in which presidential visits to North Dakota occurred. An asterisk denotes a visit by an incumbent president.

1878 – Rutherford B. Hayes (1877-1881)*
1880-1889, multiple visits – Theodore Roosevelt (1901-1909)
1883 – Ulysses S. Grant (1869-1877)
1883 – Chester A. Arthur (1881-1885)*
1899 – William McKinley (1897-1901)*
1900 – Theodore Roosevelt
1903 – Theodore Roosevelt*
1908 – William Taft (1909-1913)
1910 – Theodore Roosevelt
1911 – Theodore Roosevelt
1912 – Theodore Roosevelt
1918 – Theodore Roosevelt
1919 – Woodrow Wilson (1913-1921)*
1920 – Franklin D. Roosevelt (1933-1945)
1920 – William Taft
1934-1944, multiple visits – Franklin D. Roosevelt*
1939 – Herbert Hoover (1929-1933)
1944 – Dwight D. Eisenhower (1953-1961)
1950 – Harry S. Truman (1945-1953)*
1952 – Harry S. Truman*
1953 – Dwight D. Eisenhower*
1958 – Harry S. Truman
1958 – John F. Kennedy (1961-1963)
1960 – Lyndon B. Johnson (1963-1969)
1960 – John F. Kennedy
1963 – John F. Kennedy*
1966 – Richard M. Nixon (1969-1974)
1968 – Richard M. Nixon
1970 – Richard M. Nixon*
1975 – Ronald Reagan (1981-1989)
1976 – Ronald Reagan
1976 – James (Jimmy) Carter (1977-1981)
1979 – Ronald Reagan
1980 – Ronald Reagan

1982 – George H. W. Bush (1989-1993)
1986 – Ronald Reagan*
1989 – George H. W. Bush*
1997 – William (Bill) Clinton (1993-2001)*
2001 – George W. Bush (2001-2009)*
2005 – George W. Bush*
2014 – Barack Obama (2009-2017)*
2017 – Donald J. Trump (2017-)*
2018 – Donald J. Trump*

Rutherford B. Hayes

The first president to visit what would become North Dakota was Rutherford B. Hayes, who stopped in the state in September 1878 while traveling on an extensive western trip with his wife and three of his sons. The president made eight speeches along the journey, one of which was delivered in Fargo from the train platform. Afterward, he was taken to view the Dalrymple farms. The Northern Pacific Railroad presented President Hayes with a 930-acre farm five miles north of Bismarck; it was comprised mostly of Section 3 of Hay Creek Township. He never visited the land, and on December 17, 1885, the *Bismarck Tribune* quoted the *Chicago News* that the Hayes farm had been sold for $21,000.

Chester A. Arthur

Chester A. Arthur was the next incumbent president to visit North Dakota. He passed through the state on a much-publicized trip to Yellowstone National Park in 1883. He had scheduled the trip to regain his health, but the three-week trip was too wearying. He had planned to stop for an hour in Bismarck and take part in festivities surrounding the cornerstone of the new capitol building being laid. Sitting Bull and former President Ulysses S. Grant were also in the state for the cornerstone celebrations. However, Arthur cancelled his stop, and on the return trip, he passed from Bismarck to Fargo during the night.

William McKinley

On October 13, 1899, President William McKinley visited North Dakota. He stopped in Wahpeton first, where he spoke briefly. He arrived later in the day in Fargo. His arrival by train was delayed by two hours, so the planned parade was cancelled. He was greeted by 20,000 people, and the *Griggs Courier* noted "it was impossible for his carriage to proceed, so great was the crush to get at him." He got to the Waldorf Hotel, where he delivered a speech outlining the policy of his administration on the Philippines. Other members of his party also delivered speeches, and then he held a reception where people could shake his hand.

Theodore Roosevelt

Theodore Roosevelt visited North Dakota many times, beginning in the 1880s with his ranching operation in the Badlands. He continued to return as he became more involved with higher political offices, campaigning successfully in 1900 as

President McKinley's vice president. When McKinley was assassinated in 1901, Roosevelt became the 26th president.

In April 1903, Roosevelt visited North Dakota and made a grand tour by train, entering from South Dakota at Ellendale, proceeding through Edgeley, then to Fargo. From there, he crossed the state from east to west on the Northern Pacific route to Beach. While in Bismarck, U.S. Senator Henry Hansborough arranged for a "good horse" to await him, so he had the opportunity to ride around the city. He would return to North Dakota multiple times, but not again while in office.

Woodrow Wilson
Woodrow Wilson stopped in North Dakota near the end of his presidency, as part of an extensive national speaking tour that was supposed to promote America becoming a member of the League of Nations. He stopped in Bismarck on September 10, 1919, was driven in a motorcade through the city, spoke at the Bismarck Auditorium (now the Belle Mehus), and then toured the residential portion of the city in another motorcade. His wife was with him, and a large crowd of citizens gathered about them throughout the day, finally seeing them off to their next stop at Billings, Montana.

Franklin D. Roosevelt
Franklin Delano Roosevelt visited North Dakota several times while president. His first visit was in 1934 to Devils Lake, where he spoke to 35,000 people and surveyed the effects of drought in the area. He came to Bismarck in 1936 and viewed the drought effects first-hand once again. Parade routes were outlined in the newspapers so citizens could see him. He dedicated the fairgrounds grandstand in Grand Forks in 1937. He also came through the state in the 1940s to tour military establishments.

Harry S. Truman
President Harry S. Truman toured North Dakota in May 1950. He visited several cities, including Williston, where he gave a speech about the Garrison Dam. Thousands of citizens turned out to hear the president speak. He returned to the state in 1952 with his daughter Margaret on a whistle-stop tour across the state. They were campaigning for Adlai Stevenson, as well as for all Democrats running for Congress. During this trip, he spoke at Berthold. In 1958, Truman returned to the state once more to speak against Republican farm policies prior to the 1958 congressional elections.

Dwight D. Eisenhower
In June 1953, after becoming president, Dwight D. Eisenhower came to North Dakota to dedicate the Garrison Dam. He landed in Minot, and after speaking at the Dam Closure Ceremony, he was driven to Bismarck. His motorcade went by the capitol building, and he also visited Theodore Roosevelt's cabin.

John F. Kennedy

John F. Kennedy came to North Dakota in 1958 as a senator to speak at a fundraising dinner at the state's Democratic Convention in Minot. He also spoke in Dickinson on the anniversary of Theodore Roosevelt's birth. He returned in 1960 during a tour around the country to campaign at both Bismarck and Jamestown. In September 1963, shortly before he was assassinated, he visited Grand Forks. While there, he spoke at the University of North Dakota Resources Week Convocation and received an honorary degree.

Richard Nixon

Richard Nixon visited North Dakota before he became president, visiting in the 1950s and 1960s while he was vice president. He spoke in Bismarck in 1966 and returned to the city with his wife in 1968. He visited while in office on July 24, 1970, stopping in Fargo on his way across the country with his wife and daughter. He mainly discussed rural life and agriculture, traveling to talk to governors of less populated states. He also campaigned the same year in Grand Forks for Republican Congressman Thomas S. Kleppe, who was running for the U.S. Senate.

Ronald Reagan

Ronald Reagan campaigned and visited North Dakota several times before becoming president. He spoke to North Dakota Republicans at the Lincoln Day Dinner in Bismarck in February 1979 and came again to Bismarck in April 1980 to address the Republican State Convention during his campaign for president. As president, he came in 1986 to the University of North Dakota in Grand Forks to campaign for the re-election of Senator Mark Andrews.

George H. W. Bush

In April 1989, to celebrate the state's centennial anniversary, President George H. W. Bush came to the state capitol grounds. While there, he was greeted by an estimated crowd of 10,000. He spoke of the centennial, including that the Centennial Commission had set a goal to plant 100 million trees over the next 10 years throughout the state. As part of the ceremony, the Centennial Grove was dedicated, and Bush planted an American Elm tree, which was descended from a tree planted by John Quincy Adams on the grounds of the White House.

Bill Clinton

President Bill Clinton visited Grand Forks in April 1997 following the Red River Flood to view the damage and listen to requests for more federal funding. He landed at the Grand Forks Air Force Base, went on an hour-long helicopter tour above Grand Forks and East Grand Forks, and visited with displaced residents of the area. Clinton offered support and provided authorization for more relief money to go toward the efforts.

George W. Bush

President George W. Bush made his first of two visits to the state in March 2001, shortly after his inauguration, as part of a national speaking tour to promote his proposed tax cut program in Congress. He spoke at the Bison Sports Arena at North Dakota State University to a huge crowd. Bush returned to Fargo in 2005, this time to promote his proposed changes in the Social Security system. He spoke again at the Bison Sports Arena.

Barack Obama

President Barack Obama visited the Cannon Ball Flag Day Powwow on June 13, 2014. He told Standing Rock Sioux members that the visit was one part of his administration's commitment to improving federal and tribal relations. This was the first visit to a North Dakota reservation by a president in office, as well as the first president's visit to any reservation since 1999. While there, he spoke about improving education and economic development. He was presented with several honorifics, including a star quilt. The First Lady received a Standing Rock Sioux tribal flag.

Donald Trump

President Donald Trump made an appearance at the Andeavor Refinery in Mandan for a tax return speech in September 2017. He returned to the state in June 2018 to hold a campaign rally for Representative Kevin Cramer at the Scheels Arena in Fargo. About 6,000 people attended. In September of that year, he returned to Fargo to boost for Cramer again.

North Dakota's International Border Crossings

North Dakota's northern border covers 310 miles and follows the 49th parallel. The state shares 18 international ports with the Canadian provinces of Saskatchewan and Manitoba. The most heavily used border crossings are at Pembina, Portal, Dunseith (International Peace Garden), and Neche.

In 2018, officials from U.S. Customs and Border Protection, U.S. Department of State, U.S. General Services Administration, Federal Highway Administration, and the North Dakota Department of Transportation (NDDOT) announced the completion of border crossing upgrades at the Pembina-Emerson Port of Entry. Governor Doug Burgum stated, "the substantial improvements made to traffic flow, technology, and safety at this Port of Entry will enhance the movement of people and goods between our two countries and further strengthen North Dakota's relationship with our neighbor and number one trading partner."

The $9.7 million project included upgrades that "will allow the staff to meet the demands of the high-volume, 24/7 border crossing operation. The end result means shorter wait times for travelers and a more efficient operation for border crossing staff," said former NDDOT Director Tom Sorel.

Representatives from the U.S. congressional delegation, federal agencies, and state and local entities participated in a ribbon-cutting ceremony for border crossing upgrades at the Pembina-Emerson Port of Entry in October 2018.

Improvements concentrated on traffic flow, safety, and technology upgrades. Enhancements included new lanes to separate commercial and passenger traffic, relocation of the facility's outbound inspections and duty-free pick-up areas, construction of additional parking, a pedestrian crossing, and introduction of an Intelligent Transportation System.

Below is a listing of North Dakota's border crossings from west to east. It includes the town and road in North Dakota and the corresponding information in Canada. The data reflects incoming entry of vehicles, passengers, or pedestrians entering each North Dakota port in 2018.

Fortuna, N.D. (US 85)/Oungre, Saskatchewan (Hwy 35)
- Trucks 3,056
- Personal Vehicles 9,109
- Personal Vehicle Passengers 18,682
- Buses 4
- Bus Passengers 144

Ambrose, N.D. (ND 42)/Torquay, Saskatchewan (Hwy 350)
- Trucks 157
- Personal Vehicles 768
- Personal Vehicle Passengers 1,424

Noonan, N.D. (ND 40)/Estevan Highway, Saskatchewan (Hwy 47)
- Trucks 1,976
- Personal Vehicles 19,338
- Personal Vehicle Passengers 32,943
- Pedestrians 3

Portal, N.D. (US 52)/North Portal, Saskatchewan (Hwy 39)
- Trucks 69,141
- Trains 1,374
- Train Passengers 4,122
- Personal Vehicles 56,551
- Personal Vehicle Passengers 113,752
- Pedestrians 1,445
- Buses 100
- Bus Passengers 4090

Northgate, N.D. (ND 8)/Northgate, Saskatchewan (Hwy 9)
- Trucks 10,296
- Trains 132
- Train Passengers 324
- Personal Vehicles 9,805
- Personal Vehicle Passengers 20,012
- Pedestrians 89
- Buses 5
- Bus Passengers 197

Sherwood, N.D. (ND 28)/Carievale, Saskatchewan (Hwy 8)
- Trucks 4370
- Personal Vehicles 11,537
- Personal Vehicle Passengers 21,863
- Buses 1
- Bus Passengers 9

Antler, N.D. (ND 256)/Lyleton, Manitoba (PR 256 Pierson)
- Trucks 2097
- Personal Vehicles 5763
- Personal Vehicle Passengers 11,093

Westhope, N.D. (US 83)/Coulter, Manitoba (PTH 83 [Melita])
- Trucks 6,846
- Personal Vehicles 6,128
- Personal Vehicle Passengers 12,705

Carbury, N.D. (ND 14 [Souris])/Goodlands, Manitoba (PTH 21 [Deloraine])
- Trucks 1,462
- Personal Vehicles 9,012
- Personal Vehicle Passengers 18,977
- Buses 10
- Bus Passengers 245

Dunseith, N.D. (US 281)/Boissevain, Manitoba (PTH 10 [International Peace Garden])
    Trucks 22,000
    Personal Vehicles 44,129
    Personal Vehicle Passengers 95,413
    Buses 38
    Bus Passengers 1,414

Saint John, N.D. (ND 30)/Lena, Manitoba (PTH 18 [Killarney])
    Trucks 613
    Personal Vehicles 9,093
    Personal Vehicle Passengers 17,513
    Buses 5
    Bus Passengers 88

Hansboro, N.D. (ND 4)/Cartwright, Manitoba (PTH 5)
    Trucks 110
    Personal Vehicles 5,144
    Personal Vehicle Passengers 10,732
    Buses 13
    Bus Passengers 222

Sarles, N.D. (ND 20)/Crystal City, Manitoba (PTH 34)
    Trucks 502
    Personal Vehicles 2,822
    Personal Vehicle Passengers 5,996
    Buses 53
    Bus Passengers 410

Hannah, N.D. (91st Ave NE)/Snowflake, Manitoba (PR 242)
    Trucks 71
    Personal Vehicles 761
    Personal Vehicle Passengers 1,205

Maida, N.D. (ND 1 [Langdon])/Windygates, Manitoba (PTH 31 [Darlingford])
    Trucks 1,107
    Personal Vehicles 5,262
    Personal Vehicle Passengers 11,293

Walhalla, N.D. (ND 32)/Winkler, Manitoba (PTH 32)
    Trucks 6,026
    Personal Vehicles 28,039
    Personal Vehicle Passengers 52,403
    Buses 2
    Bus Passengers 50

Neche, N.D. (ND 18)/Gretna, Manitoba (PTH 30)
- Trucks 5,477
- Personal Vehicles 29,186
- Personal Vehicle Passengers 48,164
- Buses 1
- Bus Passengers 6

Pembina, N.D. (I-29)/Emerson, Manitoba (PTH 75)
- Trucks 168,981
- Trains 939
- Train Passengers 1,878
- Personal Vehicles 203,938
- Personal Vehicle Passengers 477,046
- Buses 644
- Bus Passengers 17,667

Visit www.cbp.gov/contact/ports/ND for the most up-to-date information on border crossings in North Dakota.

✔ World War II art by Scott Nelson may be found in the *2007-2009* and *2009-2011 North Dakota Blue Books*.

✔ Personal stories of North Dakota soldiers during wartime may be found in the *2009-2011 North Dakota Blue Book*.

✔ Information regarding laws that honor women veterans may be found in the *2011-2013 North Dakota Blue Book*.

✔ Information regarding Honor Flights may be found in the *2011-2013 North Dakota Blue Book*.

✔ Information about the *USS North Dakota* (B-29) and *USS North Dakota* (SSN-785) may be found in the *2013-2015* and *2015-2017 North Dakota Blue Books*.

✔ *USNS City of Bismarck* (T-EFP-9) information may be found in the *2017-2019 North Dakota Blue Book*.

✔ Information about unmanned aircraft systems in North Dakota may be found in the *2017-2019 North Dakota Blue Book*.

✔ North Dakota's military bases are included in the *2017-2019 North Dakota Blue Book*.

Medal of Honor Memorial Recognizes State Veterans

A memorial honoring North Dakota's Medal of Honor recipients was dedicated at Roosevelt Park in Minot on July 4, 2007. The park is named after President Theodore Roosevelt, who was a Medal of Honor recipient.

Medal of Honor Memorial.

✔ See the *2007-2009 North Dakota Blue Book* for a listing of North Dakota's Medal of Honor recipients. The latest recipient, Woodrow Wilson Keeble, is recognized in the *2015-2017 North Dakota Blue Book*.

Representation at the Federal Level

North Dakota in Congress

The United States Congress is often known as "the people's branch" of government. It is comprised of 535 members, with 435 in the House of Representatives and 100 in the Senate. Congress serves as both a representative and governing body. Responsibilities of the congressional branch include the development and passage of legislation, constituent service, oversight responsibilities for departments and agencies in the executive branch, and appropriations authority.

To obtain more information about the U.S. Congress, visit www.congress.gov. The website contains information on the federal legislative process, pending legislation, the voting records of members of Congress, and links to congressional news and information. Additional information about the federal government, including links to documents such as the U.S. Constitution, can be found at www.usa.gov/about-the-us.

United States Senators

Under Article I, Section 3, of the U.S. Constitution, "The Senate of the United States shall be composed of two senators from each state...." The Constitution originally provided that senators were to be elected by the legislatures of each state. The 17th Amendment to the Constitution, effective May 31, 1913, amended the Constitution to allow for senators to be elected by popular vote of the people. Senators serve six-year terms and are elected in staggered terms.

Extensive and timely information on the U.S. Senate can be found at www.senate.gov.

United States Representatives

Under Article I, Section 2, of the U.S. Constitution, each state elects one or more representatives to Congress. The number of representatives is based upon each state's population in relation to that of the entire nation as enumerated by the federal decennial census. In 1929, the total number of House members was limited to 435. Had this not occurred, the size of the present House of Representatives using the initial formula would now exceed 8,000 members. Based on the 2010 census, each member of the U.S. House of Representatives represents an average population of 709,760.

Extensive and timely information on the U.S. House can be found at www.house.gov.

Profile of Present Congressional Delegation

U.S. Senator

John Hoeven

Birthplace
Bismarck

Party Affiliation
Republican

Education
B.A. from Dartmouth College;
MBA from Northwestern University

Professional Experience
Bank of North Dakota, president and CEO, 1993-2000; Governor of North Dakota, 2000-2010; elected to the U.S. Senate, 2010 and 2016

Committees
- Committee on Agriculture, Nutrition, and Forestry
    - Nutrition, Agricultural Research, and Specialty Crops
    - Rural Development and Energy
    - Commodities, Risk Management, and Trade
- Committee on Appropriations
    - Agriculture, Rural Development, Food and Drug Administration, and Related Agencies (Chairman)
    - Defense
    - Energy and Water Development
    - Homeland Security
    - Military Construction, Veterans Affairs, and Related Agencies
    - Transportation, Housing and Urban Development, and Related Agencies
- Committee on Energy and Natural Resources
    - Energy
    - Public Lands, Forests, and Mining
    - National Parks
- Committee on Indian Affairs (Chairman)

U.S. Senator

Kevin Cramer

Birthplace
Rolette; raised in Kindred

Party Affiliation
Republican

Education
Graduate of Kindred High School; B.A. from Concordia College in Moorhead, Minnesota; M.A. in Management from University of Mary in Bismarck

Professional Experience
North Dakota Republican Party, chairman, 1991-1993; North Dakota State Tourism, director, 1993-1997; candidate for U.S. House of Representatives, 1996; North Dakota State Economic Development and Finance, director, 1997-2000; candidate for U.S. House of Representatives, 1998; North Dakota Public Service Commissioner, 2003-2012; elected to the U.S. House of Representatives, 2012, 2014, and 2016; elected to the U.S. Senate, 2018

Committees
- Armed Services Committee
- Environment and Public Works Committee
- Veterans' Affairs Committee
- Banking, Housing, and Urban Affairs Committee
- Budget Committee

Contact Information for North Dakota's Senators

Senator John Hoeven
https://www.hoeven.senate.gov/

Washington, D.C., Offices
338 Russell Senate Office Building
Washington, DC 20510
202-224-2551
202-224-7999 (Fax)

Bismarck District Offices
U.S. Federal Building, Room 312
220 East Rosser Avenue, P.O. Box 2579
Bismarck, ND 58502
701-250-4618
701-250-4484 (Fax)

Fargo District Offices
123 Broadway North, Suite 201
Fargo, ND 58102
701-239-5389
701-239-5112 (Fax)

Grand Forks District Offices
102 North Fourth Street, Suite 108
Grand Forks, ND 58203
701-746-8972
701-746-5613 (Fax)

Minot District Offices
U.S. Federal Building, Suite 107
100 First Street Southwest
Minot, ND 58701
701-838-1361
701-838-1381 (Fax)

Western North Dakota
Williston, ND
701-580-4535

Senator Kevin Cramer
https://www.cramer.senate.gov/

400 Russell Senate Office Building
Washington, DC 20510
202-224-2043

328 Federal Building
220 East Rosser Avenue
Bismarck, ND 58501
701-699-7020

306 Federal Building
657 Second Avenue North
Fargo, ND 58102
701-232-5094

114 Federal Building
102 North 4th Street
Grand Forks, ND 58203
701-699-7030

105 Federal Building
100 First Street Southwest
Minot, ND 58701
701-837-6141

Due to the delay in receiving mail at the Washington, D.C., locations, constituents are encouraged to mail all correspondence to the North Dakota addresses.

U.S. Congressman

Kelly Armstrong

Birthplace
Dickinson

Party Affiliation
Republican

Education
B.A. from University of North Dakota, 2001; J.D. from University of North Dakota, 2003

Professional Experience
Reichert Armstrong Law Firm, partner, 2003-2012; Armstrong Corporation, vice president, 2011-2018; North Dakota State Senator, District 36, 2013-2018; North Dakota Republican Party, chairman, 2015-2018; elected to the U.S. House of Representatives, 2018

Committees
- Committee on the Judiciary
  - Subcommittee on Constitution, Civil Rights, and Civil Liberties
  - Subcommittee on Immigration and Citizenship
  - Subcommittee on Antitrust, Commercial, and Administrative Law
- Committee on Oversight and Reform
  - Subcommittee on Environment

Contact Information for Congressman Kelly Armstrong

Representative Kelly Armstrong
https://armstrong.house.gov/

Washington, D.C., Office
1004 Longworth House Office Building
Washington, DC 20515
202-225-2611

Bismarck District Office
U.S. Federal Building, Room 228
220 East Rosser Avenue
Bismarck, ND 58501
701-354-6700

Fargo District Office
3217 Fiechtner Drive, Suite D
Fargo, ND 58103
701-353-6665

Due to the delay in receiving mail at the Washington, D.C., locations, constituents are encouraged to mail all correspondence to the North Dakota addresses.

Chronology of United States Senators from North Dakota

North Dakota was granted statehood on November 2, 1889. On this date, elections for congress and state-level officials were held. What follows is a chronology of senators elected to the U.S. Congress.

Gilbert A. Pierce (R) (1839-1901) 1889-1891
    Elected 1889; defeated for re-election 1891
Lyman R. Casey (R) (1837-1914) 1889-1893
    Elected 1889; defeated for re-election 1893
Henry C. Hansbrough (R) (1848-1933) 1891-1909
    Elected 1891, 1897, 1903; defeated for re-election 1909
William N. Roach (D) (1840-1902) 1893-1899
    Elected 1893; defeated for re-election 1899
Porter J. McCumber (R) (1858-1933) 1899-1923
    Elected 1899, 1905, 1911, 1916; defeated for re-election 1922
Martin N. Johnson (R) (1850-1909) 1909-1909
    Elected 1909; died in office October 21, 1909
Fountain L. Thompson (D) (1854-1942) 1909-1910
    Appointed December 7, 1909, to fill vacancy caused by Martin Johnson's death; resigned January 31, 1910
William E. Purcell (D) (1856-1928) 1910-1911
    Appointed February 1, 1910, to fill vacancy caused by Fountain Thompson's resignation; defeated for re-election 1911
Asle J. Gronna (R) (1858-1922) 1911-1921
    Elected 1911, 1914; defeated for re-election 1920
Edwin F. Ladd (R) (1859-1925) 1921-1925
    Elected 1920; died in office June 25, 1925
Lynn J. Frazier (R) (1874-1947) 1923-1941
    Elected 1922, 1928, 1934; defeated for re-election 1940
Gerald P. Nye (R) (1892-1971) 1925-1945
    Appointed November 14, 1925, to fill vacancy caused by Edwin Ladd's death; elected 1926, 1932, 1938; defeated for re-election 1944
William Langer (R) (1886-1959) 1941-1959
    Elected 1940, 1946, 1952, 1958; died in office November 8, 1959
John Moses (D) (1885-1945) 1945-1945
    Elected 1944; died in office March 3, 1945
Milton R. Young (R) (1897-1983) 1945-1980
    Appointed March 12, 1945, to fill vacancy caused by John Moses' death; elected in special election to fill unexpired term, 1946; elected 1950, 1956, 1962, 1968, 1974; did not seek re-election 1980
C. Norman Brunsdale (R) (1891-1978) 1959-1960
    Appointed November 19, 1959, to fill vacancy caused by William Langer's death; served until August 7, 1960

Quentin N. Burdick (D) (1908-1992) 1960-1992
   Elected June 28, 1960, to complete William Langer's unexpired term; re-elected 1964, 1970, 1976, 1982, 1988, died in office September 8, 1992
Mark Andrews (R) (1926-) 1981-1986
   Elected 1980; defeated for re-election 1986
Jocelyn Burdick (D) (1922-) 1992
   Appointed September 12, 1992, to fill vacancy caused by her husband's death; sworn in on September 16, 1992; served until December 14, 1992*
Kent Conrad (D) (1948-) 1987-2013
   Elected 1986; did not seek re-election, 1992, but following Sen. Burdick's death, won a December 4, 1992, special election to fill Burdick's unexpired term; re-elected 1994, 2000, 2006
Byron L. Dorgan (D) (1942-) 1992-2011
   Elected 1992; sworn into office December 15, 1992*, re-elected 1998, 2004; did not seek re-election 2010
John H. Hoeven (R) (1957-) 2011-present
   Elected 2010, 2016
Heidi Heitkamp (D) (1955-) 2013-2019
   Elected 2012; defeated for re-election 2018
Kevin Cramer (R) (1961-) 2019-present
   Elected 2018

* The year 1992 saw a series of unusual events that affected North Dakota's elected federal officeholders. See page 457 of the *2001-2003 North Dakota Blue Book*.

Chronology of United States House Members from North Dakota

The state of North Dakota, based on a 2010 census population of 672,591, has one at-large member of the House of Representatives. North Dakota had one representative from 1889 to 1902, two from 1903 to 1912, three from 1913 to 1932, two from 1933 to 1972, and one since 1973. House members serve for two years.

After every federal decennial (or 10-year) census, the number of House members from each state is determined by population. The U.S. Constitution guarantees every state one representative, no matter how small its population. By law, the total number of House members is set at 435. The number of members given to each state is determined by its proportion of the nation's total population as of the latest decennial census. Congressional districts are those geographical areas within each state represented by a single member of the House of Representatives. For states like North Dakota with only one House member, the entire state is considered a congressional district, referred to as a district at large.

The following is a chronology of House members elected to the U.S. Congress.

One Representative, Elected At Large (1889-1902)

Henry C. Hansbrough (R) (1848-1933) 1889-1891
    Elected 1889; did not seek re-election 1890
Martin N. Johnson (R) (1850-1909) 1891-1899
    Elected 1890, 1892, 1894, 1896; did not seek re-election 1898
Burleigh F. Spalding (R) (1853-1934) 1899-1901
    Elected 1898; did not seek re-election 1900
Thomas F. Marshall (R) (1854-1921) 1901-1903
    Elected 1900

Two Representatives, Elected At Large (1903-1912)

Thomas F. Marshall (R) (1854-1921) 1903-1909
    Elected 1902, 1904, 1906; did not seek re-election 1908
Burleigh F. Spalding (R) (1853-1934) 1903-1905
    Elected 1902; defeated for re-election 1904
Asle J. Gronna (R) (1858-1922) 1905-1911
    Elected 1904, 1906, 1908; did not seek re-election 1910
Louis B. Hanna (R) (1861-1948) 1909-1913
    Elected 1908, 1910; did not seek re-election 1912
Henry T. Helgesen (R) (1857-1917) 1911-1913
    Elected 1910

Three Representatives, Elected By District (1913-1932)

District 1
Henry T. Helgesen (R) (1857-1917) 1913-1917
    Elected 1912, 1914, 1916; died in office April 10, 1917
John M. Baer (R) (1886-1970) 1917-1921
    Elected July 10, 1917, special election to fill unexpired term of Henry Helgesen;
    elected 1918; defeated for re-election 1920
Olger B. Burtness (R) (1884-1960) 1921-1933
    Elected 1920, 1922, 1924, 1926, 1928, 1930; defeated for re-election 1932

District 2
George M. Young (R) (1870-1932) 1913-1924
    Elected 1912, 1914, 1916, 1918, 1920, 1922; resigned September 2, 1924
Thomas Hall (R) (1869-1958) 1924-1933
    Elected November 4, 1924, to fill unexpired term of George Young; elected
    1926, 1928, 1930; defeated for re-election 1932

District 3
Patrick D. Norton (R) (1876-1953) 1913-1919
    Elected 1912, 1914, 1916; defeated for re-election 1918

James H. Sinclair (R) (1871-1943)...1919-1933
    Elected 1918, 1920, 1922, 1924, 1926, 1928, 1930

Two Representatives, Elected At Large (1933-1962)

James H. Sinclair (R) (1871-1943)...1933-1935
    Elected 1932; defeated for re-election 1934
William Lemke (R) (1878-1950)...1933-1941
    Elected 1932, 1934, 1936, 1938; did not seek re-election
Usher L. Burdick (R) (1879-1960)...1935-1945
    Elected 1934, 1936, 1938, 1940, 1942; did not seek re-election
Charles R. Robertson (R) (1889-1951)..1941-1943
    Elected 1940; defeated for re-election 1942
William Lemke (R) (1878-1950)...1943-1950
    Elected 1942, 1944, 1946, 1948; died in office May 30, 1950
Charles R. Robertson (R) (1889-1951)..1945-1949
    Elected 1944, 1946; defeated for re-election 1948
Usher L. Burdick (R) (1879-1960)...1949-1959
    Elected 1948, 1950, 1952, 1954, 1956; did not seek re-election 1958
Fred G. Aandahl (R) (1897-1966)..1951-1953
    Elected 1950; did not seek re-election 1952
Otto Krueger (R) (1890-1963)...1953-1959
    Elected 1952, 1954, 1956; did not seek re-election 1958
Quentin N. Burdick (D) (1908-1992)...1959-1963
    Elected 1958; resigned August 8, 1960
Don L. Short (R) (1903-1982)...1959-1963
    Elected 1958, 1960
Hjalmer C. Nygaard (R) (1906-1963)...1961-1963
    Elected 1960

Two Representatives, Elected By District (1963-1972)

In 1959, the North Dakota Legislative Assembly created two congressional districts – East and West (Senate Bill No. 73, chapter 181, 1959 Laws of North Dakota).

East District
Hjalmer C. Nygaard (R) (1906-1963)...1963-1963
    Elected 1962; died in office July 19, 1963
Mark Andrews (R) (1926-)...1963-1973
    Elected October 22, 1963, special election to fill unexpired term of Hjalmer Nygaard; elected 1964, 1966, 1968, 1970

West District
Don L. Short (R) (1903-1982)...1963-1965
    Elected 1962; defeated for re-election 1964

Rolland Redlin (D) (1920-2011) 1965-1967
    Elected 1964; defeated for re-election 1966
Thomas S. Kleppe (R) (1919-2007) 1967-1971
    Elected 1966, 1968; did not seek re-election 1970
Arthur A. Link (D) (1914-2010) 1971-1973
    Elected 1970; did not seek re-election 1972

One Representative, Elected At Large (1973)

Mark Andrews (R) (1926-) 1973-1980
    Elected 1972, 1974, 1976, 1978; did not seek re-election 1980 (elected to Senate 1980)
Byron L. Dorgan (D) (1942-) 1981-1992
    Elected 1980, 1982, 1984, 1986, 1988, 1990, did not seek re-election 1992
Earl Pomeroy (D) (1952-) 1993-2011
    Elected 1992*, 1994, 1996, 1998, 2000, 2002, 2004, 2006, 2008; defeated for re-election 2010
Rick Berg (R) (1959-) 2011-2013
    Elected in 2010; did not seek re-election 2012
Kevin Cramer (R) (1961-) 2013-2019
    Elected 2012, 2014, 2016; did not seek re-election 2018 (elected to Senate 2018)
Kelly Armstrong (R) (1976-) 2019-present
    Elected 2018

* Earl Pomeroy was elected in November 1992 to fill Dorgan's former seat in the House of Representatives and took his oath of office with other representatives on January 3, 1993. The U.S. Constitution specifically prohibits any House member from serving by appointment. As a result, North Dakota's only House seat was officially vacant between December 15, 1992, and January 3, 1993.

United States Judicial System
Justices of the United States Supreme Court

Years of birth, states from which appointed, and periods of service:

Appointed by President Bush (1989-1993)
  Thomas, Clarence (1948-   ) DC (1991-present)

Appointed by President Clinton (1993-2001)
  Ginsburg, Ruth Bader (1933-   ) DC (1993-present)
  Breyer, Stephen (1938-   ) MA (1994-present)

Appointed by President George W. Bush (2001-2009)
  Roberts, John G. (1955-   ) DC (2005-present) Chief Justice
  Alito, Samuel Anthony (1950-   ) NJ (2006-present)

Appointed by President Obama (2009-2017)
  Sotomayor, Sonia (1954-   ) NY (2009-present)
  Kagan, Elena (1960-   ) MA (2010-present)

Appointed by President Trump (2017-present)
  Gorsuch, Neil M. (1967-   ) CO (2017-present)
  Kavanaugh, Brett M. (1965 -   ) DC (2018-present)

Judges of the Eighth Circuit Court of Appeals

Circuit Justice: Samuel A. Alito, Jr.

Active Judges

Chief Judge: Lavenski R. Smith (Little Rock, AR) appointed July 19, 2002
Judge: James B. Loken (Minneapolis, MN) appointed October 17, 1990
Judge: Steven M. Colloton (Des Moines, IA) appointed September 30, 2003
Judge: Raymond W. Gruender (St. Louis, MO) appointed June 5, 2004
Judge: Duane Benton (Kansas City, MO) appointed July 2, 2004
Judge: Bobby E. Shepherd (El Dorado, AR) appointed October 10, 2006
Judge: Jane Kelly (Cedar Rapids, IA) appointed April 24, 2013
Judge: Ralph R. Erickson (Fargo, ND) appointed October 13, 2017
Judge: L. Steven Grasz (Omaha, NE) appointed January 4, 2018
Judge: David R. Stras (Minneapolis, MN) appointed January 31, 2018
Judge: Jonathan A. Kobes (Sioux Falls, SD) appointed December 18, 2018

Senior Judges

Pasco M. Bowman (Kansas City, MO) appointed July 19, 1983
Roger L. Wollman (Sioux Falls, SD) appointed July 22, 1985
C. Arlen Beam (Lincoln, NE) appointed November 9, 1987
Morris S. Arnold (Little Rock, AR) appointed May 26, 1992
Michael J. Melloy (Cedar Rapids, IA) appointed February 14, 2002

Judges of the Eighth Circuit Court of Appeals from North Dakota

Charles J. Vogel, (1898-1980) appointed by President Dwight Eisenhower, began 1954, assumed senior status 1968.
Myron H. Bright, (1919-2016) appointed by President Lyndon Johnson, began 1968, assumed senior status 1986.
Frank J. Magill, (1927-2013) appointed by President Ronald Reagan, began 1986, assumed senior status 1998.
John D. Kelly, (1934-1998) appointed by President William Clinton, began 1998, died less than two months after assuming office.
Kermit E. Bye, (1937-) appointed by President William Clinton, began 2000, assumed senior status 2015.
Ralph R. Erickson, (1959-) appointed by President Donald Trump, began 2017.

United States District Court for the District of North Dakota Judges

Alfred D. Thomas, (1837-1896) appointed by President Benjamin Harrison, served 1890-1896.
Charles F. Amidon, (1856-1937) appointed by President Grover Cleveland, served 1896-1928.
Andrew Miller, (1870-1960) appointed by President Warren Harding, served 1922-1941.
Charles J. Vogel, (1898-1980) appointed by President Franklin D. Roosevelt, served 1941-1954.
George S. Register, (1901-1972) appointed by President Dwight Eisenhower, served 1955-1971.
Ronald N. Davies, (1904-1996) appointed by President Dwight Eisenhower, served 1955-1971.
Paul Benson, (1918-2004) appointed by President Richard Nixon, served 1971-1985.
Bruce M. Van Sickle, (1917-2007) appointed by President Richard Nixon, served 1971-1985, assumed senior status 1985.
Patrick A. Conmy, (1934-) appointed by President Ronald Reagan, served 1985-2000.
Rodney S. Webb, (1935-2009) appointed by President Ronald Reagan, served 1987-2002.
Daniel L. Hovland, (1954-) appointed by President George W. Bush, served 2002-present.
Ralph R. Erickson, (1959-) appointed by President George W. Bush, served 2003-2017.

Chief Judge
U.S. District Court

Daniel L. Hovland
Bismarck

Personal
Born 1954 in Moorhead, MN; married to Kristen, three children

Education
B.A. Concordia College (summa cum laude); J.D. University of North Dakota School of Law

Professional Experience
1979-1980, law clerk to Chief Justice Ralph J. Erickstad of the North Dakota Supreme Court; 1980-1983, Assistant Attorney General for the State of North Dakota; 1983-2002, private practice in Bismarck, ND; 2002-present, Chief Judge, U.S. District Court for the District of North Dakota

Judicial
Nominated for appointment June 27, 2002, by President George W. Bush, confirmed by Senate on November 14, 2002, sworn in November 26, 2002.

Judge
U.S. Bankruptcy Court District of North Dakota

Shon Kaelberer Hastings
Fargo

Education
B.B.A. University of North Dakota, 1986; J.D. UND School of Law, 1993

Professional Experience
1993–1995, law clerk to the Honorable Karen K. Klein, U.S. Magistrate Judge, District of North Dakota; 1995–1997, private practice in Minneapolis, MN; 1998–2011, Assistant United States Attorney, District of North Dakota

Judicial
Appointed U.S. Bankruptcy Judge, District of North Dakota, on September 9, 2011, for a 14-year term.

U.S. Commissioners and Magistrate Judges for the United States District Court for the District of North Dakota

Kenneth M. Knutson served as U.S. Commissioner in Minot from 1958 to 1970; served as part-time Magistrate Judge in Minot from 1970 to 1994.

David Kessler served as U.S. Commissioner in Grand Forks from 1959 to 1970; served as part-time Magistrate Judge in Grand Forks from 1970 to 1990.

Harry J. Pearce served as U.S. Commissioner in Bismarck in 1970; served as part-time Magistrate Judge in Bismarck from 1970 to 1977.

Everett E. Palmer served as part-time Magistrate Judge in Williston from 1970 to 1974.

Odin J. Strandness served as part-time Magistrate Judge in Fargo from 1971 to 1975.

Ted Weisenburger served as part-time Magistrate Judge in Devils Lake from 1972 to 1974.

Robert D. Hartl served as part-time Magistrate Judge in Rolla from 1970 to 1972.

Howard A. Olson served as part-time Magistrate Judge in Minnewaukan from 1970 to 1971.

John E. Rilling served as part-time Magistrate Judge in Fargo from 1970 to 1971.

Charles C. Chinquist served as part-time Magistrate Judge in Rolla from 1973 to 1975.

William A. Hill served as part-time Magistrate Judge in Fargo from 1975 to 1984.

Lewis C. Jorgenson served as part-time Magistrate Judge in Minnewaukan from 1975 to 1979.

Arne F. Boyum served as part-time Magistrate Judge in Rolla from 1976 to 1980 and 1981 to 1984.

Alan K. Grindberg served as part-time Magistrate Judge in Bismarck from 1977 to 1978.

Ronald M. Dosch served as part-time Magistrate Judge in Devils Lake from 1979 to 1985.

Dwight C. H. Kautzmann served as part-time Magistrate Judge in Bismarck from 1978 to 1994; served as part-time Magistrate Judge in Bismarck and Minot from 1994 to 1996; served as full-time Magistrate Judge in Bismarck 1996 to 2004.

Karen K. Klein served as part-time Magistrate Judge in Fargo in 1985; served as full-time Magistrate Judge in Fargo from 1985 to 2014; designated Chief Magistrate Judge in 2004.

Alice R. Senechal served as part-time Magistrate Judge in Grand Forks from 1990 to 2014; serves as full-time Magistrate Judge in Fargo from 2015 to present.

Charles S. Miller, Jr. served as full-time Magistrate Judge in Bismarck from 2004 to 2018.

Clare R. Hochhalter serves as full-time Magistrate Judge in Bismarck from 2019 to present.

Magistrate Judge
U.S. District Court

Clare R. Hochhalter
Elgin

Personal
Born in 1951, Fargo

Education
B.A. University of Jamestown, 1979; J.D. University of North Dakota, 1983

Professional Experience
1983-1987, Assistant Attorney General for the State of North Dakota; 1988-2018, Assistant U.S. Attorney for District of North Dakota; 2019 to present, Magistrate Judge, U.S. District Court North Dakota

Judicial
Appointed in 2019 for eight-year term as U.S. Magistrate Judge, chambered in Bismarck.

Magistrate Judge
U.S. District Court

Alice R. Senechal
Grand Forks

Personal
Born in 1955, Rugby

Education
B.S. North Dakota State University, 1977; J.D. University of Minnesota, 1984 (cum laude)

Professional Experience
1984-1986, law clerk to Hon. Bruce M. Van Sickle, United States District Court, District of North Dakota; 1986 to present, private practice (part-time), Grand Forks, ND

Judicial
Appointed U.S. Magistrate Judge (part-time) November 15, 1990; appointed U.S. Magistrate Judge (full-time) February 2015, chambered in Fargo.

Chapter Four
Judicial Branch

Runway 31 in Jamestown features a fresh sealcoat and paint in the mid-2010s. The Jamestown Regional Airport opened in 1938 and is one of the state's eight commercial airports.

Profile of the North Dakota Judicial System 181
North Dakota Supreme Court Justices.. 183
North Dakota Supreme Court 188
North Dakota Court of Appeals... 189
District Courts 191
Judicial Districts Map.. 192
Municipal Courts 203
North Dakota Judicial System Committees, Commissions, and Boards 203
Chronology of Justices of the North Dakota Supreme Court 208

Judiciary

Supreme Court
The Supreme Court is the appellate court of final authority in North Dakota. It consists of five justices.

Court of Appeals
The Court of Appeals is an intermittent court established to assist the Supreme Court with its caseload. Judges of this court are detailed from the ranks of retired justices or sitting district court judges.

District Court
This court is the trial court with original and general jurisdiction over all state cases. There are 51 court judgeships assigned to eight judicial districts.

Municipal Courts
This court hears violations of municipal ordinances. Appeals are heard de novo in district court. There are approximately 75 municipal judges serving 90 municipal courts.

Profile of the North Dakota Judicial System

Structure of the Court System

The original constitution of the state of North Dakota created a judicial system consisting of the Supreme Court, district courts, county courts, and such municipal courts as provided by the law. This judicial structure remained intact until 1959 when the Legislative Assembly abolished the justice of peace courts in the state.

The adoption of a new judicial article to the state constitution in 1976 significantly modified the constitutional structure of the judicial system. The new judicial article vested the judicial powers of the state in a unified judicial system consisting of a Supreme Court, district courts, and such other courts as provided by law. Thus, under the new judicial article, only the Supreme Court and the district courts retained their status as constitutional courts. All other courts in the state are statutory courts.

In 1981, the Legislative Assembly further altered the structure of the judicial system by enacting legislation that replaced the multi-level county court structure with a uniform system of county courts throughout the state. This new county court structure became effective on January 1, 1983.

With the county court system in place, the judicial system of the state consisted of the Supreme Court, district courts, county courts, and municipal courts.

This changed again as the county courts were abolished by 1991 House Bill 1517, effective January 1, 1995. The bill, with a final completion date of January 1, 2001, also transferred the jurisdictional workload to an expanded number of district judges. The 1991 total of 26 county judges and 27 district court judges had been reduced to 42 district court judges by January 1, 2001, as provided by statute. The number of judges increased to 44 in 2010, to 47 in 2013, and to 51 in 2015.

Administrative Authority

The 1976 constitutional judicial article clarified the administrative responsibilities of the Supreme Court by designating the chief justice as the administrative head of the judicial system and by granting the chief justice the authority to assign judges for temporary duty in any non-federal or tribal court in the state. It also acknowledged the Supreme Court's rulemaking authority in such areas as court procedure and attorney supervision.

Selection and Removal of Judges

All judges in North Dakota are elected in nonpartisan elections. Justices of the Supreme Court are elected for 10-year terms, district court judges for six-year terms, and municipal court judges for four-year terms.

Vacancies in the Supreme Court and the district courts can be filled either by a special election called by the governor or by gubernatorial appointment. However, before a vacancy can be filled by gubernatorial appointment, the Judicial Nominating Committee must first submit a list of nominees to the governor from which the governor makes an appointment. Whether the vacancy is filled by a special election or by appointment, the appointed judge serves for a minimum of two years and then until the next general election, at which time the office is filled by election for the remainder of the term.

If a vacancy occurs in a municipal court, it is filled by the executive officer of the municipality with the consent of the governing body of the municipality.

Under the North Dakota Constitution, only Supreme Court justices and district court judges can be removed from office by impeachment. All judges are subject to removal, censure, suspension, retirement, or other disciplinary action for misconduct by the Supreme Court upon the recommendation of the Judicial Conduct Commission. Other methods for the retirement, removal, and discipline of judges can be established by the Legislative Assembly.

Chief Justice

Gerald W. VandeWalle

Personal
Born and raised in Noonan, North Dakota.

Education
Awarded a Juris Doctor Magna Cum Laude from University of North Dakota School of Law, 1958. Editor of *North Dakota Law Review* in senior year.

Professional Experience
Served as an assistant attorney general from 1958 to 1975. Appointed first assistant attorney general in 1975. As an assistant attorney general, held portfolios for elementary, secondary, and higher education, oil and gas, and the state retirement system. Served as the North Dakota delegate to the Interstate Oil Compact Commission. Appointed to the Supreme Court in August 1978 and elected to serve the unexpired term in November 1978. Elected for a full 10-year term in 1984 and re-elected in 1994, 2004, and 2014. Elected Chief Justice in January 1993 by vote of the district court judges and Supreme Court justices. Re-elected as Chief Justice January 1995, 2000, 2005, 2010, and 2015.

Memberships and Committees
Chaired North Dakota Judicial Conference, 1985 to 1987; President of the Conference of Chief Justices, 2000 to 2001; appointed by Chief Justice Rehnquist to the Federal/State Jurisdiction Committee of the Judicial Conference of the United States; Chairperson of the Section on Legal Education and Admissions to the Bar of the American Bar Association (ABA), 2000 to 2001; recipient of the University of North Dakota Sioux Award, 1992; recipient of the North Dakota State Bar Association Distinguished Service Award, June 1998; inducted into the Warren E. Burger Society, October 2002; recipient of the National Center for State Courts Paul C. Reardon Award, 2003; American Inns of Court Professionalism Award for the Eighth Circuit, 2008; recipient of the ABA Section of Legal Education and Admissions to the Bar 2009 Robert J. Kutak Award; 42nd recipient of the North Dakota Theodore Roosevelt Rough Rider Award, 2015; recipient of National Center for State Courts Harry L. Carrico Award, 2015; recipient of National Lambda Chi Alpha Fraternity Order of Achievement, 2015; recipient of University of North Dakota Honorary Degree of Doctor of Letters, 2015; recipient of University of Mary Degree of Doctor of Leadership, 2015; and State Bar Association of North Dakota established the Gerald W. VandeWalle Medal, 2017.

Justice
Daniel J. Crothers

Personal
Born 1957 and raised in Fargo, American Samoa, and Albuquerque, New Mexico; has two children.

Education
Graduated from University of North Dakota, 1979. Major studies in Political Science and Journalism, and Minor in early American History. Earned a Juris Doctor from the University of North Dakota School of Law, 1982.

Professional Experience
Law Clerk, New Mexico Court of Appeals, Santa Fe, New Mexico, 1982 to 1983; Assistant State's Attorney, Walsh County, North Dakota, 1983 to 1984; private practice, 1983 to 1986 in Santa Fe, Grafton, and Fargo; member and partner with the Nilles Law Firm, Fargo, 1987 to 2005; appointed June 2005 to the North Dakota Supreme Court and elected to unexpired four-year term November 2008 and 10-year term in 2012.

Memberships and Committees
President of the State Bar Association of North Dakota from 2001 to 2002 and served as a member and chair of several Bar Association and Court committees relating to lawyer and judicial ethics and professional conduct. Currently serves as Chair of North Dakota's Committee on Judiciary Standards and Chair of the North Dakota Judicial Conference; member of the American Bar Association Center for Professional Responsibility Standing Committee on Professional Discipline. Past member of ABA Standing Committee on Ethics and Professional Responsibility; past chair of the ABA Standing Committee on Client Protection and Policy Implementation Committee.

Justice
Lisa K. Fair McEvers

Personal
Born in Grafton and raised in Minto, North Dakota; married to James P. McEvers; one child and three step-children.

Education
Graduated Cum Laude from the University of North Dakota with a BBA in Information Management, 1993. Awarded Juris Doctor, with distinction, from the University of North Dakota School of Law, 1997.

Professional Experience
Worked for the Northeast Judicial District in court administration prior to attending law school. After law school, law clerk to the North Dakota Supreme Court, 1997 to 1998 term; private legal practice, 1998 to 2001; Cass County Assistant State's Attorney, 2001 to 2005; appointed North Dakota Commissioner of Labor in July 2005; appointed District Judge in September 2010, and elected to the position in 2012; appointed to the North Dakota Supreme Court in 2014, and in 2016, elected to an unexpired two-year term. She was re-elected to a 10-year term in 2018.

Memberships and Committees
Served on Judicial Education Commission, 1992 to 1994; Judiciary Standards Committee, 2004 to 2009; Rough Rider Industries Prison Advisory Board, 2005 to 2013; State Bar Association's Commission for Continuing Legal Education, 2006 to 2010; Domestic Violence Benchbook Subcommittee, 2009 to 2011; Commission on the Alternatives to Incarceration, 2011 to 2017; Pattern Jury Instruction Commission, 2012 to 2013; Cass County Resource Committee on Elder Abuse, 2013; North Dakota Judges Association, 2013 to 2016; Personnel Policy Board, 2013 to 2017; and Juvenile Drug Court Advisory Committee, 2014 to 2017. Chairs Juvenile Policy Board, 2013 to present; and Joint Procedure Committee, 2017 to present. Serves on United Tribes Criminal Justice Advisory Board, 2014 to present; Court Technology Committee's File and Serve User Group Subcommittee, 2015 to present; North Dakota Attorney General's Human Trafficking Commission, 2015 to present; North Dakota Dual Status Youth Initiative Group, 2017 to present; and Executive Committee of Judicial Conference, 2017 to present.

Justice

Jerod E. Tufte

Personal
Born in Minot, North Dakota, in 1975; married to Mylynn Tufte; three children.

Education
Attended West Fargo Public Schools; BS Computer Engineering from Case Western Reserve University, Cleveland, Ohio; and Juris Doctor from Arizona State University, Tempe, Arizona.

Professional Experience
Worked as computer engineer for Motorola prior to law school. Private practice in Phoenix, Arizona, and Steele, North Dakota. Appointed Kidder County State's Attorney in 2005 and elected in 2006 and 2010. Judge Advocate, North Dakota Army National Guard, from 2008 to 2016, including overseas service in Kosovo. Legal counsel to Governor Jack Dalrymple from 2011 to 2014. Appointed District Court Judge in 2014 and elected to Supreme Court in 2016.

Membership and Committees
Chair of Court Technology Committee, Committee on Tribal and State Court Affairs, and Judicial Conference Standing Committee on Legislation. Member of Joint Committee on Attorney Standards and Personnel Policy Board. Past member of Judicial Ethics Advisory Committee.

Justice
Jon J. Jensen

Personal
Born in 1965 in Grand Forks and raised in Grand Forks, Helena, Montana, and East Grand Forks, Minnesota; married to Linda Bata.

Education
Graduated with a BS in Accounting from Minnesota State University Mankato, Mankato, Minnesota, 1987. Earned Juris Doctor from University of North Dakota School of Law, 1990.

Professional Experience
Law Clerk, North Dakota Supreme Court, Bismarck, 1990 to 1991; private practice, Grand Forks, 1991 to 2013; Northwest Airlines, Egan, Minnesota, 2000 to 2001; District Judge, Northeast Central Judicial District, Grand Forks, 2013 to 2017, appointed by Governor Jack Dalrymple in 2013 and elected to a six-year term in 2016; appointed to the North Dakota Supreme Court by Governor Doug Burgum in August 2017.

Memberships and Committees
Caseflow Management Committee, 2016 to 2017. Juvenile Drug Court Advisory Committee, 2017 to present. Pretrial Detention Workgroup, 2018 to present. Court Services Administration Committee, 2017 to present. President, Grand Forks County Bar Association, 1999. Past Chair, North Dakota CPA Taxation Committee. Chair (North Dakota), ABA Real Property Taxation Section, 1996 to 1999. Member: American Bar Association; North Dakota State Bar Association Taxation Section; Minnesota State Bar Association; Ninth Judicial District (Minnesota) Bar Association; North Dakota Society of Certified Public Accountants – Taxation Section and Public Relations Committee; Grand Forks County and Bismarck/Mandan Society of Certified Public Accountants (local chapters).

North Dakota Supreme Court

The North Dakota Supreme Court has five justices. Each justice is elected for a 10-year term in a nonpartisan election. The terms of the justices are staggered so only one judgeship is scheduled for election every two years. Each justice must be a licensed attorney and a citizen of the United States and North Dakota.

One member of the Supreme Court is elected as Chief Justice by the justices of the Supreme Court and the district court judges. The term is for five years or until the justice's elected term on the court expires. The Chief Justice's duties include presiding over Supreme Court conferences, representing the judiciary at official state functions, and serving as the administrative head of the judicial system.

Functions and Powers

The North Dakota Supreme Court is the highest court for the state. It has two major types of responsibilities: adjudicative and administrative.

In its adjudicative capacity, the Supreme Court is primarily an appellate court with jurisdiction to hear appeals from decisions of the district courts. All appeals from these courts must be accepted for review. In addition, the court also has original jurisdiction in matters, such as certain habeas corpus cases and decisions of the secretary of state in the petition process, and can issue such original and remedial writs as are necessary to exercise this authority.

The state constitution requires a quorum, composed of a majority of the justices, is necessary before the court can conduct its judicial business. It also stipulates the court cannot declare a legislative enactment unconstitutional unless four of the justices so decide. When the court decides an appeal, it is required to issue a written opinion stating the rationale for its decision. Any justice disagreeing with the majority decision may issue a dissenting opinion that explains the reasons for the disagreement with the majority.

In its administrative capacity, the Supreme Court has major responsibilities for ensuring the efficient and effective operation of all courts in the state, except federal and tribal courts; maintaining high standards of judicial conduct; supervising the legal profession; and promulgating procedural rules that allow for the orderly and efficient transaction of judicial business. Within each area of administrative responsibility, the court has general rulemaking authority.

The court carries out its administrative responsibilities with the assistance of various committees and boards. It exercises authority to admit and license attorneys through the State Board of Law Examiners. Supervision of legal ethics is exercised through the Disciplinary Board of the Supreme Court and supervision of judicial conduct is exercised through the Judicial Conduct Commission. Continuing review and study of specific subject areas within its administrative jurisdiction are provided through five advisory committees: the Joint Procedure Committee, the Joint Committee on Attorney Standards, the Judiciary Standards Committee, the Court Services Administration Committee, and the Judicial Planning Committee. Other committees, such as the Continuing Judicial Education Commission, Personnel Policy Board, and the North Dakota Legal Counsel for Indigents Commission, also provide valuable assistance to the Supreme Court in important administrative areas.

Administrative personnel of the Supreme Court also play a vital role in helping the court fulfill its administrative functions. The clerk of the Supreme Court supervises the calendaring and assignment of cases, oversees the distribution and publication of opinions and administrative rules and orders, and decides certain procedural motions filed with the court. The state law librarian supervises the operation of the state law library.

North Dakota Court of Appeals

The Court of Appeals was established in 1987 to assist the Supreme Court in managing its workload. Since it was established, the Court of Appeals has written opinions disposing of 90 cases.

Cases assigned to the Court of Appeals under Administrative Rule 27 may include family law issues, appeals from administrative agency decisions, appeals from trial court orders on motions for summary judgment, appeals involving cases originating under the Uniform Juvenile Court Act, and appeals from misdemeanor convictions.

Authorization for the Court of Appeals must be granted by the Legislature every four years.

Supreme Court Communication Information

Supreme Court
600 East Boulevard Avenue
Judicial Wing, 1st Floor
Bismarck, ND 58505-0530
Telephone: 701-328-2221
Fax: 701-328-4480
Website: www.ndcourts.gov

Sally A. Holewa
State Court Administrator
Telephone: 701-328-4216
Fax: 701-328-2092
Email: sholewa@ndcourts.gov

Penny Miller
Clerk of the Supreme Court
Telephone: 701-328-2221
Fax: 701-328-4480
Email: pmiller@ndcourts.gov
TTY: 800-366-6888

Catherine Palsgraaf
Acting Law Librarian
Telephone: 701-328-4248
Fax: 701-328-3609
Email: cpalsgraaf@ndcourts.gov

Office of State Court Administrator

Article VI, Section 3, of the North Dakota Constitution authorizes the chief justice of the Supreme Court to appoint a court administrator for the unified judicial system. Pursuant to this constitutional authority, the Supreme Court has outlined the powers, duties, qualifications, and term of the state court administrator in Administrative Rule 1. The duties delegated to the state court administrator include assisting the Supreme Court in the preparation and administration of the judicial budget, providing for judicial education services, coordinating technical assistance to all levels of courts, planning for statewide judicial needs, and administering a personnel system.

Judicial Education

The office of state court administrator, under the guidance of the Judicial Branch Education Commission and through the director of education and communication, develops and implements education programs for all judicial and non-judicial personnel. The University of North Dakota Law School provides additional materials upon request.

Research and Planning

Staff services are provided to the Judicial Planning Committee and other advisory committees of the Supreme Court by staff in the office of state court administrator. The duties of these staff personnel include research, bill drafting, rule drafting, arrangement of committee meetings, and any other tasks assigned by various committees. Specific activities and projects of the Supreme Court standing committees are provided in a latter section of this chapter.

Personnel Management

To ensure uniformity in personnel administration, personnel policies and a pay and classification plan for district court employees were developed under the direction of the state court administrator. This program is administered by the director of human resources. The Personnel Policy Board provides oversight and guidance.

Fiscal Responsibilities

One of the primary functions of the office of state court administrator is to obtain adequate financial resources for judicial operations and to manage these resources.

In viewing the judicial budget, it should be noted the state funds the Supreme Court, Judicial Conduct Commission, approximately half of the expenses of the Disciplinary Board, and district court expenses, including 14 of the clerk of district court offices. The remaining clerk offices are funded by the state through a service contract. Municipal courts are funded by the municipalities they serve.

Information Technology

The state court administrator's office is responsible for providing information technology services to the judicial branch. These services are provided through the Judicial Branch Information Technology Department.

The Judicial Branch Information Technology Department supports approximately 4,000 individuals who access court records regularly.

District Courts

There are district court services in each of the state's 53 counties. The district courts are funded by the state of North Dakota. The district courts have original and general jurisdiction in all cases except as otherwise provided by law. They have the authority to issue original and remedial writs. They have exclusive jurisdiction in criminal cases and have general jurisdiction for civil cases.

The district courts also serve as the juvenile courts in the state and have exclusive and original jurisdiction over any minor who is alleged to be unruly, delinquent, or deprived. This jurisdiction includes cases in which a female minor is seeking judicial authorization to obtain an abortion without parental consent. The responsibility for supervising and counseling juveniles who have been brought into court lies with the judicial branch of government in North Dakota.

The district courts are also the appellate courts of first instance for appeals from the decisions of many administrative agencies. Acting in this appellate capacity, district

North Dakota Administrative Units
Judicial Districts 2019

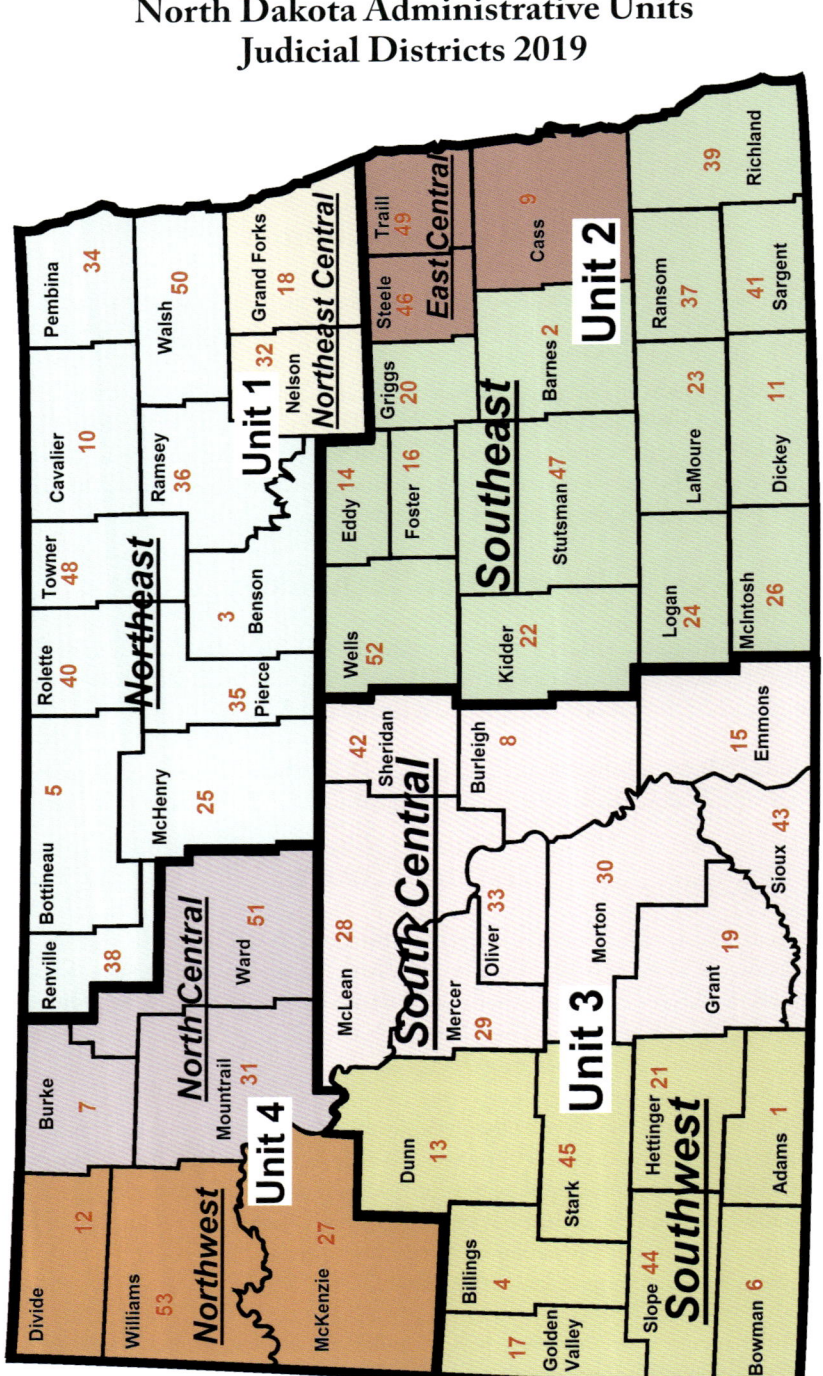

courts do not conduct a retrial of the case. Their decisions are based on a review of the record of the administrative proceeding conducted by the administrative agency.

Under the authority granted to the Supreme Court in Article VI, Section 3 of the Constitution of North Dakota, the court has organized the district courts into eight judicial districts operating within four administrative units. In each district, there is a presiding judge who oversees the courts' judicial services in the district's geographical area. The duties of the presiding judge, as established by the Supreme Court, include convening regular meetings of the judges within the judicial district to discuss issues of common concern, assigning cases among the judges of the district, and assigning judges within the judicial district in cases of demand for change of judge. The administrative unit structure consolidates the managerial and administrative functions of the courts within the districts under one trial court administrator for every two districts. The trial court administrator serves as a liaison with governmental and other agencies and is responsible for personnel, fiscal, facilities, contracts, and records management for the unit.

There are 51 district judges in the state. Nine judges in four chamber city locations serve the South Central Judicial District. Six judges in the Northwest Judicial District serve in two chamber city locations. Five judges serve the North Central Judicial District in one chamber city location. Nine judges serve the East Central Judicial District in two chamber city locations. Five judges serve the Northeast Central Judicial District in one chamber city location. Six judges serve the Northeast Judicial District in five chamber city locations. Seven judges serve the Southeast Judicial District in five chamber city locations. Four judges serve the Southwest Judicial District in one chamber city location. All district court judges are required by the state constitution to be licensed North Dakota attorneys, citizens of the United States, and residents of North Dakota.

The office of district court judge is an elected position, which is filled every six years in a nonpartisan election held in the district in which the judge will serve. If a vacancy in the office of district judge occurs, the Supreme Court must determine whether the vacancy should be filled or whether the vacant office should be abolished or transferred. If the vacancy is to be filled, the governor may either fill the vacancy by appointing a candidate from a list of nominees submitted by the Judicial Nominating Committee or by calling a special election to fill the vacancy. If the vacancy is filled by the nomination process, the appointed judge serves for a minimum of two years and then until the next general election, at which time the office is filled by election for the remainder of the term.

Northeast Judicial District – Administrative Unit 1

Presiding Judge Laurie A. Fontaine
Court Administrator Scott Johnson
Asst. Court Administrator Kelly Hutton
Pembina County Courthouse
301 Dakota Street West, #3
Cavalier, ND 58220-4100
Telephone: 701-265-8783

LAURIE A. FONTAINE, Cavalier, Presiding
Born in 1956 in Grand Forks and raised in Cavalier. BS, Mayville State University, 1978. JD, UND School of Law, 1983. Private practice in Pembina County, 1983 to 1998. Pembina County State's Attorney, 1987 to 1998. Elected District Judge in 1998; re-elected 2004, 2010, and 2016. Presiding Judge, 2013 to present.

ANTHONY SWAIN BENSON, Bottineau
Born in 1970. BUS, NDSU, 1994. JD, UND School of Law, 2000. Private practice in Bottineau, 2000 to 2015. Assistant Bottineau County State's Attorney, 2000 to 2015. Appointed District Judge in 2015; elected in 2018.

DONOVAN FOUGHTY, Devils Lake
Born in 1955 in Devils Lake. BA, UND. JD, UND School of Law, 1983. Admitted to the North Dakota Bar in 1983. County Judge, 1987 to 1994. Elected District Judge in 1994; re-elected 1996, 2002, 2008, and 2014. Presiding Judge, 2007 to 2012.

MICHAEL P. HURLY, Rugby
Born in 1976. BS, NDSU, 2000. JD, UND School of Law, 2005. Law Clerk, Montana 16th Judicial District, 2005 to 2006. Private practice in Devils Lake, 2007 to 2017. Appointed District Judge in 2017.

LONNIE OLSON, Devils Lake
Born in 1962. Graduate, Devils Lake Central High School, 1980. BA, UND, 1984. JD, UND School of Law, 1987. Private practice, 1987 to 1989. Special Assistant State's Attorney for the Lake Region Child Support Enforcement Unit, 1990. Elected Ramsey County State's Attorney, 1990. Elected District Judge in 2016.

BARBARA L. WHELAN, Grafton
Born in 1963 in Turtle Lake. BA, Concordia College, 1986. JD, University of Baltimore School of Law, 1990. Private practice in Maryland, 1990 to 1993. Private practice in Hettinger, 1993 to 1994. Private practice in Grafton, 1994 to 1998. Pembina County State's Attorney, 1999 to 2005. Walsh County State's Attorney, 2006 to 2017. Appointed District Judge in 2017.

Northeast Central Judicial District – Administrative Unit 1

Presiding Judge Donald Hager
Court Administrator Scott Johnson
Asst. Court Administrator Kelly Hutton
Grand Forks County Courthouse
124 South 4th Street
Grand Forks, ND 58201
Telephone: 701-787-2730

DONALD HAGER, Grand Forks, Presiding
Born in 1955. BSBA, Mayville State University, 1983. JD, UND School of Law, 1986. Served in the U.S. Navy, 1974 to 1980. Private practice in Larimore, 1986 to 2014. Appointed District Judge in 2014; elected in 2018. Presiding Judge, 2017 to present.

JAY D. KNUDSON, Grand Forks
Born in 1979. BA, UND, 2001. JD, UND School of Law, 2004. Private practice in Grand Forks, 2004 to 2011 and 2017. Attorney for Indigent Defense Office in Grand Forks. Judicial Referee and Magistrate, 2015 to 2016. Appointed District Judge in 2017.

JASON McCARTHY, Grand Forks
Born in 1971. BA, Minnesota State University Moorhead, 1995. JD, with distinction, UND School of Law, 1999. Served in Grand Forks County State's Attorney's Office for 13 years. Appointed District Judge in 2016.

LOLITA G. ROMANICK, Grand Forks
Born in 1956. BS, UND, 1979. JD, University of Idaho School of Law, 1983. BA, UND, 1995. Private practice in Grand Forks and Minot, 1984 to 2014. Appointed District Judge in 2014; elected in 2018.

JOHN A. THELEN, Grand Forks
Born in 1952. BS, 1978. JD, UND School of Law, 1981. Private practice, 1981 to 2009. Judicial Referee and Magistrate, 2009 to 2015. Appointed District Judge in 2015; elected in 2018.

East Central Judicial District – Administrative Unit 2

Presiding Judge Frank L. Racek
Court Administrator Rodney Olson
Asst. Court Administrator Chris Iverson
Cass County Courthouse
PO Box 2806
Fargo, ND 58108-2806
Telephone: 701-451-6940

FRANK L. RACEK, Fargo, Presiding
Born in 1957. BA, Cum Laude, St. John's University, Collegeville, MN, 1979. JD, with distinction, UND School of Law, 1982. Private practice in Fargo, 1982 to 1988. Appointed Judge of County Court, 1988. Elected District Judge in 1994; re-elected 1996, 2002, 2008, and 2014. Presiding Judge, 2010 to present. CPA certificate.

SUSAN L. BAILEY, Fargo
Born in 1963. BS, UND, 1986. MA, UND, 1988. JD, UND School of Law, 1997. Assistant Cass County State's Attorney, 2001 to 2006. Served as Administrative Law Judge, 2006 to 2014. Municipal Judge of West Fargo and Horace, 2004 to 2014. Municipal Judge of Tower City, Kindred, and Davenport, 2009 to 2014. Elected District Judge in 2014.

JOHN C. IRBY, Fargo
Born in 1956 in Warroad, MN. Graduate, Falls Senior High School, International Falls, MN. BA, Moorhead State University. JD, University of Wyoming. Legal intern for Legal Services for Southeastern Wyoming Inc., 1980. Private practice in Casselton, 1982 to 2002. Casselton City Prosecutor and Assistant City Attorney, 1982 to 2002. Appointed District Judge in 2002; elected in 2004; re-elected 2006, 2012, and 2018.

STEVEN L. MARQUART, Fargo
Born in 1954. Graduate, Moorhead High School. BA, Moorhead State University. JD, UND School of Law. Private practice in Fargo, 1979 to 2004. Law Clerk, U.S. District Court Judge Paul Benson. Elected District Judge in 2004; re-elected 2010 and 2016.

STEVEN E. McCULLOUGH, Fargo
Born in 1962. Graduate, West Fargo High School. BA, Moorhead State University. JD, UND School of Law. Private practice in Fargo, 1987 to 2004. Elected District Judge in 2004; re-elected 2010 and 2016.

THOMAS R. OLSON, Fargo
Born in 1952. BA, Augsburg College, 1976. Studied at Luther Theological Seminary, 1975 to 1976. JD, William Mitchell College of Law, 1981. Served in Clay County, MN, Attorney's Office, 1983 to 1985. Private practice in Fargo, 1985 to 2014. Appointed District Judge in 2014; elected in 2016.

STEPHANNIE N. STIEL, Fargo
Born in 1978. BA, Minnesota State University Moorhead, 2000. JD, UND School of Law, 2003. Law Clerk, North Dakota Supreme Court, 2003 to 2004. Private practice in Fargo, 2004 to 2017. Appointed District Judge in 2017.

TRISTAN J. VAN DE STREEK, Fargo

Born in 1975. BA, Minot State University, 2000. JD, UND School of Law, 2003. Private practice in Minot, 2003 to 2007. Assistant Cass County State's Attorney, 2007 to 2018. Appointed District Judge in 2018.

WADE L. WEBB, Fargo

Born in 1970 in Grafton. Graduate, Oak Grove Lutheran High School, Fargo, 1988. BA, Concordia College, Moorhead, MN, 1992. JD, UND School of Law, 1995. Law Clerk, Minnesota District Court, 1995 to 1996. Assistant Cass County State's Attorney, leading Personal Crimes Team, 1996 to 2003. Appointed District Judge in 2003; elected in 2006; re-elected 2008 and 2014.

Southeast Judicial District – Administrative Unit 2

Presiding Judge Daniel D. Narum
Court Administrator Rodney Olson
Asst. Court Administrator Chris Iverson
LaMoure County Courthouse
PO Box 128
LaMoure, ND 58458
Telephone: 701-883-6057

DANIEL D. NARUM, Ellendale, Presiding

Born in 1969. BS, NDSU, 1996. JD, UND School of Law, 1999. Private practice, 1999 to 2006. LaMoure County State's Attorney, 2001 to 2006. U.S. Navy, 1987 to 1990. Appointed District Judge in 2006; elected in 2008; re-elected 2010 and 2016. Presiding Judge, 2016 to present.

MARK T. BLUMER, Valley City

Born in 1955. Graduate, North Sargent High School, Gwinner. U.S. Navy, 1976 to 1980. BA, University of Colorado. JD, UND School of Law. Private practice, 1989 to 2016. Dickey County State's Attorney. Elected District Judge in 2016.

CHERIE L. CLARK, Jamestown

Born in 1969. BS and MA, University of South Dakota (USD), 1996 and 1997. JD, USD School of Law, 2000. Assistant County Attorney, Otter Tail County, Minnesota, 2002 to 2006. Assistant Cass County State's Attorney, 2006 to 2017. Appointed District Judge in 2017.

BRADLEY A. CRUFF, Wahpeton

Born in 1964 in Valley City and raised in rural Rogers. Graduate, Barnes County North, 1982. Graduate, Valley City State College, 1986. JD, UND School of Law, 1994. Served as Barnes County State's Attorney, City Attorney for Valley City, Municipal Judge for Valley City, and Barnes County Commissioner. Private practice in Valley City. Elected District Judge in 2012; re-elected 2018.

JAMES D. HOVEY, New Rockford
　Born in 1964. BA, UND, 1987. MA, University of Arizona, 1991. JD, with distinction, UND School of Law, 1996. Private practice in Grand Forks, 1996 to 2010. City Attorney for Larimore, 2001 to 2010. Instructor, UND Center for Legal Studies, 2002. Taught basic Russian as graduate student and completed 260 hours of language instruction at Moscow State University, Moscow, Russia. Appointed District Judge in 2010; elected in 2014; re-elected 2016.

TROY J. LeFEVRE, Jamestown
　Born in 1974 in Jamestown. Graduate, Jamestown High School, 1992. BA, UND, 1996. JD, UND School of Law, 2002. Private practice, 2002 to 2004. Law Clerk, Southeast Judicial District, 2004 to 2006. Stutsman County Chief Assistant State's Attorney, 2006 to 2016. Elected District Judge in 2016.

JAY A. SCHMITZ, Valley City
　Born in 1962 in Pierre, SD, and raised on cattle ranch near Verona. Graduate, Oakes High School, 1980. BA, Moorhead State University, 1985. JD, Southwestern University School of Law, Los Angeles, CA, 1989. Private practice in Los Angeles, 1989 to 1995. Private practice in Oakes, 2000 to 2002. Stutsman County Chief Assistant State's Attorney, Jamestown, 2003 to 2010. Member of Southeast Judicial District Caseload Management Committee. Elected District Judge in 2010; re-elected 2016.

South Central Judicial District – Administrative Unit 3

Presiding Judge Gail Hagerty
　Court Administrator Donna Wunderlich
　Burleigh County Courthouse
　PO Box 1013
　Bismarck, ND 58502-1013
　Telephone: 701-222-6682

GAIL HAGERTY, Bismarck, Presiding
　Born in 1953 in Bismarck. BA, UND, 1975. JD, UND School of Law, 1978. MJS, University of Nevada, Reno, 1994. Served as Burleigh County State's Attorney, 1982 to 1986. Served as Assistant Burleigh County State's Attorney and Assistant Attorney General. Burleigh County Judge, 1987 to 1994. Elected District Judge in 1994; re-elected 1996, 2002, 2008, and 2014. Presiding Judge, 2004 to present. President, State Bar Association of North Dakota, 2012 to 2013. Chair, North Dakota Judicial Conference, 1995 to 1997. Commissioner, National Conference of Commissioners on Uniform State Laws.

DOUGLAS A. BAHR, Bismarck
　Born in 1960. BS, Brigham Young University, 1987. JD, University of South Dakota School of Law, 1990. Judicial Clerk, Iowa Supreme Court, 1990 to 1991. Assistant Attorney General, 1991 to 1998. Director, Civil Litigation Division, North Dakota Office of Attorney General, 1999 to 2016. Private Practice, 2016 to 2018. Appointed District Judge in 2018.

DANIEL J. BORGEN, Bismarck

Born in 1972. Graduate, Devils Lake High School, 1990. U.S. Navy, 1990 to 1993. Graduate, North Dakota Police Officer Training Course, 1995. Police officer in Cando and Devils Lake, 1995 to 1997. BBA, UND, 2000. JD, UND School of Law, 2004. Private practice in Grand Forks, 2004 to 2007, and in Bismarck, 2012 to 2018. Grand Forks Public Defenders Office, 2007 to 2012. Elected District Judge in 2018.

CYNTHIA M. FELAND, Bismarck

Born in 1965. BA, UND, 1987. JD, UND School of Law, 1990. Grant County State's Attorney, 1992 to 1998, while also in private practice in Mandan. Assistant Burleigh County State's Attorney, 1999 to 2010. Elected District Judge in 2010; re-elected 2016.

JOHN W. GRINSTEINER, Mandan

Born in 1972 in Bismarck. Graduate, UND and Bismarck State College. JD, UND School of Law, 1998. Private practice in Bismarck, 1998 to 2003. Judicial Referee and Magistrate for South Central Judicial District, 2003 to 2015. Appointed District Judge in 2015; elected in 2018.

JAMES S. HILL, Mandan

Born in 1949 in Grand Forks. JD, UND School of Law, 1974. Served five years as Assistant U.S. Attorney in Bismarck. Private practice in Bismarck, 1981 to 2014. Served as representative of State Bar Association to American Bar Association House of Delegates and served on ABA Board of Governors. Chair, ABA Commission on IOLTA. Appointed District Judge in 2014; elected 2016.

DAVID E. REICH, Bismarck

Born in 1956 in Jamestown. BA, UND, 1979. JD, UND School of Law, 1982. Law Clerk, North Dakota Supreme Court, 1982 to 1983. Private practice in Bismarck, 1983 to 2006. Appointed District Judge in 2006; elected in 2008; re-elected 2014.

BRUCE A. ROMANICK, Bismarck

Born in 1960 in Washburn. BS, UND, 1982. JD, UND School of Law, 1986. Private practice in Washburn and Bismarck, 1986 to 1988. Judge Advocate, U.S. Army, Fort Carson, CO, and Kingdom of Saudi Arabia, 1989 to 1992. Private practice in Moorhead, MN, 1992 to 1994. Assistant Burleigh County State's Attorney, 1995 to 2000. Elected District Judge in 2000; re-elected 2006 and 2012.

THOMAS J. SCHNEIDER, Mandan

Born in 1950 in Dickinson. BA, UND, 1972. JD, UND School of Law, 1981. Private practice, 1981 to 1985. Mandan Municipal Judge, 1982 to 1986. Judicial Referee, South Central Judicial District, 1982 to 1986. County Judge, Morton, Grant, and Sioux Counties, 1986 to 1994. Elected District Judge in 1994; re-elected 1996, 2002, 2008, and 2014.

Southwest Judicial District – Administrative Unit 3

Presiding Judge William A. Herauf
  Court Administrator Donna Wunderlich
  Stark County Courthouse
  51 3rd Street East, Suite 202
  Dickinson, ND 58601
  Telephone: 701-227-3150

WILLIAM A. HERAUF, Dickinson, Presiding
  Born in 1957 in Dickinson. Graduate, Dickinson High School, 1975. BA, UND, 1979. JD, UND School of Law, 1982. Private practice in Dickinson, 1982 to 2006. Appointed District Judge in 2006; elected in 2008; re-elected 2010 and 2016. Presiding Judge, 2010 to present.

RHONDA R. EHLIS, Dickinson
  Born in 1968 in Bowman. Graduate, Scranton High School, 1986. BA, UND, 1990. JD, UND School of Law, 1993. Staff attorney and outreach attorney, Legal Assistance of North Dakota, Devils Lake, 1993 to 1995. Staff attorney, Regional Child Enforcement Unit, Bismarck, 1995 to 2001. Private practice in Dickinson, 2001 to 2006. Assistant Stark County State's Attorney, 2006 to 2015. Appointed District Judge in 2015; elected in 2018.

JAMES D. GION, Dickinson
  Born in 1953. Graduate, Regent High School, 1971. BA, UND, 1976. JD, UND School of Law, 1982. Private practice in Hettinger County, 1982 to 2015. Hettinger County State's Attorney, 1991 to 2015. Served as State's Attorney of Bowman and Slope Counties. Appointed District Judge in 2015; elected in 2018.

DANN E. GREENWOOD, Dickinson
  Born in 1952 in Dickinson. Earned rank of Eagle Scout in Boy Scouts of America, 1968. Graduate, Dickinson High School, 1970. Attended Dickinson State College, 1970 to 1972. Graduate, UND, 1974. JD, UND School of Law, 1977. Private practice in Dickinson, 1977 to 2012. President, North Dakota Trial Lawyers Association, 1987. President, State Bar Association of North Dakota, 1998 to 1999. Elected District Judge in 2012; re-elected in 2018.

North Central Judicial District – Administrative Unit 4

Presiding Judge Gary H. Lee
  Court Administrator Carolyn Probst
  Ward County Courthouse
  PO Box 5005
  Minot, ND 58702-5005
  Telephone: 701-857-6625

GARY H. LEE, Minot, Presiding

Born in 1955. BA, UND. JD, UND School of Law. Private practice in Minot, 1982 to 2004. Assistant Attorney General, 1980 to 1982. Elected District Judge in 2004; re-elected 2010 and 2016. Presiding Judge, 2014 to present.

TODD L. CRESAP, Minot

Born in 1961 in Valley City. BS, Minot State College, 1983. JD, UND School of Law, 1986. Admitted to practice in North Dakota, 1986. Private practice in Minot, 1986 to 2009. Appointed District Judge in 2009; elected in 2012; re-elected 2016.

RICHARD L. HAGAR, Minot

Born in 1957, Clark AFB, Pampanga, Philippines. Graduate, Santa Paula Union High School, Santa Paula, CA, 1975. Appointed to U.S. Air Force Academy by President Gerald Ford. BS, U.S. Air Force Academy, Colorado Springs, CO, 1979. JD, UND School of Law, 1988. Private practice in Minot, 1988 to 2006. Elected District Judge in 2006; re-elected 2012 and 2018.

STACY J. LOUSER, Minot

Born in 1973 in Minot. BS, UND, 1996. MS, Minot State University, 2001. JD, UND School of Law, 2007. Private practice in Minot, 2007 to 2014. Appointed District Judge in 2014; elected in 2016; re-elected 2018.

DOUGLAS L. MATTSON, Minot

Born in 1955 in Minot. Served in ND House of Representatives, 1978 to 1982. JD, UND School of Law, 1985. Worked for Federal Energy Regulatory Commission and Senator Mark Andrews in Washington, D.C., 1985 to 1986. Private practice in Minot, 1987 to 1990. Ward County State's Attorney, 1990 to 2002. Elected District Judge in 2002; re-elected 2008 and 2014.

Northwest Judicial District – Administrative Unit 4

Presiding Judge Robin A. Schmidt
Court Administrator Carolyn Probst
McKenzie County Courthouse
201 5th Street Northwest
Watford City, ND 58854
Telephone: 701-842-8237

ROBIN A. SCHMIDT, Watford City, Presiding

Born in 1976. Graduate, Sawyer High School. BS, UND, 1999. JD, UND School of Law, 2004. Judicial Clerk, North Dakota Supreme Court, 2004 to 2005. Private practice in Fargo, 2005 to 2010, and in Watford City, 2010 to 2013. Appointed District Judge in 2013; elected in 2016. Presiding Judge, 2017 to present.

DANIEL S. EL-DWEEK, Watford City
Born in 1981. BS, UND, 2003. JD, UND School of Law, 2006. Managing Attorney, Dakota Plains Legal Services, 2006 to 2010. Staff Attorney, Regional Native Public Defense Corporation, 2010 to 2013. Supervising Attorney, Williston Public Defender's Office, 2013 to 2015. Appointed District Judge in 2015; elected in 2018.

PAUL W. JACOBSON, Williston
Born in 1948 in Valley City. Graduate, Fargo North High School, 1966. BA, NDSU, 1970. JD, University of Minnesota Law School, 1973. Served in U.S. Army Judge Advocate General's Corps, 1974 to 1979. Private practice in Williston, 1979 to 1993. Assistant Disciplinary Counsel, 1993 to 1999. Disciplinary Counsel, 1999 to 2013. Appointed District Judge in 2013; elected in 2016.

BENJAMEN J. JOHNSON, Williston
Born in 1982 in Williston. BS, University of Mary, Bismarck, 2004. JD, UND School of Law, 2008. Private practice in Tioga, 2008 to 2017. Public Defender, 2012 to 2017. Assistant Burke County State's Attorney, 2008 to 2010. Prosecutor, Three Affiliated Tribes, 2010 to 2012. Burke County State's Attorney, 2010 to 2011. Served as City Attorney for Tioga, Ross, Wildrose, Flaxton, Portal, and Bowbells. Appointed District Judge in 2017.

JOSHUA B. RUSTAD, Williston
Born in 1972. Graduate, Williston High School, 1991. Graduate, UND, 1995. JD, UND School of Law, 1999. Private practice in Williston, 1999 to 2006. Supervising attorney, North Dakota Legal Counsel for Indigents Commission, Williston, 2006 to 2010. Elected District Judge in 2010; re-elected 2016.

KIRSTEN M. SJUE, Williston
Born in 1981. Graduate, Williston High School, 1999. BA, UND, 2003. JD, with distinction, UND School of Law, 2006. Law Clerk, Chief Justice Gerald W. VandeWalle, 2006 to 2007. Law Clerk, U.S. District Judge Ralph Erickson, 2007 to 2009. Private practice in Williston, 2013 to 2015. Appointed District Judge in 2015; elected in 2018.

For a listing of former district court judges, see https://www.ndcourts.gov/district-court/all-district-court-judges.

Municipal Courts

There are approximately 363 incorporated cities in North Dakota. Currently, there are 75 municipal judges serving 90 municipal courts.

Each municipality under 5,000 in population has the option of deciding whether or not to have a municipal court. Municipalities may contract with the state to provide municipal ordinance violation court services so that district judges may hear municipal ordinance violations.

Municipal judges have jurisdiction over all violations of municipal ordinances, except certain violations involving juveniles. Violations of state law are not within the jurisdiction of the municipal courts.

A municipal judge is elected for a four-year term. The judge must be a qualified elector of the city, except in cities with a population below 5,000. In cities with a population of 5,000 or more, the municipal judge is required to be a licensed attorney, unless an attorney is unavailable or not interested in serving. At present, there are approximately 18 legally-trained and 57 lay municipal judges in the state. Vacancies that occur between elections are filled by the executive officer of the municipality with the consent of the governing body of the municipality.

State law requires each new municipal judge attend two educational seminars and all others attend one course conducted by the Supreme Court in each calendar year. If a municipal judge fails to meet this requirement without an excused absence from the Continuing Judicial Education Commission, the judge's name is referred to the Judicial Conduct Commission for disciplinary action.

North Dakota Judicial System Committees, Councils, Commissions, and Boards

Advisory Committees

In the North Dakota judicial system, a system of committees has been established to develop new ideas and evaluate proposals for improving public services. These advisory committees include citizen members, legislators, lawyers, district court judges, municipal court judges, and members of the Supreme Court. Committee minutes can be found at https://www.ndcourts.gov/supreme-court/committees.

Administrative Council

The Administrative Council is established by Administrative Rule 22. Duties of the Council are to develop uniform administrative policies and procedures for the trial courts and juvenile courts and make recommendations for their implementation; to review the biennial budget proposals submitted by the trial court administrators for the respective administrative units; to review and approve for submission to the Supreme Court a proposed trial court component of the unified judicial system budget for each biennium; to monitor trial court budget expenditures; and to perform other duties as directed by the Chief Justice.

Advisory Commission on Electronic Media in the Courtroom

The Advisory Commission on Electronic Media in the Courtroom is established by Supreme Court rule and governs electronic and photographic media coverage of court proceedings. The Commission generally monitors the experience with electronic media in the North Dakota Supreme Court, district courts, and municipal courts.

Caseflow Management Committee

Established by Policy 510, the Caseflow Management Committee is developed under the auspices of the Administrative Council to provide recommendations to the Council on case management activities governing all trial courts statewide. The purpose of the Committee is to establish and monitor caseflow management practices in each judicial district of the state.

Committee on Legislation

The Committee on Legislation, a standing committee of the Judicial Conference, drafts, reviews, and tracks proposed legislation that may affect the North Dakota judicial system. During legislative sessions, the Committee provides weekly reports to the members of the conference on legislation that could affect judicial services.

Committee on Tribal and State Court Affairs

The Committee on Tribal and State Court Affairs was established following adoption of Administrative Rule 37 by the Supreme Court. The Committee is comprised of tribal and state court judges, tribal and state court support services representatives, and public members. It provides a vehicle for expanding awareness about the operation of tribal and state court systems; identifying and discussing issues regarding court practices, procedures, and administration, which are of common concern to members of the two court systems; and for cultivating mutual respect for, and cooperation between, tribal and state courts.

Court Services Administration Committee

The Court Services Administration Committee, established by Supreme Court rule, is responsible for the study and review of all rules and orders relating to the administrative supervision of the judicial system.

Court Technology Committee

The Court Technology Committee is established by Administrative Order and is responsible for the planning and implementation of information technology for the Judicial Branch. The Committee's coordinated efforts are responsible for consistent and efficient management of information technology resources.

Disciplinary Board

The Disciplinary Board was created in 1965 to provide for investigating, evaluating, and acting upon complaints alleging unethical conduct by attorneys licensed in North Dakota. The Rules of Professional Conduct are the primary guide for lawyer conduct, and the North Dakota Rules for Lawyer Discipline provide the procedural framework for the handling and disposition of complaints.

Informal Complaint Panel

The Informal Complaint Panel is established by Supreme Court rule. It provides an informal forum to address complaints or concerns about judges or other employees of the state judicial system. It is confidential, non-confrontational, and educational. It is intended to constructively influence conduct and resolve issues before they rise to the level of a formal grievance or disciplinary proceeding.

Joint Committee on Attorney Standards

The Joint Committee on Attorney Standards, established by Supreme Court rule, is comprised of members appointed by the Chief Justice and the Board of Governors of the State Bar Association. The Committee is responsible for the study and review of all rules and proposals concerning attorney supervision, including admission to the bar, attorney discipline, rules of professional conduct, and law student practice.

Joint Procedure Committee

The Joint Procedure Committee is the standing committee of the Supreme Court responsible for proposing adoption, amendment, or repeal of rules of civil procedure, criminal procedure, appellate procedure, evidence, and specialized court procedure. The Committee membership of 10 judges and 10 attorneys is appointed by the Supreme Court, except for one liaison member appointed by the State Bar Association.

Judicial Branch Education Commission

The Judicial Branch Education Commission was established by Supreme Court rule in 1993. The responsibilities of the Commission are to establish policies that affect the implementation of the mandatory education provision of the rule, develop judicial education programs for judges and court support personnel, develop and recommend a biennial budget for judicial education activities to the North Dakota Supreme Court, and develop a library of resource materials for judges and court support personnel.

Judicial Conduct Commission

The Judicial Conduct Commission was established in 1975 to receive, evaluate, and investigate complaints against any judge in the state and, when necessary, conduct hearings concerning the discipline, removal, or retirement of any judge. The Commission consists of four non-lawyers, two judges, and one lawyer. The non-lawyers are appointed by the governor, the judges are appointed by the North Dakota Judges Association, and the lawyer member is appointed by the State Bar Association.

Judicial Planning Committee

The Judicial Planning Committee is established by Supreme Court rule. The Committee studies the judicial system and makes recommendations concerning long-range and strategic planning and future improvements for the system.

Judiciary Standards Committee

The Judiciary Standards Committee, established by Supreme Court rule, studies and reviews all rules relating to the supervision of the judiciary, including judicial discipline, judicial ethics, and the judicial nominating process.

Jury Standards Committee

The Jury Standards Committee, established by Supreme Court rule, studies and oversees the operation of North Dakota's jury system. The Committee is responsible for reviewing the Uniform Jury Selection Act, studying and making recommendations concerning juror use and management, and reviewing the operation, management, and administration of the state's jury system.

Juvenile Policy Board

The Juvenile Policy Board is established by Supreme Court rule to define the mission of juvenile court services consistent with N.D.C.C. 27-20-01, to provide the administrative mechanism and authority to ensure the implementation of the policies, and to ensure the full involvement of the judges and personnel of the North Dakota judicial system in the development of juvenile court policies and procedures.

Minority Justice Implementation Committee

The Minority Justice Implementation Committee was established by Supreme Court Administrative Order 21 to oversee the implementation of the recommendations of the North Dakota Commission to Study Racial and Ethnic Bias in the Courts.

North Dakota Judicial Conference

The North Dakota Judicial Conference is established by statute for the purpose of soliciting, receiving, and evaluating suggestions relating to the improvement of the administration of justice; considering and making recommendations to the Supreme Court for changes in rules, procedures, or any matter pertaining to the judicial system; coordinating continuing judicial education efforts for judges and support staff; and establishing methods for reviewing proposed legislation, which may affect the operation of the judicial branch.

Parenting Investigator Review Board

The Parenting Investigator Review Board is established by Supreme Court rule. It addresses complaints about parenting investigators. It has nine members: three judges and one lawyer appointed by the Chief Justice, two lawyers appointed by the State Bar Association, and three parenting investigators appointed by the Chief Justice and the president of the State Bar Association acting together.

Pattern Jury Instruction Commission

The Pattern Jury Instruction Commission, established by Supreme Court rule, is composed of six lawyer-members appointed by the State Bar Association of North Dakota Board of Governors and six judge-members appointed by the chair of the Judicial Conference after consultation with the Executive Committee. In addition to revising and developing instructions corresponding to current law, the Commission is engaged in an extensive review of all pre-1986 civil and criminal instructions. A primary goal is rewriting the instructions using plain English, that is, language that is understandable by jurors without a legal background.

Personnel Policy Board

The Personnel Policy Board was established by Supreme Court Administrative Rule 33. The Board is comprised of a Supreme Court justice, district court judges, Supreme Court department heads, and employees of the supreme and district courts. The Board is tasked with the responsibility of reviewing and implementing the personnel system and developing a salary administration plan for the judiciary.

State Board of Law Examiners

The State Board of Law Examiners was created by the 1905 Legislative Assembly to assist the Supreme Court in its constitutional responsibility to regulate the admission to practice. The Board's three members must all be licensed members of the North Dakota Bar.

Chronology of Justices of the North Dakota Supreme Court

Under the provisions of the 1889 Constitution, the Supreme Court consisted of three judges elected for terms of six years. So that terms might be staggered, the first three judges elected drew lots so that there would initially be one term of three years, one of five years, and one of seven years.

Guy C.H. Corliss (R)(1858-1937) 1889-1898
  Elected 1889, received the three-year term; elected 1892; resigned April 15, 1898

Joseph M. Bartholomew (R)(1843-1901) 1889-1901
  Elected 1889, received the five-year term; elected 1894; did not seek re-election 1900

Alfred M. Wallin (R)(1836-1923) 1889-1903
  Elected 1889, drew the seven-year term; elected 1896; did not seek re-election 1902

Newton C. Young (R)(1862-1923) 1898-1906
  Appointed August 19, 1898, to replace Corliss; elected 1898, 1904; resigned August 15, 1906

David E. Morgan (R)(1849-1912) 1901-1911
  Elected 1900, 1906

John M. Cochrane (R)(1859-1904) 1903-1904
  Elected 1902; died in office July 20, 1904

Edward Engerud (R)(1869-1921) 1904-1907
  Appointed August 9, 1904, to replace Cochrane; elected 1904; resigned January 1907

John Knauf (R)(1868-1952) 1906-1906
  Appointed August 15, 1906, to replace Young; defeated in November 1906 general election

Charles J. Fisk (D)(1862-1932) 1907-1910
  Elected 1906 to fill unexpired term of Young

Burleigh F. Spalding (R)(1853-1934) 1907-1910
  Appointed January 30, 1907, to replace Engerud; elected 1908

A constitutional amendment, adopted November 3, 1908, increased the number of judges from three to five. The two new judges were appointed by Governor John Burke.

John Carmody (1854-1920) 1909-1910
  Appointed January 15, 1909; defeated in June 1910 primary election

Sidney E. Ellsworth (1862-1945) 1909-1910
  Appointed January 15, 1909; defeated in June 1910 primary election

The 1909 Legislature enacted a law providing that Supreme Court Judges should henceforth be elected on a no party ballot. This measure became effective with the 1910 elections.

David E. Morgan (1849-1912).. 1911-1911
    Incumbent; resigned October 31, 1911

Burleigh F. Spalding (1853-1934) 1911-1914
    Incumbent; defeated in June 1914 primary election

Charles J. Fisk (1862-1932)... 1911-1916
    Incumbent; defeated in June 1916 primary election

Edward T. Burke (1870-1935).. 1911-1916
    Elected 1910; defeated in June 1916 primary election

Evan B. Goss (1872-1930) 1911-1916
    Elected 1910; defeated in June 1916 primary election

Andrew A. Bruce (1866-1934).. 1911-1918
    Appointed October 31, 1911, to replace Morgan; elected 1912; did not seek re-election 1918; resigned December 1, 1918

Adolph M. Christianson (1887-1954)... 1915-1934
    Elected 1914, 1920, 1926, 1932

Luther E. Birdzell (1880-1973)... 1917-1933
    Elected 1916, 1922, 1928; resigned November 1, 1933

Richard H. Grace (1868-1929) 1917-1922
    Elected 1916; did not seek re-election 1922

James E. Robinson (1844-1933).. 1917-1922
    Elected 1916; defeated in June 1922 primary election

Harrison A. Bronson (1873-1947) 1919-1924
    Elected 1918; did not seek re-election 1924

Sveinbjorn Johnson (1883-1946).. 1923-1926
    Elected 1922; resigned November 29, 1926

William L. Nuessle (1878-1959)... 1923-1934
    Elected 1922, 1928

John Burke (1859-1937).. 1925-1934
    Elected 1924, 1930

Alexander G. Burr (1871-1951) 1926-1934
    Appointed November 29, 1926, to replace Johnson; elected 1928

George H. Moellring (1878-1935).. 1933-1934
    Appointed November 1, 1933, to replace Birdzell; defeated in November 1934 general election

A constitutional amendment approved June 25, 1930, increased the term of office to 10 years. So that terms might be staggered, this provision did not take effect until the 1934 elections, when three judges were elected. Of the three, a 10-year term went to the judge receiving the highest vote, an eight-year term to the judge receiving the second highest, and a six-year term to the judge receiving the third highest vote.

John Burke (1859-1937) 1935-1937
 Incumbent; elected 1936; died in office May 14, 1937

Adolph M. Christianson (1887-1954) 1935-1954
 Incumbent; elected 1938, 1948; died in office February 11, 1954

James Morris (1893-1980) 1935-1964
 Elected 1934 to a 10-year term; elected 1944, 1954; did not seek re-election 1964

Alexander G. Burr (1871-1951) 1935-1949
 Elected 1934 to an eight-year term; elected 1942; resigned September 2, 1949

William L. Nuessle (1878-1959) 1935-1950
 Elected 1934 to a six-year term; elected 1940; resigned December 31, 1950

P. O. Sathre (1878-1968) 1937-1938
 Appointed December 7, 1937, to replace John Burke; defeated November 1938 general election

Thomas J. Burke (1896-1966) 1939-1966
 Elected 1938 to fill unexpired term of John Burke; elected 1946, 1956; died in office March 20, 1966

Gudmunder Grimson (1878-1965) 1949-1958
 Appointed September 15, 1949, to replace Burr; elected 1950; resigned November 20, 1958, effective December 31, 1958

P. O. Sathre (1878-1968) 1951-1962
 Elected 1950 to fill unexpired term of Alexander Burr; elected 1952; did not seek re-election 1962

Nels G. Johnson (1896-1958) 1954-1958
 Appointed February 26, 1954, to replace Christianson; elected 1954 to fill unexpired term; elected 1958; died in office December 2, 1958

Obert C. Teigen (1908-1978) 1959-1974
 Appointed December 23, 1958, effective January 13, 1959, to replace Grimson; elected 1960, 1970; resigned May 1, 1974, effective July 1, 1974

Alvin C. Strutz (1903-1973) 1959-1973
 Appointed February 6, 1959, effective April 1, 1959, to replace Johnson; elected 1960 to fill unexpired term; elected 1968; died in office June 16, 1973

Ralph J. Erickstad (1922-2001) 1963-1992
 Elected 1962, 1972, 1982; did not seek re-election 1992

Harvey B. Knudson (1903-1978) 1965-1974
 Elected 1964 to 10-year term; did not seek re-election

William S. Murray (1916-1998) 1966
  Appointed April 1, 1966, to replace Thomas Burke; defeated in 1966 general election

William L. Paulson (1913-2000) 1967-1983
  Elected 1966, 1976; resigned effective September 5, 1983

Robert L. Vogel (1918-2005) 1973-1978
  Appointed June 27, 1973, to replace Strutz; elected 1974 to 10-year term; resigned effective August 11, 1978

J. Philip Johnson (1938-) 1974
  Appointed June 20, 1974, effective July 1, 1974, to replace Teigen; defeated in September 1974 primary election

Paul M. Sand (1914-1984) 1973-1984
  Elected 1974 to fill unexpired term of Vogel; re-elected 1978; died in office December 8, 1984

Vernon R. Pederson (1919-2017) 1975-1984
  Elected 1974 to fill unexpired term of Teigen; re-elected 1980; resigned November 8, 1984, effective January 7, 1985

Gerald Wayne VandeWalle (1933-) 1978-present
  Appointed July 8, 1978, effective August 13, 1978, to replace Vogel; elected to unexpired term 1978, re-elected to 10-year term in 1984, 1994, 2004, 2014

Herman F. Gierke (1943-2016) 1983-1991
  Appointed effective September 30, 1983, to replace Paulson; elected to fill unexpired term 1984; re-elected 1986; resigned November 20, 1991, effective immediately

Beryl J. Levine (1935-) 1985-1996
  Appointed January 17, 1985, to replace Sand; elected to unexpired term 1986; re-elected to 10-year term in 1988; resigned effective March 1, 1996

Herbert L. Meschke (1928-2017) 1985-1998
  Appointed January 17, 1985, to replace Pederson; elected to unexpired term 1986; re-elected to a 10-year term in 1990; resigned effective September 30, 1998

J. Philip Johnson (1938-) 1992
  Appointed February 11, 1992; defeated for election 1992

Dale V. Sandstrom (1950-) 1992-2016
  Elected 1992 to fill unexpired term of Gierke; assumed office December 31, 1992; re-elected to a 10-year term in 1996 and 2006; did not seek re-election 2016

William A. Neumann (1944-) 1993-2005
  Elected to a 10-year term in 1992 and 2002; resigned effective March 14, 2005

Mary Muehlen Maring (1951-) 1996-2013
  Appointed March 1, 1996, to replace Levine; elected to fill unexpired term in 1996; re-elected to a 10-year term in 1998 and 2008; resigned effective December 31, 2013

Carol Ronning Kapsner (1947-).. 1998-2017
  Appointed November 1, 1998, to replace Meschke; elected to a 10-year term in 2000 and 2010; retired effective July 31, 2017

Daniel J. Crothers (1957-)...2005-present
  Appointed June 10, 2005, to replace Neumann; elected to unexpired term in 2008; re-elected to a 10-year term in 2012

Lisa K. Fair McEvers (1962-)...2014-present
  Appointed November 18, 2013, to replace Maring; elected to unexpired term in 2016; re-elected to a 10-year term in 2018

Jerod E. Tufte (1976-) 2017-present
  Elected to 10-year term in 2016

Jon J. Jensen (1965-)..2017-present
  Appointed July 12, 2017, to replace Kapsner

Chapter Five
Executive Branch

A Piper Seneca II airplane contracted by the State Water Commission for use in cloud seeding sits on the ramp at the Bowman Airport in 2015.

Elected State Officials 215
Chronology of Elective State Officers Since Statehood 232
State Officials Appointed by the Governor to Head State Agencies 250
Executive Commissions and Boards 265
Agencies Headed by Gubernatorial Appointees 273
Administrative Departments under Boards and Commissions 309
North Dakota Boards and Commissions 328

Executive Branch

This chapter begins with a listing of North Dakota's 13 elected executives. Each official is pictured along with biographical information and a short summary of duties.

The 13 elected officials are the:
- Governor
- Lieutenant Governor
- Secretary of State
- State Auditor
- Attorney General
- State Treasurer
- Insurance Commissioner
- Agriculture Commissioner
- Public Service Commissioners (3)
- Tax Commissioner
- Superintendent of Public Instruction

✔ The *2001-2003 North Dakota Blue Book* contains a comprehensive overview of the duties and responsibilities of each of the 13 officials.

✔ See the *2011–2013 North Dakota Blue Book* for information regarding the 2010 Governor Transition Ceremony.

Elected State Officials

Governor
Doug Burgum

Personal
Born August 1, 1956; married to Kathryn Helgaas Burgum; two sons, Joe and Tom, and a daughter, Jesse

Party Affiliation
Republican

Education
Graduate of North Dakota State University in 1978 and Stanford University Graduate School of Business in 1980 with an M.B.A.

Professional Experience
Consultant at McKinsey & Co. in Chicago from 1980 to 1983; returned to North Dakota to join Great Plains Software in 1983 and grew it from a small startup company to an award-winning global software company; former chairman and CEO of Great Plains Software through its initial public offering in 1997 and acquisition by Microsoft Corp. in 2001; senior vice president of Microsoft through 2007; founder of Kilbourne Group, a real estate development firm committed to creating smart, healthy cities through vibrant downtowns; co-founder of Arthur Ventures, a venture capital firm that invests in ambitious, mission-driven software companies; awarded the Theodore Roosevelt Rough Rider Award in 2009; elected Governor on November 8, 2016; sworn in as Governor on January 3, 2017.

Summary of Duties
The Governor is the chief executive officer of the state and has general supervision over executive branch state agencies. He serves as commander-in-chief of the state's military forces except when they are called into service of the United States. In addition, the Governor has the authority to convene special sessions of the Legislative Assembly; veto legislation and line items on appropriations bills; recommend legislative measures; and grant reprieves, commutations, and pardons for all offenses except treason and impeachment.

The Governor chairs the Industrial Commission, Emergency Commission, Board of University and School Lands, State Board of Equalization, State Water Commission, and Indian Affairs Commission.

Lieutenant Governor
Brent Sanford

Personal
Born December 23, 1971; married to Sandi; three children, Sydney, Nicolas, and Erin

Party Affiliation
Republican

Education
Earned a degree in accounting from the University of North Dakota in 1994 and is a certified public accountant

Professional Experience
Worked at Eide Bailly in Fargo for eight years; served as chief financial officer for Transwest Trucks, a multi-location truck dealership, financing, and manufacturing operation headquartered in Brighton, Colo.; became owner and president of S & S Motors in Watford City; served as mayor of Watford City from 2010 to 2016 and as a city councilman for four years prior; served as a board member with the McKenzie County Job Development Authority; sworn in as Lieutenant Governor of North Dakota on January 3, 2017.

Summary of Duties
The Lieutenant Governor acts as chief executive in case of the Governor's death, resignation, or on other occasions when the Governor is unable to fulfill his responsibilities; serves as President of the Senate and, in the event of a tie, may cast the decisive vote; leads the North Dakota Trade Office; chairs the State Investment Board, Capitol Grounds Planning Commission, Higher Education Challenge Fund Commission, Early Childhood Education Council, and Northern Plains Unmanned Aircraft Systems Authority; and assumes other board chairmanships and functions as prescribed by the Governor.

Secretary of State
Alvin (Al) A. Jaeger

Personal
Born December 10, 1943, in Beulah, N.D.; wife, Kathy (deceased November 24, 2016); three children, Todd, Stacy, and Heidi

Party Affiliation
Republican

Education
Beulah High School; Bismarck State College, A.A.; Dickinson State University, B.S.; University of North Dakota and Montana State University, post-graduate work

Professional Experience
Military: 1966-1972, North Dakota Army National Guard; Career: 1966-1969, Killdeer High School, 1969-1971, Kenmare High School, teacher of business education; 1971-1973, Mobil Oil Corporation, marketing analyst; 1973-1992, real estate broker; 1992, elected Secretary of State, re-elected 1996, 2000, 2004 (two-year term), 2006, 2010, 2014, and 2018.

Jaeger is a member of the National Association of Secretaries of State and has served several times on the Executive Committee. He has been chair of the Awards Committee since 1994.

Summary of Duties
The Secretary of State commissions notaries public, registers lobbyists, issues contractor licenses, registers charitable organizations, regulates boxing and mixed fighting styles, maintains a central database for the recording of various security documents (e.g., uniform commercial code, crop, and livestock liens), registers and administers laws pertaining to more than 40 different business entity categories, and is the state's chief election officer.

In addition, the Secretary of State attests the official acts of the Governor and maintains a related registry, is the custodian of the Great Seal, and receives and files the original signed copies of legislative bills and resolutions.

The Secretary of State is a member of the Emergency Commission, Board of University and School Lands, State Historical Board, State Canvassing Board, Theodore Roosevelt Rough Rider Awards Committee, and State Information Technology Advisory Committee.

State Auditor
Joshua C. Gallion

Personal
Born 1979 in Spokane, Wash.; married to Rebecca (Becky); two daughters, Brooklyn and Sasha

Party Affiliation
Republican

Education
Central Valley High School, Spokane, Wash.; Bismarck State College, Associate of Arts; Dickinson State University, bachelor's degrees, accounting and business administration; University of North Dakota, Master of Business Administration

Professional Experience
U.S. Air Force, Minot Air Force Base, 1998-2002; office manager, R.W. Gallion Floors, Spokane, Wash., 2002; office manager, Fougner Engineered Sales, Bismarck, 2002-2008; transportation management officer and finance, Department of Transportation, Bismarck, 2008-2010; accounting manager, Public Service Commission, Bismarck, 2010-2016; elected as State Auditor, 2016.

Summary of Duties
The North Dakota State Auditor leads the way in providing truthful, objective, and independent information to the North Dakota State Legislature and citizens of North Dakota. The Office of the State Auditor is a valuable tool for North Dakota state agencies and local government entities, providing an opportunity to improve operations, fiscal responsibility, and taxpayer services. We are relied on for our independent, professional audits conducted in accordance with performance audit standards issued by the Comptroller General of the United States to verify compliance and improve operations. The State Auditor performs three distinct types of performance audits. The first are audits conducted as determined necessary by the State Auditor, Legislative Audit and Fiscal Review Committee, or as specified by state law. The second is referred to as operational audits and are performed on most state agencies on a biennial basis. The third type is conducted by the office's Higher Education Audit Division.

The State Auditor conducts independent, professional audits of the state's financial statements, the university system's financial statements, various state agencies, and political subdivisions. The State Auditor also audits federal funds in accordance with the Single Audit Act and federal oil and gas royalties under an agreement with the federal Office of Natural Resource Revenues. These reports, often referred to as external financial reporting, provide accountability to stakeholders outside of state government, primarily citizens, creditors, investors, and grantors.

Attorney General
Wayne Stenehjem

Personal
Born February 5, 1953, in Mohall, N.D.; married to Beth Bakke Stenehjem; one son, Andrew

Party Affiliation
Republican

Education
Graduate of Bismarck High School; A.A. from Bismarck Junior College; B.A. from University of North Dakota; J.D. from UND School of Law

Professional Experience
Formerly a partner in the Grand Forks law firm of Kuchera, Stenehjem, Walberg & Sharp. Licensed to practice law in North Dakota and North Dakota U.S. district courts since 1977. Member of the North Dakota House of Representatives from 1976 to 1980. State Senator from 1980 to 2000. Chairman of the Senate Judiciary Committee, 1995 to 2000. President Pro Tem of the Senate, 1999. Member of the Legislative Council, 1997 to 2000. Elected Attorney General 2000, re-elected 2004 (two-year term), 2006, 2010, 2014, and 2018.

Summary of Duties
The Attorney General represents the state in all legal matters, civil and criminal, where the state is named as a party or the state may have an interest in the outcome of the litigation; provides legal services and opinions to state legislators, state officials, constitutional officers, state agencies, boards, and commissions; and enforces open meetings and open records laws and consumer fraud laws. The attorney general's office issues licenses for retail alcohol beverage establishments, Class A and Class B gambling organizations, polygraph (lie detector) examiners, amusement games and devices, and concealed weapons permits; maintains the state's criminal history records and offender registration systems; performs fire safety inspections of public buildings; conducts arson investigations and criminal investigations; and is responsible for the North Dakota Lottery and the state Crime Laboratory.

The Attorney General is a member of numerous boards and commissions, including the Board of University and School Lands, Industrial Commission (which oversees all state-owned industries), Public Employees Retirement System Board, Judicial Council, and Pardon Advisory Board.

State Treasurer
Kelly L. Schmidt

Personal
Born in 1962 in Elmhurst, Ill.; married to Charles (Chuck); four sons, five grandsons

Party Affiliation
Republican

Education
Moorhead High School, Moorhead, Minn.; attended the University of Minnesota-Moorhead, and North Dakota State University, Behavioral Sciences

Professional Experience
Investment/insurance firm-brokerage manager; self-employed/contractual services; N.D. House of Representatives Appropriations Committee, 2003 legislative and special sessions. Schmidt was elected State Treasurer in 2004; re-elected 2008, 2012, 2016. She is a founding member of the State Financial Officers Foundation and elected chair in September 2014. They awarded her the SFOF Servant Leadership Award in October 2016. She has served as president of the National Association of State Treasurers and chaired its foundation. The Council of State Governments named her a "Toll Fellow" for her achievement and service to state government. The Credit Union National Association awarded her the Desjardins Financial Education Award for her leadership on behalf of financial literacy. She is a founding member of the North Dakota Jump$tart Coalition and past member of the board of directors for the National Jump$tart Coalition and the American Savings Education Council. Schmidt serves on six boards, including the State Investment Board that oversees the investment programs of several funds, including the Legacy Fund, public pensions, and insurance trust; Teachers Fund for Retirement; University and School Lands Board; State Board of Equalization; State Historical Board; and State Canvassing Board.

Summary of Duties
1. Cash Management: The management of the state "checkbook." The forecasting and cash management expertise offered by the Office of State Treasurer (OST) is necessary to ensure the availability of sufficient funds to cover state obligations while optimizing investment earnings.
2. Accounting: The State Treasurer pays all warrants or checks drawn against the state. All bank balances are reconciled daily to the state accounting system (PeopleSoft) and the Bank of North Dakota. State funds received by agencies are deposited through the OST for investment in the general fund.
3. Investments: The Treasurer serves as custodian for all state funds. The OST manages the investment of the state's general and special funds and several trust funds, including the trustee of the Veterans Postwar Trust Fund. State funds are invested as Certificate of Deposits with the Bank of North Dakota. Trust fund money is invested in banks and credit unions throughout the state.
4. Tax Collections and Distributions: The OST disburses over 30 tax distributions to political subdivisions. The web-based system TDOC, Tax Distribution Outstanding Check, pulls data from a variety of sources, which streamlines distributions and ensures greater accuracy, transparency, and efficiency. We provide analysis, data, and education of various tax distributions and state laws to legislators, employees of state agencies, officials and employees of local political subdivisions, and the public.
5. Financial Literacy: Schmidt worked collaboratively to pass legislation to promote financial literacy as a responsibility of the State Treasurer. NDCC 54-11-01 outlines the duty: "May work to promote access to financial education tools that can help all North Dakotans make wiser choices in all areas of personal financial management."

Insurance Commissioner
Jon Godfread

Personal
Born in Bismarck in 1982; married to Amanda; three children

Party Affiliation
Republican

Education
B.A., Business Administration, University of Northern Iowa, cum laude, 2005; summer session, McGeorge School of Law, University of the Pacific, 2008, including study abroad in Austria under U.S. Supreme Court Justice Anthony Kennedy; member, North Dakota Law Review, UND; J.D./M.B.A., UND School of Law, 2011

Professional Experience
Professional basketball player, Ehingen Steeples, Ehingen, Germany, October 2005-March 2006; branch manager/personal banker, Alerus Financial, Grand Forks, July 2005-August 2007; legislative intern, House Finance and Taxation Committee and House Transportation Committee, 2009 North Dakota Legislative Session; legislative aide, North Dakota Office of the State Tax Commissioner, December 2010-August 2011; vice president of governmental affairs, Greater North Dakota Chamber, August 2011-December 2016; elected Insurance Commissioner, November 8, 2016.

Summary of Duties
The Commissioner regulates insurance companies doing business in the state, which includes licensing, registering and/or approving, and examining for business conduct and financial stability. Oversight of more than 52,000 insurance agents involves the administration of continuing education and pre-licensing requirements. The Insurance Department also interprets and applies laws dealing with the insurance industry and aids policyholders in receiving fair treatment during disputes.

The Commissioner is responsible for the State Health Insurance Counseling and Prescription Connection programs and also receives and investigates inquiries and insurance fraud referrals.

Agriculture Commissioner
Doug Goehring

Personal
Born in 1965; raised on a family farm near Menoken, Burleigh County, N.D.; married to Annette; six children and eight grandchildren

Party Affiliation
Republican

Education
Graduate of Century High School, Bismarck; graduate of Bismarck State College

Professional Experience
Third generation family farmer from Burleigh County, 1990-present; president of Nodak Mutual Insurance, 2002-2008; licensed medical laboratory technician; appointed Agriculture Commissioner in 2009; elected to four-year terms in 2010, 2014, and 2018.

Summary of Duties
The Agriculture Commissioner oversees and coordinates the activities of the Department of Agriculture and represents the agricultural community in the formulation of public policy.

The Department of Agriculture is organized into seven divisions:

1. Administrative Services includes fiscal management, human resources, procurement, emergency management, IT, GIS, and wildlife services.
2. Plant Industries includes noxious weeds, plant protection, and apiary programs.
3. Livestock Industries includes dairy inspection and state meat and poultry inspection.
4. Business, Marketing, and Information includes public policy, the North Dakota Mediation Service, public information, international marketing, the Pride of Dakota program, specialty crop block grants, local foods, agricultural products utilization, and agricultural development.
5. Grain and Livestock Licensing includes grain inspection, feed inspection and registration, livestock development and licensing, livestock pollution prevention, and beef age and source verification.
6. Animal Health/State Veterinarian protects the health of domestic animals and nontraditional livestock of the state and administers all rules and orders of the State Board of Animal Health.
7. Pesticide and Fertilizer regulates pesticides, fertilizers, and anhydrous ammonia to protect human health and the environment.

The Agriculture Commissioner is a member of numerous boards and commissions, including the Industrial Commission (which oversees the North Dakota Mill, the Bank of North Dakota, the Department of Mineral Resources, and the Oil and Gas Division), the Board of Tax Equalization, the State Water Commission, and the State Board of Agricultural Research and Education.

Public Service Commissioner
Randy Christmann

Personal
Outside of government service, Randy owns a 113-year-old, third generation cattle ranch west of Hazen, N.D. He is married to Bethanie.

Party Affiliation
Republican

Education
Before graduating from Hazen High School in 1978, Christmann enlisted in the North Dakota Army National Guard. He enrolled at North Dakota State University and graduated in 1982 with a bachelor's degree in business administration.

Professional Experience
Christmann has a background in agriculture, telecommunications, and 18 years in the North Dakota Senate representing energy country. He was elected to the North Dakota Senate in 1994 and initially focused mostly on energy, taxation, and natural resources issues. Governor Ed Schafer appointed Christmann to serve as one of the two legislative appointees on the Lignite Research Council. He continued to serve in that position under Governor John Hoeven and Governor Jack Dalrymple. Senate Republicans chose Christmann to serve as Assistant Majority Leader in 2002. He was re-elected to that post every two years through 2012. He also served on the Senate Appropriations Committee. From 1999 through 2012, the members of West River Telecommunications (WRT) Cooperative elected Christmann to serve on its board of directors. Christmann was elected to the Public Service Commission in 2012 and 2018. His portfolios include coal mining and reclamation, abandoned mine lands, licensing of auctioneers and grain dealers, telecommunications, and a new portfolio, wind and solar reclamation.

Summary of Duties
Originally established as the Railroad Commission, the name was changed to the Public Service Commission in 1940. The Commission maintains jurisdiction over railroads; telecommunications companies; pipeline utilities engaged in the transportation of gas and oil; electric utilities engaged in the generation and distribution of natural, synthetic, or artificial gas; all heating utilities engaged in the distribution of heat; and all other public utilities engaged in business in the state or any of its political subdivisions.

The Abandoned Mine Lands Division administers a federal program to remove hazards and environmental problems associated with abandoned mines, investigates abandoned mine land sites, designs reclamation projects, submits applications for federal funds, and manages construction projects under public contracts.

Public Service Commissioner
Julie Fedorchak

Personal
Third generation North Dakotan; born in 1968 in Williston, N.D.; husband Mike Fedorchak of Minot; three children, Elizabeth, Nathan, and Samuel

Party Affiliation
Republican

Education
Century High School, Bismarck, 1986; University of North Dakota, bachelor's degree in journalism, 1990

Professional Experience
Julie Fedorchak was appointed to the Public Service Commission in December 2012 by Governor Jack Dalrymple and elected in 2016. She holds the pipeline, electric transmission, and energy conversion siting; railroad; and consumer affairs portfolios and is the agency's lead for issues relating to the Midwest Independent System Operations. She has led efforts to enhance the Commission's pipeline reclamation program, developed and received legislative approval for a state rail safety program, and is a tireless advocate for reliable, affordable utility services. She launched her professional career with the University of North Dakota Alumni Association and Foundation where she was director of communications and editor of alumni publications. Julie lived in Washington, D.C., and worked at the University of Maryland College Park from 1993-1995. She returned to North Dakota in 1995 to be communications director for Governor Ed Schafer, serving as a senior advisor and principal speech writer, spokesperson, and media liaison until he retired from office in 2000. For the next decade, Julie managed Liffrig Communications, a small firm that provided marketing, communications, media, and government relations services. She also published a bi-weekly column in the *Bismarck Tribune* and collaborated with her mother on two books. Upon U.S. Senator John Hoeven's election in 2010, Julie helped lead his state offices as state director.

Summary of Duties
See description of Summary of Duties on previous page.

Public Service Commissioner
Brian Kroshus

Personal
Born in 1963 in Fargo, N.D.; two daughters, Megan and Alyssa, and son-in-law, Michael

Party Affiliation
Republican

Education
Graduate of North Dakota State University, B.S.

Professional Experience
Kroshus was appointed to the Public Service Commission in March 2017 by Governor Doug Burgum and elected in 2018. He has a background in business, agriculture, and energy. His portfolio at the commission includes business operations, electric and gas economic regulation, pipeline safety and damage prevention, and weights and measures. Prior to his appointment to the Public Service Commission, Kroshus spent 30 years in business management, including 20 years (1997-2017) with Lee Enterprises, Bismarck. During his time with Lee Enterprises, he spent 17 years as publisher of *Farm and Ranch Guide*, 13 years as group publisher of Lee Agri-Media, and 10 years as publisher of *The Bismarck Tribune*. He continues to be involved with his farming and ranching operation in western North Dakota.

Kroshus has served as a board member and trustee for numerous organizations, including United Way, Bismarck-Mandan Chamber, Bismarck-Mandan Development Foundation, Sanford Health Foundation, Lewis and Clark Fort Mandan Foundation, and Bismarck State College Foundation. He served as president of the Bismarck State College Foundation in 2012-2013 and co-chaired the United Way Missouri Slope Area Wide Annual Gift Giving Campaign in 2009.

Summary of Duties
See description of Summary of Duties on page 223.

Tax Commissioner
Ryan Rauschenberger

Personal
Born in 1982 in Kenmare, N.D.; resides in Bismarck

Party Affiliation
Republican

Education
Graduate of University of North Dakota with a bachelor's degree in accounting and a master's degree in business administration

Professional Experience
Auditor for PricewaterhouseCoopers; manager of energy development for the North Dakota Department of Commerce; deputy tax commissioner, July 2009-December 2013; appointed Tax Commissioner by Governor Jack Dalrymple to fill a vacancy, effective January 2014; elected Tax Commissioner in November 2014 and 2018.

Summary of Duties
The Tax Commissioner is responsible for the fair and effective administration of the tax laws of North Dakota. As the primary revenue-producing agency for the state of North Dakota, the department collects more than 95 percent of all general fund dollars. The Office of State Tax Commissioner collects revenue from 36 tax types, such as sales and use taxes; individual and corporate income; oil and gas taxes; motor fuels; excise taxes, including motor vehicle, alcohol, and tobacco product taxes; estate; and other miscellaneous taxes. The department also issues sales and use tax permits.

The Tax Commissioner provides assistance in establishing uniformity of procedures for the administration of property taxes. The Property Tax Division makes annual tentative valuations of centrally assessed properties (railroads, utility companies, wind farms, pipelines, airlines, and telecommunications companies) for the Tax Commissioner to submit to the State Board of Equalization, which makes the final assessments.

The Tax Commissioner researches and prepares opinions answering tax-related questions; drafts proposals for changes in the tax laws; assists the Office of Management and Budget with preparing the revenue forecast; estimates the fiscal impact of all tax-related legislation; conducts all litigation for the department and the State Board of Equalization; and helps draft rules and regulations for the administration of the various state taxes.

Superintendent of Public Instruction
Kirsten Baesler

Personal
Born 1969 in Flasher, N.D.; three adult sons, Lee and twins, Mitchel and Chancellor

Education
Master's degree in education and library information technology, Valley City State University; bachelor's degree in elementary education, magna cum laude, Minot State University; associate of arts degree, Bismarck State College; associate of science degree, Bismarck State College. She has completed the Graduate School Educational Leadership Program at Harvard University. Baesler holds Valley City State University's Distinguished Alumni Award and the Rising Star Award from Bismarck State College.

Professional Experience
Baesler worked for 24 years in the Bismarck school district as an assistant principal, a library media specialist, a technology integration specialist, and as an aide to children with intellectual disabilities. She is a former top aide to the director of the North Dakota School Boards Association. In 2004, she was elected to the Mandan School Board, serving for nine years, including seven years as president. She is a former chair of the board of trustees of Morton County's public library. Baesler was elected superintendent of public instruction in November 2012 and 2016. She serves on more than a dozen boards, including the Education Standards and Practices Board, Educational Technology Council, Teachers' Fund for Retirement board, and Board of University and School Lands, which manages state land holdings and oversees a $4.2 billion trust fund that benefits North Dakota's public schools. She is one of the nine directors of the Council of Chief State School Officers, which represents state education organizations across the nation. CCSSO provides leadership, technical assistance, and advocacy on major educational issues. Baesler is one of 25 women leaders chosen from across the country for the Governing Institute's 2019 Women in Government Leadership Program, which provides training for participants to serve as mentors and advisers for other prospective female leaders. She is a member of the advisory board of the Civics Education Initiative. One of its advocacy objectives is to require high school students to pass a civics exam as a requirement for graduation. Baesler successfully advocated for the approval of this idea in the North Dakota Legislature in 2015.

Summary of Duties
The Superintendent of Public Instruction is an advocate for more than 121,000 North Dakota students in grades kindergarten through 12. The superintendent oversees compliance with state and federal laws and regulations that affect education. The job's duties include oversight of elementary and secondary education, school accreditation, review of proposed school construction projects, and the development of course content standards and assessments of student progress. The superintendent adopts rules for the credentialing of teachers and administrators. She administers state and federal programs, including state aid to schools, school breakfast and lunch programs, assistance for students who need extra help in reading and mathematics, and instruction for students who are not fluent in English. She is in charge of implementing a uniform system for accounting, budgeting, and reporting school district data and responsible for publishing yearly reports on school finance and teacher compensation. The superintendent selects the North Dakota Teacher of the Year. In addition to the Department of Public Instruction, she has charge of the State Library, School for the Deaf/Resource Center for the Deaf and Hard of Hearing in Devils Lake, and Vision Services/School for the Blind in Grand Forks.

Executive Officials Contact Information

The Constitution establishes all elective offices. This distribution of power has traditionally been seen as severely limiting the power of the Governor. However, the Governor's powers have increased over the more recent history of the state with greater control of the budgeting process and more direct appointments of the heads of the state's largest executive agencies. At the same time, North Dakota has a larger number of elected officials than most states outside of southern states.

Three elected officials – the Governor, Agriculture Commissioner, and Attorney General – exercise joint power through the Industrial Commission. This product of the industrial program of the Nonpartisan League was established to manage state-owned industries. The use of commissions and boards headed by elected officials has been common in North Dakota state government, although the Industrial Commission is a unique expression of that phenomenon.

The following is contact information and term requirements for the executive official's offices:

Governor
600 East Boulevard Avenue, 1st Floor
Bismarck, ND 58505-0001
Phone: 701-328-2200
Fax: 701-328-2205
Web: www.governor.nd.gov
[Constitution, Article V, Section 1; NDCC 54-07]

Term: four years. Qualifications: citizen of the United States, qualified elector of the state, at least 30 years old, resident of the state for five years immediately prior to the election.

Lieutenant Governor
600 East Boulevard Avenue, 1st Floor
Bismarck, ND 58505-0001
Phone: 701-328-2200
Fax: 701-328-2205
Web: www.governor.nd.gov
[Constitution, Article V, Section 2; NDCC 54-08]

Term: four years. Qualifications: same as Governor.

Agriculture Commissioner

600 East Boulevard Avenue, Dept. 602
Bismarck, ND 58505-0200
Phone: 701-328-4754
Toll Free: 800-242-7535
North Dakota Mediation Services: 701-328-4158
Fax: 701-328-4567
Web: www.agdepartment.com
Email: ndda@nd.gov
[Constitution, Article V, Section 2; NDCC 4-01]

Term: four years. Qualifications: qualified elector of the state, at least 25 years old.

Attorney General

600 East Boulevard Avenue, Dept. 125
Bismarck, ND 58505-0040
Phone: 701-328-2210
Fax: 701-328-2226
Web: www.attorneygeneral.nd.gov
Email: ndag@nd.gov
Gaming Division: 701-328-4848
Bureau of Criminal Investigation (BCI): 800-472-2185
[Constitution, Article V, Section 2; NDCC 54-12]

Term: four years. Qualifications: qualified elector of the state, at least 25 years old, licensed attorney.

State Auditor

600 East Boulevard Avenue, Dept. 117
Bismarck, ND 58505-0060
Phone: 701-328-2241
Web: www.nd.gov/auditor
Email: ndsao@nd.gov
[Constitution, Article V, Section 2; NDCC 54-10]

Term: four years. Qualifications: qualified elector of the state, at least 25 years old.

Insurance Commissioner
600 East Boulevard Avenue
Bismarck, ND 58505-0320
Phone: 701-328-2440
Toll Free: 800-247-0560 - Consumer Hotline
Fax: 701-328-4880
Web: www.nd.gov/ndins
[Constitution, Article V, Section 2; NDCC 26.1-01]

Term: four years. Qualifications: qualified elector of the state, at least 25 years old.

Superintendent of Public Instruction
600 East Boulevard Avenue, Dept. 201
Floors 9, 10 and 11
Bismarck, ND 58505-0440
Phone: 701-328-2260
Fax: 701-328-2461
Web: www.nd.gov/dpi
Facebook: www.facebook.com/NDDPI
Email: dpi@nd.gov
[Constitution, Article V, Section 4; NDCC 15.1-02-01]

Term: four years. Qualifications: qualified elector of the state, at least 25 years old, resident of North Dakota for five years preceding the election to office.

Public Service Commission
600 East Boulevard Avenue, Dept. 408
Bismarck, ND 58505-0480
Phone: 701-328-2400
Fax: 701-328-2410
TTY: 800-366-6888
Web: www.psc.nd.gov
Email: ndpsc@nd.gov
[Constitution, Article V, Section 2; NDCC 49-01]

Term: three commissioners serving six-year terms with one commissioner's term expiring every two years. Qualifications: qualified elector of the state, at least 25 years old.

Secretary of State
600 East Boulevard Avenue, Dept. 108
Bismarck, ND 58505-0500
Phone: 701-328-2900
Toll Free: 800-352-0867
Fax: 701-328-2992
TTY: 800-366-6888
Web: https://sos.nd.gov
Email: sos@nd.gov
[Constitution, Article V, Section 2; NDCC 54-09]

Term: four years. Qualifications: qualified elector of the state, at least 25 years old.

Tax Commissioner
600 East Boulevard Avenue, Dept. 127
Bismarck, ND 58505-0599
Phone: 701-328-7088
Toll Free: 877-328-7088
Fax: 701-328-3700
Relay ND: 800-366-6888
Web: www.nd.gov/tax
Email: taxinfo@nd.gov
[Constitution, Article V, Section 2; NDCC 57-01]

Term: four years. Qualifications: qualified elector of the state, at least 25 years old.

State Treasurer
600 East Boulevard Avenue, 3rd Floor, Dept. 120
Bismarck, ND 58505-0600
Phone: 701-328-2643
Fax: 701-328-3002
Web: www.nd.gov/treasurer
Email: treasurer@nd.gov
[Constitution, Article V, Section 2; NDCC 54-11]

Term: four years. Qualifications: qualified elector of the state, at least 25 years old.

Executive Branch

Chronology of Elective State Officers Since Statehood

Elected officials take office on January 1 except the Governor and Lieutenant Governor who take office on December 15. (Legislators take office on December 1.)

Governor

The office was created by the 1889 state constitution and originally provided for a two-year term. By constitutional amendment, adopted June 30, 1964, the term was increased to four years (Article V, Section 1).

John Miller (R) (1843-1908) 1889-1891
    Elected 1889; did not seek re-election 1890
Andrew H. Burke (R) (1850-1918) 1891-1893
    Elected 1890; defeated for re-election 1892
Eli C. D. Shortridge (Pop) (1830-1908) 1893-1895
    Elected 1892; did not seek re-election 1894
Roger Allin (R) (1848-1936) 1895-1897
    Elected 1894; did not seek re-election 1896
Frank A. Briggs (R) (1858-1898) 1897-1898
    Elected 1896; died in office August 9, 1898
Joseph M. Devine (R) (1861-1938) 1898-1899
    Lieutenant Governor; completed Frank Briggs' term
Frederick B. Fancher (R) (1852-1944) 1899-1901
    Elected 1898; defeated for renomination 1900
Frank White (R) (1856-1940) 1901-1905
    Elected 1900, 1902; did not seek re-election 1904
Elmore Y. Sarles (R) (1859-1929) 1905-1907
    Elected 1904; defeated for re-election 1906
John Burke (D) (1859-1937) 1907-1913
    Elected 1906, 1908, 1910; did not seek re-election 1912
Louis B. Hanna (R) (1861-1948) 1913-1917
    Elected 1912, 1914; did not seek re-election 1916
Lynn J. Frazier (R) (1874-1947) 1917-1921
    Elected 1916, 1918, 1920; recalled October 28, 1921
Ragnvold A. Nestos (R) (1877-1942) 1921-1925
    Elected 1921, 1922; defeated for re-election 1924
Arthur G. Sorlie (R) (1874-1928) 1925-1928
    Elected 1924, 1926; died in office August 28, 1928
Walter J. Maddock (R) (1880-1951) 1928-1929
    Lieutenant Governor; completed Arthur G. Sorlie's term
George F. Shafer (R) (1888-1948) 1929-1932
    Elected 1928, 1930; did not seek re-election 1932
William Langer (R) (1886-1959) 1933-1934
    Elected 1932; removed from office July 17, 1934

Ole H. Olson (R) (1872-1954) 193-1935
    Lieutenant Governor; completed William Langer's term
Thomas H. Moodie (D) (1878-1948) 1935
    Elected 1934; removed from office February 16, 1935
Walter Welford (R) (1868-1952) 1935-1937
    Lieutenant Governor; completed Thomas H. Moodie's term; defeated for
    election 1936
William Langer (R) (1886-1959) 1937-1939
    Elected 1936; did not seek re-election 1938
John Moses (D) (1885-1945) 1939-1945
    Elected 1938, 1940, 1942; did not seek re-election 1944
Fred G. Aandahl (R) (1897-1966) 1945-1951
    Elected 1944, 1946, 1948; did not seek re-election 1950
C. Norman Brunsdale (R) (1891-1978) 1951-1957
    Elected 1950, 1952, 1954; did not seek re-election 1956
John E. Davis (R) (1913-1990) 1957-1961
    Elected 1956, 1958; did not seek re-election 1960
William L. Guy (D) (1919-2013) 1961-1973
    Elected 1960, 1962, 1964, 1968; did not seek re-election 1972
Arthur A. Link (D) (1914-2010) 1973-1981
    Elected 1972, 1976; defeated for re-election 1980
Allen I. Olson (R) (1938-) 1981-1985
    Elected 1980; defeated for re-election 1984
George A. Sinner (D) (1928-2018) 1985-1992
    Elected 1984, 1988; did not seek re-election 1992

In the General Election November 4, 1986, voters approved a constitutional amendment changing the date of office for Governor and Lieutenant Governor from January 1 to December 15. (1987 Session Laws, Chapter 776). That provision is now found in Article V, Section 5, of the North Dakota Constitution.

Edward T. Schafer (R) (1946-) 1992-2000
    Elected 1992, 1996; did not seek re-election 2000
John H. Hoeven (R) (1957-) 2000-2010
    Elected 2000, 2004, 2008; resigned December 7, 2010, following election to
    U.S. Senate
John (Jack) Dalrymple (R) (1948-) 2010-2016
    Appointed in 2010 to fill unexpired term of John Hoeven; elected 2012;
    did not seek re-election 2016
Doug Burgum (R) (1956-) 2016-present
    Elected 2016

Lieutenant Governor

In 1974, voters approved a constitutional amendment requiring the Governor and the Lieutenant Governor be of the same party (joint ballot) (Article V, Section 4).

Alfred Dickey (R) (1846-1901)...1889-1890
    Elected 1889; did not seek renomination 1890
Roger Allin (R) (1848-1936)..1891-1892
    Elected 1890; defeated for renomination at 1892 Republican convention
Elmer D. Wallace (D-I) (1844-1928)...1893-1894
    Elected 1892; did not seek re-election 1894
John H. Worst (R) (1850-1945)..1895-1896
    Elected 1894; defeated for renomination at 1896 Republican convention
Joseph M. Devine (R) (1861-1938)..1897-1900
    Elected 1896, 1898; did not seek re-election 1900
David Bartlett (R) (1854-1913) 1901-1906
    Elected 1900, 1902, 1904; did not seek re-election 1906
Robert S. Lewis (R) (1856-1956)..1907-1910
    Elected 1906, 1908; did not seek re-election 1910
Usher L. Burdick (R) (1879-1960)..1911-1912
    Elected 1910; did not seek re-election 1912
Anton T. Kraabel (R) (1862-1934)..1913-1914
    Elected 1912; defeated in June 1914 Republican primary
John H. Fraine (R) (1861-1943)..1915-1916
    Elected 1914; did not seek re-election 1916
Anton T. Kraabel (R) (1862-1934)..1917-1918
    Elected 1916; defeated in June 1918 Republican primary
Howard R. Wood (R) (1887-1958)..1919-1922
    Elected 1918, 1920; did not seek re-election 1922
Frank H. Hyland (R) (1880-1934)..1923-1924
    Elected 1922; did not seek re-election 1924
Walter J. Maddock (R) (1880-1951) 1925-1928
    Elected 1924, 1926; did not seek re-election 1928
John W. Carr (R) (1874-1932)..1929-1932
    Elected 1928, 1930; died in office June 14, 1932
Ole H. Olson (R) (1872-1954) 1932-1934
    Elected 1932; defeated in June 1934 Republican primary
Walter Welford (R) (1868-1952)...1935-1936
    Elected 1934; did not seek re-election 1936
Thorstein H. H. Thoresen (R) (1885-1956)..1937-1938
    Elected 1936; did not seek re-election 1938
Jack A. Patterson (R) (1890-1971)...1939-1940
    Elected 1938; did not seek re-election 1940
Oscar W. Hagen (R) (1884-1945)..1941-1942
    Elected 1940; did not seek re-election 1942
Henry Holt (D) (1888-1944)...1943-1944
    Elected 1942; died in office March 2, 1944
Clarence P. Dahl (R) (1892-1976)..1944-1950
    Elected 1944, 1946, 1948; did not seek re-election 1950
Ray Schnell (R) (1893-1970) 1951-1952
    Elected 1950; defeated in June 1952 Republican primary

Clarence P. Dahl (R) (1892-1976) 1953-1956
    Elected 1952, 1954; did not seek re-election 1956
Francis Clyde Duffy (R) (1890-1977) 1957-1958
    Elected 1956; did not seek re-election 1958
Clarence P. Dahl (R) (1892-1976) 1959-1960
    Elected 1958; did not seek re-election 1960
Orville W. Hagen (R) (1915-2007) 1961-1962
    Elected 1960; did not seek re-election 1962
Frank A. Wenstrom (R) (1903-1997) 1963-1964
    Elected 1962; defeated in November 1964 general election
Charles Tighe (D) (1927-2004) 1965-1968
    Elected 1964; defeated in November 1968 general election
Richard F. Larsen (R) (1936-) 1969-1972
    Elected 1968; did not seek re-election 1972
Wayne G. Sanstead (D) (1935-) 1973-1980
    Elected 1972, 1976; defeated for re-election 1980
Ernest Sands (R) (1922-2012) 1981-1984
    Elected 1980; defeated for re-election 1984
Ruth Meiers (D) (1925-1987) 1985-1987
    Elected 1984; died in office March 19, 1987
Lloyd B. Omdahl (D) (1931-) 1987-1992
    Appointed April 22, 1987, eff. May 15, to complete Ruth Meiers' term; elected 1988; did not seek re-election 1992
Rosemarie Myrdal (R) (1929-) 1992-2000
    Elected 1992, 1996; did not seek re-election 2000
John (Jack) Dalrymple (R) (1948-) 2000-2010
    Elected 2000, 2004, 2008; became governor December 7, 2010
Drew H. Wrigley (R) (1965-) 2010-2016
    Appointed in 2010 to fill the unexpired term of Jack Dalrymple; elected 2012; did not seek re-election 2016
Brent Sanford (R) (1971-) 2016-present
    Elected 2016

Secretary of State

Originally a two-year term, the office became a four-year term with adoption of a constitutional amendment in June 1964 (Article V, Section 12). Voters approved a change to the Constitution at the Primary Election on June 13, 2000, that puts one-half of the elected officials on the ballot each election year. To begin that process, the Secretary of State, the Commissioner of Agriculture, the Attorney General, and the Tax Commissioner were elected for two-year terms in 2004. Those offices then returned to four-year terms (2001 Laws of North Dakota, Chapter 591).

John Flittie (R) (1856-1913) 1889-1892
    Elected 1889, 1890; did not seek re-election 1892

Christian M. Dahl (R) (1865-1923) 1893-1896
    Elected 1892, 1894; did not seek re-election 1896
Fred Falley (R) (1859-1907) 1897-1900
    Elected 1896, 1898; did not seek re-election 1900
Edward F. Porter (R) (1858-1915) 1901-1906
    Elected 1900, 1902, 1904; did not seek re-election 1906
Alfred Blaisdell (R) (1875-1946) 1907-1910
    Elected 1906, 1908; did not seek re-election 1910
Patrick D. Norton (R) (1876-1953) 1911-1912
    Elected 1910; did not seek re-election 1912
Thomas Hall (R) (1869-1958) 1913-1924
    Elected 1912, 1914, 1916, 1918, 1920, 1922; did not seek re-election 1924
Robert Byrne (R) (1886-1967) 1925-1934
    Elected 1924, 1926, 1928, 1930, 1932; defeated in June 1934 Republican primary
James D. Gronna (R) (1884-1963) 1935-1940
    Elected 1934, 1936, 1938; did not seek re-election 1940
Herman Thorson (R) (1880-1960) 1941-1942
    Elected 1940; defeated in November 1942 general election
Thomas Hall (R) (1869-1958) 1943-1954
    Elected 1942, 1944, 1946, 1948, 1950, 1952; did not seek re-election 1954
Ben Meier (R) (1918-1995) 1955-1988
    Elected 1954, 1956, 1958, 1960, 1962, 1964, 1968, 1972, 1976, 1980, 1984; did not seek re-election 1988
Jim Kusler (D) (1947-) 1989-1992
    Elected 1988; defeated for re-election 1992
Alvin A. Jaeger (R) (1943-) 1993-present
    Elected 1992, 1996, 2000, 2004, 2006, 2010, 2014, 2018

State Auditor

Originally a two-year term, the office became a four-year term with adoption of a constitutional amendment in June 1964 (Article V, Section 12).

John P. Bray (R) (1859-1917) 1889-1891
    Elected 1889, 1890; resigned September 1892
Archie Currie (R) (1860-1943) 1892-1892
    Appointed September 1892 to complete John P. Bray's term
Arthur W. Porter (D-I) (1857-1952) 1893-1894
    Elected 1892; defeated in November 1894 general election
Frank A. Briggs (R) (1858-1898) 1895-1896
    Elected 1894; did not seek re-election 1896
Nathan B. Hannum (R) (1851-1920) 1897-1898
    Elected 1896; did not seek re-election 1898
Albert N. Carlblom (R) (1865-1920) 1899-1902
    Elected 1898, 1900; did not seek re-election 1902

Herbert L. Holmes (R) (1853-1922).. 1903-1908
    Elected 1902, 1904, 1906; did not seek re-election 1908
David K. Brightbill (R) (1865-1949)..1909-1912
    Elected 1908, 1910; did not seek re-election 1912
Carl O. Jorgenson (R) (1881-1951)..1913-1916
    Elected 1912, 1914; defeated in June 1916 Republican primary
Carl R. Kositzky (R) (1876-1940)...1917-1920
    Elected 1916, 1918; defeated in June 1920 Republican primary
David C. Poindexter (R) (1891-1927)..1921-1924
    Elected 1920, 1922; defeated in June 1924 Republican primary
John Steen (R) (1874-1959)..1925-1934
    Elected 1924, 1926, 1928, 1930, 1932; did not seek re-election 1934
Berta E. Baker (R) (1875-1964)..1935-1956
    Elected 1934, 1936, 1938, 1940, 1942, 1944, 1946, 1948, 1950, 1952, 1954; did not seek re-election 1956
Curtis G. Olson (R) (1908-2004)...1957-1972
    Elected 1956, 1958, 1960, 1962, 1964, 1968; did not seek re-election 1972
Robert W. Peterson (R) (1929-2013) 1973-1996
    Elected 1972, 1976, 1980, 1984, 1988, 1992, did not seek re-election 1996
Robert R. Peterson (R) (1951-)...1997-2016
    Elected 1996, 2000, 2004, 2008, 2012; did not seek re-election 2016
Joshua C. Gallion (R) (1979-).. 2017-present
    Elected 2016

State Treasurer

Originally a two-year term, the office became a four-year term with adoption of a constitutional amendment in June 1964 (Article V, Section 12). Article V, Section 12, prohibited any person from serving more than two consecutive terms as State Treasurer; that prohibition was removed in 1996 by a vote of the people (S.L. 1995, ch. 646, HCR 3009).

Lewis E. Booker (R) (1846-1918).. 1889-1892
    Elected 1889, 1890; defeated in November 1892 general election
Knud J. Nomland (D-I) (1852-1922).. 1893-1894
    Elected 1892; defeated in November 1894 general election
George E. Nichols (R) (1856-1935)... 1895-1898
    Elected 1894, 1896; ineligible for re-election 1898
Dennis W. Driscoll (R) (1849-1905)... 1899-1900
    Elected 1898; defeated for renomination in 1900 Republican convention
Donald H. McMillan (R) (1849-unknown).............................. 1901-1904
    Elected 1900, 1902; ineligible for re-election 1904
Albert Peterson (R) (1862-1944) 1905-1908
    Elected 1904, 1906; ineligible for re-election 1908
George L. Bickford (R) (1874-1937) 1909-1910
    Elected 1908; defeated in June 1910 Republican primary

Gunder Olson (R) (1852-1948) 1911-1914
    Elected 1910, 1912; ineligible for re-election 1914
John Steen (R) (1874-1959) 1915-1918
    Elected 1914, 1916; ineligible for re-election 1918
Obert A. Olson (R) (1882-1938) 1919-1920
    Elected 1918; did not seek re-election 1920
John Steen (R) (1874-1959) 1921-1924
    Elected 1920, 1922; ineligible for re-election 1924
Chessmur A. Fisher (R) (1868-1948) 1925-1928
    Elected 1924, 1926; ineligible for re-election 1928
Berta E. Baker (R) (1875-1964) 1929-1932
    Elected 1928, 1930; ineligible for re-election 1932
Alfred S. Dale (R) (1896-1974) 1933-1934
    Elected 1932; defeated in June 1934 Republican primary
John Gray (R) (1877-1952) 1935-1938
    Elected 1934, 1936; ineligible for re-election 1938
John R. Omland (R) (1893-1970) 1939-1940
    Elected 1938; defeated in June 1940 Republican primary
Carl Anderson (R) (1897-1945) 1941-1944
    Elected 1940, 1942; ineligible for re-election 1944
Otto G. Krueger (R) (1890-1963) 1945
    Elected 1944; resigned September 7, 1945
Hjalmer W. Swenson (R) (1885-1958) 1945-1948
    Appointed October 3, 1945, to fill Otto G. Krueger's term; elected 1946; defeated in June 1948 Republican primary
Albert Jacobson (R) (1899-1958) 1949-1952
    Elected 1948, 1950; ineligible for re-election 1952
Ray Thompson (R) (1911-1957) 1953-1954
    Elected 1952; defeated in June 1954 Republican primary
Albert Jacobson (R) (1899-1958) 1955-1958
    Elected 1954, 1956; died in office October 27, 1958
Mike J. Baumgartner (R) (1895-1969) 1958
    Appointed November 1, 1958, to fill Albert Jacobson's term
John R. Erickson (R) (1905-1980) 1959-1962
    Elected 1958, 1960; ineligible for re-election 1962
Phil Hoghaug (R) (1906-1971) 1963-1964
    Elected 1962; defeated in November 1964 general election
Walter Christensen (D) (1910-1979) 1965-1968
    Elected 1964; defeated in November 1968 general election
Bernice Asbridge (R) (1919-2004) 1969-1972
    Elected 1968; defeated in November 1972 general election
Walter Christensen (D) (1910-1979) 1973-1979
    Elected 1972, 1976; died in office August 3, 1979
Robert E. Hanson (D) (1947-2015) 1979-1980
    Appointed September 28, 1979, to fill Walter Christensen's term; defeated for election 1980

John S. Lesmeister (R) (1955-2006) 1981-1984
    Elected 1980; defeated for re-election 1984
Robert E. Hanson (D) (1947-2015) 1985-1992
    Elected 1984, 1988; ineligible for re-election 1992
Kathi Gilmore (D) (1944-) 1993-2004
    Elected 1992, 1996, 2000, did not seek re-election in 2004
Kelly L. Schmidt (R) (1962-) 2005-present
    Elected 2004, 2008, 2012, 2016

Attorney General

Originally a two-year term, the office became a four-year term with adoption of a constitutional amendment in June 1964 (Article V, Section 12). Voters approved a change to the Constitution at the Primary Election on June 13, 2000, that puts one-half of the elected officials on the ballot each election year. To begin that process, the Secretary of State, the Commissioner of Agriculture, the Attorney General, and the Tax Commissioner were elected for two-year terms in 2004. Those offices then returned to four-year terms (2001 Laws of North Dakota, Chapter 591).

George F. Goodwin (R) (1849-1918) 1889-1890
    Elected 1889; defeated for renomination in 1890 Republican convention
Clarence A. M. Spencer (R) (1850-1933) 1891-1892
    Elected 1890; did not seek re-election 1892
William H. Standish (D-I) (1843-1923) 1893-1894
    Elected 1892; defeated in November 1894 general election
John F. Cowan (R) (1858-1917) 1895-1900
    Elected 1894, 1896, 1898; did not seek re-election 1900
Oliver D. Comstock (R) (1865-1945) 1901-1902
    Elected 1900; defeated for renomination in 1902 Republican convention
Carl N. Frich (R) (1867-1927) 1903-1906
    Elected 1902, 1904; did not seek re-election 1906
Thomas F. McCue (R) (1866-1938) 1907-1908
    Elected 1906; defeated in June 1908 Republican primary
Andrew Miller (R) (1870-1960) 1909-1914
    Elected 1908, 1910, 1912; did not seek re-election 1914
Henry J. Linde (R) (1879-1917) 1915-1916
    Elected 1914; defeated in June 1916 Republican primary
William Langer (R) (1886-1959) 1917-1920
    Elected 1916, 1918; did not seek re-election 1920
William Lemke (R) (1878-1950) 1921
    Elected 1920; recalled October 28, 1921
Sveinbjorn Johnson (R) (1883-1946) 1921-1922
    Elected October 28, 1921; did not seek re-election 1922
George F. Shafer (R) (1888-1948) 1923-1928
    Elected 1922, 1924, 1926; did not seek re-election 1928

James Morris (R) (1893-1980) 1929-1932
    Elected 1928, 1930; defeated in June 1932 Republican primary
Arthur J. Gronna (R) (1897-1965) 1933
    Elected 1932; resigned November 1, 1933
P. O. Sathre (R) (1878-1968) 1933-1937
    Appointed November 1, 1933, to fill Arthur J. Gronna's term; elected
    1934, 1936; resigned December 6, 1937
Alvin C. Strutz (R) (1903-1973) 1937-1944
    Appointed December 7, 1937, to fill P. O. Sathre's term; elected 1938,
    1940, 1942; did not seek re-election 1944
Nels G. Johnson (R) (1896-1958) 1945-1948
    Elected 1944, 1946; defeated in June 1948 Republican primary;
    resigned September 1, 1948
P.O. Sathre (R-NPL) (1878-1968) 1948
    Appointed September 1, 1948, to fill Nels G. Johnson's term
Wallace E. Warner (R) (1916-1994) 1949-1950
    Elected 1948; did not seek re-election 1950
Elmo T. Christianson (R) (1920-1996) 1951-1954
    Elected 1950, 1952; resigned May 5, 1954
Paul Benson (R) (1918-2004) 1954
    Appointed May 15, 1954, to fill Elmo T. Christianson's term
Leslie R. Burgum (R) (1890-1984) 1955-1962
    Elected 1954, 1956, 1958, 1960; did not seek re-election 1962
Helgi Johanneson (R) (1906-1994) 1963-1972
    Elected 1962, 1964, 1968; did not seek re-election 1972
Allen I. Olson (R) (1938-) 1973-1980
    Elected 1972, 1976; did not seek re-election 1980
Robert Wefald (R) (1942-) 1981-1984
    Elected 1980; defeated for re-election 1984
Nicholas Spaeth (D) (1950-2014) 1985-1992
    Elected 1984, 1988; did not seek re-election 1992
Mary Kathryn "Heidi" Heitkamp (D) (1955-) 1993-2000
    Elected 1992, 1996; did not seek re-election 2000
Wayne Stenehjem (R) (1953-) 2001-present
    Elected 2000, 2004, 2006, 2010, 2014, 2018

Insurance Commissioner

    Originally a two-year term, the office became a four-year term with adoption of a constitutional amendment in June 1964 (Article V, Section 12).

A. L. Carey (R) (1846-1906) 1889-1892
    Elected 1889, 1890; did not seek re-election 1892
James Cudhie (D-I) (1858-1941) 1893-1894
    Elected 1892; defeated in November 1894 general election
Frederick B. Fancher (R) (1852-1944) 1895-1898
    Elected 1894, 1896; did not seek re-election 1898

George W. Harrison (R) (1867-1931) 1899-1900
    Elected 1898; defeated for renomination at 1900 Republican convention
Ferdinand Leutz (R) (1854-1934) 1901-1904
    Elected 1900, 1902; defeated for renomination at 1904 Republican convention
Ernest C. Cooper (R) (1856-1917) 1905-1910
    Elected 1904, 1906, 1908; did not seek re-election 1910
Walter C. Taylor (R) (1870-1929) 1911-1916
    Elected 1910, 1912, 1914; defeated in June 1916 Republican primary
Sveinung A. Olsness (R) (1866-1954) 1917-1934
    Elected 1916, 1918, 1920, 1922, 1924, 1926, 1928, 1930, 1932; defeated in June 1934 Republican primary
Harold Hopton (R) (1894-1984) 1935-1936
    Elected 1934; defeated in June 1936 Republican primary
Oscar E. Erickson (R) (1884-1945) 1937-1945
    Elected 1936, 1938, 1940, 1942, 1944; died in office August 15, 1945
Otto G. Krueger (R) (1890-1963) 1945-1950
    Appointed September 7, 1945, to fill Oscar E. Erickson's term; elected 1946, 1948; did not seek re-election 1950
Alfred J. Jensen (R) (1893-1973) 1951-1962
    Elected 1950, 1952, 1954, 1956, 1958, 1960; did not seek re-election 1962
Frank Albers (R) (1909-1974) 1963-1964
    Elected 1962; defeated in June 1964 Republican primary
Kelly O. Nygaard (D) (1906-1979) 1965-1968
    Elected 1964; defeated in November 1968 general election
Joris O. Wigen (R) (1917-1987) 1969-1976
    Elected 1968, 1972; defeated for re-election 1976
Byron Knutson (D) (1929-) 1977-1980
    Elected 1976; defeated for re-election 1980
Jorris O. Wigen (R) (1917-1987) 1981-1984
    Elected 1980; did not seek re-election 1984
Earl Pomeroy (D) (1952-) 1985-1992
    Elected 1984, 1988; did not seek re-election 1992
Glenn Pomeroy (D) (1956-) 1993-2000
    Elected 1992, 1996; did not seek re-election 2000
Jim Poolman (R) (1970-) 2001-2007
    Elected in 2000, 2004; resigned August 31, 2007
Adam Hamm (R) (1971-) 2007-2016
    Appointed October 9, 2007, to fill Jim Poolman's term; elected 2008, 2012; did not seek re-election 2016
Jon Godfread (R) (1982-) 2017-present
    Elected in 2016

Commissioner of Agriculture and Labor

Originally a two-year term, the office became a four-year term with adoption of a constitutional amendment in June 1964 (Article V, Section 12). This combination office existed until 1967.

Henry T. Helgesen (R) (1857-1917) 1889-1892
   Elected 1889, 1890; did not seek re-election 1892
George E. Adams (D-I) (1859-1946)
   Elected 1892; but failed to qualify for office
Nelson Williams (D-I) (1856-1941) 1893-1894
   Appointed January 3, 1893, to fill George E. Adams' term; did not seek re-election 1894
Andrew H. Laughlin (R) (1848-1914) 1895-1896
   Elected 1894; defeated for renomination at 1896 Republican convention
Henry U. Thomas (R) (1853-1926) 1897-1900
   Elected 1896, 1898; did not seek re-election 1900
Rollin J. Turner (R) (1850-1918) 1901-1904
   Elected 1900, 1902; did not seek re-election 1904
William C. Gilbreath (R) (1851-1921) 1905-1914
   Elected 1904, 1906, 1908, 1910, 1912; did not seek re-election 1914
Robert F. Flint (R) (1872-1941) 1915-1916
   Elected 1914; defeated in June 1916 Republican primary
John N. Hagan (R) (1873-1952) 1917-1921
   Elected 1916, 1918, 1920; recalled October 28, 1921
Joseph A. Kitchen (R) (1878-1942) 1921-1932
   Elected October 28, 1921, 1922, 1924, 1926, 1928, 1930; defeated in June 1932 Republican primary
John Husby (R) (1884-1965) 1933-1934
   Elected 1932; defeated in June 1934 Republican primary
Theodore Martell (R) (1894-1967) 1935-1936
   Elected 1934; defeated in June 1936 Republican primary
John N. Hagan (R) (1873-1952) 1937-1938
   Elected 1936; did not seek re-election 1938
Matt Dahl (R) (1884-1976) 1939-1964
   Elected 1938, 1940, 1942, 1944, 1946, 1948, 1950, 1952, 1954, 1956, 1958, 1960, 1962; did not seek re-election 1964
Arne Dahl (R) (1907-1974) 1965-1966
   Elected 1964

Agriculture Commissioner

A constitutional amendment adopted June 28, 1960, authorized the Legislative Assembly, if it so chose, to separate agriculture and labor into two distinct offices. The 1965 Legislative Assembly enacted the necessary legislation, and in January 1967, the former Commissioner of Agriculture and Labor became the new Commissioner of Agriculture. Voters approved a change to the Constitution at the Primary Election on

June 13, 2000, which put one-half of the elected officials on the ballot each election year. To begin that process, the Secretary of State, the Commissioner of Agriculture, the Attorney General, and the Tax Commissioner were elected for two-year terms in 2004. Those offices then returned to four-year terms (2001 Laws of North Dakota, Chapter 591).

Arne Dahl (R) (1907-1974) 1967-1974
    Elected 1968, 1972; died in office February 2, 1974
Myron Just (D) (1941-) 1974-1980
    Appointed February 14, 1974, to fill Arne Dahl's term;
    elected 1976; did not seek re-election 1980
H. Kent Jones (R) (1926-1995) 1981-1988
    Elected 1980, 1984; 1988 on ballot as independent, defeated for re-election
Sarah Vogel (D) (1946-) 1989-1996
    Elected 1988, 1992; did not seek re-election 1996
Roger Johnson (D) (1953-) 1997-2009
    Elected 1996, 2000, 2004, 2006; resigned April 4, 2009
Doug Goehring (R) (1965-) 2009-present
    Appointed April 6, 2009; elected 2010, 2014, 2018

Labor Commissioner

Following passage of the June 28, 1960, constitutional amendment, the 1965 Legislative Assembly created the office of Commissioner of Labor, to be elected on a no-party ballot for a four-year term, beginning with the general election in 1966 (1965 S.L., ch. 236) (North Dakota Century Code Sections 34-05-01.2 and 16.1-11-08). Beginning January 1, 1999, the Governor appoints the Labor Commissioner (1995 S.L., ch. 334, amendment to NDCC 34-05-01.2).

Orville W. Hagen (1915-2007) 1967-1986
    Elected 1966, 1970, 1974, 1978, 1982; defeated for re-election 1986
Byron Knutson (1929-) 1987-1990
    Elected 1986; defeated for re-election 1990
Craig Hagen (1965-) 1991-1998
    Elected 1990, 1994; resigned August 13, 1998

Superintendent of Public Instruction

Originally a two-year term, the office became a four-year term with adoption of a constitutional amendment in June 1964 (Article V, Section 12).

William Mitchell (R) (1830-1890) 1889-1890
    Elected 1889; died in office March 10, 1890
William J. Clapp (R) (1857-1934) 1890
    Appointed April 10, 1890, to fill William Mitchell's term;
    defeated for nomination at 1890 Republican convention
John Ogden (R) (1824-1910) 1891-1892
    Elected 1890; did not seek re-election 1892

Laura J. Eisenhuth (D-I) (1858-1937) 1893-1894
    Elected 1892; defeated in November 1894 general election
Emma F. Bates (R) (1854-1920) 1895-1896
    Elected 1894; defeated for renomination in 1896 Republican convention
John G. Halland (R) (1863-1938) 1897-1900
    Elected 1896, 1898; did not seek re-election 1900
Joseph M. Devine (R) (1861-1938) 1901-1902
    Elected 1900; did not seek re-election 1902
Walter L. Stockwell (R) (1868-1950) 1903-1910
    Elected 1902, 1904, 1906, 1908; did not seek re-election 1910
Edwin J. Taylor (R) (1869-1956) 1911-1914
    Elected 1910, 1912

An act of the 1913 Legislative Assembly provided for the election of the Superintendent of Public Instruction on a no-party ballot, effective in 1914 (1913 S.L., ch. 153) (North Dakota Century Code Section 16.1-11-08).

Edwin J. Taylor (1869-1956) 1915-1916
    Elected 1914; did not seek re-election 1916
Neil C. MacDonald (1876-1923) 1917-1918
    Elected 1916; defeated in November 1918 general election
Minnie J. Nielson (1874-1958) 1919-1926
    Elected 1918, 1920, 1922, 1924; did not seek re-election 1926
Bertha R. Palmer (1880-1959) 1927-1932
    Elected 1926, 1928, 1930; defeated for re-election 1932
Arthur E. Thompson (1891-1969) 1933-1946
    Elected 1932, 1934, 1936, 1938, 1940, 1942, 1944; resigned August 31, 1946
Garfield B. Nordrum (1906-1995) 1946-1951
    Appointed August 31, 1946, to fill Arthur E. Thompson's term; elected 1946, 1948, 1950; resigned January 4, 1951
Marvell F. Peterson (1908-1996) 1951-1976
    Appointed January 4, 1951, to fill Garfield B. Nordrum's term; elected 1952, 1954, 1956, 1958, 1960, 1962, 1964, 1968, 1972; did not seek re-election 1976
Howard J. Snortland (1912-2006) 1977-1980
    Elected 1976; defeated for re-election 1980
Joseph Crawford (1944-) 1981-1984
    Elected 1980; did not seek re-election 1984
Wayne G. Sanstead (1935-) 1985-2012
    Elected 1984, 1988, 1992, 1996, 2000, 2004, 2008
Kirsten Baesler (1969-) 2013-present
    Elected 2012, 2016

Tax Commissioner

The 1919 Legislature replaced the three-member Tax Commission, created in 1911, with a single Tax Commissioner, appointed by the Governor for a six-year term with the advice and consent of the Senate. The first commissioner was to be appointed on or before the last Monday in February 1919 (S.L. 1919, Ch. 213).

George E. Wallace (1873-1952) 1919-1921
    Appointed March 3, 1919, eff. July 28, 1919; removed December 31, 1921, by Governor Nestos

C. C. Converse (1878-1961)...1922-1925
    Appointed January 3, 1922, by Governor Nestos; removed March 27, 1925, by Governor Sorlie

Thorstein H. Thoresen (1885-1956) 1925-1929
    Appointed March 28, 1925, by Governor Sorlie; removed July 1, 1929, by Governor Shafer

Iver A. Acker (1886-1969) 1929-1932
    Appointed June 24, 1929, eff. July 1, 1929, by Governor Shafer; removed December 31, 1932, by Governor Langer

F. A. Vogel (1888-1951) 1933
    Appointed January 3, 1933, by Governor Langer; resigned March 15, 1933

J. J. Weeks (1871-1936) 1933-1935
    Appointed March 15, 1933, by Governor Langer; removed from office, following extensive litigation, March 24, 1935

Lyman Baker (1886-1972)
    Appointed August 9, 1934, by Governor Olson; didn't take office due to Week's litigation

Ingram J. Moe (1872-1942)
    Appointed January 17, 1935, by Governor Moodie; didn't take office due to Week's litigation

Lee Nichols (1883-1966) 1935-1937
    Appointed March 25, 1935, by Governor Welford; removed from office, January 12, 1937, by Governor Langer

John Kenneth Murray (1882-1960) 1937
    Appointed January 13, 1937, by Governor Langer; resigned April 10, 1937

Owen T. Owen (1890-1989) 1937-1938
    Appointed April 10, 1937, eff. April 12, 1937, by Governor Langer; resigned, December 15, 1938

Claude P. Stone (1891-1946) 1938-1939
    Appointed December 27, 1938, by Governor Langer; removed from office January 3, 1939, by Governor Moses

William T. DePuy (1903-1982)...1939
    Appointed January 3, 1939, by Governor Moses; resigned, March 31, 1939

Lee Nichols (1883-1966) 1939
    Served as Acting Tax Commissioner, April 1 to May 17, 1939

John Gray (1877-1952) 1939-1940
    Appointed May 17, 1939, effective May 18, by Governor Moses

By constitutional amendment adopted June 28, 1938, the Tax Commissioner became an elected office with a term of four years. The measure also provided for the election of the Tax Commissioner on a no-party ballot and that the first commissioner would not be elected until the 1940 general election (Article V, Section 12). In 1987, the Tax Commissioner was removed from no-party ballot (1987, S.L., ch. 253) (NDCC 16.1-11-08).

Voters approved a change to the Constitution at the Primary Election on June 13, 2000, which puts one-half of the elected officials on the ballot each election year. To begin that process, the Secretary of State, the Commissioner of Agriculture, the Attorney General, and the Tax Commissioner were elected for two-year terms in 2004. Those offices then returned to four-year terms (2001 Laws of North Dakota, Chapter 591).

John Gray (1877-1952) 1941-1952
    Elected 1940, 1944, 1948; died in office July 17, 1952
Burtis B. Conyne (1890-1974) 1952
    Appointed July 22, 1952, to fill John Gray's term; defeated in 1952 general election
J. Arthur Engen (1897-1963) 1953-1963
    Elected 1952, 1956, 1960; died in office March 21, 1963
Lloyd B. Omdahl (1931-) 1963-1966
    Appointed April 15, 1963, to fill J. Arthur Engen's term; elected 1964; resigned May 1, 1966
Edwin O. Sjaastad (1903-1969) 1966-1969
    Appointed May 1, 1966, to fill Lloyd B. Omdahl's term; elected 1968; died in office March 20, 1969
Byron L. Dorgan (D) (1942-) 1969-1980
    Appointed March 31, 1969, to fill Edwin O. Sjaastad's term; elected 1972, 1976; did not seek re-election 1980
Kent Conrad (D) (1948-) 1981-1986
    Elected 1980, 1984; resigned December 2, 1986
Mary Kathryn "Heidi" Heitkamp (D) (1955-) 1986-1992
    Appointed December 2, 1986, to fill Kent Conrad's term; elected 1988; did not seek re-election 1992
Robert Hanson (D) (1947-2015) 1993-1996
    Elected 1992; defeated 1996
Rick Clayburgh (R) (1960-) 1997-2005
    Elected 1996, 2000, 2004; resigned May 31, 2005
Cory Fong (R) (1972-) 2005-2013
    Appointed June 1, 2005, to fill Rick Clayburgh's term; elected 2006, 2010; resigned December 31, 2013
Ryan Rauschenberger (R) (1982-) 2014-present
    Appointed January 2014 to fill Cory Fong's term; elected 2014, 2018

Public Service Commissioners

The Board of Railroad Commissioners, as originally created by the 1889 Constitution, consisted of three commissioners, each elected for a two-year term (Article V, Section 12).

David Barlett (R) (1854-1913) 1889-1890
    Elected 1889; defeated for renomination at 1890 Republican convention
George S. Montgomery (R) (1856-1936) 1889-1890
    Elected 1889; defeated for renomination at 1890 Republican convention
T. S. Underhill (R) (1834-1928) 1889-1890
    Elected 1889; did not seek re-election 1890
George W. Harmon (R) (1842-1902) 1891-1892
    Elected 1890; did not seek re-election 1892
Andrew Slotten (R) (1840-1902) 1891-1892
    Elected 1890; defeated for renomination at 1892 Republican convention
George H. Walsh (R) (1845-1913) 1891-1892
    Elected 1890; defeated for renomination at 1892 Republican convention
Peter Cameron (D-I) (1847-1916) 1893-1894
    Elected 1892; defeated in November 1894 general election
Nels P. Rasmussen (D-I) (1849-1909) 1893-1894
    Elected 1892; did not seek re-election 1894
Benjamin B. Stevens (D-I) (birth and death date unknown) 1893-1894
    Elected 1892; defeated in November 1894 general election
John W. Currie (R) (1847-1937) 1895-1896
    Elected 1894; defeated for renomination at 1896 Republican convention
George H. Keys (R) (1845-1935) 1895-1898
    Elected 1894, 1896; did not seek re-election 1898
John J. Wamberg (R) (1854-1915) 1895-1896
    Elected 1894; defeated for renomination at 1896 Republican convention
John R. Gibson (R) (1860-1940) 1897-1898
    Elected 1896; defeated for renomination at 1898 Republican convention
Luther L. Walton (R) (1844-1922) 1897-1900
    Elected 1896, 1898; did not seek re-election 1900
Henry Erickson (R) (1866-1924) 1899-1900
    Elected 1898; did not seek re-election 1900
John Simmons (R) (1858-1925) 1899-1900
    Elected 1898; defeated for renomination at 1900 Republican convention
Curtis J. Lord (R) (1862-1936) 1901-1904
    Elected 1900, 1902; did not seek re-election 1904
James F. Shea (R) (1856-1932) 1901-1904
    Elected 1900, 1902; did not seek re-election 1904
Joseph J. Youngblood (R) (1864-1938) 1901-1902
    Elected 1900; did not seek re-election 1902
Andreas Schatz (R) (1858-1928) 1903-1904
    Elected 1902; did not seek re-election 1904

John Christianson (R) (1862-1954) 1905-1906
    Elected 1904; did not seek re-election 1906
Christian S. Deisem (R) (1848-1919) 1905-1908
    Elected 1904, 1906; did not seek re-election 1908
Erick A. Stafne (R) (1848-1925) 1905-1908
    Elected 1904, 1906; defeated in June 1908 Republican primary
Simon Westby (R) (1876-1963) 1907-1908
    Elected 1906; defeated in June 1908 Republican primary
Olaf P. N. Anderson (R) (1872-1939) 1909-1916
    Elected 1908, 1910, 1912, 1914; defeated in June 1916 Republican primary
William H. Mann (R) (1857-1935) 1909-1916
    Elected 1908, 1910, 1912, 1914; defeated in June 1916 Republican primary
William H. Stutsman (R) (1866-1950) 1909-1916
    Elected 1908, 1910, 1912, 1914; defeated in June 1916 Republican primary
Sam J. Aandahl (R) (1869-1922) 1917-1920
    Elected 1916, 1918; did not seek re-election 1920
Charles W. Bleick (R) (1881-1964) 1917-1918
    Elected 1916; did not seek re-election 1918
Myron P. Johnson (R) (1873-1937) 1917-1918
    Elected 1916; defeated in June 1918 Republican primary
Charles F. Dupuis (R) (1865-1940) 1919-1920
    Elected 1918; defeated in June 1920 Republican primary
Frank Milhollan (R) (1885-1944) 1919-1926
    Elected 1918, 1920, 1922, 1924, 1926
William H. Stutsman (R) (1866-1950) 1921-1922
    Elected 1920; did not seek re-election 1922
Clark W. McDonnell (R) (1870-1952) 1921-1926
    Elected 1920, 1922, 1924
Fay A. Harding (R) (1875-1943) 1923-1926
    Elected 1922, 1924

By constitutional amendment, approved June 30, 1926, terms of Commissioners of Railroads were increased to six years. This took effect with the November 1926 general election. So that the terms might be staggered, the three commissioners elected that year were elected for terms of six, four, and two years (Article V, Section 12).

Frank Milhollan (R) (1885-1944) 1927-1928
    Elected 1926 for six-year term; resigned April 1, 1928
Clark W. McDonnell (R) (1870-1952) 1927-1936
    Elected 1926 for four-year term; elected 1930; defeated in June 1936 Republican primary
Fay A. Harding (R) (1875-1943) 1927-1934
    Elected 1926 for two-year term; elected 1928; defeated in June 1934 Republican primary

Ben C. Larkin (R) (1873-1949) 1928-1944
    Appointed April 1, 1928, to fill Frank Milhollan's term; elected 1932, 1938
Elmer W. Cart (R) (1891-1980) 1935-1940
    Elected 1934; defeated in June 1940 Republican primary
Simon S. McDonald (R) (1869-1956).. 1937-1942
    Elected 1936

A constitutional amendment, adopted June 25, 1940, created the Public Service Commission and transferred to it the powers and duties of the Board of Railroad Commissioners. It also provided that two commissioners would be elected at the 1940 general election, one for a six-year term and one for a four-year term.

Ben C. Larkin (R) (1873-1949) 1941-1949
    Elected 1940 for six-year term; elected 1946; died in office November 22, 1949
Clark W. McDonnell (R) (1870-1952) 1941-1950
    Elected 1940 for four-year term; elected 1944; won the June 1950 Republican primary but resigned his place on the ballot September 30, 1950
Simon S. McDonald (R) (1869-1956) 1943-1948
    Incumbent in 1940; elected 1942; defeated in June 1948 Republican primary
Elmer W. Cart (R) (1891-1980) 1949-1954
    Elected 1948; defeated in June 1954 Republican primary
Ernest D. Nelson (R) (1897-1961) 1949-1961
    Appointed December 3, 1949, to fill Ben C. Larkin's term; elected 1952, 1958; died in office September 10, 1961
Everett H. Brant (R) (1885-1954).. 1951-1954
    Elected 1950; died in office November 3, 1954
Martin Vaaler (R) (1927-2014) 1954-1962
    Appointed November 15, 1954, to fill Everett H. Brant's term; elected 1956; did not seek re-election 1962
Anson J. Anderson (R) (1905-1996) 1955-1960
    Elected 1954; did not seek re-election 1960
Richard J. Thompson (R) (1913-1973) 1961-1966
    Elected 1960; did not seek re-election 1966
E. Bruce Hagen (D) (1930-) 1961-2000
    Appointed September 19, 1961, to fill Ernest D. Nelson's term; elected 1964, 1970, 1976, 1982, 1988, 1994; did not seek re-election in 2000
Ben J. Wolf (R) (1907-1986)... 1963-1980
    Elected 1962, 1968, 1974; did not seek re-election 1980
Richard Elkin (R) (1932-) 1967-1983
    Elected 1966, 1972, 1978; resigned May 1, 1983
Leo M. Reinbold (R) (1933-2010)... 1981-2003
    Elected 1980, 1986, 1992, 1998; resigned July 31, 2003
Dale Sandstrom (R) (1950-) 1983-1992
    Appointed May 5, 1983, to complete Richard Elkin's term; elected 1984, 1990; resigned December 31, 1992

Susan Wefald (R) (1947-) 1993-2008
   Appointed effective January 1, 1993, to complete Sandstrom's term;
   elected 1996, 2002; did not seek re-election 2008
Tony Clark (R) (1971-) 2001-2012
   Elected 2000, 2006; resigned June 2012 to become Commissioner at
   Federal Energy Regulatory Commission
Bonny Fetch (I) (1943-) 2012
   Appointed July 1, 2012, to December 31, 2012, to complete Tony Clark's term;
   did not seek election in 2012
Kevin Cramer (R) (1961-) 2003-2012
   Appointed August 1, 2003, to complete Leo Reinbold's term; elected 2004,
   2010; resigned December 31, 2012
Brian Kalk (R) (1966-) 2009-2017
   Elected 2008, 2014, resigned 2017
Julie Fedorchak (R) (1968-) 2012-present
   Appointed December 2012 to complete Kevin Cramer's term; elected 2014 to
   complete term ending in 2016; elected 2016
Randy Christmann (R) (1960-) 2013-present
   Elected 2012, 2018
Brian Kroshus (R) (1963-) 2017-present
   Appointed March 2017 to fill Brian Kalk's term; elected 2018 to complete term
   ending in 2020

State Officials Appointed by the Governor to Head State Agencies

This segment of the *Blue Book* is based on the agencies that currently have gubernatorial appointed heads. (The Tourism Division of the North Dakota Department of Commerce is included because of the 2001 changes made as noted on that entry.)

Adjutants General
NDCC 37-03-01

Alan S. Dohrmann	Major General	December 13, 2015–present
David A. Sprynczynatyk	Major General	August 26, 2006–December 13, 2015
Michael J. Haugen	Major General	December 19, 2000–August 25, 2006
Keith D. Bjerke	Major General	1993–2000
Alexander P. Macdonald	Major General	1984–1993
C. Emerson Murry	Major General	1975–1984
LaClair A. Melhouse	Major General	1962–1975
Heber L. Edwards	Major General	1937–1962
Frayne Baker	Brigadier General	1935–1937
Earle R. Sarles	Brigadier General	1933–1935
G. A. Fraser	Brigadier General	1917–1933
Thomas Tharalson	Major General	1915–1917

Ira A. Berg	Major General	1913–1915
William C. Treumann	Major General	1911–1913
Amasa Peake	Major General	1909–1911
Thomas H. Poole	Major General	1907–1909
Heber M. Creel	Brigadier General	1905–1907
Eliot S. Miller	Brigadier General	1895–1905
W. H. Topping	Brigadier General	1893–1895
William A. Bentley	Brigadier General	1891–1893
William Devoy	Brigadier General	1890

Department of Corrections and Rehabilitation
NDCC 54-23.3-03

Leann K. Bertsch	Director	July 1, 2005–present
Elaine Little	Director	1989–July 1, 2005

The Department of Corrections and Rehabilitation was created in 1989 (1989 S.L., ch. 156). Prior to 1989, correctional institutions fell under the jurisdiction of the Director of Institutions. See entries for Director of Institutions for additional history.

Director of Institutions

See Department of Corrections and Rehabilitation, was NDCC 54-21-06 until repealed in 1991.

Director of Institutions

Richard L. Rayl	Director	1987–December 14, 1988
Clarence A. Bina	Director	November 25, 1985–May 31, 1986
Erwin Giegle	Acting Director	July 1, 1985–September 30, 1985
Alton L. Lick	Director	1979-1985
Edward J. Klecker	Director	July 16, 1973–1979
Isak Hystad	Acting Director	April 5, 1973–July 15, 1973
Walter R. Fiedler	Director	July 1, 1969–1973

Board of Administration

Isak Hystad	Chairman	December 1, 1964–June 30, 1969
Howard I. Henry	Chairman	October 3, 1963–September 30, 1964
H. H. Joos	Chairman	August 1, 1957–September 10, 1963
R. H. Sherman	Chairman	December 8, 1947–July 31, 1957
Mark I. Forkner	Chairman	June 15, 1939–December 1, 1947
J. D. Harris	Chairman	March 20, 1939–June 15, 1939
Jennie Ulsrud	Chairman	July 1, 1937–March 20, 1939
J. D. Harris	Chairman	August 1, 1935–June 30, 1937
Nelson Sauvain	Chairman	December 22, 1930–August 1, 1935
J. E. Davis	Chairman	July 9, 1929–December 28, 1930
R. B. Murphy	Chairman	December 1, 1922–July 9, 1929
Robert T. Muir	Chairman	May 1, 1922–November 30, 1922
George A. Totten	Chairman	July 7, 1919–April 30, 1922

Board of Control of State Institutions

James A. Brown	Chairman	December 1, 1917–June 30, 1919
R. S. Lewis	Chairman	March 1, 1913–December 1, 1917
John Carmody	Chairman	June 15, 1911–March 1, 1913

In 1991, the Legislative Assembly transferred the Director of Institutions responsibilities to other agencies, including the Department of Corrections and Rehabilitation (1991 S.L., ch. 592).

In 1969, the Legislative Assembly established a Director of Institutions and abolished the Board of Administration (1969 S.L., ch. 440).

In 1919, the Legislative Assembly combined the Board of Control, Board of Education, and Board of Regents into the Board of Administration (1919 S.L., ch. 71).

In 1911, the Legislative Assembly created the Board of Control of State Institutions (1911 S.L., ch. 62).

Department of Transportation
NDCC 24-02-01.3

Ron Henke	Interim Director	April 27, 2019–present
Thomas Sorel	Director	August 7, 2017–April 26, 2019
Grant Levi	Director	May 22, 2013–May 31, 2017
Francis Ziegler	Director	October 5, 2006–May 21, 2013
Grant Levi	Interim Director	August 28, 2006–October 4, 2006
David A. Sprynczynatyk	Director	January 1, 2001–August 25, 2006
Tom D. Freier	Director	March 2, 2000–December 31, 2000
Marshall W. Moore	Director	January 4, 1993–February 29, 2000
Richard J. Backes	Director	January 16, 1989–December 14, 1992

On January 1, 1990, the North Dakota Highway Department became the Department of Transportation – "Commissioner" became "Director" (1989 S.L., ch. 72).

Walter R. Hjelle	Commissioner	January 14, 1985–December 31, 1988
Duane R. Liffrig	Commissioner	January 1, 1982–January 7, 1985
Walter R. Hjelle	Commissioner	January 3, 1961–January 31, 1981

The North Dakota State Highway Department was created in 1953 (1953 S.L., ch. 177).

One-Man Highway Commission

A. W. Wentz	Commissioner	April 1, 1957–January 3, 1961
S. W. Thompson	Commissioner	May 1, 1951–April 1, 1957
M. P. Wynkoop	Commissioner	January 2, 1951–May 1, 1951

N. O. Jones	Commissioner	April 2, 1945–December 31, 1950
J. S. Lamb	Commissioner	January 18, 1939–April 2, 1945
P. H. McGurren	Commissioner	January 19, 1937–January 18, 1939
W. J. Flannigan	Commissioner	April 21, 1935–January 18, 1937
Ole H. Olsen	Commissioner	January 17, 1935–April 21, 1935
T. G. Plomasen	Commissioner	September 13, 1934–January 17, 1935
Bert M. Salisbury	Commissioner	July 21, 1934–September 13, 1934
F. A. Vogel	Commissioner	March 15, 1933–July 22, 1934

In 1933, the office of Highway Commissioner was established, abolishing the commission. The commissioner was appointed by the Governor (1933 S.L., ch. 125).

Chief Highway Commissioner and Two-Man Highway Commission Members

Chief Highway Commissioner
A. D. McKinnon
July 30, 1931– March 14, 1933

Members
C. D. King
February 1, 1933–March 14, 1933

J. A. Dinnie
July 30, 1931–January 30, 1933

H. R. Lapman
July 30, 1931–March 14, 1933

In 1931, the Legislative Assembly established the commission, three members appointed by the Governor, one of whom was appointed Chief Highway Commissioner (1931 S.L., ch. 153).

Three-Man Highway Commission With Executive Secretary

Governor	Executive Secretary	Two Appointed Members
George Schafer January 1, 1929– July 20, 1931	H. C. Frahm April 1, 1929– July 29, 1931	I. J. Moe March 15, 1927– July 29, 1931
	Joe J. Ermatinger March 15, 1927– April 1, 1929	J. A. Dinnie February 15, 1929– July 29, 1931
	Ray S. Ashley March 15, 1927 to February 14, 1929	
Walter Maddock August 30, 1928– December 31, 1928	Joe J. Ermatinger March 15, 1927– April 1, 1929	I. J. Moe March 15, 1927– July 29, 1931
	Ray S. Ashley March 15, 1927– February 14, 1929	

A. G. Sorlie March 15, 1927– August 29, 1928	Joe J. Ermatinger March 15, 1927– April 1, 1929	I. H. Moe March 15, 1927– July 29, 1931
		Ray S. Ashley March 15, 1927– February 14, 1929

In 1927, the membership of the Highway Commission changed to include the Governor and two members appointed by the Governor (1927 S.L., ch. 158).

In 1927, the Department of State Highways was created (1927 S.L., ch. 159).

Five-Man Highway Commission

Governor	State Engineer	Commissioner of Agriculture and Labor	Two Members Appointed by Governor
A. G. Sorlie January 9, 1925– March 14, 1927	H. C. Frahm September 14, 1925– March 14, 1927	Joseph H. Kitcher November 23, 1921– March 14, 1927	I. J. Moe April 15, 1925– March 14, 1927
	W. G. Black April 2, 1923– September 13, 1925		Herman Hardt April 15, 1925– March 14, 1927
			Ormanzo A. Brown April 15, 1923– April 14, 1925
			Joseph Poupore April 2, 1923– April 14, 1925
R. A. Nestos November 23, 1921– January 8, 1925	W. G. Black April 2, 1923– September 13, 1925	Joseph H. Kitcher November 23, 1921– April 15, 1923	Ormanzo A. Brown March 14, 1927– April 14, 1925
	W. H. Robinson October 26, 1918– April 1, 1923		Joseph Poupore April 2, 1923– April 14, 1925
			Herman Hardt May 13, 1921– April 14, 1923
			Benton Baker November 23, 1921– April 1, 1923

Lynn J. Frazier
April 20, 1917–
November 22, 1921

W. H. Robinson
October 26, 1918–
April 1, 1923

John N. Hagan
April 20, 1917–
November 22, 1921

Herman Hardt
May 13, 1921–
April 14, 1923

Jay W. Bliss
April 20, 1917–
October 25, 1918

J. J. Marquart
April 4, 1919–
May 12, 1921

Two Members Appointed by Governor

Frayne Baker
July 15, 1919–
November 22, 1921

Theodore Andrew
April 20, 1917–
April 3, 1919

Ed White
April 20, 1917–
November 18, 1918

In 1917, the membership of the commission was changed to include the Governor, State Engineer, Commissioner of Agriculture and Labor, and two members appointed by the Governor (1917 S.L., ch. 131).

Three-Man State Highway Commission
January 14, 1914

Governor	**State Engineer**	**One Member Appointed by Governor**
Louis B. Hanna	Jay W. Bliss	C. A. Grow

In 1913, the State Highway Commission was created to consist of the Governor, the State Engineer, and one other member appointed by the Governor (1913 S.L., ch. 179).

Game and Fish Department
NDCC 20.1-02-01

Terry Steinwand	Director	January 1, 2006–present
Dean Hildebrand	Director	1996–December 31, 2005
K. L. Cool	Director	1993–1996
Lloyd A. Jones	Director	1989–1993
Dale Henegar	Commissioner	1981–1989
Larry Kruckenberg	Commissioner	1979–1981
Russell Stuart	Commissioner	1961–1979
Dr. I. G. Bue	Commissioner	1957–1961

H. R. Morgan	Commissioner	1948–1957
Wm. J. Lowe	Commissioner	1938–1948
O. W. Hulterstrom	Commissioner	1936–1938
A. I. Swenson	Commissioner	1934–1936
Thoralf Swenson	Commissioner	1932–1934
Burnie Maurek	Commissioner	1930–1932

Commissioner changed to director. References removed to commissioner and made instead to Game and Fish Department and its director (1991 S.L., ch. 231).

Information Technology Department
NDCC 54-59-03

Shawn Riley	Chief Information Officer	April 17, 2017–present
Daniel Sipes	Interim Chief Information Officer	December 15, 2016–April 16, 2017
Mike Ressler	Chief Information Officer	October 10, 2013–December 31, 2016
Mike Ressler	Interim Chief Information Officer	May 20, 2013–October 9, 2013
Lisa Feldner	Chief Information Officer	May 8, 2006–May 19, 2013
Mike Ressler	Acting Chief Information Officer	January 1, 2006–May 7, 2006
Curtis L. Wolfe	Chief Information Officer	October, 1999–December 31, 2005

Job Service North Dakota
NDCC 52-02-01

Bryan Klipfel	Interim Executive Director	January 2019–present
Michelle Kommer	Executive Director	December 2017–December 2018
Michelle Kommer	Interim Executive Director	September 2017–December 2017
Cheri Giesen	Executive Director	July 2014–August 2017
Darren Brostrom	Interim Director	October 2013–June 2014
Maren Daley	Executive Director	2000–2013
Jennifer Gladden	Executive Director	1996–2000
Gerald Balzer	Executive Director	1993–1996
Michael Deisz	Executive Director	1985–1992
Shirley Peterson	Executive Director	1981–1984
Therman Kaldahl	Executive Director	1977–1981
Martin Gronvold	Executive Director	1965–1976

In 1979, Job Service North Dakota was created (1979 S.L., ch. 522). The Employment Security Bureau was created in 1965 (1965 S.L., ch. 333).

Department of Commerce
NDCC 54-60-03

Michelle Kommer	Commissioner	January 1, 2019–present
Shawn Kessel	Interim Commissioner	October 1, 2018–December 31, 2018
Jay Schuler	Commissioner	February 27, 2017–October 1, 2018
Al Anderson	Commissioner	May 2, 2011–December 31, 2016
Paul Govig	Acting Commissioner	January 1, 2011–May 2, 2011
Shane Goettle	Commissioner	December 1, 2005–December 31, 2010
Lee Peterson	Commissioner	July 1, 2001–November 30, 2005
Lee Peterson	Director	December 2000–June 30, 2001
Kevin Cramer	Director	June 1, 1997–December 2000

Ron Rauschenberger	Interim Director	May 22, 1997–May 30, 1997
Charles (Chuck) W. Stroup	Director	January 1, 1993–May 15, 1997
Mitchell Bohn	Director	January 6, 1992–January 1, 1993
Bill Davis	Director	September 1, 1991–January 5, 1992
Carol Jean Larsen	Acting Director	May 1, 1991–August 31, 1991
Joe Cascalenda*	Director	May 1, 1991–December 1991
Fred A. Haeffner	Director	August 1990–May 1, 1991
William S. Patrie	Director	September 1986–June 30, 1990
Robert Whitney	Director	May 1985–September 1986
Sylvan Melroe	Director	April 9, 1984–May 24, 1985
Edwin Becker	Director	November 1980–February 29, 1984
Bruce L. Bartch	Director	April 10, 1969–November 1980
Fred P. Brandt	Acting Director	March 1969
Robert H. Huey	Director	1961–February 1969
Lawrence A. Schneider	Director	1957–September 1961

In 2001, the North Dakota Department of Commerce was created, placing the agency under a commissioner of commerce (2001 S.L., ch. 488).

In 1991, Growing North Dakota legislation abolished the Economic Development Commission by establishing in its place the Department of Economic Development and Finance (1991 S.L., ch. 95). The Governor was given authority to appoint the department's director. The Governor appointed Fred Haeffner to the position.

In 1987, the Legislative Assembly moved the appointment of the agency director to the Economic Development Commission (1987 S.L., ch. 622).

In July 1987, the Economic Development Commission named William Patrie its director. Governor George Sinner had, prior to the 1987 change, appointed William Patrie as director of the Economic Development Commission.

In 1981, the name reverted to Economic Development Commission (1981 S.L., ch. 528).

In 1969, the Business and Industrial Development Department replaced the Economic Development Commission (1969 S.L., ch. 446).

In 1957, the Legislative Assembly created the Economic Development Commission (1957 S.L., ch. 343).

*Governor Sinner hired Joe Cascalenda, Minnesota consultant, to find Fred Haeffner's replacement, as well as to design the organizational structure for the newly created Department of Economic Development and Finance.

Department of Human Services
NDCC 50-06-01.3

Christopher D. Jones	Executive Director	February 27, 2017–present
Maggie Anderson	Interim Executive Director	December 1, 2016–February 26, 2017
Maggie Anderson	Executive Director	April 29, 2013–December 1, 2016
Carol K. Olson	Executive Director	July 1997–April 28, 2013
Henry C. "Bud" Wessman	Executive Director	February 1993–June 1997
John A. Graham	Executive Director	February 1984–December 1992
Dale E. Moug	Executive Director	January 1982–December 1983
Thorfin N. Tangedahl	Executive Director	December 1972–December 1981
Leslie O. Ovre	Executive Director	October 1962–June 1972
Carlyle D. Onsrud	Executive Director	July 1944–October 1962
E. A. Wilson	Executive Director	May 1935–June 1944

The North Dakota Department of Human Services was created in 1981 (1981 S.L., ch. 486).

In 1971, the Public Welfare Board became the Social Service Board of North Dakota (1971 S.L., ch. 465).

The State Board of Public Welfare was established in 1935 (1935 S.L., ch. 221).

Department of Labor and Human Rights
NDCC 34-05-01.2

Erica Thunder	Commissioner	June 3, 2019–present
Michelle Kommer	Interim Commissioner	January 1, 2019–June 2, 2019
Michelle Kommer	Commissioner	December 19, 2016–January 1, 2019
Troy T. Seibel	Commissioner	October 1, 2014–November 23, 2016
Bonnie Storbakken	Commissioner	May 16, 2013–September 30, 2014
Tony J. Weiler	Commissioner	September 7, 2010–May 15, 2013
Lisa K. Fair McEvers	Commissioner	July 25, 2005–August 31, 2010
Leann K. Bertsch	Commissioner	September 1, 2004–June 30, 2005
Mark Bachmeier	Commissioner	January 1, 2001–August 18, 2004
Tony Clark	Commissioner	September 16, 1999–December 14, 2000
Mark Bachmeier	Interim Commissioner	August 14, 1998–September 15, 1999

During the 2013 Legislative Session, the name of the Labor Department was changed to the Department of Labor and Human Rights (HB 1369).

In 1995, the Legislative Assembly made the position appointive by the Governor, beginning January 1, 1999 (1995 S.L., ch. 334). The last elected Commissioner of Labor, Craig Hagen, resigned the position effective August 13, 1998.

Indian Affairs Commission
NDCC 54-36-02

Scott J. Davis	Standing Rock Sioux Tribe	Executive Director	April 2009–present
Cheryl M. Kulas	Oglala Lakota Nation	Executive Director	April 2001–April 2009
Cynthia A. Mala	Spirit Lake Nation	Executive Director	January 1998–March 2001
Deborah A. Painte	Three Affiliated Tribes	Executive Director	January 1991–January 1998
Juanita Helphrey	Three Affiliated Tribes	Executive Director	March 1975–December 1990
Earl Azure	Turtle Mountain Band of Chippewa	Executive Director	August 1971–February 1975
Rev. Austin Engel		Executive Director	January 1965–August 1971
Hans Walker, Jr.	Three Affiliated Tribes	Executive Director	February 1962–January 1965
Edward A. Milligan		Executive Director	October 1960–January 1962
John B. Hart		Executive Director	August 1949–September 1960

Office of Administrative Hearings
NDCC 54-57-01

Timothy J. Dawson	Director	January 1, 2016–present
Wade C. Mann	Director	January 1, 2014–December 31, 2015
Allen C. Hoberg	Director	July 1, 1991–December 31, 2014

Office of Management and Budget
NDCC 54-44-03

Joe Morrissette	Director	March 2018–present
Pam Sharp	Director	June 2003–February 2018
Pam Sharp	Acting Director	January 2003–June 2003
Rod Backman	Director	December 15, 1992–January 2003
Charles Mertens	Director	January 3, 1992–December 15, 1992
Richard Rayl	Director	January 1, 1985–December 1992
Lee M. Stenehjem	Director	August 1, 1983–December 31, 1984
Robert B. Melland	Director	January 1, 1983–May 1983
Darrell R. Ohlhauser	Acting Director	January 1982–December 31, 1982
Dale Moug	Director	January 1, 1981–December 31, 1981
Dean L. Conrad	Director	December 1, 1976–December 31, 1980
Dale Moug	Acting Director	September 9, 1976–November 30, 1976
Lloyd Omdahl	Director	1975–1976
Ralph Dewing	Director	January 1961–1975

In 1981, the Office of Management and Budget was created (S.L. Chapter 534).
In 1959, the Department of Accounts and Purchases was created (S.L. Chapter 372).

Parks and Recreation Department
NDCC 55-08-01.2

Melissa Baker	Director	2017–present
Jesse Hanson	Interim Director	2016–2017
Mark Zimmerman	Director	2011–2016
Douglass A. Prchal	Director	1994–2010
Douglas K. Eiken	Director	1981–1994
Robert Horne	Director	1978–1981
Gary Leppart	Director	1975–1977
Einar Johnson	Director	1973–1975
David L. O'Brien	Director	1968–1972
James R. Kittle	Director	1964–1967

In 1993, the agency name reverted back to Parks and Recreation Department as tourism became its own department (1993 S.L., ch. 80).

In 1991, the Legislative Assembly created the Parks and Tourism Department with the director of the Parks and Outdoor Recreation Division and the director of the Tourism Division being appointed by the Governor (1991 S.L., ch. 640).

In 1977, the Parks and Recreation Department was created, combining the Park Service and State Outdoor Recreation Agency (1977 S.L., ch. 503).

In 1965, the North Dakota Park Service was created (1965 S.L., ch. 379).

State Department of Health
NDCC 23-01-05

Mylynn Tufte	State Health Officer	February 17, 2017–present
Avry Smith	Co-Acting State Health Officer	December 15, 2016– February 16, 2017
David Glatt	Co-Acting State Health Officer	December 15, 2016– February 16, 2017
Terry L. Dwelle, M.D.	State Health Officer	October 23, 2001– December 15, 2016
Robert A. Barnett	Interim State Health Officer*	December 15, 2000– October 23, 2001
Murray G. Sagsveen	State Health Officer	February 1, 1998– December 14, 2000
Robert A. Barnett	Interim State Health Officer*	September 8, 1997– January 31, 1998
Jon R. Rice, M.D.	State Health Officer	February 22, 1993– August 31, 1997
Robert A. Barnett	Interim Director*	December 15, 1992– February 21, 1993
Robert M. Wentz, M.D.	State Health Officer	January 11, 1985– December 14, 1992
Gene A. Christianson	Acting Administrator*	December 1, 1984– January 10, 1985

M. A. K. Lommen, M.D.	State Health Officer	January 1, 1982–November 30, 1984
Gene A. Christianson	Acting Administrator*	January 6, 1981–December 31, 1981
Joan G. Babbott, M.D.	State Health Officer	July 1, 1980–January 5, 1981
Gene A. Christianson	Acting Administrator*	October 4, 1979–July 1, 1980
Thomas Campbell	Executive Officer*	October 1, 1979–October 4, 1979
Jonathan B. Weisbuch, M.D.	State Health Officer	June 1, 1976–September 30, 1979
Willis Van Heuvelen	Executive Officer*	January 1, 1975–May 31, 1976
James R. Amos, M.D.	State Health Officer	September 1, 1961–December 31, 1974
Willis Van Heuvelen	Executive Officer*	June 1, 1957–August 31, 1961
Jerome H. Svore	Director of Public Health*	July 1, 1953–May 31, 1957
Russell O. Saxvik, M.D.	State Health Officer	July 1, 1947–June 30, 1953
William M. Smith, M.D.	Acting State Health Officer	1946–June 30, 1947
George F. Campana, M.D.	State Health Officer	1944–1946
Frank J. Hill, M.D.	Acting State Health Officer	1942–1944
Maysil M. Williams, M.D.	State Health Officer	1933–1942
Arthur A. Whittemore, M.D.	State Health Officer	1923–1933
Harley E. French, M.D.	Secretary–Superintendent of Health	1921–1923
Charles J. McGurren, M.D.	Secretary–Superintendent of Health	1913–1921
James Grassick, M.D.	Secretary–Superintendent of Health	1907–1913
Herbert H. Healy, M.D.	Secretary–Superintendent of Health	1901–1907
Amos Flaten, M.D.	Superintendent, State Board of Health	1897–1901
John Montgomery, M.D.	Superintendent, State Board of Health	1895–1997
Francis H. DeVaux, M.D.	Superintendent, State Board of Health	1893–1995
Harry D. Quarry, M.D.	Superintendent, State Board of Health	1891–1993
J. G. Millspaugh, M.D.	Superintendent, State Board of Health	1890–1991

*State Health Officer position vacant

In 1995, the name reverted back to the State Department of Health (1995 S.L., ch. 243).

The 1987 Legislative Assembly changed the agency's name to State Department of Health and Consolidated Laboratories (1987 S.L., ch. 263).

In 1923, the State Department of Health was created with a state health officer as its head (1923 S.L., ch. 227).

The State Board of Health was created in 1890.

Department of Environmental Quality
NDCC 23.1

L. Dave Glatt Director April 29, 2019-present

In 2017, the Legislative Assembly passed legislation splitting the Environmental Health Section from the Department of Health to create a new Department of Environmental Quality, which became an independent agency on April 29, 2019 (2017 S.L., ch. 199).

State Department of Financial Institutions
NDCC 6-01-08

Lisa Kruse	Commissioner	2017–present
Bob Entringer	Commissioner	2011–2017
Timothy J. Karsky	Commissioner	2001–2010
Gary D. Preszler	Commissioner	1986–2001
Jane M. Lundberg	Commissioner	1985–1986
Marilyn Foss	Commissioner	1983–1985
L. M. Stenehjem, Jr.	Commissioner	1981–1983
LeRoy Gilbertson	Commissioner	1977–1981
G. W. Ellwein	Commissioner	1969–1977
H. L. Thorndal	State Examiner	1966–1969
Eugene Rich	State Examiner	1961–1966
G. H. Russ, Jr.	State Examiner	1956–1961
John A. Graham	State Examiner	1939–1956
Adam A. Lefor	State Examiner	1933–1939
Gilbert Semingson	State Examiner	1921–1933
O. E. Loftus	State Examiner	1919–1921
J. R. Waters	State Examiner	1917–1919
G. J. Johnson	State Examiner	1915–1917
S. G. Severtson	State Examiner	1913–1915
Oliver Knudson	State Examiner	1907–1913
D. K. Brightbill	State Examiner	1905–1907
Evan S. Tyler	State Examiner	1903–1905
R. E. Wallace	State Examiner	1901–1903
H. A. Langlie	State Examiner	1895–1901
Kemper Peabody	State Examiner	1893–1895
R. E. Wallace	State Examiner	1891–1893
Wm. G. Hayden	Public Examiner	1889–1891

In 2001, the State Department of Financial Institutions was created (2001 S.L., ch. 88).

In 1969, the Legislative Assembly created the Department of Banking and Financial Institutions with the commissioner known as the State Examiner (1969 S.L., ch. 96).

The Department of Banking came into existence in 1911 (1911 S.L., ch. 55).

In 1905, the State Banking Board was created (1905 S.L., ch. 165).

In 1893, the position of State Examiner was created (1893 S.L., ch. 95). Prior to that time, the office of Public Examiner had been established in 1887 and given duties to audit/examine the county records in the new state of North Dakota in 1890 (1890 S.L., ch. 116).

State Highway Patrol
NDCC 39-03-02

Brandon Solberg	Superintendent	2018–present
Michael Gerhart	Superintendent	2014–2018
James Prochniak	Superintendent	2009–2014
Mark Nelson	Superintendent	2007–2009
Bryan R. Klipfel	Superintendent	2003–2007
James M. Hughes	Superintendent	1993–2003
Brian C. Berg	Superintendent	1985–1992
Norman D. Evans	Superintendent	1981–1985
James D. Martin	Superintendent	1978–1981
Ralph M. Wood	Superintendent	1961–1978
Clark J. Monroe	Superintendent	1953–1961
E. M. Klein	Superintendent	1943–1953
John Jeffery	Superintendent	1941–1943
Archie O'Connor	Superintendent	1939
Frank Putman	Superintendent	1939–1941
H. G. Lund	Superintendent	1937–1938
Frank Putman	Superintendent	1935–1937

In 1951, the Governor was granted authority to appoint the superintendent (1951 S.L., ch. 237). Prior to that time, the highway commissioner, with the Governor's consent, made the appointment (1935 S.L., ch. 148).

State Securities Department
NDCC 10-04-03

Karen Tyler	Commissioner	September 1, 2001–present
Syver Vinje	Commissioner	January 1, 1998–August 31, 2001
Harold P. Kocher	Acting Commissioner	November 17, 1997–December 31, 1997
Calvin Hoovestol	Commissioner	February 15, 1993–November 16, 1997
Harold P. Kocher	Acting Commissioner	January 1, 1993–February 14, 1993
Glenn A. Pomeroy	Commissioner	March 1, 1988–December 31, 1992
Harold P. Kocher	Acting Commissioner	December 29, 1987–February 28, 1988
Peter A. Quist	Commissioner	May 6, 1983–January 31, 1988
Dale Sandstrom	Commissioner	May 1, 1981–May 5, 1983
Arly Richau	Commissioner	May 7, 1977–April 30, 1981
Peter A. Quist	Acting Commissioner	December 27, 1976–May 6, 1977
Robert Holte	Commissioner	January 1, 1976–December 24, 1976
Donald R. Holloway	Commissioner	March 12, 1968–December 31, 1975
Wallace E. Warner	Commissioner	July 1, 1965–March 11, 1968
Charles L. Hughes	Commissioner	July 1, 1959–June 30, 1965

In 1961, the Legislative Assembly gave the Governor the authority to appoint the commissioner (1961 S.L., ch. 116).

In 1951, the Securities Commission was abolished and agency functions placed under the state examiner in the Department of Banking (1951 S.L., ch. 106).

The Securities Commission was created in 1923 (1923 S.L., ch. 182).

Division of Tourism
NDCC 54-60-02

Sara Otte Coleman	Director	2003–present
Allan Stenehjem	Director	2001–2002
Bob Martinson	Director	1997–2000
Kevin Cramer	Director	1993–1997
James Fuglie	Director	1985–1992
Michael Foster	Director	1981–1985
Wally Reber	Director	1977–1981
Joe Satrom	Director	1968–1977
James Hawley	Director	1962–1967

In 2001, the North Dakota Tourism Department again became a division, this time within the North Dakota Department of Commerce (2001 S.L., ch. 488). The statutory language provided that until August 1, 2005, the Governor appointed the director of the Tourism Division. After that date, the appointment was made by the commissioner of the North Dakota Department of Commerce.

In 1993, the Legislative Assembly created the North Dakota Tourism Department with its director appointed by the Governor (1993 S.L., ch. 80).

In 1991, Tourism was merged with Parks to become the Department of Parks and Tourism with the director of tourism portion of the agency being appointed by the Governor (1991 S.L., ch. 640).

In 1981, the Tourism Division was placed under the Economic Development Commission (1981 S.L., ch. 528).

The Travel Division was created as part of the North Dakota State Highway Department in 1953 but did not have its own budget/funding until 1961 (1953 S.L., ch. 177), (1961 S.L., ch. 205).

Executive Commissions and Boards

Emergency Commission
Phone: 701-328-2900 (Secretary of State)
[NDCC 54-16]

The 1915 Legislative Assembly established the Emergency Commission. From the beginning, its function has been to respond to natural disasters or unforeseen events and funding circumstances when the legislature is not in session and which were not contemplated during the legislative session. For example, it considers and approves requests from state agencies to transfer spending authority between appropriated line items; the accepting and authorization to disburse federal funds; the accepting and authorization to disburse funds received from other sources; approving expenditures from a contingency fund appropriated to the Commission; and granting borrowing authority from the Bank of North Dakota in response to a disaster declaration by the Governor.

The original members were the Governor, Secretary of State, and State Auditor. In 1919, the State Auditor was replaced by the Commissioner of Agriculture and Labor. The 1949 Legislature added the respective chairmen of the House and Senate Appropriations Committees if the amount being considered was more than $10,000.

In 1967, the title of the Commissioner of Agriculture and Labor was changed to the Commissioner of Agriculture. That position was removed in 1995 and replaced with the Chairman of the Legislative Council. During the same session, the respective chairman of the Appropriations Committees became full members of the Commission, regardless of the dollar amount of the request being considered. In 2005, the chairman of the Legislative Council was replaced by the respective majority leaders in the House and the Senate.

Currently, the Commission consists of the Governor, Secretary of State, and four members from the legislature. The Secretary of State also serves as the Commission's secretary.

Equalization, State Board of
Phone: 701-328-7088, option 6
[NDCC 57-13-01]

The State Board of Equalization consists of the Governor, State Treasurer, State Auditor, Agriculture Commissioner, and State Tax Commissioner. The Governor acts as chair and the Tax Commissioner as secretary.

The Board equalizes the valuation and assessment of property throughout the state and has the power to equalize assessments between assessment districts of the same county and between the different counties of the state.

Industrial Commission

600 East Boulevard Avenue
Bismarck, ND 58505-0840
Phone: 701-328-3722
Fax: 701-328-2820
Web: www.nd.gov/ndic
Email: ndicinfo@nd.gov
[NDCC 54-17]

The Industrial Commission consists of the Governor as chairman, the Attorney General, and the Agriculture Commissioner. In addition to an Executive Director and Secretary, the Commission employs other staff as the public interest dictates. As the management authority for all utilities, industries, enterprises, and business projects owned, administered, and operated by the state, the Commission has under its jurisdiction the Bank of North Dakota, North Dakota Mill and Elevator Association, North Dakota Housing Finance Agency, North Dakota Public Finance Authority, North Dakota Student Loan Trust, North Dakota Building Authority, North Dakota Transmission Authority, and North Dakota Pipeline Authority. In addition to the business entities, the Commission has regulatory responsibilities through the Department of Mineral Resources, which consists of the North Dakota Oil and Gas Division and North Dakota Geological Survey. The Commission also provides research grants through the Lignite Research, Development, and Marketing Program; Oil and Gas Research Program; and Renewable Energy Program. In 2013, the Industrial Commission was given oversight of the Outdoor Heritage Fund and the industrial water sales of the Western Area Water Supply Authority.

The Bank of North Dakota (BND) was established to promote agriculture, commerce, and industry in the state. It is the only legal depository for all state funds. As of December 31, 2018, the bank's assets were $7 billion, including loans of approximately $4.5 billion. The bank's tier 1 capital was $851 million. The bank's profits in 2018 exceeded $158 million; in 2017, the profits were $145 million. BND serves as a central clearinghouse for many North Dakota financial institutions and partners with financial institutions to provide loan programs for businesses, as well as agriculture and residential loans. BND also administers special loan programs established by the Legislature or the Industrial Commission. The Industrial Commission has directed the bank to serve as the Farm Finance Agency to facilitate first-time farmer loans. For more advanced agriculture producers, BND provides loans for financing real estate, equipment, and livestock. Businesses in North Dakota are supported through a variety of economic development programs, such as PACE (Partnership in Assisting Community Expansion), Flex PACE, Beginning Entrepreneur Programs, and Export Enhancement Programs. Through its mortgage programs, BND provides a secondary market for mortgage loans and assists rural financial institutions in originating loans if they do not have a mortgage department. Helping North Dakota residents meet their postsecondary education goals is a critical component of BND fulfilling its mission. BND takes a cradle-to-career approach by encouraging saving for college by offering two match programs through the state's 529 plan, College SAVE, which it administers. Online and face-to-face education to help students prepare for college is provided through the website, videos posted on social media, College Application Month, North Dakota Dollars for Scholars, financial literacy presentations, and Career Discovery ND. BND offers student loans with preferred rates and no fees while in college to fill the funding gaps and a refinancing option for North Dakota residents when their education is complete. BND's profits are used to support the state's economic development, community infrastructure, and disaster assistance programs. Since 2015, the Legislature has appropriated over $180 million of BND profits for these types of programs. In addition, BND administers more than $500 million of legislative-mandated programs, including the Infrastructure Revolving Loan Program, School Construction Assistance Revolving Loan Fund, and Medical Assistance Infrastructure Loan Fund. BND can also be called upon by the Legislature to provide General Fund appropriations. Since the Bank's inception, over $800 million has been appropriated to the General Fund. The Industrial Commission appoints the Bank President. Phone: 701-328-5600, 800-472-2166; Fax: 701-328-5632; TYY: 800-366-6888; Web: www.bnd.nd.gov; Mailing Address: PO Box 5509, Bismarck, ND 58506-5509; Street Address: 1200 Memorial Highway, Bismarck.

The Mill and Elevator Association is located in Grand Forks. The Mill and Elevator Association was established for the purpose of encouraging and promoting agriculture, commerce, and industry by engaging in the business of manufacturing and marketing farm products. The North Dakota Mill is the largest single site wheat flour mill in the United States and the seventh largest wheat-durum-rye milling company in the United States, with sales of more than $338 million in FY2018. The Mill is primarily a spring-wheat mill, shipping 93 percent spring wheat products and 7 percent durum products. The Mill and Elevator Association currently has the capacity to produce 4.95 million pounds of finished product per day and a terminal elevator with total available storage of more than 5 million bushels of grain. The Mill and Elevator Association processes up to 100,000 bushels of top quality North Dakota spring and durum wheat per day, adding value to more than 33 million bushels per year. Eighty percent of all products are shipped in bulk trucks or railcars, with 20 percent shipped in bags or totes. A portion of the Mill's profits are appropriated each biennium to the state's General Fund. The Industrial Commission appoints a President and CEO to oversee operations. Phone: 701-795-7000; Web: www.ndmill.com; Mailing Address: PO Box 13078, Grand Forks, ND 58208-3078.

The Commission, acting as the North Dakota Student Loan Trust, acquires and holds in trust U.S. government or North Dakota guaranteed student loans. The creation of the North Dakota Student Loan Trust enabled the state of North Dakota to obtain low cost funds (through the sale of tax-exempt and taxable bonds) and use those funds for purchasing student loans from the Bank of North Dakota. In the past, the Trust provided funding for the North Dakota Guarantee Agency, and the Legislature has appropriated funds from the Trust for certain North Dakota University System programs and other education-related programs. The Commission's Executive Director/Secretary serves as the authorized officer for the trust. Financial audits of the Trust are available on the Industrial Commission website at www.nd.gov/ndic/ic-public.htm. Phone: 701-328-3722.

The North Dakota Housing Finance Agency (NDHFA) is a self-supporting and mission-driven agency dedicated to creating and sustaining decent, safe, and affordable housing for all North Dakotans. NDHFA offers affordable home financing and down payment assistance for low- to moderate-income families by issuing bonds and generating funds to purchase mortgage loans originated by local lenders. Since 1982, NDHFA has purchased more than 45,000 loans valued at more than $3.8 billion. NDHFA administers the Housing Incentive Fund and federal financing programs to construct or rehabilitate rental housing unique to each community, ensuring the continued availability of more than 18,000 units statewide for households of modest means. The agency also administers rental subsidies and provides regulatory oversight for privately-owned rental units for low-income households. Responding to household and community needs, the agency funds competitive grant and loan programs fostering new development and enabling seniors and persons with disabilities to remain in their home. The Commission appoints the Executive Director. Phone: 701-328-8080, 800-292-8621; Fax: 701-328-8090; TTY: 800-366-6888; Web: www.ndhfa.org; Mailing Address: PO Box 1535, Bismarck, ND 58502.

The North Dakota Public Finance Authority (NDPFA), formerly the Municipal Bond Bank, was established to make loans to political subdivisions by issuing bonds and using the proceeds to purchase municipal securities issued by the borrowing political subdivisions. In addition to its general financing programs for political subdivisions, the NDPFA issues industrial revenue bonds for projects that qualify under the IRS definition of small issue manufacturing. The NDPFA also acts as the financial administrator of the state's Revolving Loan Fund established by the state in conformity with the federal Clean Water and Safe Drinking Water Acts. The NDPFA operates and is managed under the control of the Commission. The Executive Director is appointed by the Commission. Phone: 701-328-7100, 800-526-3509; Fax: 701-328-7130; Web: www.nd.gov/pfa; Mailing Address: PO Box 5509, Bismarck, ND 58506; Street Address: 1200 Memorial Highway, Bismarck.

In its role as the North Dakota Building Authority, the Commission, as authorized under North Dakota Century Code Chapter 54-17.2, provides financing through the issuance of bonds for acquiring, constructing, altering, repairing, and maintaining certain projects as directed by the Legislative Assembly. The Authority has been directed to finance $130 million of North Dakota University System projects during the 2019-2021 biennium. The Commission has appointed three authorized officers to administer this program – the Commission's Executive Director/Secretary, Public Finance Authority Executive Director, and Office of Management and Budget Director. Phone: 701-328-3722; Fax: 701-328-2820; Web: www.nd.gov/ndic/ba-info.htm; Mailing Address: See Industrial Commission office address.

The Commission administers the Lignite Research, Development, and Marketing Program established in 1987 as a partnership between the private and public sectors. By executive order, a Lignite Research Council, consisting of 30 members, advises the Commission on the administration of this program. The Commission approves or disapproves research, development, and marketing projects and activities; accepts and distributes funds; and enters into contracts for the various projects. Phone: 701-328-3722; Web: www.nd.gov/ndic/lrc-infopage.htm; Mailing Address: See Industrial Commission office address.

The Industrial Commission has jurisdiction over the investigation and publication of geological information and the regulation of coal exploration, geophysical exploration, geothermal energy, paleontology resources, subsurface minerals, and the production of oil and gas in North Dakota through the Department of Mineral Resources Geological Survey and Oil and Gas Division. The Industrial Commission appoints the Director of the Department of Mineral Resources, who serves as Director of the Oil and Gas Division and appoints the State Geologist and Assistant Director of the Oil and Gas Division.

The Geological Survey of North Dakota serves as the primary source of geological information in the state, conducts research relative to the state's mineral resources, and conducts programs to promote better public understanding of the state's natural resources, along with a variety of regulatory duties. The Geological Survey was originally established under the trustees of the University of North Dakota by the Legislative Assembly in 1895 with the "professor of geology" at the university as ex-officio State Geologist. Early work of the Survey included studies of water supplies and lignite resources. In 1953, the Industrial Commission was given jurisdiction and authority over Survey enforcement of North Dakota oil and gas conservation laws. The relationship of the State Geologist and the Industrial Commission was tied closer by a series of legislative acts until 1989, when the Legislative Assembly placed the Geological Survey under the North Dakota Industrial Commission and the Survey offices were moved from the University of North Dakota in Grand Forks to Bismarck. The Survey is headed by the State Geologist, who is appointed by the Director of the Department of Mineral Resources. Phone: 701-328-8000; TTY 800-366-6888; Fax: 701-328-8010; Web: www.dmr.nd.gov/ndgs/; Mailing Address: 600 East Boulevard Avenue, Bismarck, ND 58505; Physical Address: 1016 East Calgary, Bismarck.

The Oil and Gas Division, headed by the Director, was formed in 1981 to provide field supervision, engineering, geological, and legal analysis necessary for the Industrial Commission to effectively and efficiently enforce the Commission's statutory responsibilities and jurisdiction over rules, regulations, and orders pertaining to production and drilling of oil and gas, geophysical exploration, geologic storage of carbon dioxide, development, reclamation of lands disturbed by oil and gas development, and proper disposal of oil field brine and other oil field wastes in North Dakota. The Division facilitates electronic storage of and provides access to oil and gas production, carbon dioxide storage, reservoir, well, and geophysical exploration data for use by industry, royalty owners, other governmental agencies, and citizens. In 2013, regulation of underground gathering pipeline infrastructure was added to the Oil and Gas Division's responsibilities. In 2015, this authority was broadened to include bonding requirements on underground gathering pipelines. The Oil and Gas Division currently has primary regulatory authority (primacy) over both Class II and Class IV underground injection wells. Phone: 701-328-8020; Fax: 701-328-8022; Web: www.dmr.nd.gov/oilgas; Mailing Address: State Capitol, 600 East Boulevard Avenue, Bismarck, ND 58505; Physical Address: 1016 East Calgary, Bismarck.

In 2003, the Legislature established the Oil and Gas Research Fund to promote the growth of the oil and gas industry through research and education. The Industrial Commission is assisted in the administration of the Oil and Gas Research Program by a nine-member Oil and Gas Research Council. The Commission approves or disapproves research and education projects and enters into contracts for the various projects that promote the program's mission. The Director of the Oil and Gas Research Program is appointed by the Industrial Commission. Phone: 701-425-1237; Web: www.nd.gov/ndic/ogrp-infopage.htm; Mailing Address: See Industrial Commission office address.

The Outdoor Heritage Fund was established in 2013 to provide access to private and public lands for sportsmen, including projects that create fish and wildlife habitat; improve, maintain, and restore water quality, soil conditions, plant diversity, animal systems, and other practices of stewardship to enhance farming and ranching; develop, enhance, conserve, and restore wildlife and fish habitat on private and public lands; and conserve natural areas for recreation through the establishment and development of parks and other recreation areas. The Industrial Commission is assisted by a 16-member Advisory Board (12 voting members). After receiving recommendations from the Advisory Board, the Commission acts on their recommendations and, if funding is awarded, contracts are entered into with the applicant. Web: www.nd.gov/ndic/outdoor-infopage.htm; Phone: 701-328-3722; Fax: 701-328-2820; Mailing Address: See Industrial Commission office address.

The North Dakota Transmission Authority was established on August 1, 2005, to serve as a catalyst for developing transmission infrastructure in North Dakota, offer an alternative source of financing, partner with investors and transmission providers, foster the development of transmission corridors, and serve as a transmission developer as a builder of last resort. The Director of the Transmission Authority is appointed by the Industrial Commission. The annual reports of the Transmission Authority are available on the Industrial Commission website at www.nd.gov/ndic/ic-public.htm Phone: 701-328-3722; Fax: 701-328-2820; Address: See Industrial Commission office address.

The North Dakota Pipeline Authority was established on April 10, 2007, to diversify and expand the North Dakota economy by facilitating development of pipeline facilities to support the production, transportation, and utilization of North Dakota energy-related commodities. Similar to the Transmission Authority, the

Pipeline Authority may offer an alternative source of financing, partner with investors and pipeline providers, and serve as a pipeline developer as a builder of last resort. The Director of the Pipeline Authority is appointed by the Industrial Commission. Web: www.dmr.nd.gov/pipeline/; Phone: 701-328-3722; Fax: 701-328-2820; Mailing Address: See Industrial Commission office address.

In 2007, the Legislature established the Renewable Energy Development Fund and the Renewable Energy Program to promote the growth of renewable energy industries through research, development, marketing, and education. The Industrial Commission is assisted in the administration of the Renewable Energy Program by a seven-member Renewable Energy Council and staff from the Department of Commerce. The Commission approves or disapproves projects and enters into contracts for the various projects that promote the program's mission. Phone: 701-328-3722; Web: www.nd.gov/ndic/renew-infopage.htm; Mailing Address: See Industrial Commission office address.

In 2013, the Legislature directed that the Industrial Commission receive monthly reports on revenues and expenditures and establish rates for industrial water sales made by the Western Area Water Supply Authority (Authority). The Authority's Board of Directors oversees the operations of the Authority for their domestic and industrial water sales, but additional reporting on industrial water sales must be provided to the Industrial Commission. The Commission's Executive Director/Secretary works with the Authority's Executive Director in preparing the information for the Commission's review. Phone: 701-774-6605; Web: http://wawsp.com/; Mailing Address: PO Box 2343, Williston ND 58802; Street Address: 1117 E Broadway, Williston.

Department of Trust Lands
(University and School Lands, Board of)
Phone: 701-328-2800
Fax: 701-328-3650
Web: https://land.nd.gov
Email: dtlrequest@nd.gov
[Constitution, Article IX, and Section 21 of Article X; NDCC 15-01 through 15-08.1, 15-68, 15.1-36, 47-30.1, 57-62, 57-51.1-07.5, and 61-33-07]

The Governor, Secretary of State, State Treasurer, Attorney General, and Superintendent of Public Instruction make up the Board of University and School Lands. The Governor serves as chair and the Secretary of State as vice chair. The Commissioner, who is appointed by the Board, serves as the Department Director and as the Board's Secretary.

The primary responsibility of the Department of Trust Lands is to manage the permanent educational trust funds and assets under the control of the Board of University and School Lands in a manner that preserves the purchasing power of the funds and provides stable distributions to fund beneficiaries. Revenues are generated through prudent management of trust assets, consisting of more than 706,000 surface acres, 2.6 million mineral acres, and $5.1 billion in permanent trust financial assets. The surface acres are leased to ranchers and farmers across the state. The mineral acres are offered for oil, gas, coal, gravel, and scoria leasing. Trust Fund revenues are invested in a diversified portfolio that includes farm loans, U.S. Treasury notes and bonds, real estate, corporate stocks and bonds, and other financial assets. According to Article IX of the Constitution, biennial distributions from the permanent trust funds must be 10 percent of the five-year average value of the trust financial assets. Distributions are made to schools (public grades K-12), higher education institutions, and other public institutions at specific intervals throughout the biennium.

Besides management of the permanent trust assets, the Department has three additional major functions that include:

1. Operation of the State Unclaimed Property Division, which serves as the repository for financial accounts, cash assets, and securities that have been not claimed by the rightful owners or their heirs and successors. Acting as a custodian, the Department manages financial assets (no real estate) received from businesses referred to as "holders" and works to reunite owners with those assets. Assets that go unclaimed are invested and support the Common Schools Trust Fund.

2. Management of the Energy Infrastructure and Impact Office, which is a statutory division within the Department, is responsible for administering the coal impact loan fund and the oil and gas impact grant fund. The Office provides financial assistance through the oil and gas impact grant fund to local units of government that are impacted by oil and gas activity. The Office works with an Advisory Committee, whose members have been appointed by the Land Board, to make recommendations to the Land Board. The Land Board reviews the recommendation from the Advisory Committee and makes the final determination on the grants. Recent biennial grant authority follows:

   - $6 million – 2007-2009 Biennium
   - $8 million – 2009-2011 Biennium
   - $135 million – 2011-2013 Biennium
   - $240 million – 2013-2015 Biennium
   - $140 million – 2015-2017 Biennium
   - $40 million – 2017-2019 Biennium
   - $2 million – 2019-2021 Biennium

3. Oversight and management of four important state trust funds:

   a) The Strategic Investment and Improvements Fund (SIIF) holds the assets and revenues earned from 800,000 sovereign mineral acres, including those formerly owned by the Bank of North Dakota and State Treasurer and minerals located under navigable rivers and lakes. The SIIF also receives

a portion of the oil and gas production and extraction taxes collected by the state. This fund may be expended by the Legislature for one-time expenditures relating to improving state infrastructure or for initiatives to improve the efficiency and effectiveness of state government.
b) The Coal Development Trust Fund is a permanent fund administered by the Board to provide loans to coal-impacted counties, cities, and school districts as provided in section 57-62-03 and for loans to school districts pursuant to chapter 15.1-36.
c) The Capitol Building Fund was created under Article IX of the North Dakota Constitution for the construction and maintenance of public buildings at the capitol. This fund is not permanent; the balance of the fund is subject to legislative appropriation each biennium.
d) The Indian Cultural Education Trust was created in 2003 for the purpose of generating income to benefit the Mandan, Hidatsa & Arikara Nation Cultural Education Foundation.

Agencies Headed by Gubernatorial Appointees

Consolidation of governmental responsibilities in a number of areas has increased the scope of activity under agencies headed by direct gubernatorial appointees. Since at least 1942, there have been calls for a greater consolidation of state government, with fewer agencies and more direct control by the Governor. While general efforts to consolidate all of state government have failed, individual efforts to establish multi-functional departments have been more successful.

Administrative Hearings, Office of
2911 North 14th Street – Suite 303
Bismarck, ND 58503
Phone: 701-328-3200
Fax: 701-328-3254
Email: oah@nd.gov
Web: https://www.nd.gov/oah/
[NDCC 54-57-01]

Established in 1991, the office is administered by a director who is appointed by the Governor for a term of six years and whose appointment is confirmed by the Senate. The director must be a licensed attorney in good standing.

The director or appointed administrative law judges preside at administrative hearings as requested by agencies. With specified exceptions, all administrative hearings must be conducted by this office. The office is to assure all proceedings are conducted in a fair and impartial manner.

There is a State Advisory Council for Administrative Hearings, which is a committee of the State Bar Association appointed by its president. The committee is to meet with the director at least semi-annually and advise on rules and policy matters.

Adjutant General and North Dakota National Guard

Fraine Barracks
P.O. Box 5511
Bismarck, ND 58506-5511
Phone: 701-333-2000
Fax: 701-333-2017
Website: www.ndguard.com
[NDCC 37-03-01]

Appointed by the Governor, the Adjutant General must have been a federally recognized commissioned officer of the National Guard for a period of at least three years immediately preceding the appointment, be in the rank of lieutenant colonel or higher, and must have completed the educational requirements for appointment as a federally recognized general officer. The Adjutant General serves as Commander of the State Army and Air National Guard. The Governor is Commander-in-Chief of this military establishment, except portions called to service in a Title 10 Federal Status in support of the United States.

The North Dakota National Guard is organized into three major commands: the Joint Force Headquarters, Army Command, and Air Command. Located in Bismarck at Fraine Barracks, the North Dakota National Guard's Joint Force Headquarters is comprised of the Adjutant General's Office; the Deputy Adjutant General's Office, which includes the Director of Intelligence (J-2), Director of Training and Military Operations (J-3/7), Director of Strategic Plans and Outreach (J-5/9), and Chief Information Office (J-6); and United States Property and Fiscal Office. The Adjutant General's Office also includes the special staff offices of the Chaplain, State Surgeon, Staff Judge Advocate, Public Affairs Office, Environmental Services, and Facilities Engineering. The Adjutant General's Personal Staff includes the Inspector General, Government Affairs Officer, and Senior Enlisted Leader. The Joint Headquarters provides command, control, and supervision of the two military service components. It receives, manages, and provides support to civil authorities by activating units and providing resources during domestic operations and state emergencies as directed by the Governor.

The North Dakota Army National Guard provides personnel (soldiers) to the Army Command, which provides a full range of military support to fulfill federal, state, and community missions. The Army Command is headquartered at the Raymond J. Bohn Armory in Bismarck and consists of five major subordinate commands: the 141st Maneuver Enhancement Brigade (Fargo); the 68th Troop Command (Bismarck); the Recruiting & Retention Command (Bismarck); and the 164th Regiment (Regional Training Institute) and Camp Grafton Training Center, both located at Devils Lake.

The North Dakota Air National Guard provides personnel (airmen) to the Air Command and the 119th Wing, nicknamed "The Happy Hooligans." The 119th Wing, headquartered at Hector Field in Fargo, provides personnel and military assets in support of federal, state, and community missions and is divided into four groups: Operations Group; Mission Support Group; Medical Group; and the Intelligence, Surveillance, and Reconnaissance Group. Primary missions include gathering and utilizing intelligence to perform target system analysis and target development, missile field security at Minot Air Force Base, medical, logistics, security forces, engineering, communications, personnel, and services support.

In addition to commanding the North Dakota National Guard, the Adjutant General serves as the Director of the North Dakota Department of Emergency Services (NDDES) and is the Chairman of the Department of Emergency Services Advisory Committee. NDDES provides 24/7 emergency communications through the Divisions of State Radio and Homeland Security in collaboration with more than 50 lead and support agencies, private enterprise, and voluntary organizations to assist local jurisdictions in disaster and emergency response and planning activities. NDDES supports response and recovery coordination with emergency managers in each county and tribal nation within the state of North Dakota, as well as the cities of Bismarck and Fargo. The department administers several federal disaster recovery programs and the Homeland Security Grant Programs.

Additionally, NDDES administers the Hazardous Chemicals Preparedness and Response Program and works in collaboration with the North Dakota State and Local Intelligence Center (NDSLIC) to manage homeland security information, such as threats to critical infrastructure, so appropriate actions can be implemented to protect citizens. NDDES also manages the Emergency Management Assistance Compact (EMAC) that serves as a national clearinghouse through which member states may request and provide mutual aid assistance.

Commerce Department
1600 E. Century Ave., Suite 2
Bismarck, ND 58503
Phone: 701-328-5300
Fax: 701-328-5320
Web: www.nd.gov
Email: commerce@nd.gov

Division of Community Services
Phone: 701-328-5300
Fax: 701-328-2308

Division of Economic Development and Finance
Phone: 701-328-5300
Fax: 701-328-5320

Division of Workforce Development
Phone: 701-328-5345
Fax: 701-328-5320

Division of Tourism
Phone: 701-328-2525
Toll Free: 800-HELLO-ND
Fax: 701-328-4878
Web: www.NDtourism.com
Email: tourism@nd.gov

The North Dakota Department of Commerce is the lead agency charged by the Governor and Legislature to attract, retain, and expand wealth in North Dakota. The Department of Commerce serves businesses and communities statewide through four divisions: Community Services, Economic Development and Finance, Tourism, and Workforce Development. The agency has hundreds of partners – local, state, federal, public, tribal, private, and nonprofit – and is the primary facilitator for all entities involved in the economic and community development process.

The North Dakota Department of Commerce was created in 2001, absorbing four previous state entities. The Department is headed by a Commissioner, appointed by the Governor with the advice and counsel of the North Dakota Economic Development Foundation. The Department of Commerce must consist of a Division of Community Services; a Division of Economic Development and Finance; a Division of Tourism; a Division of Workforce Development; and any other divisions the Commissioner determines necessary. It must also encompass the Office of Renewable Energy and Energy Efficiency, Office of International Business and Trade, North Dakota Women's Business Development Office, and Rural Development Office. The Commissioner appoints the directors of the divisions.

The North Dakota Economic Development Foundation, also created in 2001, is composed of a minimum of 15 and a maximum of 30 members appointed by the Governor for two-year terms. Appointment of the foundation members must ensure a cross section of business, tourism, and economic development representation and must ensure that at least one member represents rural concerns. The foundation members elect an executive committee with a minimum of five and a maximum of seven foundation members. The executive committee members elect a chairman, vice chairman, and secretary. The foundation is to seek funding for administrative expenses from private sector sources and seek and distribute private sector funds for use in commerce-related activities. The purpose of the foundation is to provide the Governor advice and counsel in selecting the Commissioner; serve in an advisory role to the Commissioner; administer a strategic plan for economic development in the state and set accountability standards, measurements, and benchmarks to evaluate the effectiveness of the Department in implementing the strategic plan; and monitor economic development activities and initiatives of the Department.

The Department of Commerce manages programs that lead to growth and innovation within the state's economy. These include the Main Street Initiative, Research North Dakota, and Innovate North Dakota programs. The Research North Dakota program was established in 2013 to build upon earlier efforts in the Centers of Excellence and Centers of Research Excellence programs and is governed by the Centers of Excellence Commission with staff services provided by the Department. The program supports research, development, and commercialization of North Dakota projects and ideas by partnering private sector businesses with North Dakota's research universities.

The Main Street Initiative gives community leaders a direct access point to a variety of resources, helping capitalize on strengths and make sound planning decisions. These efforts will help create vibrant communities poised to attract and retain a 21st century workforce, helping North Dakota compete and succeed in a global economy.

The Innovate North Dakota program is a statewide economic development initiative designed to help entrepreneurs turn business ideas into viable new business ventures. It is coordinated by the Department of Commerce in partnership with the University of North Dakota Center for Innovation, North Dakota State University Research and Technology Park, IDEA Center in Bismarck, and Severson Entrepreneurship Academy at Minot State University. Through expert guidance from business coaches and extensive leadership courses, Innovate ND provides the entrepreneurial community of North Dakota the resources needed to help turn an innovative idea into a profitable business.

The Division of Economic Development and Finance [NDCC 54-34.3] assumes the functions of the Department of the same name, which was created in 1991 to assume the functions, powers, and duties of the Economic Development Commission. The Economic Development Commission was created in 1957 and consisted of the Governor as chair and nine members, one from each of the eight planning districts and one at-large member representing minorities. A predecessor agency, the North Dakota Research Foundation, existed from 1943 to 1957.

The mission of the division includes attracting and creating new wealth-generating enterprises in the state; promoting economic diversification and innovation within targeted industries and economic sectors; promoting increased productivity and value-added products and processes; maintaining and revitalizing economically depressed rural areas; supporting partnerships with sources of financial and intellectual capital; and identifying state statutes, rules, and policies which impede economic development. The Division of Economic Development and Finance works closely with the Bank of North Dakota and is broken down into three major areas: Business Development, Research, and Finance, which includes the North Dakota Development Fund (NDDF).

The North Dakota Development Fund, Inc., [NDCC 10-30.5] is a statewide nonprofit development corporation that has authority to take equity positions in, provide loans to, or use other innovative financing mechanisms to provide capital for new and expanding businesses in North Dakota or for relocating businesses in North Dakota. The Governor appoints the eight members who comprise the Board of Directors to serve three-year terms. The Board must include at least one member enrolled in a North Dakota tribe and one member from a rural area.

The Division of Workforce Development [NDCC 54-60-09] was established in the 2001 legislation that created the Department. The division is responsible for monitoring local, regional, and national workforce initiatives and leading the development and implementation of the state's talent and workforce intelligence coordination strategies. Its goals are to ensure North Dakota employers have access to a skilled talent pool to meet their workforce needs, encourage young people to remain in state for career opportunity, and support volunteerism in the state.

Programs administered by the division include the AmeriCorps state formula program, Operation Intern, Relocation Program, Youth Office, Area Health Education Center Grant, and Tribal College Grants. The division administers the Early Childhood Education Grant Program in cooperation with the Department of Public Instruction. The division also provides administrative support to the North Dakota State Commission on National and Community Service.

The Division of Tourism [NDCC 54-34.4] began as the Tourist Promotion Bureau in the State Highway Department in 1965. The bureau was transferred to the Economic Development Commission in 1981, merged with the Department of Parks and Recreation in 1991, and established as a separate agency in 1993. The Tourism Division became part of the North Dakota Department of Commerce in 2001.

The division fosters and promotes tourism to, and within, the state; promotes the full development of the state's tourism resources; and serves as a planning and coordinating agency for tourism-related programs of the state and the state's political subdivisions. The Legislative Assembly established a state tourism policy in 1993, which was updated during the 2011 Legislative Session.

The mission of the Tourism Division is to bring new wealth to North Dakotans by increasing the number of out-of-state visitors who choose the state as a travel destination and to enhance North Dakota's image.

Program areas within the Tourism Division include: General Leisure Tourism Marketing, Group Travel Marketing, Outdoor Promotion, International Marketing, Public and Media Relations, and Tourism Development.

The division continues to strengthen its partnerships with the hospitality industry and local tourism organizations, as well as numerous state and federal agencies in the following areas:

- Cooperative marketing programs
- Brochure distribution programs
- Trade show and sales mission participation
- Familiarization tour opportunities
- Access to the division's comprehensive photo library and research
- Hospitality training
- Merchandise sales
- Marketing and infrastructure grants
- Packages and education vacation marketing
- Complimentary website and publication listings

The division has also used research to create compelling advertising to attract regional visitors and adventure tourists from across the United States interested in activities like mountain biking, golfing, fishing, and birding. The research drives the creative strategy and the types of media purchased. In addition, it measures the return on investment the state receives for all advertising investment. The $3.17 million 2016 advertising campaign generated 354,000 new trips to North Dakota and $328.3 million in visitor spending. That means for every $1 invested, North Dakota businesses and government entities received $104 back. Additional research showed, in 2015, North Dakota hosted 22 million visitors, and they spent $3.1 billion.

Tourism is the third-largest economic driver and impacts all 53 counties. Tax revenue of $323 million was generated through visitor activity.

The Division of Community Services [NDCC 54-44.5] provides technical assistance to local governments, state agencies, and the executive branch in the areas of community and rural planning and development, policy research and development, and grant program implementation.

The division provides the people of North Dakota with effective, efficient, and customer-oriented administration of federal and state programs for Community Development, Energy Efficiency and Renewable Energy, Housing, and Low Income Programs. These programs help create a quality of life that makes North Dakota a good place in which to live, work, and do business. The Division of Community Services consists of four different program areas: Community Development, Office of Renewable Energy and Energy Efficiency, Low Income Programs, and Technical Assistance.

The Division of Community Services' primary partners for administering grant programs are the Community Action Agencies and the Regional Planning Councils. They are directly involved in the implementation of the Community Services Block Grant, Community Development Block Grant, Emergency Solutions Grants, HOME program, Neighborhood Stabilization Program, North Dakota Homeless Grant, weatherization programs, and Renaissance Zone Program. Other partners assisting in implementing programs include such entities as the North Dakota Building Officials Association, Interstate Compact on Industrialized Buildings, North Dakota Manufactured Housing Association, North Dakota Association of Builders, Institute for Building Technology and Safety, and each city with a Renaissance Zone.

The Department of Commerce also works with other strategic partners, such as the North Dakota Trade Office, Impact Dakota, Center for Technology and Business, Small Business Development Center (SBDC), and North Dakota Rural Development Council.

The purpose of the North Dakota Trade Office is to increase exports of North Dakota products to international markets. The office's goal of increasing exporting strengthens and diversifies the economy with new money; creates new, interesting career opportunities; and prepares businesses to become more globally competitive with higher growth.

The office assists North Dakota businesses in expanding exports to international markets by:

- Advocating for exporters;
- Offering export educational opportunities to North Dakota businesses;
- Researching and raising awareness of export opportunities, issues, and challenges impacting North Dakota businesses;
- Assisting North Dakota businesses in identifying, developing, and cultivating international markets for products; and
- Organizing and carrying out trade missions that seek to facilitate contact and communication between North Dakota businesses and international markets.

Impact Dakota is organized as a nonprofit organization [501(c)(3)] and is an affiliate of the Manufacturing Extension Partnership (MEP) – the nation's largest assistance network dedicated to developing domestic manufacturing. It has a Board of Directors representing progressive North Dakota businesses and the state of North Dakota (through the North Dakota Department of Commerce). As an MEP affiliate, Impact Dakota is able to introduce world-class best practices complemented by objective assessment, technical assistance, and training services locally to manufacturers, other new wealth creating companies, and related industries in order to strengthen their economic vitality and that of the region and nation. Services provided by Impact Dakota include leadership and people development, strategic and business planning, process improvement, and accelerating growth and innovation.

The Center for Technology and Business (CTB) delivers the services of the Women's Business Development Office and the Rural Development Office. These programs are involved with computer education, rural outreach, rural housing, childcare, and the North Dakota Young Professionals Network.

The Small Business Development Center (SBDC) provides high-quality business assistance in the form of counseling, training, and research to existing and prospective small businesses.

Corrections and Rehabilitation, Department of
3100 Railroad Avenue
PO Box 1898
Bismarck, ND 58502-1898
Phone: 701-328-6390
Fax: 701-328-6651
Web: docr.nd.gov

Created in 1989, the Department of Corrections and Rehabilitation (DOCR) is responsible for the direction and general administrative supervision, guidance, and planning of adult and juvenile correctional facilities and programs within the state. The Director is appointed by the Governor. The Director's qualifications include a minimum of a bachelor's degree from an accredited college or university and at least five years' experience in a management position in correctional or related work.

The Board of Control was established in 1911 to manage the state's charitable, reformatory, and penal institutions; it was succeeded by the Board of Administration in 1919. In turn, the Director of Institutions replaced that Board in 1969. The office of the Director of Institutions was abolished in 1989. The Department of Corrections and Rehabilitation was created in 1989 and consists of the Adult Services Division and Juvenile Services Division.

The Division of Adult Services manages almost 9,100 adult individuals. It has organized itself in a manner that effectively transitions individuals through the adult corrections system while enhancing public safety. Adult correctional assets are organized as follows:

Transitional Planning implements strategies that best utilize DOCR resources when managing individual movement throughout the DOCR. This unit provides administrative support for the Parole Board and Pardon Advisory Board, development of the Department's correctional sentencing report, management of the men's classification and movement, coordination for the transportation of individuals throughout the system, victim services, and discharge coordination, as well as coordination for the Department's adult individual case planning committee and legal records.

The maximum security facility for men residents, known as the North Dakota State Penitentiary (NDSP), provides housing for 800 maximum and medium custody residents. The men orientation unit, an administrative segregation unit, and medical infirmary are also located at NDSP.

The medium security facility for men residents, known as the James River Correctional Center (JRCC), provides housing for 440 residents in Jamestown. The Special Assistance Unit (SAU) located within JRCC is a 24-bed housing unit for individuals with serious mental illness or other special needs.

More than 500 men and women residents are housed across the state in transitional and prison facilities that are managed by the Division of Adult Services. Transitional Facilities consists of a 196-bed minimum security facility known as the Missouri River Correctional Center. This facility includes a 36-bed transitional housing unit allowing men residents to live in an apartment-type setting which facilitates efficient and effective reintegration. Transitional Facilities also includes residential treatment programs located at the Tompkins Rehabilitation and Corrections Center on the State Hospital campus in Jamestown; a transition assessment program located at the Bismarck Transition Center in Bismarck; and residential re-entry programs located at Lake Region Reentry Center in Devils Lake, as well as Centre, Inc., facilities, located in Mandan, Grand Forks, and Fargo.

The 2003 Legislative Assembly passed House Bill No. 1271, which directed the North Dakota Department of Corrections to contract with county entities for the housing of women residents sentenced to the DOCR. The Southwest Multi-County Correctional Center was awarded the contract and has been housing women residents at their facility in New England (Dakota Women's Correctional Rehabilitation Center) since November 2003. DWCRC is a 126-bed women's prison, consisting of a 70-bed minimum unit, 40-bed medium unit, five-bed special management unit, and 16-bed orientation unit. Following a period of orientation and assessment at the prison, women residents are classified and designated to the appropriate housing units. Roughly 75 percent of women residents are serving sentences for non-violent offenses, allowing for large numbers of women residents to serve their sentences in minimum security housing at DWCRC or residential treatment programs and halfway houses. In addition to DWCRC, classified women residents are housed at the Tompkins Rehabilitation and Corrections Center in Jamestown and at halfway houses in Devils Lake, Bismarck, Mandan, and Fargo.

The Behavioral Health Division delivers individual and group programming using the evidence of what works to reduce recidivism and improve psychosocial outcomes. People in prison participate in comprehensive behavioral health assessment to determine their specific needs. They may be referred for Thinking for a Change, substance use disorder treatment, conflict resolution or domestic violence programming, and sexual offender treatment, as well as individual counseling and psychiatric services. The behavioral health staff also provides referrals for people leaving prison to access necessary community-based resources. One such resource is Free Through Recovery, which provides care coordination and peer support services for people on community supervision through a collaboration with the Department of Human Services.

The Industry Training Program is commonly referred to as Rough Rider Industries and operates within all three institutional facilities. The program helps provide vocational learning and employment skills training to incarcerated individuals enrolled in the training program. It also helps reduce resident idleness by giving individuals an opportunity to participate in productive work activities. These activities help lessen both security and behavioral situations while instilling transferrable job skills necessary in helping make a successful transition back into the community.

The Education Division provides appropriate educational, vocational, employment skills, post-secondary, and training opportunities for residents to assist them in re-entering into the community successfully. Education has a number of programs that have been established to assist residents with personal and career development at all three institutions. Residents go through an assessment to determine their education and literacy levels and needs. Education programs include but are not limited to Adult Basic Education, General Education Development (GED), Computer Literacy Programs, Read Right, AutoCAD, Construction Technology, Welding Technology, Career Readiness, and Post-Secondary.

The Division of Parole and Probation is responsible for teaching, coaching, and holding accountable over 7,000 people on supervision to make positive changes in order to improve their lives and desist from crime. In doing so, this contributes to improving the health, safety, and vitality of communities in a cost-effective manner. The Division utilizes evidence-based practices to help identify risks and strengths to formulate case plans that serve as a roadmap for individual's behavior change. The division also collaborates with numerous public and private stakeholders throughout the state to share information and resources in order to improve outcomes. The strength of the organization rests in the innovative, motivated, and hard-working staff that work towards the mission of the department. The Division operates many specialized programs, including parole specialists, drug court, sex offense specialists, domestic violence specialists, and mental health specialists to target specific needs of the clientele.

The Division of Juvenile Services (DJS) [NDCC 27-21] is responsible for the custody of delinquent and unruly children placed in its care, custody, and control by the District Courts. The Division includes the operation of the North Dakota Youth Correctional Center and Community Services, which operates through eight regionalized offices.

Community Services (in cooperation with the Department of Human Services, North Dakota Association of Counties, and Department of Public Instruction) provides a continuum of placement options and an array of services for committed youth. Among the programs are Intensive In-Home (family therapy services); Day Treatment (providing assessment, counseling, cognitive intervention programming, behavior management, and academic remediation); Restorative Justice programming (providing accountability conferences, victim empathy seminars, and restorative councils); and Attendant Care (statewide detention support services designed to reduce the number of juveniles held in adult jails).

The North Dakota Youth Correctional Center (NDYCC) opened southwest of Mandan in 1903 with a land grant of 40,000 acres. The Center assumes responsibility for the detention, rehabilitation, and education of juveniles legally committed to the Division by the courts. Individual and group interventions are focused on reducing risk for future crime, along with helping individuals learn skills to manage criminogenic need areas, including substance use, violence, and sexual offending. A variety of academic and vocational programs are provided. The Youth Correctional Center has a fully accredited high school and middle school called Marmot Schools.

The Division of Juvenile Services utilizes an integrated approach across its system. During the intake phase, youth undergo assessment at NDYCC while Community

Services staff assesses the home and family. A treatment plan is developed based on the assessment findings. Placement is fluid, and youth move across the system based on their changing needs for level of structure and individualized treatment requirements.

Financial Institutions, Department of

2000 Schafer St., Suite G
Bismarck, ND 58501-1204
Phone: 701-328-9933
Fax: 701-328-0290
Web: www.nd.gov/dfi
Email: dfi@nd.gov
[NDCC 6-01]

Established in 1969, the Department is headed by the Commissioner. The State Examiner was established in 1893. The Department of Financial Institutions was established in 1969, and the title of the agency's head changed from State Examiner to Commissioner.

The Commissioner is appointed by the Governor and confirmed by the Senate for a four-year term. The Commissioner must be a skilled accountant and may not be an incumbent of any other public office. The Commissioner may not own, hold, or control any stocks, capital, or bonds or hold the office of trustee, assignee, officer, agent, or employee of any financial institution under his jurisdiction or of any corporation engaged in the business of guarantying or ensuring the fidelity or faithful performance of duties or the solvency of public officers or of public depositories.

The Department executes all laws relating to state banks; trust companies; building and loan associations; mutual investment corporations; mutual savings corporations; banking institutions; other financial corporations, exclusive of the Bank of North Dakota; and all credit unions, organized or doing business under the laws of this state. The Commissioner chairs the State Banking Board and the State Credit Union Board.

Additionally, the Department issues licenses to money brokers, mortgage loan originators, collection agencies, consumer finance, debt settlement providers, deferred presentment service providers, and money transmitter businesses. The Department is responsible to the depositors and creditors of the financial institutions by determining the soundness of the financial institutions and monitoring compliance with applicable rules and regulations.

The State Banking Board consists of the Commissioner and six members appointed by the Governor to terms of five years. Four members must be in an executive capacity in management of a state bank for five years; one member in an executive capacity in management of a state bank or national bank for five years; and one member is from the public. The Board may adopt rules for the government of financial corporations to the extent the rules do not conflict with any law of this state or of the United States. The Board makes and enforces orders necessary or proper to protect the public and the depositors or creditors of state financial corporations and institutions.

The State Credit Union Board has the same powers with respect to credit unions as the State Banking Board has to other financial institutions. The State Credit Union Board consists of the Commissioner and four members appointed by the Governor for terms of five years. Two members must have at least three year's experience as an officer, director, or committee member of a North Dakota state-chartered credit union; one member must have at least three year's experience as an officer, director, or committee member.

Game and Fish Department
100 North Bismarck Expressway
Bismarck, ND 58501-5095
Phone: 701-328-6300
Fax: 701-328-6352
Report All Poachers (RAP): 800-472-2121
Web: www.gf.nd.gov
Email: ndgf@nd.gov
[NDCC 20.1-02]

Game and fish laws were first established in Dakota Territory in 1861, but it was not until 1893, when the Superintendent of Irrigation and Forestry was designated as Game Commissioner, that a Game and Fish Department was formed. In 1909, the Game and Fish Board of Control was established. The Board continued to function as the agency controlling fish and game until 1929, when legislation was passed providing for a single commissioner charged with administering a Game and Fish Department.

The Game and Fish Director is appointed by the Governor. The Director names a deputy director, chief game warden, district game wardens, biologists, technicians, and other staff to enforce game laws, establish hunting and fishing seasons, and perform other duties.

The Department consists of five divisions:

- Administrative Services, which performs accounting and basic operations, data processing, licensing, and planning.
- Enforcement, which enforces game and fish laws and rules necessary for proper management of fish and game resources.
- Fisheries, which is responsible for the programs of fish production, sport fish research, and lake and stream management and access.

- Conservation and Communications, which is divided into the program areas of hunter education, fish and wildlife information and education, and boating education. It also includes environmental project review and the Department's nongame wildlife program.
- Wildlife, which is divided into the program areas of wildlife management area maintenance and development, private land habitat and access improvement, and game management.

Health, Department of
600 East Boulevard Avenue
Bismarck, ND 58505-0200
Phone: 701-328-2372
Fax: 701-328-4727
Web: www.ndhealth.gov
Email: health@nd.gov
[NDCC 23-01]

The Territorial Board of Health was created in 1885. At the time of statehood in 1889, the State Board of Health was established. In 1923, the Legislative Assembly authorized the State Department of Health. Among administrative changes made in 1933 was the transfer of public health laboratories previously connected with the University of North Dakota to the State Health Department. In 1947, the State Health Department was reorganized to provide for hospital registration and licensure.

In 1987, the State Department of Health and the State Laboratories Department were consolidated to form the State Department of Health and Consolidated Laboratories. The name was shortened to its present form in 1995, and the Department was designated the primary environmental agency for the state. In April 2019, the North Dakota Department of Health Environmental Health Section separated and became the Department of Environmental Quality because of 2017 legislation.

The North Dakota Department of Health is dedicated to ensuring North Dakota is a healthy place to live and each person has an equal opportunity to enjoy good health. It is committed to the promotion of healthy lifestyles, protection and enhancement of health and the environment, and provision of quality health care services for the people of North Dakota.

It advances its mission by networking, facilitating local efforts, collaborating with partners and stakeholders, and providing expertise in developing creative public health solutions.

The administrative head of the Department is the State Health Officer appointed by the Governor. If the Governor does not appoint as State Health Officer a physician licensed in this state, the Governor shall appoint at least three licensed physicians recommended by the state medical association to serve as an advisory committee to the State Health Officer. The State Health Officer carries out the rules and recommendations of the State Health Council; oversees operations of the agency; and serves as the primary spokesperson and authority on health issues, voicing public health policies on behalf of the Governor.

The State Health Council consists of nine members appointed by the Governor for three-year terms. These members include four persons from the health care field and five persons representing consumer interests.

The State Health Council establishes standards and rules for the maintenance of public health, including sanitation and disease control; develops, establishes, and enforces basic standards for hospitals and related medical institutions; holds hearings related to licensing of medical facilities; and advises the State Health Officer to do all things required in the proper performance of the various responsibilities placed upon the State Department of Health.

The Department consists of the following sections: Emergency Preparedness and Response, Fiscal and Operations, Health Resources, Healthy and Safe Communities, and Medical Services.

The Emergency Preparedness and Response Section is responsible for improving and maintaining public health response to disasters and large-scale emergencies. The overall goal is to promote a state of emergency readiness and response. Activities improve public health infrastructure for the detection and mitigation of chemical threats, naturally occurring phenomena such as tornadoes and floods, and other disasters and emergencies. The section includes the following divisions: Emergency Medical Systems, Public Health Preparedness, Education Technology, and Hospital Preparedness.

The Fiscal and Operations section provides services to support the Department's activities and programs. Within Fiscal and Operations are the Division of Accounting, Communications Division, Information Technology Coordinator, State Epidemiologist, Field Medical Officer, Division of Vital Records, Office of Human Resources, and Division of Medical Marijuana.

The Health Resources Section consists of three divisions: Health Facilities, Food and Lodging, and Life Safety and Construction. These divisions work to promote quality care and services for the people of North Dakota.

The goal of the Healthy and Safe Communities section is to improve the health of North Dakota citizens by working actively to promote healthy behaviors and prevent disease and injury. Many of the services are provided through local public health units. The section includes the divisions of Community and Health Systems, Family Health and Nutrition, Health Promotion, Injury and Violence Prevention, and Special Health Services.

The goal of the Medical Services Section is to promote health and prevent illness and disease. The section includes the Office of the State Forensic Examiner, Microbiology Lab, and Division of Disease Control.

Environmental Quality, Department of
918 East Divide Avenue
Bismarck, ND 58505-1947
Phone: 701-328-5150
Fax: 701-328-5200
Web: www.deq.nd.gov
Email: deq@nd.gov
[NDCC 23.1]

During the 2017 legislative session, lawmakers passed, and Governor Doug Burgum signed, Senate Bill 2327. This bill separated the Environmental Health Section from the North Dakota Department of Health to create a stand-alone North Dakota Department of Environmental Quality (NDDEQ). The bill gave the Department of Health's Environmental Health Section until July 1, 2019, to obtain the approvals and amend agreements necessary to ensure that North Dakota maintained primacy over all federal and state environmental regulations.

Primacy means that the NDDEQ has the ability and legal authority to implement many federal environmental laws, as well as the authority to enforce those laws and related regulations. The NDDEQ has primacy on all lands within the state borders except tribal and reservation lands where the U.S. Environmental Protection Agency (EPA) has jurisdiction for federal environmental regulations.

On April 29, 2019, the NDDEQ became an independent agency after all programs completed the EPA review and approval process. The state process for transition was also fully implemented, and environmental laws and rules that previously fell under the jurisdiction of the Department of Health were transferred to the NDDEQ. The transition did not change the requirements of existing laws and rules, but citations to those laws and rules were amended to reflect the establishment of the new agency.

The NDDEQ was created to streamline government and acknowledge the importance of environmental protection in North Dakota by elevating that responsibility to a cabinet-level agency. The Director of the NDDEQ is appointed by and reports directly to the Governor.

The vision of the NDDEQ is a sustainable, high quality environment for current and future generations. Its mission is to conserve and protect the quality of North Dakota's air, land, and water resources following the science and the law. The department works with the general public, industry, and government at all levels to create an awareness of the importance of protecting North Dakota's natural resources. Protective programs and standards are implemented to help maintain and improve environmental quality.

The NDDEQ will seek input from a 13-member Environmental Quality Review Advisory Board. Board members will consist of the state engineer, state geologist, director of the North Dakota Game and Fish Department, and 10 members to be appointed by the Governor. Board members will include representatives of crop agriculture, the livestock industry, agronomy/soil sciences, energy industries, and local government.

The NDDEQ has about 160 employees – including engineers, scientists, chemists, microbiologists, legal personnel, and administrative support staff. These employees work in the Office of the Director and the agency's five divisions: Air Quality, Chemistry, Municipal Facilities, Waste Management, and Water Quality.

Staff members in the Office of the Director work with all divisions in the NDDEQ to ensure proper administration and implementation of environmental protection programs, as well as assist with public education and outreach. These efforts include interacting with various federal, state, and local government agencies; industry; private entities; and the public to achieve common goals. The Office of the Director helps coordinate emergency response efforts, enforcement of environmental regulations, computer and data management activities, quality management processes, staff training, and internal and external communication.

The Division of Air Quality is responsible for protecting North Dakota's air quality and for ensuring the control of radiation. Staff scientists, engineers, and technicians oversee compliance of state and federal air and radiation rules. They also provide technical assistance addressing environmental issues and emergency response efforts. Enforcement of state and federal environmental laws is accomplished through permitting, licensing, sampling, analytical services, inspections, and monitoring activities.

The Division of Chemistry laboratory provides analytical chemistry data for environmental protection, public health, and agricultural and petroleum regulatory programs in the state. The laboratory also maintains a certification program for North Dakota laboratories that provide environmental testing services. Laboratory data is used throughout the NDDEQ to monitor and/or regulate solid and hazardous waste; municipal wastewater; agricultural runoff; surface, ground, and drinking water quality; petroleum products; and other media of environmental or public health concern.

The Division of Municipal Facilities works with political subdivisions, businesses, and industries to safeguard public health and the environment in the areas of potable water supply and wastewater collection/treatment. Enforcement of state and federal laws and rules is accomplished through monitoring of public water systems; certification and training of operators of public water and wastewater systems; inspections of public water and wastewater facilities; and the provision of financial assistance to construct or upgrade public drinking water and wastewater infrastructure.

The primary responsibilities of the Division of Waste Management include overseeing the handling, storage, transport, treatment, and disposal of waste and enforcing Resource Conservation and Recovery Act Subtitles C (hazardous solid waste) and D (non-hazardous solid waste) regulations. The division coordinates with the other divisions on significant issues involving air and water quality, municipal facility infrastructure, and data sampling and analysis. The division also works to encourage waste reduction, recycling, and beneficial reuse.

The focus of the Division of Water Quality is safeguarding and improving water quality for all statutorily defined uses. This includes protecting groundwater, streams, rivers, wetlands, and lakes; permitting wastewater discharges; enforcing Clean Water Act regulations; investigating spills; and providing technical assistance on remediation. Enforcement of state and federal environmental laws is accomplished through permitting, inspection, sampling, analytical services, and monitoring activities.

Highway Patrol
600 East Boulevard Avenue, Department 504
Bismarck, ND 58505-0240
Phone: 701-328-2447
After Hours: 800-472-2121
Fax: 701-328-1717
Email: ndhpinfo@nd.gov
Web: www.nd.gov/ndhp

The North Dakota Highway Patrol was created in 1935. During the first years of the organization, the State Highway Commissioner appointed the Superintendent of the Highway Patrol. In 1951, the Legislative Assembly gave the responsibility of appointing the Superintendent to the Governor. All officers are appointed by the Superintendent.

The Patrol is divided into two main components: Field Operations and Administration. The Field Operations component includes four geographic regions and motor carrier operations. The administration component includes the finance section and two divisions, support services and administrative services.

The Patrol enforces criminal and traffic laws, including those governing commercial motor vehicles on roadways open to the public. Other primary responsibilities include investigating vehicle crashes, promoting safe driving practices, assisting other law enforcement agencies, inspecting school buses, and administering a federal commercial vehicle safety inspection program. In addition, the Patrol has jurisdiction on state-owned and leased property, such as the Capitol grounds. The Patrol is responsible for providing security and protection for the Governor, the Governor's family, the Legislative Assembly while in session, and the Supreme Court.

The Law Enforcement Training Academy provides basic and advanced training to members of the public safety community. Certification and curriculum offered by the Law Enforcement Training Academy, located in Bismarck, must meet criteria established by the Peace Officer Standards and Training Board.

Human Services, Department of
600 East Boulevard, 3rd Floor-Judicial Wing
Bismarck, ND 58505-0250
Phone: 701-328-2310
Fax: 701-328-1545
Toll Free: 800-472-2622
TTY: 800-366-6888
Web: www.nd.gov/dhs

Established in 1981, the Department of Human Services consolidated programs formerly operated under multiple agencies. The Department's Executive Director is appointed by and serves at the pleasure of the Governor. The Department serves as the official agency for administration of federal social and rehabilitation programs in the areas of medical services, economic assistance, community services, and vocational rehabilitation. The role of the Department is to provide services that help people who are vulnerable or experiencing poverty. This role is carried out directly and through partnerships with county social service offices and contracts with an array of public and private providers.

The Department is structured into these organizational areas: Administrative Support Services, Aging Services, Behavioral Health, Child Support, Children and Family Services, Developmental Disabilities, Economic Assistance, Field Services, Medical Services (Medicaid, Medicaid Expansion, Children's Health Insurance Program, Autism Services, and Home and Community-based Services Administration Unit [provider enrollment and payment processing]), and Vocational Rehabilitation. Department divisions are responsible for receiving, distributing, and monitoring the use of state and federal funds; providing direction and technical assistance for implementing programs, setting standards and policy for service delivery, and providing training. For some areas, division staff members are involved directly in service delivery, including determining eligibility for services, paying provider claims, distributing benefits, and conducting assessments.

The Department's Field Services area provides direct client services and is comprised of eight regional human service centers located in Bismarck, Devils Lake, Dickinson, Fargo, Grand Forks, Jamestown, Minot, and Williston; the North Dakota State Hospital in Jamestown; and the Life Skills and Transition Center (LSTC) in Grafton.

- The North Dakota State Hospital, established in 1884 and continuously accredited by the Joint Commission since 1956, provides acute, sub-acute, and specialized rehabilitative hospital services for individuals with severe and persistent mental illnesses and substance use disorders. The hospital also provides specialized residential addiction services for the justice-involved and specialized residential services for individuals committed as sexually dangerous.

- The LSTC became a part of the Department in 1989. The LSTC is a state-operated comprehensive support agency for people with intellectual and developmental disabilities. It is accredited by the Council on Quality and Leadership and certified as an Intermediate Care Facility. It provides specialized services including residential, vocational, and outreach services to meet the unique needs of individuals with intellectual and developmental disabilities residing on campus, in supported living arrangements in Grafton, and in communities across the state. Outreach services that support individuals in their homes and communities include clinical and direct support consultation and services and behavioral analyst assessment and intervention services.
- Human service centers provide a comprehensive set of community-based services, including a continuum of behavioral health care services for individuals with severe mental illnesses and substance use disorders, either directly or through contracts. Other community services include vocational rehabilitation, developmental disability services, and vulnerable adult protective services. In addition, staff members provide direction and oversight of services offered through county social service offices and other providers, such as child care licensing and child welfare services.

Indian Affairs Commission, North Dakota
Phone: 701-328-2428
Fax: 701-328-1537
Email: ndiac@nd.gov
[NDCC 54-36]

The North Dakota Indian Affairs Commission consists of the Governor as Chairman; three members appointed by the Governor from the state at large, two of whom must be of Indian descent, must be enrolled members of a tribe, and must be current voting residents of the state of North Dakota; and the chairperson or the chairperson's designee of the Standing Rock Sioux Tribe; Spirit Lake Tribe; Three Affiliated Tribes of the Fort Berthold Reservation; Turtle Mountain Band of Chippewa Indians; and Sisseton-Wahpeton Oyate of the Lake Traverse Reservation. The Commission meets quarterly or as otherwise agreed. Members of the Commission or the chairperson's designee are entitled to receive mileage and expenses for attending each meeting as are allowed other state officers. The Governor appoints the Executive Director of the Commission after consultation with the members of the Commission. The Executive Director serves at the pleasure of the Governor.

The Indian Affairs Commission has the power to assist and to mobilize the support of state and federal agencies in assisting Indian individuals and groups in North Dakota, especially the five tribal councils, as they seek to develop their own goals, project plans for achieving those goals, and implement those plans. The Commission's duties are to:

- Investigate any phase of Indian affairs and to assemble and make available the facts needed by tribal, state, and federal agencies to work effectively together.

- Assist tribal, state, and federal agencies in developing programs whereby Indian citizens may achieve more adequate standards of living.
- Assist tribal groups in developing increasingly effective institutions of self-government.
- Work for greater understanding and improved relationships between Indians and non-Indians.
- Seek increased participation by Indian citizens in local and state affairs.
- Confer with and coordinate officials and agencies of other governmental units and congressional committees with regard to Indian needs and goals.
- Encourage and propose agreements and accords between federal, state, and local agencies and the several tribal governments, and, pursuant to NDCC 54-40.2, to assist in monitoring and negotiating agreements and accords when asked by an affected tribe.

Information Technology Department
4201 Normandy Street
Bismarck, ND 58503-1324
Telephone: 701-328-3190
Fax: 701-328-3000
TYY: 701-328-2001

The North Dakota Information Technology Department (ITD) supports the IT needs of state government, K-12, and higher education. Because of the diverse needs of state entities, ITD provides varied amounts of support to its customers. While some entities have their own IT departments that partner with ITD for necessary services, others utilize ITD for all of their IT needs. In all situations, it is ITD's vision to be a leader and trusted business partner for strategic IT services within government and education.

ITD provides a wide range of services, broken into four categories: infrastructure, professional services, information management, and communication. Some of these services include: help desk management, software development, hosting, network infrastructure, records management, email, and video conferencing.

In addition to ITD's core service offerings, the organization houses or has representatives in a number of statewide alliances. Statewide alliances are programs made up of stakeholders from various government entities working toward a common goal. For example, the Educational Technology Council (ND ETC) is a state board responsible for developing technology systems and coordinating their use to enhance and support the educational opportunities for elementary and secondary education. The board is made up of representatives from ITD, the Department of Public Instruction, University System, and State Board of Career & Technical Education, among other stakeholders. Other statewide alliances include the Statewide Longitudinal Data System (SLDS), Graphic Information System Hub (GIS), and Health Information Technology (HIT).

To learn more about ITD, statewide alliances, and the progress of information technology within North Dakota State Government, visit www.nd.gov/itd.

Job Service North Dakota

1000 East Divide Avenue
PO Box 5507
Bismarck, ND 58506-5507
Phone: 701-328-2825
Fax: 701-328-4000
TTY: 800-366-6888
Web: www.jobsnd.com
Webmaster Email: JSNDweb@nd.gov
[NDCC 52-02]

Job Service North Dakota, the state's workforce agency and administrator of the unemployment insurance program, delivers state and federally-funded workforce services, as well as programs funded through a competitive bidding process. The Governor appoints the Job Service North Dakota Executive Director.

Job Service North Dakota serves a customer base that is vast and includes employers, employees, job seekers, and unemployment insurance claimants. The agency's mission is to provide customer-focused services to meet the current and emerging workforce needs of the state.

Job Service North Dakota:
- Helps businesses find workers and job seekers find jobs.
- Accepts and processes unemployment insurance claims.
- Gathers and publishes in-depth labor market information and analysis to provide employers and job seekers detailed employment, wage, job growth, and other valuable workforce data.
- Helps businesses develop a cost containment strategy for unemployment insurance.
- Provides 24-hour access to workforce and unemployment information via jobsnd.com.
- Assists businesses to address short-term and long-term workforce needs and skill development.
- Processes unemployment insurance benefits and subsequently applies statute to assign unemployment insurance tax rates.
- Collects and administers unemployment insurance taxes.
- Gives priority of service to veterans.
- Provides online access to local, state, and national job openings.
- Provides a variety of workshops to help job seekers learn and develop job search and job retention skills.
- Partners with businesses and local communities to host job fairs.

Through various federal and state partnerships, Job Service North Dakota has administered and continues to be involved with many workforce programs.

The unemployment insurance program provides temporary financial benefits to unemployed workers who lose their jobs through no fault of their own. Benefits paid to claimants come from monies held in the North Dakota unemployment insurance trust fund, which is funded through unemployment insurance taxes paid by employers. A key component in the administration of the unemployment insurance program is maintaining a sound trust fund balance.

The federal Workforce Innovation and Opportunity Act (WIOA) was signed into law in 2014 to increase participant employment, retention, earnings, and skill levels with the ultimate goal of improving the quality of the workforce, reducing welfare dependency, and enhancing productivity and competitiveness. Funding through the WIOA allows Job Service North Dakota to provide specialized services to targeted groups (adults, dislocated workers, and youth). Services focus on job seeking, skills identification, and work readiness. Wagner-Peyser Act programs provide a public labor exchange service to help businesses find workers and workers find jobs.

The North Dakota New Jobs Training Program is a state-funded program that provides incentives to businesses that are creating, expanding, or locating employment opportunities within the state.

Trade Adjustment Assistance (TAA) and Alternative Trade Adjustment Assistance (ATAA) help workers who have lost their jobs as a result of increased imports or jobs outsourced to other countries. Certified individuals who are found eligible for the programs may be entitled to benefits such as reemployment assistance, training, income support, and more.

Job Service North Dakota delivers services to Temporary Assistance to Needy Families (TANF) recipients through the Job Opportunities and Basic Skills (JOBS) program in two locations in North Dakota. This program is designed to get TANF recipients back to work and help them become self-sufficient quickly and for the long term.

The Parental Responsibility Initiative for the Development of Employment (PRIDE) program is a nationally-recognized and an award-winning program administered by Job Service North Dakota. PRIDE addresses the unemployment and underemployment of noncustodial parents through one-on-one case management employment services. The PRIDE program helps individuals obtain employment, resulting in more frequent and more substantial child support payments.

The Jobs for Veterans State Grant provides services to veterans in North Dakota. Services from the grant include assistance from staff who are veterans and understand the many changes that veterans experience from military to civilian life.

Staff provides one-on-one assistance to help veterans work through employment barriers. In addition to providing individual services, routine outreach services are conducted throughout the state.

The Work Opportunity Tax Credit (WOTC) is a federal income tax credit incentive provided to private sector employers. An employer may be eligible for WOTC when they hire from certain target groups of job seekers who face employment barriers. The WOTC tax credit is a one-time tax credit for each new hire – and there is no limit to the number of new hires who can qualify an employer for a tax credit. The requirements for this program are set by the Internal Revenue Service and the U.S. Department of Labor, Employment, and Training Administration.

Labor and Human Rights, Department of
600 East Boulevard Avenue, Department 406
State Capitol, 1st Floor Judicial Wing
Bismarck, ND 58505-0340
Phone: 701-328-2660
Toll Free within ND: 800-582-8032
TTY (Relay ND): 800-366-6888 or -6889
Fax: 701-328-2031
Web: www.nd.gov/labor
Email: labor@nd.gov
[NDCC 34-01–34-14, 14-02.4, 14-02.5, and NDAC 46-02-07]

In 1889, the North Dakota Constitution created the Department of Agriculture and Labor. In 1960, North Dakota citizens approved a constitutional amendment authorizing the legislature to establish a Department of Labor separate from the Department of Agriculture, which the legislature did in 1965.

The Department is administered by the Commissioner of Labor. The Commissioner was originally elected statewide to a four-year term. In 1995, the Legislature changed the office to gubernatorial appointee effective January 1, 1999. Today, the Commissioner of Labor is appointed by and serves at the pleasure of the Governor.

The original primary responsibilities of the Commissioner of Labor were to promote the welfare of wages earners and industries, to promote friendly relations between employers and employees, and to prescribe and enforce standards relating to wages and working conditions of employment in the state. These responsibilities continue today. In addition, legislative action in 1983, 1999, and 2001 added responsibilities to the Department relating to the enforcement of anti-discrimination laws in North Dakota.

Today, the Department has two primary divisions: the Wage and Hour Division and the Human Rights Division. The Wage and Hour Division carries out the traditional responsibilities of the Department relating to wage and working conditions of employment. The division administers and enforces state labor laws and regulations, such as those relating to child labor, minimum wage, overtime compensation, breaks, paid time off, and deductions from pay. The division also investigates and enforces claims for unpaid wages and educates the public about the rights and responsibilities of employers and employees.

The Human Rights Division is responsible to receive and investigate complaints alleging discriminatory practices in the areas of employment, housing, public services, public accommodations, and credit transactions. In addition, the division educates the public about rights and responsibilities under the state's human rights laws and studies the nature and extent of discrimination in the state.

In addition to its two main divisions, the Department licenses employment agencies, makes determinations regarding the independent contractor status of workers, and issues sub-minimum wage licenses.

Management and Budget, Office of
600 East Boulevard Avenue, Department 110
Bismarck, ND 58505-0400
Phone: 701-328-2680
Fax: 701-328-3230
Web: www.nd.gov/omb
Email: omb@nd.gov

The 1941 Legislative Assembly appointed a governmental survey commission to study the field of governmental reorganization and make recommendations.

Among the recommendations was a single agency to handle the state's fiscal affairs. That study was reviewed by directive of the 1957 Legislative Assembly. The 1959 Legislative Assembly established the Department of Accounts and Purchases to become operative in 1961. In 1981, the agency became the Office of Management and Budget (OMB).

The Director is appointed by and serves at the will of the Governor. As agency head, the Director is vested with control and supervision of the fiscal administration of the executive branch of state government. There are five divisions within the OMB. The directors of two of the divisions are appointed by and serve at the pleasure of the OMB Director. The remaining three division directors are classified employees.

The Fiscal Management Division is responsible for budget preparation and the monitoring of spending after legislative appropriations are made, preparing revenue forecasts, preparing the statewide Comprehensive Annual Financial Report (CAFR), managing the state purchasing card program, maintaining the state transparency website for higher education and state government, and managing the statewide financial and payroll systems. The Division maintains the integrity, integration, and configuration of statewide financial systems in compliance with policies, procedures, laws, and rules. The Director of OMB and budget analysts prepare the Governor's executive recommendation for submission to the Legislative Assembly. As the sole financial plan for providing state services, the executive budget recommendation is presented to the Legislative Assembly prior to the convening of each session. Part of the budget process involves fiscal management staff appearing at hearings for each agency budget request, on-site visits, and comparative analyses. Once the executive budget recommendation has been submitted, the office works closely with the Legislative Assembly and its committees by explaining the budget or by providing information on other fiscal concerns. During both the Legislative Session and the Legislative Management's interim study period, the OMB assists legislators and other key policymakers in resolving budget-related issues. Phone: 701-328-2680; Email: omb@nd.gov.

The Human Resource Management Services Division provides consultative services to agencies on a multitude of human resource issues including, but not limited to, recruitment, screening, and selection of applicants; performance management; classification; salary administration; discipline; grievances; investigations; appeals; and federal and state employment requirements. In addition, the Division develops, coordinates, and conducts training programs; plans, coordinates, and leads activities for the statewide human resource information system; provides mediation services; and administers a cooperative education and internship program. The Division provides services related to establishing and maintaining a unified system of human resource management for the classified service. The Division and the State Personnel Board were created by executive order in 1974 and by the Legislative Assembly in 1975. The 2003 Legislative Assembly changed the name of the Central Personnel Division to the North Dakota Human Resource Management Services Division. The Division establishes and maintains the statewide classification and compensation plans, as well as general policies and rules, which are binding on the agencies with employees in the classified service. In 1995, the administration of the merit system function was decentralized to those agencies required to have a merit system of personnel administration. The Human Resource Management Services Division maintains the merit system auditing function. Phone: 701-328-3290; TTY: 800-366-6888; Email: hrms@nd.gov.

The Central Services Division provides service to the state of North Dakota and state government agencies: central duplicating, mailroom, central supply, state procurement, surplus property, and vendor registry. Central duplicating provides printing and mailing services. The mailroom is the central mail service for the capitol complex. Central supply orders and houses office supplies. State procurement provides comprehensive purchasing services, maintains the state's bidders list and online solicitation database, and provides procurement training to state government agencies. Surplus property acquires and distributes state and federal surplus property to qualified recipients and provides electronic waste recycling services. Vendor registry manages the state payee database, provides 1099 reporting services, and manages the purchasing module software. Phone: 701-328-1726; Email: csd@nd.gov.

The Facility Management Division was created July 1, 1991, with the elimination of the Director of Institutions office. The Division manages the physical plant operations, provides capitol tours, and coordinates event scheduling for all of the buildings located on the 132-acre capitol complex. The Division is also responsible for providing space management services for the state agencies located on the capitol complex through its state planner. Phone: 701-328-2471; Email: facmgt@nd.gov.

The Risk Management Division was established in 1995 in response to a North Dakota Supreme Court decision that eliminated the state's sovereign immunity for tort claims. The Division's objectives are to implement proactive loss control practices to address the state's exposures to loss and to appropriately administer claims and lawsuits. The 2001 Legislative Assembly established the Risk Management Workers Compensation Program and assigned the Division the duty of administering the single workers' compensation account that consolidated all state agency accounts and authorized a $100,000 deductible per claim and a cross agency return-to-work program. Phone: 701-328-7584; Email: rminfo@nd.gov.

Parks and Recreation Department
1600 East Century Avenue
Bismarck, ND 58503
Phone: 701-328-5357
Toll Free: 800-807-4732 (for reservations at state parks)
Fax: 701-328-5363
Web: www.parkrec.nd.gov
Email: parkrec@nd.gov
[NDCC 55-08]

Before 1965, all state parks were under the jurisdiction of the State Historical Society of North Dakota. In 1965, the North Dakota Park Service and the State Outdoor Recreation Agency were established as separate entities. In 1977, the State Outdoor Recreation Agency was joined with the Park Service. The Department's Director is appointed by the Governor.

The North Dakota Parks and Recreation Department consists of four divisions: Administrative Services, State Parks Division, Planning and Natural Resources Division, and Recreation Division.

The Administrative Division provides fiscal management, human resources management, information technology, and public information.

The State Parks Division manages 13 state parks and five recreation areas. State parks include Beaver Lake, Cross Ranch, Fort Abraham Lincoln, Fort Ransom, Fort Stevenson, Grahams Island, Icelandic, Lake Metigoshe, Lake Sakakawea, Lewis and Clark, Little Missouri, Sully Creek, and Turtle River. The recreation areas are Butte Saint Paul, Crow Flies High, Indian Hills, Little Metigoshe, and Pelican Point. The

Parks Division also oversees the Campground Host program, Campsite Reservation program, and the Friends of Recreation and Parks.

The Planning and Natural Resources Division includes park planning, development, capital construction, and major repairs in support of all Department lands, facilities, and infrastructure. The Division also manages programs associated with North Dakota's Natural Areas and Nature Preserve Act.

The Nature Preserves and Natural Areas Program, mandated in 1975, required the Department to establish a system of natural areas and nature preserves for public use and to promote the protection of natural areas throughout the state. Nature preserves include the Gunlogson Nature Preserve (Icelandic State Park), Head of the Mountain Nature Preserve in Sargent County, Sentinel Butte in Golden Valley County, H.R. Morgan State Nature Preserve in Ransom County, and Cross Ranch Nature Preserve in Oliver County. Natural Areas include the Stumpf Fossil Site in Morton County, Missouri River Natural Area in Morton County, and Smokey Lake in Pierce County.

The Recreation Division manages the federal outdoor recreation grant programs, off-highway vehicle and snowmobile programs, recreation trails, statewide outdoor recreation planning, the Pembina Gorge State Recreation Area, and the Lewis and Clark Interpretive Center and Fort Mandan.

Securities Department
600 East Boulevard Avenue
State Capitol, 5th Floor
Bismarck, ND 58505-0510
Phone: 701-328-2910
ND Toll Free: 800-297-5124
Fax: 701-328-2946
Web: www.nd.gov/securities
Email: ndsecurities@nd.gov
[NDCC 10-04-10]

The Securities Commissioner is appointed by the Governor and confirmed by the Senate for a four-year term. To protect the investing public, the Commissioner regulates the offer and sale of investment securities and advice in the state. Companies issuing their own securities to raise capital, broker-dealers, securities agents, investment advisors, and investment advisor representatives are required to comply with the statutory registration process. When necessary, the Commissioner investigates violations of the Securities Act and may bring injunctive administrative or civil action against persons who violate the state's securities laws and rules, and refer those violators for criminal prosecution as appropriate. The Commissioner also administers the franchise investment law and those statutes regulating pre-need funeral services.

Transportation, Department of

608 East Boulevard Avenue
Bismarck, ND 58505-0700
Phone: 701-328-2500
Toll Free: 855-637-6237
Fax: 701-328-1427
Web: www.dot.nd.gov
Email: dot@nd.gov
[NDCC 28-32-02.1]

The North Dakota State Highway Department was created in March 1917 and became the North Dakota Department of Transportation (NDDOT) in 1990. At that time, the State Highway Department and Motor Vehicle Department were consolidated. The first Highway Commission, consisting of the Governor as the chair, the State Engineer, and one member appointed by the Governor, was established in 1913. In 1917, the Commission was expanded to five members and given authority to designate a state highway system and take advantage of federal aid. In 1933, the Commission was abolished and the first independent Highway Commissioner was named.

Mission – Safely move people and goods.

Vision – North Dakota's Transportation Leader Promoting: Safe Ways, Superior Service, and Economic Growth.

Strategic Focus Areas and Goals
Safety – Provide a safe and secure transportation system and workplace.
Team – Recruit, develop, and retain a high performing workforce that results in everyone working together to achieve our mission and vision.
Service – Be proactive and adaptive to provide superior external and internal services, products, and programs.
Innovation – Promote a culture of innovation to enhance external and internal services, products, and programs.
Assets – Preserve and enhance assets managed by NDDOT.

Overview
As of December 2018, NDDOT maintained 8,622 roadway miles, including interstate and national highways. North Dakota has more miles of road per capita than any state in the nation.
NDDOT oversees the development of surface transportation (highways, bridges, transit, pedestrian and bikeway paths, and safe routes to school) in the state.

Organization
NDDOT is led by a Director appointed by the Governor. The Department also has two Deputy Directors: one for Engineering, and one for Business Support and Driver and Vehicle Services. The NDDOT Director's responsibility is to oversee the

activities of the Department and provide an integrated state highway system, built on sound engineering, with full regard for the interest and wellbeing of the entire state. The Highway Distribution Fund is to be spent in the following order: (1) maintenance of the state highway system; (2) cost of construction and reconstruction in an amount necessary to ensure that federal aid match is available to the state; and (3) other construction, improvement, or maintenance purposes. The Governor has designated the Director to act on his behalf in administering the National Highway Safety Act of 1966.

The Director oversees the entire department and the following divisions:

- The Communication Division is responsible for media relations, public information, public relations, and public involvement, as well as all internal NDDOT communications. The Communication Division also includes video, photography, graphic art, and website design services.
- The Financial Management Division is responsible for the Department's accounting and reporting functions, budgeting, payroll, procurements, revenue forecasting, central supply, cash management, and the disposal of highway equipment and materials.
- The Legal Division is responsible for providing legal services to NDDOT in all areas, with emphasis on pre-litigation, risk management, driver's license administrative matters, contract development/negotiation/drafting/administration assistance, administration of non-construction contracts, legislation, and administrative rulemaking.

The NDDOT provides service to the traveling public in three areas, which include Engineering, Business Support, and Driver and Vehicle Services.

The Deputy Director for Engineering is responsible for completing the planning, project development, construction, and maintenance as needed to meet the public needs on the state's roadways. Engineering also consists of the following offices, divisions, and districts:

- District Offices are located in eight cities throughout North Dakota, including Fargo, Valley City, Devils Lake, Grand Forks, Bismarck, Dickinson, Williston, and Minot. Each district also has a number of local maintenance sections and shops located throughout the state. The districts are responsible for highway construction, engineering, administration, roadway and bridge maintenance, roadside maintenance, rest area/visitor center maintenance, materials testing, equipment and vehicle maintenance, traffic engineering, and highway sign maintenance.
- The Office of Operations encompasses the following divisions: Construction Services Division is responsible for administering highway construction bid openings, contracts, bonds, records, and contractor payments. The Maintenance Division is responsible for coordinating district maintenance efforts, employee safety, health and emergency responses, Roadway Weather Information System (RWIS), Intelligent Transportation Systems (ITS), and providing load

restriction and road condition reports. The Civil Rights Division is responsible for EEO/affirmative action, labor and contract compliance, disadvantaged business enterprise, workplace investigations, and mediation.
- The Office of Project Development encompasses the following divisions: The Bridge Division is responsible for the overall planning, design, and upkeep of state bridges. The Design Division is responsible for designing improvements for rural highways and some urban highways, performs right-of-way activities, and deals with billboards. The Environmental and Transportation Services Division includes cultural resource compliance, environmental documentation, consultant agreement services, technical services, and right of way. The Materials and Research Division tests and researches soil and materials on highway projects.
- The Office of Transportation Programs encompasses the following divisions: the Local Government Division is responsible for general administration of all county, urban, and transit federal aid programs and projects. The Planning and Asset Management Division is responsible for administering rail programs, data collection, data management, analysis, and mapping activities. The Programming Division is responsible for coordinating the development of the Statewide Transportation Improvement Program, managing federal funds, implementing the Department's scoping process, and completing traffic operations activities.

The Deputy Director for Business Support and Driver and Vehicle Services is responsible for the following divisions:

- The Drivers License Division tests drivers, grants licenses, and maintains drivers' records.
- The Safety Division is responsible for analyzing and compiling data for the annual crash report book and creating and implementing traffic safety programs.
- The Motor Vehicle Division is responsible for registering and titling vehicles, collecting fees and excise taxes, and maintaining motor vehicle records.
- The Audit Services Division is responsible for performing and overseeing Internal Audit functions, such as an annual DOT Inventory Review and annual review of physical inventory of NDDOT fixed assets and inventoried materials as required by NDDOT policy and North Dakota Century Code.
- The Human Resources Division provides staffing for the Department through the following: recruitment and selection, employment records, performance reviews, training, discipline, staffing plans, employment law compliance, workplace investigations, personnel policies, and payroll. The Division also coordinates Department position classifications and implements salary plans.
- The Information Technology Division is responsible for all automated devices hardware and software and other technology support, information processing, records management, internet and intranet development and maintenance, printing and mail operations, telecommunications/radio, and Transportation Building physical security and maintenance.

- The State Fleet Services Division is responsible for aviation services and state fleet vehicles, liability and property damage insurance, alcohol and controlled substance testing for state employees and commercial drivers, statewide refueling program, and risk management.

Services

Transportation infrastructure is the backbone of our state and the nation's economy. The NDDOT team members work hard to serve the residents of North Dakota to provide a transportation system to safely move people and goods. Listed here are some of NDDOT's projects achieved in 2017 and 2018.

Vision Zero – The NDDOT and its partners launched Vision Zero in 2018 as the state's primary traffic safety initiative. The comprehensive, multi-agency effort's goal is to continually work toward zero motor vehicle fatalities and serious injuries on North Dakota roads. This initiative emphasizes personal responsibility and encourages motorists to buckle up and obey the law to help attain the goal of zero fatalities on our state roadways.

Construction Program – The NDDOT completed approximately $700 million of work on North Dakota's transportation infrastructure during the 2017 and 2018 construction seasons.

Track-A-Plow – The NDDOT launched a new pilot program called "Track-A-Plow" in 2018. The pilot program utilizes technology to track the location of designated state snowplows and provides the information to the public online.

Motor Vehicle Kiosks – North Dakota residents renewed more than 31,000 motor vehicle registrations through a kiosk in 2018. NDDOT expanded the use of fully automated kiosks or self-service terminals for motor vehicle registration renewals in a number of major cities across North Dakota, including Bismarck, Fargo, Dickinson, Minot, Williston, and Grand Forks. These stations dispense license plate renewal registration cards and motor vehicle tabs on the spot without visiting a Motor Vehicle Branch Office.

Driver's License Online – Nearly 5,000 drivers renewed their Driver's License online in 2018 with a new customer focused online service program. This tool makes it easier for citizens to renew their driver's license on their home computer, saving them a trip to the Driver's License office. Residents can also make appointments online to schedule visits to a physical office.

Water Commission, State

State Office Building
900 East Boulevard Avenue, Department 770
Bismarck, ND 58505-0850
Phone: 701-328-2750
Fax: 701-328-3696
TTY: 800-366-6888
Web: www.swc.nd.gov
Email: swc@nd.gov
[NDCC 61-02-04]

The Office of State Engineer was created in 1905 to administer an irrigation program passed that same year. In 1937, the State Water Conservation Commission came into being. Through 1983 legislation, the agency became known as the State Water Commission.

The State Water Commission consists of the Governor as Chairman, the Agriculture Commissioner as an ex-officio member, and seven members who are appointed by the Governor to serve terms of six years each. The Commission appoints a Secretary (the State Engineer) as its executive officer, who employs a staff as needed to carry out the work of the State Water Commission. Agency staff are organized into six divisions: Administration Services, Atmospheric Resources, Planning and Education, Regulatory, Water Appropriations, and Water Development.

The Administrative Services Division provides agency operational support, including accounting, human resources, records management, and legal support coordination for all agency projects and programs.

The Atmospheric Resources Division is responsible for the administration of cloud seeding activities in the state, conducts atmospheric research, and performs weather-related data collection and analysis.

The Planning and Education Division develops and maintains the State Water Plan and the agency's Strategic Plan; manages economic and life cycle cost analyses processes; and manages the agency's information and education programs, including public outreach and water education.

The Regulatory Division is responsible for floodplain and sovereign lands management; the Silver Jackets program; dam safety; and the processing of dam, dike, and drainage permits.

The Water Appropriations Division is responsible for the processing of water permit applications, water rights evaluations, hydrologic data collection, water supply investigations, and economic development support activities.

The Water Development Division is responsible for project engineering, construction, and maintenance; Municipal, Rural, and Industrial water supply programs; State Water Supply Program administration; flood response and recovery; cost-share program administration; Southwest Pipeline and Northwest Area Water Supply project management; and Devils Lake outlets construction and operations.

Workforce Safety and Insurance
1600 East Century Avenue, Suite One
Bismarck, ND 58504-5685
Phone: 701-328-3800
Toll Free: 800-243-3331 (Safety and Fraud Hotline)
Fax: 701-328-3820
TDD: 701-328-3786
Email: ndwsi@nd.gov
[NDCC 65-02]

In 1919, the 16th Legislative Assembly created the Workmen's Compensation Bureau. Its purpose was to provide "sure and certain relief regardless of questions of fault to the exclusion of every other remedy, proceeding or compensation." The intent of the law was to provide relief to workers injured while on the job. This relief would be in the form of compensation for lost earnings and payment of medical bills incurred. It was anticipated that the law would help employers by eliminating the risk of damaging lawsuits by injured employees.

Today, Workforce Safety & Insurance (WSI) remains an exclusive, employer financed, no-fault insurance state fund covering workplace injuries, illnesses, and death. WSI is the sole provider and administrator of the workers' compensation system in North Dakota. North Dakota is one of four "exclusive" state funds in the country (the other three are Ohio, Washington, and Wyoming). This means that all employers, except those authorized to self-insure, must purchase workers' compensation insurance from the state fund, rather than from private insurance companies. In the other 46 states and the District of Columbia, employers have options to buy workers' compensation insurance from private insurance companies, competitive state funds, or to self-insure. In November 2008, voters in North Dakota returned control of WSI back to the Governor, who now appoints the agency's Executive Director, while leaving the Board as quasi-advisory.

The 11-member Board of Directors is appointed by the Governor with members serving four-year terms. Six members represent employers that maintain active accounts with WSI, three members represent employees, one member is a member of the North Dakota Medical Association, and one is appointed as an at-large member.

As administrator of workers' compensation laws, WSI collects premiums from employers and adjusts rates of premium for each classification to assure the solvency of the organization. WSI also provides workers' compensation for injured employees, cooperates in making arrangements for rehabilitation of persons injured in employment, provides safety grants and incentives to employers, and classifies types of employment with respect to degree of hazard.

Workforce Safety & Insurance is administered by the Director and consists of Employers Services, Injury Services, and Administrative Services functions.

Injury Services

The Claims Department processes new injured worker claims that are filed. Injured workers, employers, and medical providers can file claims either by mail, over the telephone, or online. The claims technicians work closely with the claim adjusters to provide clerical support and assistance in the collection of required documentation needed in the processing of claims. Benefit levels for injured workers are tied to the state's average annual wage as reported by Job Service North Dakota. The maximum disability benefit an injured worker may receive is 125 percent of the state's average weekly wage. Return-to-Work Services assists injured workers and employers to coordinate stay-at-work or a return-to-work plan quickly and safely. Medical Services administers the managed care and medical bill audit programs and the medical and hospital fee schedules. The department administers the medical dispute resolution process for disputes arising out of managed care recommendations. WSI uses the Official Disability Guidelines-Treatment in Workers' Comp (ODG) as developed by Work Loss Data Institute, an independent database company focusing on workplace health and productivity. ODG is a nationally recognized, evidence-based treatment and disability guideline to evaluate the necessity and/or effectiveness of medical care. The department also provides technical support to the claims and rehabilitation department in the processing of medical bills and in computer and claim form functions. Provider Relations works to ensure good communication is taking place between WSI and medical providers. A pharmacy benefit management system has allowed WSI to continue to provide for the medication needs of injured workers, while addressing the issue of continued rising costs in the pharmaceutical area. Injury Services also oversees the Customer Service Call Center, which receives and answers more than 700 calls per day.

Employer Services

Policyholder Services manages employer insurance accounts, develops annual rate and classification structures (in consultation with WSI's actuarial consultant), rates employer loss experience, determines coverage status, and manages extraterritorial agreements with other states. The department's field representatives audit employer accounts and investigate uninsured employers. The Safety and Loss Prevention Department assists employers with safety and loss prevention program design, implementation, and training; conducts workplace safety inspections; and investigates industrial accidents. The department works with employers to establish their own safety programs and provides opportunities through matching grants to purchase safety intervention to eliminate hazards in the workplace. WSI offers safety grant and discount programs aimed at further reducing the frequency of workplace injuries.

These programs can reduce a qualifying employer's premium by up to 25 percent. In addition, associations and employee organizations may qualify for grants to help promote safety through training and education.

Other Administrative Services

- Communications: The department's primary efforts are designed to maintain close relationships with the news media and the public they serve, as well as contact with the legislature and other governmental leaders. It also works to enhance the agency's internal communications.
- Facility Management: Operates Century Center, WSI's home since May 2003. The building was formally dedicated in September 2003. Century Center is also the home for North Dakota's Department of Commerce, Parks and Recreation Department, Council on the Arts, Risk Management, and Human Service's Child Support Enforcement and Provider Audit Divisions.
- Finance: Monitors, records, and reports on all WSI financial activity to ensure WSI resources are used effectively and efficiently and WSI fund solvency is maintained.
- Human Resources: Administers the personnel functions of WSI and maintains the performance management system of WSI.
- Information Services: Provides support and services for all computers, software, and telephones for the WSI staff at the Century Center building and remote facilities and offices.
- Internal Audit: Plans, directs, and completes internal audits and compliance reviews to ensure WSI departments and major programs are properly functioning and operating in accordance with applicable laws, rules, and Board outcomes.
- Legal: Provides support services to legal counsel and assistance to the staff of injury services, employer services, and other administrative departments.
- Special Investigations Unit: Provides WSI's Claims, Employer Services, and Medical Services departments with investigation resources for claims adjudication, employer and medical provider non-compliance, and fraud.
- Quality Assurance: Ensures the continual improvement of WSI operations by statistically tracking performance and identifying areas that need improvement and new initiatives that would serve to improve the overall efficiency and cost effectiveness of WSI.
- Office Services: Provides support services to all of WSI through mail processing, document imaging, claims registration, fax and photocopying services, forms processing, medical and non-medical bill entry, records retention, and off-site storage.
- Decision Review Office: Established by the North Dakota Legislature in 1995 in response to two needs: providing injured workers with a no-cost, speedy claims dispute resolution alternative to litigation and reducing the amount of attorney fees paid by the agency.

Administrative Departments under Boards, Commissions, Committees, and Councils

Traditionally the most common form of executive agency, many agencies operate under the authority of a board or commission. The boards or commissions are most frequently appointed by the Governor and often have ex-officio members. The board or commission is then responsible for appointing a chief executive officer. Although traditionally seen as a check or limitation upon the power of the Governor, the Governor has the authority to replace the membership of most boards under his appointing authority upon assuming office. However, in some cases, boards have multiple appointing authorities or ex-officio membership, which provides a degree of independence from any single official.

Aeronautics Commission

Bismarck Municipal Airport – General Aviation Terminal
2301 University Drive – Building 22
Bismarck, ND 58504
Phone: 701-328-9650
Fax: 701-328-9656
Web: https://aero.nd.gov
[NDCC 2-05]

The North Dakota Aeronautics Commission was established in 1947 by the State Legislature to provide representation of the state in aviation matters and to provide responsibility for the state's aviation programs and regulatory framework. The Governor appoints five members to the Aeronautics Commission for terms of office of five years. The Commission appoints an Executive Director to administer the agency and to oversee the agency's support staff. The office is currently located at the general aviation pilot terminal on the Bismarck Municipal Airport (KBIS).

The Commission supports aviation activities in the state through communication with state, local, and Federal Aviation Association (FAA) officials; congressional offices; and national aviation groups. The Commission is responsible for administering North Dakota's laws regarding the registration of aircraft, aircraft dealers, aerial applicators, and the collection of aircraft excise tax. The Commission provides grant funding for airport infrastructure projects and manages aviation education initiatives and programs throughout the state. The office also provides airport planning services, helps to maintain the state's Automated Weather Observation Systems (AWOS), and provides airport inspections for general aviation airports.

The Commission works to maintain and update publicized planning documents to help maintain and grow North Dakota's aviation transportation system. Statewide airport capital improvement plans, aviation economic impact studies, airport directories, state aviation system plans, and pavement condition index studies are a few examples of these documents.

The Executive Director also serves as an ex-officio member of the Northern Plains UAS Test Site Authority, Upper Great Plains Transportation Institute Advisory Board, Atmospheric Resource Board, and North Dakota Aviation Council.

Animal Health, State Board of
Phone: 701-328-2655
Fax: 701-328-4567
Email: doa-bah@nd.gov
Web: www.nd.gov/ndda
[NDCC 36-01-01; 36-01-08]

The State Board of Animal Health consists of nine members appointed by the Governor for seven-year terms. Two members are licensed, practicing veterinarians and seven are livestock operators, each representing a different segment of the livestock industry: dairy cattle, commercial beef cattle, swine, sheep, bison, non-traditional livestock, and registered purebred beef cattle. Recommendations for appointments are made by the professional and industry associations represented.

The Agriculture Commissioner, with the consent of the board, appoints the State Veterinarian and Deputy State Veterinarian who graduated from a recognized college or university in veterinary medicine and surgery. As the State Veterinarian, the executive officer is not a member of the board. A veterinarian on staff at North Dakota State University is chosen to act as consulting veterinarian to the board.

The board protects the health of animals in the state and determines and employs the most efficient and practical means for the prevention, suppression, control, and eradication of dangerous, contagious, and infectious diseases among the domestic animals and non-traditional livestock of this state. In the interest of public and animal health, the board may restrict the importation, sale, and distribution of infected domestic and non-traditional livestock. The board is also empowered to impose quarantines and to kill animals infected with contagious diseases. The board also registers feedlots and inspects livestock in transit for ownership identification and health verification.

Arts, Council on the
Phone: 701-328-7590
Fax: 701-328-7595
Email: comserv@nd.gov
Web: www.nd.gov/arts
[NDCC 54-54-02]

The nine-member Board of Directors of the North Dakota Council on the Arts is appointed by the Governor and broadly represents all fields of the performing and fine arts. Members appointed for five-year terms are North Dakotans known for their competence and experience in the arts. The Governor names a chair from the board membership. The Council appoints an Executive Director to administer the agency and oversee the agency's full-time staff.

The Council functions as a community partner and a catalyst for artists and organizations. It regrants National Endowment for the Arts funds and state-appropriated funds to North Dakota communities, schools, individuals, and nonprofit organizations through its grant programs. Educational opportunities and technical advice are offered, arts information is collected and disseminated, and the Council serves as the state's foremost arts supporter. Its mission is to support, preserve, and champion the arts within our state and beyond our borders.

Canvassing Board, State
Phone: 701-328-2900 (Secretary of State)
[NDCC 16.1-15-33]

The State Canvassing Board meets after each statewide election to canvass the election results received from each county and to officially certify those results for statewide and district (legislative, judicial, soil conservation) candidates and statewide measures.

Its members are the Clerk of the Supreme Court, the Secretary of State, the State Treasurer, and the chairman, or chairman's designee, of the two political parties which cast the highest vote for Governor in the last general election at which the office of the Governor was on the ballot.

Capitol Grounds Planning Commission
Phone: 701-328-2471
(Office of Management and Budget, Facility Management Division)
[NDCC 48-10]

In addition to the Lieutenant Governor, who serves as the chairman, the Capitol Grounds Planning Commission has eight members. Selected biennially for a two-year term, the Governor appoints two citizens, one licensed architect, and one representative from the State Historical Society. The President of the Senate appoints two Senators, and the Speaker of the House appoints two Representatives.

Among its duties, the Commission may confer with the state Council on the Arts regarding the artistic value of monuments, memorials, or works of art to be constructed on the capitol grounds; work with consultants to select sites for buildings, facilities, monuments, memorials, or works of art to be constructed on the capitol grounds; develop and modify long-term plans for the development of the capitol grounds; and approve or disapprove the basic style and exterior construction of any building, facility, monument, memorial, or work of art constructed on the capitol grounds.

The Commission meets whenever major interior changes, including new construction, remodeling, or renovation of any kind, are proposed or considered for the buildings or facilities on the capitol grounds. It must also be consulted before the purchase or installation of furniture or fixtures in the public areas of the capitol and other buildings on the capitol grounds.

Career and Technical Education, State Board for
Phone: 701-328-3180
Fax: 701-328-1255
Email: cte@nd.gov
Web: www.nd.gov/cte
[NDCC 15-20.1-02]

The State Board for Career and Technical Education consists of the six members of the State Board of Public School Education, the Superintendent of Public Instruction, the executive director of Job Service North Dakota, and the chancellor of the University System or the chancellor's designee. The board appoints a director and executive officer of the Department of Career and Technical Education.

The six members, one from each of the six districts described in the governing statute, are appointed by the Governor for six-year terms and come from a list of nominees. The list of nominees for each vacant position is submitted by a committee comprised of the president of North Dakota United, the president of the North Dakota Council of Educational Leaders, and the president of the North Dakota School Boards Association.

The Board's authority includes administering state legislation passed in conformity with acts of Congress relating to career and technical education; administering funds provided by the state and federal government for career and technical education; formulating plans for the promotion of career and technical education in subjects taught in the public schools; providing for the preparation and prescribing the qualification and certification of teachers and directors; making studies relating to career and technical education; and promoting and aiding in the establishment of schools, departments, or classes. Effective July 1, 2019, the Board will have authority over the operations of the North Dakota Center for Distance Education.

Career and Technical Education, Department of
Phone: 701-328-3180
Fax: 701-328-1255
Email: cte@nd.gov
Web: www.nd.gov/cte
[NDCC 15-20.1-02]

The Department of Career and Technical Education (CTE) is governed by the State Board for Career and Technical Education and carries out the policies of the Board. The Department works with other education agencies and business and industry in planning, conducting, and evaluating career and technical education programs. Business and industry involvement is present in all CTE programs through local advisory committees. Beyond ensuring high school students have career and technical education opportunities, the Department develops career and technical education programs in cooperation with the State Board of Higher Education and the state's post-secondary institutions. To assist adults in upgrading skills or in retraining for employment, the Department offers such programs as farm business management and short-term adult classes. The Department administers all federal and state legislation affecting career and technical education, including congressional and Legislative Assembly appropriations.

Credit Review Board
Phone: 701-328-4158
[NDCC 6-09.10-02]

The Credit Review Board consists of six members. The Governor, Attorney General, and Agriculture Commissioner each appoint two members to the Board. The Governor and Attorney General each appoints one member with experience as a director or officer of a financial institution and one member actively engaged in farming in the state. The Agriculture Commissioner appoints two members who are actively engaged in farming in the state. No member of the Board may hold state office or serve in state office or state government in any capacity at any time of appointment or during service on the Board. The Credit Review Board members serve terms of two years. The Board establishes policy for the North Dakota Mediation Service and recommends policies and procedures to the Industrial Commission regarding farm loan programs to the Bank of North Dakota.

Education Commission of the States
[NDCC 15-64]

The Education Commission of the States (ECS) – created by states for states in 1965 to improve student success across the nation – is an unbiased organization that does not advocate for specific education policies. ECS tracks state policy trends, provides research-based advice, and creates opportunities for state leaders to learn from one another. It brings together governors, state legislators, K-12 leaders, higher education officials, and other education leaders to work on education issues along the full spectrum – from pre-K to postsecondary and beyond. Elected officials, members of the media, and the public can access ECS resources on the web (www.ecs.org) or through its information hotline (303-299-3675). The North Dakota delegation of commissioners includes the Governor, two legislators, and four gubernatorial appointees.

Fair Association, State
Phone: 701-857-7620
Email: ndsf@minot.com
Web: www.ndstatefair.com
[NDCC 4.1-45]

The North Dakota State Fair Association consists of three members from each county in the state chosen for one-year terms. One member from each county is selected by the county fair board, the second by the board of county commissioners, and the third by the county agent. The Board of Directors, which manages the affairs of the Association, consists of nine members elected to three-year terms from the Association membership. The Association conducts an annual state fair at Minot to exhibit agricultural, horticultural, industrial, mechanical, mining, stock breeding, and other products and resources of North Dakota. The Association also cooperates in year-round promotion of 4-H, FFA, and agricultural and industrial enhancements in order to make the state fair a North Dakota showcase.

Firefighters' Association
1502 Grumman Lane
P.O. Box 6127
Bismarck, ND 58506-6127
Phone: 701-222-2799
Fax: 701-222-2899
Email: rknuth@nd.gov
Web: www.ndfa.net
[NDCC 18-03]

The North Dakota Firefighters' Association is made up of dues-paying fire departments in the state. It is governed by a 10-member executive board and has been given the responsibility of conducting fire service training throughout the state by the North Dakota Legislature. The Association hosts an annual fire school and offers regional fire schools, specialized training, and other firefighting training following national standard recommendations. Firefighting training is held to promote the safety and welfare of the Association members through uniform and established training following national standards. Firefighting training conveys information to members on safety, health, and equipment issues based on the duties that firefighters are expected to perform on the fire ground. New skills are required for the ever-changing demands placed on fire departments.

Forest Service
307 1st Street East
Bottineau, ND 58318-1100
Phone: 701-228-5422
Fax: 701-228-5448
Email: forest@nd.gov
Web: www.ndsu.edu/ndfs
[NDCC 4.1-21]

The NDSU North Dakota Forest Service is organized under the North Dakota Board of Higher Education. The agency is administered by a State Forester who reports to the president of North Dakota State University at Fargo and supports the land grant mission in public service. The mission of the North Dakota Forest Service is to "care for, protect, and improve forest resources to enhance the quality of life for present and future generations."

A wide variety of customers depend on the North Dakota Forest Service for technical, financial, and educational forestry assistance. The State Forester administers forestry programs serving communities, rural landowners, soil conservation districts, rural fire districts, schools, and citizens of North Dakota. All the programs utilize a voluntary, educational, and incentives-based approach to address forestry and related natural resource needs and customer requests.

The agency also operates a nursery at Towner that annually produces one-million conifer (evergreen) seedlings in more than 30 different species and stock types for distribution to landowners. The trees are used for farmstead, living snow fence, field windbreaks, wildlife, forestry, and other conservation plantings. The agency also owns and manages 13,290 acres of state forestlands.

Garrison Diversion Conservancy District
Phone: 701-652-3194
Toll free: 800-532-0074
Fax: 701-652-3195
Email: gdcd@gdcd.org
Web: www.garrisondiversion.org
[NDCC 61-24]

The Garrison Diversion Conservancy District was created by the North Dakota State Legislature in 1955 to contract with the federal government for the development and operation of the Garrison Diversion Unit. The Board of Directors held its first meeting on July 18, 1955, in Harvey, N.D., with representatives from 22 counties.

Over the years, federal legislation has evolved Garrison Diversion Conservancy District's focus from strictly irrigation to a more multi-purpose effort. In 1965, legislation enacted called for the construction of the Garrison Diversion Unit Principal Supply Works. It also reduced the number of acres for irrigation development in North Dakota, originally authorized in the 1944 Flood Control Act, from 1.2 million to 250,000 acres. A focus on municipal and industrial water, fish and wildlife development, and recreation was also added.

The Garrison Diversion Unit Reformulation Act of 1986 further reduced authorized acres for irrigation development to 130,940 acres. In addition, the act authorized a $200 million grant program to facilitate municipal, rural, and industrial water service.

The Dakota Water Resources Act of 2000 authorized a $200 million increase in municipal, rural, and industrial project funding, $200 million to meet the Indian water needs, and $200 million to provide reliable, high-quality water to areas in eastern North Dakota. In addition, $31.5 million was authorized for recreation and wildlife facilities and programs in North Dakota.

The Dakota Water Resources Act further reduced the number of acres authorized for irrigation development to 75,480 acres. In 2011, Garrison Diversion completed the 3,500-acre McClusky Canal Mile Marker 7.5 Irrigation Project. Additional projects have since been added, bringing the total to nearly 7,000 irrigated acres.

The Garrison Diversion Conservancy District headquarters are located in Carrington, with additional operations and maintenance offices in McClusky, New Rockford, and Oakes. The district consists of 28 counties. Each member county elects a citizen to a four-year term on a no-party ballot at the general election to serve on the Garrison Diversion Conservancy District Board of Directors. The Board of Directors elects a chairman, vice chairman, and second vice chairman. An Executive Committee is elected from the board. Any county may petition to join the district upon application of its board of county commissioners.

Garrison Diversion's mission is "to provide a reliable, high quality, and affordable water supply to benefit the people of North Dakota." Garrison Diversion Conservancy District is responsible for the development and operation of the Garrison Diversion Unit. The district has the power of eminent domain and may levy, to cover expenses, a tax not to exceed one mill on each dollar of taxable valuation within the district. The district also acts as fiscal agent on behalf of the federal government in connection with any Garrison Diversion Unit business.

Higher Education, State Board of
All public colleges and universities
Phone: 701-328-2960
Fax: 701-328-2961
Email: ndus.office@ndus.edu
Web: www.ndus.edu/
[Constitution, Article VIII, Section 6; NDCC 15-10-02]

The State Board of Higher Education consists of eight members. Seven members must be qualified electors and state residents for at least five years preceding appointment; one must be a full-time resident student in good academic standing at an institution under the jurisdiction of the Board. All members except the student are appointed by the Governor for four-year terms and confirmed by the Senate. Members are limited to serving two terms. The student member, appointed by the Governor upon recommendation of the North Dakota Student Association, serves a one-year term. The student member cannot serve more than two consecutive terms. The seven appointments outside of the student member are made from a list of names selected by action of at least four of the following five people: the president of

North Dakota United, the Chief Justice of the North Dakota Supreme Court, the Superintendent of Public Instruction, the President Pro Tempore of the Senate, and the Speaker of the House of Representatives. In addition, the Council of College Faculties selects one nonvoting advisor for a one-year term, and the North Dakota Staff Senate selects one nonvoting staff advisor for a one-year term.

The Constitution provides that the Board employ an individual as the Commissioner of Higher Education. The Commissioner serves as Chancellor of the North Dakota University System and as the chief executive officer of the Board and University System. Under Board policy, the president of each institution of higher education governed by the Board is responsible to the Chancellor and through the Chancellor to the Board.

All public colleges and universities in North Dakota are under the Board's jurisdiction. The Board seeks appropriations through the executive and legislative budget review process.

In coordinating and planning development of North Dakota's state higher education, the Board approves all new programs of instruction, research, and public service, including the establishment of a college, school, division, department, or other unit. Plans for all capital improvements also are subject to the Board's approval.

Historical Society of North Dakota, State
Phone: 701-328-2666
Fax: 701-328-3710
Email: histsoc@nd.gov
Web: www.history.nd.gov
Web: www.statemuseum.nd.gov
Web: www.ndstudies.gov
[NDCC 55-01]

A State Historical Commission and authorization for a State Historical Society were established in 1895. In 1905, the Legislative Assembly provided an appropriation and facilities in the Capitol and named the Society trustee for the state. The Society remained a quasi-public institution until 1965, when legislative action created the State Historical Board as the governing body of the agency. In 1967, the private membership organization was severed from official connection with the state agency. The Legislative Assembly, in 1987, authorized the State Historical Society of North Dakota to create a new membership adjunct without voice in governance of the agency.

The Society is governed by a 12-member State Historical Board. Seven members of the board are appointed by the Governor for three-year terms. The remaining members are ex-officio: Commissioner of Commerce, Director of the Department of Transportation, Secretary of State, Director of Parks and Recreation Department, and State Treasurer. From among the appointed members, the Board elects a president, vice president, and secretary. The Board appoints the Director of the State Historical Society of North Dakota to administer the agency and carry out policies and directives. The agency is organized into four divisions:

The Administration Division is headed by the Assistant Director and is responsible for overall agency support, budgeting and fiscal matters, human resources, IT operations, store operations, and security. The North Dakota Heritage Center, the agency headquarters, is accredited by the American Alliance of Museums and serves as the state's federal repository in all collection areas.

The Archaeology and Historic Preservation Division protects and manages cultural resources by identifying and recording sites related to North Dakota's prehistory; surveying, identifying, and recording structures and sites eligible for listing on the North Dakota Historic Sites Registry; and nominating structures and sites for listing on the National Register of Historic Places. The Director of the State Historical Society of North Dakota serves as the State Historic Preservation Officer. The Director of the Archeology and Historic Preservation Division is the Deputy Historic Preservation Officer. The Division also preserves and manages 57 state-owned historic sites ranging in size from nearly 200 acres to less than one-tenth acre and spans 10,000 years of history.

The Visitor Engagement and Museum Division produces public and educational programs and events for adults and children at the North Dakota Heritage Center and other locations; provides liaison services to North Dakota's 170 county and local historical societies; produces publications including a biannual journal, *North Dakota History*, and a quarterly newsletter, *Plains Talk*; and coordinates visitor services for the Heritage Center. The Division collects and manages artifact collections representative of North Dakota history and culture and designs and mounts interpretive exhibits at the North Dakota Heritage Center and 10 branch museums.

The State Archives Division collects, manages, and references documentary resources relating to state history and culture. The Division is the official state archives, preserving North Dakota government records of enduring value. Its extensive collections also include the state's official newspapers, books, photographs, maps, manuscript collections, and audiovisual materials. The Director of the Division is also the North Dakota State Archivist.

State Historical Society of North Dakota activities are headquartered in the North Dakota Heritage Center and State Museum on the Capitol grounds.

Indian Scholarships, State Board for North Dakota
Phone: 701-328-2964
Fax: 701-328-2979
Web: www.ndus.edu/students/paying-for-college/grants-scholarships/#NDIS
[NDCC 15-63-01]

The Board is comprised of the Executive Director of the North Dakota Indian Affairs Commission as secretary, the Chancellor or Chancellor's designee of the North Dakota University System as chair, and an American Indian appointed by the Governor.

The Board awards scholarships each year for North Dakota residents who are members of federally recognized Indian tribes. The scholarships may be used to attend any North Dakota institution of higher learning or state career and technical education program. The scholarship funding is appropriated through the biennial budget request of the North Dakota University System.

Investment Board, State
Phone: 701-328-9885
Toll Free: 800-952-2970
Fax: 701-328-9897
Email: rio@nd.gov
Web: www.nd.gov/rio
[NDCC 21-10-01]

The State Investment Board consists of the Governor (or designee), State Treasurer, Commissioner of University and School Lands, Director of Workforce Safety & Insurance (or designee), Commissioner of Insurance, three members of the Teachers' Fund for Retirement board, and three members of the Public Employees Retirement System board. One member of the Legacy and Budget Stabilization Fund Advisory Board, as selected by that board, serves as a nonvoting member. The Board appoints an investment director. The State Investment Board serves as the administrative board to the Retirement and Investment Office, an agency of the state of North Dakota.

The Board administers the investment programs for the following funds in accordance with their stated investment goals and objectives: Statutory – State Bonding Fund, State Fire and Tornado Fund, Insurance Regulatory Trust Fund, Petroleum Tank Release Compensation Fund, Public Employees Retirement System Fund, Risk Management Fund, Risk Management Workers Compensation Fund, Teachers' Fund for Retirement, Workforce Safety & Insurance, Budget Stabilization Fund, Cultural Endowment Fund, and the Legacy Fund; and Contractual – City of Bismarck Employees Retirement Fund, City of Bismarck Police Retirement Fund, City of Bismarck Deferred Sick Leave Fund, City of Fargo Fargo Dome Permanent Fund, North Dakota Association of Counties Fund, North Dakota Job Service Retirement Fund, Public Employees Retirement System Group Health Insurance Fund, Public

Employees Retirement System Retiree Health Insurance Fund, City of Grand Forks Pension Fund, City of Grand Forks Park District Pension Fund, North Dakota Board of Medicine, and North Dakota Parks and Recreation.

Judicial Nominating Committee
Phone: 701-255-1404
[NDCC 27-25]

Six members of the Judicial Nominating Committee are appointed for three-year terms as follows: two by the Governor, two by the Chief Justice, and two by the president of the State Bar Association. In each case, one appointee is to be a judge or attorney and the other is to be a citizen who is not a judge, former judge, or attorney. The Committee of six sits to consider nominees for Supreme Court vacancies. For district court vacancies, each appointing authority appoints an additional temporary member from the judicial district with a vacancy to serve on the committee until the vacancy is filled. The Executive Director of the State Bar Association serves as nonvoting Secretary for the Judicial Nominating Committee. The Governor appoints the chairman.

The committee recruits, screens, nominates, and submits to the Governor a list of two to seven nominees for each vacancy in a district court or the Supreme Court. The Governor then may fill the vacancy by appointment from the list, call a special election to fill the vacancy, or return the list of nominees to the committee with directions to reconvene. Any gubernatorial appointment made from the list of nominees submitted by the Committee continues for at least two years and until the next general election immediately following those two years, at which time the office will be filled by election for the remainder of the term.

Milk Marketing Board
410 E. Thayer Avenue
Bismarck, ND 58501
Phone: 701-328-9588
[NDCC 4.1-26]

The Milk Marketing Board consists of five members appointed by the Governor for five-year terms. The Governor appoints one Grade A dairy farmer selling to a processor, one processor, one retailer, and two consumers not engaged in the milk business. The Board meets at the call of the chairman.

The Board promotes the North Dakota dairy industry through the following means. The Board establishes a minimum Grade A dairy farmer hundredweight price and wholesale and retail prices as a result of public hearings. The Board licenses all Grade A dairy farmers, processors, distributors, and retailers in the marketing area. The Board regulates disruptive trade practices.

Natural Resources Trust, Inc.
Phone: 701-223-8501
Fax: 701-223-6937
Email: kathy@naturalresourcestrust.com
Web: www.ndnrt.com
[Garrison Diversion Unit Reformulation Act of 1986 and Dakota Water Resources Act of 2000]

The Trust is dedicated to the preservation, enhancement, restoration, and management of wetlands and associated wildlife habitat, grasslands, and riparian areas in the state of North Dakota. The director of the Game and Fish Department is an ex-officio member. Three members are appointed by the Governor for terms of two years. Three additional members represent the North Dakota Chapter of The Wildlife Society, National Audubon Society, and National Wildlife Federation.

Parole Board, State
Phone: 701-328-6664
Web: www.nd.gov/docr/parole/board.html
[NDCC 12-59-01]

The State Parole Board consists of six members appointed by the Governor for three-year terms: one member must be experienced in law enforcement; one must be a licensed attorney; and four must be qualified by special experience, education, or training. The Board is the sole authority for all parole-related decisions in North Dakota. Department of Corrections and Rehabilitation-Division of Adult Services staff are designated to serve as clerk for the Board and provide all administrative support including docketing, information gathering, and execution of the Board's orders.

Personnel Board, State
Web: https://www.nd.gov/omb/state-employee/employment-and-compensation/state-personnel-board
[NDCC 54-44.3.03]

The State Personnel Board is composed of the Director of the North Dakota Human Resource Management Services Division of the Office of Management and Budget, who serves as chair; two members appointed by the Governor, one who must have a professional human resource background; and two members elected by state employees in classified positions. The Board meets at least once a year, and except for the chair, terms are for six years.

The primary responsibilities of the Board are to review classification and pay grade appeals, promulgate rules, and approve positions not to be included in the classified service.

Protection and Advocacy, Committee on
Phone: 701-328-2950
Toll Free: 800-472-2670
Fax: 701-328-3934
Relay ND: 711TTY
Email: panda@nd.gov
Web: www.ndpanda.org
[NDCC 25-01.3-02]

The Committee on Protection and Advocacy consists of seven members, two of whom are appointed by the Governor and two by the Legislative Management. The Arc of North Dakota, a North Dakota nonprofit advocacy group for people with disabilities, and the Mental Health Association in North Dakota, Inc., each appoint one member. Members appointed by the Governor and the Legislative Management serve two-year terms.

The Committee appoints a director who serves at the will of the Committee. The Committee oversees the North Dakota Protection and Advocacy Project, which provides advocacy and legal services to persons with all types of disabilities so they may realize the rights and services to which they are entitled.

Public Employees Retirement System Board
400 East Broadway, Suite 505
PO Box 1657
Bismarck, ND 58502
Phone: 701-328-3900
Toll Free: 800-803-7377
Fax: 701-328-3920
Email: ndpers-info@nd.gov
Web: https://ndpers.nd.gov/
[NDCC 54-52]

The NDPERS Board of Trustees is the governing authority of the Public Employees Retirement System and consists of nine members. A North Dakota citizen who is neither a state or political subdivision employee is appointed by the Governor to serve as Chairman of the Board. A member of the Attorney General's legal staff and the State Health Officer are also appointed to serve on the Board. One Board member is elected by retired PERS members and the remaining three Board members are elected from active employees currently contributing to PERS. Two members, one member from the majority party and one member from the minority party, are appointed by Legislative Management.

NDPERS manages six defined benefit retirement plans and two defined contribution retirement plans. In addition to the retirement programs, the system administers the group health plan, dental plan, vision plan, employee assistance plan, and life insurance program for public employees. The Board is also responsible for the administration of the state Flex Comp program.

NDPERS investments are under the supervision of the State Investment Board, pursuant to investment policies and asset allocations approved by the Board of Trustees.

Public School Education, State Board of
Phone: 701-328-2283
[NDCC 15.1-01]

The State Board of Public School Education consists of the Superintendent of Public Instruction and one qualified elector from each of six groups of counties that are specified in the governing law. The Superintendent is the Board's Director and Executive Secretary. The six members serve six-year terms. They are appointed by the Governor and come from a list of nominees submitted by a committee made up of the presidents of North Dakota United, North Dakota Council of Educational Leaders, and the North Dakota School Boards Association. Two members must belong to the North Dakota School Boards Association.

Retirement and Investment Office
Phone: 701-328-9885
Toll Free: 800-952-2970
Fax: 701-328-9897
Email: rio@nd.gov
Web: www.nd.gov/rio
[NDCC 54-52.5]

The North Dakota Retirement and Investment Office (RIO) was established in 1989 to coordinate the activities of the State Investment Board (SIB) and the Teachers' Fund for Retirement (TFFR).

The administrative board for the agency is the State Investment Board, which consists of the Governor (or designee), State Treasurer, Commissioner of University and School Lands, Director of Workforce Safety and Insurance (or designee), Commissioner of Insurance, three members of the Teachers' Fund for Retirement board, and three members of the Public Employees Retirement System board. One member of the Legacy and Budget Stabilization Fund Advisory Board, as selected by that board, serves as a nonvoting member. The Board appoints an executive director.

Seed Department, State
Phone: 701-231-5400
Fax: 701-231-5401
Email: ndseed@ndseed.ndsu.edu
Web: www.ndseed.com
[NDCC 4.1-52]

The State Seed Commission is the governing board for the North Dakota State Seed Department. The nine-member group is comprised of members from various industries the Department serves and represents a broad cross-section of agricultural commodities grown in this state and region. Established in 1931 by the state legislature, the Department is the state-designated authority for seed certification and seed regulatory and laboratory testing services to North Dakota producers and the agriculture industry. A self-funded agency of government, it derives its revenues from fees for services provided and receives no general fund revenues from the state of North Dakota.

Headquartered at North Dakota State University in Fargo, it maintains close working relationships with a variety of affiliates in North Dakota and surrounding states, including the North Dakota Crop Improvement Association, North Dakota Certified Seed Potato Growers Association, North Dakota State University Foundation Seedstocks Project, and numerous other public associations and private businesses.

Soil Conservation Committee, State
Phone: 701-328-9715
Fax: 701-328-9721
Email: bruce.schmidt@ndsu.edu
Web: www.ag.ndsu.edu/ndssc
[NDCC 4.1-20-03]

Of the seven members on the State Soil Conservation Committee, two are appointed by the Governor and five are elected by supervisory board members of their soil conservation districts. Committee members serve three-year terms. Representatives from the following agencies serve in an advisory capacity to the committee: State Association of Soil Conservation Districts, North Dakota Extension, Natural Resources Conservation Service, State Water Commission, Agriculture Commissioner, and Game and Fish Department.

The Committee encourages conservation of soil and soil resources. It may offer assistance to supervisors of soil conservation districts in the carrying out of their programs; facilitate exchange of advice and experience between districts; coordinate the programs of several conservation districts; secure the cooperation and assistance of state, federal, regional, and other agencies with conservation districts; and review programs and agreements affecting soil conservation districts. All surface mining operators (other than coal) file an annual detailed report of their activities with the Committee which, in turn, transmits the information to the district.

Teachers' Fund for Retirement
Phone: 701-328-9885
Toll Free: 800-952-2970
Fax: 701-328-9897
Email: rio@nd.gov
Web: www.nd.gov/rio
[NDCC 15-39.1]

The Teachers' Fund for Retirement (TFFR) is a trust fund established to provide retirement income for all public schools and state educators. The Teachers' Fund for Retirement, formerly the Teachers' Insurance and Retirement Fund, dates back to 1913. In 1971, a new law created the Teachers' Fund for Retirement.

Responsibility for the administration of the fund is assigned to a seven-member board of trustees. This board consists of the State Treasurer, the Superintendent of Public Instruction, and five members appointed by the Governor: one full-time school administrator; two full-time classroom teachers; and two retired members of the fund.

The State Investment Board is responsible for the investment of the assets of TFFR. The TFFR program and State Investment program are administered by the Retirement and Investment Office.

Theodore Roosevelt Rough Rider Award
[NDCC 54-02-07]

The Theodore Roosevelt Rough Rider Award is the highest recognition given by the state of North Dakota. It is awarded to present or former North Dakotans who have been influenced by the state in achieving national recognition in their fields of endeavor, thereby reflecting credit and honor upon the state and its citizens. Presented in the name of the Legislative Assembly and the citizens of this state, the award is not for momentary success, but for genuine achievements of lasting significance. The Governor bestows the award upon the concurrence of the Secretary of State and the Director of the State Historical Society.

Upper Great Plains Transportation Institute
Phone: 701-231-7767
Email: info@ugpti.org
Web: www.ugpti.org

The Upper Great Plains Transportation Institute conducts applied and advanced research in highway, transit, rail, air, and waterway transportation that addresses the critical issues of the state, region, and nation. It educates the transportation workforce of tomorrow through multidisciplinary curricula that focus on transportation economics, management, infrastructure planning, mobility, and supply chain logistics.

The Institute also improves the skills and knowledge of the existing workforce through training, technical assistance, and the transfer of research results to practitioners. The Institute is a research and outreach education center at North Dakota State University. It is guided, in part, by an advisory council made up of members designated by North Dakota Century Code who represent various organizations, industries, and agencies affecting or affected by transportation.

Veterans Affairs, Administrative Committee on
Phone: 701-239-7165
Fax: 701-239-7166
Toll Free: 866-634-8387
[NDCC 37-18.1]

Fifteen members with equal representation from the American Legion, Veterans of Foreign Wars, Disabled American Veterans, AMVETS, and the Vietnam Veterans of America are appointed by the Governor for three-year terms to the Committee. Appointments are made from lists of nominees submitted to the Governor by the respective organizations. From the 15, the Governor names a chair and a secretary on an annual basis. Ex-officio committee members include the Adjutant General, Center Director of Veterans Administration, and the Executive Director of Job Service North Dakota. The chairman and secretary, acting jointly, shall appoint: a seven-member governing board for administration of the Veterans Home, from within or outside the Committee, subject to ratification of a majority vote of the Committee; and a subcommittee to be responsible for supervision and government of the Department of Veterans Affairs. Each nominating organization listed in section 37-18.1-01 must have at least one voting member nominated by the organization serving on the subcommittee.

The governing board has the power to establish qualifications for the selection of an administrator (for the Veterans Home) who serves at the pleasure of the governing board. The Committee appoints the commissioner of the Department of Veterans' Affairs who serves at the pleasure of the Committee. The commissioner serves as the executive secretary for the subcommittee.

Veterans Affairs, Department of
Phone: 701-239-7165
Fax: 701-239-7166
Toll Free: 866-634-8387
[NDCC 37-18]

The Department's mission is to ensure that every veteran in the state of North Dakota who has served in the military receives every benefit to which he or she may be entitled from the U.S. Department of Veterans Affairs (VA), allied agencies, and the state of North Dakota. The Department has the responsibility of training and assisting the work of the Tribal Service Officers and County Veterans Service Officers (who service 53 counties), appointed by their respective County Board of Commissioners.

The Department of Veterans Affairs is governed by a subcommittee appointed by the chairman and secretary of the Administrative Committee on Veterans Affairs. The Administrative Committee appoints the Commissioner of Veterans Affairs and sets the salary. The Commissioner serves at the pleasure of the board. The Commissioner also acts as Executive Secretary of the Subcommittee on Veterans Affairs.

Veterans Home
Phone: 701-683-6500
Fax: 701-683-6550
[Constitution, Article IX, Section 13; NDCC 37-15]

In operation since 1893, the North Dakota Veterans Home is located on a 90-acre tract of land adjacent to the Sheyenne River in Lisbon, N.D. The chairman and secretary of the Administrative Committee on Veterans Affairs appoint a Governing Board consisting of seven members to oversee administration of the Home. Day-to-day management is the responsibility of the Administrator, who is hired by the Governing Board.

The Home provides care and service to veterans and their spouses. Services at the Home include activities, housekeeping, dietary, medical care, therapy services, and social services. The North Dakota Veterans Home has an in-house pharmacy that provides services for eligible veterans. The Basic Care Unit has 98 beds and requires that potential residents have total independence with personal care needs, such as bathing, dressing, eating, ambulating (walking), toileting, and transferring. The Skilled Care Unit has 52 beds and requires that a potential resident meet the North Dakota criteria for nursing home placement.

North Dakota Boards and Commissions

A number of boards and commissions exist in North Dakota to regulate or license occupations and professions. Others provide agencies with advice and expertise, plans, and recommendations relating to a broad range of issues. Others coordinate activities and planning among entities in a common area. Some are established under state law, while others are required by federal laws or rules. Most members of state boards and commissions generally serve without compensation.

North Dakota's boards and commissions are coordinated by the Governor's Office. For more information on boards and commissions, and for a listing of current members, call 701-328-2202 or visit the website at www.governor.nd.gov/boards.

A number of boards and commissions are listed in the profiles in this chapter. The name and a contact phone number of others not mentioned elsewhere in this chapter are listed below.

Abstracters' Board of Examiners	701-271-8500
Accountancy, State Board of	701-775-7100
Addiction Counseling Examiners, Board of	701-255-1439
Aging, Committee on	701-328-4613
Agricultural Products Utilization Commission	701-328-5350
Air Pollution Control Advisory Council	701-328-5188
Architecture and Landscape Architecture, State Board of	701-223-3540
Athletic Trainers, North Dakota Board of	701-237-0922
Atmospheric Resource Board, North Dakota	701-328-2788
Audiology and Speech-Language Pathology, Board of Examiners on	701-775-7165
Autism Spectrum Disorder Task Force	701-328-1603
Bank of North Dakota, Advisory Board of Directors to the	701-328-5600
Banking Board, State	701-328-9933
Barber Examiners, Board of	701-837-0826
Beef Commission, North Dakota	701-328-5120
Behavioral Health Planning Commission	701-328-8920
Brain Injury Advisory Council	701-777-5200
Cares, North Dakota	701-333-2012
Children's Behavioral Health Task Force	701-328-8824
Chiropractic Examiners, State Board of	701-213-0476
Clinical Laboratory Practice, North Dakota Board of	701-530-0199
Cosmetology, State Board of	701-224-9800
Counselor Examiners, Board of	701-667-5969
Credit Union Board, State	701-328-9933
Crop Protection Product Harmonization and Registration Board	701-328-2980
Dairy Promotion Commission, North Dakota	701-712-1488
Dental Examiners, State Board of	701-258-8600
Development Fund, Incorporated, Board of Directors for North Dakota	701-328-5334
Developmental Disabilities, State Council on	701-328-4847
Devils Lake Outlet Management Advisory Committee	701-328-4942
Dietetic Practice, Board of	701-838-0218
Drug Use Review Board	701-328-4023
Drugs and Alcohol, Governors Prevention Advisory Council on	701-328-8824

Early Childhood Education Council, North Dakota	701-328-4646
Economic Development Foundation, North Dakota	701-328-5311
Education Factfinding Commission	701-290-0593
Education Standards and Practices Board	701-328-9646
Educational Technology Council, North Dakota	701-451-7407
Electrical Board, State	701-328-9520
Energy Policy Commission (EmPower North Dakota Commission)	701-328-5311
Engineers and Land Surveyors, State Board of Registration for Professional	701-258-0786
Funeral Service, State Board of	701-776-6222
Game and Fish Advisory Board, State	701-328-6305
Gaming Commission, State	701-328-4849
Health Council	701-328-2372
Health Information Technology Advisory Committee	701-328-1991
Hearing Aid Specialists, Board of	701-500-3107
Higher Education Grant Review Committee	701-328-4129
Historical Board, State	701-328-3710
Historical Records Advisory Board, State	701-328-2090
Homelessness, Interagency Council on	701-328-8072
Humanities, North Dakota	701-255-3360
Initiated and Referred Measure Study Commission	710-328-3208
Innovative Education Task Force	701-328-1048
Integrative Health Care, State Board of	218-791-0908
Interagency Coordinating Council	701-328-8936
Intergovernmental Relations, Advisory Commission on	701-258-8988
International Peace Garden, Inc., Board of Directors of the	701-263-4390
Interstate Adult Offender Supervision, North Dakota State Council for	701-328-6616
Interstate Juvenile Supervision, North Dakota Council for	859-721-1062
Interstate Oil and Gas Compact Commission (IOGCC)	701-328-3722
Judicial Conduct Commission	701-328-3925
Juvenile Justice Advisory Group	701-328-7320
Legal Counsel for Indigents, Commission on	701-845-8632
Library Coordinating Council, North Dakota	701-328-4654
Lignite Research Council	701-328-3722
Marriage and Family Therapist Licensure Board, North Dakota	701-400-2696
Massage, North Dakota Board of	701-363-2206
Medical Facility Infrastructure Loan Task Force	701-224-9732
Medical Imaging and Radiation Therapy Board of Examiners, North Dakota	701-425-0861
Medical Marijuana Advisory Committee	701-328-2372
Medicine, State Board of	701-328-6500
Midwest Interstate Passenger Rail Compact Commission	630-810-0210
Midwestern Higher Education Commission	612-626-8288
Military Interstate Children's Compact Commission	701-226-1777
Military Issue in North Dakota, Governor's Task Force (TF MIND)	701-333-2172
National and Community Service, State Commission on	701-328-6048
Military Promotions and Strategic Sustainment (ND COMPASS), North Dakota Commission on	701-665-7644
Nursing Home Administrators, State Board of Examiners for	701-222-4881
Nursing, State Board of	701-328-9777

Occupational Therapy Practice, Board of	701-250-0847
Oil and Gas Research Council	701-328-3722
Oilseed Council, North Dakota	701-328-5107
Olmstead Commission	701-328-2538
Outdoor Heritge Fund Advisory Board, North Dakota	701-328-3722
Optometry, North Dakota State Board of	701-690-7937
Pardon Advisory Board	701-328-6712
Petroleum Tank Release Compensation Advisory Board	701-328-9606
Pharmacy, State Board of	701-328-9535
Physical Therapy, North Dakota Board of	701-352-0125
Plumbing, State Board of	701-328-9977
Podiatric Medicine, North Dakota Board of	701-390-7190
Prison Industries Advisory Committee	701-328-6129
Private Investigative and Security Board	701-222-3063
Psychologist Examiners, State Board of	701-214-5580
Racing Commission, North Dakota	701-328-4633
Real Estate Appraiser Qualifications and Ethics Board, North Dakota	701-222-1051
Real Estate Commission, North Dakota	701-328-9737
Reflexology, North Dakota Board of	701-331-2435
Rehabilitation Council, State	701-328-8926
Renewable Energy Council	701-426-9827
Respiratory Care, State Board of	701-222-1564
Rural Development Council	701-223-0707
Small Business Air Pollution Compliance Advisory Board	701-328-5188
Social Work Examiners, North Dakota Board of	701-222-0255
Soil Classifiers, State Board of Registration for Professional	701-952-9049
State Employees Compensation Commission	701-328-4904
State Information Technology Advisory Committee	701-328-1001
Statewide Independent Living Council	701-328-8926
Statewide Longitudinal Data System Committee	701-328-1000
Status of Women, Commission on	701-327-2372
STOP Violence Against Women Advisory Committee	701-328-3340
Task Force for Higher Education Governance	701-328-2201
Task Force for Veterans Affairs	701-328-2289
Teachers' Fund for Retirement, Board of (TFFR)	701-328-9895
Unemployment Insurance Advisory Council	701-328-2843
Uniform State Laws, Commission on	312-450-6606
Veterinary Medical Examiners, State Board of	701-328-9540
Water Pollution Control Board, State	701-667-2492
Water Well Contractors, State Board of	701-328-3440
Western Interstate Commission for Higher Education	303-541-0200
Wheat Commission, North Dakota State	701-328-5111
Workforce Development Council, North Dakota	701-328-3105
Workforce Safety and Insurance Board	701-328-3856
Workforce Safety and Isurance Coordinating Committee	701-328-2440

✔ See the *1997-1999 North Dakota Blue Book* for a more detailed description of the duties of the Boards, Commissions, Committees, and Councils.

✔ See the *2011-2013 North Dakota Blue Book* for the Guide to North Dakota Statutes on Licensing, Certification, Registration, and Permits.

Chapter Six
Legislative Branch

A J-5 airplane belonging to Capital Aviation taxies along a rural road in the 1940s.

Legislative Branch 332
Members of the 66th Legislative Assembly 334
How a Bill Becomes a Law 386
North Dakota's Revenue Forecasting and Budgeting Process 388
Legislative Documents and Resources 393
Citizen Involvement 395
Legislative Management 396
Legislative Compensation 398
The Role of the Legislature in Achieving Women's Right to Vote 401
The 66th Legislative Assembly 404

Legislative Branch

The Legislative Assembly of the State of North Dakota is the bicameral legislative body established and governed by the Constitution of North Dakota as the Legislative Branch of North Dakota State Government. As the policy making branch for the state, the Legislative Assembly enacts laws and appropriates money for state government operations; conducts oversight on state and local government spending and authority; places proposed constitutional amendments before North Dakota voters; voices opinions on behalf of North Dakota to federal agencies, other states, and interstate organizations; and provides constituent services to assist North Dakotans in their interactions with government entities.

Redistricting

Every 10 years the Legislative Assembly redistricts itself based upon the decennial census. The most recent legislative district boundaries are in effect following a November 2011 special session for redistricting. The Legislative Assembly will undertake the redistricting process again following completion of the 2020 census.

Elections

The Legislative Assembly currently comprises 47 senators and 94 representatives, with one senator and two representatives serving each legislatively apportioned district. Voters in the state elect one-half of each chamber biennially to four-year terms: elections for odd-numbered district seats took place in 2018, and even-numbered district seats will be on the 2020 general election ballot.

Legislator Qualifications

Article IV, Section 5, of the Constitution of North Dakota specifies, "Each person elected to the legislative assembly must be, on the day of the election, a qualified elector in the district from which the member was chosen and must have been a resident of the state for one year immediately prior to that election. An individual may not serve in the legislative assembly unless the individual lives in the district from which selected."

Legislative Sessions

A legislator formally begins service to constituents on December 1 following election. The regular biennial session of the Legislative Assembly commences the first Tuesday after the third day in January, or as prescribed by law, but no later than the 11th day of January. The state constitution limits the session to 80 natural, but not necessarily consecutive, days per biennium and specifies neither chamber may recess or adjourn for more than three days without the consent of the other chamber. Legislators also meet for a three-day organizational session in December of even-numbered years, for committee meetings throughout the biennium, and if necessary, for special sessions called by the Governor or for impeachment proceedings.

Presiding Officers

The President of the Senate and the Speaker of the House are the presiding officers of their respective bodies. The presiding officers conduct legislative floor sessions, issue rulings on procedures, and sign all bills and resolutions passed by the Legislative Assembly. North Dakota's Lieutenant Governor serves as the President of the Senate and may cast a vote if there is a tie vote among senators voting on a procedural or substantive matter. The Senate elects one of its members to be a fully voting President Pro Tempore in times of absence of the President of the Senate. The House of Representatives chooses its Speaker from its membership, and the Speaker votes on all questions before the House.

Chamber Leadership

Majority and minority leaders, assistant majority and minority leaders, caucus chairmen, and committee chairmen and vice chairmen serve as party leadership within the Legislative Assembly. The majority and minority leaders are senior party members who promote their respective party policies and platforms and who influence legislative workflow through decisions about committee membership and leadership, bill assignment and consideration, and legislative procedures. The assistant leaders of each caucus work to unify caucus members for votes on important issues, and the assistant majority leader assists the presiding officer in coordinating floor sessions and states most procedural motions. The caucus chairmen develop party cohesion through formal and informal caucuses at which members discuss positions and strategy and participate in politically oriented social events. Committee chairmen direct committee workflow and appoint conference committees, and their vice chairmen support them in organizing committee activities.

Committees

Committees meet throughout session to receive testimony, to deliberate, and to recommend legislative action. During the regular session of the Legislative Assembly, standing committees make policy and appropriation recommendations to their respective houses, select committees consider special matters such as confirmation of executive nominees, and procedural committees address the Legislative Assembly's working mechanics in terms of committee appointments and room arrangements, journal revisions and corrections, delayed bills, employment, inaugural planning, and rules. Special committees also may convene in extraordinary circumstances, as they did during the regular session of the 66th Legislative Assembly to implement Article XIV of the Constitution of North Dakota, relating to ethics. Conference committees, comprising like committees from the Senate and the House, meet toward the end of legislative sessions to resolve chamber discrepancies on, and to produce final versions of, bills and resolutions. When the Legislative Assembly is not in session, interim committees of the Legislative Management conduct studies as directed by the Legislative Assembly and develop legislation.

Members of the 66th Legislative Assembly - 2019
Convened January 3, 2019; Adjourned April 26, 2019

Senate

Lieutenant Governor Brent Sanford, President
David Hogue (R), President Pro Tempore
Rich Wardner (R), Majority Leader
Joan Heckaman (D), Minority Leader
Shanda Morgan, Secretary

District	Name	County	Post Office
8	Howard C. Anderson, Jr.	Pt. Burleigh, Pt. McLean	Turtle Lake
43	*JoNell A. Bakke	Pt. Grand Forks	Grand Forks
1	Brad Bekkedahl	Pt. Williams	Williston
5	Randy Burckhard	Pt. Ward	Minot
16	David A. Clemens	Pt. Cass	West Fargo
34	Dwight Cook	Pt. Morton	Mandan
41	Kyle Davison	Pt. Cass	Fargo
32	Dick Dever	Pt. Burleigh	Bismarck
26	*Jim Dotzenrod	Pt. Dickey, Pt. Ransom, Pt. Richland, Sargent	Wyndmere
47	Michael Dwyer	Pt. Burleigh	Bismarck
36	Jay Elkin	Pt. Dunn, Pt. Hettinger, Pt. Morton, Pt. Stark	Taylor
28	Robert Erbele	Pt. Burleigh, Pt. Dickey, Emmons, Pt. LaMoure, Logan, McIntosh	Lehr
19	Robert O. Fors	Pt. Grand Forks, Pt. Walsh	Larimore
12	*John Grabinger	Pt. Stutsman	Jamestown
23	*Joan Heckaman	Pt. Benson, Eddy, Griggs, Nelson, Steele	New Rockford
21	*Kathy Hogan	Pt. Cass	Fargo
38	David Hogue	Pt. Ward	Minot
17	Ray Holmberg	Pt. Grand Forks	Grand Forks
4	Jordan Kannianen	Pt. Dunn, Pt. McKenzie, Pt. McLean, Pt. Mercer, Pt. Mountrail, Pt. Ward	Stanley
14	Jerry Klein	Pt. Benson, Kidder, Pierce, Sheridan, Wells	Fessenden
40	Karen K. Krebsbach	Pt. Ward	Minot
42	Curt Kreun	Pt. Grand Forks	Grand Forks
3	Oley Larsen	Pt. Ward	Minot
30	Diane Larson	Pt. Burleigh	Bismarck
22	Gary A. Lee	Pt. Cass	Casselton
13	Judy Lee	Pt. Cass	West Fargo
20	Randy D. Lemm	Pt. Cass, Pt. Grand Forks, Traill	Hillsboro
25	Larry Luick	Pt. Cass, Pt. Richland	Fairmount
9	*Richard Marcellais	Rolette	Belcourt
11	*Tim Mathern	Pt. Cass	Fargo

District	Name	County	Post Office
18	Scott Meyer	Pt. Grand Forks	Grand Forks
10	Janne Myrdal	Cavalier, Pembina, Pt. Walsh	Edinburg
35	*Erin Oban	Pt. Burleigh	Bismarck
15	Dave Oehlke	Ramsey, Towner	Devils Lake
20	Arne Osland	Pt. Cass, Pt. Grand Forks, Traill	Mayville
39	Dale Patten	Adams, Billings, Bowman, Pt. Dunn, Golden Valley, Pt. McKenzie, Slope	Watford City
44	*Merrill Piepkorn	Pt. Cass	Fargo
7	Nicole Poolman	Pt. Burleigh	Bismarck
24	*Larry J. Robinson	Barnes, Pt. Cass, Pt. Ransom	Valley City
46	Jim P. Roers	Pt. Cass	Fargo
27	Kristin Roers	Pt. Cass	Fargo
2	David S. Rust	Burke, Divide, Pt. Mountrail, Pt. Williams	Tioga
31	Donald Schaible	Grant, Pt. Hettinger, Pt. Morton, Sioux	Mott
45	Ronald Sorvaag	Pt. Cass	Fargo
33	Jessica Unruh	Pt. Mercer, Pt. Morton, Oliver	Beulah
6	Shawn Vedaa	Bottineau, McHenry, Renville	Velva
29	Terry M. Wanzek	Foster, Pt. LaMoure, Pt. Stutsman	Jamestown
37	Rich Wardner	Pt. Stark	Dickinson

House

Lawrence R. Klemin (R), Speaker
Chet Pollert (R), Majority Leader
Josh Boschee (D), Minority Leader
Buell J. Reich, Chief Clerk

District	Name	County	Post Office
43	*Mary Adams	Pt. Grand Forks	Grand Forks
2	Bert Anderson	Burke, Divide, Pt. Mountrail, Pt. Williams	Crosby
6	Dick Anderson	Bottineau, McHenry, Renville	Willow City
41	*Pamela Anderson	Pt. Cass	Fargo
27	Thomas Beadle	Pt. Cass	Fargo
7	Rick Becker	Pt. Burleigh	Bismarck
38	Larry Bellew	Pt. Ward	Minot
42	Jake G. Blum	Pt. Grand Forks	Grand Forks
9	*Tracy Boe	Rolette	Mylo
30	Glenn Bosch	Pt. Burleigh	Bismarck
44	*Josh Boschee	Pt. Cass	Fargo
28	Mike Brandenburg	Pt. Burleigh, Pt. Dickey, Emmons, Pt. LaMoure, Logan, McIntosh	Edgeley
27	*Ruth Buffalo	Pt. Cass	Fargo
10	Chuck Damschen	Cavalier, Pembina, Pt. Walsh	Hampden
8	Jeff Delzer	Pt. Burleigh, Pt. McLean	Underwood
23	Bill Devlin	Pt. Benson, Eddy, Griggs, Nelson, Steele	Finley
11	*Gretchen Dobervich	Pt. Cass	Fargo
7	Jason Dockter	Pt. Burleigh	Bismarck

43	*Matt Eidson	Pt. Grand Forks	Grand Forks
26	Sebastian Ertelt	Pt. Dickey, Pt. Ransom, Pt. Richland, Sargent	Lisbon
4	Clayton Fegley	Pt. Dunn, Pt. McKenzie, Pt. McLean, Pt. Mercer, Pt. Mountrail, Pt. Ward	Berthold
5	Jay Fisher	Pt. Ward	Minot
12	Jim Grueneich	Pt. Stutsman	Jamestown
11	*Ron Guggisberg	Pt. Cass	Fargo
21	*LaurieBeth Hager	Pt. Cass	Fargo
44	*Karla Rose Hanson	Pt. Cass	Fargo
1	Patrick Hatlestad	Pt. Williams	Williston
29	Craig Headland	Foster, Pt. LaMoure, Pt. Stutsman	Montpelier
32	Pat D. Heinert	Pt. Burleigh	Bismarck
20	*Richard G. Holman	Pt. Cass, Pt. Grand Forks, Traill	Mayville
3	Jeff A. Hoverson	Pt. Ward	Minot
22	Michael Howe	Pt. Cass	West Fargo
6	Craig Johnson	Bottineau, McHenry, Renville	Maxbass
15	Dennis Johnson	Ramsey, Towner	Devils Lake
45	Mary Johnson	Pt. Cass	Fargo
24	Daniel Johnston	Barnes, Pt. Cass, Pt. Ransom	Kathryn
4	Terry B. Jones	Pt. Dunn, Pt. McKenzie, Pt. McLean, Pt. Mercer, Pt. Mountrail, Pt. Ward	New Town
45	Tom Kading	Pt. Cass	Fargo
35	Karen Karls	Pt. Burleigh	Bismarck
46	Jim Kasper	Pt. Cass	Fargo
47	George Keiser	Pt. Burleigh	Bismarck
39	Keith Kempenich	Adams, Billings, Bowman, Pt. Dunn, Golden Valley, Pt. McKenzie, Slope	Bowman
24	Dwight Kiefert	Barnes, Pt. Cass, Pt. Ransom	Valley City
47	Lawrence R. Klemin	Pt. Burleigh	Bismarck
16	Ben Koppelman	Pt. Cass	West Fargo
13	Kim Koppelman	Pt. Cass	West Fargo
33	Gary Kreidt	Pt. Mercer, Pt. Morton, Oliver	New Salem
8	Vernon Laning	Pt. Burleigh, Pt. McLean	Bismarck
37	Mike Lefor	Pt. Stark	Dickinson
2	Donald W. Longmuir	Burke, Divide, Pt. Mountrail, Pt. Williams	Stanley
5	Scott Louser	Pt. Ward	Minot
28	Jeffery J. Magrum	Pt. Burleigh, Pt. Dickey, Emmons, Pt. LaMoure, Logan, McIntosh	Hazelton
16	Andrew Marschall	Pt. Cass	Fargo
35	Bob Martinson	Pt. Burleigh	Bismarck
20	Aaron McWilliams	Pt. Cass, Pt. Grand Forks, Traill	Hillsboro
32	Lisa Meier	Pt. Burleigh	Bismarck
25	*Alisa Mitskog	Pt. Cass, Pt. Richland	Wahpeton
18	*Corey Mock	Pt. Grand Forks	Grand Forks
10	David Monson	Cavalier, Pembina, Pt. Walsh	Osnabrock
30	Mike Nathe	Pt. Burleigh	Bismarck
14	Jon O. Nelson	Pt. Benson, Kidder, Pierce, Sheridan, Wells	Rugby

9	*Marvin E. Nelson	Rolette	Rolla
42	Emily O'Brien	Pt. Grand Forks	Grand Forks
17	Mark S. Owens	Pt. Grand Forks	Grand Forks
3	Bob Paulson	Pt. Ward	Minot
19	Gary Paur	Pt. Grand Forks, Pt. Walsh	Gilby
29	Chet Pollert	Foster, Pt. LaMoure, Pt. Stutsman	Carrington
34	Todd Porter	Pt. Morton	Mandan
22	Brandy Pyle	Pt. Cass	Casselton
1	David Richter	Pt. Williams	Williston
46	Shannon Roers Jones	Pt. Cass	Fargo
31	Karen M. Rohr	Grant, Pt. Hettinger, Pt. Morton, Sioux	Mandan
38	Dan Ruby	Pt. Ward	Minot
40	Matthew Ruby	Pt. Ward	Minot
17	Mark Sanford	Pt. Grand Forks	Grand Forks
12	Bernie Satrom	Pt. Stutsman	Jamestown
36	Mike Schatz	Pt. Dunn, Pt. Hettinger, Pt. Morton, Pt. Stark	New England
13	Austen Schauer	Pt. Cass	West Fargo
31	Jim Schmidt	Grant, Pt. Hettinger, Pt. Morton, Sioux	Huff
21	*Mary Schneider	Pt. Cass	Fargo
40	Randy A. Schobinger	Pt. Ward	Minot
25	Cynthia Schreiber-Beck	Pt. Cass, Pt. Richland	Wahpeton
36	Luke Simons	Pt. Dunn, Pt. Hettinger, Pt. Morton, Pt. Stark	Dickinson
26	Kathy Skroch	Pt. Dickey, Pt. Ransom, Pt. Richland, Sargent	Lidgerwood
37	Vicky Steiner	Pt. Stark	Dickinson
41	Michelle Strinden	Pt. Cass	Fargo
34	Nathan Toman	Pt. Morton	Mandan
19	Wayne A. Trottier	Pt. Grand Forks, Pt. Walsh	Northwood
33	Bill Tveit	Pt. Mercer, Pt. Morton, Oliver	Hazen
18	Steve Vetter	Pt. Grand Forks	Grand Forks
23	Don Vigesaa	Pt. Benson, Eddy, Griggs, Nelson, Steele	Cooperstown
14	Robin Weisz	Pt. Benson, Kidder, Pierce, Sheridan, Wells	Hurdsfield
15	Greg Westlind	Ramsey, Towner	Cando
39	Denton Zubke	Adams, Billings, Bowman, Pt. Dunn, Golden Valley, Pt. McKenzie, Slope	Watford City

(*) Democrats - All other Republicans

On the following pages, contact information and short biographies for all senators and representatives are listed by legislative district. Maps of North Dakota cities that include multiple legislative districts are included at the end of this section.

DISTRICT #1

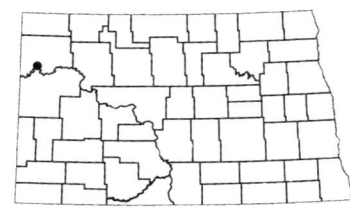

BRAD BEKKEDAHL
418 12th Avenue West, Williston, ND 58801-4730; bbekkedahl@nd.gov; (R) Pt. Williams • Dentist • BA, University of Jamestown; BS, U of M; DDS, U of M School of Dentistry • US Army Reserves, 1996-2002; ND National Guard, 2002-present, Rank: Col. • Williston Park Board, 1988-1996; Williston City Finance Commissioner, since 1996; USA Hockey Director Emeritus • Senate since 2015
APPROPRIATIONS

PATRICK HATLESTAD
P.O. Box 1342, Williston, ND 58802-1342; phatlestad@nd.gov; (R) Pt. Williams • Retired, Part-time Teacher • BA, Western Washington University; MEd. EA, UND • Past President, TriCounty ED Board; Past President, Williston Chamber of Commerce; President, Williston Rotary; Board, USND; Board, Williams County Social Service; Board, Northwest Human Services; TrainND, Instructor; Past President, ND Elks Association; PER Williston Elks; Renaissance Zone Committee; RC&D Board; Marketplace 4 Kids; Shrine; API • Married (Durelle); 2 Children • House since 2007
FINANCE AND TAXATION; POLITICAL SUBDIVISIONS

DAVID RICHTER
2414 22nd Street West, Williston, ND 58801-6500; dwrichter@nd.gov; (R) Pt. Williams • Retired, Education Administration • BA, MSU; MA, Wayne State College • Williston Public School Board; ND State Board of Public Education; ND State Board for Career and Technical Education; Williston Old Armory Board • Married (Debbie); 3 Children • House since 2019
AGRICULTURE; INDUSTRY, BUSINESS AND LABOR

DISTRICT #2

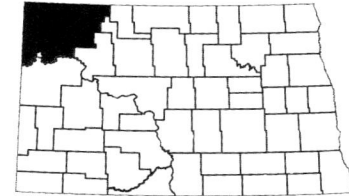

DAVID S. RUST
P.O. Box 1198, Tioga, ND 58852-1198; drust@nd.gov; (R) Burke, Divide, Pt. Mountrail, Pt. Williams • Retired Superintendent, Tioga Public School • BS, VCSU; MA, Bowling Green State University; EDS, NDSU • Past President, Western Dakota Energy Association; Past President, ND Council of Educational Leaders; Past Chairman, Tioga Community Medical Center; Tioga EDC Board; ND Superintendent of the Year, 1996; First Baptist Church of Tioga • Married (Claudia); 4 Children; 9 Grandchildren • House 2009-2014; Senate since 2015
EDUCATION; TRANSPORTATION

BERT ANDERSON
P.O. Box 604, Crosby, ND 58730-0604; bertanderson@nd.gov; (R) Burke, Divide, Pt. Mountrail, Pt. Williams • Business Owner • Lake Region College; Northwest Bible College • Mayor of Crosby; Crosby City Council; Board, St. Luke's Hospital; Crosby Assembly of God • Married (Diane); 2 Children; 4 Grandchildren • House since 2015
APPROPRIATIONS; APPROPRIATIONS - HUMAN RESOURCES DIVISION

DONALD W. LONGMUIR
P.O. Box 1191, Stanley, ND 58784-1191; dlongmuir@nd.gov; (R) Burke, Divide, Pt. Mountrail, Pt. Williams • Retired, Small Business Owner • BS, Business Economics, NDSU • Stanley Public School Board, 21 years; Past President, ND Land Title Assoc.; Past President, ND Planning Assoc.; Lions International Melvin Jones Fellow; ND Emergency Managers Assoc. Achievement Award; Stanley Lions Club; Stanley Boy Scouts Troop Committee; Stanley Boy Scout Trust Committee; Stanley Area Community Foundation; Trinity Health Foundation; Stanley American Lutheran Church • Married (Connie); 2 Children; 7 Grandchildren • House since 2017
EDUCATION; POLITICAL SUBDIVISIONS

DISTRICT #3

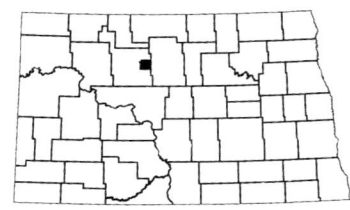

OLEY LARSEN
11051 20th Avenue SE, Minot, ND 58701-2658; olarsen@nd.gov; (R) Pt. Ward • Self Employed, Insurance • Diesel Technology, WSC; BA, Vocational Education, VCSU; MS, Educational Leadership, NDSU • Young Educator of the Year, NDACTE; Teacher of the Year; VFW; EAA Skills-USA; Member, Kluane First Nation • Married (Elizabeth); 2 Children • Senate since 2011
AGRICULTURE; HUMAN SERVICES

JEFF A. HOVERSON
1300 72nd Street SE, Minot, ND 58701-9377; jahoverson@nd.gov; (R) Pt. Ward • Pastor • Masters of Divinity • Married (JoAnn); 6 Children • House since 2019
EDUCATION; GOVERNMENT AND VETERANS AFFAIRS

BOB PAULSON
9801 Highway 52 South, Minot, ND 58701-2426; bpaulson@nd.gov; (R) Pt. Ward • Retired, Navy Pilot; Rancher • BBA, Evangel University • US Navy • Married (Sheryll); 10 Children • House since 2019
JUDICIARY; TRANSPORTATION

DISTRICT #4

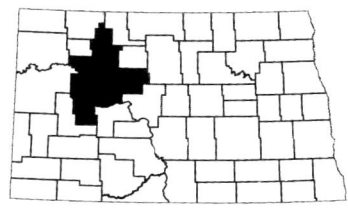

JORDAN KANNIANEN
8011 51st Street NW, Stanley, ND 58784-9562; jkannianen@nd.gov; (R)
Pt. Dunn, Pt. McKenzie, Pt. McLean, Pt. Mercer, Pt. Mountrail, Pt. Ward
• Electrical Contractor • BS, MS, Management, MSU • Director, Sikes Township Board; President, Belden Finnish Cemetery Assoc.; Sunday School Counselor, The Church of Jesus Christ of Latter-day Saints
• Married (Elizabeth); 9 Children • Senate since 2017
FINANCE AND TAXATION; POLITICAL SUBDIVISIONS

CLAYTON FEGLEY
10801 240th Street NW, Berthold, ND 58718-9619; cfegley@nd.gov; (R)
Pt. Dunn, Pt. McKenzie, Pt. McLean, Pt. Mercer, Pt. Mountrail, Pt. Ward
• Farmer; Ambulance Squad Leader • NDSCS • Past, Township Supervisor; Ward Co. Planning & Zoning; Ward Co. Emergency Management; Board, First Western Bank & Trust • Married (Holly); 4 Children; 7 Grandchildren • House since 2018
HUMAN SERVICES; POLITICAL SUBDIVISIONS

TERRY B. JONES
P.O. Box 1964, New Town, ND 58763-1964; tbjones@nd.gov; (R) Pt. Dunn, Pt. McKenzie, Pt. McLean, Pt. Mercer, Pt. Mountrail, Pt. Ward • Farmer, Rancher, Contractor • AS, Business • Married (Kelly); 6 Children • House since 2017
JUDICIARY; TRANSPORTATION

DISTRICT #5

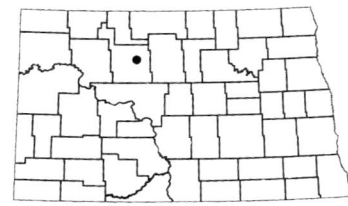

RANDY BURCKHARD
1837 15th Street SW, Minot, ND 58701-6158; raburckhard@nd.gov; (R) Pt. Ward • Retired, SRT Communications Executive • Past President, Minot CVB and MSU Alumni Association; Past Chair, Minot Area Chamber of Commerce; Minot Area Development Corporation; Souris Valley United Way; Task Force 21 Executive Committee; AF Global Strike Command Civic Leaders' Program; MSU Board of Regents; MSU Alumni Golden Award; Rotary Club; Past Member, Minot City Council; Catholic • Married (Pat); 3 Children; 9 Grandchildren • Senate since 2011
INDUSTRY, BUSINESS AND LABOR; POLITICAL SUBDIVISIONS

JAY FISHER
1828 15th Street SW, Minot, ND 58701-6159; jayfisher@nd.gov; (R) Pt. Ward • Agronomist, Fisher Research LLC • BS, MS, NDSU • Past Director, NDSU Central Research Extension Center; Our Lady of Grace Catholic Church • Married (Marlys); 4 Children • House since 2019
AGRICULTURE; FINANCE AND TAXATION

SCOTT LOUSER
400 Fourth Street SW Minot, ND 58701-4315; sclouser@nd.gov; (R) Pt. Ward • Realtor/Owner; NextHome Legendary Properties • BS & MS, MSU • VP, National Association of Realtors, 2012 • Married (Alexa); 3 Children • House since 2011
ETHICS; GOVERNMENT AND VETERANS AFFAIRS; INDUSTRY, BUSINESS AND LABOR

DISTRICT #6

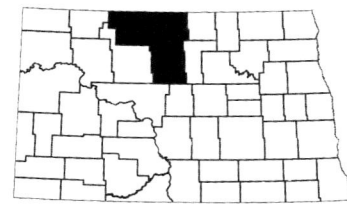

SHAWN VEDAA
P.O. Box 550, Velva, ND 58790-0550; svedaa@nd.gov; (R) Bottineau, McHenry, Renville • Small Business Owner • Attended MSU • ND Army National Guard • Board, ND Grocers Association; Souris Basin Planning Council; Souris Valley Care Center/Valley View Manor; Velva Community Development Corporation; Velva Association of Commerce; Velva Clinic • Married (Geneil); 5 Children • Senate since 2017
GOVERNMENT AND VETERANS AFFAIRS; INDUSTRY, BUSINESS AND LABOR

DICK ANDERSON
1187 77th Street NE, Willow City, ND 58384-9109; dickanderson@nd.gov; (R) Bottineau, McHenry, Renville • Farmer • BA, UND • District Advisor, ND Game and Fish Dept.; Board, Rugby Airport Authority; Board, Rugby Farmers Elevator; Board, North Central Experiment Station; Board, Heart of America Medical Center; Board, All Seasons Water Users; Normal Town Board; Harvest Bowl Award; NDSU McHenry County Extension; McHenry County Conservation Award, 2013 • Married (Susan); 2 Children • House since 2011
ETHICS; ENERGY AND NATURAL RESOURCES; HUMAN SERVICES

CRAIG JOHNSON
8080 17th Avenue NW, Maxbass, ND 58760-9769; craigjohnson@nd.gov; (R) Bottineau, McHenry, Renville • Farmer and Rancher • BS, Agricultural Engineering, NDSU • Clerk/Treasurer, Chatfield Township; Bottineau County Farmers Union; Trinity Lutheran Church • Married (Julia); 2 Children • House since 2017
GOVERNMENT AND VETERANS AFFAIRS; INDUSTRY, BUSINESS AND LABOR

DISTRICT #7

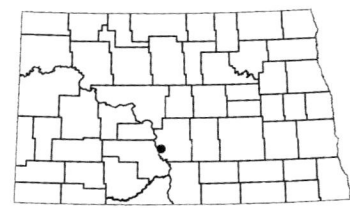

NICOLE POOLMAN
3609 Bogey Drive, Bismarck, ND 58503-9195; npoolman@nd.gov; (R) Pt. Burleigh • English Teacher, Century High School; Small Business Owner • BS, Education, English and Secondary Education, UND • Board, Anne Carlsen Center; Chair, Protection and Advocacy Board; Lottery Commission • Married (Jim); 3 Children • Senate since 2013
APPROPRIATIONS; ETHICS

RICK BECKER
6140 Ponderosa Avenue, Bismarck, ND 58503-9156; rcbecker@nd.gov; (R) Pt. Burleigh • Plastic Surgeon • BS, UND; MD, UND School of Medicine • Married (Anne); 4 Children • House since 2013
ETHICS; JUDICIARY; TRANSPORTATION

JASON DOCKTER
4433 Cumberland Loop, Bismarck, ND 58503-8504; jddockter@nd.gov; (R) Pt. Burleigh • Small Business Owner • BSC; UND • ND Army National Guard • Lions; Faith Lutheran Church • 2 Children • House since 2013
FINANCE AND TAXATION; POLITICAL SUBDIVISIONS

DISTRICT #8

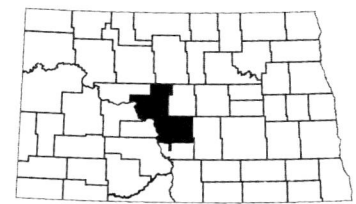

HOWARD C. ANDERSON, JR.
2107 Seventh Street NW, Turtle Lake, ND 58575-9667; hcanderson@nd.gov; (R) Pt. Burleigh, Pt. McLean • Retired Executive Director, ND State Board of Pharmacy; HC Anderson Consulting • Pharmacy, NDSU • Honorary President, NABP; Rotary; Masons; Eagle Scout; State Health Council; ND Pharmacists Association; Lifetime NRA; DU; Methodist Church • Married (Joan); 4 Sons; 9 Grandchildren • Senate since 2013
ETHICS; HUMAN SERVICES; POLITICAL SUBDIVISIONS

JEFF DELZER
2919 Fifth Street NW, Underwood, ND 58576-9603; jdelzer@nd.gov; (R) Pt. Burleigh, Pt. McLean • Farmer • Attended Dawson Community College • House 1991-1992, since 1995
APPROPRIATIONS

VERNON LANING
4121 78th Avenue NE, Bismarck, ND 58503-6396; vrlaning@nd.gov; (R) Pt. Burleigh, Pt. McLean • Retired • BS, Mechanical Engineering, NDSU • US Army Active Duty 1971-1974 • Mayor of Stanton; City Councilman; Park Board; Chairman, Mercer County Planning and Zoning Commission • Married (Rose); 4 Children • House since 2013
GOVERNMENT AND VETERANS AFFAIRS; INDUSTRY, BUSINESS AND LABOR

DISTRICT #9

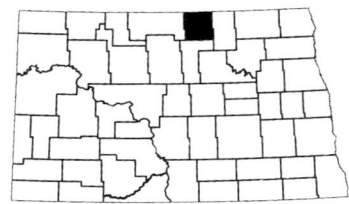

RICHARD MARCELLAIS
301 Laite Loop NE, Belcourt, ND 58316-3877; rmarcellais@nd.gov; (D) Rolette • AAS, Business Administration; Structural Drafting Degree • US Army, Vietnam Veteran • Board, Turtle Mountain Community; President, NISMA; Chairman, Turtle Mountain Band of Chippewa, 2008-2010; Vice Commander, American Legion Central Region; American Legion Post #262; VFW Post 4516; NARFE Chapter #2168; ND Native American Hall of Honor • Married (Betty); 2 Children; 9 Grandchildren • Senate since 2007
EDUCATION; GOVERNMENT AND VETERANS AFFAIRS

TRACY BOE
5125 89th Street, Mylo, ND 58353-9438; tboe@nd.gov; (D) Rolette • Farmer • President, Northern Plains Electric Cooperative; ND Farm Bureau; ND Farmers Union; ND Grain Growers; Our Saviors Lutheran Church • Married (Sandy) • House since 2003
APPROPRIATIONS; APPROPRIATIONS - EDUCATION AND ENVIRONMENT DIVISION

MARVIN E. NELSON
P.O. Box 577, Rolla, ND 58367-0577; menelson@nd.gov; (D) Rolette • Agricultural Consultant • AS, Agriculture, NDSU; BBIF, BS, Entomology, NDSU • ND Farm Bureau; ND Farmers Union; ND Agricultural Consultant's Association; AHEC; ND Stockmen's Association; Church of the Lutheran Brethren in America; Ebenezer Lutheran Brethren Church • Married (Susan); 2 Children • House since 2011
INDUSTRY, BUSINESS AND LABOR; TRANSPORTATION

DISTRICT #10

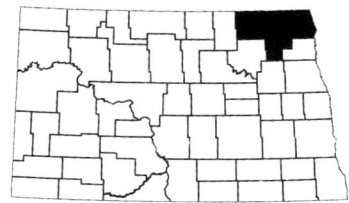

JANNE MYRDAL
P.O. Box 153, Edinburg, ND 58227-0153; jmyrdal@nd.gov; (R) Cavalier, Pembina, Pt. Walsh • Homemaker; Farmer • ND Rural Development Council; Co-chair, President Trump`s Agriculture Advisory Team; Midwest Regional Director, National Foundation for Women`s Legislators; Board, Concerned Women for America; ALEC Rural Caucus; ALEC Energy, AG Taskforce; Member, SARL • Married (Mark); 3 Children • Senate since 2017
AGRICULTURE; JUDICIARY

CHUCK DAMSCHEN
9461 80th Street NE, Hampden, ND 58338-9351; cdamschen@nd.gov; (R) Cavalier, Pembina, Pt. Walsh • Supervisor, Storlie Township • Hampden High School • Board, Cavalier County Water Resource; Member, Pembina County JDA; Ex-officio Director, LAND; Zoar Lutheran Church • Married (Alice); 3 Children • House since 2005
ENERGY AND NATURAL RESOURCES; HUMAN SERVICES

DAVID MONSON
P.O. Box 8, Osnabrock, ND 58269-0008; dmonson@nd.gov; (R) Cavalier, Pembina, Pt. Walsh • Farmer; Retired School Administrator; Retired Insurance Agent/Owner • AA, UND-Williston; BS, UND; MEd, UND • Speaker of the House - 2007-2009; Asst. Majority Leader - 1997-2009; Boards: Pres., Family Mutual Ins. Co.; Pres., Dovre Lutheran Church; North American Industrial Hemp Council; ND Atmospheric Resource Board; NE ND Heritage Assoc.; Past Boards: Prairie Public Broadcasting; Pres., North Central Council of School TV; Pres., Upper Valley Special Education Unit; Pres., Osnabrock School District; Memberships: Past Grand Chancellor, Knights of Pythias - Life Member; Eagles; ND Pulse Growers; Farm Bureau; Northern Canola Growers; NRA - Life Member; National Wildlife Federation - Life Member; Legislator of the Year: ND Township Officers - 2011; ND Career and Technical Education - 2007 • Married (Mary); 3 Sons, 5 Grandchildren • House since 1993
APPROPRIATIONS; APPROPRIATIONS - EDUCATION AND ENVIRONMENT DIVISION

DISTRICT #11

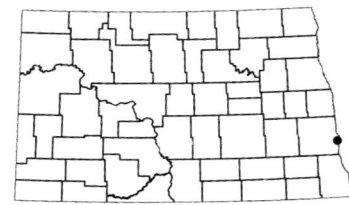

TIM MATHERN
433 16th Avenue South, Fargo, ND 58103-4329; tmathern@nd.gov; (D) Pt. Cass • Director of Public Policy, Prairie St. John's • BA, NDSU; MSW, University of Nebraska; MPA, Harvard University • Advisory Council, UND School of Medicine and Health Sciences; CSG Health and Human Services Committee; Board, Prairie Roots Food Cooperative; YMCA Child Care Committee; Commissioner of ND National and Community Service; Board, Prairie Roots Community Fund; National Association for Behavioral Healthcare Advocacy Award; Council of Educational Leaders Golden Apple Award; Affordable Housing Hero Award; Emergency Management Systems Association Vision Award; Roman Catholic • Married; 4 Children; 9 Grandchildren • Senate since 1987
APPROPRIATIONS; ETHICS

GRETCHEN DOBERVICH
1625 23rd Street South, Fargo, ND 58103-3722; gdobervich@nd.gov; (D) Pt. Cass • Policy Project Manager, American Indian Public Health Resource Center, NDSU • BSW, MSU; Attending NDSU • Dacotah Chapter, Daughters of the American Revolution; American Legion Auxiliary Post 151 Harry W Lindberg; Board, CHI Health and Home; Past Chair, ND Rural Health Association; American Public Health Association; ND Public Health Association; ND Farmers Union; Trustee, Awesome Foundation Cass Clay; Pierce Congregational Church • Married (Eric) • House since 2016
AGRICULTURE; HUMAN SERVICES

RON GUGGISBERG
1621 17th Street South, Fargo, ND 58103-4027; rguggisberg@nd.gov; (D) Pt. Cass • Fire Department Captain • AAS, Liberal Arts, MSCTC; pursuing Economics Degree, NDSU • Certified Firefighter 1&2, EMT-B, Rescue Technician; Past President, Fargo Firefighter's Local 642; Professional Fire Fighters of ND; Governor's 2020 and Beyond Task Force; Senior Executives in State and Local Government Program, Harvard Kennedy School; Bush Foundation Leadership Fellow; BILLD • Married (Gayle); 2 Children • House since 2011
EDUCATION; POLITICAL SUBDIVISIONS

DISTRICT #12

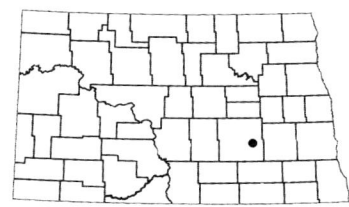

JOHN GRABINGER
1008 Eighth Avenue NE, Jamestown, ND 58401-3507; jgrabinger@nd.gov; (D) Pt. Stutsman • Owner, Grabinger Marine • Jamestown High School • Lifetime/Honorary Member, Jamestown Volunteer Fire Department; Jamestown City Council; Former President, St. John's Academy School Board; St. James Basilica Church • Married (Debra); 1 Child • Senate since 2013
APPROPRIATIONS

JIM GRUENEICH
3051 83 1/2 Avenue SE, Jamestown, ND 58401-9600; jgrueneich@nd.gov; (R) Pt. Stutsman • Business Owner • Alexandria Tech College • US Air Force • Elks; Shriners; Jamestown Clowns • Married (Naomi); 3 Children • House since 2017
FINANCE AND TAXATION; TRANSPORTATION

BERNIE SATROM
P.O. Box 950, Jamestown, ND 58402-0950; blsatrom@nd.gov; (R) Pt. Stutsman • President, Maranatha • BS, Business Finance, Montana State University • Civil Justice Task Force; Criminal Justice Task Force; American Legislative Exchange Council; Salvation Army Advisory Board; Gideons Jail Ministry; Elder, Temple Baptist Church • Married (Dianne); 4 Children • House since 2017
AGRICULTURE; JUDICIARY

DISTRICT #13

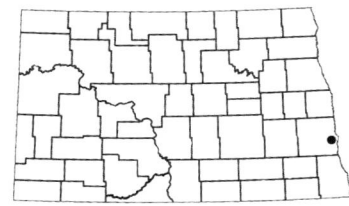

JUDY LEE
1822 Brentwood Court, West Fargo, ND 58078-4204; jlee@nd.gov; (R) Pt. Cass • Retired Real Estate Broker • BS, Medical Technology, UND • Board, UND Masters in Public Health; Board, Vocational Training Center; Board, Eventide; President Pro Tempore, 2007; Board, Comprehensive Health Association of ND; First Lutheran Church • 2 Children; 3 Grandchildren • Senate since 1995
HUMAN SERVICES; POLITICAL SUBDIVISIONS

KIM KOPPELMAN
513 First Avenue NW, West Fargo, ND 58078-1101; kkoppelman@nd.gov; (R) Pt. Cass • President/CEO, Koppelman & Associates, LLC • NDSCS • BILLD Fellow; Toll Fellow; Past National Chairman, Council of State Governments (CSG); Chairman, CSG Suggested State Legislation Committee; Past: City Councilman; Executive Committee, NCSL and CSG; Committee Chair, MLC, CSG Public Safety & Justice Task Force; Co-Chairman, Interstate Compact on Transmission Line Siting; Founder/Chairman, National Interbranch Summit of the States; Founder/Chairman, Interbranch Working Group; R Street Board; ALEC; Chairman, VCLA Board; Church Elder/Chairman; Legislative Awards: NDSAA, SBAND; Stueben Eagle Leadership Award; CSG Champion Award; NDFA Champion Award • Married (Torey); 3 Children • House since 1994
ETHICS; JUDICIARY; POLITICAL SUBDIVISIONS

AUSTEN SCHAUER
110 West Beaton Drive, West Fargo, ND 58078-2657; aschauer@nd.gov; (R) Pt. Cass • Business Development Manager, ProSource Professional Recruiters • AA, DSU; BA, UND • Youth Ministry; Prison Ministry; Salvation Army • Married (Angela); 3 Children; 9 Grandchildren • House since 2019
GOVERNMENT AND VETERANS AFFAIRS; INDUSTRY, BUSINESS AND LABOR

DISTRICT #14

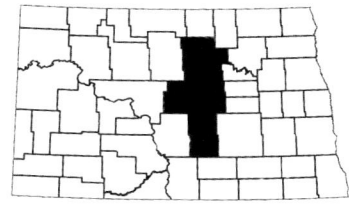

JERRY KLEIN
P.O. Box 265, Fessenden, ND 58438-0265; jklein@nd.gov; (R) Pt. Benson, Kidder, Pierce, Sheridan, Wells • Retired Grocery Store Owner, 35 years • BSC; U of Mary • Assistant Majority Leader, 2013; President Pro Tempore, 2009-2011; Past Board, Carrington Health Center; Member, Harvey Knights of Columbus; President, Fessenden Economic Development; Past Chair, ND Grocers Association; Past President, Civic & Commerce Association; ND Grocer of the Year, 2005; Fessenden Fire Department; Past Jaycees; Past Kiwanis; St. Augustine Catholic Church • Married (Bev); 4 Children; 10 Grandchildren • Senate since 1997
AGRICULTURE; INDUSTRY, BUSINESS AND LABOR

JON O. NELSON
420 Sixth Avenue SE, Rugby, ND 58368-2320; jonelson@nd.gov; (R) Pt. Benson, Kidder, Pierce, Sheridan, Wells • Farmer • Attended MSU & Dakota College at Bottineau • Executive Committee, ND Rural Water Association; ND Farm Bureau; State Public Finance & Education Committee; Board, All Seasons Water Users; Wolford Wildlife Club; Wolford School Board, 12 years; Moving the Marble Award, American Cancer Society; Past Board, Heart of America Hospital; Wolford Lutheran Church Council • Married (Shirley "Sid"); 3 Children • House since 1997
APPROPRIATIONS; APPROPRIATIONS - HUMAN RESOURCES DIVISION

ROBIN WEISZ
2639 First Street SE, Hurdsfield, ND 58451-9029; rweisz@nd.gov; (R) Pt. Benson, Kidder, Pierce, Sheridan, Wells • Farmer, Businessman • Attended UND • Chairman, Lynn Township; BILLD Fellowship, 1999; Legislator of the Year, NDEMSA, 1999, 2011; Legislator of the Year, NDTOA, 2003, 2009; Legislator of the Year, MHA, 2006; Henry Toll Fellow, 2006; Farm Bureau • Married (Lori); 2 Children • House since 1997
HUMAN SERVICES; TRANSPORTATION

DISTRICT #15

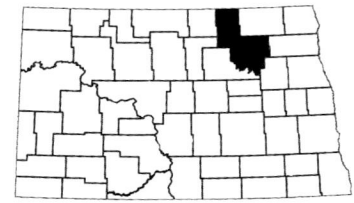

DAVE OEHLKE
125 Woodlea Drive, Devils Lake, ND 58301-8545; doehlke@nd.gov; (R) Ramsey, Towner • Insurance Agent, CIC • BA, Concordia College • Master Graduate of Rapport Leadership Int'l; Lake Region Search & Rescue Team; Elks; Rotary • Married (Vicki); 2 Children • Senate since 2007
APPROPRIATIONS

DENNIS JOHNSON
7871 45th Street NE, Devils Lake, ND 58301-9089; djohnson@nd.gov; (R) Ramsey, Towner • Farmer • Vietnam Veteran; US Navy Seabees • MHEC, Commissioner; Farm Bureau; Farmers Union; ND Stockmen's Association; ND Grain Growers; American Legion; VFW • Married (Donna); 3 Children; 3 Grandchildren • House since 1993
AGRICULTURE; EDUCATION

GREG WESTLIND
205 13th Street, Cando, ND 58324-6613; gwestlind@nd.gov; (R) Ramsey, Towner • Retired Farmer/Businessman • AA, Agriculture Science; BA, Arts, Brooks Institute of Photography, Santa Barbara, CA • National Guard • Cando School Board; Board, Towner County Medical Center, Board, Heartview Foundation • Married (Janet); 2 Children • House since 2016
HUMAN SERVICES; TRANSPORTATION

DISTRICT #16

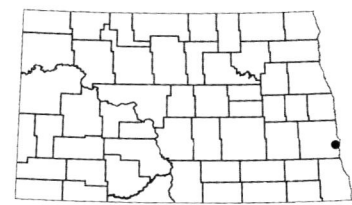

DAVID A. CLEMENS
1682 Oakwood Drive, West Fargo, ND 58078-4315; dclemens@nd.gov; (R) Pt. Cass • Owner, Clemens Transport • BS, Industrial Engineering, NDSU • US Army, Vietnam Veteran • Chairman, Republican Party District 16, 2012-16; VFW; American Legion; NRA • Married (Jody); 4 Children • Senate since 2017
HUMAN SERVICES; TRANSPORTATION

BEN KOPPELMAN
205 36 1/2 Avenue Place East, West Fargo, ND 58078-7931; bkoppelman@nd.gov; (R) Pt. Cass • Building Contractor • Attended NDSU • West Fargo School Board, 2008-2012; School Board President, 2011-2012 • Married (Julie); 2 Children • House since 2013
FINANCE AND TAXATION; GOVERNMENT AND VETERANS AFFAIRS

ANDREW MARSCHALL
4469 Santiago Boulevard South, Fargo, ND 58103-1069; amarschall@nd.gov; (R) Pt. Cass • Small Business Owner, Three Lyons Pub • BS, Occupational Education; MA, Business, Automotive Tech • Air National Guard, 2.5 Years; Air Force; 24.5 Years Total Military Service • DAV; VFW; American Legion; NRA • 1 Child • House since 2017
EDUCATION; ENERGY AND NATURAL RESOURCES

DISTRICT #17

RAY HOLMBERG
621 High Plains Court, Grand Forks, ND 58201-7717; rholmberg@nd.gov; (R) Pt. Grand Forks • Retired School Counselor • Chairman, WICHE; Member, GF Chamber • 2 Children; 5 Grandchildren • Senate since 1977
APPROPRIATIONS

MARK S. OWENS
5865 Fountain Vista Drive, Grand Forks, ND 58201-2820; mowens@nd.gov; (R) Pt. Grand Forks • Associate Vice President, Transportation Services, Iteris Inc. • BS, Troy State; MS, Central Michigan University • USAF Retired • Lifetime Member, Disabled American Veterans and NRA; Vice Chairman, First Liberty Federal Credit Union; Past President, Board, Grand Forks Optimist Club; Grace Baptist Church • Married (Judith); 5 Children; 3 Grandchildren • House 2005-2008, since 2011
EDUCATION; TRANSPORTATION

MARK SANFORD
675 Vineyard Drive, Grand Forks, ND 58201-2904; masanford@nd.gov; (R) Pt. Grand Forks • Retired School Administrator • BS, Math and History, MSU; MEd. EA, UND; Ed.D. School Leadership, UND • Married (Gloria); 2 Children • House since 2011
APPROPRIATIONS; APPROPRIATIONS - EDUCATION AND ENVIRONMENT DIVISION

DISTRICT #18

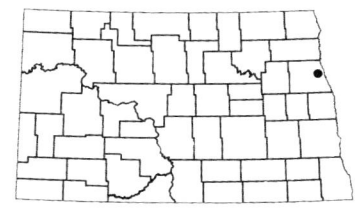

SCOTT MEYER
Grand Forks, ND; scottmeyer@nd.gov; (R) Pt. Grand Forks • Loan Officer, Benchmark Mortgage • BS, Psychology, UND • Sertoma • Senate since 2017
FINANCE AND TAXATION; GOVERNMENT AND VETERANS AFFAIRS

COREY MOCK
P.O. Box 12542, Grand Forks, ND 58208-2542; crmock@nd.gov; (D) Pt. Grand Forks • Business Owner; Business and Leadership Development Consultant • BA, History (Magna Cum Laude), UND • Board, Kennedy Memorial Foundation; Grand Forks/East Grand Forks Chamber of Commerce; Sons of Norway; Rotary International; ND Farmers Union; American Legion Boys State Senior Staff; Former Board of Trustees, Grand Forks Public Library; BILLD Fellow (2011); State Legislative Leadership Foundation, Emerging Leaders Program Fellow (2011); Global Bridges Alumni (2015); Council of State Governments Henry Toll Fellow (2018); Minority Leader, 2015-18; Assistant House Minority Leader, 2013-15 • Married (Jeannie); 2 Children • House since 2009
APPROPRIATIONS; APPROPRIATIONS - GOVERNMENT OPERATIONS DIVISION; ETHICS

STEVE VETTER
804 South 17th Street, Grand Forks, ND 58201-4241; smvetter@nd.gov; (R) Pt. Grand Forks • Real Estate Appraiser • BS, Business Administration, Organizational Leadership, U of Mary • House since 2017
GOVERNMENT AND VETERANS AFFAIRS; JUDICIARY

DISTRICT #19

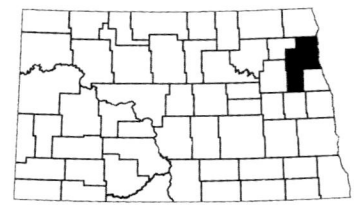

ROBERT O. FORS
P.O. Box 413, Larimore, ND 58251-0413; rfors@nd.gov; (R) Pt. Grand Forks, Pt. Walsh • Retired • NDSCS • Retired, US Air Force • Larimore School Board • Married (Sharon); 2 Children • Senate since 2019
EDUCATION; TRANSPORTATION

GARY PAUR
2710 28th Street NE, Gilby, ND 58235-9706; gpaur@nd.gov; (R) Pt. Grand Forks, Pt. Walsh • Retired, Farmer • UND • Past President, Northarvest Bean Growers Association; Knights of Columbus; Past Chairman, District 19 Republicans; Farm Bureau; St. Timothy's Catholic Church • Married (Ruth); 3 Children • House since 2011
JUDICIARY; TRANSPORTATION

WAYNE A. TROTTIER
115 North Lincoln Street, Northwood, ND 58267-4010; wtrottier@nd.gov; (R) Pt. Grand Forks, Pt. Walsh • Auctioneer • AS, Animal Science, NDSU • US Army • Past Board, North Dakota State Fair; Past Commissioner, City Council; Past Legion Commander • Married (Gladys); 1 Child; 2 Grandchildren • House since 2011
AGRICULTURE; FINANCE AND TAXATION

DISTRICT #20

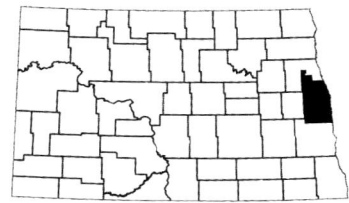

ARNE OSLAND
Mayville, ND; aosland@nd.gov; (R) Pt. Cass, Pt. Grand Forks, Traill
• Retired Farmer/Businessman • BS, Mayville State • Traill County Commissioner; ND Society of CPA; American Institute of CPAs; Goose River Masons; Kem Shriner; ND Farm Bureau; ND Stockmen's Assoc.
• Married (Pat); 4 Children • Senate 2017-2019
AGRICULTURE; JUDICIARY

RANDY D. LEMM
623 166th Avenue SE, Hillsboro, ND 58045-9263; rlemm@nd.gov; (R) Pt. Cass, Pt. Grand Forks, Traill • Senate since 2019
AGRICULTURE; JUDICIARY

RICHARD G. HOLMAN
622 153rd Avenue NE, Mayville, ND 58257-9000; rholman@nd.gov; (D) Pt. Cass, Pt. Grand Forks, Traill • Retired Math Teacher, Farmer, College Professor • BS, Mayville State; MS, Bemidji State; EdD, UND • Board, AHEC; Board, Center for Rural Health RN to BSN Nursing Program; MSU Distinguished Alumni and Professor Emeritus; Hillsboro; Kiwanis; Goose River Masonic Lodge; Gran Lutheran Church • Married (Marilyn); 3 Children • House since 2009
APPROPRIATIONS; APPROPRIATIONS - HUMAN RESOURCES DIVISION

AARON MCWILLIAMS
16148 First Street SE, Hillsboro, ND 58045-9169; amcwilliams@nd.gov; (R) Pt. Cass, Pt. Grand Forks, Traill • Business Owner • Married (Sara); 1 Child • House since 2017
AGRICULTURE; JUDICIARY

DISTRICT #21

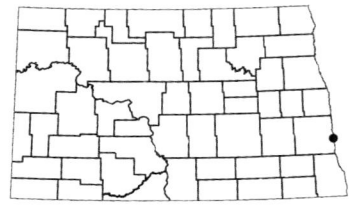

KATHY HOGAN
710 South University Drive, Fargo, ND 58103-2632; khogan@nd.gov;
(D) Pt. Cass • Retired • BS, Jamestown College; MS, NDSU • ASSITIV,
Presentation Associates; St Anthony of Padua • Married (Dennis);
2 Children • House 2009-2018; Senate since 2019
AGRICULTURE; HUMAN SERVICES

LAURIEBETH HAGER
920 Ninth Street South, Fargo, ND 58103-3146; lbhager@nd.gov; (D) Pt.
Cass • Former College Student Affairs Counselor/Administrator
• BS, Psychology, Honors Program, UND; MS, Ed Counselor Education,
NDSU • Married (Pete); 1 Child • House since 2019
EDUCATION; TRANSPORTATION

MARY SCHNEIDER
1011 Eighth Street South, Fargo, ND 58103-2725; mschneider@nd.gov;
(D) Pt. Cass • Attorney • NUI Galway; Emory University School of
Law; UND School of Law; BS, Sociology, NDSU • Bush Foundation
Fellow, 2004-2005; MN State Assembly Delegate; President, County Bar
Association; National ABA Delegate; YWCA Lifetime Achievement
Award; Champion of Justice Award; Human Rights Award; Soroptimists
International • Married (Mark); 2 Children • House since 2015
GOVERNMENT AND VETERANS AFFAIRS; HUMAN SERVICES

DISTRICT #22

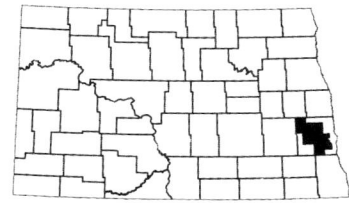

GARY A. LEE
P.O. Box 3, Casselton, ND 58012-0003; galee@nd.gov; (R) Pt. Cass
• Retired • BA, NDSU • Vietnam Veteran • President Pro Tempore,
2017; Casselton City Council; Central Cass School Board; Past Director,
Cass Rural Water Users; EFC Church • Married (Joan); 2 Children; 5
Grandchildren • Senate since 2001
APPROPRIATIONS

MICHAEL HOWE
1011 Westport Parkway, West Fargo, ND 58078-8291; mchowe@nd.gov;
(R) Pt. Cass • Farmer/Business Owner • BS, NDSU • ND Grain Growers;
ND Corn Growers; ND Farm Bureau • House since 2017
APPROPRIATIONS; APPROPRIATIONS - GOVERNMENT
OPERATIONS DIVISION

BRANDY PYLE
P.O. Box 337, Casselton, ND 58012-0337; bpyle@nd.gov; (R) Pt. Cass
• Self Employed • Carlson School of Management, University of
Minnesota • MN Army National Guard • Cass County Park Board;
RLND Class VII; Casselton Business Association; Global Bridges Fellow;
CSG BILLD Fellow; Westminster Presbyterian Church • Married
(Nicholas); 4 Children • House since 2017
EDUCATION; POLITICAL SUBDIVISIONS

DISTRICT #23

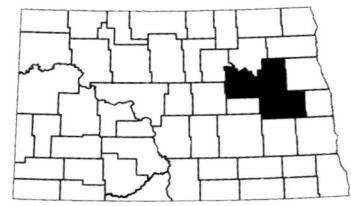

JOAN HECKAMAN
322 Second Avenue North, New Rockford, ND 58356-1712; jheckaman@nd.gov; (D) Pt. Benson, Eddy, Griggs, Nelson, Steele • Retired Teacher • BS, Ed, VCSU; MS, Special Education, MSU • Governor's Autism Task Force; Legislative Procedures and Arrangements; Eastern Star; New Rockford Book Club; Eagles Auxiliary; First Lutheran Church • Married (Dewey); 4 Children; 10 Grandchildren • Senate since 2007

BILL DEVLIN
P.O. Box 505, Finley, ND 58230-0505; bdevlin@nd.gov; (R) Pt. Benson, Eddy, Griggs, Nelson, Steele • Former Newspaper Publisher • Attended Mayville State College • Director, Nodak Insurance Company; Past County Commissioner; Past President, ND Newspaper Association; Member, North Dakota Newspaper Association Hall of Fame; Distinguished Service Award, ND Long Term Care Association; 2017 Outstanding Rural Health Legislator of the Year; BILLD Fellow, CSG Midwest; Speaker of the House, 2013 Session • Married (Margie); 2 Children; 5 Grandchildren • House 1997-2006, since 2011
ENERGY AND NATURAL RESOURCES; HUMAN SERVICES

DON VIGESAA
P.O. Box 763, Cooperstown, ND 58425-0763; dwvigesaa@nd.gov; (R) Pt. Benson, Eddy, Griggs, Nelson, Steele • Auto Dealer • BS, Business Economics, NDSU • Farm Bureau; Elder, Zion Lutheran Church • Married (Cheryl); 3 Children; 8 Grandchildren • House since 2003
APPROPRIATIONS; APPROPRIATIONS - GOVERNMENT OPERATIONS DIVISION

DISTRICT #24

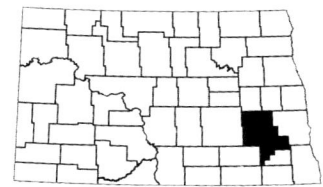

LARRY J. ROBINSON
3584 Sheyenne Circle, Valley City, ND 58072-9545; lrobinson@nd.gov; (D) Barnes, Pt. Cass, Pt. Ransom • Executive Director, University Advancement, VCSU • BS, VCSU; MS, NDSU • Past President, Valley City Area Chamber of Commerce; Barnes County Wildlife Federation; Valley City Area Chamber of Commerce; Governor's Alcohol & Drug Prevention Advisory Task Force; Legislative Council, 1991-2014; Member, VCSU-V-500; Century Club Scholarship; Organizations: Elks; Eagles; Knights of Columbus; Kiwanis; St. Catherine's Catholic Church • Married (Mary Lee); 2 Children; 3 Grandchildren • Senate since 1989
APPROPRIATIONS

DANIEL JOHNSTON
5807 Valley Road, Kathryn, ND 58049-9308; dljohnston@nd.gov; (R) Barnes, Pt. Cass, Pt. Ransom • Self Employed • BA, Interdisciplinary Studies, Accounting/Religion; MA, Public Policy-Public Administration • Army • VFW Post #2764; DAV Post #24; NRA; Eagles Post #2192; ND Farm Bureau Legion • Married (Wendi); 8 Children • House since 2017
EDUCATION; GOVERNMENT AND VETERANS AFFAIRS

DWIGHT KIEFERT
3721 115th Avenue SE, Valley City, ND 58072-9312; dhkiefert@nd.gov; (R) Barnes, Pt. Cass, Pt. Ransom • Farmer, Contractor • Valley City High School • Married (Robbin); 3 Children • House since 2013
AGRICULTURE; HUMAN SERVICES

DISTRICT #25

LARRY LUICK
17945 101st Street SE, Fairmount, ND 58030-9522; lluick@nd.gov; (R) Pt. Cass, Pt. Richland • Farmer, Excavation Contractor • AAS, Diesel Mechanic, NDSCS • Board, Red River Human Services; NCSL Ag Task Force; NCSL Natural Resources Committee; Past President, Fairmount Public School Board; Past Director, OCIA; Past Member, OCIA Internal Review Committee; Past Director, SE Education Cooperative; Vice-chair, Agriculture Interim Committee, 2014; Water Topics Interim Committee, 2014; ND Representative, US Ag Summit, 2012-2015; International Legislative Forum, Steering Committee Director; Red River Basin Commission; SARL; NDSU Rural Leadership Program • Married (Yolanda); 5 Children • Senate since 2011
AGRICULTURE; JUDICIARY

ALISA MITSKOG
1504 Oakwood Avenue, Wahpeton, ND 58075-3553; amitskog@nd.gov; (D) Pt. Cass, Pt. Richland • Chiropractor • NDSCS; UND; Logan College of Chiropractic • Board, BreckenridgeWahpeton Community Foundation; SE Senior Services/Wahpeton, Senior Center Board; Red River Human Services Foundation; Past President, Wahpeton City Council • Married (Allen); 3 Children • House since 2015
ENERGY AND NATURAL RESOURCES; ETHICS; FINANCE AND TAXATION

CYNTHIA SCHREIBER-BECK
1251 Pegasus Road, Wahpeton, ND 58075-4868; cschreiberbeck@nd.gov; (R) Pt. Cass, Pt. Richland • Business Owner • BS, Speech Language Pathology • ND Aeronautics Commission; American College of Norway Foundation, USA; Executive Director, ND Agricultural Aviation Association • 1 Child • House since 2015
AGRICULTURE; EDUCATION

DISTRICT #26

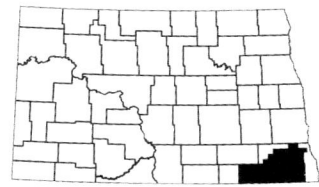

JIM DOTZENROD
P.O. Box 69, Wyndmere, ND 58081-0069; jdotzenrod@nd.gov; (D) Pt. Dickey, Pt. Ransom, Pt. Richland, Sargent • Farmer • BS, Engineering, NDSU • Air Force; ND Air National Guard • American Legion; 2018 Candidate, ND Agriculture Commissioner; Wyndmere Lutheran Church • 2 Children • Senate 1978-1994, since 2009
FINANCE AND TAXATION; POLITICAL SUBDIVISIONS

SEBASTIAN ERTELT
906 Ash Street, Lisbon, ND 58054-4316; sertelt@nd.gov; (R) Pt. Dickey, Pt. Ransom, Pt. Richland, Sargent • Quality Engineer • MBA, Management, U of Mary; BS, Mechanical Engineering, NDSU • House since 2017
FINANCE AND TAXATION; POLITICAL SUBDIVISIONS

KATHY SKROCH
10105 155th Avenue SE, Lidgerwood, ND 58053-9761; kskroch@nd.gov; (R) Pt. Dickey, Pt. Ransom, Pt. Richland, Sargent • Farmer/Rancher; Restorative Nurse/CNA; School Bus Route/Activity Driver; Co-Manager/Owner, Vinnie's Mud Bog, LLC • CNA Certification, Moorhead Technical College • Lidgerwood Public School Board; Board President, Lidgerwood Ambulance; ND Long Term Care Assoc. Certificate of Recognition; Nominated, CNA of the Year 2016; American Legion Auxiliary • Married (Michael); 7 Children • House since 2017
AGRICULTURE; HUMAN SERVICES

DISTRICT #27

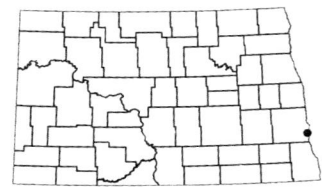

KRISTIN ROERS
4240 31st Avenue South, Fargo, ND 58104-8725; kroers@nd.gov; (R) Pt. Cass • Nursing Practice Specialist • BS, Business Economics, SDSU; BS, Nursing, SDSU; MS, Nursing and Healthcare Systems Administration, U of Minnesota • Senate since 2019
GOVERNMENT AND VETERANS AFFAIRS; HUMAN SERVICES

THOMAS BEADLE
4266 Russet Avenue South, Fargo, ND 58104-8429; tbeadle@nd.gov; (R) Pt. Cass • Business Development Manager, Super Studio; Commercial Broker, KW Commercial Real Estate • BA, Business Economics, Concordia College • Board, ND Autism Center; State Debate Coach of the Year, NDHSAA, 2009 • Married (Shana) • House since 2011
APPROPRIATIONS; APPROPRIATIONS - GOVERNMENT OPERATIONS DIVISION

RUTH BUFFALO
P.O. Box 9763, Fargo, ND 58106-9763; rbuffalo@nd.gov; (D) Pt. Cass • Independent Consultant, Small Business Owner • BA, Criminal Justice; MA, Management; MBA, Business Administration; MPH, Public Health • Fargo Native American Commission (2016-18); National Native American Boarding Healing Coalition; National Center for American Indian Enterprise Development (2016) "40 under 40" • Married (Brian); 4 Children • House since 2019
AGRICULTURE; JUDICIARY

DISTRICT #28

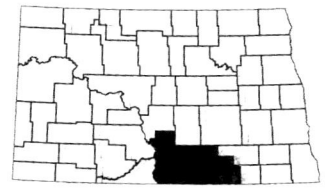

ROBERT ERBELE
6512 51st Avenue SE, Lehr, ND 58460-9149; rerbele@nd.gov; (R) Pt. Burleigh, Pt. Dickey, Emmons, Pt. LaMoure, Logan, McIntosh • Rancher • University Studies, Ag Econ, Animal Science and Music, NDSU • ND Stockmen's Association; President, Prairie Bible Camp (Lehr); WICHE Veterinary Advisory Council; UND Medical Advisory Board; Lay Leader, United Methodist Church • Married (Susan); 4 Children • Senate since 2001
APPROPRIATIONS

MIKE BRANDENBURG
8044 County Road 34, Edgeley, ND 58433-9761; mbrandenburg@nd.gov; (R) Pt. Burleigh, Pt. Dickey, Emmons, Pt. LaMoure, Logan, McIntosh • Farmer • Edgeley High School • ND National Guard • Trump Ag Advisory Group; Nora Township Supervisor; Board, ND Chemical Harmonization; Board, Dakota Prairie Ag; Board, LaMoure County Farm Bureau; Farmers Union; Lions Club; Zion Lutheran Church Council • Married (Lovice); 6 Children; 15 Grandchildren • House 1997-2002, since 2005
APPROPRIATIONS; APPROPRIATIONS - GOVERNMENT OPERATIONS DIVISION

JEFFREY J. MAGRUM
P.O. Box 467, Hazelton, ND 58544-0467; jmagrum@nd.gov; (R) Pt. Burleigh, Pt. Dickey, Emmons, Pt. LaMoure, Logan, McIntosh • Self Employed, Businessman, Rancher • Environmental Systems, NDSSS • Licensed Master Plumber; Licensed Water Well Contractor; ND Class A Contractor; Beaver Valley Horse Club; Voices for Lake Oahe; Past Mayor, City of Hazelton; Past, Emmons County Commissioner; Past Board, Emmons County Social Service • Married (Donna); 2 Children • House since 2017
JUDICIARY; POLITICAL SUBDIVISIONS

DISTRICT #29

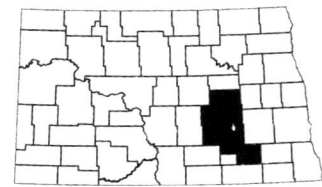

TERRY M. WANZEK
900 Seventh Avenue SW, Jamestown, ND 58401-4542; tmwanzek@nd.gov; (R) Foster, Pt. LaMoure, Pt. Stutsman • Farmer; Rancher; Businessman • Cum Laude BA, Jamestown College; Texas A&M TEPAP Graduate • Board, Global Farmers Network; Board, Nodak Insurance Co.; Board, Jamestown Regional Medical Center; Community Leadership Award, GNDC; Kernel Award, NDGGA; Past President, ND Grain Growers; Knights of Columbus; Farm Bureau; NAWG; Basilica of St. James Catholic Church • Married (Janice); 3 Children; 4 Grandchildren • House 1993-94; Senate 1995-2002, since 2007
APPROPRIATIONS

CRAIG HEADLAND
4950 92nd Avenue SE, Montpelier, ND 58472-9630; cheadland@nd.gov; (R) Foster, Pt. LaMoure, Pt. Stutsman • Farmer • Attended MSU Moorhead and NDSU • Elks Club; El Zagal Shriners; Montpelier Lutheran Church • Married (Dawn); 1 Child • House since 2003
AGRICULTURE; ETHICS; FINANCE AND TAXATION

CHET POLLERT
151 Crossroads Estates Drive, Carrington, ND 58421-8919; cpollert@nd.gov; (R) Foster, Pt. LaMoure, Pt. Stutsman • Owner/Operator of G & R Grain and Feed, New Rockford • Trinity Lutheran Church • Married (Jo) • House since 1999

DISTRICT #30

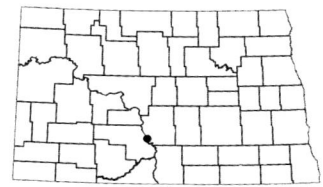

DIANE LARSON
2525 Larson Road, Bismarck, ND 58504-8926; dklarson@nd.gov; (R) Pt. Burleigh • Retired, Youth Worker, Bismarck Police Department • AA, BSC; BS, Education, UND • National Conference of State Legislatures: Co-chair, Law, Criminal Justice and Public Safety Committee; Ex Officio Member, ND State Council for Interstate Juvenile Supervision; Interstate Commission on Juveniles; Supreme Court's Judiciary Standards Committee; Governor's Juvenile Justice Advisory Group • Married (Greg); 2 Children; 4 Grandchildren • House 1989-90, 2013-16; Senate since 2017
JUDICIARY; POLITICAL SUBDIVISIONS

GLENN BOSCH
4117 Downing Street, Bismarck, ND 58504-8848; gdbosch@nd.gov; (R) Pt. Burleigh • Retired, Executive VP, AVI Systems; Co-Owner, Bismarck Larks Baseball Club • AAS, Electronic Technology, BSC • Trustee, BSC Foundation; Corpus Christi Catholic Church • Married (Julie); 2 Children • House since 2017
ENERGY AND NATURAL RESOURCES; INDUSTRY, BUSINESS AND LABOR

MIKE NATHE
3723 Lockport Street, Bismarck, ND 58503-5537; mrnathe@nd.gov; (R) Pt. Burleigh • Owner, Bismarck Funeral Home • BS, Mortuary Science, U of M • Kiwanis; NRA; NFIB; CANA; BILLD; DMORT • Married (Karen); 3 Children • House since 2009
APPROPRIATIONS; APPROPRIATIONS - EDUCATION AND ENVIRONMENT DIVISION

DISTRICT #31

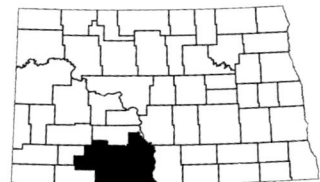

DONALD SCHAIBLE
9115 Highway 21, Mott, ND 58646-9200; dgschaible@nd.gov; (R) Grant, Pt. Hettinger, Pt. Morton, Sioux • Farmer • AS, Agriculture, NDSU • Past President, Mott/Regent School Board; EMT-1, Mott Ambulance Service; FFI, Mott Volunteer Fire Brigade; Trustee for Zoar Congregational Church • Married (Carmen); 4 Children • Senate since 2011
EDUCATION; ENERGY AND NATURAL RESOURCES

KAREN M. ROHR
1704 Fourth Street NE, Mandan, ND 58554-3814; kmrohr@nd.gov; (R) Grant, Pt. Hettinger, Pt. Morton, Sioux • Bioethics and Faculty Formation Director • PhD, Nursing Research; MSN, Nursing Administration & Board Certified Nurse Practitioner • 3 Children • House since 2011
ETHICS; GOVERNMENT AND VETERANS AFFAIRS; HUMAN SERVICES

JIM SCHMIDT
5165 Highway 1806, Huff, ND 58554-8721; jeschmidt@nd.gov; (R) Grant, Pt. Hettinger, Pt. Morton, Sioux • Retired, USDA; Farmer; Small Business Owner • BS, Utah State University • Morton County Water Resource Board; Board, Missouri West Water Systems; Board, Morton County Soils Committee; Member, Jacobson Memorial Hospital Foundation • 2 Children • House since 2011
APPROPRIATIONS; APPROPRIATIONS - EDUCATION AND ENVIRONMENT DIVISION

DISTRICT #32

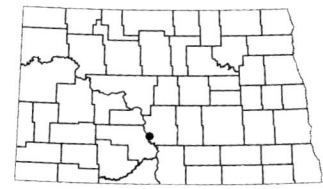

DICK DEVER
1416 Eastwood Street, Bismarck, ND 58504-6226; ddever@nd.gov; (R)
Pt. Burleigh • Self Employed; DEVCO; Manufacturers Representative
• UND • US Army • PERS Board; Chair, Legislative Veteran`s Caucus;
BILLD Fellow; 2004 ND Small Business Champion of the Year, NFIB;
Life Member, VFW & AmVets; Bis-Man Chamber; Legislator of the Year,
MHA, 2007; Elder, Shepherd of the Valley Lutheran Church • Married
(Pam); 3 Children; 12 Grandchildren • Senate since 2001
APPROPRIATIONS; ETHICS

PAT D. HEINERT
1501 Eastwood Street, Bismarck, ND 58504-6230; pdheinert@nd.gov; (R)
Pt. Burleigh • Retired Sheriff, Burleigh County • BA, Management, MA,
Management, U of Mary • Knights of Columbus; Elks • Married (Lynn);
2 Children • House since 2017
EDUCATION; ENERGY AND NATURAL RESOURCES; ETHICS

LISA MEIER
1713 South Third Street, Bismarck, ND 58504-7114; lmeier@nd.gov; (R)
Pt. Burleigh • Sales and Interior Designer • AS, BSC • Board, KNDR
Radio; District Commissioner, Boy Scouts; Board, Pride Industries;
Delegate, American Council of Young Political Leaders, South Korea,
2001; Delegate, Asian Summit in Tokyo, Japan, 2006; Participant,
Government of Canada's Rising State Leader Program, 2007; Board, ND
State Commission of National and State Community Service • Married
(Dennis); 1 Son; 3 Stepsons; 6 Grandchildren • House since 2001
APPROPRIATIONS; APPROPRIATIONS - HUMAN RESOURCES
DIVISION

DISTRICT #33

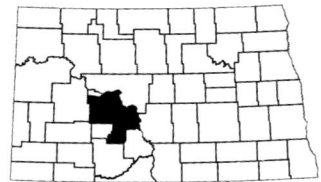

JESSICA UNRUH
1224 First Avenue NE, Beulah, ND 58523-6301; jkunruh@nd.gov; (R) Pt. Mercer, Pt. Morton, Oliver • Environmental Manager, Coyote Creek Mining Company • BS, Natural Resources Management, Economics, NDSU • Member, Energy Council since 2013; Mercer County Economic Development Board; Beulah Wellness Center Foundation; State Council for Interstate Adult Offender Supervision • Single; 2 Children • Senate since 2013
ENERGY AND NATURAL RESOURCES; ETHICS; FINANCE AND TAXATION

GARY KREIDT
3892 County Road 86, New Salem, ND 58563-9406; gkreidt@nd.gov; (R) Pt. Mercer, Pt. Morton, Oliver • Nursing Home Administrator; Farmer • Past President, West River Transportation; Past President, New Salem School Board; Past President, NDLTCA; Past Secretary/Treasurer, New Salem Development Corporation; Past Region VI Vice President, American Healthcare Association; Elks; Peace Church New Salem • Widower (Judy); 5 Children; 10 Grandchildren; 6 Greatgrandchildren • House since 2003
APPROPRIATIONS; APPROPRIATIONS - HUMAN RESOURCES DIVISION

BILL TVEIT
610A Hazen Bay Road, Hazen, ND 58545-9483; btveit@nd.gov; (R) Pt. Mercer, Pt. Morton, Oliver • Retired, Farm Equipment Owner/Dealer • NDSCS • US Army 1968-71 • Past Chair, Mercer County Commissioner; Past Chair, Dakota Central Social Services; Past President, ND John Deere Dealer Group; 65th Session, Senate Deputy Sergeant at Arms; Interdenominational Riverdale Community Church • Married (Laurel); 3 Children; 10 Grandchildren • House since 2019
AGRICULTURE; HUMAN SERVICES

DISTRICT #34

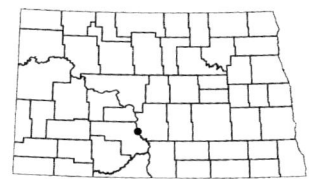

DWIGHT COOK
1408 17th Street SE, Mandan, ND 58554-4895; dcook@nd.gov; (R) Pt. Morton • Retired Small Business Owner • Chair, Morton County Housing Authority; Kiwanis; American Legion; Lutheran • Married (Shirley); 3 Children; 8 Grandchildren • Senate since 1997
ENERGY AND NATURAL RESOURCES; FINANCE AND TAXATION

TODD PORTER
4604 Borden Harbor Drive SE, Mandan, ND 58554-7961; tkporter@nd.gov; (R) Pt. Morton • Owner/Paramedic, Metro-Area Ambulance Service Inc. • Century College (Paramedic Program) • Chair, Bismarck/Burleigh County 911 Center; Elks; Pheasants Forever; Rocky Mountain Elk Foundation; Bismarck/Mandan Chamber of Commerce; Bismarck/Mandan Development Association; Greater North Dakota Chamber • Married (Shirley); 2 Children • House since 1999
ENERGY AND NATURAL RESOURCES; HUMAN SERVICES

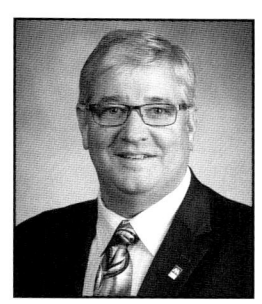

NATHAN TOMAN
203 Fourth Avenue NW, Mandan, ND 58554-3135; nptoman@nd.gov; (R) Pt. Morton • Information Systems, Ducks Unlimited Inc. • AA, BSC • Married (Jessica); 5 Children • House since 2013
FINANCE AND TAXATION; POLITICAL SUBDIVISIONS

DISTRICT #35

ERIN OBAN
1319 Apache Street, Bismarck, ND 58501-2632; eoban@nd.gov; (D) Pt. Burleigh • District Manager, Junior Achievement • BS, Mathematics Education, U of Mary • Co-chair, ND Sportsmen's Caucus; 2015 BILLD Fellow; Governing Institute Women in Government Class of 2015; '40 under 40,' Bismarck Tribune, 2014; Board, Designer Genes and YouthWorks; Good Shepherd Lutheran Church • Married (Chad); 1 Son • Senate since 2015
EDUCATION; ETHICS; GOVERNMENT AND VETERANS AFFAIRS

KAREN KARLS
2112 Senate Drive, Bismarck, ND 58501-1978; kkarls@nd.gov; (R) Pt. Burleigh • Retired • BS, Medical Technology, MSU • Board Secretary, Bis-Man Rifle & Pistol Association; NRA; Chair, District 35 Republicans, 22 years; ND Council on Educational Opportunity for Military Children; Protection & Advocacy; Board, Volunteer Caregivers for the Elderly; Cathedral of the Holy Spirit • Married (Ken); 4 Children • House since 2007
GOVERNMENT AND VETERANS AFFAIRS; JUDICIARY

BOB MARTINSON
2749 Pacific Avenue, Bismarck, ND 58501-2513; bmartinson@nd.gov; (R) Pt. Burleigh • Independent Landman • BSC; BS, U of Mary • Retired NDARNG, Lt. Col. • Majority Leader, 1993-95; ND Tourism Director, 1997-2000; American Legion; AMVETS; Elks; Moose; Eagles • Married (Jodi) • House 1973-97, since 2001
APPROPRIATIONS; APPROPRIATIONS - EDUCATION AND ENVIRONMENT DIVISION

DISTRICT #36

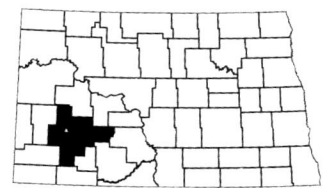

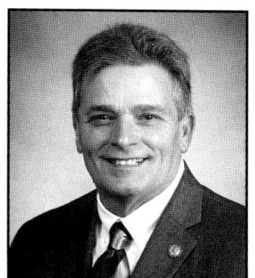

JAY ELKIN
3489 94th Avenue SW, Taylor, ND 58656-9645; jayelkin@nd.gov; (R) Pt. Dunn, Pt. Hettinger, Pt. Morton, Pt. Stark • Farmer; Rancher • Attended BSC; Attended NDSU • Stark County Commissioner; Taylor Lions; Dickinson Elk Lodge; St. Mary`s Church • Married (Anita) • Senate since 2019
EDUCATION; GOVERNMENT AND VETERANS AFFAIRS

MIKE SCHATZ
400 East Ninth Street, New England, ND 58647-7528; mischatz@nd.gov; (R) Pt. Dunn, Pt. Hettinger, Pt. Morton, Pt. Stark • Businessman • MSU • Former Vice President, Education Standards & Practices Board; Former President, New England Park Board; Lifetime Member, Past ND Coaches Association; NRA; ND Stockmen's Association • Married (Patti); 4 Children; 2 Grandchildren • House 1989-90, since 2009
APPROPRIATIONS; APPROPRIATIONS - EDUCATION AND ENVIRONMENT DIVISION

LUKE SIMONS
11509 27th Street SW, Dickinson, ND 58601-8238; lsimons@nd.gov; (R) Pt. Dunn, Pt. Hettinger, Pt. Morton, Pt. Stark • Rancher • Married (Aliesha); 5 Children • House since 2017
JUDICIARY; POLITICAL SUBDIVISIONS

DISTRICT #37

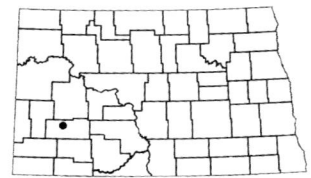

RICH WARDNER
1042 12th Avenue West, Dickinson, ND 58601-3654; rwardner@nd.gov; (R) Pt. Stark • Retired Educator; Former Executive Director, Dickinson Area Chamber of Commerce • BS, DSU; MS, Northern State University • Past President Pro Tempore of the Senate; Chairman, Sunrise Youth Bureau; Chair, Midwest Legislative Conference; Member, Legislative Management; Elks; Rotary • Married (Kayleen); 2 Children • House 1991-1998; Senate since 1999

MIKE LEFOR
P.O. Box 1347, Dickinson, ND 58602-1347; mlefor@nd.gov; (R) Pt. Stark • President, Blackridge Enterprises LLC • DSU Graduate • President, Dickinson Park Board, 2006-2014; Chairman, CHI St. Joseph Hospital, 2008-2014; City Commission, 2016; Chairman, Planning and Zoning Commission, 1993-2003 • Married (Sherryl); 3 Children • House since 2015
ENERGY AND NATURAL RESOURCES; ETHICS; INDUSTRY, BUSINESS AND LABOR

VICKY STEINER
859 Senior Avenue, Dickinson, ND 58601-3755; vsteiner@nd.gov; (R) Pt. Stark • Owner, Big Sky Condos • BS, MSU Moorhead • Vision West ND; Badlands Advisory Group; DSU Community Committee; Rotary; ND Right to Life; St. Patrick's Church Building Committee • Married (Calvin); 4 Children; 8 Grandchildren • House since 2011
ETHICS; FINANCE AND TAXATION; GOVERNMENT AND VETERANS AFFAIRS

DISTRICT #38

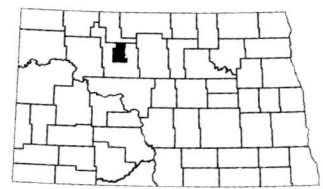

DAVID HOGUE
P.O. Box 1000, Minot, ND 58702-1000; dhogue@nd.gov; (R) Pt. Ward
• Attorney • BA, Cornell College; U.S. Army War College; JD, UND
• Veteran • Married (Paula); 2 Children • Senate since 2009
APPROPRIATIONS; ETHICS

LARRY BELLEW
812 Bel Air Place, Minot, ND 58703-1751; lbellew@nd.gov; (R) Pt. Ward
• AA, Horticulture • Board, Minot Commission on Aging; Kalix; Dakota Family Services • Married (Carol); 4 Children • House since 2001
APPROPRIATIONS; APPROPRIATIONS - GOVERNMENT OPERATIONS DIVISION

DAN RUBY
4620 46th Avenue NW, Minot, ND 58703-8710; druby@nd.gov; (R) Pt. Ward • Circle Sanitation Inc.; Noonan Landfill LLC • Married (Lori); 10 Children; 17 Grandchildren • House since 2001
ETHICS; INDUSTRY, BUSINESS AND LABOR; TRANSPORTATION

DISTRICT #39

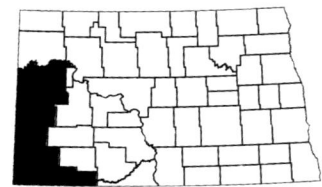

DALE PATTEN
P.O. Box 812, Watford City, ND 58854-0812; dpatten@nd.gov; (R) Adams, Billings, Bowman, Pt. Dunn, Golden Valley, Pt. McKenzie, Slope • Retired, Banker • BS, Animal Science, NDSU • McKenzie County Commission, 2000-2012 • Married (Joy); 2 Children • Senate since 2019
FINANCE AND TAXATION; TRANSPORTATION

KEITH KEMPENICH
9005 151st Avenue SW, Bowman, ND 58623-8857; kkempenich@nd.gov; (R) Adams, Billings, Bowman, Pt. Dunn, Golden Valley, Pt. McKenzie, Slope • Rancher; Crop Adjuster; Owner, Box K Trucking • Black Hills State • Farm Bureau; Farmers Union; AOPA • Married (Melinda); 3 Children • House since 1993
APPROPRIATIONS; APPROPRIATIONS - GOVERNMENT OPERATIONS DIVISION

DENTON ZUBKE
P.O. Box 927, Watford City, ND 58854-0927; dzubke@nd.gov; (R) Adams, Billings, Bowman, Pt. Dunn, Golden Valley, Pt. McKenzie, Slope • Retired CEO, Financial Institution • Chairman, McKenzie County Water RD; Director, Past Chairman, Western Area Water Supply Project; McKenzie County Job Development Authority; Watford City Chamber of Commerce; Midwest Federal Corporate Credit Union • Married (Margaret); 5 Children; 3 Grandchildren • House since 2015
EDUCATION; ENERGY AND NATURAL RESOURCES

DISTRICT #40

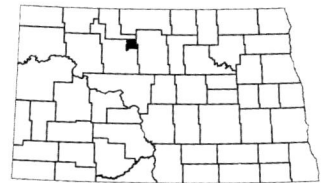

KAREN K. KREBSBACH
P.O. Box 1767, Minot, ND 58702-1767; kkrebsbach@nd.gov; (R) Pt. Ward • President, Krebsbach Realty Co. Inc. • BS, MSU • Board of Regents, MISU; MISU Foundation; Board, Trinity Health; TR Medora Foundation; Norsk Hostfest Association; Minot Community Ambulance; Past Chair, Minot Area Development Corporation; Minot Area Chamber of Commerce; Greater North Dakota Chamber; Minot Job Service Employer's Committee; Souris Valley United Way; SBA Advisory Committee; President Pro Tempore, 2001; First Lutheran Church • 2 Children; 4 Grandchildren • Senate since 1989
APPROPRIATIONS

MATTHEW RUBY
315 Fourth Street NW, Minot, ND 58703-3129; mruby@nd.gov; (R) Pt. Ward • Owner, 5R Construction • 7 Years, SGT, 815th Engineer, Edgeley • Apathy Original Motorcycle Club; American Legion; St. John's Catholic Church • Married (Dana); 3 Children • House since 2017
ENERGY AND NATURAL RESOURCES; HUMAN SERVICES

RANDY A. SCHOBINGER
Minot, ND; rschobinger@nd.gov; (R) Pt. Ward • Insurance Agent • Economics, MSU • Senate 1995-2006; House since 2017
APPROPRIATIONS; APPROPRIATIONS - HUMAN RESOURCES DIVISION

DISTRICT #41

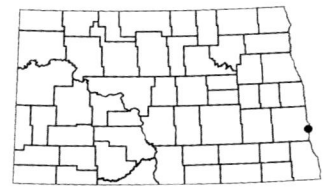

KYLE DAVISON
4918 Meadow Creek Drive South, Fargo, ND 58104-7116; kdavison@nd.gov; (R) Pt. Cass • Executive Director, South East Education Cooperative • BS, Business Administration, VCSU • Married (Laura); 3 Children • Senate since 2015
EDUCATION; GOVERNMENT AND VETERANS AFFAIRS

PAMELA ANDERSON
3001 40th Avenue South, Unit H, Fargo, ND 58104-4406; pkanderson@nd.gov; (D) Pt. Cass • Retired; Sr. Vice President, Regional Trust Manager, Wells Fargo • BA, MA, Economics, UND • Board, Thoreson & Steffes Trust Company; Board, Union State Bank; Board, NDPERS; Past Board, Bethany Retirement Living; MeritCare; FM Symphony; Sanford Health System; YWCA; FM Community Theatre • 3 Children; 4 Grandchildren • House since 2015
GOVERNMENT AND VETERANS AFFAIRS; INDUSTRY, BUSINESS AND LABOR

MICHELLE STRINDEN
245 Prairiewood Drive South, Fargo, ND 58103-4625; mstrinden@nd.gov; (R) Pt. Cass • BS, Secondary Education, UND; MS, Counseling, MSUM • Atonement Lutheran Church • Married (Tom); 4 Children • House since 2019
EDUCATION; POLITICAL SUBDIVISIONS

DISTRICT #42

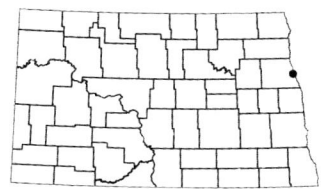

CURT KREUN
3111 Longbow Court, Grand Forks, ND 58203-2193; ckreun@nd.gov; (R) Pt. Grand Forks • Retired Small Business Owner • BS, Education, Mayville State College • Chair, Grand Forks Housing Authority; Vice Chair, Alerus Commission; Grand Forks Chamber of Commerce; Past: City Council; School Board; EGF Technical College; Chair, Salvation Army; Chair, AM Rotary; Prairie Harvest Foundation; Lake Agassiz Water Authority • Married (Linda); 2 Children • House 2011-14; Senate since 2017
ENERGY AND NATURAL RESOURCES; INDUSTRY, BUSINESS AND LABOR

JAKE G. BLUM
401 Hamline Street, Apt. #3, Grand Forks, ND 58203-2801; jblum@nd.gov; (R) Pt. Grand Forks • Political Science, Criminal Justice, UND • Former Deputy Communications Director, Kevin Cramer for Senate; Former State Field Director, Congressional Leadership Fund Super PAC; Former State Director, Students for Trump; Former Government Affairs Commissioner, UND • House since 2017
AGRICULTURE; FINANCE AND TAXATION

EMILY O'BRIEN
2002 University Avenue, Apt. #3, Grand Forks, ND 58203-3346; eobrien@nd.gov; (R) Pt. Grand Forks • Self Employed • Entrepreneurship and Business Management, UND • 1 Child • House since 2017
INDUSTRY, BUSINESS AND LABOR; TRANSPORTATION

DISTRICT #43

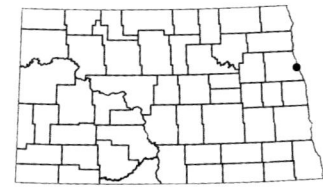

JONELL A. BAKKE
1498 Norchip Circle, Grand Forks, ND 58201-3702; jbakke@nd.gov; (D) Pt. Grand Forks • Retired, Special/Elementary Teacher • BA, Elementary/Special Education, UND; MA, Special Education • Chair, District 43, DemNPL Party; President, Grand Forks Education Association (6 years); NDEA Board of Directors (6 years); Chair, ND Women's Network (5 years); Vice Chair, ND Human Rights Coalition Board of Directors (5 years); Chair, AHEC Advisor Board (6 years); NCATE Board of Examiners; ND State Board of Examiners; State Mentoring Trainer for Teacher Support System • Married (Greg); 4 Children; 5 Grandchildren • Senate 2007-10; since 2019
JUDICIARY; TRANSPORTATION

MARY ADAMS
1942 Prairie Rose Court, Grand Forks, ND 58201-5896; mkadams@nd.gov; (D) Pt. Grand Forks • Realtor • Grand Forks Noon Rotary • Married (Steven); 2 Children • House since 2019
INDUSTRY, BUSINESS AND LABOR; POLITICAL SUBDIVISIONS

MATT EIDSON
2750 South 38th Street, Apt. #121, Grand Forks, ND 58201-5969; meidson@nd.gov; (D) Pt. Grand Forks • Graduate Teaching Assistant, UND • BA, English, UND; pursuing MA, English, UND; MA, Government, Johns Hopkins University • US Marine Corps Veteran, 2008-2015, former Sergeant (E5), deployments, Iraq and Afghanistan • House since 2019
ENERGY AND NATURAL RESOURCES; FINANCE AND TAXATION

DISTRICT #44

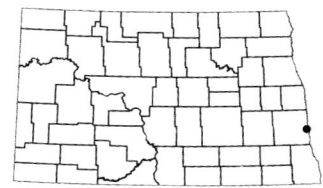

MERRILL PIEPKORN
1321 Third Street North, Fargo, ND 58102-2728; mpiepkorn@nd.gov; (D) Pt. Cass • President, Prairie Airwaves Inc.; Producer, Dakota Air: The Radio Show, film, television, and radio projects; Radio Stars Band • BA, Concordia College • Horace Mann Area Neighborhood Assoc.; Messiah Lutheran Church's "Hour of Worship" telecast • Married (Connie) • Senate since 2017
ENERGY AND NATURAL RESOURCES; INDUSTRY, BUSINESS AND LABOR

JOSH BOSCHEE
517 First Street North, Fargo, ND 58102-4540; jboschee@nd.gov; (D) Pt. Cass • Sales Manager, Realtor, Hatch Realty • BA, Political Science, NDSU; MEd., Educational Leadership, NDSU • Partnered • House since 2013

KARLA ROSE HANSON
1114 Fifth Street North, Fargo, ND 58102-3713; krhanson@nd.gov; (D) Pt. Cass • Small Business Owner • BA, NDSU • 2013 Woman of the Year, ND Women's Network; Fargo Theatre • Married (Shawn); 2 Children • House since 2017
JUDICIARY; TRANSPORTATION

DISTRICT #45

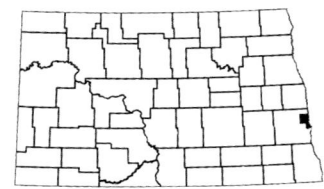

RONALD SORVAAG
3402 Birdie Street North, Fargo, ND 58102-1201; rsorvaag@nd.gov; (R) Pt. Cass • Small Business Owner • BA, Sociology, Concordia College • Past Commissioner, Fargo Park District; Past Director, Prosper Farmers Elevator; Member, Fargo/Moorhead/West Fargo Chamber of Commerce • Married (Carla); 2 Children • Senate since 2011
APPROPRIATIONS

MARY JOHNSON
3407 Birdie Street, Fargo, ND 58102-1203; marycjohnson@nd.gov; (R) Pt. Cass • Controller, Valley Bus, LLC • BS, Accounting, MSUM; JD, UND School of Law • Fargo Park Board • Married (David); 2 Children • House since 2015
EDUCATION; POLITICAL SUBDIVISIONS

TOM KADING
7205 County Road 31, Fargo, ND 58102-6117; tkading@nd.gov; (R) Pt. Cass • Attorney; Entrepreneur • BS, Civil Engineering, NDSU; JD, UND; MA, Business Administration, UND • Salem Evangelical Free Church • Married (Ashley) • House since 2015
FINANCE AND TAXATION; TRANSPORTATION

DISTRICT #46

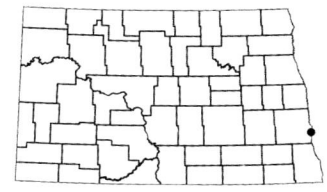

JIM P. ROERS
200 45th Street South, Fargo, ND 58103-0907; jroers@nd.gov; (R) Pt. Cass • Owner, Roers Companies • BS, Agriculture, NDSU • 2016 Service Award, NDSU Foundation; NDSU Alumni Assoc.; The Chamber; NDSU Foundation; Valley Prosperity Partnership • Married (Sandra); 5 Children • Senate 2012, since 2017
ENERGY AND NATURAL RESOURCES; INDUSTRY, BUSINESS AND LABOR

JIM KASPER
1128 Westrac Drive, Fargo, ND 58103-2342; jkasper@nd.gov; (R) Pt. Cass • President, Asset Management Group Inc. • Business Economics, NDSU • US Army Reserve • Business Champion Legislator, GNDC, 2011; Friend of Farm Bureau, 2011 and 2009; Distinguished Friend of ND Pharmacy Award, 2010; Keynote Speaker, ACLI, Boston, 2008; Keynote Speaker, Mealey's Conference, NY City Harvard Club, 2007; Keynote Speaker, Life Settlements Conference, Orlando, 2007; Outstanding Legislator, NDAIFA, 2007; Testified, US Senate Banking Committee, Privacy Matters, 2002; F-M Life Underwriter of the Year; 44-Year Member MDRT; Bethel Evangelical Free Church • Married (Sandy); 2 Sons • House since 2001
ETHICS; GOVERNMENT AND VETERANS AFFAIRS; INDUSTRY, BUSINESS AND LABOR

SHANNON ROERS JONES
5948 Silverleaf Drive South, Fargo, ND 58104-7127; sroersjones@nd.gov; (R) Pt. Cass • Attorney • BA, Business, College of St. Benedict; MBA, U of St. Thomas; JD, UND • Married (Ross); 3 Children • House since 2017
ENERGY AND NATURAL RESOURCES; JUDICIARY

DISTRICT #47

MICHAEL DWYER
1754 Santa Gertrudis Drive, Bismarck, ND 58503-0862; madwyer@nd.gov; (R) Pt. Burleigh • Attorney/Farmer • BA, St. Olaf College; JD, UND • Upper Missouri Water Distinguished Service, Presidents Award, National Water Resources Association; Williston Area Development Ambassador Award; Commodore, ND Mythical Navy; ND Water Wheel; Red River Steamboat, GNDA Natural Resources Award; Bismarck Optimist Friend of Youth; Charity Lutheran Church; FCA; Upper Missouri Ministries; NFIB; Farm Bureau • Married (Patricia); 6 Children • Senate since 2019
JUDICIARY; TRANSPORTATION

GEORGE KEISER
422 Toronto Drive, Bismarck, ND 58503-0276; gkeiser@nd.gov; (R) Pt. Burleigh • Owner, Quality Printing Service • PhD, University of Utah • US Army • Past Bismarck City Commissioner • Married (Kathy); 4 Children • House since 1993
ENERGY AND NATURAL RESOURCES; INDUSTRY, BUSINESS AND LABOR

LAWRENCE R. KLEMIN
3929 Valley Drive, Bismarck, ND 58503-1729; lklemin@nd.gov; (R) Pt. Burleigh • Lawyer, Schweigert, Klemin & McBride PC • BA, English, UND; JD, UND • US Army, Vietnam Veteran, 101st Airborne Division (Air Assault) • Commission on Uniform State Laws; State Council for Interstate Adult Offender Supervision; Who's Who in American Law; American Legion; Elks; Eagles; Optimist Club; National Uniform Law Commission; Church of Corpus Christi • Married (Rita); 2 Children • House since 1999

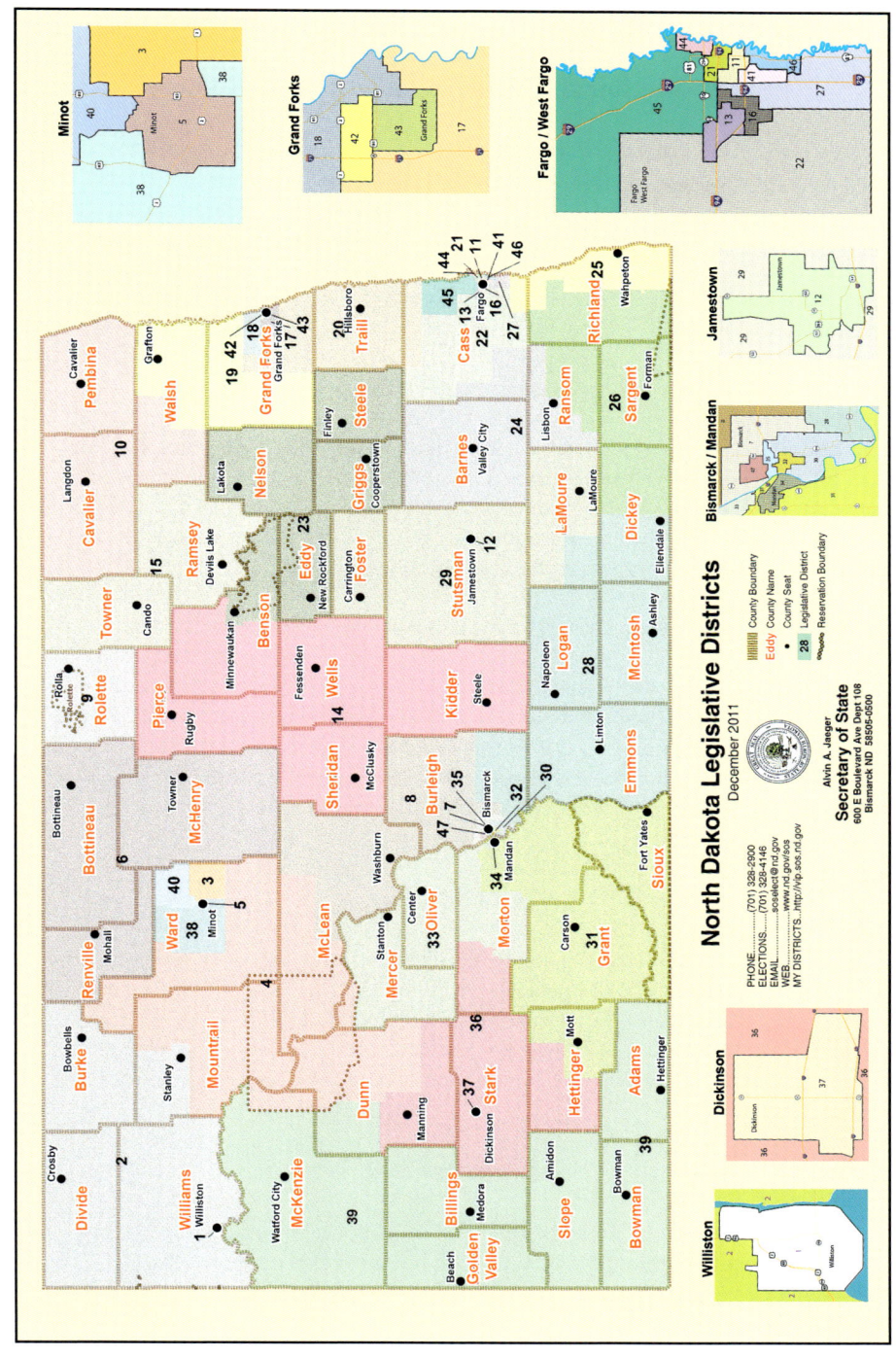

How a Bill Becomes a Law

Introduction and Standing Committee Referral

Legislative Assembly members, standing committees, and the Legislative Management sponsor bills that conform to statutory requirements and legislative rules. The presiding officer of a bill's chamber of origin refers each bill to an appropriate standing committee unless the body by motion assigns it to a select or other standing committee or to the Committee of the Whole in the case of the House of Representatives. A journal entry records the bill's official introduction, title, and committee referral.

Committee Hearing

The committee chair designates and posts a hearing date, time, and place for each bill assigned. The committee convenes as scheduled, and the chairman calls the committee to order and announces the bill under consideration. The committee receives testimony and other information from interested parties such as the bill's author, concerned citizens, and state agency representatives.

Committee Consideration and Recommendation

A standing committee makes its final decision in an executive session, and committee staff members prepare a report for chamber submission conveying the committee's recommendation. A standing committee either reports a bill favorably, unfavorably, or without recommendation. Where applicable, a committee may recommend amendment or rereferral of a bill in addition to one of the foregoing options.

Amendment

The Senate and House first consider a bill's recommended amendments on the sixth order of business prior to placing the bill on the daily calendar for second reading and final passage. The House considers all amendments on the calendar simultaneously unless a representative requests that an amendment be voted upon separately, whereas the Senate deliberates and votes upon each recommended amendment in turn.

Engrossment

The legislative rules deem a bill amended in its house of origin properly engrossed upon amendment adoption, but an amended bill must also undergo a formal engrossment process of inserting all adopted amendments into place to produce a new official version of the bill.

Second Reading and Final Passage

Second reading and final passage occurs on the eleventh order of business in a bill's chamber of origin and on the fourteenth order of business in the opposite chamber. Prior to voting on final passage, the Senate may amend a bill from the floor or rerefer it to a committee for further action, and the House may rerefer a bill to a standing committee or to the Committee of the Whole, amend a bill's title, or by unanimous consent otherwise amend a bill. To obtain final passage, a bill requires a favorable majority vote, and amendment or repeal of any law initiated or referred within the past seven years requires a favorable two-thirds vote, of the members-elect. Each chamber must record and print in its journal any vote on a bill's final passage.

Secondary House Procedure

A bill successfully passed by its house of origin goes through the same series of steps in the opposite house as in its house of origin. If the opposite house amends a bill, the house of origin must concur or refuse to concur with the proposed amendments. If the opposite house passes a bill without change, or if the house of origin agrees to the opposite house's amendments, the originating chamber may enroll the bill.

Conference Committee

If the house of origin does not concur in the opposite house's amendments, each chamber may organize a committee to meet in conference with a like committee from the other chamber to further discuss the bill. Conference committees may agree to recede from the opposite house's amendments, accede to the opposite house's amendments, recede and propose new amendments, accede and propose further amendments, or state an inability or unwillingness to agree. In the latter case, chambers may reappoint conference committee members or appoint entirely new conference committees.

Enrollment

The enrollment process involves final bill proofreading and editing, code section clean-up, line number removal, replacement of the words "A Bill for . . . " with the words "An Act . . . ," and printing of an official bill version for signatures.

Presiding Officer's Signature

The constitution requires the presiding officer of each house to sign all bills the Legislative Assembly passes and each chamber to enter the fact of such signing in the journal. As a formal procedure, the Chief Clerk of the House and the Secretary of the Senate also sign these bills before messaging them to the Governor for consideration.

Governor's Signature or Veto

The Legislative Assembly must present to the Governor for consideration every bill they pass. If the Governor approves a bill by signing it, the bill becomes law on its effective date. If the Governor vetoes a bill or any parts of a bill, the items approved become law and the portions disapproved are void unless subsequently enacted through a veto override by the Legislative Assembly. If during session the Governor neither signs nor vetoes a bill within three business days, the bill becomes law on its effective date without the Governor's signature. If the Legislative Assembly adjourns within three days after the Governor receives a bill, the bill becomes law automatically unless the Governor files it in the office of the Secretary of State within 15 business days after adjournment of the Legislative Assembly along with a veto message detailing the Governor's objections to the bill.

Veto Consideration

If the Governor vetoes part or all of a bill during session, the Governor must return it to its house of origin along with a veto message detailing the Governor's objections to the bill. If the originating house chooses to reconsider the bill or the applicable bill items and two-thirds of its members-elect agree to override the Governor's veto, the bill or bill items together with the Governor's objections thereto proceed to the opposite house for reconsideration. If two-thirds of the members-elect of the opposite house also override the Governor's veto, the bill becomes law.

Effective Date

Following filing with the Secretary of State, the effective dates of bills are as follows: July 1 for appropriation measures for the support and maintenance of state departments and institutions, for tax measures that change tax rates, or for measures that impose a fee for any purpose or which authorize an entity or public official to determine the level of a fee; August 1 for all other bills that do not specify other effective dates; and the effective date specified for bills containing approved emergency or delayed effective clauses.

North Dakota's Revenue Forecasting Process

Office of Management and Budget (1)

The Executive Budget Office (Office of Management and Budget) has primary authority for revenue forecasting in North Dakota. Historically, during each biennium, the Office of Management and Budget issues three revenue forecasts:

Preliminary	July	Issued in the year prior to the start of the legislative session
Executive Budget	December	Presented, along with the executive budget recommendations, to the Budget Section and organizational session of the Legislative Assembly
Revised	March	Updated and presented to the Appropriations Committees

Tax Department (2)

The Tax Department is responsible for the basic methodology for forecasting the following general fund tax types: sales, motor vehicle excise, individual income, corporation income, financial institution, oil extraction, oil and gas production, cigarette and tobacco, coal conversion, and wholesale liquor taxes.

Moody's Analytics (3)

The Office of Management and Budget contracts with Moody's Analytics to provide economic projections for the state of North Dakota. Moody's Analytics provides tax-based forecasts for each of the major taxable sectors. Reports prepared by Moody's Analytics include analyses and forecasts of sweet crude oil prices and production. As needed, Moody's Analytics also provides analyses and forecasts of North Dakota's major crops and livestock, including farm income and cash receipts for livestock and other agricultural commodities.

Revenue Advisory Committee (4)

The Revenue Advisory Committee, created by the Office of Management and Budget, is a committee generally consisting of private sector members, at least two legislators, and other public officials. The Revenue Advisory Committee meets before the issuance of each forecast to review the economic projections and resulting tax-based forecasts.

Legislative Assembly (5)

Legislative Management appoints an interim Legislative Revenue Advisory Committee to study state revenues and state revenue forecasts. The committee contracts with IHS Markit to develop a state revenue forecast for the Legislative Assembly to consider along with the revenue forecast prepared by the Office of Management and Budget and by Moody's Analytics. The Legislative Assembly receives and reviews the revenue forecast from the Office of Management and Budget during its organizational session in December, the revenue forecast from IHS Markit in January, and an updated forecast from the Office of Management and Budget and IHS Markit in March during the regular session. The Appropriations Committees may adopt one of the forecasts as presented or change the forecast amounts prior to adopting the official legislative revenue forecast.

Forecasting Process

2	Updates the historical tax base statistics and provides the results to Moody's Analytics.
3	Processes the historical data through forecasting models, adjusting forecast equations or "drivers" as needed.
1 2 3	Participate in conference calls to discuss views on the United States and North Dakota economies.
3	Creates North Dakota's tax-based forecasts for each of the next two fiscal years.
4 5	Reviews the tax-based forecasts and recommends modifications.
2	Applies the appropriate tax rates and statutory distributions through the use of inhouse tax revenue models to produce the tax revenue forecast, which the Tax Department supplies to the Office of Management and Budget.

North Dakota's Budgeting Process

North Dakota's Legislative Assembly meets for up to 80 legislative days beginning in January and usually concluding in April of each odd-numbered year. By the close of each regular legislative session, the Legislative Assembly approves North Dakota's biennial budget, which takes effect on July 1 of that year and ends on June 30 of the following odd-numbered year.

North Dakota's budgeting process begins in March of the year prior to the legislative session with state agencies and institutions preparing and submitting their biennial budget requests to the Office of Management and Budget. The Office of Management and Budget holds executive budget hearings, attended by the legislative budget analyst and auditor's staff, which allow agencies an opportunity to explain and justify their budget requests for inclusion in the Governor's budget recommendations to the Legislative Assembly.

The Governor develops the executive budget recommendation using revenue forecast information based on data provided by the Tax Department, input from the Advisory Council on Revenue Forecasting, and an analysis by the economic forecasting firm under contract with the state. The Legislative Assembly also uses this revenue information, as well as revenue forecasting information provided by the Legislative Management's revenue forecasting consultant and updated revenue information provided in March during the legislative session, as it develops the legislative budget.

The Legislative Assembly receives the Governor's executive budget recommendation during its organizational session in December preceding the legislative session, and the Legislative Management's Budget Section meets afterward to receive more detailed information about the recommendation. Prior to the legislative session, the Legislative Council fiscal staff prepares a comprehensive analysis of the executive budget, presents this analysis to the Appropriations Committee of each house, and makes it available to all members of the Legislative Assembly for the members' use in developing the legislative budget.

The Appropriations Committees introduce base level appropriations bills for each agency containing the ongoing legislative appropriations for the agency for the current biennium as a starting point for the legislative budget development process during the session. The Office of Management and Budget submits draft appropriations bills containing the Governor's budget recommendations to the Legislative Assembly for informational purposes and for the Appropriations Committees to consider as they develop the state budget. Individual legislators may also introduce bills affecting state revenues or appropriations for an agency, and the Legislative Assembly may consider bills for deficiency appropriations relating to the current biennium. As it develops the legislative budget, the Legislative Assembly considers the Governor's recommendations and information received through public hearings held in each chamber on each appropriations and revenue bill.

The rules of the Legislative Assembly require that the Senate and the House of Representatives refer each bill having an appropriation of $5,000 or more and each bill with a fiscal note indicating a fiscal impact of $50,000 or more to their respective Appropriations Committee. The Senate Appropriations Committee (14 members in 2019) forms ad hoc subcommittees to consider specific issues or funding levels for select agencies. The House Appropriations Committee (21 members in 2019) organizes itself into three formal divisions: Education and Environment, Human Resources, and Government Operations. These subdivisions hold budget hearings on assigned agencies, develop budget recommendations, and report their recommendations to the full Appropriations Committee.

The Legislative Council fiscal staff serves the Appropriations Committees and all members of the Legislative Assembly by conducting research, analyzing budgets, preparing amendments, and monitoring the status of revenues, appropriations, and fund balances included in the legislative budget. The fiscal staff also publishes the "budget status" report throughout the legislative session, which provides the updated status of general fund revenues, appropriations, and ending general fund balance for the next biennium's budget.

The Legislative Assembly approves approximately 75 appropriations bills each session, providing for the operations of state government for the subsequent biennium. Once passed by both chambers of the Legislative Assembly, each bill moves from its originating chamber to the Governor for signature, and when signed, the bill becomes law. Unless otherwise indicated, appropriations bills or tax measure bills become effective on July 1 following the legislative session, and other bills become effective on August 1.

If defined unforeseen circumstances arise following an appropriation, North Dakota Century Code Chapter 54-16 grants authority to the state's Emergency Commission to approve agency requests for line item transfers, for acceptance of additional federal or other funds, and for use of state contingencies appropriations. Transfer or additional spending of federal or other funds exceeding $50,000 requires Budget Section approval.

Documents in the Budget Process

Planning, preparing, and managing a state budget is a continuous process throughout which the Office of Management and Budget (OMB) and the Legislative Council produce a variety of budget documents that provide information about state revenues and appropriations. Following is a chart of North Dakota's budget publications produced each biennium.

	Date	Publication	Author	Description
Even-numbered years	March or April	*Guidelines for Preparation of Biennium Agency Operating and Capital Budget Requests*	Governor and OMB	Agency guidelines for the preparation of the next biennium's budget
	By July 15	Budget Requests	State Agencies	Agency/institution budget requests, narratives of functions and programs, and appropriations for the last two biennia
	December	*Budget Message of the Governor and Executive Budget Summary*	Governor and OMB	Governor's budget recommendations and message delivered to the Legislative Assembly
Odd-numbered years	By January	*Executive Budget Detail*	OMB	Agency budget requests and details about the Governor's budget recommendations
		Supplement to the Report of the Legislative Council, Budget Section: Analysis of . . . Executive Budget	Legislative Council	Narrative and schedules analyzing the executive budget recommendations
	Crossover	*Analysis of Changes to Base Funding Levels*	Legislative Council	List and explanation of legislative changes made through crossover to agency budgets for the upcoming biennium
	After legislative session adjournment	*Changes to Agency Base Budgets for the . . . Biennium*	Legislative Council	List and explanation of legislative changes made to agency budgets for the upcoming biennium
		Report on Appropriations and Estimated Revenues for the Biennium . . .	Legislative Council	Final budget status report showing Legislative Assembly changes and final agency/institution appropriations from the general fund and special funds; comparison of agency/institution appropriations changes listed by bill number
		State Budget Actions . . . Biennium	Legislative Council	Comparison of total legislative appropriations, executive budget recommendations, and the previous biennium's agency/institution appropriations; analyses of special funds and FTE positions; pie graphs and schedules on general fund revenues and appropriations
		Legislative Appropriations for the . . . Biennium	Governor and OMB	Summary of and Governor's policies relating to the budget passed by the Legislative Assembly; agency/institution total appropriations

	Date	Publication	Author	Description
Odd-numbered years	Between legislative sessions	*Biennium Report on Compliance with Legislative Intent*	Legislative Council	Report on agency/institution compliance with legislative intent included in appropriations measures; information on the status of selected special funds
		Audit Reports	State Auditor	Report on agencies' use of appropriated funds
	End of the biennium	*Biennium Budget and Actual Detail (Budgetary Basis)*	OMB	Individual agency/institution revenues and expenditures; information on each agency's/institution's total approved, adjusted, spent, and unspent or uncollected appropriations for the biennium
	End of the fiscal year	*Comprehensive Annual Financial Report for the Fiscal Year Ended June 30, . . .*	OMB	Financial statements on the state's revenues, expenditures, and funding sources; section defining all special funds

Legislative Documents and Resources

Legislative documents and resources related to a particular Legislative Assembly, including most of the materials listed in this section, are available by clicking on the applicable link online at www.legis.nd.gov/assembly.

	Resource	Description
General	*Constitution of North Dakota*	Supreme legal document of the state of North Dakota
	North Dakota Century Code	North Dakota's codification of general and permanent law, first published between 1959 and 1960 and named to commemorate the 100th anniversary of the establishment of Dakota Territory in 1861
	Legislative events calendar	List of legislative session dates, interim committee meeting dates, and other dates important to the legislative process
	News page	Key information about the legislative branch, such as announcements about upcoming meetings and updates on legislator activities

	Resource	Description
Session	Bill action pages	Date and chamber information, descriptions, and journal links for legislative measures
	Bill version pages	Official amendments, fiscal notes, and versions for legislative measures
	Senate and House Legislative Manual	Procedural guidelines for floor sessions of the Senate and House of Representatives and a legislative directory
	Legislative deadlines	List of important session dates such as bill filing, introduction, rereferral, and reporting deadlines and crossover
	Legislative calendars	Legislative floor session agendas
	Committee hearing schedules	Meeting information organized by date and time, committee, room, bill number, and legislator
	Journals of the Senate and House of Representatives	Records mandated by the state constitution of the actions of the Legislative Assembly
	Standing and conference committee minutes	Summaries of committee deliberation on bills and resolutions and attached testimony showing support for, opposition to, and additional information about each bill
	Major topics index	List of proposed legislation by category, with links to bill status and bill version pages as well as a short descriptive heading for each bill or resolution
	North Dakota *Session Laws*	Compilation of a given biennium's enacted laws, adopted resolutions, gubernatorial vetoes, and ballot measures
Interim	*Legislative Management Final Report* and interim committee memoranda, notices, agendas, minutes, and bill drafts	Information about interim study research, deliberation, and recommendations
	North Dakota Administrative Code	Administrative rules through which state boards, departments, and commissions classified as administrative agencies implement their statutory responsibilities

✔ See the 2011-2013, 2013-2015, and 2017-2019 editions of the *North Dakota Blue Book* for details on reconvened and special sessions.

Citizen Involvement

Research

During sessions of the Legislative Assembly, members of the public may obtain legislative documents, including bills and resolutions; committee hearing schedules; and daily calendars, journals, and bill status reports through the bill and journal room or through the Legislative Document Subscription Service. Additional information about the Legislative Assembly, pending legislation, and other related topics is available when the Legislative Assembly is in session through the *North Dakota Legislative Daily* app or at the first floor information kiosk and on the legislative branch website (http://www.legis.nd.gov).

Visit

High school and junior high school classes may arrange for student tours by contacting the legislative tour coordinator, and members of the general public are welcome to tour the Capitol complex throughout the year. Information on legislative meeting times is available via standing committee hearing and meeting, conference committee meeting, and legislative session schedules published in hard copy, on electronic signs located throughout the Capitol, or online on the legislative branch website.

Participate

North Dakota has one of the most open legislatures in the nation. Constituents may contact legislators during a legislative session through the legislative branch website or by leaving a message at the legislative telephone message center and may contact legislators throughout the biennium by telephone, mail, or email. North Dakota citizens have the right to testify during scheduled committee hearings on any bill or resolution before the Legislative Assembly, may request that legislators introduce bills or resolutions on their behalf for consideration by the Legislative Assembly, and may refer or initiate measures to the state's electorate for their vote in a primary or general election.

Serve

The Legislative Assembly encourages students to participate in the "page for the day" program and offers a number of legal internships, as well as a fiscal internship and a library internship, to students enrolled in North Dakota institutions of higher education. Qualified individuals also may participate in the chaplain for the day or the doctor of the day programs, apply for Legislative Council or session employment opportunities, or run for legislative office.

Legislative Management

The Legislative Assembly created the Legislative Research Committee in 1945 and renamed it the Legislative Council in 1969 and the Legislative Management in 2009. By statute, Legislative Management membership includes the majority and minority leaders of both houses, the Speaker of the House, and six senators and six representatives appointed based on the proportionate representation of each party in the Senate and the House. At least two senators and two representatives must represent the minority party.

Following each regular legislative session, the Legislative Management prioritizes interim studies and assigns each legislator to serve on one or more interim committees in the period between legislative sessions. Several interim committees, including the Administrative Rules, Budget Section, Employee Benefits Programs, Energy Development and Transmission, Information Technology, Legacy and Budget Stabilization Fund Advisory Board, Legislative Audit and Fiscal Review, Committee on Tribal and State Relations, Water Topics Overview, and Workers' Compensation Review committees function under statutory authority. Interim committees allow citizen legislators to keep up with rapidly changing developments in complex fields such as the Budget Section, which receives the Governor's executive budget just prior to each legislative session, and the Administrative Rules Committee, which monitors executive branch rules. The Legislative Management names and assigns other interim committees, and if the need arises, the Chairman of the Legislative Management may assign additional studies to interim committees.

Between sessions, interim committees hold hearings, take testimony, and review information provided by the Legislative Council, state agencies, and interested parties as the committees consider alternative approaches to issues raised by studies. The Legislative Council staff handle the vast majority of work associated with interim studies, although the Legislative Management occasionally contracts with universities, consulting firms, or outside professionals on specialized studies and projects.

In November of each even-numbered year, the Legislative Management meets to consider the results of all interim committee work and may accept, reject, or amend committee reports. The Legislative Management then presents its recommendations, together with bills and resolutions necessary for implementation, to the Legislative Assembly.

The Legislative Management interim studies over the past 74 years have influenced nearly every facet of state government. The Legislative Management is, in a sense, the Legislative Assembly working between sessions.

Legislative Council

Providing continuity between legislative sessions, the Legislative Management, through its attorneys, accountants, and other personnel known as the Legislative Council, provides a wide range of services to legislators, other state agencies, and the public, including:

- Staffing interim study committees.
- Drafting bills and resolutions.
- Providing fiscal and budget analyses.
- Supervising the publication of the *Laws of North Dakota* (Session Laws), the *North Dakota Century Code*, and the *North Dakota Administrative Code*.
- Providing legal advice on legislative matters to legislators and legislative committees.
- Considering problems of statewide significance that arise during the interim.
- Handling financial administration for the legislative branch.
- Developing and managing information technology services for the Legislative Assembly.
- Reviewing information technology in all three branches of state government.
- Representing the Legislative Assembly in interstate organizations, such as the National Conference of State Legislatures, Council of State Governments, and National Conference of Commissioners on Uniform State Laws.
- Encouraging coordination between the Legislative Assembly and other branches of state government.
- Responding to informational needs of legislators and their constituents.
- Handling miscellaneous interim business for the Legislative Assembly.
- Maintaining a library of contemporary and historical legislative reference sources.
- Preparing and submitting to the Secretary of State the estimated fiscal impact of an initiated measure, then tracking and reporting on actual fiscal impact if voters approve the initiated measure.
- Providing technical expertise to budget and appropriations committees.
- Reviewing audit reports for the Legislative Audit and Fiscal Review Committee (LAFRC).
- Assisting LAFRC in conducting studies designed to improve the state's fiscal practices.

Legislative Compensation

The 1889 Constitution of North Dakota entitled legislators to compensation of $5 per day during a legislative session and 10 cents per mile for travel to and from the capitol. As the cost of serving in the Legislative Assembly rose, expense reimbursements gradually increased.

In 1969, the Legislative Assembly established the Legislative Compensation Commission, a five-member committee of gubernatorial appointees tasked with determining appropriate rates of expense allowance and compensation for legislators. The Legislative Assembly repealed this commission in 1979 but reinstated it in 1983 following voter approval of a constitutional amendment that repealed the 1889 constitutional provision of $5 per day, authorized the Legislative Assembly to set compensation levels, provided legislators' expenses could not exceed those of other state employees, and prohibited the practice of unvouchered expense reimbursements (Article XI, Section 26 of the Constitution of North Dakota).

In 2011, the Legislative Assembly repealed the Legislative Compensation Commission once again and amended North Dakota Century Code (NDCC) Section 54-03-20 to require the Legislative Management to make recommendations and submit any necessary legislation to adjust legislative compensation amounts prior to each regular legislative session. Since 2011, legislator compensation has increased by the same percentage as state employee compensation.

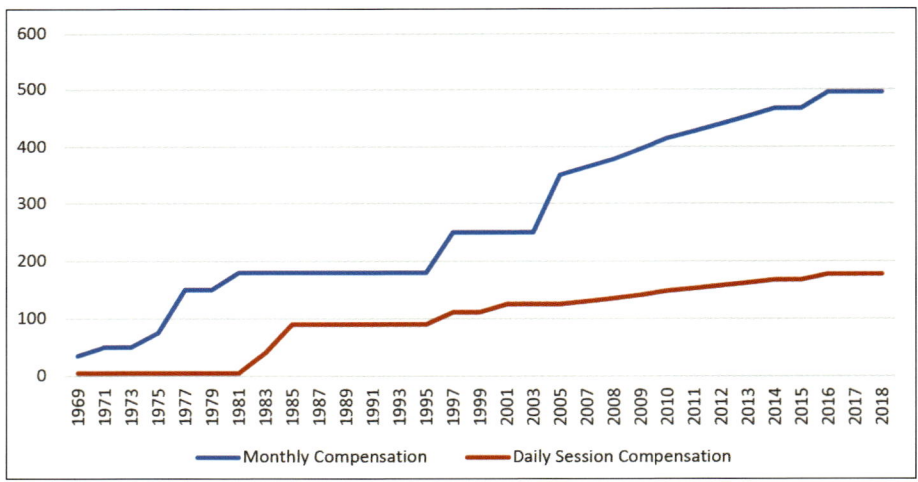

Legislative Compensation 1969-2018

Salary and Other Reimbursement Legislators Receive under Current Law (as of October 2018)

Compensation During Term of Office (NDCC § 54-03-20)

- Compensation paid monthly to legislators during term of office $495 per month

- Additional compensation for majority leaders, minority leaders, and chairman of the Legislative Management $355 per month

Compensation for Regular, Special, or Organizational Sessions

- Salary (NDCC § 54-03-20) $177 per calendar day

- Additional compensation (NDCC § 54-03-10)
  - Speaker of the House, majority leaders, and minority leaders $15 per calendar day
  - Substantive standing committee chairmen, assistant majority leaders, and assistant minority leaders $10 per calendar day

Expense Reimbursement for Regular, Special, or Organizational Sessions

- Lodging (NDCC § 54-03-20)
  Actual expenses, not to exceed 90 percent of the $83.70 daily lodging rate established by the General Services Administration (GSA) plus any additional applicable state or local taxes, subject to the maximum monthly session reimbursement of 30 times 70 percent of the daily lodging rate, or $1,758 per month

- Mileage
  Mileage reimbursement rate established by the GSA of 58 cents per mile applied to one round trip per calendar week for each legislator who resides outside of Bismarck to travel to and from the meeting of the Legislative Assembly

Compensation for Interim Meetings (NDCC § 54-35-10)

- Compensation for attendance at meetings of the Legislative Management and its committees $177 per day

- Additional compensation for the chairman of the Legislative Management and committee chairmen $5 per day

Expense Reimbursement for Interim Meetings

- Meals (NDCC § 44-08-04)
  Up to $35 per day in state; an amount equal to the federal per diem meals rate for out-of-state travel

- Lodging (NDCC § 44-08-04)
  Actual expenses, not to exceed 90 percent of the $84.60 daily lodging rate established by the GSA plus any applicable state or local taxes for in-state travel; actual expenses for out-of-state travel

- Mileage (NDCC § 54-06-09)
  Rate of 58 cents per mile by motor vehicle in state and up to 300 miles out of state; 18 cents per mile by motor vehicle more than 300 miles out of state; 82 cents per mile by private airplane

The Role of the North Dakota Legislature in Achieving Women's Right to Vote

For more than 30 years, from statehood in 1889 to 1920, only men could serve in the North Dakota Legislative Assembly. Until 1917, North Dakota women could merely vote in school elections and on education issues. Therefore, when women wanted the right to vote and run for office in municipal, state, and national elections, they needed the support of their male state legislators.

From 1889 through 1919, the Legislative Assembly considered suffrage bills at almost every session. In 1913, 1917, and 1919, the Legislative Assembly passed important legislation that assisted women in achieving the right to vote and hold office.

The 1889 Constitution of North Dakota gave women the right to vote in school elections and on education issues. In 1892, both men and women voters elected Laura Eisenhuth as the Superintendent of Public Instruction, the first woman in the United States to hold statewide office. Superintendent Eisenhuth was followed by Superintendent Emma Bates, who was elected in 1894.

To be able to vote for other elected officials, women had to work with the Legislative Assembly to change either the state constitution or state suffrage laws. Both were politically challenging. A proposed constitutional amendment had to be approved by two consecutive Legislative Assemblies and then receive a majority vote at a general election. To change state suffrage law, only one Legislative Assembly had to approve a bill to expand women's suffrage (the voting rights of women), but it then had to be adopted "by a majority of the electors of the state voting at a general election."

In 1913, during the 13th Legislative Assembly, two important bills passed regarding women's suffrage. The North Dakota Votes for Women League (NDVWL) was organized in June 1912 to promote women's suffrage. As the *Grand Forks Evening Times* reported, "This question of equal suffrage has come before practically every legislative session in the history of the state, but this is the first time the forces favoring the bill have been so thoroughly organized." Clara Darrow, president of the NDVWL; Elizabeth Preston Anderson, president of Women's Christian Temperance Union (WCTU); and members of their respective organizations were very active during the legislative session. Five states in the west had recently approved equal suffrage.

Several legislators introduced measures relating to women's suffrage, including Senator Harrison A. Bronson of Grand Forks, who sponsored the two that passed in the final days of the session. Senate Bill No. 8 included simple changes to election laws allowing most women to vote for all officials. The second, a resolution, proposed the same changes to the state constitution. Neither would go into effect until

Governor Lynn Frazier signing women's suffrage bills in 1917.

approved by male voters at a general election. These were the first women's suffrage bills that had passed the Legislative Assembly since statehood, and Governor Louis Hanna arranged for a signing ceremony on March 7, 1913. Clara Darrow and Elizabeth Preston Anderson were happy to be a part of the signing ceremony and considered it a "splendid victory."

However, after an energetic and time-consuming campaign to convince men to vote for full women's suffrage, male voters in November 1914 did not approve changing the state law. Women in favor of suffrage suffered another setback during the 14th Legislative Assembly (1915) when legislators did not approve a concurrent resolution for the women's suffrage amendment to the Constitution of North Dakota. Supporters were disappointed because they wanted the measure on the ballot in 1916. The State Anti-Suffrage Association, led by Ida Young, and the Personal Liberty League of the German American Alliance of North Dakota led the campaigns against women's suffrage.

However, in 1917 during the 15th Legislative Assembly, women's suffrage achieved significant progress in a short time. WCTU President Elizabeth Preston Anderson asked Robert M. Pollock of Fargo to draft a bill that allowed women to vote for President of the United States and to vote for municipal offices. The Legislative Assembly may have been more receptive to this proposal since it did not allow women to vote for any state officials, including legislators, or for U.S. Senators or Representatives to Congress. The state Legislative Assembly could pass the bill, and it would go into effect without any referral vote. Both the NDVWL and the WCTU favored this legislation, as well as the constitutional amendment legislation.

Senator Oscar Lindstrom of Burke County introduced both bills, which passed by large majorities in both houses. On January 23, 1917, new Governor Lynn Frazier held a bill signing ceremony and invited many people, including legislators and representatives of women's groups who supported women's suffrage.

By 1919, women's suffrage legislation attracted little attention. Senator Richard McCarten of Sargent County, President Pro Tempore of the Senate, sponsored Senate Bill No. 81, which supported, for the second time, an amendment to the Constitution of North Dakota allowing full suffrage for women. The 16th Legislative Assembly quietly passed this bill, and voters would vote on this "elective franchise" amendment in November 1920.

However, in June 1919, Congress voted to propose the women's suffrage amendment to the Constitution of the United States, which had to be ratified by 36 states. Governor Frazier called a special session of the Legislative Assembly in November 1919 to consider ratifying the amendment to the Constitution of the United States, as well as other matters. On November 26, 1919, the Senate approved a joint resolution ratifying the proposed amendment and the House followed on December 1, 1919. Frazier signed the joint resolution in a special ceremony attended by legislators and supporters of women's suffrage on December 5, 1919.

On August 26, 1920, the 19th Amendment became part of the Constitution of the United States, and women were now eligible for full suffrage. North Dakota men and women voted in the November 1920 election and approved the "elective franchise" amendment to the Constitution of North Dakota by a vote of 135,370 in favor and 60,772 opposed.

The 66th Legislative Assembly
Regular Session: Thursday, January 3 – Friday, April 26, 2019 (76 Legislative Days)

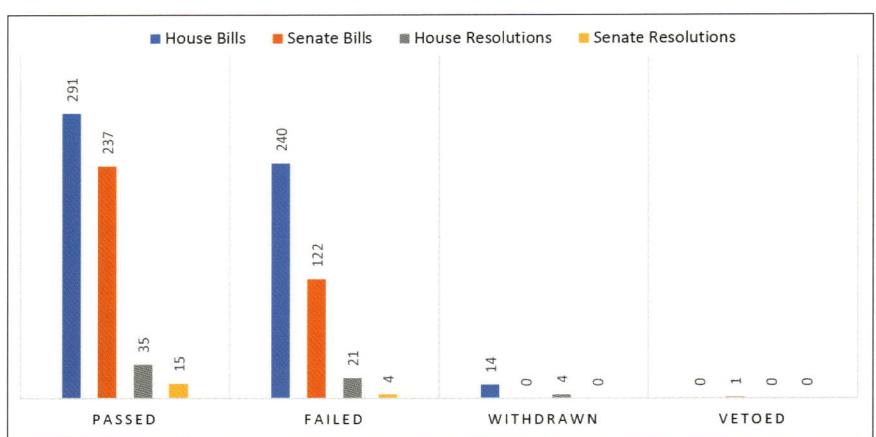

Composition

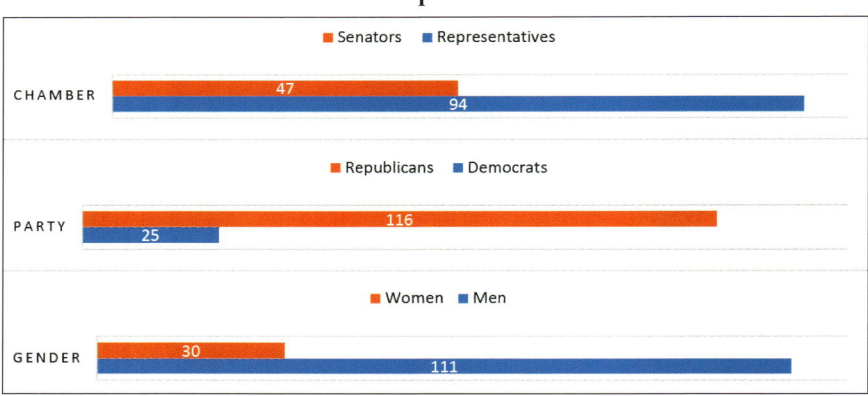

Leadership

Position	Senate	House
President President Pro Tempore Interim President Pro Tempore	Lt. Governor Brent Sanford Senator David Hogue Senator Oley Larsen	
Speaker		Representative Lawrence R. Klemin
Majority Leader	Senator Rich Wardner	Representative Chet Pollert
Assistant Majority Leader	Senator Jerry Klein	Representative Scott Louser
Minority Leader	Senator Joan Heckaman	Representative Josh Boschee
Assistant Minority Leader	Senator John Grabinger	Representative Karla Rose Hanson
Republican Caucus Leader	Senator David Hogue	Representative Shannon Roers Jones
Democratic Caucus Leader	Senator Erin Oban	Representative Gretchen Dobervich

Budget Overview

General Fund

The Legislative Assembly projected general fund revenues for the 2019-21 biennium of $4.89 billion – an increase of $159 million, or 3.4%, compared to the revised 2017-19 biennium revenues. Major areas of tax and fee revenue change as compared to the revised revenue forecast for the 2017-19 biennium included an estimated increase of $95.99 million, or 5.4%, in sales and use tax collections; an estimated increase of $35.49 million, or 4.6%, in individual income tax collections; an estimated decrease of $47.64 million, or 26.5% in corporate income tax collections; and an estimated decrease of $37.38 million, or 33.9%, in insurance premium tax collections.

The Legislative Assembly provided general fund appropriations of $4.84 billion – $417.7 million, or 9.4%, more than the 2017-19 legislative appropriations. Major general fund appropriation increases included $285.8 million for the Department of Public Instruction, $123.4 million for the Department of Human Services, $15.3 million for the Department of Corrections and Rehabilitation, $10.5 million for the Department of Career and Technical Education, $8.0 million for the Information Technology Department, and $7.5 million for the Housing Finance Agency. Major general fund appropriation decreases related to the Department of Transportation ($10.5 million), the Governor ($14.5 million), higher education ($18.9 million), and the Department of Commerce ($19.9 million). Please note the decreases result from the Legislative Assembly providing 2017-19 biennium supplemental appropriations during the 2019 legislative session. See the 2017-19 Supplemental Appropriations section below.

Special Funds

The Legislative Assembly provided special funds appropriations of $9.85 billion – $593.2 million, or 6.4%, more than the 2017-19 legislative appropriations. Major special funds appropriation increases included $279.4 million for higher education, $246.0 million for the State Water Commission, $191.7 million for the Department of Transportation, $96.5 million for the Information Technology Department, $70.3 million for the Department of Human Services, $46.2 million for the Department of Environmental Quality, and $38.8 million for the Aeronautics Commission. Major special funds appropriation decreases related to the Department of Health ($34.1 million), Adjutant General ($79.6 million), Department of Public Instruction ($80.0 million), and Department of Trust Lands ($228.0 million).

Summary of Selected Appropriations

Higher Education: $660.5 million – ($18.9 million), or 2.8%, decrease (reflecting 2017-19 supplemental appropriations)
- $30 million added to campus base funding formula distributions
- $10.7 million for student residency positions at the University of North Dakota School of Medicine and Health Sciences
- $9.4 million for the higher education challenge fund to provide matching grants for academic enhancements to North Dakota University System institutions
- $250,000 to provide matching grants of $1 for every $2 of private funds for the University of North Dakota School of Law

Elementary and Secondary Education: $2.18 billion – $165.8 million increase
- $2.098 billion for integrated formula payments
- $56.5 million for transportation aid
- $24 million for special education contracts
- $10.5 million in grant funding
- $5.5 million for PowerSchool
- $3 million for rapid enrollment grants
- $1.2 million for a rewrite of the Department of Public Instruction's school district data collection system
- $800,000 for music grants to school districts
- $300,000 for a Pre K-12 Education Vision Steering Committee
- $200,000 to rewrite the state school aid formula computer program
- $189,000 for an Education Coordination Council
- $108,000 for national board certification

Human Services: $1.46 billion – $123.8 million, or 9.2%, increase
- $173.7 million for a county social and human services program
- $64.6 million added for provider inflationary increases
- $56.5 million for cost, caseload, utilization, rate, and other changes in programs
- $20.3 million to replace a reduction in federal funds for Medicaid Expansion due to a declining federal matching percentage
- $7.1 million for a Medicaid management information system technology stack upgrade
- $5.4 million for supporting the Self-Service Portal and Consolidated Eligibility System
- $1.25 million for a child welfare technology project

Capital Construction: $1.82 billion
- $815.1 million for transportation-related projects
- $528.4 million for water projects
- $434 million for major capital projects
- $33.1 million for extraordinary repairs
- $10.7 million for bond payments
- $1.8 million for other projects

State Employees
- The 2019-21 biennium FTE level of 15,805.77 is an overall decrease of 41.61 FTE positions compared to the 2017-19 authorized level, including a decrease of 157.89 FTE positions in higher education and an increase of 116.28 FTE positions in all other state agencies.
- $84.9 million for salary increases
- $69.2 million for a health insurance premium increase

Corrections: $229.7 million – $15.3 million, or 7.2%, increase
- Added 54.5 new FTE positions
- $20.2 million for contract housing and programming
- $11.9 million for female inmate contract housing
- $3.9 million to contract with the State Hospital for up to 30 addiction treatment beds

Information Technology: $226.6 million for state agency information technology projects, including:
- $120 million to the Information Technology Department for the statewide interoperable radio network
- $22.5 million for a driver's license system rewrite project
- $17.58 million for the unemployment insurance computer modernization project for Job Service North Dakota
- $11.4 million for cybersecurity tool set modernization for the Information Technology Department
- $11.2 million for voting system replacement and e-poll book implementation projects
- $9 million to the Retirement and Investment Office for a Teachers' Fund for Retirement pension administration system modernization project
- $7.1 to the Department of Human Services for a Medicaid management information system technical stack upgrade
- $7 million to Workforce Safety and Insurance for releases 7, 8, 9, and 10 of the claims and policy system replacement project

Economic Development
- $8.8 million for North Dakota Tourism operating expenses
- $5 million for the unmanned aircraft systems (UAS) program
- $4 million for the Agricultural Products Utilization Commission in the Department of Agriculture

- $3 million for enhanced use lease grants
- $2.95 million for entrepreneurship grants and vouchers, also known as Innovate ND
- $2 million for workforce training in the Department of Career and Technical Education
- $1.89 million for adult farm management grants in the Department of Career and Technical Education
- $1.6 million for the North Dakota Trade Office
- $1.5 million for homeless shelter grants in the Department of Commerce
- $1 million for a Census 2020 program for marketing and advocating to transient and low-population county individuals in the 2020 census
- $855,000 to the Department of Commerce for Operation Intern, a program providing matching funds to help expand the number of internship, work experience, and apprenticeship positions with North Dakota employers
- $500,000 for a nonresident nurse employment recruitment program, which requires the Department of Commerce to provide up to $4,000 in incentives for each nonresident licensed nurse who signs a written agreement to work at least four years in a North Dakota licensed health care facility
- $500,000 to the Department of Commerce for providing workforce grants to tribally controlled community colleges in North Dakota

Infrastructure
- $874.5 million for water projects
- $819.7 million, including $702.9 million from federal funds, for road projects
- $45.8 million for airport grants
- (see also Aid to Political Subdivisions)

Aid to Political Subdivisions: $3.95 billion – $430 million, or 12.2%, increase
- $115 million to the municipal infrastructure fund
- $115 million to the county and township infrastructure fund
- $18 million for fire department payments

Military-Related Programs
- $4,782,072 for the National Guard tuition assistance program
- $1,051,168 for the reintegration program to support National Guard members and their families
- $210,916 for rental payments and project costs for city-owned armories

2017-19 Supplemental Appropriations
- $49.9 million for higher education capital projects
- $28 million for a beyond visual line of sight UAS program
- $15 million for the Theodore Roosevelt Presidential Library and Museum endowment fund
- $8.1 million to townships in non-oil-producing counties for the maintenance and improvement of township roads and bridges

Summary of Selected Legislation

House Bill No. 1018, the agency appropriation for the Department of Commerce, authorizes the department to establish and administer a program for the design, purchase, implementation, and operating costs of a beyond visual line of sight unmanned aircraft system.

House Bill No. 1039 changes the age of culpability for the commission of a criminal offense from 7 to 10 years of age.

House Bill No. 1045 defines "blockchain technology" and "smart contract;" recognizes blockchain technology and smart contracts, electronic transaction definitions, and reporting requirements for limited liability companies and publicly traded corporations; allows the use of blockchain technology to sign and secure records; and specifies smart contracts are valid and enforceable.

House Bill No. 1050 removes the criminal penalty for a person 21 years of age or older who intentionally ingests, inhales, injects, or otherwise internally uses marijuana. The bill amends the criminal penalty associated with the possession of marijuana to an infraction for possession of less than one-half ounce, to a Class B misdemeanor for possession of at least one-half ounce but not more than 500 grams, and to a Class A misdemeanor for possession of more than 500 grams and reduces the penalty associated with possession of marijuana paraphernalia to an infraction.

The bill authorizes the Department of Corrections and Rehabilitation to place a person, sentenced to the legal and physical custody of the department as the result of an offense relating to the unlawful possession of drug paraphernalia, into a drug and alcohol treatment program; and, upon successful completion of the program, directs the department to release the person from imprisonment to begin any court-ordered probation, or if the person is not subject to court-ordered probation, authorizes the court to order the person to serve the remainder of the sentence of imprisonment on supervised probation subject to the terms and conditions imposed by the court.

The bill gives a court the discretion to order an individual sentenced to the legal and physical custody of the Department of Corrections and Rehabilitation who successfully completes an alcohol treatment program designated by the department to serve the remainder of the sentence of imprisonment on supervised probation.

The bill also authorizes a court to sentence an individual convicted of an infraction as though convicted of a Class B misdemeanor if the individual has within one year before the commission of the infraction been convicted at least twice of the same offense classified as an infraction.

House Bill No. 1053 provides an income tax deduction equal to the amount of a veteran's military retirement pay to veterans or surviving spouses who receive military retirement benefits for service in the armed forces of the United States, a reserve component of the armed forces, or the National Guard.

House Bill No. 1058 repeals the law prohibiting an individual from leaving a parked motor vehicle unattended with the engine running.

House Bill No. 1066 creates the municipal infrastructure fund to provide grants to cities located in non-oil-producing counties for essential infrastructure projects; the county and township infrastructure fund to provide grants to non-oil-producing counties and to townships located in non-oil-producing counties for road and bridge infrastructure projects; and the airport infrastructure fund to provide grants to airports for infrastructure projects.

The bill modifies the oil and gas gross production tax distribution formula by moving allocations to political subdivisions previously under the one-fifth side of the revenue allocation formula to the four-fifths side of the revenue allocation formula.

Allocations under the one-fifth side of the formula include 8 percent to the outdoor heritage fund, up to $20 million per fiscal year; 4 percent to the abandoned oil and gas well plugging and site reclamation fund, up to $7 million per fiscal year but not exceeding a total fund balance of more than $100 million; and all remaining amounts to the legacy fund to meet the constitutional obligation to deposit 30 percent of oil and gas revenue in the legacy fund.

Allocations under the four-fifths side of the formula include distribution of the first $5 million received from each county back to the county, a portion of which the formula allocates to the hub city funding pool, hub city school district funding pool, and the supplemental school district funding pool, and the remainder, which the formula allocates 60 percent to the county general fund, 20 percent to non-hub cities in the county, 9 percent to hub cities, 5 percent to non-hub city school districts in the county, 4 percent to townships in the county, and 2 percent to hub city school districts. The formula allocates all remaining revenue 30 percent to the county and 70 percent to the hub city funding pool, the hub city school district funding pool, the supplemental school district funding pool, and the legacy fund to meet the constitutional obligation to deposit 30 percent of oil and gas revenue in the legacy fund.

The bill modifies distributions of the state's share of oil and gas gross production tax and oil extraction tax revenue to increase the second round of allocations to the state general fund from $100 million to $200 million; to replace the previous $100 million allocation split between the strategic investment and improvements fund and the lignite research fund with a $10 million allocation to the lignite research fund; to provide an allocation of up to $30,375,000 to the municipal infrastructure fund; to provide a $400 million allocation to the strategic investment and improvements fund; to provide an allocation equal to the amount deposited in the municipal infrastructure fund to the newly created county and township infrastructure fund; to provide an allocation of $169,250,000 divided equally between the municipal infrastructure fund and the county and township infrastructure fund; and to provide an allocation of $20 million to the airport infrastructure fund.

House Bill No. 1101 requires the Adjutant General to establish and operate a North Dakota National Guard member, veteran, family, and survivor support program and provides for a continuing appropriation for that purpose.

House Bill No. 1106 authorizes the Insurance Commissioner to pursue a Section 1332 State Innovation Waiver to establish an invisible reinsurance pool for the individual health insurance market. Under the waiver, the reinsurance program would cover 75 percent of paid claims totaling between $100,000 and $1 million. A portion of the funding for the program would come from the federal government due to the reduction in advanced premium tax credits being passed back to the state, and a portion of the funding would come from assessments against the group health insurance market, with a premium tax credit for the amount of the assessment paid by the insurer. The bill provides for the establishment of the Reinsurance Association of North Dakota (RAND) as a nonprofit legal entity and for the establishment of a RAND Board of Directors.

House Bill No. 1113 revises the definition of marijuana to exclude industrial hemp and, as recommended by the State Board of Pharmacy, adds several substances to the list of controlled substances.

House Bill No. 1117 provides if the law requires a legal notice to be published in a newspaper, the newspaper must also publish the notice on a statewide legal notices website and on the newspaper's website in a location open and free to the public. The bill provides if an insubstantial error in the notice occurs due to placement on the website and if the error is the newspaper's fault, the error does not affect the notice's validity and effectiveness.

House Bill No. 1135 designates a parking space as reserved for the mobility impaired if it has two of the following indications: blue paint on the curb or edge adjacent to a space; a sign bearing the symbol of accessibility for the mobility impaired; or notice unauthorized use of the parking space is subject to a fee of $100.

House Bill No. 1174 provides an income tax deduction for the amount of social security benefits subject to federal income tax for individual taxpayers with federal adjusted gross income of $50,000 or less and married couples filing jointly with federal adjusted gross income of $100,000 or less and adjusts marriage penalty income tax credit calculations accordingly. The bill also provides income includes the full amount of an individual's social security benefits for purposes of calculating the homestead property tax credit regardless of any exclusions for purposes of calculating income tax liability.

House Bill No. 1194 directs the Department of Human Services to facilitate care coordination agreements, which are agreements between health care providers and tribal health care organizations that will result in 100 percent federal funding for eligible medical assistance provided to American Indians; creates a tribal health care coordination fund into which the department must deposit 60 percent of any federal funding received in excess of the state's regular share of federal medical assistance funding that results from care coordination agreements; directs the department to distribute money from the fund to tribal governments in proportion to the federal funding received from the care coordination agreement requests for services originating from that tribal nation; and provides tribal governments must use the money distributed from the fund for health-related purposes.

House Bill No. 1256 authorizes an individual to petition the court to seal a criminal record, replaces "expunge" with "seal" in statutory language where applicable, and includes sealed records of arrests and convictions of adults in the records the Bureau of Criminal Investigation may review in determining whether an applicant for a concealed weapons license has been or is a danger to self or others.

House Bill No. 1275 prohibits an administrative agency from adopting, without statutory authorization, a rule that prescribes a criminal penalty.

House Bill No. 1287 establishes criteria for approved alternative teacher certification programs and for teacher licensure and teacher license renewal via these programs.

House Bill No. 1296 makes it a Class C felony for the driver of a motor vehicle to willfully flee or attempt to elude a pursuing police vehicle during or after the commission of a felony. The bill also makes it a Class C felony for the driver of a motor vehicle to willfully flee or attempt to elude a pursuing police vehicle if at any time during the flight or pursuit, the driver willfully operates the vehicle in a manner constituting an inherent risk of death or serious bodily injury to a third person.

House Bill No. 1335 prohibits the board of a school district from establishing a dress code policy that prohibits students from wearing traditional tribal regalia or objects of cultural significance during a graduation ceremony.

House Bill No. 1336 provides a physician or physician's agent, as a part of the informed consent requirements before the performance of an abortion, must inform the patient it may be possible to reverse the effects of an abortion-inducing drug and the printed materials provided to her include further information and assistance. The bill similarly expands the information the State Department of Health must include in these printed materials.

House Bill No. 1345 provides cosmetology, for State Board of Cosmetology regulation purposes, does not include natural hair braiding or threading.

House Bill No. 1349 creates a new Century Code chapter to regulate the production and licensure of hemp, repeals the chapter related to industrial hemp, and replaces statutory references accordingly. The bill also establishes a licensing procedure for any person desiring to grow or process hemp and amends the definition of medical marijuana to exclude hemp.

House Bill No. 1393 creates an offense for domestic violence separate from the offense of simple assault and provides a definition for "family or household member," the elements for the offense of domestic violence, and the penalties associated with a violation of the offense. This bill also revises the type of Class B misdemeanor offenses criminal justice agencies must report to the Bureau of Criminal Investigation to include offenses of domestic violence under the newly created section.

House Bill No. 1396 establishes a minimum mandatory sentence of one year imprisonment for an offender who has pled guilty or nolo contendere to, or has been found guilty of, felony child abuse and restricts such offenders from participating in electronic home detention or home-based global positioning system monitoring if a minor is present in the home.

House Bill No. 1400 defines meat as the edible flesh of an animal born and harvested for the purpose of human consumption; prohibits the misrepresentation, advertising for sale, packaging, or sale of cell-cultured protein products as meat; and requires labeling of cell-cultured protein products as such.

House Bill No. 1404 designates State Highway 22 as the Veterans Memorial Highway.

House Bill No. 1433 limits the circumstances under which a hospital may use maintenance of certification status in determining whether to grant a physician staff privileges, clarifies the circumstances under which a hospital may consider maintenance of certification status, and prohibits a hospital from considering maintenance of certification participation or status as a standard of care consideration in the course of a quality improvement assessment.

The bill also provides a health care insurer may not deny reimbursement to a physician, prevent a physician from being a preferred provider, or discriminate with respect to reimbursement levels based solely on a physician's decision to not participate in maintenance of certification.

House Bill No. 1439 provides a sales and use tax exemption for materials used to construct or expand a system used to compress, gather, collect, store, transport, or inject carbon dioxide for secure geologic storage.

The bill provides a 10-year property tax exemption for pipeline property and necessary associated equipment used to transport or store carbon dioxide for secure geologic storage. The bill classifies any carbon dioxide capture system or equipment located at a coal conversion facility and used for secure geologic storage of carbon dioxide as personal property, exempt from property tax.

The bill also expands the oil extraction tax exemption for incremental production from a tertiary recovery project from 5 to 10 years from the date incremental production begins for a project drilled within the Bakken and Three Forks Formations and from 10 to 20 years from the date incremental production begins for a project drilled outside the Bakken and Three Forks Formations if more than 50 percent of the injected carbon dioxide is from coal production.

House Bill No. 1461 requires public elementary schools developing and processing assessments and reading screenings to ensure those evaluations include the core components of phonetic awareness, decoding, and spelling. The bill also creates a dyslexia screening pilot program to be implemented in eligible school districts, regional education associations, and special education units that meet certain requirements.

House Bill No. 1521 creates a new Century Code chapter establishing the North Dakota Ethics Commission, as required by the Constitution of North Dakota following November 2018 voter approval of Initiated Measure No. 1. The new chapter provides for commission member terms, compensation, and duties and establishes the procedures for making complaints, the procedures for conducting investigations, and the penalties for violations.

Several sections of the bill implement the new constitutional article's transparency requirements by amending Century Code sections regarding campaign finance reporting. The bill provides new definitions and reporting requirements, guidelines for adjusting reporting thresholds for inflation, and new penalties for failing to comply with reporting requirements.

The bill also adds "commission," which it defines as the North Dakota Ethics Commission, to various references throughout the Administrative Agencies Practice Act and requires the commission to comply with the Act with respect to certain rulemaking and adjudicative proceedings.

House Bill No. 1531 amends a Century Code section regarding specialty area teacher qualifications to allow an individual who meets specified requirements to teach in any subject, except in the subject areas of elementary education, special education, mathematics, science, language arts, and social studies, and provides criteria for the board of a school district to authorize such an individual to teach for one year at a time, up to a maximum of three years.

House Bill No. 1546 makes it a Class C felony for an individual to intentionally perform a human dismemberment abortion except in the case of a medical emergency. The bill provides the prohibition on human dismemberment abortions becomes effective on the 30th day after the adoption of an amendment to the U.S. Constitution that, in whole or in part, restores to the states the authority to prohibit abortion; on the 30th day after the Attorney General certifies to the Legislative Council the issuance of the judgment in any decision of the U.S. Supreme Court or the Eighth Circuit Court of Appeals that would allow enforcement of the prohibition on human dismemberment abortions; or the issuance of the judgment in any decision of the U.S. Supreme Court that, in whole or in part, restores to the states authority to prohibit abortion. The bill also amends the effective date of a 2007 Session Laws chapter relating to the prohibition of the performance of abortions and providing a penalty.

Senate Bill No. 2001, the agency appropriation for the Governor's office, creates the Theodore Roosevelt Presidential Library and Museum endowment fund for the purpose of using the interest and earnings to pay interest expenses on a loan from the Bank of North Dakota. The bill also authorizes the Governor to provide grants to a private entity for the construction, operation, and maintenance costs of the presidential library.

Senate Bill No. 2044 prohibits an individual from causing a substantial interruption or impairment of a critical infrastructure facility; provides a definition for "critical infrastructure facility;" and provides for a fine, not to exceed $100,000, for an organization that acts as a conspirator with an individual who causes a substantial interruption or impairment of a critical infrastructure facility or a public service.

Senate Bill No. 2051 adopts the Uniform Nonparent Custody and Visitation Act, which specifies criteria for a nonparent to seek and a court to award nonparent custody or visitation of a child. The bill also repeals a Century Code section relating to grandparental rights of visitation to an unmarried minor child.

Senate Bill No. 2110 creates definitions for "cybersecurity" and "cybersecurity strategy" and directs the Information Technology Department to advise and oversee cybersecurity for all executive branch agencies, including institutions under the control of the State Board of Higher Education, counties, cities, school districts, and other political subdivisions that advise and consult with the legislative and judicial branches regarding cybersecurity strategy.

Senate Bill No. 2124 shifts delivery of social services from counties to human service zones; revises the duties of county social service boards, human service zones, and the Department of Human Services as those duties relate to the delivery of certain social services; and updates applicable statutory terminology and references accordingly. The bill provides for the creation of up to 19 human service zones to provide lines of accountability between state program and policy and the administration of social services; provides for zone directors to report to and participate in a Department of Human Services human service zone leadership team; provides for zone boards with representation from each county in a zone; provides the department establish consistent budgeting guidelines, human resource policies, and policies and guidelines for standard and consistent program delivery; and provides for full-time equivalent position transfer authority.

The bill also provides the manner in which legislative property tax relief associated with the state takeover of social service costs must be calculated and displayed on property tax statements, eliminates the county's 20-mill levy authority for human services purposes, and removes base year property tax adjustment language relating to state-paid social services costs.

Senate Bill No. 2157 authorizes a student to enroll in a driver's training course through a high school program if the student will be at least 14 years of age by the completion date of the classroom portion of the course and prohibits a student from participating in the behind-the-wheel portion of the course until the student is at least 14 years of age.

Senate Bill No. 2196 directs the Forensic Pathology Department at the University of North Dakota School of Medicine and Health Sciences to appoint a drug fatalities review panel to review individuals' deaths identified as, or pertaining to a trend or pattern of deaths identified as, drug or alcohol overdoses. The bill directs the State Department of Health and the School of Medicine and Health Sciences to provide for or arrange for administrative services to assist the panel.

Senate Bill No. 2225 requires each parent and every adult child of an adult who is unable to support oneself to maintain that adult to the extent each is able. The bill outlines when a creditor may recover for furnishing necessary health services to an adult who is unable to support oneself under the familial duty of support for health services.

The bill also repeals the law that provided a parent or child of an individual eligible for county general assistance had the duty to support that individual and provided a county could recover from the parent or adult children of an indigent individual for necessaries furnished by the county.

Senate Bill No. 2230 prohibits qualifications for eligibility for public school board membership in a school district located on tribal land from being less restrictive than eligibility qualifications prescribed by tribal law or resolution for public office and defines "tribal land."

Senate Bill No. 2257 authorizes the Governor, in consultation with the Tax Commissioner, to enter an agreement with the governing body of any tribe in this state for the collection and administration of the alcoholic beverages and tobacco products wholesale taxes and the alcoholic beverages gross receipts tax. The bill also repeals the existing chapter of Century Code relating to sales, use, and gross receipts tax agreements entered between the Governor and the Standing Rock Sioux Tribe.

Senate Bill No. 2258 authorizes the Governor, in consultation with the Tax Commissioner, to enter an agreement with the governing body of any tribe in this state for the collection and administration of sales, use, alcoholic beverages gross receipts, and farm machinery gross receipts taxes. The bill also repeals the existing chapter of Century Code relating to sales, use, and gross receipts tax agreements entered between the Governor and the Standing Rock Sioux Tribe.

Senate Bill No. 2265 requires the Superintendent of Public Instruction to create a process to reinstate and recertify Title I credentials for certain individuals; requires school districts to provide for a minimum number of instructional hours for students; increases professional days in a school calendar from two to three days; requires schools to make up certain instructional hours for school dismissal due to weather; requires school districts to apply for a waiver if the district intends to operate under a school calendar that consists of four days of instruction per week; adds behavior prevention or mitigation techniques to the list of categories from which a school district may offer youth behavioral health professional development training to teachers and administrators; amends a new Century Code section, relating to a prohibition on qualifications for eligibility for public school board membership in a school district located on tribal land from being less restrictive than eligibility qualifications prescribed by tribal law or resolution for public office, to restrict the applicability of the section to qualifications for public office relating to criminal convictions; allows an individual, under certain circumstances, to teach any subject except elementary education, special education, mathematics, science, language arts, and social studies if the individual meets certain teaching requirements; amends requirements for high school unit instructional time to replace hours of instruction with hours of student engagement; prohibits the Superintendent from forwarding state aid payments to school districts until enrollment reports have been filed with the Superintendent; makes factor adjustments in the section relating to the determination of average daily membership for school districts to add a factor for the number of students by which the fall enrollment of a school district exceeds the average daily membership of the prior year, to increase the factor for the number of students by which the fall enrollment of a school district exceeds the average daily membership of the prior year, and to provide for annual increases in the factor; amends various factors in the calculation of the state aid baseline funding formula; requires the deduction of 60 mills from the state school aid formula beginning in the 2025-26 school year; increases the deduction for local property tax in the state school aid formula; allows the board of a school district to determine the length of an instructional period, day, and week and requires the school district to reschedule hours if the district falls below the minimum hours due to weather-related closures; requires the Superintendent to pay the cost of cross-border attendance from funds appropriated by the Legislative Assembly for state aid to schools; and requires school districts that admit students from another school district and meet certain criteria to charge 200 percent of the tuition payment required or $4,000, whichever is greater. The bill also repeals provisions relating to a school district's ability to apply to the Superintendent for permission to reconfigure the number of required instructional days.

Senate Bill No. 2306 revises the law regarding the occupational and professional licensure of military spouses, providing a board shall grant a provisional license or temporary permit to a military spouse who is licensed by a foreign jurisdiction; expands the definition of the term "board" as it applies to the law regulating the occupational or professional practice of foreign practitioners and the practice of military members and military spouses; and requires a board to inquire whether an applicant for licensure is a member of the military or a military spouse.

The bill also specifies provisional teaching license requirements for military spouses and requires the Education Standards and Practices Board to grant a teaching license to an applicant who is a military spouse, if the individual meets certain requirements for licensure of military spouses.

Senate Bill No. 2312 changes the allowable revenue sharing split for a state-tribal oil and gas revenue sharing agreement. The bill modifies the previous 50/50 state-tribal oil and gas revenue sharing split to require the tribe receive 80 percent of the oil and gas revenue attributable to trust lands and 20 percent of the oil and gas revenue from all other production, with the state receiving the remainder.

The bill removes the revenue sharing agreement requirements of Legislative Assembly confirmation and of expiration within 16 years of its effective date.

The bill also suspends the Committee on Tribal and State Relations until July 31, 2021.

Senate Bill No. 2320 requires the State Board of Higher Education and the institutions under the board's control to adopt policies to protect students' rights to free speech, assembly, and expression; to permit institutions to establish and enforce reasonable and constitutional time, place, and manner restrictions on these rights; to permit students, faculty, or student organizations to invite guest speakers or groups to present regardless of the viewpoint or content of the anticipated speech of the guest speaker or group; and to protect the academic freedom and free speech rights of faculty while adhering to guidelines established by the American Association of University Professors.

Senate Bill No. 2362 clarifies oil extraction tax revenue allocated to the state pursuant to the terms of a state-tribal revenue sharing agreement is subject to allocation among the resources trust fund, common schools trust fund, foundation aid stabilization fund, legacy fund, and general fund. The bill also provides for an additional one-half percent oil extraction tax revenue allocation to the resources trust fund, beginning with allocations in August 2019 and continuing until the additional allocations total $128,740,000.

Chapter Seven
Tribal-State Relationships

In May 2015, David Diebel and Carson Nordgaard of D&N Cinematics in Bismarck operated a camera drone to capture imagery of Fort Abraham Lincoln State Park near Mandan.

Native American Hall of Honor 420
North Dakota Tribal Nations 446
North Dakota Tribal Colleges 452
North Dakota Tourism Partners with Native American Tourism 455
North Dakota Native Tourism Alliance 455
First Nations Day 456
Indian Youth Leadership Academy 457
Native American Youth Leadership Summit 457
Woodrow Keeble Award 457

Native American Hall of Honor

The North Dakota Native American Hall of Honor is an annual program that recognizes traditional and contemporary achievements of Native Americans who have gone above and beyond representing their tribes and cultures. Scott Davis, executive director of the North Dakota Indian Affairs Commission, and a committee of representatives from North Dakota were instrumental in moving the North Dakota Native American Hall of Honor from a dream to a reality in partnership with the State Historical Society of North Dakota and the State Historical Society of North Dakota Foundation.

The grand opening and first inductee ceremony of the North Dakota Native American Hall of Honor was held on September 8, 2016. The event was attended by the inductees and their families, along with many other individuals who filled the Russell Reid Auditorium at the North Dakota Heritage Center and State Museum as well as overflow areas. Approximately 350 people attended the event and enjoyed a traditional meal with bison stew provided free of charge by United Tribes Technical College. Davis served as emcee for the inaugural event. During the induction ceremony, videos created by Makoché Studios were premiered, which showcased the accomplishments of each honoree. Each inductee then shared comments, followed by an honor song and celebration of the new exhibit.

The Native American Hall of Honor provides a place where the public can honor and commemorate significant achievements of Native Americans in North Dakota. The program recognizes the achievements of the chosen inductees in four categories: Leadership, Veterans, Culture and Arts, and Athletics. Information, selected personal objects, and a video about each chosen honoree are placed on exhibit for one year in the Native American Hall of Honor at the North Dakota Heritage Center and State Museum.

Nominations for the award can be made of people who are living or in memory of those who have passed away. Up to two people per category are considered for acceptance into the Hall of Honor each year. The selection of inductees is done by a committee with membership representation from all the tribal nations in North Dakota. A description of the nominee's accomplishments, a biography, photos, other documentation, and two letters of reference are also used to determine those chosen for induction into the Native American Hall of Honor.

The criteria for each category include:

Leadership

Individuals, groups, elected leaders, community leaders, grassroots leaders, elders, spiritual leaders, teachers, and educational leaders can be nominated for this award. Nominees considered have made innovative contributions to their field, community, or state and have distinguished themselves as models in leadership. Also considered in the selection process are awards received and volunteer service.

Military/Veteran

An individual or group can be nominated who was honorably discharged, served during war time or peace time, and demonstrated a positive impact in and around their community or state. Also considered during the selection process are awards and medals received by the nominee and volunteer service.

Culture/Arts

Those eligible for this award include dancers, drum groups, singers, writers, artists in all forms of media art, poets, and designers who have had an impact on the preservation of the culture and art of their specific tribe and state. Also considered in the selection process are other awards received and volunteer service.

Sports/Teams

An individual or group can be nominated who has shown sportsmanship, dedication, and character and made contributions to team, charity, and athletic achievements. Nominees are considered that have provided leadership and support, displayed qualities of an active role model, have distinguished themselves as models in personal and professional conduct, and have performed volunteer services to the local community and state. Also considered during the selection process are other awards received.

To nominate an individual or group for the North Dakota Native American Hall of Honor, visit http://indianaffairs.nd.gov/hall-of-honor. For additional information, call 701-328-2428.

Harriett Skye
Standing Rock Sioux Tribe

Induction Year:
2016

Category:
Leadership

Harriett Skye, Ph.D., (1931-2018) dedicated her life to the advancement of Native endeavors. She was an educator, activist, journalist, mentor, poet, student, and filmmaker, often at the same time.

From 1972 to 1982, as the director of the Office of Public Relations at United Tribes Technical College (UTTC), Skye hosted the local KFYR television program *Indian Country Today*. The program placed prominent Native Americans before the public to talk about issues from a tribal point of view.

At age 55, "too young to retire, and too old to train," she picked up the phone and called a community college. She received her doctorate in ethnic studies from the University of California-Berkley in 2003. She returned to North Dakota and retired in 2011 as Vice President Emeritus of Intertribal Programs at UTTC.

Other significant accomplishments include directing the documentary *The Right to Be*, which was screened at the Sundance Film Festival in 1994, serving as editor of the *Standing Rock Star* and *United Tribes News*, and serving on a North Dakota advisory board to the U.S. Commission on Civil Rights.

In addition to her accomplishments, Skye was honored in the Native American Hall of Honor for showing leadership at a time when it was difficult for Native communities to have a voice.

Marcellus Red Tomahawk
Standing Rock Sioux Tribe

Induction Year:
2016

Category:
Leadership

Marcellus Red Tomahawk, *Tacanipiluta* (1849-1931), was born in Montana Territory as a member of the Hunkpapa-Tanktonai tribe. He was 24 when he moved to the Standing Rock Sioux Reservation. He served as an Indian Police Duty Sergeant and First Lieutenant for 18 years. In 1890, under order of James McLaughlin, he participated in the arrest of Sitting Bull.

In 1911, Red Tomahawk became the first Tribal Chairman of the Standing Rock Sioux Tribe. He served on the Tribal Council repeatedly over many years, always striving to improve the welfare of his tribe. He was recognized as a peace negotiator, working to educate and create awareness about Native culture among the public. Representing the tribe, he frequently met with dignitaries, including President Theodore Roosevelt.

For more than 90 years, his profile was recognized across the state as the symbol on North Dakota highway signs. The North Dakota Highway Patrol also adopted his profile as its emblem and continues to use it.

A friend of all people, Red Tomahawk is recognized as one of North Dakota's great historical leaders.

U.S. Army Corporal Nathan Goodiron
Mandan, Hidatsa, and Arikara Nation and Standing Rock Sioux Tribe

Induction Year:
2016

Category:
Military/Veteran

Corporal Nathan J. Goodiron (1981-2006) served with the 1st Battalion, 188th Air Defense Artillery, North Dakota National Guard. He died November 23, 2006, when his unit came in contact with enemy forces using small-arms fire and rocket-propelled grenades in Qarabagh, Afghanistan.

He was a fourth generation of Goodiron military veterans, beginning with his great-grandfather, who served as a code talker with the U.S. Army during World War I. Goodiron carried warrior names since infancy; his maternal great-grandmother named him "Young Eagle" and "Distant Thunder."

A high achiever in academics and sports, he played basketball for the Mandaree Warriors, continuing his education at Minot State University and Fort Berthold Community College. Enfolded by the Hidatsa way, he participated in ceremonies, powwows, giveaways, and honorings.

A family member wrote that Corporal Goodiron "represents the ancient way of the Hidatsa people and their willingness to give all [so] that our people remain safe, true to our traditions, and free in this land that is now the United States of America."

He was honored in the Native American Hall of Honor for his military endeavors and for the honor, humility, and compassion he showed toward his community.

Richard Marcellais
Turtle Mountain Band of Chippewa

Induction Year:
2016

Category:
Military/Veteran

Senator Richard Marcellais (b. 1947) served in the U.S. Army from 1968 to 1971. From 1971 to 1994, he was a computer specialist with the U.S. Veterans Administration, Bureau of Indian Affairs, and Indian Health Services. Marcellais serves in the North Dakota Senate (2006-present) and was Tribal Chairman for the Turtle Mountain Band of Chippewa (2008-2010).

A colleague describes him as "a man of integrity, respect, common sense, and someone who represents his state, his district, and his people with pride and distinction." Another praises his "colorful dress and humor. He understands that occasional independence from convention and laughter can be soothing to his spirit and the spirit of others."

Marcellais was honored in the Native American Hall of Honor for his ongoing work with Native American veterans throughout various communities in North Dakota.

Anthony McDonald
Spirit Lake Nation

Induction Year:
2016

Category:
Culture/Arts

A member of the Spirit Lake Nation, Anthony McDonald (b. 1937) was the first Native American to be ordained a deacon of the Roman Catholic Church in North Dakota.

Ordained in 1983, McDonald has dedicated his life to serving people with prayer and support. He held healing services combining Native culture with Catholic faith to bring about better understanding of both worlds. Abstaining from alcohol himself, he remains a role model for those seeking support and help with addiction through counseling and treatment programs.

A fluent Dakota speaker, McDonald taught Dakota culture and language class to elementary school students. He established an Indian club for children to learn dancing and singing to promote positive self-worth and pride in their ancestry. He also served on local school boards, mentored young cowboys in the rodeo club, and, along with his family, coordinated community events to honor veterans.

In addition to his endeavors in the field of arts and culture, McDonald has shown great leadership in sharing his culture with dignity, humility, and compassion.

Arnold Charging, Sr.
Mandan, Hidatsa, and Arikara Nation

Induction Year:
2016

Category:
Sports/Teams

Arnold Charging, Sr. (1933-2011) was a stellar athlete, excelling in both football and basketball, who played during the golden years of the Elbowoods Warriors in North Dakota.

Charging competed in football, basketball, and track, but football was his favorite. He played fullback when the Warriors won the 1950 Conference Championship. He was also on the Warriors team that won its way to third place in the 1951 State Class B Basketball Tournament.

During his senior year of high school, Charging was named to the All-State Basketball Team. That year he was also nominated to the National High School All-American All-Star Football Team and invited by the Winnipeg Blue Bombers football team to tryouts. Offered athletic scholarships from several universities, he enrolled at Dickinson State College on a scholarship in 1952. He left college to assist his family and others in the massive relocation caused by the completion of the Garrison Dam.

Robert Eaglestaff
Standing Rock Sioux Tribe

Induction Year:
2016

Category:
Sports/Teams

Robert "Bob" Eaglestaff (1953-1996) excelled at both academics and basketball. A member of the National Honor Society at Standing Rock High School, he set several basketball scoring records, including the most points in one game (69) and the individual scoring record (1,792 points), which is still unbroken. He chose college over playing professional basketball. Recruited to Brigham Young University, he later transferred to the University of North Dakota (UND). During his time as starting forward, the team won the conference title for three consecutive years. He was inducted into the UND Hall of Fame in 2004.

After graduating with a bachelor's degree from UND in 1976, Eaglestaff attended the University of South Dakota, earning a master's degree in education administration in 1980.

From 1983 until 1996, Eaglestaff worked as an educator in Washington, leading the American Indian Heritage School in Seattle from a place of little hope to a proud community of high-achieving students.

Eaglestaff was honored in the North Dakota Native American Hall of Honor, not only for his endeavors in sports, but for setting an example for all young athletes in Native communities.

David Gipp
Standing Rock Sioux Tribe

Induction Year:
2017

Category:
Leadership

David M. Gipp (b. 1946) has provided a lifetime of service for Native American people, not only in North Dakota but across the country. His activism was fueled, in part, by the positions he held, friendships across the country, and stories from the students of United Tribes Technical College.

His lengthy career included serving as one of the first tribal planners, writing the first proposal for the development of what is now Sitting Bull College, and working to establish United Tribes Technical College and United Tribes of North Dakota. He was the first permanent executive director of the American Indian Higher Education Consortium and has been an officer and member of the boards of the American Indian Higher Education Consortium and the American Indian College Fund.

Dr. Gipp served as president of United Tribes Technical College for nearly 37 years and led the intertribal college to its initial accreditation by the North Central Association's Higher Learning Commission. Under his leadership, the college grew from a one-year certificate-granting employment training institution to a community college granting two- and four-year degrees. Throughout his career, his main focus has remained on Indian education and equality for Native Americans. He has testified on legislation to state legislators advocating for Native American rights and concerns.

Gipp has been the recipient of many awards, including the Martin Luther King, Jr. Award in 1991. He has served on numerous boards and commissions. He also served in the North Dakota and Colorado National Guards and was trained as a military journalist.

Leigh Jeanotte
Turtle Mountain Band of Chippewa

Induction Year:
2017

Category:
Leadership

Leigh Jeanotte (b. 1948) officially began his work at the University of North Dakota (UND) in 1972 after completing his bachelor's degree in elementary education. While completing his master's in education degree in school administration, he worked as the field coordinator for the Teacher Corps Program at UND, providing academic support and personal advisement to American Indian students. In 1978, Jeanotte was appointed director of Native American Programs and has held that position ever since. He has 43 years of service in education working for American Indian people throughout North Dakota and the region. Jeanotte has various publications to his credit, including his doctoral dissertation completed in 1981. He has done consultation and program evaluation work for many organizations and written grant proposals.

Jeanotte has served as a member, chair, or officer of many organizations and programs that impact higher education for American Indian students, including the National Indian Education Association, North Dakota Indian Education Association, Higher Education Resource Organization for Students, Department of Public Instruction, North Dakota University System, and numerous advisory committees. He has also served as a board member of Turtle Mountain Community College in Belcourt and the Grand Forks Northeast Human Service Center. Jeanotte was instrumental in applying for and raising many millions of dollars in grant funding for programs that impact American Indian students and their tribal communities. His expertise in the area of Indian education has been utilized nationwide.

Jeanotte is well known as a friend, more so than an administrator, and one who always has time for his family. He is extremely proud of his three grown daughters, two sons-in-law, and six grandchildren. There are two weeks out of the year that Jeanotte particularly looks forward to: one is North Dakota deer hunting season, and the other is UNDIA Annual Time Out and Wacipi.

Dan Jerome
Turtle Mountain Band of Chippewa

Induction Year:
2017

Category:
Culture/Arts

Dan Jerome (b. 1930) was born on the Turtle Mountain Indian Reservation. His formal education began in the Belcourt school system, and he attended Haskell Institute (now Haskell Indian Nations University) in Lawrence, Kansas. He interrupted his studies to join the U.S. Navy, but received an honorary diploma from Haskell in 2009.

Jerome served in the U.S. Navy for four years during the Korean Conflict, with 20 of those months aboard ship in the Pacific and Korean waters. After his discharge, he attended the University of North Dakota in 1954 and was one of three Native students enrolled at the time. After graduation in 1960, he began teaching mathematics in North Dakota public schools. After teaching for five years, he returned to Belcourt. He became the first superintendent of schools of what is now Belcourt School District 7.

After retiring in 1990, Jerome ran for the North Dakota State Senate and became the first Native American senator in North Dakota. After his term in the Senate, he continued his native art crafts of making flutes, bows and arrows, Red River Carts, dog sleds, snowshoes, rattles, war clubs, drums, and cultural works. Jerome has professionally recorded two discs of flute music and recently wrote and illustrated 14 Ojibwa Legends booklets. At the age of 87, he complied *Warriors of Turtle Mountain Band of Chippewa: Those Who Have Served in the United States Armed Forces*. The book lists more than 1,700 veterans who served in World War I, World War II, Korea, Vietnam, and into the present time. All that Jerome does is for the preservation of the history, culture, and art of the people of the reservation.

Mary Louise Defender Wilson
Standing Rock Sioux Tribe

Induction Year:
2017

Category:
Culture/Arts

Born on the Standing Rock Reservation near Shields, Mary Louise Defender Wilson (b. 1930) was surrounded by the culture and storytelling of her Dakotah-speaking family and was particularly influenced by the cultural knowledge of her grandfather, Tall Man See the Bear. Storytelling was her main form of traditional education and, by age 11, she became a storyteller herself. With her ability to speak three languages (Dakotah, Hidatsa, and English), Wilson began a lifetime of sharing the stories she carried with others.

In 1949, Wilson met her husband, William, a U.S. Marine who served as a code talker in the South Pacific during World War II. She moved to his Navaho Reservation in the 1970s and worked with Native American-related government agencies and continued to expand her knowledge of traditional storytelling. She returned to Standing Rock in 1976 and sought out elders who would teach her more stories. During the 1980s, she taught tribal culture and language at Sitting Bull College in Fort Yates, North Dakota. In 1999, Wilson released her first spoken word album. She continues public appearances sharing her knowledge and stories to this day.

Wilson has received the National Endowment for the Arts' National Heritage Fellowship, the country's highest honor for a traditional artist. She received the Bush Foundation's prestigious Bush Artist Fellowship and the Enduring Vision Award, two of the country's largest artist fellowships. In 2015, she was the first North Dakotan to ever receive the coveted USA Artist Fellowship, another of the country's most prestigious recognitions.

Wilson has performed at the Kennedy Center for Performing Arts, the Library of Congress's Great Hall, and the American Indian Museum in Washington, D.C. She lives her art. Wilson has demonstrated patience, grace, commitment, and unsurpassed artistry for eight decades.

1973 Fort Yates Warriors Basketball Team
Standing Rock Sioux Tribe

Induction Year
2017

Category:
Sports/Teams

The Fort Yates Warriors gave North Dakota sports fans perhaps the most exciting State Class A Boys Basketball championship game of all time. Coached by Clark Swisher, Jr., the Warriors made a breathtaking comeback in regulation time, eventually winning the 1973 championship game in triple overtime, by defeating Minot, one of the largest schools in the state. Fort Yates had the smallest population of any school in the tournament. It was an inspiring victory that fans and foes across the state remember to this day and has been a source of Native pride ever since.

Team members were Jerry Grey Bear, Tony Bobtail Bear, Oliver Eagleman, Verle Red Tomahawk, Gus Claymore, Jesse Taken Alive, Albert Gipp, Kenny Walks, Darrell Eaglestaff, Roger Goudreaux, Bill Eaglestaff, Victor Goudreaux, Gary Little Dog, and Wyman Archambault. The team also included student managers Kevyn Heck and Sheldon Speigleman; head coach Clark Swisher, Jr.; assistant coach Sherman Laubach; and cheerleaders Julie McLaughlin, Nadine Claymore, and Rosie Treetop.

The persistence displayed on the championship court in 1973 carried over into the adult lives of the Warrior athletes. They became family men, some served in the military, and they had jobs and careers. They were successful citizens and served their communities and the tribe. They credited their experience in 1973 as a guiding influence in their lives and became mentors and role models for young people who are still respected in the community.

The 1973 team was born of a dynasty of teams of athletic men who practiced hard and battled eagerly on the court for the joy of the game and the respect of their opponents. They had inherited the determination to compete and bring honor to the People. Throughout the season and in that championship game, they played together as a team, never giving up, even as time was running out. They demonstrated the Lakota value of fortitude.

Pete Fredericks
Mandan, Hidatsa, and Arikara Nation

Induction Year:
2017

Category:
Sports/Teams

Pete Fredericks (b. 1936) was born in Elbowoods, North Dakota. His Indian name is Charging Eagle. He grew up and attended school on the Fort Berthold Indian Reservation until the completion of Garrison Dam submerged Elbowoods and forced its people to relocate. Fredericks transferred to Watford City for his last two years of high school. During his sophomore year in Elbowoods, Fredericks won the National High School Bareback Championship, and in his senior year, he won the National High School All-Around Championship and the National High School Saddle Bronc Championship. He continued his education at New Mexico State in Las Cruces, New Mexico, transferring after two years to Dickinson State College, where he developed a rodeo club and started the Dickinson State College Rodeo team, which went on to win at the National College Finals at Penn Rose Stadium in Colorado Springs, Colorado. Fredericks has been a strong advocate for young cowboys and cowgirls, on and off the reservation, enabling them to pursue their dreams. Fredericks has shown dedication and contributed to the sport of rodeo.

In 1967, Fredericks organized the Indian National Finals Rodeo (INFR) Commission, which held the first INFR Championship Rodeo at Salt Palace in Salt Lake City, Utah. He remains on the INFR Board of Commissioners, which now stages the INFR annually in Las Vegas, Nevada. In 1999, Fredericks was inducted into the North Dakota Cowboy Hall of Fame in Medora, North Dakota, and in 2012, he was inducted into the Rodeo Hall of Fame at the National Cowboy & Western Heritage Museum in Oklahoma City, Oklahoma. In 2011, Fredericks was recognized for playing an integral part in Indian rodeo history and was inducted into the INFR Hall of Fame in Las Vegas.

Fredericks continues to serve his community of Twin Buttes. He has served as a chairman of the Twin Buttes Catholic Church, an MHA Elder's board member, and chairman of the Twin Buttes Community Board multiple times.

Patrick Gourneau
Turtle Mountain Band of Chippewa

Induction Year:
2018

Category:
Leadership

Patrick Gourneau (1904-1989) was born on February 11 in 1904 or 1905. His childhood and youth were spent in Indian boarding schools and the Turtle Mountains looking for labor jobs to help his family. Gourneau was among the first group of Turtle Mountain Reservation students to attend the Wahpeton Indian School. In 1919, he went to Indian school at Fort Totten. He continued his education at Haskell Institute in Kansas and Wahpeton Indian School.

Gorneau traveled through several states in search of labor. After marrying the daughter of a large-scale market gardener, Gourneau worked with him for two years. He returned to the reservation and purchased land to develop his own business. Through his efforts, the William Langer Jewel Bearing Plant (now Microlap Technologies Inc.) was established, providing jobs to generations of tribal members and surrounding communities.

Gourneau served as tribal chairman from July 1953 to January 1959. He was involved in the revival of traditional Indian ceremonies and dances and wrote a condensed history of the Turtle Mountain Band. His image in Native dance regalia appeared on the front of the North Dakota highway map and on booklets to promote tourism. As Tribal Advisory Committee chairman in March 1954, his testimony before a congressional committee saved the tribe from termination and a loss of federal support. He worked to bring the four tribes of North Dakota into an intertribal alliance (United Tribes of North Dakota), and his efforts resulted in an appointment to the National Committee of Civil Rights.

During his term of office, Gourneau refused a salary and the use of an automobile to conduct tribal business and brought about the repeal of Indian liquor laws. Due to his efforts, rural electrification was brought to the reservation and provided Indians the advantages of electricity and phone services. In 1986, he was awarded the North Dakota Heritage Profile Honor Award.

Betty Gress
Mandan, Hidatsa, and Arikara Nation

Induction Year:
2018

Category:
Leadership

Betty L. (Fredericks) Gress (b. 1945) was the youngest of nine children born to John Sr. and Catherine (Medicine Stone) Fredericks. She was born on the Fort Berthold Indian Reservation in Elbowoods, North Dakota. Gress grew up on the reservation, attending grade school in Elbowoods and Halliday and finishing eighth grade at Twin Buttes School. She attended Killdeer High School and graduated from Halliday High School in 1963. She attended Minot State College and the University of North Dakota and graduated from Northern Arizona University in Flagstaff, Arizona, with a bachelor of science degree in psychology and minors in sociology and education. Gress also attended workshops at Georgetown University in Washington, D.C., and the John F. Kennedy School of Government at Harvard University in Boston.

Gress's professional experience includes girls advisor/counselor, director for adult education, director of a family development center, Title I counselor, associate executive director for the Coalition of Indian Controlled School Boards, Inc., and 23 years of federal service for the Office of Native American Programs of the U.S. Department of Housing and Urban Development. Through her efforts with the Coalition, a cornerstone achievement was reached with the securing of monies for the startup of the Title VI Indian Education Act and programs.

Gress joined the board of directors of the Denver Indian Health and Family Services (DIHFS) in 1988, was elected board chairperson in 1995, and continues to serve in this capacity. On April 18, 2018, DIHFS held an open house celebrating 40 years of service and the opening of a new clinic, which doubled the size of the facility. It was named "The Betty Gress Clinic" to honor her years of service and dedication to Native people in the Denver area. Gress has also served as a trustee for the North Dakota Cowboy Hall of Fame and Native American Heritage Center in Medora, North Dakota.

1941-1942 Elbowoods Warriors Basketball Team Mandan, Hidatsa, and Arikara Nation

Induction Year:
2018

Category:
Sports/Teams

The Elbowoods Warriors of 1941-1942 was the first Indian team to gain a berth in the North Dakota State Class B Basketball tournament in Minot. The Warriors were awarded the first-place title 60 years after the championship game was played. Team members were Harry Grady, Issac Fox, Sidney Fox, Charlie Blake, Leon Fox, John Rabbithead, Duane Charging, Raymond Weikum, and Harold Oderman.

With the start of the 1942 tournament play, the Warriors were 22-2. They defeated the New England Tigers 29-27 and Sacred Heart Academy 29-28. On March 21, they played the Lakota Raiders for the championship. Their star guard, John Rabbithead, turned 20 on March 21, and tournament rules made him ineligible to play. Coach Leon Wall had planned on using two substitutes instead of playing Rabbithead. The game ended with a 31-32 win for the Lakota Raiders.

Wall later received a letter from the Lakota High School superintendent, informing him that Lakota had played an ineligible player and was forfeiting the entire season. The North Dakota High School Activities Association (NDHSAA) in April 1942 disagreed about how to handle the issue. One member moved to declare the title vacant and another to award it to Elbowoods, but no action was taken.

It was not until January 2002, after several meetings and negotiations by Mark Fox (Isaac's son) and others, that a motion was approved by NDHSAA to name the Elbowoods Warriors as the 1942 State Champions. On March 28, 2002, a victory celebration was held at the Four Bears Lodge in New Town. Oderman and Weikum, the two members of the team still living at the time, were in attendance, along with family members of departed teammates.

The team's experience is intertwined with World War II. All the Indian team members served honorably during the war. Upon their return to Fort Berthold, they helped rebuild a strong agriculture and cattle ranching economy on their lands. They served as leaders in federal and tribal governments and in community institutions, such as schools and churches. All were forced to leave their homes and relocate to higher grounds in the mid-1950s when the waters of the Garrison Dam covered the school, dormitory, small gymnasium, and display cases that held the athletic trophies won by the Elbowoods Warriors.

Martin Cross
Mandan, Hidatsa, and Arikara Nation

Induction Year:
2019

Category:
Leadership

Martin Old Dog (1906-1964) (Yellow Eagle) was born on the Fort Berthold Reservation to Chief Old Dog and his wife Many Dances. He was educated at Wahpeton and Flandreau Indian schools.

As a young man, he enjoyed the carefree life of a cowboy. He traveled the local rodeo circuit at Minot, Beulah, Yucca, and Strawberry Lake. In 1928, he married Dorothy Bartell and settled on the Old Dog allotment near the Missouri River, raising cattle, crops, and 10 children. In 1942, he enlisted in the U.S. Army Air Corps and changed his name from Old Dog to Cross. He served for six months before being honorably discharged and was an active member of the Joseph Young Hawk American Legion Post and served as both commander and adjutant.

In 1944, Cross was elected chairman of the Tribal Business Council. For the next 20 years, he served four terms as chairman and two terms as councilman. He was frequently called upon to represent the people and speak on their behalf in matters concerning their welfare and land, making several trips to Washington, D.C.

Cross served his tribe in the time of their greatest need, during the building of the Garrison Dam. He was elected as chairman in 1944, the year the Flood Control Act was passed by Congress. The next 12 years would be a time of resistance and negotiations and eventually the massive relocation and displacement of more than 90 percent of the people from their beloved homeland. He provided leadership during those turbulent years. He served with numerous other organizations, including the National Congress of American Indians, Joseph Young Hawk Post, Fort Berthold Livestock Association, Fort Berthold Inter-Agency Committee, Governors' Interstate Indian Council, InterTribal Council of North Dakota, National Inter-Tribal Institute, and Fort Berthold Inter-Agency Committee.

Cross represents that generation of Indian leaders who answered the call to serve their people when they were needed, and they did so without hesitation.

Chief Little Shell III
Turtle Mountain Band of Chippewa

Induction Year:
2019

Category:
Leadership

Chief Little Shell III (c. 1825-1901) is the iconic image of the Turtle Mountain Chippewa tribal license plates, flag, Great Seal, and many other tributes. He provided for future generations by fighting for established land claims and just compensation for lands taken, refusing to sign the 1882 "Ten Cent Treaty" McCumber Agreement that drastically reduced the reservation by taking the best quality lands.

Chief Little Shell was among the Ojibwe leaders who signed the Old Crossing Treaty near Red Lake Falls, Minnesota, in 1863, surrendering rights to land in Minnesota and a strip of land in North Dakota along the Red River. After this, he and his band became nomadic hunters, fishers, and trappers and did not want to be settled down and confined to a tiny area on the Plains.

Chief Little Shell is the model for the official Massachusetts Commonwealth seal. The legislature of Massachusetts approved the seal on June 5, 1885, and it is also on the Commonwealth flag.

Chief Little Shell ranged far and wide providing for his people and interacting with state and federal governments, as well as church and civic officials, other tribes, and non-Indians. His efforts initiated legal processes and encouraged others to persevere in seeking justice and compensation for the loss of lands and livelihood, providing for future generations who finally received some compensation through the Indian Claims Commission and subsequent proceedings based on the legal case he made.

Chief Little Shell is photographed wearing a Peace Medal and is sometimes described as "the Peace Chief" as he did not resort to violence against the settlers and hostile usurpers, quelling near-incidents, always seeking to keep the peace and thinking first of his people whose lands and lives were at stake in future negotiations.

With the death of Chief Little Shell III, Congress quickly ratified an amended McCumber Agreement, which required the Turtle Mountain Band to release all claims against the United States as a prerequisite to obtaining their much-needed annuities from the government.

Charles Murphy
Standing Rock Sioux Tribe

Induction Year:
2019

Category:
Leadership

Charles William Murphy (b. 1948) served the Standing Rock Sioux Tribe for 36 years as tribal chairman and tribal councilman. He was born to Rita Murphy and Frank Brave Bull in Fort Yates. Murphy served his country during the Vietnam War and received the Bronze Star, National Defense Ribbon, and Good Conduct and Military Merit Service medals.

Murphy began his career in tribal government and leadership when he was elected to Tribal Council in 1981-1983 as the Porcupine Tribal Council representative. He was first elected chairman of the Standing Rock Sioux Tribe for 1983-1987 and re-elected for 1987-1991, 1994-1997, 1997-2001, and 2001-2005. In 2009, he was elected to his sixth term. While in office, Murphy testified before Congress on the social and economic impact of the Oahe Reservoir on Standing Rock tribal lands. In 1991, he was appointed a member of the federal task force for the reorganization of the Bureau of Indian Affairs.

Murphy has served as chairman of the board of directors for United Tribes Technical College and the Great Plains Tribal Chairman Association, as well as on various committees and boards.

Murphy addressed the 59th Legislative Assembly for the State of the Tribal-State Relationship in 2005. In 2006, he was appointed by Governor John Hoeven to the North Dakota State Board of Higher Education. He was presented with an honorary bachelor's degree from Sitting Bull College in 2014.

He married Caroline "Kay" Ogg in 1973 and had three sons. Kay lost her battle to cancer in 1993. He then married Ernesdean Shade Murphy, and they have a blended family of four sons and six grandchildren. Murphy is retired and enjoys traveling, volunteering for the Catholic Church in Fort Yates, gardening, attending horticulture enrichment classes, and spending time with his family.

John Smith
Mandan, Hidatsa, and Arikara Nation

Induction Year:
2019

Category:
Military/Veteran

John Smith (1898-1977), son of Conrad and Mary Red Feather Smith, was 19 years old when the United States declared war on Germany in 1917. He was living in Shell Village on the Fort Berthold Reservation and was the first solider from the reservation to enlist on August 11.

Smith survived many battles on French soil. He was discharged on September 24, 1919, with the rank of sergeant. He was cited for Conspicuous Gallantry in Action and entitled to wear the Silver Star. He served with the 1st Infantry Division of the U.S. Army.

Returning home, he continued to represent his nation and his people in military, community, and family matters. Smith was the first Hidatsa to enlist in the 2nd North Dakota National Guard Regiment in 1917. He served in Company M, 26th Infantry with Alphonse Bear Ghost and Louis Latraille. All three men from Indian Country were cited for gallantry and were eligible for the silver Citation Star. He also received the French Fourragere. Smith was rated by his commanding officer as a "very good scout and leader of men."

After war, Smith filled out a report for Joseph Dixon, in which he wrote: "After his discharge and his return to the Reservation, John helped establish the Joseph Young Hawk Post 253, the first American Legion Post on the Fort Berthold Reservation. In 1944, Congress passed the Flood Control Act, which resulted in the Garrison Dam being built on the Missouri River. The reservoir flooded 155,000 acres of the tribal land and 90 percent of the family homes, resulting in a massive relocation of the Fort Berthold people to higher ground. The Joseph Young Hawk Post, along with the rest of the tribal people, objected valiantly to the taking of the land but was unable to stop the building of the dam and the resultant large body of water now known as Lake Sakakawea."

Smith and his family moved to Poplar, Montana, after the Garrison Dam was built.

Seven Vietnam War Marines and Soldiers
Standing Rock Sioux Tribe

Induction Year:
2019

Category:
Military/Veteran

Seven men from the Standing Rock Sioux Tribe lost their lives while serving in the U.S. Army and U.S. Marine Corps during the Vietnam War.

Five of the men served in the U.S. Marine Corps. Ronald "Christy" Good Iron (casualty date February 2, 1968) and Gary Frederick Myers (casualty date May 13, 1968) were from Porcupine District, North Dakota. Kenneth Robert Jamerson (casualty date February 5, 1967) grew up in Running Antelope District, South Dakota. Randolph Scott Hutchinson (casualty date December 30, 1966) was from Standing Rock, South Dakota. Conrad Lee Flying Horse (casualty date August 13, 1970) grew up in Long Solider District, North Dakota.

Lawrence Dean Brown Otter (casualty date November 18, 1967), from Rock Creek District, South Dakota, served in the U.S. Army. Loren Dallas Lebeau (casualty date February 1, 1971) was also a soldier and grew up in Standing Rock, South Dakota.

All of the men attended school on Standing Rock and had special interests in music, sports, hobbies, and cultural ways. All graduated from high school. Each of them chose to serve their communities in a positive way, and all had an impact in their communities.

Their decision to enlist in the U.S. military was their choice to serve their country. This is a cultural tradition as warriors to protect and serve their people, home, and land.

Keith Bear
Mandan, Hidatsa, and Arikara Nation

Induction Year:
2019

Category:
Culture/Arts

Keith Bear (b. 1995) (O'Mashi! Ryu Ta – Bright Lights That Wave in the North Sky) is a Mandan and Hidatsa traditional artist enrolled with the Three Affiliated Tribes in Fort Berthold. He is the son of Christine and John Bear of the Nagadawi Clan. He spent much of his childhood in foster homes but always had contact with family members. As a young adult, he moved from place to place working oil rigs and boxing.

While working at the Flagstaff Medical Center as an orderly, Bear noticed patients were not only physically hurting, but also emotionally hurting, too. He traded with a traditional man for a flute, and he played for the patients. Bear says, "It was powerful. The flute brought tears and healing. It was then I knew the power of the flute to heal and transform. Later, as my mother was dying, I made a promise to her to return home and to return to the People through the 'sacred branch of the Tree of Life,' the flute, that told me, 'You are a child and must learn to walk a new way.'"

Through his family, he learned traditional songs, beadwork, porcupine quillwork, flute music, and traditional stories. He also performs the sacred Buffalo Dance, a ceremony only honored tribal members may perform. As an artist, he makes flutes, play flutes, sings traditional songs, and tells traditional stories. He is one of the few men who have permission to do quillwork. He learned songs and stories from many relatives, as well as how to make war bonnets, headdresses, and buffalo headdresses for the sacred Buffalo Dance.

The stories that Bear has been taught are living stories. Now, when he teaches stories and flute making to children on the reservation, it helps them to know and remember who they are. When he tells the same stories to children from other cultures, it helps them know and remember who they are, too. This is because these stories contain lessons of humanity, loss, survival, love, and anger that all people have.

Wallace Thunder Hawk
Standing Rock Sioux Tribe

Induction Year:
2019

Category:
Culture/Arts

Wallace "Butch" Thunder Hawk (b. 1946) is an enrolled citizen of the Standing Rock Lakota/Dakota Nation and grew up in Cannonball and Bismarck. He earned a bachelor's degree in physical education from Dickinson State College and studied graphic design at California College of Arts in Oakland.

Since joining United Tribes Technical College in 1973, Thunder Hawk has specialized in the interpretation and creation of plains tribal objects and art. As the college's tribal arts instructor, he is a beloved figured on campus and an accomplished and well-known artist in many forms, ranging from drawings and paintings to stain-glassed, textiles, bones and hide work, and feathers.

Thunder Hawk has been a visiting curator and mentor at the Peabody Museum, Harvard University, and was awarded a Harvard Fellowship. He co-curated and assisted with the design of a Lewis and Clark exhibit and a Wiyohpiyata (the West), a Ledger Art exhibit, both at the Peabody.

He has been commissioned for many projects: by Harvard University to create a Horse Memorial effigy for display and permanent collection; by the James Monroe House Museum, Ash Lawn-Highland Charlottesville, Virginia, to create two major art pieces for their Native American collection; by Thomas Jefferson's Monticello, to create 20 traditional Native items as replicas of those President Jefferson received from Lewis and Clark; and by the North Dakota Cowboy Hall of Fame for a major art piece for fundraising and display in the museum in Medora.

Thunder Hawk was awarded a Fine Arts Fellowship by his alma mater, Dickinson State University. His work is in private and public collections across the country and abroad.

Turtle Mountain High School Wrestling Team
Turtle Mountain Band of Chippewa

Induction Year:
2019

Category:
Sports/Teams

Under the leadership of wrestling coach Marlin Shalager, the 1967-68 Belcourt Braves had four wins and five loses. They placed third in the conference and in the regional tournament. Four wrestlers participated in the state tournament that year, establishing the Braves as firm contenders for the coming season.

In 1968-69, the Braves had a good season, taking first in the conference, second in the regional, and sixth in the state tournament. The Braves sent four wrestlers to state: Larry Azure, Ray Trottier, Gerald Champagne, and Gerald Davis. Davis placed first in all three championships. Trottier was the conference and regional champion and placed fourth at state. Champagne was conference champion and placed second in the region. Azure placed third in the conference and second in the regional.

In 1969-70, the Braves were conference and regional champions. At state, they tied for third place. Gerald Champagne captured a first place in his weight class, Logan Davis placed second, Ray Trottier won third, and George Falcon placed fourth. William Hoff, Isaiah Trottier, and Fred Schindler also qualified for the state competition.

In 1970-71, the Belcourt Braves were the state wrestling champions. They won 13 matches in a row before losing to two Class A schools under wrestling coach George Shalager. State champions in their weight class included Duane Falcon, Logan Davis, and Mickey Decoteau. Gerald Davis was the regional champion and took second at state. Larry Azure took third place at the state tournament, and George Falcon took fourth. Regional champions included Howard Azure, Pat Delorme, Victor Baker, and Fred Schindler. Steve Peltier took third in the regional tournament, and Alec Albert placed fourth in the conference tournament.

In the 1971-72 school year, the Braves placed third in the state tournament. The wrestlers set good examples in their field of work. At school, they were great role models, and on the mat, they were excellent sportsmen. Several are active volunteers, and they all seem to be willing to give a helping hand.

North Dakota Tribal Nations

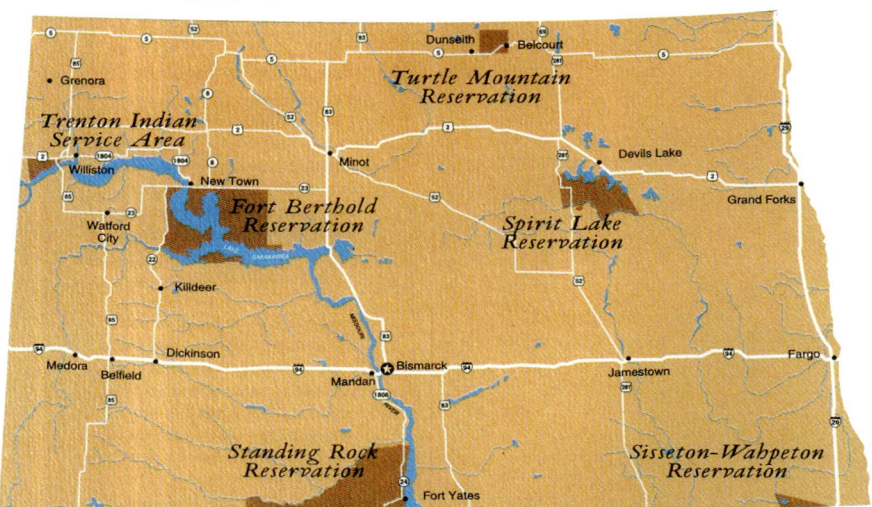

Spirit Lake Nation
816 3rd Avenue North
Fort Totten, ND 58335
701-766-1219
www.spiritlakenation.com

Demographics
- Tribal Enrollment   7,992 (Spirit Lake Enrollment Office 2018)
- Population   4,403 (American Community Survey 2013-2017)

Government

The reservation was created by the "Treaty with the Sioux – Sisseton and Wahpeton Bands" in February 1867. The treaty provided for the establishment of Lake Traverse Reservation in eastern South Dakota, and another reservation south of Devils Lake in North Dakota for the Cut-Head bands of Yanktonai Sioux who did not go to Lake Traverse.

The Spirit Lake Tribe operates under a constitution approved on February 3, 1944. Originally known as the Devils Lake Sioux Tribe, the name was changed to Spirit Lake Tribe in May 1995 by a general referendum vote of its members.

The Tribal Council is made up of six members, including a chairman and secretary, elected at large by the tribal membership residing on the reservation. One district representative is elected from each of the four districts of Fort Totten, Mission (St. Michael), Woodlake, and Crow Hill. Council members serve four-year terms, and elections are held once every two years in May.

The reservation is located in east-central North Dakota. The topography of the reservation is generally consistent with the Northern Plains region, with flat terrain, rolling hills, and some wooded areas. The major surface water feature of the reservation is Devils Lake, which comprises 90,000 acres of area stretched over 200 miles. There are also numerous small lakes on the reservation, including Twin Lakes, Spring Lake, Free Peoples Lake, Elbow Lake, and Skin and Bone Lake.

The Spirit Lake Tribe Indian Reservation covers approximately 405 square miles. It is located primarily in Benson County, but its southern boundary is in Eddy County, its eastern boundary is in Nelson County, and its northern boundary is in Ramsey County. Its total acres are as follows: total tribally owned, allocated trust land – 26,283 acres; trust – 34,026 acres; U.S. government and state – 375 acres; and fee land – 184,451 acres. Total acres within the exterior boundaries equal 245,141 acres.

The major river surface water body is the Sheyenne River, which forms the southern boundary of the reservation. The portion of the Sheyenne within the reservation is approximately 50 miles long. Ultimately the Sheyenne River discharges into the Red River, which flows north between North Dakota and Minnesota into Manitoba, Canada. Numerous small streams and springs within the reservation also contribute flows to the Sheyenne River. In addition, the rivers and streams of the reservation have substantial areas of associated wetlands and prairie potholes.

Turtle Mountain Band of Chippewa Indians
PO Box 900
Highway 5 West
Belcourt, ND 58316
701-477-2600
tmbci.org

Demographics
- Tribal Enrollment   32,591 (Turtle Mountain Enrollment Office 2018)
- Population   9,232 (American Community Survey 2013-2017)

Government

The Turtle Mountain Reservation lies entirely in Rolette County in the extreme north-central portion of North Dakota, about seven miles from the Canadian border and near the exact geographic center of the North American continent. The reservation is almost equally divided between tribally owned and individually allotted lands. The terrain ranges in elevation from 200 to 2,300 feet above sea level and is dotted with lakes, rolling hills, and a relative abundance of trees. The unincorporated town of Belcourt is the only community on the Turtle Mountain Reservation. Near the reservation are the towns of Rolla, Rolette, Dunseith, and St. John.

The reservation was established by the Executive Orders of December 21, 1882, and March 29, 1884, on an area of 72,000 acres of land. The 72,000 acres proved to be inadequate for the population of the reservation. Consequently, the U.S. government, as specified in an 1892 Treaty Agreement, provided public domain land in western North Dakota and eastern Montana consisting of approximately 69,860 acres. The land was available to Turtle Mountain Chippewa who were willing to relocate and homestead in that area. The treaty agreement assured services would be provided to the relocated membership as if they resided on reservation land.

The Turtle Mountain Tribe's governing body, the Tribal Council, consists of a chairman and eight members elected to two-year terms. The chairman is elected at large by the general membership; the vice-chairman is elected by the eight council members at the first meeting of each newly elected council. The tribal government is organized according to a 1959 constitution and bylaws. In 1976, the tribe adopted a Tribal Code, covering criminal and civil law.

An elected board of directors consisting of a chairperson and six representatives now governs the Trenton Indian Service Area (TISA). Election of directors is held every four years, and terms are staggered. TISA has been divided into three districts (Williston, Trenton, and Montana), with two representatives from each district.

The Chippewa proudly referred to themselves as Anishinabe, meaning "The Original People." The Turtle Mountain Band of Chippewa is primarily a member of the Pembina Band of Chippewa. Ancestry may include intermarriage with other Chippewa bands, Cree, and other nations who make up the membership of the Turtle Mountain Band.

The name Chippewa, a mispronunciation of Ojibwa, Ojibway, Ojibwe, Saulteaux, and Anishinabe, are all nations that refer to the same group of people. The term "Chippewa" is used after European contact.

The Ojibway are members of the Algonquin language group, which are located from Newfoundland to the Rocky Mountains and from Hudson Bay to North Carolina. Other tribes in this language group are the Cree, Ottawa, Sauk, Fox, Menominee, Potawatomi, Miami, Shawnee, Delaware, Cheyenne, Blackfeet, and Arapaho. Scholars have established this classification by language, but this does not mean the tribes were closely related or that they were allies.

Mandan, Hidatsa, and Arikara Nation
(Three Affiliated Tribes)
404 Frontage Road
New Town, ND 58763
701-627-4781
www.mhanation.com

Demographics
- Tribal Enrollment   16,124 (Three Affiliated Enrollment Office 2018)
- Population   7,304 (American Community Survey 2013-2017)

Government

The reservation was established under the Fort Laramie Treaty of 1851 and modified over the years, resulting in the final establishment of the reservation by the Executive Order of April 12, 1870. Congressional acts and executive orders gradually reduced the reservation to its present size from the initial 12.5 million acres. In 1972, a federal court ruling determined that land lost to homesteaders through the 1910 Homestead Act had, in fact, always been part of the reservation.

The constitution for the Three Affiliated Tribes was adopted on May 15, 1936. The Tribal Council is made up of seven members, including a chairman elected at-large by the tribal membership and one representative from each of the reservation's six districts of Four Bears, Mandaree, Little Shell (New Town), Lucky Mound (Parshall), Twin Buttes, and White Shield. Council members serve four-year terms. Elections are held once every two years in November.

The Fort Berthold Reservation spans approximately one million acres of both flat prairie land and rolling terrain in west-central North Dakota, southeast of Minot and northwest of Bismarck. The reservation is intersected by the Missouri River. About 11 percent of the total surface area is covered by Lake Sakakawea, the reservoir formed behind the Garrison Dam. While there are Indian families living throughout the reservation, the majority live in the local communities of Mandaree, White Shield, Twin Buttes, Four Bears (location of the tribal headquarters), and the incorporated towns of Parshall and New Town (location of the Bureau of Indian Affairs headquarters).

The U.S. Government, as defined by the U.S. Constitution, has governmental relationships with international, tribal, and state entities. The tribal nations have a government-to-government relationship with the United States. The tribes signed treaties in the 1800s with the United States, which are the legal documents that established boundaries and recognized their rights as a sovereign government. The tribal government maintains jurisdiction within the boundaries of the reservation including all rights-of-way, waterways, water courses, and streams running through any part of the reservation and to such other lands as may hereafter be added to the reservation under the laws of the United States.

The tribal government operates under a constitution consistent with the Indian Reorganization Act of 1934 and a Business Council approved by the tribal membership of the Three Affiliated Tribes. The Business Council consists of a chairman, vice-chairman, secretary, treasurer, and three additional council members who are elected by the tribal members. The chairman is the administrative head of the tribe. The chairman and officers serve a four-year term and are elected at large with the three members elected from their districts.

At the time of initial contact with Euro-American culture (around 1790), the three tribes lived along the Missouri River, hunting buffalo and growing squash, corn, and beans. Contact brought some predictable consequences, notably a devastating smallpox epidemic in 1837. To escape the disease, a group of Hidatsa moved up the Missouri River in 1845 and established the village of Like-A-Fishhook. Eventually they were joined by the other two tribal bands, and by 1862, formal unification of the tribes had begun.

Though the Treaty of Fort Laramie granted the three tribes more than 12 million acres, executive orders and allotments eventually reduced the reservation's size to less than one million acres, its approximate size today. During 1954, the tribes lost another 152,300 acres, along with innumerable natural resources, due to the U.S. Army Corps of Engineers' filling of the Garrison Reservoir (which is now Lake Sakakawea). The flooding destroyed long-established Indian population centers, and families who had supported themselves by ranching and farming along the fertile Missouri bottomlands watched the land become dry, windy uplands. Though the tribes received $12 million in compensation for their flooded land, an independent evaluator placed the loss at more than $20 million.

Today, the reservation continues to support limited farming and ranching, but the tribes have been more successful in establishing or attracting businesses in electronics manufacturing, construction, and gaming. Traditional culture has also seen an increase, with Native American church ceremonies, sweat lodges, and the use of native languages all making a comeback. The tribes continue to maintain discreet tribal identities through the preservation of language, customs, and residence.

Standing Rock Sioux Tribe
PO Box D
Fort Yates, ND 58538
701-854-8500
www.standingrock.org

Demographics
- Tribal Enrollment   15,782 (Standing Rock Enrollment Office 2018)
- Population   8,616 (American Community Survey 2013-2017)

Government

The Standing Rock Reservation was established by the 1851 Fort Laramie Treaty and was a part of the Great Sioux Nation. The center of the reservation was the Black Hills, the "paha sapa," sacred to all Lakota. The size of the reservation has been reduced through various ways. The 1868 Fort Laramie Treaty broke the Great Sioux Nation and divided the land for some of the tribes, but took the Black Hills. The series of allotment acts that began in 1868 and ended in 1915 divided the land even further, assigning to individuals and families timber allotments to provide for fuel and home sites. Finally, nearly one million acres of western reservation lands were opened for white settlement.

The Standing Rock Reservation is situated in southwest North Dakota on the North Dakota-South Dakota border. The reservation encompasses all of Sioux County in North Dakota, and all of Corson County and small portions of Dewey and Ziebach Counties in South Dakota. The size of the reservation is more than 2.3 million acres. As of 2015, approximately 925,000 acres of this land is Indian-owned trust land. The remainder of the land is more than 1.4 million acres of fee land, primarily non-Indian owned lands, school and township lands, and approximately 50,000 acres that was a result of the creation of the Oahe Reservoir.

The Tribal Council, as the Standing Rock Sioux Tribe's supreme governing body, is constitutionally empowered to enter into negotiations with the federal, state, and local governments on the tribe's behalf; employ attorneys and protect tribal land and political rights; appoint tribal officials, boards, and organizations; evict non-enrolled people whose presence may be detrimental to the tribe; administer the tribal budget; regulate property; and pass laws and establish courts for the administration of justice. Although the Standing Rock Sioux Tribe has considerable authority, federal law mandates the Secretary of the Interior approve or disapprove certain council actions.

The people of each of the eight districts on the Standing Rock Reservation comprise a local district council which elects officers to consult, make recommendations to and advise the Tribal Council, Bureau of Indian Affairs agency superintendent, and Secretary of the Interior on all matters of local or tribal interest. Tribal Council members are obligated to attend local district council meetings and report tribal business to the local people, ensuring input on a local level.

North Dakota Tribal Colleges

The 1970s brought the establishment of five two-year tribal colleges. Created to retain students on the reservations and prepare them for the job market, the colleges provide both academic and vocational training.

The schools and the year they were established are United Tribes Technical College, Bismarck, 1969; Turtle Mountain Community College, Belcourt, 1972; Nueta Hidatsa Sahnish College, New Town, 1973; Sitting Bull College, Fort Yates, 1973; and Cankdeska Cikana (Little Hoop) Community College, Fort Totten, 1974.

Tribal College Fall 2018 Enrollment

Cankdeska Cikana Community College	178
Nueta Hidatsa Sahnish College	198
Sitting Bull College	284
Turtle Mountain Community College	567

Cankdeska Cikana Community College

214 1st Avenue
Fort Totten, ND 58335
701-766-4415
www.littlehoop.edu

Mission

To provide higher education opportunities at the community college level, including vocational and technical training. As a tribal college, we emphasize the teaching and learning of Dakota culture and language toward the perpetuation of the Spirit Lake Dakota Nation. The goal is student independence and self-sufficiency through academic achievement.

Vision

Through the education and training of its residents, we are maintaining a strong and viable Dakota community that enjoys physical, mental, emotional, and spiritual wellness and growth.

Nueta Hidatsa Sahnish College

PO Box 490
220 8th Avenue North
New Town, ND 58763
701-627-4738
https://nhsc.edu

Mission

The Nueta Hidatsa Sahnish College will provide quality cultural, academic, and vocational education and services for the Mandan, Hidatsa, and Arikara Nation.

Values

Nueta Hidatsa Sahnish College's values are illustrated through the earth lodge, which is the common home to the Nueta, Hidatsa, and Sahnish people. Unity, being the key value, is located in the center (fire pit), which the rest of the values are built around. Spirituality, people, culture, and future are the four domains represented by the four main posts. The outer 12 posts represent values within each of the four domains.

Sitting Bull College

1341 92nd Street
Fort Yates, ND 58538
701-854-8000
www.sittingbull.edu

Mission

Sitting Bull College is an academic and technical institution committed to improving the levels of education and training, economic, and social development of the people it serves while promoting responsible behavior consistent with the Lakota/Dakota culture and language.

Vision

Catching the spirit to fulfill a dream through culture, academics, technical training, and responsible behavior for now and the future.

Turtle Mountain Community College

PO Box 340
BIA Highway #7 North
Belcourt, ND 58316
701-477-7862
www.tm.edu

Mission
Turtle Mountain Community College is committed to functioning as an autonomous Indian-controlled college on the Turtle Mountain Chippewa Reservation focusing on general studies, undergraduate education, career and technical education, scholarly research, and continuous improvement of student learning. By creating an academic environment in which the cultural and social heritage of the Turtle Mountain Band of Chippewa is brought to bear throughout the curriculum, the college establishes an administration, faculty, and student body exerting leadership in the community and providing service to it.

Institutional Philosophy
Turtle Mountain Community College is a tribal community college with obligations of direct community service to the Turtle Mountain Chippewa Tribe. Under this unifying principle, the college seeks to maintain, seek out, and provide comprehensive higher education services in fields needed for true Indian self-determination.

United Tribes Technical College

3315 University Drive
Bismarck, ND 58504
701-255-3285
www.uttc.edu

Mission
United Tribes Technical College is dedicated to providing American Indians with postsecondary and technical education in a culturally diverse environment that will provide self-determination and economic development for all tribal nations.

Vision
United Tribes Technical College (UTTC) is a premiere college, a leader in tribal education, arts, cultural preservation, technology, research, and the humanities. UTTC foresees a campus community with state-of-the-art facilities. UTTC aspires to be self-sustaining in line with its mission for tribal self-sufficiency and self-determination. Most importantly, UTTC envisions skilled, knowledgeable, culturally-grounded, healthy graduates who will achieve their educational goals; empower their communities; and preserve the environment, tribal land, water, and natural resources.

North Dakota Tourism Partners with Native American Tourism

North Dakota Tourism continues to work alongside Native American tourism providers to promote tribal tourism in North Dakota. In 2016, the North Dakota Native Tourism Alliance was revived under the leadership of each of the state's five tribal tourism departments, George Washington University, and Mike Mabin at Agency MABU in Bismarck. Together, they are presenting North Dakota's vibrant Native American culture to visitors from around the world.

North Dakota Tourism has always been a supporter of events, attractions, and activities showcasing the history and culture of Native people in and around the state. The Tourism Division shares information with media and travel trade around the globe. The Tourism Division also works alongside individual committees to showcase events and activities on its website (NDtourism.com), travel guide, and advertising, as well as through press trips and tourism product development trips to the attractions.

North Dakota Native Tourism Alliance

The mission of the North Dakota Native Tourism Alliance (NDNTA) is to protect, promote, preserve, and educate the world about the culture, history, and environment of our sovereign nations. NDNTA will use sustainable tourism to promote, educate, and develop economic opportunities for our people and nations.

NDNTA works hand-in-hand with North Dakota Tourism and other partners to tell the stories of our tribal nations from our perspective. We are the first state in the nation to organize our tribal nations to develop tourism packages as part of the Great American West partnership. The Great American West states, including North Dakota, South Dakota, Montana, Wyoming, and Idaho, work collaboratively to market and promote tourism worldwide.

The Turtle Mountain Band of Chippewa Indians (TMBCI) initiated its tribal tourism efforts in 2009 with preliminary funding from the tribal Pathways to Prosperity Program. The tourism project led to the development of a Tribal Tourism Plan, which included tabulating tourism survey results, identifying and mapping key tourism sites, conducting cost/benefit analysis, and facilitating a tribal Scenic Byway Plan. TMBCI Tourism efforts led to the development of the North Dakota Native Tourism Alliance, a statewide collaboration of all North Dakota tribes.

Tribal Tourism Websites
- Turtle Mountain Band of Chippewa – www.tmchippewa.com
- Three Affiliated Tribes – www.mhanation.com
- Standing Rock Sioux Tribe – www.sittingbull.edu/visitors-center
- Spirit Lake Nation – www.spiritlakenation.com

- Sisseton Wahpeton Oyate – www.swo-nsn.gov
- Native American Travel – www.nativeamerica.travel
- North Dakota Native Tourism Alliance – https://www.facebook.com/NDNTA/

Primary contacts for NDNTA are Les Thomas, 701-278-1167, lesthomas52@yahoo.com, and Darian Morsette, 701-627-2243, dmorsette@mhanation.com.

First Nations Day

First Nations Day, held annually in October, recognizes North Dakota's indigenous peoples and their unique role in shaping the history and culture of the state, as well as the history and culture of the nation. It also recognizes the role American Indian people play in shaping the future of the state and nation by making important and distinctive contributions to culture and society, as well as the critical role American Indian people, tribal governments, colleges, and businesses play in strengthening their communities and growing North Dakota's economy.

The 2016 First Nations Day celebration, "Preserving Our Culture," was held on October 7 at the North Dakota Heritage Center and State Museum. The event included a flag presentation by the United Tribes Technical College Honor Guard and the Wise Spirit Singers. In addition, opening remarks were made by Scott Davis, executive director of the North Dakota Indian Affairs Commission, and a keynote address was presented by Dakota Goodhouse, a writer, editor, and artist, as well as instructor at United Tribes Technical College. The First Nations Day celebration also included the Governor's and the city of Bismarck's First Nations Day proclamations. A traditional meal was provided by United Tribes Technical College.

The focus of First Nations Day in 2017, "Justice for Murdered and Missing Indigenous Women Across the United States and Canada," brought people from law enforcement and tribal entities together to address the issue of missing and murdered indigenous women. The issue was of particular importance because of the murder of Savanna Greywind in Fargo on August 19, 2017.

The focus of First Nations Day 2018 was "Resiliency of the Great Plains Indians," with programming on the history and culture of the Plains Indians, criminal justice, child welfare/juvenile justice, education, healthcare and history, behavioral health, workforce, and urban Indians and housing.

First Nations Day continues to be celebrated on the first Friday in October at the North Dakota Heritage Center and State Museum.

Indian Youth Leadership Academy

The North Dakota Indian Youth Leadership Academy, held each year in June, creates and fosters an environment for Native youth to learn and develop leadership skills, which will open doors for them in their local communities, the state of North Dakota, and throughout the United States. The academy is a peer-to-peer mentorship program that utilizes current college students and/or former youth leadership academy attendees to help participants learn about pursuing a career or expanding on their educational aspirations. Participants are challenged by motivational speakers and mentors, visit college campuses, learn about military opportunities, and have multiple opportunities to talk about the challenges they face. The Leadership Academy celebrated its 10th anniversary in 2019.

Native American Youth Leadership Summit

The North Dakota Native American Youth Leadership Summit, held during the United Tribes Technical College Tribal Leaders Summit in September, offers youth leaders from around the state an opportunity to talk about issues in their communities. The event includes group discussions and an opportunity to present issues to tribal leaders.

Woodrow Keeble Award

The Woodrow W. Keeble "Je Suis Pret (I Am Ready)" Award is presented to any member or former member of the North Dakota National Guard (NDNG). This award is in honor of the actions of MSG Woodrow "Woody" W. Keeble, a NDNG 164th Infantry Regiment member who received the Medal of Honor for his extraordinary courage, selfless service, and devotion to duty in the Korean War.

Keeble also served with the 164th at Guadalcanal in World War II, where he was awarded the Silver Star, the Bronze Star, two Purple Hearts, and the Combat Infantry Badge. Keeble epitomized the values of humility, compassion, strength, selfless service, bravery, and honor in keeping with the finest traditions of the NDNG 164th Regiment's history, reputation, and motto, "Je Suis Pret."

The act performed must have been one displaying personal courage, fortitude, and determination to protect/defend life, limb, or property. This may include, but is not limited to, providing lifesaving measures, performing evacuation efforts (e.g., fire), assisting with a vehicle accident, etc. Acts performed while in a deployed combat zone are not eligible. Acts performed during sanctioned emergency service operations may qualify for additional recognition with this award.

The first MSG Woodrow W. Keeble Award Ceremony was held on February 8, 2019, at the Circle of Nations School in Wahpeton, North Dakota, to recognize 20 recipients.

Graduation at United Tribes Technical College.

Chapter Eight
Elections

North Dakota National Guard Soldiers of the 1st Battalion, 112th Aviation Regiment train in "hoist" operations with a UH-72A Lakota helicopter on June 6, 2018, at the Army Aviation Support Facility in Bismarck. Operating the hoist is Staff Sgt. Aaron Reich, while Army medic Staff Sgt. Colton Benmore practices evacuation procedures.

Vote of the People 460
Amending the Constitution 460
1971-1972 Constitutional Convention 461
Initiating and Referring Laws 462
Special Elections 464
Summary of Initiative and Referendum Activity 466
North Dakota Measures before the Voters 2018 to Present 467
2018 General Election Report of Vote Totals 468
2020 North Dakota Election Calendar 469

Vote of the People

Since the adoption of the North Dakota Constitution on October 1, 1889, four types of questions have been submitted to the electorate for approval or rejection:

1. Amendments to the constitution as proposed by the Legislative Assembly or as proposed by the people through a petition procedure.
2. Statutory proposals initiated by the people through a petition procedure.
3. Acts of the Legislative Assembly referred to the electorate by a petition procedure.
4. A proposed new constitution, with four alternate propositions to certain sections, submitted by a Constitutional Convention (April 28, 1972).

Amending the Constitution

The original North Dakota Constitution provided for submission of amendments to the people after approval of two consecutive sessions of the Legislative Assembly. A majority vote of the legislators was required. In 1918, the constitution was amended to require a majority vote in only one legislative session before submission of the amendment to the people.

On the crest of the "Progressive Party" reform movement, North Dakota changed its constitution in 1914 to provide for an amendment through a procedure of petition by the people. Petitions proposing amendments were to be filed with the Secretary of State at least six months before the election. Those petitions carried the signatures of at least 25 percent of the legal voters in at least one-half of the counties of the state. If the people approved the amendment, it was then referred to the Legislative Assembly for consideration. If the Legislative Assembly adopted the amendment, it became a part of the North Dakota Constitution. If the Legislative Assembly did not approve, the measure returned to the ballot for another test at the polls. If approved again by the people, it became a part of the constitution.

This cumbersome procedure met its fate at the polls in 1918 when the people approved a new initiative procedure calling for petitions with 20,000 signatures to be filed 120 days before the election. Approval by a majority of the voters made the measure a part of the constitution. The Legislative Assembly was no longer involved in the initiative process.

On four occasions, the Legislative Assembly has submitted proposed amendments to the people for an increase in the required number of signatures to initiate constitutional amendments:

- On March 15, 1932, the people voted 104,953 to 51,459 against increasing the number of signatures from 20,000 to 40,000.

- On June 30, 1942, a proposed increase from 20,000 to 30,000 signatures was defeated by a vote of 69,904 to 52,275.

- On November 4, 1958, the people defeated by a vote of 127,290 to 47,814 a proposal to change from 20,000 signatures to the number of signatures equal to 10 percent of the vote cast for governor at the last general election.

- On November 7, 1978, the people approved by a vote of 102,182 to 75,413 proposal that required a petition to carry signatures equal to four percent of the population based on the last federal census.

1971-72 Constitutional Convention

On April 28, 1972, when the people voted on a proposed new constitution, they approved by a vote of 76,585 to 71,062 the alternate proposition to increase the number of signatures required for initiating constitutional amendments. The increase would have changed from 20,000 required signatures to a number of signatures equal to four percent of the state's population, or around 25,000 signatures. The increase did not occur because none of the four alternate propositions on the ballot took effect if the proposed constitution was defeated, and it was.

Initiating and Referring Laws

Even though "initiative" and "referendum" are different types of political action(s), they have been treated as companion procedures since their original adoption in 1914.

The 1914 amendment to the constitution called for petitions proposing new laws to be signed by at least 10 percent of the legal voters in a majority of counties, then submitted to the Secretary of State at least 30 days before the Legislative Assembly convened. When the Legislative Assembly met, the Secretary of State would then present the measure for its consideration. The Legislative Assembly had the option of adopting the measure, submitting it to the people for a vote, rejecting it, or offering a counter proposal. If the Legislative Assembly failed to act or rejected the proposal, the measure went on the ballot at the next election. If the Legislative Assembly offered a counter proposal, both the counter proposal and the original measure appeared together on the ballot; the measure receiving the highest number of votes won.

The power of "referendum" was included in the 1914 constitutional amendment. Acts, or parts of the acts of the Legislative Assembly, would be referred when a petition was signed by 10 percent of voters from a majority of counties. Petitions were filed within 90 days of adjournment of a Legislative Assembly. A referendum could also be held if a majority of legislators decided to submit legislation to a vote of the people. Measures pertaining to preservation of the public peace, health, or safety that passed both houses by a two-thirds majority could not be referred.

Mired down in cumbersome and unworkable machinery, reformers proposed an amendment on November 5, 1918, which greatly simplified both the initiative and referendum processes. This amendment eliminated the Legislative Assembly from the process and simply required petitions signed by 10,000 qualified electors to be filed no later than 90 days before an election. The referendum was changed to require 7,000 signatures to place the measure on the next election ballot or 30,000 signatures to force a special election.

	For	Against
October 1, 1889 Article XV established requirements for future amendments to the North Dakota Constitution	27,441	8,107
November 3, 1914 Signatures of 10 percent of legal voters in majority of counties to initiate or refer measures	48,783	19,964
November 5, 1918 10,000 signatures to initiate 7,000 signatures to refer	47,447	32,598

The Legislative Assembly has on numerous occasions asked the voters to make the provisions of the initiative and referendum more stringent.

	For	Against
March 15, 1932	50,967	105,581
30,000 signatures to initiate		
25,000 signatures to refer		
June 24, 1936	41,500	127,511
20,000 signatures to initiate or refer		
June 25, 1940	61,573	64,636
15,000 signatures to initiate or refer		
June 30, 1942	53,925	70,927
20,000 signatures to initiate		
30,000 signatures to refer		
40,000 signatures to force special election – referring emergency measures		
November 4, 1958	47,814	127,290
10 percent of votes cast for governor to initiate		
Seven percent of votes cast for governor to refer		
November 8, 1966	69,116	84,131
Three percent of population to initiate		
Two percent of the population to refer		

In addition to the increases proposed by the Legislative Assembly, the Constitutional Convention of 1971–1972 submitted to the people the question of increasing the required signatures for the initiative and the referral to the number of signatures equal to two percent of the population, or around 12,500 signatures. This proposal was approved by a vote of 76,585 to 71,062, but did not become effective because the proposed constitution itself was defeated.

On November 7, 1978, the people approved by a vote of 102,182 to 75,413 a proposal to amend the constitution to initiate or refer laws by petition. The petitions required signatures equal to two percent of the population based on the last federal decennial census to refer and initiate statutory changes and four percent to initiate constitutional change(s).

Special Elections

The first special election involving referred measures occurred on June 26, 1919, after the Non-Partisan League (NPL) successfully passed legislation creating the Industrial Commission, Bank of North Dakota, and State Mill and Elevator. Voters approved the NPL programs.

The second special election, called because of recall petitions filed against the NPL Governor, Attorney General, and Commissioner of Agriculture and Labor, meant the defeat of nine different measures – some designed to hobble the NPL program. The program was sustained, but the three primary NPL architects were turned out of office as a result of the recall election of October 28, 1921. This was the first recall of state officials in the United States.

In 1933, the Legislative Assembly adopted a sales tax to bolster the state's waning finances through the tough Depression era. However, the proposal was referred, and another special election was required on September 22 of that year. The measure was defeated 41,241 to 113,807. There were actually seven measures for voter consideration at this special election.

In 1935, the Legislative Assembly passed another sales tax measure, and it was referred. At a July 15 special election, the measure was adopted by a vote of 75,166 to 65,890.

At a July 11, 1939, special election, voters considered four measures, one of which would have established a two percent income tax on businesses and professions. The measure was defeated 36,117 to 168,976.

The 1963 Legislative Assembly's tax program was referred and submitted to a vote of the people on July 17. The program, presented as several measures, was defeated by margins of five to one.

In 1965, the Legislative Assembly passed another tax program. It was referred, and on September 21 was defeated by a vote of 37,886 to 99,269.

In 1971, a special election brought before voters the referred measure that appropriated funds for the operation of the Department of Accounts and Purchases. Voters upheld the appropriation on a 61,342 to 39,076 vote.

On April 28, 1972, voters considered a proposed new constitution and four alternate propositions submitted by the 1971–1972 Constitutional Convention. The new constitution was defeated and as a result made null the votes on the four alternate propositions.

In 1973, the legislative apportionment plan was referred, and a constitutional amendment requiring single-member Senate and House districts initiated. Both measures considered in a special election on December 4 were defeated. The apportionment plan lost by a vote of 44,363 to 50,729, and the initiated constitutional amendment lost by a vote of 43,178 to 53,831.

In 1987, the people voted on two measures. The first dealt with the effective date of measures dealing with appropriations. The second provided for increases in state income tax with mandatory withholding. Both measures were approved on March 18, 1987.

On December 5, 1989, the people considered eight measures. The first, a proposed constitutional amendment, dealt with the reorganization of state government. The other measures referred 1989 legislation, including increases in motor fuel tax, state sales tax and state income tax, use of seatbelts, use of electronic video gaming devices, a retirement plan for legislators, and health care education in the schools. All measures were defeated by the voters.

In 1990, the people voted on a measure that would have provided for a one percent increase in state sales and use tax, motor vehicle excise tax, and aircraft excise tax to support elementary, secondary, adult, and vocational education. The measure was defeated by a vote of 52,610 to 74,207.

On November 3, 1992, the people voted on a measure that would establish water development objectives and impose a one-half of one percent sales and use tax. The measure was defeated by a vote of 110,045 to 181,960.

Summary of Initiative and Referendum Activity in North Dakota

Since statehood in 1889 through the end of the 2018 election cycle, approximately 514 measures have been placed on the ballot for consideration by North Dakota's voters. These have included constitutional measures resulting from legislative action, initiated constitutional measures, initiated statutory measures, and referred measures.

While the greatest plurality (233 of 510) of measures voted upon have been those resulting from legislative action or the Constitutional Convention, more than half (269, or 52 percent of 510) of all measures voted upon represent initiated or referred measures that required petitions to be circulated and signatures gathered. Of those, 141 have been initiated statutory measures, and 49 have been initiated constitutional measures. Actions of the Legislative Assembly have been referred to the voters of North Dakota 79 times. The 510 measures that have been considered by North Dakota voters include the four alternate propositions from the 1972 special election to approve a new constitution.

It is also important to note that the power to initiate and refer laws was not adopted in North Dakota until 1914. Since 1914, 482 measures have been placed on the ballot for consideration by North Dakota's voters. This demonstrates that 55 percent (269 of 489) of all ballot measures voted upon since the adoption of the initiative and referendum process in 1914 represent ballot measures that have required petitions to be circulated and signatures gathered. These statistics strengthen the percentage of measures that have gained ballot access in North Dakota through the initiative and referendum process versus through legislative action.

These statistics support the fact that North Dakota's initiative and referendum laws generally have not created overwhelming hurdles or obstacles to the initiative process. Rather, the statistics demonstrate the citizens of North Dakota have taken advantage of the initiative and referendum process more than the state's Legislative Assembly has taken advantage of its authority to propose constitutional change through the ballot box.

✔ A complete chronology of all measures before the voters since statehood is found in the *2009–2011 North Dakota Blue Book*. In subsequent elections, updates from each election will be published to ensure a complete ongoing listing.

North Dakota Measures Before the Voters 2018 to Present

	For	Against	Action
511. General 2018 (November 6) **Const. Amend. (Initiative)** Relating to establishment of an ethics commission.	169,676	146,709	Accepted
512. General 2018 (November 6) **Const. Amend. (Initiative.)** Relating to qualified electors.	208,499	107,751	Accepted
513. General 2018 (November 6) **Statutory (Initiative)** Relating to legalization of marijuana.	132,199	193,837	Rejected
514. General 2018 (November 6) **Statutory (Initiative)** Relating to personalized vehicle plates for volunteer first responders.	203,634	112,964	Accepted

2018 General Election Report of Vote Totals

United States Senator
Kevin Cramer, Republican.. **179,720**
Heidi Heitkamp, Democratic-NPL 144,376

Representative in Congress
Kelly Armstrong, Republican **193,568**
Mac Schneider, Democratic-NPL..114,377
Charles Tuttle, Independent 13,066

Secretary of State
Alvin A. Jaeger, Independent *(Letter of Support from Republican Party)*........ **145,275**
Josh Boschee, Democratic-NPL..120,475
Michael Coachman, Independent 40,590

Attorney General
Wayne Stenehjem, Republican.. **215,633**
David Clark Thompson, Democratic-NPL 102,869

Agriculture Commissioner
Doug Goehring, Republican... **213,689**
Jim Dotzenrod, Democratic-NPL..100,914

Public Service Commissioner
Randy Christmann, Republican.. **190,792**
Jean Brandt, Democratic-NPL..118,122

Public Service Commissioner Unexpired 2-Year Term
Brian K. Kroshus, Republican.. **187,939**
Casey Buchmann, Democratic-NPL..117,235

Tax Commissioner
Ryan Rauschenberger, Republican **183,283**
Kylie Oversen, Democratic-NPL 128,806

Justice of the Supreme Court
Lisa K. Fair McEvers, No Party... **178,124**
Robert V. Bolinske Sr., No Party 92,088

(Candidates indicated in bold letters were elected.)

2020 North Dakota Election Calendar
Offices to be Filled in 2020

Federal Congressional Offices (Party)
Representative in Congress .... Two-year Term

Statewide Offices (Party)
Governor and Lt. Governor .... Four-year Term
State Auditor .... Four-year Term
State Treasurer .... Four-year Term
Public Service Commissioner .... Six-year Term

Statewide Offices (No Party)
Superintendent of Public Instruction .... Four-year Term
Justice of the Supreme Court .... Ten-year Term

Judicial District Offices (No Party)
Judges of the District Courts .... Six-year Term

State Legislative Seats (Party)
North Dakota Senate .... Four-year Term
(even-numbered districts)
North Dakota House of Representatives .... Four-year Term
(even-numbered districts)

County Offices (No Party)
Commissioners .... Four-year Term
Director, Southwest Water Authority .... Four-year Term
Supervisor, Soil Conservation District .... Six-year Term
Director, Garrison Diversion Conservancy District .... Four-year Term

Election Dates
Townships .... March 17, 2020
School Districts .... Between April 1 and June 30, 2020
Cities .... June 9, 2020
Statewide Primary .... June 9, 2020
Statewide General .... November 5, 2020

Note: Cities with home rule charters may have different election dates.

Voters at the Bismarck Event Center.

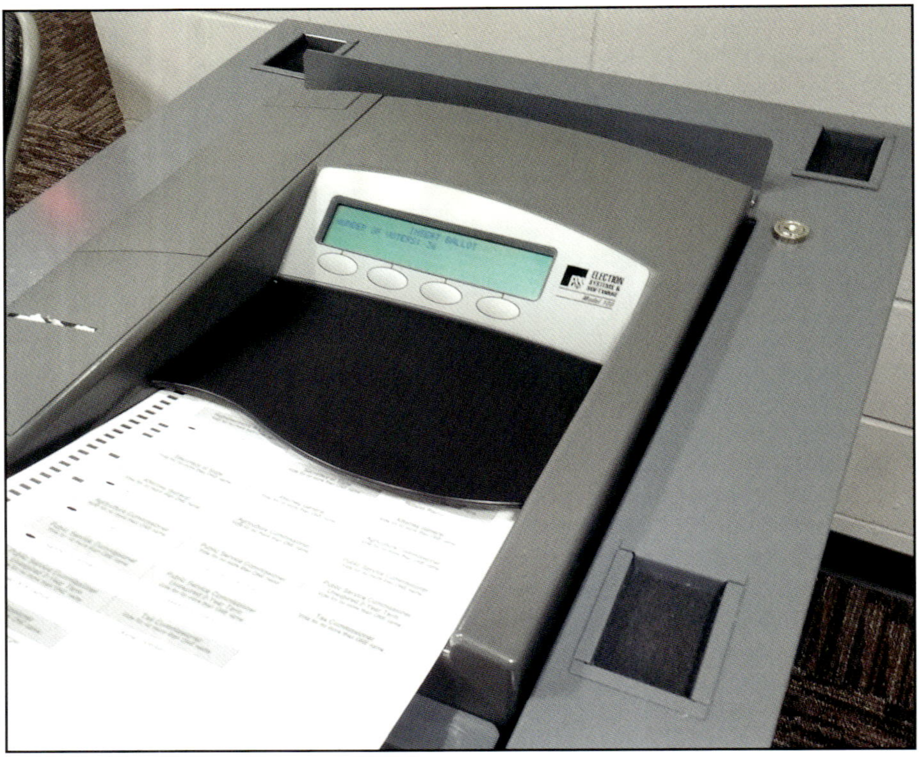

An election machine.

Chapter Nine
Education

Children gather for the Aviation Camp Experience (ACE) in 2014 at the Dakota Territory Air Museum in Minot. This was the first year of the museum's ACE and Passport Aviation Camp Experience (PACE) programs, which work to expand aerospace education opportunities for the state's youth.

North Dakota State Teacher of the Year... 473
North Dakota School Data 474
Computer Science and Cybersecurity Instruction 475
Seal of Biliteracy... 476
Milken Awards 476
School Safety... 477
Higher Education in North Dakota.. 478
Governance of Public Institutions of Higher Education 483
North Dakota University System 484
North Dakota Colleges and Universities 487
National Athletic Championships... 500

North Dakota Education

✔ To review additional history of education in our state, refer to past editions.

- The *1995 North Dakota Blue Book* gives a short history of public education in the state and includes material about the early private colleges in North Dakota.

- The *1997-1999 North Dakota Blue Book* features more detailed information about the history of education and Native American education in North Dakota.

- The *1999-2001 North Dakota Blue Book* includes an institutions of higher education location map, as well as North Dakota Rhodes Scholars and U.S. Senate Youth Winners.

- The *2001-2003 North Dakota Blue Book* lists supplemental federal and state programs provided to school districts, along with home education information and profiles of Department of Public Instruction's Division of Independent Study, Schools for the Blind and the Deaf, and alternative education.

- The *2003-2005 North Dakota Blue Book* lists teacher compensation for school year 2001-2002 and describes private and public residential school facilities for special needs students and at-risk children.

- The *2005-2007 North Dakota Blue Book* contains summaries of educational trends, open enrollment, reorganization trends, joint powers, and the Education Fact Finding Commission.

- The *2007-2009 North Dakota Blue Book* describes education funding established in 2007, the number of schools and students served by the Department of Career and Technical Education, and descriptions of the North Dakota School for the Deaf and North Dakota Vision Services/School for the Blind.

- The *2009-2011 North Dakota Blue Book* highlights the programs at state colleges and universities that have a global impact.

- The *2011-2013 North Dakota Blue Book* provides a list of North Dakota Teachers of the Year from 1978-2011. It also provides a chronology of the chief executive officers of North Dakota's colleges and universities.

- The *2017-2019 North Dakota Blue Book* provides an overview of Career and Technical Education and lists Career and Technology Centers and 21st Century Community Learning Centers.

Teacher of the Year Program

Nominations for North Dakota Teacher of the Year may come from a teacher, school administrator, school board member, education association, parent, or student. The Department of Public Instruction encourages each of the state's 178 public school districts to nominate a candidate. A group of eight regional Teacher of the Year candidates are named, followed by the selection of four finalists. An eight-member committee reviews application materials, interviews candidates, and selects the Teacher of the Year. The superintendent of public instruction honors each of the finalists during a visit to his or her school, followed by a ceremony at which the superintendent and governor announce the Teacher of the Year selection.

A candidate must have the respect and admiration of their colleagues, students and parents, and the community, and:

- Be an expert in their field who guides students of all backgrounds and abilities to help them to achieve excellence;
- Collaborate with colleagues, students, and families to create a school culture of respect and success;
- Connect the classroom and key stakeholders to foster a strong community;
- Embody lifelong learning by demonstrating leadership in and outside of the classroom; and
- Express themselves in an engaging and articulate way.

North Dakota State Teacher of the Year
2012 to Present

Year	Teacher	School	Year	Teacher	School
2012	Brenda Werner	Bismarck High School, Bismarck	2013	Andrea Noonan	Cheney Middle School, West Fargo
2014	Aaron Knodel	West Fargo High School, West Fargo	2015	Dean Aamodt	Wahpeton Public, Wahpeton
2016	Amy Neal	Lewis & Clark Elementary School, Minot	2017	Nanci Jo Dauwen	Sheyenne High School, West Fargo
2018	Leah Juelke	South High School, Fargo	2019	Kayla Delzer	Mapleton Elementary School, Mapleton

✔ See the *2011-2013 North Dakota Blue Book* for the North Dakota State Teacher of the Year list from 1978 to 2011.

2019 North Dakota Teacher of the Year Kayla Delzer (left) and Kirsten Baesler (right), state superintendent of public instruction, with Delzer's students at Mapleton Elementary School in Cass County.

North Dakota School Data

School Year 2018-2019

Number of Public School Districts
High School Districts 147
Elementary Districts 23
One-Room Rural Districts 5
Non-Operating Districts 3

Number of Non-Public Schools
Approved Non-Public Schools 54
K-12 Enrollment 6,722
Licensed Staff 685

Accreditation Status of Schools
Approved Public High School Units 165
Approved Public Middle School Units in High School LEAs 33
Approved Public Middle School Units in Graded Elementary LEAs 2
Approved Public Elementary School Units in High School LEAs 252
Approved Public Elementary School Units in Graded Elementary LEAs 25
Approved Public Elementary School Units in Rural LEAs 5
Approved Non-Public High School Units 15
Approved Non-Public Middle School Units 4
Approved Non-Public Elementary School Units 49
Non-Approved Non-Public Elementary School Units 1
Approved BIE/Grant High School Units 1
Approved BIE Elementary School Units 5
Approved State Institution High School Units 2
Approved State Institution Middle School Units 1
Approved State Institution Elementary School Units 2

Schools Using Advanced for Education Review Process
Elementary Schools 293
Middle/Junior High Schools 35
High Schools 175

Enrollment by Type of System – Fall 2018
Kindergarten 9,316
One-Room Rural 49
Elementary 70,047
Secondary 31,430
Total K-12 Public Enrollment 110,842

Cost of Education and Average Cost Per Pupil – 2018

	Cost of Education	Cost Per Pupil
Preschool Special Education	$15,971,428	$13,810
Kindergarten	$93,990,973	$10,021
Elementary 1-6	$633,954,243	$11,953
Elementary 7-8	$197,109,684	$11,638
Elementary 1-8	$831,063,928	$11,877
Elementary K-8	$925,054,900	$11,658
Secondary 9-12	$420,021,452	$13,223

Cost of education figures include per pupil cost expenditures from public school districts, multi-district special education units, and career and technology education centers. They are based on average daily membership.

Type of School Plants in Session – Fall 2018
Elementary Schools 172
Middle Level/Junior High Schools 27
Senior High Schools 34
Elementary/Secondary Combination 131
One-Teacher Schools 8

Computer Science and Cybersecurity Instruction

A team of 18 North Dakota educators developed the nation's first set of K-12 computer science and cybersecurity learning standards, which North Dakota's schools began using in fall 2019.

The standards are part of a multipronged approach to promoting computer science and cybersecurity instruction. To accompany the new standards, the 2019 Legislature gave the Department of Public Instruction authority to establish a professional teaching credential for computer and cyber science.

Kirsten Baesler, state superintendent of public instruction, is working with technology industry groups to raise funds to train more North Dakota educators to teach computer science and cybersecurity. Public opinion polls show a large majority of parents want their children to learn computer science, which has become foundational knowledge in K-12 education – almost on a par with reading, writing, and mathematics.

"Today's students must have a basic understanding of how the internet works, how to use and test an algorithm, how to create an app, and how to develop computational thinking," Baesler said. "It is this computational thinking that allows students to look at problems differently and to develop problem-solving skills that can be applied to any situation."

Seal of Biliteracy

To recognize North Dakota students who are proficient in more than one language, and to encourage others to take up the challenge of learning a second language, the Department of Public Instruction approved a "seal of biliteracy" for high school diplomas, beginning in spring 2019.

Students who demonstrate the ability to speak, write, and understand English and another language may apply for a gold or silver seal that will be affixed to their diploma. The gold seal demonstrates stronger language skills.

State School Superintendent Kirsten Baesler said North Dakota students who are native English speakers and have learned a second language may qualify for the seal, as may students who are not native speakers and have gained a good command of English – such as new Americans who have emigrated to North Dakota from Nepal, Bosnia, Somalia, and other countries.

Baesler said speakers of Native American tribal languages and students who are skilled at American Sign Language could also qualify for a seal of biliteracy. American Sign Language is used to communicate with people who are deaf or hard of hearing.

"North Dakota's adoption of the Seal of Biliteracy sets a standard of the value in learning world languages, as well as maintaining native and heritage languages and cultures in our schools, homes, and communities," Baesler said.

Milken Awards

The Milken Educator Awards, which honor top educators around the country with $25,000 prizes, did not have any North Dakota recipients for eight years.

This changed in 2017, when Jamestown High School Principal Adam Gehlhar was selected for the honor, and in 2019, when Brittany Larson, a first-grade teacher at Century Elementary School in Grafton, was chosen. Both awards were announced in front of cheering students during assemblies at the two schools.

Robert Lech, superintendent of the Jamestown school district, called Gehlhar "a brilliant educator" and "a very innovative principal, and I think what's important about how he innovates is that he understands how change needs to happen. He focuses first on making the case about why change needs to happen. That's a really important piece that is missed sometimes."

Larson said a teacher "is the only thing I ever wanted to be." One of Larson's colleagues, Stacey Gaustad, called the Milken Award "a wonderful honor for (Larson), and good for the school and the community. She makes it fun to come to work every day."

School Safety

A coalition of organizations representing schools, law enforcement, and state agencies for education, human services, and emergency management hosted community forums in Bismarck, Dickinson, Williston, Fargo, Valley City, and Rugby during the summer of 2018 to listen to public opinions about school safety measures to present to the 2019 Legislature.

Participants in the forums advocated safety improvements to school buildings; hiring more school resource officers, who are law enforcement officers stationed at schools; and greater student access to counselors and behavioral health specialists.

The 2019 Legislature approved a bill that requires each school to designate a behavioral health resource coordinator and ordered the Department of Public Instruction to keep a coordinator database. Lawmakers extended North Dakota's anti-bullying law in schools to cover bullying by electronic devices, whether on or off school property.

Lawmakers gave school districts the authority to ask voters for a property tax increase of up to five mills to pay for a school safety plan that would be crafted by the local school board.

The legislature also approved a proposal to allow individuals who are not law enforcement officers to serve as "armed first responders" in schools. During the previous three sessions, lawmakers had rejected the idea of making it legal for someone who was not a law officer to bring a gun into a school.

Under the law, local school districts will decide whether to employ an armed first responder. The person will be required to have extensive training in firearms and emergency response, pass a criminal background check and a physical and mental health exam, and have a North Dakota Class 1 permit for carrying a concealed weapon. A Class 1 North Dakota permit requires its holder to demonstrate shooting proficiency.

Higher Education in North Dakota
The Beginnings

As North Dakota moved from territorial days to statehood in the last quarter of the 19th century, several institutions of higher education were established to meet the educational needs of citizens. These early institutions were a mix of denominational, private, and public schools and colleges and included "normal" schools designed to give instruction in the science and art of teaching. Some survived only a short period of time.

The public higher education system of today began when North Dakota became a state on November 2, 1889. The North Dakota State Constitution, which was approved by a vote of the people on October 1, 1889, provided the framework. Article VIII: Education, Section 6 said:

1. A board of higher education, to be officially known as the state board of higher education, is hereby created for the control and administration of the following state educational institutions, to wit:
    a. The state university and school of mines, at Grand Forks, with their substations.
    b. The state agricultural college and experiment station, at Fargo, with their substations.
    c. The school of science, at Wahpeton.
    d. The state normal schools and teachers colleges, at Valley City, Mayville, Minot, and Dickinson.
    e. The school of forestry, at Bottineau.
    f. And such other state institutions of higher education as may hereafter be established.

Chandler Hall was the oldest building at the University of North Dakota in Grand Forks until it was demolished in summer 2018.

North Dakota Institutions of Higher Education Established in the 19th Century

Institution	Dates	Notes
Arvilla Academy and North Dakota School of Music	1886-1893	The first private college in the state to maintain a music department; designated a normal school by the territorial superintendent of public instruction in 1888. Its building was destroyed by fire in 1893 and never rebuilt.
Bruflat Academy (Portland)	1889-1920	Normal school designated by the territorial superintendent of public instruction, also known as Portland Normal School and Business College.
Dakota College (Lisbon)	1891-1895	Baptist; operated for two years in a converted hotel building, which burned down in February 1895.
Fargo College	1887-1922	Congregationalist; Fargo College had a sizable campus and three brick buildings, but massive debt put it out of business in 1922.
Grand Forks College (later Northwestern College)	1891-1912	Norwegian Lutheran; moved to Velva in 1910, due to a change in synodical boundaries, and changed its name to Northwestern College. The college closed in 1912.
Jamestown College (now University of Jamestown)	1883-1893, 1909-present	Presbyterian; normal school. Jamestown was formally chosen as the site for the college on October 31, 1883, and first opened its doors on September 28, 1886. The college closed in the spring of 1893 because of financial problems, but was able to reopen on September 22, 1909, thanks to good organization and strong local support.
Milnor Normal School	1887-1890	Normal school designated by the territorial superintendent of public instruction.
Red River Valley University (Wahpeton)	1891-1905	Methodist; moved from Wahpeton to Grand Forks in 1905 and affiliated itself with the University of North Dakota as Wesley College.
Rolla University	1889-1892	Normal school designated by the territorial superintendent of public instruction.
School of Forestry (Bottineau)	1889-present	Established in the state constitution.
State Agricultural College and Experiment Station (Fargo) (now North Dakota State University)	1889-present	Established in the state constitution.
State Normal Schools (Dickinson, Mayville, Minot, Valley City)	1889-present	Established in the state constitution.
State School of Science (Wahpeton)	1889-present	Established in the state constitution; moved into the building vacated by Red River Valley University in 1905.
Tower University (Tower City)	1886-1888	Baptist; classes began in the fall of 1886 with 30 students enrolled the first year. Enrollment fell to 20 in 1887, and officials closed the school at the end of the school year.
University of North Dakota (Grand Forks)	1883-present	North Dakota's first university was founded in 1883, well before the 1889 state constitution affirmed that the state university and school of mines would be located in Grand Forks.

20th Century and Beyond

Junior Colleges

During the 22nd Legislative Assembly, Senator Lynn Sperry (R-Burleigh County) sponsored Senate Bill 209 to authorize the establishment of junior colleges in the state. The bill was signed into law on March 11, 1931, and led to the establishment of Bismarck Junior College (1939), Devils Lake Junior College (1941), and University of North Dakota – Williston (1957). These three colleges became part of the North Dakota University System in 1984.

Denominational Schools

Three denominational schools were established in the mid-20th century:

- Assumption College (1961, Richardton, Catholic; closed in 1971)
- Mary College (1955, Bismarck, Catholic; now University of Mary)
- Trinity Bible College (1948, Devils Lake, Assemblies of God; now Trinity Bible College & Graduate School, Ellendale)

Tribal Colleges

In the late 1960s and early 1970s, five two-year tribal colleges were established to provide academic and vocational training for the state's Native peoples under their own governance. They included:

- Fort Berthold Community College (1973, New Town; now Nueta Hidatsa Sahnish College)
- Little Hoop Community College (1974, Fort Totten; now Cankdeska Cikana Community College)
- Sitting Bull College (1973, Fort Yates)
- Turtle Mountain Community College (1972, Belcourt)
- United Tribes Employment Training Center (1969, Bismarck; now United Tribes Technical College)

United Tribes Technical College was the nation's second tribal college and was a founding member of the American Indian Higher Education Consortium (AIHEC).

North Dakota Colleges and Universities Today

North Dakota now has six four-year public institutions, three four-year private institutions, five two-year public colleges, and five two-year tribal colleges. The 11 public institutions make up the North Dakota University System.

Four-Year Public Institutions

Institution	Original Name	Date Established/Created
Dickinson State University	Dickinson State Normal School	1916
Mayville State University	Mayville Normal School	1889
Minot State University	Minot Normal School	1889
North Dakota State University (Fargo)	North Dakota Agricultural College	1889
University of North Dakota (Grand Forks)	University of North Dakota	1883
Valley City State University	Valley City Normal School	1889

Four-Year Private Institutions

Institution	Original Name	Date Established/Created
Trinity Bible College & Graduate School (Ellendale)	Trinity Bible College	1948
University of Jamestown	Jamestown College	1883
University of Mary (Bismarck)	Mary College	1955

Two-Year Public Colleges

Institution	Original Name	Date Established/Created
Bismarck State College	Bismarck Junior College	1939
Dakota College at Bottineau	School of Forestry	1889
Lake Region State College (Devils Lake)	Devils Lake Junior College and Business School	1941
North Dakota State College of Science (Wahpeton)	School of Science (in state constitution), which became North Dakota Academy of Science	1889
Williston State College	University of North Dakota - Williston	1957

Two-Year Tribal Colleges (see Chapter 7 for complete information)

Institution	Original Name	Date Established/Created
Cankdeska Cikana Community College (Fort Totten)	Little Hoop Community College	1974
Nueta Hidatsa Sahnish College (New Town)	Fort Berthold Community College	1973
Sitting Bull College (Fort Yates)	Sitting Bull College	1973
Turtle Mountain Community College (Belcourt)	Turtle Mountain Community College	1972
United Tribes Technical College (Bismarck)	United Tribes Employment Training Center	1969

✔ A summary of the names changes of North Dakota colleges and universities can be found in the *2015-2017 North Dakota Blue Book*.

Chief Executive Officers – North Dakota Colleges and Universities

Institution	President	Starting Date
Bismarck State College	Larry C. Skogen, Ph.D.	March 2007 – June 30, 2013; July 2015 (*served as Interim NDUS Chancellor, July 2013– June 2015*)
Cankdeska Cikana Community College (Fort Totten)	Cynthia Lindquist Mala, Ph.D.	October 2003
Dakota College at Bottineau	Steven Shirley, Ph.D.	July 2014
Dickinson State University	Thomas Mitzel, Ph.D.	December 21, 2015
Lake Region State College (Devils Lake)	Doug Darling, Ph.D.	March 8, 2013
Mayville State University	Brian Van Horn, Ed.D.	August 2018
Minot State University	Steven Shirley, Ph.D.	July 2014
North Dakota State College of Science (Wahpeton)	John Richman, Ph.D.	July 2007
North Dakota State University (Fargo)	Dean L. Bresciani, Ph.D.	June 2010
Nueta Hidatsa Sahnish College (New Town)	Twyla Demaray-Baker, Ph.D	September 2014
Sitting Bull College (Fort Yates)	Laurel Vermillion, Ph.D.	May 1, 2006
Trinity Bible College & Graduate School (Ellendale)	Paul Alexander, Ph.D.	June 2012
Turtle Mountain Community College (Belcourt)	James L. Davis, D.Ed.	2005
United Tribes Technical College (Bismarck)	Leander "Russ" McDonald	October 30, 2014
University of Jamestown	Polly L. Peterson, Ph.D.	March 2018
University of Mary (Bismarck)	Monsignor James Patrick Shea	July 2009
University of North Dakota (Grand Forks)	Joshua Wynne, M.D., M.B.A., M.P.H.	June 2019 (Interim)
Valley City State University	Alan LaFave, D.M.A	December 17, 2018
Williston State College	John S. Miller, Ph.D.	June 27, 2017

Governance of North Dakota's Public Institutions of Higher Education

Prior to 1911, all public colleges – and the university – were governed by independent boards of trustees whose members were appointed by the Governor. In that year, the State Board of Normal School Trustees was created specifically to administer the affairs of the normal schools (or teacher colleges). This board consisted of three gubernatorial appointees serving staggered four-year terms and the Superintendent of Public Instruction, who served as ex-officio president.

In 1915, the State Board of Regents was created and given authority over all public colleges, including the normal schools, and the university. This board consisted of five members appointed by the Governor for six-year terms.

The 1919 Legislative Assembly abolished the Board of Regents and placed the administration of the public colleges and the university under a new agency, the Board of Administration. This board consisted of three gubernatorial appointees, as well as the Superintendent of Public Instruction and Commissioner of Agriculture and Labor, serving as ex-officio members. Since the board was charged with "the general supervision and administration of all state penal, charitable and educational institutions of the state, and the general supervision of the public and common schools," the situation was not altogether a satisfactory one.

The controversy surrounding the charges of political interference in the administration of the North Dakota Agriculture College and the firing of its president and seven high-ranking faculty members in 1937 precipitated a movement to create an independent board to govern the state's institutions of higher learning. A constitutional amendment was initiated to create a board of higher education, which was approved by voters in June 1938. The new board consisted of seven members, each appointed by the Governor for seven-year terms, under a carefully outlined procedure intended to remove the board members as far as possible from political influence. The new law also required the board to appoint a Commissioner of Higher Education to serve as its chief executive officer. The board's first meeting took place in Bismarck on July 6, 1939.

Commissioners of Higher Education who served from inception until the creation of the North Dakota University System (NDUS) in 1990:

Robert Murphy	1940 to December 1942
Albert Arnason	December 1942 to September 1957
Arthur Mead	October 1957 to November 1963
Kenneth Raschke	July 1964 to September 1978
Kent Alm	September 1978 to September 1981
John Richardson	September 1981 to May 1990

North Dakota University System

In February 1990, the Board of Higher Education created a one-university system, the North Dakota University System (NDUS), which it governs. The commissioner of higher education was replaced with a chancellor, who serves as the system's chief executive officer.

Mission
To enhance the quality of life for all those we serve and the economic and social vitality of North Dakota through the discovery, sharing, and application of knowledge.

Vision
Leading the nation in educational attainment through access, innovation, and excellence.

NDUS Chancellor

The chancellor serves as the chief executive officer of the NDUS and leads the NDUS staff in support of its mission. The chancellor's office supports the State Board of Higher Education in developing public policy for the governance of the NDUS and in advocating on its behalf.

The presidents of the individual institutions report to and are responsible to the chancellor. Presidents are the chief executive officers of their respective institutions and retain their authority in managing campus affairs.

The chancellor's cabinet includes the chancellor, vice-chancellors, the NDUS chief information officer, institution presidents, and Dakota College at Bottineau (DCB) dean. The cabinet is intended to enable presidents to advise the chancellor and facilitate discussion and consensus-building concerning recommendations to the board, institution administration, and other matters. Presidents and the DCB dean are expected to solicit input from and inform institution officers and faculty about topics on cabinet agendas.

Chancellors, 1990 to present, include:

John Richardson	May to September 1990
Thomas Clifford	October 1990 to July 1991
Douglas Treadway	July 1991 to February 1994
Larry Isaak, co-chancellor	February to July 1994
Gene Kemper, co-chancellor	February to July 1994
Larry Isaak	July 1994 to November 2003
Michael Hillman, interim chancellor	November 2003 to June 2004
Robert L. Potts	July 2004 to August 2006

Eddie Dunn	August 2006 to June 30, 2007
William Goetz	July 1, 2007 to June 30, 2012
Hamid A. Shirvani	July 1, 2012 to June 20, 2013
Larry C. Skogen, interim chancellor	June 20, 2013 to June 30, 2015
Mark R. Hagerott	July 1, 2015 to present

State Board of Higher Education

The State Board of Higher Education (SBHE) is the policy-setting and advocacy body for the NDUS and the governing body for North Dakota's 11 publicly supported colleges and universities. Decisions on issues with systemwide implications are made by the board and chancellor in consultation with the chancellor's cabinet. The SBHE also oversees the NDSU Extension and Agricultural Research Stations, Northern Crops Institute, State Forest Service, and Upper Great Plains Transportation Institute.

The SBHE is comprised of eight voting members. Seven citizen members are nominated by the governor and approved by the North Dakota Senate. Citizen members serve four-year terms with a two-term limit. One student member, appointed by the governor, serves a one-year term. The Council of College Faculties selects the board's non-voting faculty advisor. The NDUS Staff Senate selects the board's non-voting staff advisor.

SBHE Members

Name	Appointment Date	Term Ends
Nick Hacker, Chair	January 12, 2015	June 30, 2023
Don Morton	July 1, 2012	June 30, 2020
Kathleen Neset	June 20, 2012	June 30, 2021
Casey Ryan	July 1, 2017	June 30, 2021
Daniel M. Traynor	July 1, 2018	June 30, 2022
Jill Louters	July 1, 2018	June 30, 2022
Timothy Mihalick	January 11, 2019	June 30, 2023
Kaleb Dschaak, Student Member	July 1, 2019	June 30, 2020
Retha Mattern, Staff Advisor	July 1, 2019	June 30, 2020
Deborah Dragseth, Faculty Adviser	July 1, 2019	June 30, 2020

Chancellor Mark R. Hagerott, Ph.D.

Dr. Mark R. Hagerott is chancellor for the North Dakota University System. Prior to his move back home to North Dakota, Hagerott served on the faculty and held numerous academic leadership roles at the U.S. Naval Academy. He also served as a planning and strategy director in one of the largest U.S. Army educational organizations, NATO Training Mission, which included the Afghanistan army, police, air force, and medical school programs. Hagerott served as distinguished professor and deputy director of the Center for Cyber Security Studies at the Naval Academy and served on the Defense Science Board summer study of unmanned systems from 2014-2015. He is a commissioner on the American Council on Education, Midwestern Higher Education Compact, and Western Interstate Commission for Higher Education.

Hagerott's research and writing are focused on the evolution of technology, education, and changes in technical career paths, and he is the author of multiple articles and book chapters, with a recent emphasis on unmanned systems. He served as a non-resident cyber Fellow of the New America Foundation from 2015-2017.

Prior to his transition to an academic career path, Hagerott held numerous leadership positions in the U.S. Navy, both aboard ships and in administrative positions in the Department of Defense. A certified naval nuclear engineer in power generation and distribution, he served as chief engineer for a major environmental project defueling of two atomic reactors. Hagerott also ran tactical data networks for the Navy and rose to ship command prior to his career in higher education. He also served in both Bush administrations, as a White House Fellow in the first Bush administration and in the office of the Deputy Secretary of Defense in the second Bush administration.

Hagerott holds a B.S. from the U.S. Naval Academy, an M.A. in political science and economics from Oxford University where he attended as a Rhodes Scholar, and a Ph.D. in history from University of Maryland.

The chancellor hails from a multi-generation North Dakota family of farmers and energy producers. The Hagerott-Brandenburg family homesteaded in Center and Mandan before statehood, where his father continues work on the fourth-generation farm, and his mother's family came with the first Bakken oil boom.

Contact information:
Website: www.ndus.edu
Email: mark.hagerott@ndus.edu
Phone: 701-328-2963
Fax: 701-328-2961

NDUS Fall 2018 Enrollment

Four-Year

Dickinson State University	1,392
Mayville State University	1,184
Minot State University	3,189
North Dakota State University	13,796
Valley City State University	1,547
University of North Dakota	13,847

Two-Year

Bismarck State College	3,778
Dakota College at Bottineau	996
Lake Region State College	2,072
North Dakota State School of Science	2,957
Williston State College	1,124

NDUS Four-Year Institutions

Dickinson State University

291 Campus Drive
Dickinson, ND 58601-4896
701-483-2507
800-279-HAWK
www.dickinsonstate.edu

President: Thomas Mitzel, Ph.D.
Nickname: Blue Hawks

University Mission Statement
    Dickinson State University is a regional four-year institution within the North Dakota University System, whose primary role is to contribute to the intellectual, social, economic, and cultural development, especially to southwestern North Dakota. The university's mission is to provide high-quality, accessible programs; to promote excellence in teaching and learning; to support scholarly and creative activities; and to provide service relevant to the economy, health, and quality of life of the citizens of the State of North Dakota.

History

The "College on the Hill" began as Dickinson State Normal School when it was established by a constitutional amendment in 1916. Classes began in 1918 with a two-year program designed to train elementary and secondary school teachers. One hundred four students attended the first classes at Dickinson High School because the new normal school had no buildings. The sessions were free of charge, although students paid their own room and board. Subsequent classes were held at the historic Elks Building until May Hall was completed in 1924. In 1931, four-year degrees were offered for the first time under the school's new name, Dickinson State Teachers College. In 1963, the name was changed to Dickinson State College, and university status was granted in 1987.

Mayville State University

330 Third Street Northeast
Mayville, ND 58257
701-788-4687
800-437-4104
www.mayvillestate.edu

President: Brian Van Horn, Ed.D.
Nickname: Comets

Mission

Mayville State University is dedicated to excellence in teaching, service, and scholarship in dynamic, inclusive and supportive learning environments that are individually focused. We offer quality undergraduate and master's programs enriched with practical experiences to prepare all learners for a global economy.

Purposes

- To provide academic programs and services that address contemporary career and workforce opportunities.
- To maintain collaborative relationships with schools, employers, and communities which contribute to the economic growth and social vitality of North Dakota.
- To deliver flexible programs, instruction, and student services to meet the needs of the individual.
- To cultivate an environment that supports creativity, intellectual curiosity, lifelong learning, service, and an appreciation of diversity.

History

Mayville Normal School, located in the heart of the Red River Valley in east-central North Dakota, was established in 1889, and classes began in 1890. Funds for a building, Old Main, were provided in 1891, and classes were held there beginning in 1893. The school became Mayville State Teachers College in 1925, Mayville State College in 1963, State University of North Dakota – Mayville on April 1, 1987, and finally, Mayville State University on April 27, 1987.

Minot State University

500 University Avenue West
Minot, ND 58707
701-858-3000
800-777-0750
www.minotstateu.edu

President: Steven Shirley, Ph.D.
Nickname: Beavers

Mission

Minot State University is a public university dedicated to excellence in education, scholarship, and community engagement achieved through rigorous academic experiences, active learning environments, commitment to public service, and a vibrant campus life.

Vision

Minot State University will:
- Deliver high-quality education where, when, and how it is needed to a diverse, multi-generational student population.
- Prepare students and the institution for the evolving social and technological challenges of the world.
- Inspire scholarship and creative activity among students, faculty, and staff.
- Empower graduates with a distinctive combination of professional expertise and broad-based education to support varied careers and productive lives.

History

Minot State University is a regional public institution located in Minot (the "Magic City") in the northwest region of the state. It began as Minot Normal School when it was created by popular vote in November 1910 when the state constitution was amended. The first classes met in September 1913 in the city armory. The school's first building, Old Main, came into use in April 1914.

North Dakota State University

1340 Administration Avenue
PO Box 6050
Fargo, ND 58108-6050
701-231-8011
800-488-NDSU (6378)
www.ndsu.edu

President: Dean Bresciani, Ph.D.
Nickname: Bison

Mission
With energy and momentum, North Dakota State University addresses the needs and aspirations of people in a changing world by building on our land-grant foundation.

Vision
We envision a vibrant university that will be globally identified as a contemporary metropolitan land-grant institution.

History
The 1889 state constitution located North Dakota Agricultural College at Fargo, an action ratified by the 1890 Legislature, which established it as North Dakota Agricultural College. The first classes met in January 1891. The first building, College Hall (now called Old Main), was completed in 1892. In 1960, the institution's name was changed to North Dakota State University. Today, it is a student-focused, land-grant, research university located in the northwest part of Fargo. The university also has a major presence in Fargo's downtown area.

University of North Dakota
3501 University Avenue, Stop 8357
Grand Forks, ND 58202
701-777-3000
800-CALL-UND
www.und.edu

Interim President: Joshua Wynne, M.D., M.B.A., M.P.H.
Nickname: Fighting Hawks

Piercing Vision
Our mission is to provide transformative learning, discovery, and community engagement opportunities for developing tomorrow's leaders.

Strategic Plan
The University of North Dakota One UND Strategic Plan emphasizes seven main goals to accomplish by 2022. As the Chief Opportunity Engine for North Dakota and our students, we strive to be the Premier Flagship University in the Northern Plains. The One UND Strategic Plan is the product of a process that involved more than 900 individuals coming together to craft the future of the University of North Dakota. This plan is truly an illustration of One UND, touching all corners of the university: research, enrollment, online education, creation of 21st century programs, alumni relations, and so much more. Our aim is for this process to be observable and evident in all actions made by UND in the years ahead.

Goals
- Goal 1 – Liberal Arts – Provide a strong undergraduate liberal arts foundation.
- Goal 2 - Graduation Rates – Increase undergraduate, graduate, and professional retention and graduation rates.
- Goal 3 – Enrollment – Deliver more educational opportunities online and on-campus.
- Goal 4 – Research – Enhance discovery at a level consistent with the most research-intensive universities (Carnegie R1).
- Goal 5 – Inclusive – Foster a welcoming, safe, and inclusive campus climate.
- Goal 6 – Serving Military – Meet educational needs of active-duty military personnel, veterans, and their families.
- Goal 7 – Engaging Alumni – Attract support for the university by actively engaging alumni and donors.

Core Values
- Community – A spirit of collaboration and connectedness across the University and beyond
- Discovery – An enthusiasm for inquiry, creativity, and innovation
- Diversity – An understanding and appreciation of diverse people, experiences, and ideas
- Inclusivity – A welcoming, inclusive, and supportive environment for all
- Liberal Arts – An educational foundation essential for living an intellectually curious, personally fulfilling, and socially responsible life
- Lifelong Learning – A passion for learning, civic engagement, and community leadership

History
An act of the 1883 Dakota Territory legislature created the University of North Dakota (the first use of the name "North Dakota") six years before statehood was achieved. Unlike most state institutions of higher education west of the Mississippi, the University of North Dakota did not begin as an agricultural school or only as a teachers' college. Instead, it was organized as a College of Arts & Sciences with a Normal School for the education of teachers. The first classes met in September 1884 when the first building was completed. The university's location at Grand Forks was recognized in North Dakota's 1889 Constitution.

Valley City State University
101 College Street Southwest
Valley City, ND 58072
800-532-8641
www.vcsu.edu

President: Alan LaFave, D.M.A
Nickname: Vikings

Mission

Valley City State University is a public, regional university offering exceptional programs in an active, learner-centered community that promotes meaningful scholarship, ethical service, and the skilled use of technology. As an important knowledge resource, the university offers programs and outreach that enrich the quality of life in North Dakota and beyond. Through flexible, accessible, and innovative baccalaureate and master's programs, Valley City State University prepares students to succeed as educators, leaders, and engaged citizens in an increasingly complex and diverse society.

Vision

As an innovative university, we deliver distinctive, learner-centered experiences.

History

The 1889 State Constitution located a normal school at Valley City, and the school was established by the 1890 Legislature. Valley City Normal School opened in October 1890 above a downtown business and occupied its first building in December 1892. In 1921, the school began granting a bachelor of arts degree in education and changed its name to State Teachers College in Valley City. The name was changed to Valley City State College (1963); State University of North Dakota-Valley City (January 1, 1987); and, finally, to Valley City State University (April 27, 1987). The university has been a leader in applying technology to enhance learning. In 1996, it was the second university in the nation to become a laptop university, which means that every full-time student has access to their own laptop computer, provided by Valley City State University. In 2005, the university was authorized to offer its first master's degree program, a master of education.

NDUS Two-Year Institutions

Bismarck State College

P.O. Box 5587
1500 Edwards Avenue
Bismarck, ND 58506
701-224-5400
800-445-5073
www.bismarckstate.edu

President: Larry C. Skogen, Ph.D.
Nickname: Mystics

Mission

Bismarck State College, an innovative community college, offers high quality education, workforce training, and enrichment programs reaching local and global communities.

Vision
A national model for innovative education and workforce training.

History
Created in 1939 in response to a community need for a local college, Bismarck State College was originally known as Bismarck Junior College. Classes began on September 4, 1939, on the third floor of Bismarck High School. By the late 1940s, a new location became urgent as college enrollments soared with returning GIs. In 1951, the Legislature granted the college 15 acres on the Capitol grounds, and Bismarck Junior College moved into its own building at 900 Boulevard Avenue in 1955. The college quickly outgrew the site. In 1959, Harold Schafer, local entrepreneur and founder of the successful Gold Seal Company, offered the college land overlooking the Missouri River at the northwest edge of Bismarck. Classes began on the new campus in the fall of 1961. Part of the Bismarck Public Schools for many years, the college became part of NDUS in 1984. The college's name was changed to Bismarck State Community College on January 1, 1987, and then to Bismarck State College on April 27, 1987.

Dakota College at Bottineau
105 Simrall Boulevard
Bottineau, ND 58318
800-542-6866
701-228-5488
www.dakotacollege.edu

President: Steven Shirley, Ph.D.
Campus Dean: Jerry Migler, Ph.D.
Nickname: Lumberjacks and Ladyjacks

Mission
Dakota College at Bottineau provides students with a quality education in a caring environment. The institution values diversity and personal enrichment by promoting engaged learning for employment and university transfer. With the help of a supportive community, Dakota College at Bottineau emphasizes nature and technology to accomplish its mission through an array of curricula, programs, and services.

- Liberal arts education provides students the knowledge and tools to continue their education, to serve as good stewards of the environment, and to function as responsible citizens.
- Career/technical education provides students with the knowledge and skills required to succeed by utilizing natural, human, and technological resources.
- Distance delivery provides students increased access to education and career opportunities.
- Community education provides diverse lifelong learning experiences.
- Support services provide opportunities for individual growth and success.
- Campus activities provide for interpersonal development.
- Campus outreach provides area schools and groups access to college resources.

- Workforce training and development provides the human resources for economic development.
- All programs provide a greater understanding of human diversity.

Dakota College at Bottineau's curricula, programs, and services take students *beyond nature and technology* and leave them with an ethic of concern and care for the natural world.

Vision
Dakota College at Bottineau is rooted in the past and grows towards the future by combining the best from the *Past, Present, and Future* to provide students with innovative educational opportunities. The campus will emphasize a knowledge and appreciation of *Nature*, implement a rapidly changing *Technology*, and prepare students to go *Beyond* and improve the quality of life.

History
The 1889 constitution located a School of Forestry within the counties of McHenry, Ward, Bottineau, or Rolette; a popular vote in November 1894 placed it at Bottineau. The 1897 Legislature formally established the North Dakota School of Forestry, although the school did not begin operations until 1907. The school closed briefly during 1923-1925 when the Legislature refused to provide funding and reopened primarily as a junior college. In 1968, the school was attached to North Dakota State University for administrative purposes and is now administratively attached to Minot State University. Effective August 1, 2009, the college's name was changed to Dakota College at Bottineau. The Minot State University president oversees operations at both sites, and the chief executive officer at the college is the campus dean. The campus is located on the north side of Bottineau, a city near the Turtle Mountains in north-central North Dakota.

Lake Region State College

1801 College Drive North
Devils Lake, ND 58301
701-662-1600
800-443-1313
www.lrsc.edu

President: Doug Darling, Ph.D.
Nickname: Royals

Mission
We enhance lives and community vitality through quality education.
- Academic Education: Provides academic courses and programs that lead to an associate in arts degree, meeting the NDUS general education requirements, and allows for seamless transfer to baccalaureate-granting institutions.
- Vocational/Technical Training: Provides courses and programs in vocational and technical career training that lead to a certificate of completion, a diploma,

or an associate in applied science degree preparing students for an immediate career, advancement in specific occupations, or transfer to an articulated technical baccalaureate program.
- Workforce Training: Develops linkages with businesses, industry, and organizations to encourage economic development.
- Educational Outreach Opportunities: Provides educational outreach opportunities for individuals who are time and/or place bound.
- Lifelong Learning: Provides opportunities for continuing and lifelong learning in the form of cultural, educational, occupational, social, athletic, and vocational programs, courses, workshops, and institutes. The college is committed to being a responsive diverse institution, which prepares students for successful living and citizenship in a rapidly changing local, national, and world community.

History

In July 1941, Devils Lake residents voted to create Devils Lake Junior College and Business School, a two-year college to operate as an extension of the public school system. Classes began in September 1941 in a former high school building, and the college moved to its present 35-acre campus in 1966. In 1963, the name was changed to Lake Region Junior College, and in 1981, to Lake Region Community College. On July 1, 1984, the college joined NDUS, with administrative supervision transferred to the North Dakota State College of Science in Wahpeton in 1985. The college became affiliated with the University of North Dakota in 1987, operating as a branch campus under the name UND-Lake Region. On July 1, 1999, the college attained independent status within NDUS as Lake Region State College.

North Dakota State College of Science

NDSCS Wahpeton: 800 Sixth Street North
Wahpeton, ND 58076
800-342-4235 or 701-671-2401
NDSCS Fargo: 1305 19th Avenue North
Fargo, ND 58012
701-231-6900
www.ndscs.edu

President: John Richman, Ph.D.
Nickname: Wildcats

Mission

The North Dakota State College of Science (NDSCS) is a comprehensive, associate degree-granting college founded on a tradition of quality and integrity. We deliver learner-focused education through a unique and evolving collegiate experience. Using innovative delivery strategies, NDSCS anticipates and responds to statewide and regional needs by providing access to occupational/technical programs, transfer programs, and workforce training.

Vision Statement

To enrich people's lives through responsive lifelong learning in a dynamic educational and technological environment.

History

The constitution of the state of North Dakota directed that a state scientific school be located in Wahpeton. The first classes met in 1903, making the institution one of the oldest public two-year colleges in the United States. In 1987, the North Dakota State School of Science changed its name to the North Dakota State College of Science. In 1997, NDSCS established a regional workforce training center in Fargo. The college offers a variety of face-to-face, distance education, and online courses, as well as workforce training. NDSCS offers degrees, certificates, and diplomas in traditional career and technical studies, as well as liberal arts. The college's 125-acre campus is located on the north side of Wahpeton, and the NDSCS-Fargo location is in north Fargo.

Williston State College

1410 University Avenue
Williston, ND 58801
701-774-4200
888-863-9455
www.willistonstate.edu

President: John Miller, Ph.D.
Nickname: Tetons

Mission

The mission of WSC, "Where the People Make the Difference," is to provide accessible, affordable, life changing, and life-long educational pathways to residents of North Dakota, the Upper Plains, and beyond.

Vision

We are committed to student excellence. We embrace quality student experiences, open communication, and actionable data that enrich personal relationships among our college, faculty, and students. We believe that people make the difference; that the college is the heart of the communities we serve; that our facilities are a needed, neutral, and central community space; and that our faculty and staff serve multiple and diverse needs in a global environment. We strive for a strong student presence on-campus, expanded offerings, fiscal sustainability, modern facilities, current technologies, and continuous improvement as a result of both our master and strategic plans.

History

From its beginning as an extension center, Williston State College (WSC) now provides educational opportunities to the greater Williston area in northwest North Dakota. The University of North Dakota (UND) first offered extension classes in

Williston during the fall of 1957. In 1961, WSC, then known as the UND Williston Center, founded its own resident campus, faculty, and curricula through a contractual arrangement between UND and Williston School District #1. This arrangement continued until July 1, 1984, when the North Dakota State Board of Higher Education assumed responsibility for the college, and the institution was renamed UND-Williston. In 1999, legislative action expanded the college's mission to include workforce training, and UND-Williston then became an autonomous campus renamed Williston State College.

Private Colleges and Universities

Trinity Bible College and Graduate School

50 Sixth Avenue South
Ellendale, ND 58436
800-523-1603
www.trinitybiblecollege.edu

President: Paul R. Alexander, Ph.D.
Nickname: Lions

Mission

Trinity Bible College and Graduate School is committed to training and educating people with theological reflection and missional passion, in order that people and communities everywhere will hear the good news of Jesus and see his love demonstrated.

Vision

Over the coming years, Trinity Bible College and Graduate School will continue to develop its role as a leading Pentecostal Bible college in the USA and beyond. We will champion the cause of raising and training well equipped leaders and prepare our students to be effective, skilled individuals fitted for service in today's world. We will emphasize lifelong learning, spiritual vitality and life skills, ensuring that our graduates make a Christ-centered contribution to the communities in which they live and work. We will always take seriously the diverse world in which we live. From the view that accepts the Christian Gospel as the fundamental under-girding for life, we will ensure that our students are trained and encouraged to serve Jesus Christ authentically while handling complexity and diversity effectively. We will seek to pioneer the development of innovative training, scholarly understanding and critical awareness in order to prepare people to plant churches, enter cross-cultural ministry or the workplace in such a way as to build churches and communities that truly show the life changing power of Jesus Christ. We will be adaptive to changes in our society and culture by ensuring the development of talented, highly skilled and motivated staff, effective governance, management and leadership. We will achieve this through the provision of well-resourced facilities and a commitment to network in an unthreatened way with churches and institutions that share our vision for a better world through the sending and placing of well-trained Christian leaders.

History
This private school, operated by the Assemblies of God denomination, was founded in 1948 as Lakewood Park Bible School in Devils Lake. It moved to Aberdeen, South Dakota, in 1960, where it became Hub City Bible Institute. In the fall of 1967, it moved to the former Trinity Hospital in Jamestown and was renamed Trinity Bible Institute. When the University of North Dakota-Ellendale Branch (Ellendale State Teachers College) closed, Trinity moved to that facility and offered its first classes there in October 1972. The present name was adopted in 1983.

University of Jamestown
Jamestown Campus
6000 College Lane
Jamestown, ND 58405
701-252-3467
www.uj.edu

President: Polly L. Peterson, Ph.D.
Nickname: Jimmie

Mission
University of Jamestown is a community dedicated to the development of wholeness in our students. We adhere to a curriculum of academic excellence which balances the ideals of the liberal arts tradition and sound professional preparation. Our Christian tradition encourages an atmosphere of self-discipline, responsibility, and concern for the continuing growth of the individual.

Vision Statement
University of Jamestown will be nationally recognized for preparing professional and community leaders through a total experience that is student-centered and character focused. Students will be engaged academically through close interaction with faculty in a curriculum that integrates the liberal arts with sound professional programs.

Statement of Values
As an institution of higher education in the Presbyterian tradition, we celebrate God through the use of our minds and the exercise of reason, believing that God is the source of all truth.

You shall love the Lord our God with all your heart, and with all your soul, and with all your mind (Matthew 22:37).

Our Christian and Reformed tradition embraces the liberal arts and the ongoing search for knowledge and truth as a way of liberating the human spirit and of understanding the world we share with others. University of Jamestown promotes education as a means to improve lives, search for vocation, and create lifelong seekers of truth and wisdom. We value the life of the mind and the life of the spirit and therefore hold that faith and reason reinforce each other and that through mind, heart, and hands one can honor God and serve humanity.

Historically, this strong belief that learning and the search for truth are closely connected to faith formed the basis for the Presbyterian Church's early and significant commitment to higher education. As a result, prior to the Civil War, one-fourth of the colleges in the United States were Presbyterian. In 1883, when the Presbyterian Church extended its mission into the Dakota Territory's frontier, Jamestown College was founded in a newly incorporated city ninety miles west of Fargo.

University of Jamestown is a fully independent, self-governing institution that shares a historic relationship with the Presbyterian Church (USA). We are non-sectarian and welcome students of all faiths and beliefs. Our Latin motto, "Lux et Veritas," proclaims to all that the pursuit of truth lights our journey today as it has since 1883.

History

The University of Jamestown was founded as Jamestown College on October 31, 1883, by the Presbyterian Church. In September 1886, the college held its first classes at the North Side School House, a local public school building. The college was forced to close in spring 1893 because of hard financial times throughout the country. It reopened on September 22, 1909, when things improved. On August 21, 2013, the name was changed to University of Jamestown "to better reflect the breadth of its educational offerings at all levels – bachelor's, master's, and doctoral – and to recognize significant growth and change in its 130-year history."

University of Mary
7500 University Drive
Bismarck, ND 58504
701-355-8030
800-288-6279 (MARY)
www.umary.edu

President: Monsignor James Shea
Nickname: Marauders

Statement of Mission and Identity

The University of Mary exists to serve the religious, academic, and cultural needs of the people in this region and beyond. It takes its tone from the commitment of the Sisters of Annunciation Monastery. These sisters founded the university in 1959 and continue to sponsor it today. It is Christian, it is Catholic, and it is Benedictine.

History

The University of Mary was founded in 1955 as Mary College, a two-year institution, by the Roman Catholic Benedictine Sisters of Annunciation Priory. It became a four-year college in 1959 and was renamed University of Mary when it achieved university status in 1986. In 2010, the university opened its first international campus in Rome, Italy. In 2012, the university entered into a collaborative agreement with Arizona State University to offer ASU students the opportunity to take courses in theological studies and Catholic studies. In 2015, the university opened its second international campus in Arequipa, Peru. The 150-acre home campus is located on a site overlooking the Missouri River Valley southeast of Bismarck and adjacent to the Annunciation Priory.

National Athletic Championships

North Dakota's college and university athletes have a history of national success at both the individual and team levels.

Team Championships

Dakota College at Bottineau

- NJCAA, Men's Ice Hockey – 1986, 1991, 1998, 2003, 2007, 2008, 2009, 2010, 2016, 2017

Dickinson State University

- NAIA, Men's Outdoor Track & Field – 2004, 2005, 2006
- NAIA, Women's Volleyball – 2000

Minot State University

- NAIA, Men's Cross Country – 2002, 2003

North Dakota State University

- NCAA, FCS, Football – 2011, 2012, 2013, 2014, 2015, 2017, 2018
- NCAA, Division II, Football – 1983, 1985, 1986, 1988, 1990
- Football – 1965 (Pecan Bowl), 1968 (Pecan Bowl), 1969 (Camellia Bowl)
- NCAA, Division II, Women's Indoor Track and Field – 2002
- NCAA, Division II, Wrestling – 1988, 1998, 2000, 2001
- NCAA, Division II, Women's Softball – 2000
- NCAA, Division II, Women's Basketball – 1991, 1993, 1994, 1995, 1996
- NCAA, Division II, Men's Cross Country – 1972

Trinity Bible College and Graduate School

- NBCAA, Women's Volleyball – 1986, 1987, 1989

University of Mary

- NAIA, Division II, Women's Basketball – 2000

University of North Dakota

- NCAA, Division I, Men's Ice Hockey – 1959, 1963, 1980, 1982, 1987, 1997, 2000, 2016
- NCAA, Division II, Football – 2001
- NCAA, Division II, Women's Basketball – 1997, 1998, 1999

Williston State College

- NJCAA, Men's Ice Hockey – 2013, 2014

Individual Championships and Achievements

Bismarck State College

NJCAA Wrestling, Men
- Individual Champion
  - 123-126-133 Pounds
    - 1974 - Rhett Hilzendeger
    - 1978 - Kent Ness
  - 157-152-158-165 Pounds
    - 1973-1974 - Gary Hoffman
  - 191-190-197 Pounds
    - 1976 - Robert Ayres
    - 1982 - Mike Blaske
  - Heavyweight
    - 1998 - Brock Lesnar
- NJCAA Outstanding Wrestler - Ernest B. Gould Award
  - 1998 - Brock Lesnar
- NJCAA Man of the Year (NJCAA Wrestling Coaches Association)
  - 1984 - Ed Kringstad
- NJCAA Wrestling Coach of the Year
  - 1974, 1986 - Ed Kringstad

Dickinson State University

NAIA Wrestling, Men
- Individual Champion
  - 118 Pounds
    - 1983 - Randy Burwick
  - 137 Pounds
    - 1964 - Dean Buchmeier
  - 165 Pounds
    - 2005 - Tyson Springer
  - 174 Pounds
    - 2003 - Larry Johnson
  - 197 Pounds
    - 2006-2008 - Justin Schlecht
    - 2014 - Jesse Hellinger
  - Heavyweight
    - 1981 - Kurt Lesser

NAIA Indoor Track and Field, Men
- 400-Meter Dash
  - 2007-2009 - Ramon Miller
  - 2010 - Sean Pickstock
- 55-Meter Dash
  - 2003-2004 - Derrick Atkins
- 200-Meter Dash
  - 2009 - Ramon Miller
- 1000-Meter Run
  - 2013 - Dante Carter
- 35-Pound Weight Throw
  - 2005 - Ross Walker
- Long Jump
  - 2005-2006 - Trevor Berry
  - 2008 - Dominic Goodman
- High Jump
  - 2005-2006 - Trevor Barry
- 1600-Meter Relay
  - 2006 - Francisco Rose, Ramon Miller, Trevor Barry, Aaron Cleare
  - 2008 - Allan Ayala, John Ingram, Sean Pickstock, Ramon Miller
  - 2009 - Allan Ayala, Sean Pickstock, Ian Smith, Ramon Miller
- Harry Gill Outstanding Performer
  - 2006 - Trevor Barry
- Most Valuable Performance (based on national meet total points scored)
  - 2009 - Ramon Miller

NAIA Outdoor Track and Field, Men
- 100-Meter Dash
  - 2003-2005 - Derrick Atkins
- 200-Meter Dash
  - 2004-2005 - Derrick Atkins
- 400-Meter Dash
  - 2002, 2004-2006 - Aaron Cleare
  - 2008-2009 - Ramon Miller
  - 2010 - Sean Pickstock
- 400-Meter Hurdles
  - 2008-2010 - Allan Ayala
- 4x100-Meter Relay
  - 2009 - Ramon Miller, John Ingraham, Kurt McCormack, Jamal Forbes
- 4x400-Meter Relay
  - 2008 - Allan Ayala, John Ingraham, Sean Pickstock, Ramon Miller
  - 2009 - Sean Pickstock, John Ingraham, Allan Ayala, Ramon Miller
- Long Jump
  - 2004-2006 - Trevor Barry
- Triple Jump
  - 2007 - Dominic Goodman
- Shot Put
  - 2006 - Ross Walker
- Decathlon
  - 2005 - Ben Knight
- Coach of the Year
  - 2003-2006 - Pete Stanton

NAIA Indoor Track and Field, Women
- 800-Meter Run
  - 2004 - Tara McAvena
- Pole Vault
  - 2008, 2010 - Kelsey Aide

NAIA Outdoor Track and Field, Women
- Discus
  - 2001-2002 - Amanda Anderson
- Pole Vault
  - 2007, 2009 - Kelsey Aide
- Javelin
  - 1990 - Cathy Carlson

NAIA Volleyball, Women
- NAIA National Championship Coach of the Year
  - 2000 - Dave Moody
- NAIA/AVCA (American Volleyball Coaches Association) Player of the Year
  - 2000 - Nesilhan Yilmaz

Minot State University

NAIA Cross Country, Men
- Coach of the Year
  - 1999 - Dave Zittleman
  - 2002-2003 - Scott Simmons

NAIA Indoor Track and Field, Men
- Triple Jump
  - 2003 - Travis Hanson
- 3000-Meter Run
  - 2002 - Brad Tighe

NAIA Indoor Track and Field, Women
- 3000-Meter Run
  - 2007 - Genevieve Binsfeld
- 3000-Meter Race Walk
  - 2003 - Magda Spyra
- Shot Put
  - 1998-1999 - Donelle Carter
- 20-Pound Weight Throw
  - 1999 - Donelle Carter

NAIA Outdoor Track and Field, Women
- Shot Put
  - 1998-1999 - Donelle Carter
- Discus
  - 1999 - Donelle Carter
- Javelin
  - 2005 - LeeAnn Pekovitch

North Dakota State College of Science

NJCAA Wrestling, Men
- Individual Champion
  - 177-184 Pounds
    - 1988 - Lloyd Huyck

North Dakota State University

NCAA Wrestling, Men
- **Individual Champion**
  - 118 Pounds
    - 1993-1995 - Brian Kapusta

- 126 Pounds
    - 1973 - Phil Reimnitz
    - 1988 - Rick Goeb
- 133 Pounds
    - 2000 - Kris Nelson
- 134 Pounds
    - 1983 - Steve Carr
    - 1992 - Lloyd Wurm
    - 1997 - George Thompson
- 142 Pounds
    - 1973 - Lee Petersen
    - 1982 - Mike Langlais
- 150 Pounds
    - 1984 - Mike Langlais
- 157 Pounds
    - 2000 - Wayne Mooney
    - 2003 - Paul Carlson
- 158 Pounds
    - 1998 - Mark Pazdernik
- 167 Pounds
    - 1998 - Steve Saxlund
- 171 Pounds
    - 1971-1972 - Bill Demaray
- 174 Pounds
    - 2000-2002 - Todd Fuller
- 184 Pounds
    - 2000-2001 - Steve Saxlund
- 190 Pounds
    - 1971 - Bob Backlund
    - 1975 - Brad Rheingans
    - 1995 - Ryan Wolters
- Heavyweight
    - 2001-2002 - Nick Severson

NCAA Cross Country, Men
- 1971-1972 - Mike Slack
- 1977 - Mike Bollman
- 1988, 1990 - Doug Hanson

NCAA Indoor Track and Field, Men
- 5000 Meters
    - 1989-1990 - Doug Hanson
- Pole Vault
    - 1996 - Ryan McGlynn

NCAA Outdoor Track and Field, Men
- 800 Meters
  - 1998 - Heith Janke
- 10,000 Meters
  - 1988-1989, 1991 - Doug Hanson
- 3000-Meter Steeplechase
  - 1979-1980 - Curt Bacon
- Decathlon
  - 2003-2004 - Nathan Schmidt

NCAA Indoor Track and Field, Women
- 800 Meters
  - 2004 - Kinsey Coles
- 3000 Meters
  - 1985 - Nancy Dietman
- 1600 Meter Relay
  - 2002 - Kinsey Coles, Nicole Rieck, Jill Theeler, Tamara Brudy
  - 2004 - Nicole Rieck, Sarah Klein, Kiki Smith, Kinsey Coles
- High Jump
  - 1993 - Penny Ensrud
  - 1996 - Andrea Jeseritz
- Triple Jump
  - 2002, 2004 - Amanda Thieschafer
- Weight Throw
  - 2001 - Diandra Bauer

NCAA Outdoor Track and Field, Women
- 800 Meters
  - 2004 - Kinsey Coles
- 400-Meter Hurdles
  - 2003 - Kinsey Coles
- Triple Jump
  - 2003 - Amanda Thieschafer
- Hammer Throw
  - 2001 - Diandra Bauer

University of Jamestown

NAIA Wrestling, Men
- Individual Champion
  - 150 Pounds
    - 1984 - Paul Syvrud
  - 158 pounds
    - 1985-1986 - Paul Syvrud
  - 190 Pounds
    - 1983 - David Marshall

NAIA Indoor Track and Field, Men
- Pole Vault
  - 1997 - Chad Stadler

NAIA Outdoor Track and Field, Men
- 3000-Meter Steeplechase
  - 1983 - Brad Braunberger
- Pole Vault
  - 1997 - Chad Stadler
- Javelin
  - 1988 - Jon Claymore

NAIA Indoor Track and Field, Women
- 600-Meter Run
  - 1997 - Erin Boziel

NAIA Outdoor Track and Field, Women
- 800-Meter Run
  - 1985 - Teresa Lloyd
- 1500-Meter Run
  - 1986 - Teresa Lloyd
- 3000-Meter Steeplechase
  - 2011 - Katie Conlon
- Marathon
  - 1995 - Shawna Doty

University of Mary

NAIA Wrestling, Men
- Individual Champion
  - 118 Pounds
    - 1997 - Joe Tezak
  - 125 Pounds
    - 2003 - Aaron Hartnell
  - 126 Pounds
    - 1993-1994 - Kerry Boumans
  - 133 Pounds
    - 2001 - Brian Biel
  - 142 Pounds
    - 1992 - Monte Trusty
  - 158 Pounds
    - 1995-1996 - Mike Seeger
  - 184 Pounds
    - 1999-2001 - Jeremy Engelhardt
  - 190 Pounds
    - 1994 - Jim Cudney

- 197 Pounds
  - 2005 - Jesse Laber
- Heavyweight
  - 1997 - Dan Hughes

NAIA Indoor Track and Field, Men
- NAIA, High Jump
  - 2000 - Shane Yates

NAIA Outdoor Track and Field, Men
- Marathon
  - 2002 - Pawel Oboz
- Triple Jump
  - 2000 - Rob Renschler

NAIA Indoor Track and Field, Women
- 1600-Meter Relay
  - 2004 - Latasha Rudolph, Femi Kehinde, Mollie Hoff, Bukky Hassan
- High Jump
  - 1999 - Mandy Schroeder
- Shot Put
  - 1991 - Tiffany Johnson
- Pole Vault
  - 2000, 2002 - Kari Wilson
  - 2004 - Kristin Schwehr
- Long Jump
  - 1997 - Jamey Mulske
- Pentathlon
  - 1996 - Cindy Leingang
  - 1997 - Jamey Mulske
  - 1998-1999 - Mandy Schroeder
  - 2002 - Annie Goodson
- Outstanding Performer
  - 1997 - Jamey Mulske
- Coach of the Year
  - 2000, 2002 - Mike Thorson

NAIA Outdoor Track and Field, Women
- Marathon
  - 2000 - Shandi Hertz
- 100-Meter Hurdles
  - 2002 - Karla Fandrich
- 400-Meter Hurdles
  - 1998 - Jamey Mulske
  - 2005 - Shawn Kern

- Long Jump
  - 1997-1998 - Jamey Mulske
- High Jump
  - 1998 - Mandy Schroeder
- Heptathlon
  - 1996-1998 - Jamey Mulske
  - 2002 - Annie Goodson
- Hebert B. Marett Outstanding Performer
  - 1997-1998 - Jamey Mulske
- Coach of the Year
  - 1997, 1999 - Mike Thorson

University of North Dakota

NCAA Wrestling, Men
- Individual Champion
  - 158 Pounds
    - 1987-1988 - Kory Mosher
    - 1989 - Tim Briggs

NCAA Cross Country, Men
- 1967 - Arjan Gelling

NCAA Indoor Track, Men
- 55-Meter Dash
  - 1987-1988 - Norm McGee
- Shot Put
  - 1985 - Dave Levos

NCAA Outdoor Track, Men
- 100-Meter Dash
  - 1987-1989 - Norm McGee
- 10,000-Meter Run
  - 1969 - Arjan Gelling
- Discus Throw
  - 1986 - Dave Levos
- Javelin Throw
  - 2008 - Matt Litzinger

NCAA Swimming, Men
- 100-Yard Butterfly
  - 2004-2005 - Fernando Alves
- 200-Yard Butterfly
  - 2004 - Fernando Alves
  - 2006 - Dan Zabler

- 500-Yard Freestyle
  - 2005 - Rodrigo Cintra
- 1650-Yard Freestyle
  - 2002 - Rodrigo Cintra
- 100-Yard Backstroke
  - 2004-2007 - Rodrigo Ferreira
- One-Meter Diving
  - 2004 - Kasey Moseley
- Three-Meter Diving
  - 2004 - Mike Hahn
- 200-Yard Freestyle Relay
  - 2004 - Fernando Alves, Andy Burckhard, Jason Mraule, Rodrigo Ferreira
  - 2005 - Rodrigo Ferreira, Eric Knight, Pedro Pereira, Jason Mraule
  - 2007 - Anthony Buhr, Eric Knight, Pedro Pereira, Per Westergren
- 400-Yard Freestyle Relay
  - 2004 - Jeff Schneider, Fernando Alves, Jason Mraule, Sebastian Andersson
  - 2006 - Adam Rollins, Rodrigo Ferreira, Eric Knight, Per Westergren
  - 2007 - Daniel Moraes, Rodrigo Ferreira, Per Westergren, Eric Knight
- 800-Yard Freestyle Relay
  - 2007 - Daniel Moraes, Dan Zabler, Shaun Seaburg, Per Westergren
- 200-Yard Medley Relay
  - 2001 - Jacob Mills, Mats Linden, Vesa Nurmiviita, Sebastian Anderson
  - 2002 - Jacob Mills, Andy Burckhard, Vesa Nurmiviita, Mats Liden
  - 2006 - Rodrigo Ferreira, Jeff Schneider, Jared Peters, Eric Knight
  - 2007 - Rodrigo Ferreira, Pedro Pereira, Per Westergren, Eric Knight
- 400-Yard Medley Relay
  - 2002 - Jacob Mills, Mats Liden, Mike Walz, Sebastian Anderson
  - 2003 - Jake Mills, Jeff Schneider, Fernando Alves, Sebastian Andersson
  - 2006 - Rodrigo Ferreira, Pedro Pereira, Jared Peters, Per Westergren
  - 2007 - Rodrigo Ferreira, Pedro Pereira, Dan Zabler, Eric Knight

NCAA Indoor Track, Women
- 800-Meter Run
  - 1994 - Marie Crep

NCAA Outdoor Track, Women
- 1500-Meter Run
  - 2008 - Heidi Evans

NCAA Swimming, Women
- 50-Yard Freestyle
  - 1984 - Kimber Edwards
  - 1990 - Janine Etchepare
  - 2008 - Carissa Gormally
- 100-Yard Freestyle
  - 2008 - Carissa Gormally
- 100-Yard Backstroke
  - 2004 - Jenny Bachmeier
- 100-Yard Breaststroke
  - 1990 - Marion Warner
  - 1999, 2002 - Beth Morris
- 200-Yard Breaststroke
  - 1993 - Tisha Yantzer
  - 2002 - Janice Berry
- 100-Yard Butterfly
  - 1985 - Mary Beth Dunlevy
  - 1990 - Marion Warner
  - 1992-1993 - Shelly Ebbighausen
  - 1994 - Andrea Rudser
  - 1997 - Tania Younkin (Note: Tied with Nida Zuhal, Drury University)
- 200-Yard Butterfly
  - 1994 - Andrea Rudser
- 400-Yard Individual Medley
  - 1999 - Rebecca Fischer
  - 2002 - Janice Berry
- Three-Meter Diving
  - 2003 - Erin Borgshatz
- 200-Yard Freestyle Relay
  - 1985 - Kimber Edwards, Janine Owens, Margaret Schmidt, Mary Beth Dunlevy
- 200-Yard Medley Relay
  - 1989 - Michelle Puetz, Marion Warner, Kristin McClocklin, Janine Etchepare
  - 1990 - Michelle Puetz, Jodie Schwartz, Marion Warner, Janine Etchepare
  - 1991 - Marion Warner, Jodie Schwartz, Shelly Ebbighausen, Janine Etchepare
  - 1998 - Tara Bruels, Katherine Poole, Tania Younkin, Sarah Doeden
  - 1999 - Brook McKee, Beth Morris, Holly Skarsgard, Sarah Doeden
  - 2000 - Brook McKee, Beth Morris, Barb Colbert, Marie Buckhard
- 400-Yard Medley Relay
  - 1990 - Michelle Puetz, Jodie Schwartz, Marion Warner, Janine Etchepare
  - 1999 - Brook McKee, Beth Morris, Holly Skarsgard, Trish Stoutenberg
  - 2000 - Brook McKee, Beth Morris, Barb Colbert, Trish Stoutenberg

Valley City State University

NAIA Wrestling, Men
- Individual Champion
  - 158 Pounds
    - 1990 - Casey Schweitzer
    - 1992 - Duey Yliniemi
  - 190 Pounds
    - 1979-1980 - Tony Huck

NAIA Indoor Track and Field, Men
- 35-Pound Weight Throw
  - 2013 - Darien Moore

NAIA Outdoor Track and Field, Men
- Marathon
  - 1989 - Gary Schafer
- Hammer Throw
  - 2012 - Darien Moore

NAIA Outdoor Track and Field, Women
- Javelin
  - 2017 - Seri Geisler

Chapter Ten
Agriculture

Due to the vast size of the state and limited rural transit options, aviation continues to be a critical method of transportation in North Dakota. Many rural airports in North Dakota, like the Glen Ullin Airport pictured in approximately 2012, provide important access to commercial, private, agriculture, and medical aviation services.

Barley, Hops, and Craft Breweries 514
North Dakota's Agriculture Profile 524
North Dakota's Rank Among the States 526
North Dakota's Top Agricultural Exports 527
North Dakota's Cash Receipts 528
North Dakota's Leading Commodities 529
North Dakota's Dairy Ambassadors 530

Barley, Hops, and Craft Breweries

Barley, water, hops, and yeast. These basic ingredients make up one of humankind's most ancient potables – beer. More and more entrepreneurs are trying a hand at brewing beer, with new craft breweries and microbreweries opening every year.

According to the North Dakota Barley Council, craft beers have been growing by 12 percent per year for the past 10 years. There are now more than 4,000 craft breweries today as compared with roughly 500 in the mid-1990s. Craft brewers are seeking to reach 20 percent market share in the United States by 2020.

North Dakota is no exception. Although it only boasts 26 craft breweries, it ranks 29th in breweries per capita (per 100,000 age 21+ adults). With North Dakota's status as a leading agriculture state, it only makes sense to use local ingredients as they become available to add value for grower, brewer, and customer.

Hops: Small but Mighty

Freshly harvested hop cones.

A crop that used to be grown in North Dakota before prohibition now has a small presence again. Hops (*Humulus lupulus*) are grown primarily for use as a bittering and flavoring agent in beer, but they also have anti-microbial properties and act as a preservative.

The North Dakota State University Williston Research Extension Center (WREC), which conducts research to increase agricultural productivity, started a pilot study of hops in 2009 with six cultivars. WREC received a specialty crop block grant in 2014, as well as additional funding, which allowed them to study 12 cultivars through June 2019. Kyla Splichal, WREC horticulture research specialist, said they will continue to grow hops, regardless of funding.

According to Splichal, there were hundreds of varieties from which to choose for the study. WREC narrowed them down based on brew usage – some were chosen for aroma, some chosen for bittering value, and some chosen were dual-purpose. They also chose one from the United Kingdom and one from Germany.

Growing hops is not without challenges. Hops are long bines (climbing stems) grown on high trellises and are labor intensive. They are a perennial that must be trained each year onto vertical strings, which are then cut at the end of the season. Hops need up to a gallon of water each day and must be irrigated. They use a lot of nitrogen and are also prone to diseases. At the end of the season, the hop cones are either harvested by hand, or a mechanical harvester is used. Mechanical harvesters are expensive and currently not easily available in North Dakota. After harvest, the cones are dried and, most of the time, are pelleted as that is what the breweries prefer.

Hop bines grow up a trellis, which is typically 18-25 feet high.

It takes three to five years for hop plants to reach maximum production. Hops may produce for many years, but cultivars are the driving force in the market as breweries want a certain type of beer. This may cause hop growers to pull out plants and start a new variety. The current top states for hops are Idaho, Oregon, and Washington. North American commercial hop production in 2015 was 45,488 total acres between the United States and Canada.

WREC has a small research plot with three rows of 150 feet each – about one-tenth of an acre. Splichal believes there are less than five acres total in the state. She provides information and gives seminars to producers interested in growing hops and says the North Dakota climate can support it, but the state will need some serious growers and serious investments to get into larger-scale production.

One of the growers in the state is Ostlie's Sunnyside Acres, run by Lindsay and Mike Ostlie of Carrington, North Dakota. They have been growing hops since 2014 and have one-half of an acre. Mike said that "they've talked about increasing their acreage but at this point are holding steady," due to the intensity it takes to raise them. He said even one-half of an acre is not possible without mechanization and the support of family and friends. The family owns a hop harvester and pelletizer and does custom pelleting for other hop farmers.

Ostlie said they started hops before they knew about the trials at the WREC but did visit to learn more about commercial harvesting. They spent a lot of time researching hops production and attending sessions on hops before they started. They were able to qualify for a grant from the Agricultural Products Utilization Commission to help set up for harvesting and pelleting. They hold an annual "Hops Day" in which they do tours of their hopyard and demonstrate their equipment, including the hop harvester.

Kyla Splichal inspecting hop cones as they come through the harvester at the Williston Research Extension Center.

Ostlie's Sunnyside Acres has sold hops to three breweries: Fargo Brewing Company, Kilstone Brewing, and Laughing Sun Brewery. All three breweries have made a North Dakota beer. The most widely available is the fresh hop ale made by the Fargo Brewing Company, which has been canned for the last two years. Fargo Brewing Company brews it within 24 hours of the hops being harvested and has even participated in the harvest. The other North Dakota beers are seasonal and use pelleted hops.

Ostlie estimated there are only a handful of hop producers in the state, other than home brewers. He said there are a number of people at the early stages of commercialization, but he only knows of three other hop growers that have delivered to microbreweries. Due to the time that hops take to mature, commercial production takes time to develop. Recent declines in pricing for some hop varieties may stall any immediate plans for new startups.

Ostlie said there are many factors to consider if someone is thinking about getting into hops production, such as the need for irrigation, trellising, plant sourcing, and more. One of the challenges is a source of sufficient water for irrigation. Even though hops will use less water than corn over a growing season, they need to be watered

Freshly pelleted hops.

Hop bines being fed into a hop harvester.

daily due to their shallow root system. The bottom line is setup is not cheap and the return on investment is several years out. However, it is easier with good wells, the equipment to install trellis poles, and the ability to get to the top of an 18- to 25-foot trellis.

A Long History of Barley

Barley has been grown in North Dakota as long as there have been records. The U.S. Department of Agriculture's National Agriculture Statistics Service (USDA-NASS) shows barley being grown in North Dakota since 1882. North Dakota currently represents approximately 36 percent of U.S. barley production, which provides an average value of $250 million each year in economic value to the state.

Barley is typically grown for one of three purposes: malting barley, used in brewing beer; feed barley, used in feeding livestock; and barley for human food, such as pearled barley for soup mixes. Barley has also been used in pet food.

Barley used to be traded as a commodity but now is procured as an ingredient, mostly under contract with the malting and brewing industry. Malting barley is the only crop that must be delivered in a "living state" as it must germinate to make

Close up of two-row barley growing on the Stober farm near Goodrich, North Dakota.

malt. It also is subject to specifications such as maximum allowable protein content, percentage of plump seeds, etc. Both two- and six-row barley can be used to make beer. The numbers refer to how many rows of kernels are found around the head of a barley stalk.

Historically, North Dakota has produced six-row barley for the malting and brewing industry. Six-row barley accounted for 80 percent of state acres in 2005 and 65 percent in 2015. However, efficiencies in brewing technology, coupled with an increase in craft brewing, has resulted in increased production of two-row barley, displacing the amount of six-row historically produced. Two-row barley is projected to account for about 80 percent of barley acres in the state in 2019. Two-row barley provides higher levels of malt extract, thus allowing for brewing greater quantities of beer, but it is a little more challenging to grow.

Farmers have had the benefit of breeders developing new and better six-row varieties over the years, as well as their own experience in raising it. Two-row is a completely different crop with different needs. For example, six-row should be planted as early as possible, but two-row cannot handle frost and should be planted after the last frost. Two-row is also more prone to sprout damage and lodging. Breeders have already started working on two-row varieties to better suit the area, but it will take some time to develop.

Adding Value Locally

One company that is growing two-row barley is Two Track Malting Company of Lincoln, North Dakota. Jared Stober, Donovan Stober, John Stober, Greg Kessel, and Chris Fries head the company, which has been around since June 2016. They currently grow a total of 550 acres of barley, most on the sixth-generation Stober farm near Goodrich, North Dakota. They also source some from a part-owner in Belfield, North Dakota, and want to work with additional farmers.

Two Track is able to trace the barley to the field in which it was grown. The name reflects that traceability, as well as the two-track roads commonly used by farmers. Using a QR code printed on coasters, people drinking beer made with Two Track barley can find information about the farmer that grew the barley, the growing conditions, view a satellite image of the field, and more.

Two Track currently produces six malt recipes and ships malt to 24 states and 70 breweries across the country, including most in North Dakota.

The company's locally-grown two-row barley goes through the malting process of steeping, germinating, and kilning in Lincoln. They make about 15 tons of malt each week but may expand in the future.

The Two Track Malting Company team with bags of their finished product. Pictured left to right: Greg Kessel, Donovan Stober, Chris Fries, and Jared Stober.

Two Track coasters display a QR code, which allows patrons to find out information about the farmer that grew the barley, the growing conditions, and even a satellite image of the field.

The Malting Process

Steeping is the first stage of the malting process in which the grain is submerged in water to increase the moisture content from 12 percent to between 42 and 48 percent. The process takes approximately two to three days, during which the grain is submerged, drained, and repeated. This starts the growth process and once chit, or rootlets, start to emerge, it is time to move to the germination stage.

Unloading finished malt from the germination kiln vessel at Two Track Malting Company.

Germination is the next stage in the malting process where chitted grain is transferred to a germination kiln vessel or GKV. Germination allows for the development of malt enzymes needed for brewing and takes three to five days.

Kilning is the final step in the malting process and turns the modified grain into malt. The specific type of malt being produced will determine how long the grain is left in the kiln. The kiln dries out the grain using heat and gives the malt its flavor and color. After about 24 hours, the malt is finished and is then cleaned and packaged.

Putting It All Together

North Dakota's longest-running brewery, Laughing Sun Brewing Company, started because the two founders had a passion for brewing great beer. Todd Sattler began brewing with his father, Dale, in the 1980s when he was still in high school. Mike Frohlich took a job with Rattlesnake Creek Brewery in Dickinson while attending college in the 1990s and learned to brew there.

When Laughing Sun opened in Bismarck, North Dakota, in 2012, there were no other breweries operating in the state. The owners knew the time was right when they noticed that a few of the local bars had begun to sell one or two craft beers and believed they could create a following for a local brand that was high quality and tasted great.

Laughing Sun uses malt from Two Track Malting and also sources fruit, honey, and other adjuncts from local suppliers. Their "I ♥ ND" golden ale uses only North Dakota malt. Sattler said once there are commercial-sized hop growers in North Dakota, they plan to have several all-North Dakota ingredient beers.

Two Track malted barley is added to the mill for a batch at Laughing Sun Brewing Company.

Laughing Sun has brewed more than 100 different beers since they opened. They brew one 20-barrel batch (620 gallons) at a time in a process that takes about two weeks before kegging or canning. Then they repeat the process with another batch.

The fermenters at Laughing Sun Brewing Company.

Laughing Sun recently expanded from a storefront location in downtown Bismarck to a large warehouse-style building a few blocks away, which allowed upgrades to its brewing capacity and production. They now distribute kegs and cans of Laughing Sun beer to all four corners of North Dakota and everywhere in between.

Another longtime brewery in the state is the Fargo Brewing Company in Fargo, North Dakota. Aaron Hill and Jared Hardy started the brewery. Hardy lived in Oregon for a few years and experienced the "Beervana" culture and wanted to bring some of that to North Dakota. They were young, had minimal obligations, and wanted to do something meaningful. Hill said, "[W]e were naïve enough to believe we could do it, and we received enough encouragement around us to go for it." They started talking to business contacts, who asked how they could invest, and a brewery was born.

Fargo Brewing Company currently sources most of their hops from Oregon, Washington, and Europe and most of their malt from Idaho, Montana, and Europe. They do, however, create the fresh hop beer every fall that uses local hops and malt. This past year, it was called "Farm Fresh," and previously it has been called "Super Green."

Fargo Brewing currently distributes throughout all of North Dakota, South Dakota, and parts of Minnesota and Wisconsin.

The Brewing Process

Brewing starts with mashing the grains, typically barley. Mashing means steeping in hot, but not boiling, water for about an hour. This activates enzymes in the grains and causes it to break down and release its sugars. After that is done, the water is drained from the mash and that liquid is called wort. The wort is boiled for about an hour while hops and other spices are added. Hops add bitterness to balance out the sugar, provide flavor, and also act as a preservative. The wort is then cooled, strained, filtered, and put into a fermenting vessel with yeast. The beer stays there for approximately two weeks before kegging or canning. That time period allows the yeast to metabolize the sugars and produce alcohol and carbon dioxide as waste products, thereby making beer.

According to the Brewers Association, craft brewer sales continued to grow at a rate of five percent by volume in 2017, reaching 12.7 percent of the U.S. beer market by volume. Retail dollar sales of craft beer increased eight percent, up to $26 billion and now account for more than 23 percent of the U.S. beer market. The future certainly looks promising for more value-added agriculture products in North Dakota like pelletized hops, malted barley, and craft beer.

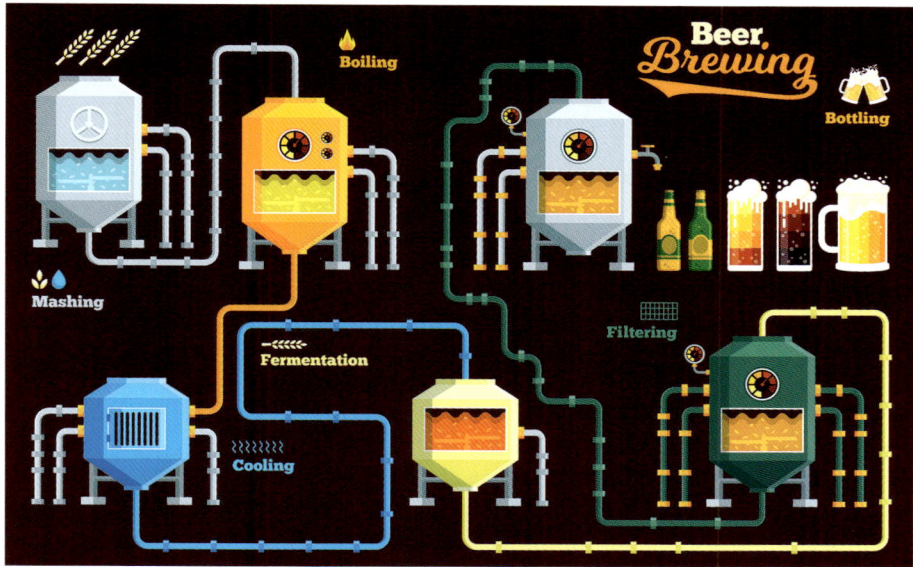

The brewing process.

References

1. "Hops." North Dakota State University Williston Research Extension Center, 27 March 2017, www.ag.ndsu.edu/willistonrec/horticulture-program-1/current-research-1/hops.
2. Hill, Aaron. "Re: A few questions for story on craft breweries, barley, and hops." Received by Michelle Mielke, 18 January 2019.
3. "How Beer is Made." Beeriety, 6 July 2009, blog.beeriety.com/2009/07/06/how-beer-is-made/.
4. Knutson, Jonathan. "Area barley industry switching to two-row." AgWeek, 24 December 2018, www.agweek.com/business/agriculture/4546792-area-barley-industry-switching-two-row.
5. North Dakota Barley Council. www.ndbarley.net/. Accessed 19 November 2018.
6. "North Dakota Craft Beer Sales Statistics, 2017." Brewers Association, 2019, www.brewersassociation.org/statistics/by-state/?state=ND.
7. "National Beer Sales and Production Data." Brewers Association, 2019, www.brewersassociation.org/statistics/national-beer-sales-production-data/.
8. Ostlie, Mike. "Re: Story that includes hops." Received by Michelle Mielke, 14 January 2019.
9. Ostlie's Sunnyside Acres. www.ostlieacres.com/. Accessed 14 December 2018.
10. Sattler, Todd. "Re: Story on barley, hops, and craft breweries." Received by Michelle Mielke, 15 January 2019.
11. Splichal, Kyla. Personal interview. 9 January 2019.
12. Stober, Jared. Personal interview. 8 January 2019.
13. Two Track Malting Company. twotrackmalting.com/. Accessed 3 January 2019.

Agriculture Is North Dakota's Leading Industry

- North Dakota agriculture reached $7.8 billion in cash receipts in 2017 with crop production totaling $6.6 billion and animals and products totaling $1.2 billion.
- The largest sector in North Dakota's economy, production agriculture makes up almost 25 percent of the state's economy.
- North Dakota agriculture supports nearly one-fourth of the state's workforce, including farmers and ranchers.
- North Dakota's 29,900 farms and ranches occupy 39.1 million acres. The average farm size is 1,308 acres.

North Dakota's Agriculture Profile

Number of Farms	29,900
Land in Farms (acres)	39,100,000
Percent of Land in Farms	89%
Average Size of Farm in Acres	1,308
Average Age of Operator	57
Primary Occupation of Operator	
Farming	17,509
Other	13,452
Gender of Primary Operator	
Male	27,728
Female	3,233

Sources: 2012 Census of Agriculture and U.S. Department of Agriculture.

Ag Production Facts

- It takes a combine nine seconds to harvest enough wheat to make 70 loaves of bread.
- A pig can run a seven-minute mile.
- An ear of corn contains approximately 800 kernels.
- Approximately 72 billion pounds of edible food is thrown away in the United States each year.
- Only 7.8 cents of every dollar spent on food goes to farmers and ranchers.
- Around 53 cents of every food dollar are spent on food prepared outside the home.

U.S. Food-at-Home and Away-from-Home Expenditures 1960-2017

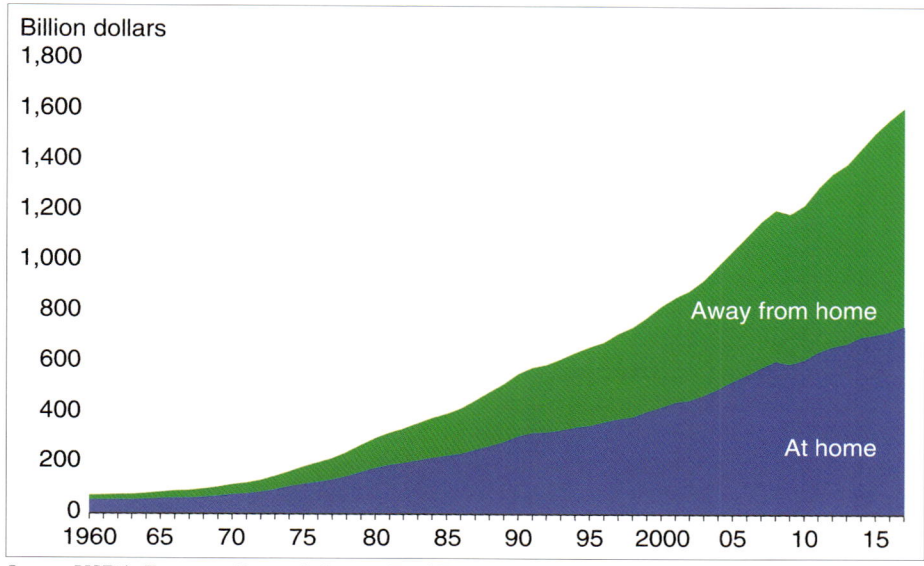

Source: USDA, Economic Research Service, Food Expenditure Series.

2016 Food Dollar (Nominal): Industry Group

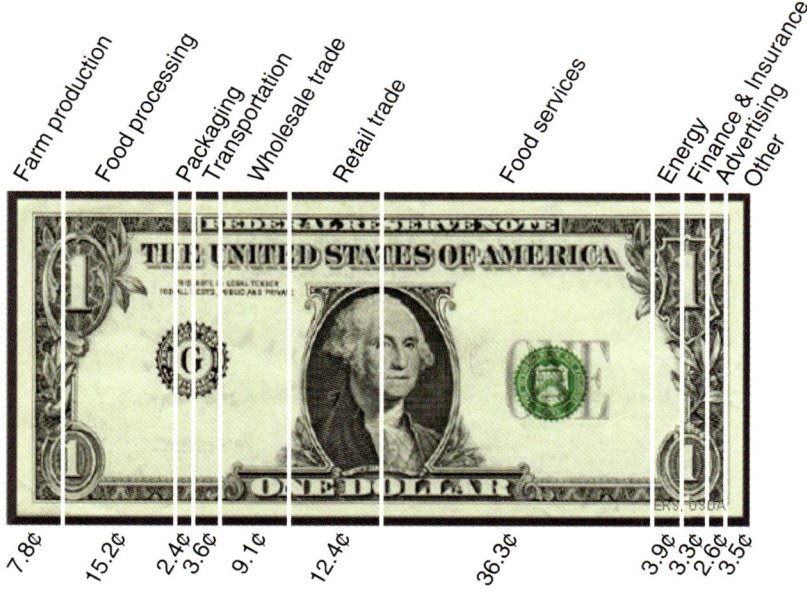

Note: "Other" includes two industry groups: agribusiness plus legal and accounting.
Source: USDA, Economic Research Service, Food Dollar Series.

North Dakota's 2018 Rank Among the States

North Dakota's farmers and ranchers maintained the state's number one ranking in the production of dry edible, navy, and pinto beans; canola; flaxseed; dry edible peas; and durum and spring wheat in 2018. North Dakota oat production increased to number one in 2018. North Dakota also continued to be the leading producer of honey in the United States.

2018 U.S. Rank	Commodity	Percent of Nation's Production
#1	Beans, All Dry Edible	28.8%
	Beans, Navy	39.7%
	Beans, Pinto	60.9%
	Canola	85.6%
	Flaxseed	84.9%
	Honey	25.0%
	Oats	15.3%
	Peas, Dry Edible	50.4%
	Wheat, All	19.3%
	Wheat, Durum	54.9%
	Wheat, Spring	51.0%
#2	Beans, Black	28.2%
	Beans, Cranberry	14.6%
	Lentils	28.5%
	Sunflower, All	34.9%
	Sunflower, Non-Oil	33.8%
	Sunflower, Oil	35.1%
#3	Barley	18.6%
	Sugarbeets	17.3%
#5	Bison	6.6%
	Potatoes, All	5.1%
#6	Hay, Alfalfa	4.7%
	Safflower	4.4%
#9	Soybeans	5.4%
	Beef Cows, All	3.1%
#11	Corn for Grain	3.1%
	Hay, All	3.6%
#13	Calf Crop	2.6%
#14	Hay, Other	2.7%
#15	Cattle and Calves	1.9%
#16	Corn for Silage	2.1%
	Wool	1.7%

Source: U.S. Department of Agriculture
National Agriculture Statistics Service, North Dakota Field Office
PO Box 3166, Fargo, ND 58108-3166

North Dakota's Top Ag Exports 2017

	Rank Among States	Value (millions)
Soybeans	9	$1,133.8
Wheat	1	$1,070.6
Other Oilseeds and Products*	1	$602.2
Corn	11	$260.6
Feeds and Other Grain**	11	$235.6
Soybean Meal	9	$206.2
Vegetable Oils	6	$205.8
Grain Products	7	$204.4
Other Plant Products	27	$166.4
Vegetables, Processed	6	$161.8
Total Exports	**9**	**$4,535.3**

*Other oilseeds and products include peanuts (oilstock), other oil crops, corn meal, other oilcake and meal, protein substances, bran, and residues.
**Feeds and other feed grains include processed feeds, fodder, barley, oats, rye, and sorghum.
Source: USDA-ERS State Fact Sheet 2017 Estimates.

North Dakota's Top Producing Counties 2017

Four North Dakota counties are the largest producers in the nation of the following products:

County	Products
Williams	Spring, Durum Wheat
Cavalier	Canola
Cass	Soybeans
Ward	Flaxseed

Source: USDA – NASS North Dakota Field Office 2017.

North Dakota's Organic Production 2016

Number of Certified Organic Farms	114
North Dakota's Rank in Number of Farms	25
Number of Certified Organic Acres	116,305
North Dakota's Rank in Number of Acres	12
Total Value of All Organic Products Sold in N.D.	**$22,741,000**

Source: USDA-NASS Organic Survey 2016.

North Dakota's Cash Receipts 2013-2017

Year	Value
2013	$8,840,653,000
2014	$8,677,655,000
2015	$7,090,528,000
2016	$8,116,204,000
2017	$7,868,950,000

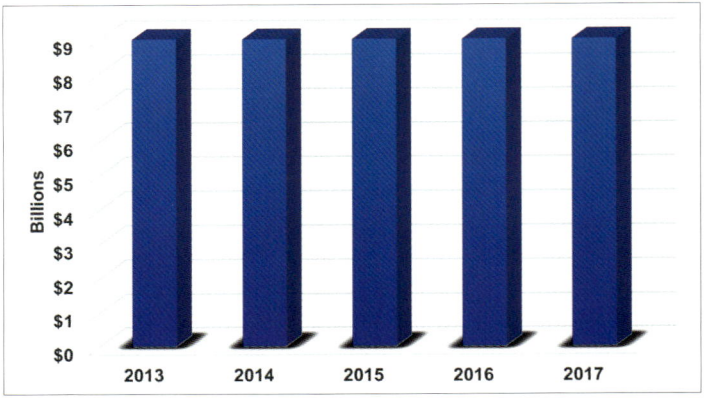

Source: USDA-ERS Cash Receipts by Commodity Dataset 2017.

North Dakota's Commodities

Source: USDA National Agricultural Statistics Service.

Many commodities are produced across North Dakota. This map shows the highest concentrations throughout the state.

North Dakota's Leading Commodities 2017

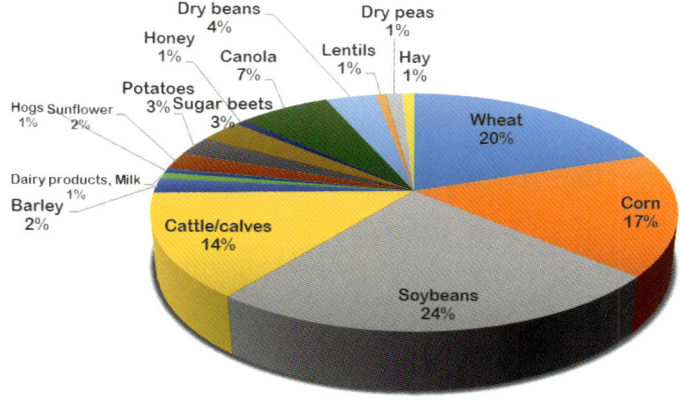

Commodity	Value of Receipts
All Commodities	$7,868,950,000
Crops	$6,628,084,000
Animals and Products	$1,240,867,000
Soybeans	$1,895,617,000
Wheat	$1,532,145,000
Corn	$1,303,730,000
Cattle and Calves	$1,010,830,000
Canola	$516,256,000
Dry Beans	$285,198,000
Sugarbeets	$241,060,000
Potatoes	$202,512,000
Sunflowers	$180,344,000
Barley	$161,247,000
Dry Peas	$93,726
Hay	$68,120
Honey	$63,636
Dairy Products, Milk	$59,840
Lentils	$57,638
Hogs	$56,826

Source: USDA-ERS Farm Income and Wealth Statistics: Cash Receipts by Commodity 2010-2017; 2017 USDA – Census of Agriculture: State Data.

North Dakota's Dairy Ambassadors

Midwest Dairy introduced new dairy ambassadors at the 52nd Annual North Dakota Dairy Convention in 2019. Zach Gebeke of Arthur, North Dakota, and Elli Peterson of Finlayson, Minnesota, are both students at North Dakota State University and active members of the Bison Dairy Club.

In their roles as North Dakota dairy ambassadors, Gebeke and Peterson will be representing North Dakota dairy farmers at events throughout the year. The new North Dakota Dairy Ambassador program provides students with leadership opportunities to connect with consumers and share their dairy story while networking with their peers and industry professionals.

North Dakota is the leading producer of honey in the United States.

Chapter Eleven
Natural Resources

A Cessna 152 flies over the Missouri River near Williston in approximately 2013. North Dakota has experienced a recent resurgence in the number of pilots and aircraft based in the state due to economic growth and airport improvements.

Climate	532
Weather Facts	535
Water Facts	535
Water Resources	536
Water Use	538
Sovereign Lands	539
Aquatic Nuisance Species	539
Threatened or Endangered Species	540
Fishing and Hunting Licenses	541

Climate

Since North Dakota's settlement days, the state has experienced extreme weather patterns from the drought during the "Dirty Thirties" to the extended wet cycle that led to the rise of Devils Lake, beginning in 1993. More recently, the state has experienced record floods in 2009 and 2011 and exceedingly dry years in 2012 and 2017.

North Dakota spans a region that often swings from "too wet" to "too dry." This range of climate varies not only geographically, east to west, but over time as well. It is not uncommon for the state to experience extreme drought in one place and severe flooding in another – sometimes at the same time.

30 Year (1989 - 2018) Average Rainfall (April - September)

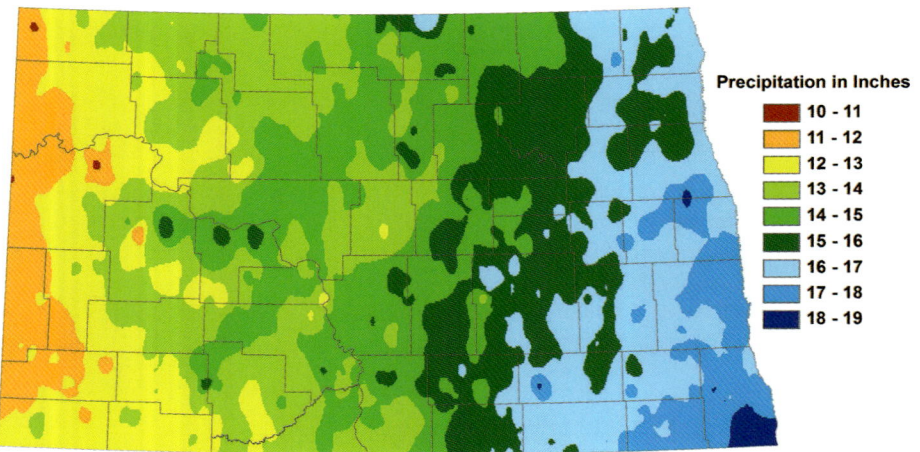

The state has experienced an extended wet cycle beginning in 1993 that has increased average annual precipitation statewide (Courtesy NDARB).

The 100th Meridian line of longitude roughly splits the state in half. East of this line, there is generally more precipitation in the form of snow and rain than there is the uptake of water by plants and evaporation. West of the 100th Meridian, water loss generally exceeds precipitation. Recent fluctuations in climate have shown this artificial boundary between wet and dry shifts slightly east or west, depending on larger climatic patterns. Geological evidence indicates this boundary can shift even more dramatically.

Drought

Drought has often been a defining aspect of climate in North Dakota, from the many problems caused by drought in the 1930s through several shorter dry cycles experienced as recently as 2017. Drought can cause crops to fail, stress municipal water supplies, impact recreation, and create challenges for anyone who makes their living from the land.

April-September 2017 Percent of Normal Rainfall

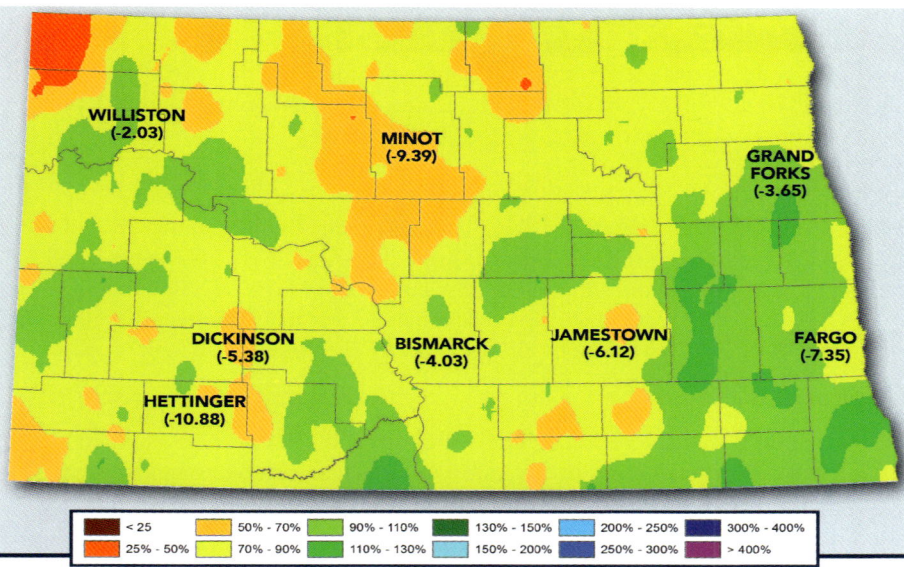

Source: NDARB Cooperative Observer Network.

The drought of 2017 had a pronounced effect on North Dakota. Its origins began in February 2017 when snowfall tapered off, and growing season rains were scarce through mid-summer. In addition to below normal precipitation, the state experienced above normal temperatures from late winter through mid-summer, further exacerbating dry conditions.

Drought certainly is not new to the region. The most severe dry periods recorded were in the 1930s and the 1980s. Studies of isolated lakebeds in several places in North Dakota show extreme fluctuations in the pattern of excessive precipitation and drought are normal. Studies found, in the case of lakes, a variation between wet cycles and dry cycles has existed for thousands of years. Lakebed records indicate, since the glaciers receded, droughts and wet cycles lasting more than 100 years have occurred.

While in an "average" year there is often sufficient precipitation, historical and paleoclimatological records indicate there will be periods of time when there is not nearly enough moisture.

Flooding

While droughts are common in the northern Great Plains, it is also true the region experiences wet cycles. Climatologists believe North Dakota is currently in a wet cycle that began in 1993, which has led to flooding throughout the state. It is useful to note, although the state is believed to be in a long-term wet cycle, mini-droughts can be experienced within this cycle.

Flooding in the Red River Valley in 1997 was one of the most severe in recorded history. Parts of the Red River Valley experienced a record-breaking 12 feet of snow, followed by a severe spring ice storm and rapid melt. These factors, along with ice jams in several key areas, led to the catastrophic flooding that most visibly impacted the city of Grand Forks. Partial records indicate a flood more severe than the 1997 event occurred prior to settlement.

With regard to the Devils Lake Basin, many in the state were concerned the fishery was in imminent danger of dying off in 1992 due to high salinity related to low lake levels caused by the late 1980s drought. In 1993, all of that changed, and with significant rainfall and snow runoff, the lake began to rise. The flooding of Devils Lake has been relentless, rising more than 30 feet in a little over 20 years, with only a couple of dry years, evaporation, and operations of the Devils Lake outlets causing appreciable reductions in lake levels.

Two significant and very damaging floods impacted most of the state in 2009 and 2011. Most of the major cities in the state were affected, with Minot and Bismarck especially impacted. In Minot, the 2011 flood impacted one-third of the city's homes.

Climate Trends

Several studies of lake sediment in North Dakota have demonstrated the state is subject to long-term climatic variation, alternating between extended wet and dry cycles. Evidence has shown the state does not really have a "normal" climate.

In recent years, climate change and global warming have gained greater attention. While the root causes of climate change, whether natural or human-induced, are still very much under debate, recent data does indicate global temperatures have increased slightly. If warming trends continue, it is uncertain what effects North Dakota will experience.

Climatological data inferred from lake core samples that provide a picture of climate in the region since the termination of the last ice age indicate when global temperatures are warmer, North Dakota's climate may not react in a predictable manner. With a wet cycle that has lasted for more than two decades and models indicating a likelihood that current patterns could persist for decades more, regular flooding may become the new normal for much of the state.

Weather Facts

- Highest temperature: 121 degrees, Steele, July 6, 1936.
- Lowest temperature: 60 degrees below zero, Parshall, February 15, 1936.
- Largest rainfall event in 24-hour period: 10.05 inches, Gilby, June 2000.
- Largest snowfall event in 24-hour period: 29.7 inches, Fullerton, May 1922.
- The average first day of frost occurs in mid-September in northern parts of the state.
- The average last day of frost occurs in mid- to late-May.
- North Dakota receives a higher percentage of possible sunshine and more hours of sunshine annually than any other state along the Canadian border. On an annual basis, the state receives 58 to 62 percent of total possible sunshine.
- July is the sunniest month, when approximately three-quarters of possible sunshine is recorded.
- July and August will record about twice as many sunshine days as any other month of the year.
- Average yearly rainfall ranges from 24 inches in the southeastern portion of the state to 14 inches in the far west.
- When compared to the period from 1907-1992, average annual precipitation has increased during the "wet cycle" period of 1993-2016 by approximately 29 percent in Fargo, 28 percent in Bismarck, and 11 percent in Dickinson.
- North Dakota's greatest source of atmospheric moisture is the Gulf of Mexico.

Water Facts

- There are five major hydrologic subdivisions in North Dakota: the Missouri River Basin, the James River Basin, the Red River Basin, the Devils Lake Basin, and the Mouse River Basin.
- Lakes and reservoirs total about 863,000 acres.
- There are 90,640 total river miles.
- There are 427 river border miles.
- The longest river completely within the state is the Sheyenne at 591 miles.
- There are about 2.5 million acres of wetlands.
- Average daily stream flow of the Missouri River at Bismarck is 22,680 cubic feet per second (cfs); the Red River at Drayton is 4,393 cfs; the Mouse River at Westhope is 269 cfs; and the James River at LaMoure is 163 cfs.
- The lowest elevation in the state is 750 feet above mean sea level (amsl) where the Red River crosses the border into Canada.
- Devils Lake is the largest natural lake in the state. At an elevation of 1,454 feet amsl, it covers about 205,000 acres, including Stump Lake.
- Lake Sakakawea is the largest reservoir and body of water in the state. At a maximum operating pool (elevation 1,854 feet amsl), it covers 380,000 acres.
- At its normal operating pool elevation of 1,837.5 feet amsl, Lake Sakakawea has more shoreline (1,340 miles) than California has coastline (840 miles).
- Garrison Dam is 210 feet high and 11,300 feet (2.1 miles) long.
- It is estimated 60 million acre-feet of ground water is stored in the major unconsolidated aquifers in the state.

Water Resources

Surface Water Resources

North Dakota is separated by a continental divide running from the northwest to the southeast corners of the state. The northeastern portion of the state drains into Hudson Bay and includes the Mouse (Souris), Devils Lake, and Red River basins. The southwestern part is drained by the Missouri and James River basins to the Gulf of Mexico.

Flow in all North Dakota streams and rivers are seasonably and annually variable. Runoff is generally greatest in early spring as a result of snowmelt water and spring rainfall. Many smaller streams experience little or no flow for extended periods during summer months. Dramatic flow variations in river discharges can be caused by changes in weather patterns, isolated storm events, evaporation rates, and snow pack conditions.

In North Dakota in 2016, there were almost 715,967 acres of natural lakes and reservoirs (239,237 acres and 476,730 acres respectively) and about 3,206,820 acres of wetlands. In the state, there are 21,108 waterbodies of at least 10 acres or greater in size.

The state's four largest reservoirs (Sakakawea, Oahe, Audubon, and Ashtabula) comprise about 10 percent of North Dakota's total water surface acres, accounting for a surface area of 397,467 acres. The majority of these acres are contained within the two mainstem Missouri River reservoirs (Lake Sakakawea and Lake Oahe) at their normal operating pool elevations.

North Dakota Drainage Basins

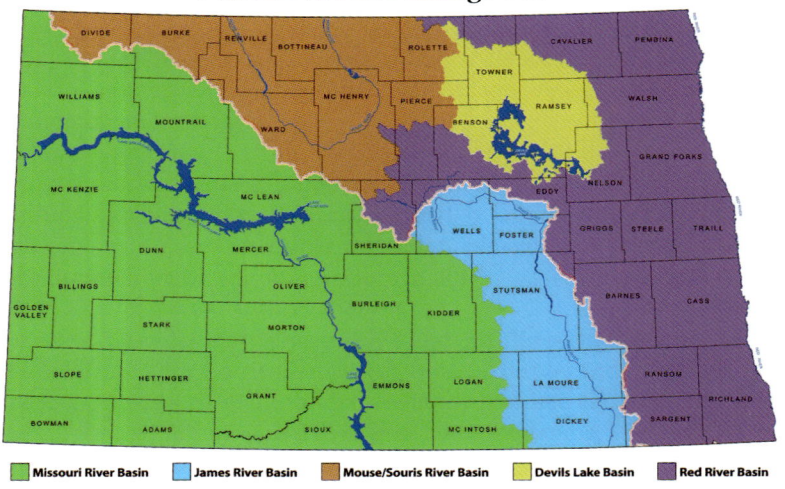

Ground Water Resources

Ground water underlies the land surface throughout the state and generally occurs in two major types of rock – unconsolidated deposits and bedrock.

Unconsolidated deposits are loose beds of gravel, sand, silt, or clay of glacial origin. Bedrock aquifers consist primarily of shale, sandstone, and lignite.

Aquifers of glacial origin are generally more productive than aquifers in the underlying bedrock. Bedrock aquifers underlie the entire state and tend to be more continuous and widespread than aquifers in the unconsolidated deposits.

It is estimated 60 million acre-feet of water are stored in major unconsolidated aquifers in the state. The amount of water available in the major bedrock aquifers is estimated to be approximately 435 million acre-feet.

In recent years, the development of technologies such as horizontal drilling and aquifer recharge and recovery (previously called artificial recharge) could also prove to be a vital tool in mitigating the boom-bust nature of precipitation the state frequently experiences.

Atmospheric Water Resources

Mean annual precipitation ranges from a maximum of nearly 24 inches in the southeast corner of the state to just over 14 inches in the extreme west. It is worth noting the maximum mean annual rainfall in southeast North Dakota has increased from just over 21 inches to 24 inches due to the extended wet cycle, which started in 1993 and continues through the present.

During North Dakota's growing season (April-September), precipitation ranges from approximately 18 inches in the southeast part of the state to about 10 inches in the far west. This distribution results in generally adequate moisture for dry land farming in the east, but less reliable supplies in the semi-arid west.

Precipitation is largely dependent upon an adequate supply of airborne moisture, both visible (clouds) and invisible (water vapor). The primary atmospheric water source for North Dakota is the warm, humid air originating from the Gulf of Mexico.

While westerly flow from the Pacific Ocean does initially move atmospheric moisture toward the state, the repeated lifting and cooling of the air as it passes over the Rocky Mountains causes much of the moisture to precipitate from the air before it reaches the plains. Moisture from the Gulf of Mexico faces no such impediments.

The capacity of the atmosphere to hold moisture is largely governed by its temperature. Warm summer air can hold enough moisture to allow a thunderstorm to generate several inches of rainfall in a short period of time, whereas cold arctic air from the Canadian prairies can scarcely support any precipitation. As such, the warm season accounts for more than three-quarters of the state's total annual precipitation.

Depending on the season, the total water contained in the atmosphere above North Dakota ranges from approximately 350,000 acre-feet in the winter to 5.5 million acre-feet in the summer. Most of the water passes through the state borne by winds aloft. On any given day, nature converts a small fraction of the available water to clouds and sometimes precipitation.

Water Use

Water in North Dakota is used in a variety of ways. While the traditional uses of "mining, irrigating, and manufacturing" found in the North Dakota Constitution in Article XI, Section 3, still remain prevalent, new diverse uses and needs are continually being created.

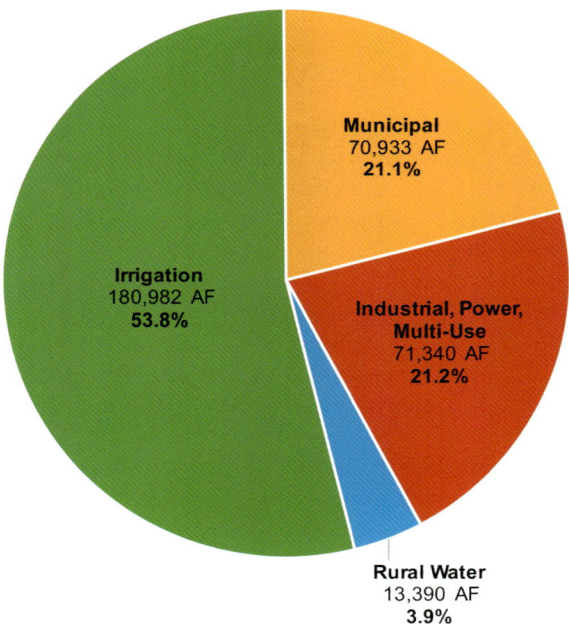

2008-2017 Average Annual Consumptive Water Use = 336,645 Acre-Feet

- Municipal: 70,933 AF, 21.1%
- Irrigation: 180,982 AF, 53.8%
- Industrial, Power, Multi-Use: 71,340 AF, 21.2%
- Rural Water: 13,390 AF, 3.9%

Historically, and through today, the greatest percentage of consumptive water use is for irrigation. When comparing the state's consumptive water use to the rest of the states in the country, North Dakota ranks fifth lowest at 0.13 percent of total consumptive water use.

Sovereign Lands

North Dakota's sovereign lands are those areas, including the beds of waterbodies and islands, lying within the ordinary high watermark of navigable lakes and streams. The state engineer is responsible for administering the state's non-mineral interests in North Dakota's sovereign lands.

The state engineer is responsible under the Public Trust Doctrine to use prudent judgment in identifying all rivers and lakes throughout the state that should be included on the state's list of navigable waters.

The state of North Dakota has ownership to the ordinary high watermark of the state's navigable waters. The delineation of the ordinary high watermark is a critical component of sovereign land management because it identifies the specific areas in and around the state's navigable waters that are under the jurisdiction of the state engineer. The ordinary high watermark delineates the boundary between the uplands owned by the riparian landowners and the state-owned sovereign lands.

Aquatic Nuisance Species

Aquatic nuisance species (ANS), whether they are animals, such as the zebra mussel or common carp, or plants, such as curly-leaf pondweed, threaten fishing, boating, swimming, and other water-based activities. In states where they have become established, ANS are expensive to combat and difficult or impossible to control or eliminate.

In 2015, adult zebra mussels were confirmed in the Red River for the first time. No additional discoveries of zebra mussels have occurred through the end of 2018. The current list of ANS that exist in North Dakota is as follows:

Animals
Zebra mussel
Silver carp
Common carp

Plants
Curly-leaf pondweed
Eurasian water milfoil

Other ANS are found in nearby states, and numerous regulations are in place to help prevent their introduction into North Dakota waters. The 2019 Legislature passed a law creating an ANS program fund, which established additional fees for boats registered in North Dakota and in other states that are using North Dakota waters, as well as a surcharge on resident and nonresident fishing licenses.

Threatened and Endangered Species

Since 2017, one species has been declared endangered in North Dakota and added to the list maintained by the U.S. Fish and Wildlife Service in accordance with the Endangered Species Act of 1973. The Rusty Patched Bumble Bee (Bombus affinis) is endangered; it is a species of bumble bee that lives in colonies, including a single queen and female workers. In late summer, males are produced, and only males and workers have a rusty reddish patch on the back.

North Dakota does not have a state threatened or endangered species list. Only those species listed by the federal Endangered Species Act are considered threatened or endangered in North Dakota. A total of 12 species are currently listed in North Dakota, although not all species are known to have populations in the state. There are several species that have been petitioned to be listed, such as the monarch butterfly and moose, as well as two more bumble bee species. The process for determining if a listing is warranted can take several years.

The U.S. Fish and Wildlife Service has primary oversight of threatened and endangered species. For additional information, contact the North Dakota Ecological Services Field Office in Bismarck at 701-250-4481 or northdakotafieldoffice@fws.gov.

Current List of Threatened or Endangered Species in North Dakota

Common Name	Scientific Name	Type	Status	Date Added to ESA List
Whooping Crane	Grus americana	Bird	Endangered	3/11/1967
Least Tern (Interior)	Sterna antillarum	Bird	Endangered	5/28/1985
Piping Plover	Charadrius melodus	Bird	Threatened	12/11/1985
Red Knot (Rufa)	Calidris canutus rufa	Bird	Threatened	1/12/2015
Black-footed Ferret	Mustela nigripes	Mammal	Endangered	3/11/1967
Northern Long-eared Bat	Myotis septentrionalis	Mammal	Threatened	5/4/2015
Gray Wolf	Canis lupus	Mammal	Endangered	3/9/1978
Pallid Sturgeon	Scaphirhynchus albus	Fish	Endangered	9/6/1990
Dakota Skipper	Hesperia dacotae	Insect	Threatened	11/24/2014
Poweshiek Skipperling	Oarisma poweshiek	Insect	Endangered	11/24/2014
Rusty Patched Bumble Bee	Bombus affinis	Insect	Endangered	3/21/2017
Western Prairie Fringed Orchid	Platanthera praeclara	Plant	Threatened	9/28/1989

Fishing and Hunting Licenses
Fishing License Increase

For the first time in state history, starting with the 2012-2013 licensing year, more than 200,000 resident and nonresident anglers have purchased North Dakota fishing licenses each year. The all-time record of more than 220,000 occurred in 2015-2016. Much of this sustained increase in participation is due to a significant increase in the number of fishing waters, along with aggressive fish management in those waters, continuing to provide excellent fishing opportunities in many places where fisheries did not exist historically.

At the end of 2018, North Dakota had more than 425 fishing waters, compared to less than 200 in 1993 when the current wet cycle started.

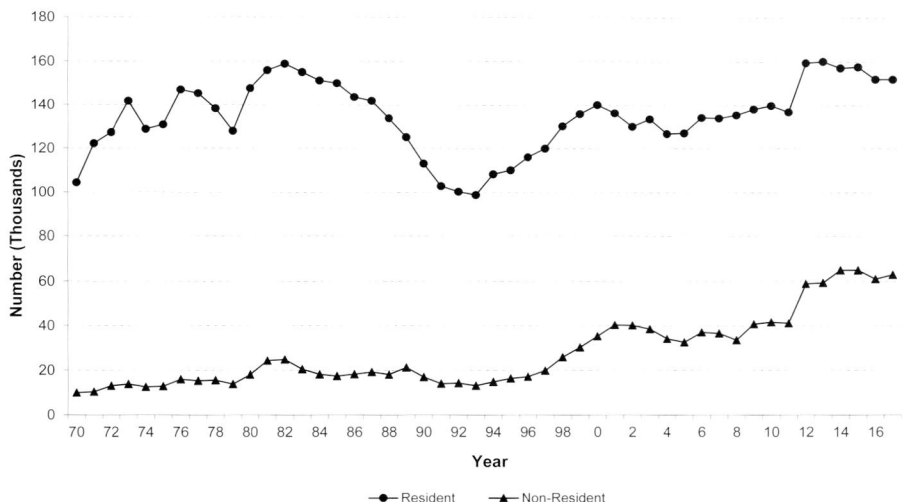

North Dakota Fishing License Sales

Hunting License Decline

North Dakota resident and nonresident hunting license sales have gradually declined since peaking in 2007. This decline is largely attributed to reduced pheasant and deer populations related to several severe winters over the last decade or more combined with the loss of approximately 2 million acres of Conservation Reserve Program grasslands since 2007.

The pheasant harvest has declined from more than 900,000 in 2007 to roughly 300,000 in 2017. Deer gun license availability fell from more than 140,000 in 2007 to about 43,000 in 2015. By 2018, the number of deer gun licenses had inched back up to about 55,000.

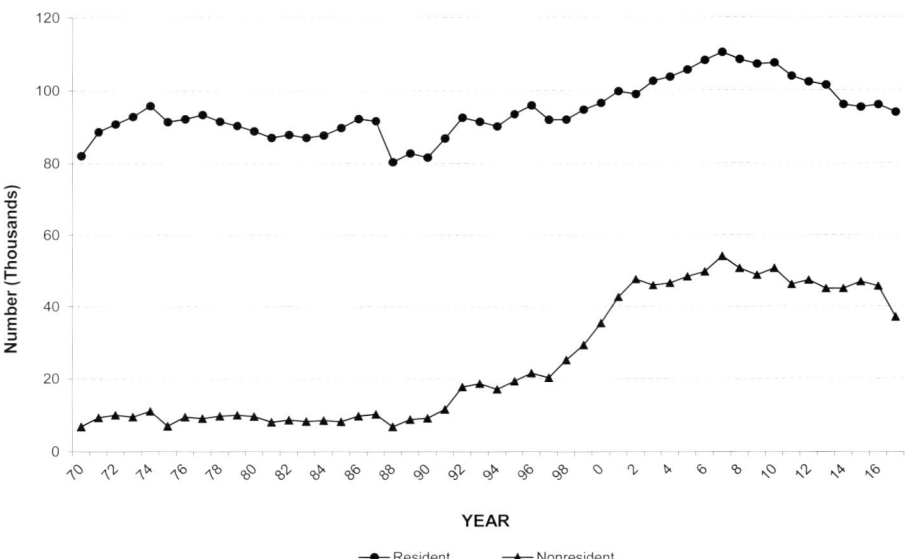

North Dakota General Game License Sales

Chapter Twelve
Energy

The North Dakota Geological Survey drone is pictured in the Badlands in October 2017 during sample collection and field-mapping activities. The drone has proven beneficial in collecting real-time aerial imagery for landslide mapping and infrastructure siting, as well as extending the geologists' observational ranges by quickly obtaining high-resolution photos of land-surface features that are distant or inaccessible due to terrain.

Project Tundra: Energy Industry Looks to Reduce Carbon Footprint 544
North Dakota's Total Energy Production 546
Biofuel 547
Biomass 548
Energy Efficiency 548
Ethanol 549
Lignite 549
Natural Gas 550
Oil 550
Petroleum Marketing 551
Refining 552
Solar, Geothermal, Hydrogen, and Hydro Power 552
Transmission 553
Wind 553
Getting a Charge Out of North Dakota 554

Project Tundra: Energy Industry Looks to Reduce Carbon Footprint

Lignite coal has been a source of low-cost power generation in North Dakota for six decades. Through that time, power companies have worked and invested to maintain a history of compliance with federal clean air regulations. In the past, there have been successful efforts to remove sulfur dioxide, nitrogen dioxide, and mercury from combustion emissions.

More recently, the North Dakota lignite industry has been challenged by the federal mandates of the Clean Power Plan (CPP), finalized in 2015, to reduce carbon dioxide (CO_2) emissions. While a stay in the implementation of the CPP was subsequently issued by the U.S. Supreme Court, the industry is positioning itself for a low-carbon energy future by searching for an economically feasible way to remove CO_2 while continuing to provide low-cost energy to consumers. A plan named Project Tundra was developed to join the proven technologies of carbon capture, utilization, and storage (CCUS) with lignite-based energy production by creating a new enhanced oil recovery (EOR) industry and reducing the amount of CO_2 released into the atmosphere.

In late 2018, the North Dakota Industrial Commission approved a $15 million funding request for Project Tundra for the study of a commercial-sized CO_2 capture system to be retrofitted onto Unit 2 at the Milton R. Young Station located near Center, North Dakota. Another $15 million will be requested from the U.S. Department of Energy.

Project Tundra will benefit from the knowledge gained during the design, construction, and operation of the United States' first commercial-scale CCUS operation, named Petra Nova, located at a coal-fired power plant near Houston and transporting captured CO_2 via 80 miles of pipeline to support EOR at a Texas oil field. Operations to capture more than 90 percent of the CO_2 from 240 megawatts of power production (more than 5,000 tons of CO_2 per day) began in December 2016. With EOR, oil production has increased from 500 to 7,000 barrels per day.

Petra Nova captures carbon from the combustion of semibituminous coal from the Powder River Basin of Wyoming. Part of the Project Tundra study will include testing efficiencies of the solvent used to remove CO_2 from a North Dakota lignite-sourced flue gas stream, as well as the differences that may arise due to the colder climate.

Carbon capture and storage adds to the cost of power production and consumes additional energy in order to be accomplished. Finding or creating a utilization market for the CO_2 improves the economics of these endeavors. The oil industry has proven EOR can substantially increase oil production volumes, although large

Milton R. Young Station located near Center, North Dakota.

supplies of CO_2 are often not available near the oil fields. Like Texas, North Dakota possesses the necessary setting to make a project like this work as there is potential for beneficial use of large volumes of captured CO_2 in the revitalization of oil fields regionally near the lignite power plants where the CO_2 would be produced. Sales of CO_2 would offset the cost of carbon capture at the power plant, while increasing production for the oil producer. Project Tundra proposes to move CO_2 through a 120-mile pipeline to the Foreman Butte oil field in McKenzie County. When captured carbon volumes exceed market sale volumes, excess CO_2 will be permanently stored, or sequestered, underground via injection wells located near the power plant.

During the EOR process, carbon dioxide is injected into a hydrocarbon reservoir where it interacts with and displaces trapped oil. Once mobilized, the oil along with CO_2 is extracted by nearby production wells. At the surface, a recycling process separates CO_2 from the oil, which is then reinjected in continuing EOR operations. Not all of the injected CO_2 is extracted with the enhanced oil production; a portion becomes sequestered in the reservoir formation deep below the surface. Currently, EOR operations are suitable only at conventional oil fields with vertical wells, but with further innovation may someday also be applied to fields of the Bakken shale.

Benefits of Project Tundra may not be limited to only the lignite and oil industries. Project Tundra could lay a foundation of carbon capture and utilization that can also be applied to other energy industries, such as natural gas and ethanol.

These developments coincided with the U.S. Environmental Protection Agency granting the North Dakota Oil and Gas Division primary regulatory authority, or primacy, over underground injection of carbon dioxide for long-term storage in April 2018. North Dakota is the first state in the nation to be approved for this authority.

North Dakota's Total Energy Production

According to the U.S. Energy Information Administration, North Dakota ranks sixth in the nation for total energy production – a total of 3,498 trillion BTU. The state ranks fourth in the country for total energy consumption per capita at 776 million BTU.

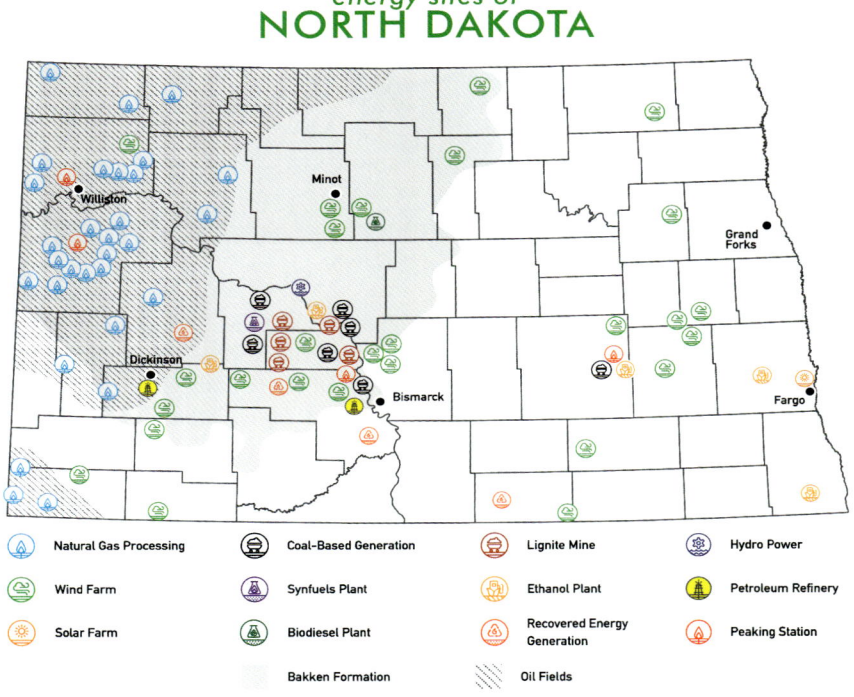

+ Map courtesy of Bismarck State College National Energy Center of Excellence.

EmPower North Dakota
www.business.nd.gov/energy/EmPowerNorthDakota/

Through the EmPower North Dakota Commission, leaders from all major energy industries in North Dakota meet regularly with one common goal: to be critical thinkers for the development of the state's energy resources. The strategic partnerships between North Dakota's long-standing and emerging energy industries enable all sectors of the industry to work together as they meet the state's and country's energy needs without government mandates. North Dakota is proactive and aggressive in addressing energy development. It serves as a model for America in fostering innovative, long-term energy strategies to meet the nation's growing energy demand and need for energy security in an environmentally responsible manner.

Great Plains Energy Corridor
www.energyND.com

The Great Plains Energy Corridor, housed at Bismarck State College's National Energy Center of Excellence, works with partners in government, education, and the private sector to promote and enhance North Dakota's energy development. These entities provide information, education, outreach programs, and special events on a wide range of energy topics.

Highlights from the 2018 edition of the Great Plains Energy Corridor's *Spotlight on North Dakota Energy* include:

- The development of wind projects in North Dakota continues. The state has some of the best wind resources in the nation. Over the past 15 years, more than 3,000 megawatts of wind generation have been installed. Federal tax credits continue to be an additional factor for wind energy development in North Dakota.
- It is anticipated that North Dakota's natural gas production will exceed 4 billion cubic feet per day. The development and expansion of natural gas processing plants will allow North Dakota to catch up on processing capacity through 2021, but additional plants or expansions will be needed in the future.

Biofuel

Biofuel production has grown in North Dakota in recent years. Strides are also being made in the development of the next generation of technologies and feedstocks for the biofuels industry. Biofuel producers are eligible for several state incentive programs, including the Ethanol Production Incentive Program and the Biofuels PACE Program.

Highlights include:

- E15 (85 percent gasoline, 15 percent ethanol) is for use in all 2001 and newer cars and light-duty vehicles, as well as flex-fuel vehicles. These vehicles make up nearly 90 percent of the light-duty vehicles on the road today.
- North Dakota is a national leader in the installation of flex-fuel blender pumps, which allow most vehicle owners the option of a 15 percent ethanol blend and higher percentage ethanol blends for owner/operators of flex-fuel vehicles. There are 40 locations statewide that offer E15-E85 fuel blends, with more than 20 of those locations offering E15 fuel specifically. Nearly all retail gasoline dealers offer E10 fuel.
- North Dakota's only biodiesel production facility is located near Velva. The ADM plant has the potential to produce 85 million gallons of biodiesel per year. The facility is currently producing biodiesel with canola oil provided by an adjacent crushing plant. Because of low in-state usage, most of the produced biodiesel is shipped to other states or to Canada.

Biomass

North Dakota is an agricultural state with significant land area in working farms and ranches, and there are many opportunities for agriculture-related energy production. Biomass includes all plant and animal matter, such as wood waste, energy crops, crop residues, and other forms of organic waste. Harvested biomass may be used to generate various forms of energy, such as heat, electricity, and biofuels. Utilizing biomass for energy production may have many benefits, including improved national security, increased economic growth, and broad-based environmental benefits.

Highlights include:

- At the Marathon oil refinery in Dickinson, production began in June 2018 to co-process renewable feedstock along with Bakken crude oil to produce a five percent renewable diesel blend. A retrofit of the plant allows co-processing of up to 16,800 gallons per day of renewable feedstock using regionally sourced soybean oil and distillers corn oil from ethanol plants.
- Research is being done on biomass availability from crop residues, and the potential use of oilseed crops like carinata, canola, and camelina to produce jet fuel for military and commercial aviation uses. The field research is being conducted at the USDA Northern Great Plains Research Laboratory in Mandan.

Energy Efficiency

Energy efficiency continues to be a high priority in public buildings around the state and in North Dakota homes and is promoted by the North Dakota Department of Commerce Office of Renewable Energy and Energy Efficiency.

Highlights include:

- According to the North Dakota Department of Commerce, 600 housing units were weatherized in North Dakota in 2017. Homeowners achieve an average of 7-18 percent lower energy costs (about $283/year). Clients can expect savings of more than $4,000 during the lifetime of the measures installed. Additional health benefits bring the total savings to more than $13,000.
- The North Dakota Department of Commerce administers the Energy Conservation Grant, which is funded by one-half of 1 percent of the oil extraction tax deposited in the Resources Trust Fund up to $200,000 for the current biennium. Grants can be used for energy efficiency projects in public buildings. To date, 68 completed projects have received funding, at an average project cost of $33,265.
- The North Dakota Industrial Commission awarded a contract in December 2018 to Fargo's Smart Energy Ramp project. The objective is to demonstrate how a Smart Clean Energy Package that includes renewable energy and

artificial intelligence can add value, cost-effectively attract tenants, and enhance economic development while making efficient use of the utility grid in a public-private partnership.

Ethanol

The five North Dakota ethanol plants have the capacity to produce more than 525 million gallons of ethanol per year, which is more than five times the production a decade ago. The state's ethanol industry generates nearly $625 million in economic activity each year and directly employs more than 230 workers in rural communities across the state.

Highlights include:

- Each North Dakota ethanol plant is located in a community with a population of less than 2,500 and contributes an average of 46 jobs and an average annual payroll of $3.3 million to the community.
- North Dakota ethanol plants use 160-180 million bushels of corn annually, with 80 percent coming from North Dakota farmers. Each bushel of corn processed produces 2.8 gallons of ethanol, 18 pounds of livestock feed (dried distillers grains), 18 pounds of carbon dioxide, and up to 1 pound of corn oil.
- One-third of every bushel of grain used for ethanol production returns to the animal feed market in the form of dried distillers grains (DDGs). More than 1.5 million tons of DDGs are produced in the state annually.

Lignite

North Dakota's lignite industry is a vital part of the state's economy with an economic impact of more than $5.7 billion. The state supports 4,000 megawatts of lignite and other coal generation at seven locations, providing low-cost, reliable, and clean electric power. The lignite industry is North Dakota's fifth largest industry behind agriculture, oil and gas, tourism, and manufacturing.

Highlights include:

- North Dakota's power plants have invested around $2 billion in new technology to reduce emissions and increase efficiencies. These investments account for 20 to 30 percent of a power plant's costs.
- North Dakota is currently one of only 15 states that meets all of the U.S. Environmental Protection Agency's federal ambient air quality standards.
- The lignite industry employs 3,800 workers directly and another 10,200 indirect workers.
- Great River Energy's Stanton Station near Stanton was shut down in February 2017 and demolition began that fall. The restoration (reclamation) phase of the project should be mostly complete by late 2019.

Natural Gas

North Dakota's natural gas industry has worked hard to connect more than 2,100 new wells to gas plants. There are 30 natural gas processing plants operating in western North Dakota, and six new facilities are planned or under construction. A challenge of the petroleum industry is capturing the natural gas co-produced with oil.

Highlights include:

- According to the North Dakota Department of Mineral Resources, private industry has invested more than $13 billion in additional natural gas gathering and processing infrastructure to reduce flaring, and another $3.3 billion is planned in the coming years.
- Since 2010, natural gas processing capacity in North Dakota has grown nearly 387 percent, increasing from 491 MMCFD to 2,400 MMCFD at year-end 2018.
- The North Dakota Pipeline Authority recently updated its natural gas forecast, which estimates North Dakota could be producing 4.5-5.5 billion cubic feet of natural gas each day in the late 2030s. This is up from the 2018 natural gas production of roughly 2.5 billion cubic feet per day.

Oil

From 2008-2018, oil and gas extraction and production taxes have raised almost $18 billion for North Dakota, which accounts for almost 44 percent of the total tax revenues collected by the state during that period. Over the last five years, oil and gas extraction and production taxes accounted for more than 50 percent of all tax revenues collected by the state. The necessary job skills continue to broaden as the oil industry moves from the exploration phase toward the development phase.

Highlights include:

- North Dakota is the second largest oil-producing state in the nation and among the top 20 producers in the world.
- North Dakota has 17 active oil and gas producing counties. An oil and gas producing county has had oil and gas production in the last five calendar years. This designation is reviewed for each county at the beginning of each calendar year and adjusted as necessary. Four counties are considered core oil and gas producing counties. Core counties must be top oil and gas producers and, when combined, account for at least 75 percent of North Dakota's oil and gas production. The remaining 13 non-core counties generate 25 percent or less of North Dakota's oil and gas production.
- Average rig count in 2018 was 62 rigs, an increase of 11 from the previous year. The all-time high was 218 rigs in May 2012. Newer, more advanced rigs operating today are able to drill more wells faster. Each rig can drill about twice

as many wells in a year compared to 2012. More than 99 percent of drilling takes place in the Bakken and Three Forks formations.

North Dakota's Oil and Gas Counties

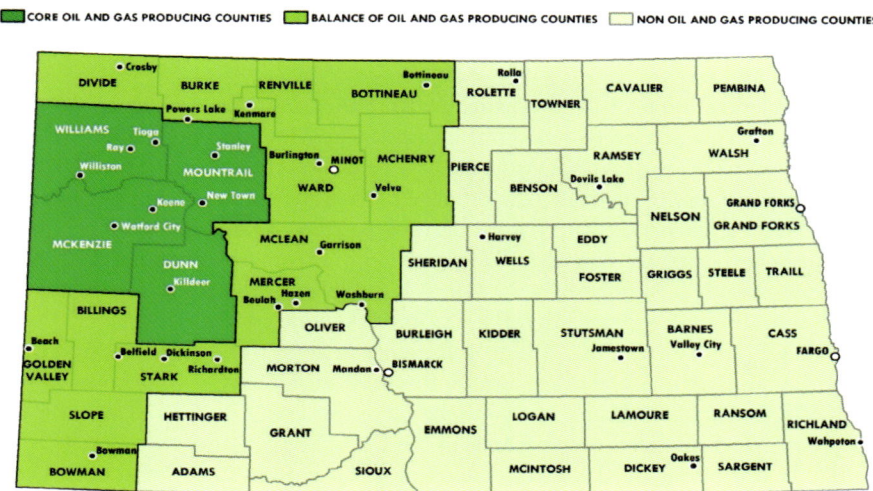

Petroleum Marketing

North Dakota petroleum marketers are dedicated to providing quality product and great customer service and continue to be strong community leaders and supporters. Consumer demand always has and always will dictate what a petroleum retailer offers its customers. The unprecedented economic growth in the state has been very good for the retail petroleum industry.

Highlights include:

- According to the North Dakota Petroleum Marketers Association, there are more than 400 petroleum marketers in North Dakota. The list includes service station dealers, convenience stores, and truck stops. These operations deal in every aspect of refined petroleum and renewable fuel products, ranging from wholesale and supply to the numerous retail outlets scattered across the state.
- North Dakota petroleum marketers also supply another fuel critical to the state – propane. Propane is a 100 percent domestic fuel, serving to fortify national and energy security. Propane supplies have grown dramatically in recent years because of the numerous oil shale plays in the United States. Propane serves a variety of residential, commercial, and industrial needs. It is used as the prime heating source in 13.4 percent of homes in North Dakota. In 2018, the state's propane marketers sold roughly 165.4 million gallons of propane.

Refining

There are two oil refineries in North Dakota – one is in Mandan, the other is near Dickinson. North Dakota's refining capacity continues to expand with the continued growth of Bakken oil production.

Highlights include:

- The Mandan refinery is now owned by Marathon Petroleum Corp. It was previously owned by Tesoro and then Andeavor. Marathon purchased the refinery from Andeavor in April 2018. It began operations in 1954 and is the largest refinery in the state. The refinery has a crude oil processing capacity of 71,000 barrels per day (bpd). One barrel is equal to 42 gallons.
- Marathon employs more than 275 people in the Bismarck-Mandan area and more than 100 employees in western North Dakota and eastern Montana with the Andeavor Logistics High Plains Crude pipeline system.
- Marathon purchased its Dickinson Refinery in 2018 from Andeavor (its original name was Dakota Prairie Refining). That refinery was constructed by WBI Energy and subsequently purchased by Andeavor in 2016. It was the first greenfield diesel refinery built in the United States since the late 1970s and came online in May 2015. The refinery can process 19,000 bpd of Bakken crude oil into diesel fuel and other petrochemical components.

Solar, Geothermal, Hydrogen, and Hydro Power

North Dakota has invested in research for hydrogen, solar, and geothermal applications.

Highlights include:

- Verendrye Electric Cooperative, Velva, has the largest solar program in North Dakota with more than 290 solar-powered water pumps throughout its service territory, including 19 systems installed in 2018. The pumps are primarily used in pasture wells in remote areas where building power lines is cost prohibitive.
- Bismarck State College has an 8-kW PV solar array on campus composed of both crystalline and thin panel solar systems so students have the opportunity to study both.
- The University of North Dakota Petroleum Research Center continues to study the feasibility of using oil well sites in the Bakken to generate up to 300 MW of electricity using geothermal energy.
- Since the National Center for Hydrogen Technology was formed in fall 2004, the University of North Dakota Energy & Environmental Research Center has received contracts totaling more than $60 million in hydrogen and hydrogen-related funded projects with more than 85 partners.
- The Garrison Dam on the Missouri River, with a capacity of 583 MW, is North Dakota's only producer of hydroelectric power.

Transmission

The development of new transmission in North Dakota continues as companies construct lines to support new load growth, as well as connect new generation to the electric grid. Studies to identify impacts of new load on existing transmission systems and identify new lines needed for the future continue at individual companies and at regional transmission planning entities.

Highlights include:

- Otter Tail Power Company and Montana-Dakota Utilities Co. constructed the 163-mile Big Stone South to Ellendale Transmission Line. The 345-kV line connects the new Big Stone South Substation near Big Stone City, South Dakota, to the new Ellendale Substation near Ellendale. The line was energized in February 2019.
- Xcel Energy partnered in early 2017 with the Federal Aviation Administration to further study safe operation of unmanned aircraft system (drone) technology to inspect transmission lines for damage. Xcel Energy has been working the past few years with the University of North Dakota and other partners to conduct test flights in North Dakota using drones.

Wind

North Dakota is known for being windy, and the potential for wind energy is great. In per-capita terms, North Dakota has the highest wind installed electricity capacity, according to the National Renewable Laboratory's 2016 Renewable Energy Data Book.

Highlights include:

- North Dakota has more than 3,000 megawatts of wind energy capacity installed throughout the state, consisting of more than 1,500 wind turbines.
- North Dakota ranks 11th for installed wind capacity, getting 27 percent of its net electricity generation from wind resources.
- While the national wind capacity factor averaged 37 percent in 2017, North Dakota wind farms typically see higher rates between 40-50 percent.

Getting a Charge Out of North Dakota

Many North Dakotans feel they are envisioning the future as they purchase electric cars. Unless someone is already driving a Tesla, Nisan Leaf, Chevy Bolt, Chevy Spark, or Ford Focus Electric, most people are likely unaware of a quiet revolution that is building electric infrastructure across North Dakota.

There are two basic types of electric vehicles: all-electric vehicles and plug-in hybrid electric vehicles (PHEVs). Charging an electric vehicle requires connecting to the electric grid, whereas hybrids will reclaim unused energy from the car's operation. There are three major categories of chargers based on the maximum amount of power the charger provides to the battery. Charging times range from less than 30 minutes to 20 hours or more, based on the type of electric equipment used as well as the type of battery, how depleted it is, and its capacity.

- Level 1
  - Provides charging through 120 volt AC plugs and does not require installation of additional charging equipment.
  - Can deliver 2 to 5 miles of range per hour of charging.
  - Found most often in homes.
- Level 2
  - Provides charging through 240 volt (for residential) or 208 volt (for commercial) plugs and requires the installation of additional charging equipment.
  - Can deliver 10 to 20 miles of range per hour of charging.
  - Found in homes and at workplaces.
- DC Fast Charge
  - Provides charging through 480 volt AC input and requires highly-specialized, highly-powered equipment, as well as special equipment in the vehicle itself.
  - Can deliver 60 to 80 miles of range in 20 minutes of charging.
  - Found most often in public charging stations, especially along high-traffic corridors.

According to Auto Alliance, North Dakota's ranking of electrical vehicle sales for 2016 was 48th in the nation with .04 percent of the market. While electric vehicles are not commonplace in North Dakota, there are 47 public charging stations around the state.

References
1. Baker, Marvin. "Getting a charge out of N.D." Message to Shari Mosser. 21 December 2018. Email.
2. ChargeHub. 2018 December 27. *Charging Stations*. Retrieved from https://chargehub.com/en/charging-stations-map.html.
3. Great Plains Energy Corridor and Bismarck State College. "Spotlight on Energy: 2018 Annual Report."

Chapter Thirteen
United Tribes Technical College

At the request of the North Dakota National Guard, two UH-72A "Lakota" helicopters were given names during a ceremony September 4, 2012, in the grassy expanse near the United Tribes Powwow dance arena. Standing Rock culture-carrier George Iron Shield dubbed one "Eagle" and the other "Turtle," symbolizing spirituality and hope, along with protection and healing, for their safe operation by personnel of the Army Aviation facility located nearby at the municipal airport.

Mission
United Tribes Technical College provides quality post-secondary education and training to enhance knowledge, diversity, and leadership for all indigenous nations.

Motto
Leadership Begins Here

Vision
Striving to build cultural, educated, and healthy leaders who empower their communities.

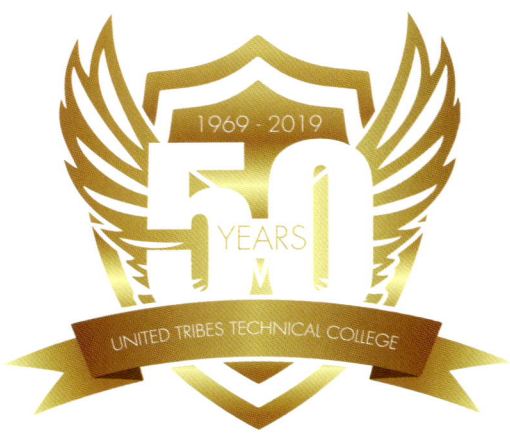

50-Year Winter Count

A traditional winter count is a series of drawings. Each is of a memorable event in the life of a tribal group. Each image tells a story. And each contributes to a timeline, chronicling remarkable experiences. Today, these are historical records that document the past from a tribal point of view. They reflect observations and values from within the culture. It shows how Native people viewed events, what was important to them, and what they thought was worth remembering for the future.

This winter count expresses its content in writing and photographs. In 2019, United Tribes Technical College reached 50 years as a tribal college. People involved with marking the anniversary considered the many events that shaped the college's progress and success and chose these to present as the *United Tribes Technical College 50-Year Winter Count*.

United Tribes got its start in the early 1960s. Four North Dakota tribes actively resisted government policies aimed at diminishing tribes and terminating their existence: Devils Lake Sioux Tribe, Standing Rock Sioux Tribe, Three Affiliated Tribes, and Turtle Mountain Band of Chippewa Indians. Working together, they prevented the state from assuming greater jurisdiction on reservations. Other mutual concerns (economic development, tribal planning, and career training) led to the formation of the United Tribes of North Dakota Development Corporation in 1968. When Bismarck's Fort Lincoln became available, they secured the 105-acre former military post as a training center for Indian families. The facility they established became United Tribes Employment Training Center, later named United Tribes Technical College.

1969
The United Tribes of North Dakota Board selected the Bendix Field Engineering Corporation of Owings Mills, Maryland, to operate an Indian family training center on the site that was formerly Fort Lincoln in Bismarck. Contract operations began

An estimated 200 local residents attended the United Tribes dedication program September 6, 1969, along with Native people from the center's governing tribes and government officials. Entertainment featured the Harmonettes, a group of singing nuns from Watertown, S.D.

July 1; the first group of trainees arrived in late August. United Tribes Employment Training Center was formally dedicated September 6 during a public program. Job training instruction began within days for the first cohort of student-trainees.

1970

Powwows first started at United Tribes. Trainees and staff held one April 11. The first one to which the public was invited took place July 24-26 as the highlight of United Tribes Days. An open house for the local community, it was a huge public relations success. Lee Fox, a student from Three Affiliated Tribes, conceived and promoted the event with the help of staff and other student-trainees. His 17-year-old daughter, Sharon, was selected Miss United Tribes.

1971

Having planned to end the start-up contract with Bendix, United Tribes assumed full tribal control and supervision of all aspects of its vocational training programs July 1. The ratio of Native staff changed from 40 percent to 63 percent Indian, as the character of the organization became more "Indian-oriented."

1972

United Tribes recruited a new executive director, Warren W. Means (Oglala Lakota). His academic, administrative, and legal background bolstered confidence in the new organization among federal agencies. Means initially concentrated on streamlining the organization and developing support for Indian vocational programs.

1973

Theodore Jamerson Elementary School (TJES) began serving the children of student-trainees. It was named for Theodore "Tiny Bud" Jamerson, the center's first director. North Dakota U.S. Senator Milton R. Young, who was considered the "primary motivating force" in establishing the center, honored the campus with a visit.

1974

Two United Tribes students, Effie Fighting Bear (Crow Agency) and Joe Benson (Three Affiliated), became the first couple married on campus. The Rev. Lester Kills Crow officiated in the United Tribes Chapel. Photos were taken by W.L. "Bill" Miller, photography instructor.

United Tribes Employment Training Center hosted the Great Plains Indian Rodeo Association finals at the center's rodeo grounds.

1975

The United Tribes of North Dakota Development Corporation and its United Tribes Employment Training Center merged into one organization with a new name, United Tribes Educational Technical Center (UTETC). The change broadened the scope of service to allow for two-year associate degree programs. A redesigned logo featured five diamonds instead of four, signifying the addition of Sisseton-Wahpeton to the governing board.

1976

Planning moved forward on new campus facilities after United Tribes and the city of Bismarck resolved two years of discord over the city's recommendation to relocate UTETC to make way for expansion of the Bismarck airport.

United Tribes hosted a training workshop for its American Indian Curricula Development Program (AICDP) started in 1972. AICDP resulted in educational materials prepared from tribal sources that reflected a Native worldview.

UTETC Executive Director David M. Gipp, center right meeting with staff, relied in part on a systems approach when his long leadership tenure began in 1977.

The first cohort of United Tribes practical nursing program students graduated in 1979.

1977
New construction began on campus following groundbreaking for a $3.5 million vocational skills center and receipt of a $300,000 grant for a daycare facility.

Standing Rock educator David M. Gipp, 30, took over as UTETC's executive director. He began work on improving operations, attaining accreditation, and upgrading training programs beyond the certificate level.

1978
United Tribes received candidate status for accreditation at the certificate-granting level from the North Central Association of Colleges and Schools.

Two new buildings were dedicated on campus, completing the first major expansion of facilities since the center was established almost a decade earlier.

1979
United Tribes conducted a capping ceremony for the center's first cohort of practical nursing students. Harlan Horned Eagle, Wagner, South Dakota, was the only male among the first 10 UTETC nursing grads.

1980
UTETC hosted the center's first cultural arts show in June; more than 600 people viewed the work of 29 artists in the new Skill Center Building.

1981
UTETC adopted a new academic calendar, moving from a 12-month continuous operation to a system of quarters. Gone was the monthly entry and exit system, replaced by three terms per year – fall, winter, and spring – each 12 weeks in length.

1982

United Tribes created an endowment fund in response to federal budget cuts of 47 percent. Three Affiliated Tribes made the first contribution. To remain open, the center cut back to a four-day work week, released half the staff, and discontinued two educational programs.

The North Central Association of Colleges and Schools accredited UTETC at the certificate-granting level.

1983

Congress addressed funding cuts by approving line-item status for UTETC in the Bureau of Indian Affairs annual budget.

The Thunderbird Theatre of Haskell Indian Junior College was featured during the annual powwow.

1984

United Tribes hosted the annual conference of the American Indian Higher Education Consortium and the Second Annual National Indian Athletic Conference Basketball Championships.

Student athletes competed in their second season of intercollegiate cross-country competition under Coach Dave Archambault Sr.

Minority Business Enterprise Director James K. Laducer was named Minority Advocate of the Year by the U.S. Small Business Administration.

The 1984-1985 United Tribes Thunderbirds basketball squad posed with Coach/Athletic Director Dave Archambault Sr. (far left). The popular nickname came about under his tenure.

1985
Russell Hawkins of Sisseton-Wahpeton presented the first of the State of the Tribal-State Relationship speeches at the State Capitol in Bismarck. Planning involved UTETC leaders and board members and the state Indian Affairs Commission. The idea for a formal talk to lawmakers came from Brian Palecek of the North Dakota Peace Coalition, later a noted United Tribes instructor.

1986
One of the earliest contests that ignited the long-running, cross-town basketball rivalry between United Tribes and Bismarck Junior College occurred in the final game of the state junior college tournament. The 58-69 loss by UTETC's Thunderbirds, in their second season of intercollegiate play, to the Bismarck Junior College's Mystics was considered a big accomplishment for a new program and a preview of exciting games to come.

1987
The United Tribes amended its articles of incorporation to change the center's name to United Tribes Technical College (UTTC).

UTTC hosted an accreditation site visit and received approval for the school's first two-year associate of applied science degree programs: medical records and licensed practical nursing.

The college modified the cycle of its academic year, switching from quarters to semesters.

1988
A basketball squad from United Tribes pulled off a remarkable victory in junior college play. The Thunderbirds defeated North Dakota State University Bottineau 84-81 with only three T-Bird players on the court at the end of regulation.

UTTC's Indian Business Development Center was heralded for its outstanding work by the U.S. Department of Commerce Minority Business Development Agency.

1989
United Tribes was well represented in the crowd that welcomed President George H.W. Bush to the State Capitol to mark the North Dakota Centennial. Theodore Jamerson Elementary School students had front row seats and several shook hands with the president.

Faculty member Wallace "Butch" Thunder Hawk designed the North Dakota Centennial Native American logo.

A 20th Anniversary Reunion for all alumni and staff was part of the festivities of the United Tribes Powwow.

1990

UTTC received initial funding under the Federal Carl Perkins Vocational and Technologies Act of 1990.

The powwow dance arena at the center of campus was named Lone Star Arena after UTTC President David M. Gipp's Indian name. An honoring for Gipp recognized his commitment to tribal higher education and acknowledged his receipt of an honorary doctorate from North Dakota State University.

1991

Native servicemen and women in Operation Desert Storm were honored for their service by posting 176 flags in Lone Star Arena. Each flag named an American Indian from UTTC's governing tribes who served.

UTTC students won the American Indian Higher Education Consortium Knowledge Bowl at the annual student competition.

1992

Research and Development Director Jack Barden led the planning for UTTC professional development. Supported by a Bush Foundation grant, the effort focused on general education, state-of-the-art work in the vocations, work skills across the curriculum, and the connection between elementary and postsecondary components of the institution.

1993

UTTC received general authority to offer associate of applied science degrees for all of its vocational and academic programs.

1994

During UTTC's silver anniversary year, America's Tribal Colleges and Universities (TCUs) became Land Grant institutions. TCUs gained access to resources and benefits previously reserved for state institutions and historically black colleges and universities. These TCUs, nicknamed "1994s," received endowment funds and grants for equity, extension programs, and research to improve the lives of tribal students and the self-sufficiency of Native communities.

1995

United Tribes entered the era of distance education, offering classes for the first time over the North Dakota Interactive Video Network. A Skill Center classroom was equipped with telecommunications equipment to interact with instruction originating from North Dakota University System campuses and other tribal colleges and state institutions.

1996

Seventy Native American visual artists from around the country displayed their works at the United Tribes Indian Arts Expo. The two-day event at the Bismarck Civic Center was held for the first time in the spring, separating it from the powwow held in the fall.

1997

A cultural group from United Tribes participated in President Bill Clinton's inaugural parade.

UTTC published a student yearbook for the first time.

A grant from the W.K. Kellogg Foundation launched the Northern Plains Bison Education Program to assist in developing and managing bison herds on tribal homelands.

1998

The UTTC automotive technology program was certified by the National Institute for Automotive Service Excellence.

Newly-appointed Assistant Secretary for Indian Affairs Kevin Gover visited United Tribes in the company of North Dakota U.S. Senator Kent Conrad.

1999

United Tribes received funding to strengthen institutional operations and services to students through Title III of the Tribally Controlled Colleges and Universities Act.

For the second year in a row, the Thunderbird men's team earned a trip to the National Junior College Athletic Association (NJCAA) basketball finals.

The college instituted a "no smoking" policy in campus buildings.

2000

With financial support from the American Indian College Fund, UTTC purchased 132 acres to the south for future development. The adjacent parcel more than doubled the size of campus, empowering the vision to increase institutional capacity and expand the student population.

A groundbreaking ceremony blessed a new building on the north side of campus, a Cultural Interpretive Arts Center.

2001

The Higher Learning Commission of the North Central Association of Colleges and Schools granted United Tribes 10 years of continuing accreditation, without stipulation, as a two-year degree and certificate-granting institution.

Students, staff, and friends from the community gathered at the campus Medicine Wheel to pray and smudge for American lives lost on 9/11.

2002

United Tribes dedicated its newly constructed student center to a man who avoided the spotlight. The Jack Barden Student Life and Technology Center featured computers, high-tech instructional equipment, the college bookstore, and meeting space.

A last-minute shot in double overtime lifted the Thunderbird men into the junior college national tournament for the third time in five years.

2003

After 30 years of continuous occupation, UTTC received unrestricted title to the property that was formerly Fort Lincoln.

Strategic planning was underway to expand the campus and to double enrollment.

Two reports illustrated the college's positive economic impact in the local community and the value of investing tax dollars in tribal college students.

An exhibit about the internment period of World War II opened on campus with public programs.

War in Iraq claimed the life of a former TJES student Pfc. Sheldon R. Hawk Eagle, 21.

2004

The Parade of Champions and Bismarck-Mandan's Folk Fest Parade merged into one community cultural event on powwow weekend.

A UTTC group marched in the grand procession of Native nations to open the National Museum of the American Indian in Washington, D.C.

The first in a series of public art sculptures by UTTC art students was dedicated near the Missouri River multi-use pathway.

During Operation Teddy Bear, teacher education students collected more than 2,000 stuffed animals to send to children in Iraq.

2005

During spring commencement, the number of UTTC graduates topped the century mark for the first time. Among the 114 grads was the first cohort of five elementary education students to earn bachelor's degrees, conferred in partnership with Sinte Gleska University.

The United Tribes campus, seen in 2008, is a family-oriented learning community. Several economic impact studies confirmed that transforming Bismarck's former military post into a tribal higher education facility is both an economic boon to the community at large and the highest and best use of the public resource.

2006

UTTC named its new wellness center for the late Lewis Goodhouse, chairman of the Devils Lake Sioux Tribe and one of the college founders.

A new apartment complex was built with student and staff labor, providing much-needed on-campus housing. It was later named for August Little Soldier, chairman of the Three Affiliated Tribes and also a college founder.

2007

United Tribes marked David M. Gipp's 30th year as its leader with honoring events and the establishment of a scholarship fund in his name.

Lobbying by North Dakota's tribal college presidents paid off with a long-sought victory in the state legislature. A new law provided funding for non-beneficiary (non-Indian) students attending tribal colleges.

2008

David M. Gipp addressed the Democratic National Convention in a speech titled "Renewing America's Promise to American Indians."

UTTC art students sculpted an eagle dubbed "The Keeper," the fifth and final public art piece in a series commissioned by the local park board.

The college previewed a vision for the future at a dedication overlooking the college's new south campus.

The metal sculpture of an eagle, titled "The Keeper," was dedicated September 4, 2008, in Bismarck's Sertoma Park. It was the fifth and final public art piece in a series created by UTTC art/art marketing students along the city's multi-use trail near the Missouri River.

2009

An intertribal group organized by United Tribes marched in President Barack Obama's Inaugural Parade.

Tribal arts instructor Butch Thunder Hawk co-curated an exhibit about Lakota culture at Harvard's Peabody Museum.

UTTC began using the social media platform Facebook.

Ground was broken for a new science and technology building, the first structure on the college's south campus.

Fireworks thundered over the powwow, marking the college's 40th anniversary.

The Curriculum Committee approved the college's first-ever upper division course, early childhood special education.

2010

Canadian actor Gary Farmer, who played the warm-hearted Philbert in the movie "Powwow Highway," was a big hit when he visited UTTC.

The campus hosted the Fort Lincoln Planning Conference about the internment era during WWII.

Two outstanding former basketball players, Tanner Albers and Jason Logg, were inducted into the Thunderbird Hall of Fame.

2011

United Tribes became a four-year college with Higher Learning Commission approval of three bachelor-degree programs: elementary education, business administration, and criminal justice. Ten years of accreditation included associate degree programs and degrees earned online.

The North Dakota Education and Practices Board approved UTTC teacher education for preparing graduates for teacher licensure in elementary education.

2012

The Educational Outreach program launched a dual enrollment program to start tribal high school students on the path to college.

UTTC's Skill Center was designated as a polling site for local and state elections.

The once-popular welding vocation that went dormant was revived as part of TCC DeMaND, a workforce training program UTTC coordinated with four tribal colleges.

Billi Jo Beheler Gravseth, Standing Rock, was the first student to graduate with a bachelor's degree from UTTC.

The United Tribes welding program, revived in 2012 as part of a workforce training initiative, later became an accredited test facility of the American Welding Society.

2013

UTTC's teacher education staff arranged for world-class presenters from the Smithsonian Institution to present at the workshop Prairie Traditions for pre-service teachers.

The Tribal Leader's Summit commemorated the 50th anniversary of Robert F. Kennedy's visit to Bismarck.

UTTC became the first tribal college in the state to be a Tobacco Free campus.

2014

United Tribes experienced a transition in executive leadership. After nearly 37 years at the helm, David M. Gipp became the college's president emeritus. Following eight months of interim leadership by Academic Vice President Phil Baird, the College Board selected Leander "Russ" McDonald as the new UTTC president.

One entire team and nine individuals were inducted into the Thunderbird Hall of Fame.

U.S. Attorney General Eric H. Holder Jr. keynoted the fourth annual Tribal Consultation Conference at UTTC.

2015

UTTC adopted single-stream recycling throughout campus, co-mingling recyclables that previously went to the landfill.

Dr. Leander R. McDonald, top row at center, became the new UTTC president in October 2014, in time to preside over the college's fall graduation ceremony.

A very active UTTC chapter earned first place in the Portfolio Competition at the annual American Indian Business Leaders Conference.

Campus teams raised and donated more than $6,770 to the American Cancer Society during the college's first-ever Mini Relay for Life.

2016

United Tribes began a pilot program offering tuition waivers for Native students who were enrolled members of federally-recognized tribes.

Shawn Craig and Trevor Shavehead earned national acclaim as the two remaining Thunderbird players in a wild, double-overtime conference basketball game.

For the first time ever, the UTTC women went all the way to the NJCAA Division II national basketball tournament.

The welding program was certified as an accredited test facility of the American Welding Society.

UTTC became the first tribal college in the country to earn designation as a Tree Campus USA.

The college hosted a Prayer for Peace gathering for unity in resolving community friction over the Dakota Access Pipeline.

UTTC received approval from the Higher Learning Commission to offer its fourth bachelor's degree: environmental science and research.

2017

United Tribes instituted a student work repayment program to help settle unpaid bills that accumulated while attending the college.

UTTC became a certified third-party biller for medical care provided at the college's wellness center.

The powwow arena overflowed with family descendants of WWI-era Native servicemen from the college's governing tribes. The sacrifices of those who served in the Great War in Europe were honored.

2018

Legislation initiated by the North Dakota Congressional delegation helped UTTC avert the loss of federal Pell Grant eligibility. The measure excused high student loan default rates at colleges located in high poverty areas.

After a two-year trial, the Native Student Tuition Waiver became a permanent program.

The college received a combination U.S. Department of Agriculture grant/loan to construct a storm water system on the campus.

At the outset of the annual powwow, the newly renovated dance arbor was re-dedicated with a slightly new name, Lone Star Veterans Arena.

Learn more from the *United Tribes Technical College Chronology* posted at www.uttc.edu.

The UTTC powwow in 2018 took place in the college's newly renovated dance arena that changed the main entrance to face east.

Index

Symbols

4 Bears Casino and Lodge   *See* 2013-15 Blue Book
4-H Youth Development, Center for   *See* 2007-09 Blue Book
1981 State Capitol Addition 72

A

A. Kirk Lanterman Investment Center   *See* 2007-09 Blue Book
Aandahl, Fred G. 169, 233
   See also 2001-03 Blue Book
Abraham, Jerome   *See* 2003-05 Blue Book
Academy of Science, North Dakota 60
Adams County   *See* 2001-03, 2005-07, 2013-15 and 2015-17 Blue Books
Adams, Mary 335, 380
Adjutant General 35, 250-251, 274-275, 326, 411
Administrative Council 203-204
Administrative Hearings, Office of 259, 273
Administrative Offices and Tower, State Capitol 71-72
Advanced Traffic Analysis Center   *See* 2007-09 Blue Book
Advisory Commission on Electronic Media in the Courtroom 204
Aerial Application 4, 14
Aeronautics Commission, North Dakota 3, 6, 12-13, 15, 32, 35, 40, 309-310
Ag Coalition   *See* 2001-03 Blue Book
Ag Foundation   *See* 2001-03 Blue Book
Agard, Aljoe   *See* 2003-05 Blue Book
AgBiotechnology, Center of Excellence for Oilseed Development   *See* 2007-09 Blue Book
Aging, Committee on 328   *See also* 2001-03 Blue Book
Agricultural Experiment Station, North Dakota   *See* 2007-09 Blue Book
Agricultural Hall of Fame 63
Agricultural Mediation Service, North Dakota   *See* 2007-09 Blue Book
Agricultural Policy and Trade Studies, Center for   *See* 2007-09 Blue Book
Agricultural Products Utilization Commission 328   *See also* 2001-03 and 2007-09 Blue Books
Agricultural Statistics, North Dakota 524-529
Agricultural Weather Network Center, North Dakota   *See* 2007-09 Blue Book
Agriculture - History   *See* 1999-2001 Blue Book
Agriculture Commissioner 222, 229, 242-243
Air Commerce Act of 1926 2
Air National Guard 1, 5-6, 27-29, 130
   See also National Guard, North Dakota
Air Service, North Dakota 12-15
Air Taxi Service Center   *See* 2007-09 Blue Book
Air Toxic Metals, Center for   *See* 2007-09 Blue Book
Airport Association of North Dakota 6
Airport Authority Act 4
Albers, Everett C. Humanities Center   *See* 2007-09 Blue Book
Allin, Roger 232, 234   *See also* 2001-03 Blue Book
Ambassadors Program, North Dakota   *See* 2007-09 Blue Book
Amberland Foods   *See* 2017-19 Blue Book
American Crystal Sugar   *See* 2013-15 Blue Book
American Elm 46, 54
American Indian Student Services Center   *See* 2007-09 and 2017-19 Blue Books
American Renewable Oil Association   *See* 2001-03 Blue Book
Amerman, Bill   *See* 2015-17 Blue Book
Amidon, Charles F. 172   *See also* 2017-19 Blue Book
Anderson, Andy   *See* 2005-07 Blue Book
Anderson, Bert 335, 339
Anderson, Dick 335, 343
Anderson, Jr., Howard C. 334, 345
Anderson, Pamela 335, 378
Andrist, John M.   *See* 2013-15 Blue Book
Andrist, Steve   *See* 2003-05 Blue Book
Animal Health, State Board of 310

Anne Carlsen Center   *See* 2003-05 Blue Book
Aquatic Nuisance Species   539
Aquifers   535   *See also* 1997-99 Blue Book
Arikara   *See* Three Affiliated Tribes
Armstrong, Kelly   164-165, 468
Army National Guard   25-27, 130
   See also National Guard, North Dakota
Art Museum, State   58
Artists, North Dakota   *See* 2003-05 Blue Book
Arts and Humanities   *See* 2007-09 Blue Book
Arts, North Dakota Council on the   310
   See also 2017-19 Blue Book
Ashley Beth Pottery   *See* 2017-19 Blue Book
Assiniboine   *See* 2013-15 Blue Book
Association of Counties, North Dakota   *See* 2013-15 Blue Book
Astronauts, North Dakota   *See* 1997-99 Blue Book
Atkinson, Myron Sr.   *See* 2011-13 Blue Book
Atmospheric Resource Board, North Dakota   328   *See also* 2007-09 Blue Book
Attorney General   219, 229, 239-240
Auditor, State   218, 229, 236-237
Audubon, John James   *See* 2007-09 Blue Book
Authors, North Dakota   135
   See also 2003-05 Blue Book
Aviation   1-42   *See also* 1999-2001 Blue Book
Aviation Council, North Dakota   6, 8, 35, 310
Aviation Hall of Fame, North Dakota   40-41
Axness, Tyler   *See* 2015-17 Blue Book

B

Bad Gun   *See* 2003-05 Blue Book
Badlands   *See* 2001-03 Blue Book
Baesler, Kirsten   227, 244, 474-476
Bagg Bonanza Farm   *See* 2007-09 Blue Book
Bahmer, Dr. Robert Henry   93
Bahr, Douglas A.   198
Bailey, Susan L.   196
Baird, Phil   *See* 2013-15 Blue Book
Bakke, JoNell A.   334, 380

Bakken Formation   414, 551   *See also* 2011-13 and 2015-17 Blue Books
Bank of North Dakota   147-148, 266-267, 313, 415, 464   *See also* 2005-07, 2007-09 and 2011-13 Blue Books
Bank of North Dakota, Advisory Board of Directors   328
Baptiste, Jean   *See* 1999-2001 Blue Book
Barley   514-523, 526, 529   *See also* 2001-03 and 2011-13 Blue Book
Barley and Malt Sciences, Institute of   *See* 2007-09 Blue Book
Barley Council, North Dakota   514
   See also 2001-03 Blue Book
Barn Guy, The   *See* 2017-19 Blue Book
Barnes County   *See* 2001-03, 2013-15 and 2015-17 Blue Books
Bartholomew, Joseph   208   *See also* 2003-05 Blue Book
Basic Sciences Imaging Center   *See* 2007-09 Blue Book
Beadle, Thomas   335, 364
Beans, Dry Edible   526-529   *See also* 2001-03 and 2009-11 Blue Books
Beans, Navy   526   *See also* 2009-11 Blue Book
Beans, Pinto   526   *See also* 2009-11 and 2011-13 Blue Books
Bear Chief   *See* Iron Bear
Bear, Floyd   *See* 2003-05 Blue Book
Bear, Keith   443
Bear, Robert "Bobby" Jr. (Swift Hawk)   *See* 2003-05 Blue Book
Bear, Robert Sr. (Neetaan Taka Ta)   *See* 2003-05 Blue Book
Beauchamp, Peter Jr.   *See* 2003-05 Blue Book
Becker, Rich S.   *See* 2017-19 Blue Book
Becker, Rick   335, 344
Beef Commission, North Dakota   328
   See also 2001-03 Blue Book
Beef Systems Center of Excellence   *See* 2007-09 Blue Book
Beekeepers Association, North Dakota   *See* 2001-03 Blue Book
Beetle, Japanese   *See* 2015-17 Blue Book
Bekkedahl, Brad   334, 338
Bellew, Larry   335, 375
Belter, Wesley R.   *See* 2015-17 Blue Book

Benson County   See 2001-03, 2005-07, 2013-15 and 2015-17 Blue Books
Benson, Anthony Swain   194
Bentonite Beds   See 2001-03 Blue Book
Berg, Rick   170   See also 2011-13 Blue Book
Berry, Spencer D.   See 2013-15 Blue Book
Better Farming Association   See 2013-15 Blue Book
Big Hill of Home, The   See 2003-05 Blue Book
Big Iron   See 1997-99 and 2013-15 Blue Books
Big Thief (Mar-toh-tah)   See 2003-05 Blue Book
Biking   See 2005-07 Blue Book
Billings County   See 2001-03, 2005-07, 2009-11, 2013-15 and 2015-17 Blue Books
Bio-Imaging and Sensing Center   See 2007-09 Blue Book
Biodiesel   See 2007-09 Blue Book
Biofuel   547
Biomass   548   See also 2007-09 Blue Book
Biomedical Research and Pathophysiology and Neurodegeneration Disease, Center for   See 2007-09 Blue Book
Biomedical Research, Center for   See 2007-09 Blue Book
Bird Watching   See 2005-07 Blue Book
Birdzell, Luther E.   209   See also 2003-05 Blue Book
Bismarck Municipal Airport   9, 43, 149
Bismarck State College   480-482, 492-493, 501
Bison   See 2001-03 and 2013-15 Blue Books
Bison Center of the Northern Plains   See 2007-09 Blue Book
Bison Trails   See 1999-2001 Blue Book
Blackhoop, F. David   See 2003-05 Blue Book
Blind, North Dakota School for the   See Vision Services/School for the Blind, North Dakota
Blue Flint Ethanol   See 2011-13 Blue Book
Blum, Jake G.   335, 379
Blumer, Mark T.   197
Boards and Commissions, North Dakota   328-330
Boating   See 2005-07 Blue Book

Boating Access   See 2005-07 Blue Book
Boating Waters   See 2005-07 Blue Book
Bobcat Company   See 2011-13 Blue Book
Bodine, Elizabeth   100
Bodmer, Karl   See 2007-09 and 2009-11 Blue Books
Boe, Tracy   335, 346
Boiler and Pressure Vessel Inspectors   See 2001-03 Blue Book
Bolinske Sr., Robert V.   468
Bonanza Farms   See 1999-2001, 2007-09 and 2013-15 Blue Books
Books (Poem)   See 2003-05 Blue Book
Borealosuchus   See 2011-13 Blue Book
Borgen, Daniel J.   199
Bosch, Glenn   335, 367
Boschee, Josh   335, 381, 468
Bottineau County   See 2001-03, 2005-07, 2009-11, 2013-15 and 2015-17 Blue Books
Bottineau, John Baptist   See 2003-05 Blue Book
Bowman Airport   213
Bowman, Bill   See 2017-19 Blue Book
Bowman County   See 2001-03, 2005-07, 2009-11, 2013-15 and 2015-17 Blue Books
Braaten, Karen K.   See 2013-15 Blue Book
Brabandt, Roger   See 2017-19 Blue Book
Brandenburg, Mike   335, 365
Brandt, Jean   468
Breweries   514-523
Bridges   See 2007-09 Blue Book
Briggs, Frank A.   232   See also 2001-03 Blue Book
Bronson, Harrison A.   209   See also 2003-05 Blue Book
Brontotheres   See 2011-13 Blue Book
Bruce, Andrew A.   209   See also 2003-05 Blue Book
Bruflat Academy   See 2007-09 Blue Book
Brunsdale, C. Norman   166, 233   See also 2001-03 Blue Book
Buchanan, President James   44
Buchmann, Casey   468
Buckwheat   See 2001-03 and 2003-05 Blue Books
Budgeting Process, North Dakota's   390-393
Buffalo Boulders   See 1999-2001 Blue Book
Buffalo Gals Mercantile   See 2017-19 Blue Book

Buffalo, Ruth 335, 364
Building Authority, North Dakota 268
Bullion Creek Formation   *See* 1999-2001 Blue Book
Bulls Eye   *See* 2003-05 Blue Book
Burckhard, Randy 334, 342
Burgum, Doug 120, 154, 215, 233, 288
Burial Mounds   *See* 2001-03 Blue Book
Burke, Andrew H. 232   *See also* 2001-03 Blue Book
Burke County   *See* 2001-03, 2005-07, 2013-15 and 2015-17 Blue Books
Burke, Edward T. 209   *See also* 2003-05 Blue Book
Burke, John 79, 209-210, 232   *See also* 2001-03 and 2003-05 Blue Books
Burke, Thomas J. 210   *See also* 2003-05 Blue Book
Burleigh County   *See* 2001-03, 2007-09, 2013-15 and 2015-17 Blue Books
Burr, Alexander G. 209   *See also* 2003-05 Blue Book
Business and Economic Research, Bureau of   *See* 2007-09 Blue Book
Business and Industry Development, Institute for   *See* 2007-09 Blue Book
Business - Assistance   *See* 2001-03 Blue Book
Business - Climate   *See* 2003-05 and 2007-09 Blue Books
Business Innovator of the Year   *See* 2007-09 Blue Book
Business - Services   *See* 2001-03 Blue Book
Bye, Kermit Edward 172

C

Cambrian Period   *See* 2011-13 Blue Book
Camp Grafton 26-27, 50, 130, 274
Cankdeska Cikana Community College 452, 480-482   *See also* 2005-07, 2007-09, 2009-11 and 2011-13 Blue Books
Cannonball Formation   *See* 2011-13 Blue Book
Canoeing   *See* 2005-07 Blue Book
Canola 526-529
Canola Growers Association, Northern   *See* 2001-03 Blue Book
Canvassing Board, State 311   *See also* 2011-13 Blue Book

Capitol Grounds Arboretum Trail 75
Capitol Grounds Planning Commission 311
Capitol Grounds Prairie Trail 75
Carbon Sequestration 544-545   *See also* 2009-11 Blue Book
Career and Technical Education   *See* 2007-09 and 2017-19 Blue Books
Career and Technical Education, Department of 312-313
Career and Technical Education, State Board for 312
Career and Technology Centers   *See* 2017-19 Blue Book
Carlisle, Ron   *See* 2015-17 Blue Book
Carlsen, Dr. Anne H. 91
Carlson, Al   *See* 2017-19 Blue Book
Carmody, John 208   *See also* 2003-05 Blue Book
Caseflow Management Committee 204
Casinos   *See* 2011-13 Blue Book
Casper, Jonathan   *See* 2017-19 Blue Book
Cass County   *See* 2001-03, 2005-07, 2013-15 and 2015-17 Blue Books
Cassowaries   *See* 2001-03 Blue Book
Catlin, George   *See* 2007-09 Blue Book
Cattle 526, 528-529   *See also* 2001-03 and 2007-09 Blue Books
Cavalier Air Force Station 23-24   *See also* 2017-19 Blue Book
Cavalier County   *See* 2001-03, 2005-07, 2013-15 and 2015-17 Blue Books
Cavalier County Museum, Dresden   *See* 2009-11 Blue Book
Cavalry   *See* 1999-2001 Blue Book
Celebrations, North Dakota   *See* 2013-15 Blue Book
Cell Biology Center   *See* 2007-09 Blue Book
Cenozoic Era   *See* 2011-13 Blue Book
Centennial Farms Program   *See* 2009-11 Blue Book
Centennial Grove 75, 79   *See also* 2011-13 Blue Book
Centennial, North Dakota 1, 5-6   *See also* 1989 and 1995-97 Blue Books
Center for Innovation   *See* 2007-09 Book
Centers of Excellence   *See* 2007-09 Blue Book

Central Grasslands Research Extension
   Center   *See* 2007-09 Blue Book
Chahinkpapa Zoo   *See* 2009-11 and 2017-19
   Blue Books
Champion Tree Program, North
   Dakota   *See* 2013-15 Blue Book
Chancellor, North Dakota University System
   484-486
Charbonneau, Toussaint   *See* 1999-2001
   Blue Book
Charging Eagle   *See* Bad Gun
Charging, Sr., Arnold   427
Chickpeas   *See* 2001-03 Blue Book
Chief Executive Officers, North Dakota
   Colleges and Universities   482
Child Development, Center for   *See* 2007-09
   Blue Book
Children and Family Services Training
   Center   *See* 2007-09 Blue Book
China   *See* 2009-11 Blue Book
Chippewa Indians   *See* Turtle Mountain
   Band of Chippewa Indians
Chokecherry   55
Christianson, Adolf M.   209   *See also*
   2003-05 Blue Book
Christmann, Randy   223, 250, 468
   See also 2011-13 Blue Book
Christopher, Warren   112
Clark, Cherie L.   197
Clark, Donald L.   *See* 2011-13 Blue Book
Clark, Tony   250, 258
Clark, William   *See* 1999-2001 Blue Book
Clemens, David A.   334, 353
Clifford, Thomas J.   115
Climate   532-535   *See also* 1997-99 and
   2013-15 Blue Books
Climate Change and CO2 Sequestration,
   Center for   *See* 2007-09 Blue Book
Clinker   *See* 2001-03 Blue Book
Cloud Modification Project, North
   Dakota   *See* 2007-09 Blue Book
Cloud Seeding   *See* 2001-03 Blue Book
Cloverdale Foods   *See* 2009-11 Blue Book
Coachman, Michael   468
Coal Ash Research Center   *See* 2007-09
   Blue Book
Coal   *See* Lignite
Coal-Fired Power Plants   *See* 2003-05 and
   2007-09 Blue Books

Coal Utilization Technologies
   Center   *See* 2007-09 Blue Book
Cochrane, John M.   208   *See also* 2003-05
   Blue Book
Code, North Dakota Revised   *See* 2011-13
   Blue Book
Codification of North Dakota Law
   See 2011-13 Blue Book
Cold War and Cold War Era   *See* 2011-13
   Blue Book
Collin, Andrea Winkjer   *See* 2003-05 Blue
   Book
Columbia   *See* 2009-11 Blue Book
Commerce   *See* 2003-05 Blue Book
Commerce, North Dakota Department
   of   256-257, 264, 275-280
Committee on Legislation   204
Committee on Tribal and State Court Affairs
   204
Communication   *See* 1999-2001 Blue Book
Community Vitality, Center for   *See* 2007-09
   Blue Book
Compiled Laws of North Dakota 1913 with
   1925 Supplement   *See* 2009-11 Blue Book
Computational Research Center
   See 2007-09 Blue Book
Computer Science and Cybersecurity
   Instruction   475-476
Computer Systems Institute   *See* 2007-09
   Blue Book
Conflict Resolution Center   *See* 2007-09
   Blue Book
Congressional Medal of Honor   *See* Medal
   of Honor Recipients
Conklin, Tom   *See* 2011-13 Blue Book
Conrad, Kent   167, 259
Constitution of North Dakota   51, 181-182,
   460-461, 478   *See also* 1989 and 2011-13
   Blue Books
Constitutional Amendments   460-461   *See
   also* 2009-11 Blue Book
Constitutional Convention 1889   *See* 1989
   Blue Book
Constitutional Convention 1971-72   461
   See also 1989 and 2011-13 Blue Books
Construction Projects, State
   Government   *See* 2011-13 Blue Book
Continental Divide   128   *See also* 2009-11
   Blue Book

INDEX   575

Cook, Dwight 334, 371
Corliss, Guy C. H. 208   *See also* 2003-05 Blue Book
Corn 524, 526-529
Corn Growers Association, North Dakota   *See* 2001-03 and 2011-13 Blue Books
Corn Utilization Council, North Dakota   *See* 2001-03 Blue Book
Corps of Discovery   *See* Lewis and Clark Expedition
Corrections and Rehabilitation, Department of 251-252, 280-284, 409
Corridor of Time, North Dakota   *See* 2011-13 Blue Book
Coteau Slope   *See* 1999-2001 Blue Book
Counties, History of   *See* 1999-2001, 2001-03, 2013-15 and 2015-17 Blue Books
Country Woman of the Year, North Dakota   *See* 2013-15 Blue Book
County Government   *See* 2001-03 and 2013-15 Blue Books
County Map   *See* 2003-05 Blue Book
Courage (Poem)   *See* 2003-05 Blue Book
Court Improvement Project Committee   *See* 2017-19 Blue Book
Court of Appeals, North Dakota 180, 189
Court Services Administration Committee 204
Court Technology Committee 205
Cowboy Hall of Fame, North Dakota   *See* 2013-15 Blue Book
Crambe   *See* 2001-03 Blue Book
Cramer, Kevin 162-163, 167, 170, 250. 256, 264, 468
Credit Review Board 313
Cresap, Todd L. 201
Cretaceous Period   *See* 2011-13 Blue Book
Crop Improvement and Seed Association, North Dakota   *See* 2001-03 Blue Book
Crop Production Maps   *See* 2007-09 Blue Book
Crops, Specialty   *See* 2015-17 Blue Book
Cross, Martin 438   *See also* 2003-05 Blue Book
Cross Ranch State Park   *See* 1997-99 Blue Book
Crothers, Daniel J. 184, 212
Crow Chief   *See* 2003-05 Blue Book

Crow Flies High, Rose (Eda-Awa-Ge'dah)   *See* 2003-05 Blue Book
Crows Paunch   *See* 2003-05 Blue Book
Cruff, Bradley A. 197
Crystals from North Dakota (Poem)   *See* 2003-05 Blue Book
Curling   *See* 2005-07 Blue Book
Custer, George Armstrong   *See* 2003-05 Blue Book
Custody Investigator Review Board   *See* 2011-13 Blue Book
Customized Business Solutions, Institute for   *See* 2007-09 Blue Book

D

Dahl, Eugene 126
Dahl, Stacey   *See* 2011-13 Blue Book
Dairy   *See* 2001-03 Blue Book
Dairy Ambassadors, North Dakota 530
Dairy Princess, State   *See* 2017-19 Blue Book
Dakota 45
Dakota Boys Ranch   *See* 2003-05 Blue Book
Dakota College at Bottineau 478-482, 493-494, 500
Dakota Cowboy Poetry Gathering   *See* 1997-99 Blue Book
Dakota Dinosaur Museum   *See* 2011-13 Blue Book
Dakota Magic Casino and Hotel   *See* 2011-13 Blue Book
Dakota Territory 44, 48
Dakota Territory Air Museum 5, 31-32, 471
Dakota the Dinomummy   *See* 2011-13 Blue Book
Dakota Water Resource Act   *See* 2001-03 Blue Book
Dakota Zoo   *See* 2017-19 Blue Book
Dalmatian Toadflax   *See* 2005-07 Blue Book
Dalrymple, Jack 35, 233, 235   *See also* 2015-17 Blue Book
Damschen, Chuck 335, 347
Data Center, North Dakota State   *See* 2007-09, 2009-11 and 2011-13 Blue Books
Daughter of the Northern Plains   *See* 2003-05 Blue Book
Davies, Ronald N. 104
Davis, John E. 233, 251   *See also* 2001-03 Blue Book

Davis, Scott 259, 420, 456
Davison, Kyle 334, 378
Dead-Ice Moraine *See* 2001-03 Blue Book
Deaf, North Dakota School for the *See* 2001-03, 2007-09 and 2009-11 Blue Books
Death, Leading Causes in North Dakota 129
Decisionmakers, Dakota *See* 2005-07 Blue Book
Decoteau, Raphael John *See* 2003-05 Blue Book
Deep Creek Encounter *See* 2003-05 Blue Book
Deer Hunter's Paradise *See* 2005-07 Blue Book
Delmore, Lois *See* 2017-19 Blue Book
Delzer, Jeff 64, 335, 345
Designs by Krista Marie *See* 2017-19 Blue Book
Dever, Dick 334, 369
Devils Lake *See* 2003-05 Blue Book
Devils Lake Basin 534-536
Devils Lake Regional Airport 9
Devils Lake Sioux Tribe *See* Spirit Lake Nation
Devine, Joseph M. 232, 234, 244 *See also* 2001-03 and 2007-09 Blue Books
Devlin, Bill 335, 360
Dickey, Alfred 234 *See also* 2001-03 Blue Book
Dickey Bridge *See* 2007-09 Blue Book
Dickey County *See* 2001-03, 2005-07, 2009-11, 2013-15 and 2015-17 Blue Books
Dickinson State University 478-482, 487-488, 500, 502-503
Dickinson State University - Research Institutes *See* 2007-09 Blue Book
Dickinson Theodore Roosevelt Regional Airport 9
Dickinson, Angie 107
Diffuse Knapweed *See* 2005-07 Blue Book
Disaster *See* 2001-03 Blue Book
Disciplinary Board 205
District Courts 180, 191-202
Divide County *See* 2001-03, 2005-07, 2009-11, 2013-15 and 2015-17 Blue Books
Dmitri, Ivan 86
Do It Monday - If It's Monday (Poem) *See* 2003-05 Blue Book

Dobervich, Gretchen 335, 348
Dockter, Jason 335, 344
Dohrmann, Alan S. 26, 250
Dosch, Mark A. *See* 2015-17 Blue Book
Dotzenrod, Jim 334, 363, 468
Double Ditch Indian Village State Historic Site *See* 1999-2001 Blue Book
Drags Wolf *See* 2003-05 Blue Book
Dromaeosaurids *See* 2011-13 Blue Book
Drones *See* Unmanned Aircraft Systems
Drovdal, David *See* 2013-15 Blue Book
Drumlins *See* 1999-2001 Blue Book
Duhamel, Josh 138
Dunbar, Carl O. *See* 2011-13 Blue Book
Duncan, Lieutenant Cecil "Dunk" *See* 2009-11 and 2011-13 Blue Books
Dunes *See* 2001-03 Blue Book
Dunn County *See* 2001-03, 2005-07, 2013-15 and 2015-17 Blue Books
Durick, Brad *See* 2005-07 Blue Book
Durum Growers Association, U.S. *See* 2001-03 Blue Book
Dwyer, Michael 334, 384

E

Eagle Feather (Ankedoucharo) *See* 2003-05 Blue Book
Eaglestaff, Robert 428
Earthquakes *See* 1999-2001 Blue Book
Eco-Tourism, North Dakota *See* 2005-07 Blue Book
Ecological Studies, Institute for *See* 2007-09 Blue Book
Economic Development *See* 2001-03, 2003-05 and 2007-09 Blue Books
Economic Development in Life Sciences and Advanced Technologies, Center of Excellence for *See* 2007-09 Blue Book
Economic Development in UAVs and Simulation Applications, Center of Excellence for 33 *See also* 2007-09 Blue Book
Economic Development - Vision 2000 *See* 2001-03 Blue Book
Eddy County *See* 2001-03, 2005-07, 2013-15 and 2015-17 Blue Books
Edmontosaurus *See* 2011-13 Blue Book
Education Commission of the States 313

Education Services and Applied Research, Bureau of   See 2007-09 Blue Book
Education, Higher   See Higher Education
Education, History   See 1997-99 Blue Book
Education, Indian   See 1997-99 Blue Book
Education, K-12   474-477
Ehlis, Rhonda R.   200
Eidson, Matt   336, 380
Eielson, Carl Ben   2, 41, 111
El-Dweek, Daniel S.   202
Elbowoods Warriors Basketball Team, 1941-42   437
ElboWoods Works   See 2007-09 Blue Book
Election Calendar, 2020 North Dakota   469
Election Report of Vote Totals, 2018 General   468
Elections   460-470   See also Previous Blue Books
Electric Vehicles   554
Elk   See 2001-03 Blue Book
Elkin, Jay   334, 373
Ellison, Doug   See 2003-05 Blue Book
Ellsworth, Sidney E.   208   See also 2003-05 Blue Book
Emergency Commission   265
Emily P. Reynolds Historic Costume Collection   See 2007-09 Blue Book
Emission Control Technologies Center   See 2007-09 Blue Book
Emmons County   See 2001-03, 2005-07, 2009-11, 2011-13, 2013-15 and 2015-17 Blue Books
EmPower North Dakota   546   See also 2011-13 Blue Book
Emu   See 2001-03 Blue Book
Enabling Act   See 1989 Blue Book
Endangered Species   540
Energy   543-554   See also 2007-09 Blue Book
Energy and Environmental Research Center   See 2007-09 Blue Book
Energy Efficiency   548-549
Engerud, Edward   208   See also 2003-05 Blue Book
Engineering Services   See 2001-03 Blue Book
Entrepreneur Hall of Fame, North Dakota   See 2007-09 Blue Book

Entrepreneurship and Rural Revitalization, Center for   See 2007-09 Blue Book
Environmental Quality, North Dakota Department of   262, 288-290
Environmental Training Institute   See 2007-09 Blue Book
Eocene Chadron Formation   See 2011-13 Blue Book
Equalization, State Board of   265
Equine, Honorary   66
Era Bell Thompson Cultural Center   See 2007-09 Blue Book
Erbele, Robert   334, 365
Erdrich, Louise   122
Erickson, Ralph   172
Erickstad, Ralph J.   210   See also 2003-05 Blue Book
Ertelt, Sebastian   336, 363
Ethanol   549   See also 2007-09 and 2011-13 Blue Books
Ever and Always (Poem)   See 2003-05 Blue Book
Every Student Succeeds Act   See 2017-19 Blue Book
Exports   See 2007-09 Blue Book
Extended Learning, Center for   See 2007-09 Blue Book
Extension Service, NDSU   See 2013-15 Blue Book

F

Fair Association, North Dakota State   142, 314
Fairview Lift Bridge   See 2007-09 Blue Book
Family Medicine, Center for   See 2007-09 Blue Book
Family Therapy Center   See 2007-09 Blue Book
Fancher, Frederick B.   232, 240   See also 2001-03 and 2007-09 Blue Books
Fargo Air Museum   32-33
Fargo Brewing Company   516, 522
Fargo Hector International Airport   9
Farm Bureau, North Dakota   See 2001-03 Blue Book
Farm Service Agency   See 2001-03 Blue Book

Farmers Union, North Dakota   See 2001-03 Blue Book
Farms   524, 527   See also 2001-03 Blue Book
Farms, Centennial   See 2009-11 Blue Book
Federal Government   See 2001-03 Blue Book
Federal Grants   See 2001-03 Blue Book
Federal Land Ownership   See 2001-03 Blue Book
Fedorchak, Julie   224, 250
Fegley, Clayton   336, 341
Fehr, Alan   See 2015-17 Blue Book
Feland, Cynthia M.   199
Fetal Alcohol Syndrome Center, North Dakota   See 2007-09 Blue Book
Field Bindweed   See 2005-07 Blue Book
Finance   See 2001-03 Blue Book
Financial Institutions, State Department of   262, 284-285
Firefighters' Association   314
First Nations Day   65, 456
Fischer, Tom   See 2011-13 and 2013-15 Blue Books
Fish   See 1997-99 Blue Book
Fish, North Dakota Record   See 2015-17 Blue Book
Fisher, Jay   336, 342
Fishing   541   See also 2005-07 Blue Book
Fishing Waters   See 2005-07 Blue Book
Fisk, Charles J.   208   See also 2003-05 Blue Book
Flag, Governor's   50
Flakoll, Tim   See 2015-17 Blue Book
Flat Bear   See 2003-05 Blue Book
Flax   526-527   See also 2001-03 and 2011-13 Blue Books
Flickertail March   61
Flickertail State   45
Floyd, Sergeant Charles   See 1999-2001 Blue Book
Foley, James W.   55, 136   See also 2003-05 Blue Book
Fong, Cory   246
Fontaine, Laurie A.   194
Forest Service, North Dakota   75, 314-315
Fors, Robert O.   334, 356
Fort Abercrombie State Historic Site   See 1999-2001 and 2009-11 Blue Books
Fort Abraham Lincoln State Park   See 1999-2001 and 2009-11 Blue Books
Fort Berthold Community College   See Nueta Hidatsa Sahnish College
Fort Berthold Reservation   449-450
Fort Buford State Historic Site   See 1999-2001 Blue Books
Fort Clark State Historic Site   See 1999-2001 Blue Book
Fort Clatsop   See 1999-2001 Blue Book
Fort Mandan and Lewis and Clark Interpretive Center   64
Fort Mandan   See 1999-2001 and 2009-11 Blue Books
Fort Seward Wagon Train   See 1997-99 Blue Book
Fort Totten State Historic Site   See 1999-2001 and 2009-11 Blue Books
Fort Union Trading Post   See 1997-99, 1999-2001 and 2009-11 Blue Books
Fort Yates Warriors Basketball Team, 1973   433
Fossil Digs, Public Participation   See 2005-07 and 2011-13 Blue Books
Foster County   See 2001-03, 2005-07, 2009-11, 2013-15 and 2015-17 Blue Books
Foughty, Donovan   194
Four Bears Bridge   See 2007-09 Blue Book
Four Bears (Mah-ta-to-pe)   See 2003-05 Blue Book
Four Dances   See 2003-05 Blue Book
Fox Hills Formation   See 2011-13 Blue Book
Fox, Robert (Roaming Wolf)   See 2003-05 Blue Book
Fraine, John H.   49, 234   See also 1999-2001 Blue Book
Frantsvog, Robert   See 2015-17 Blue Book
Frazier, Lynn J.   166, 232, 255, 403
Freborg, Layton   See 2011-13 Blue Book
Fredericks, Pete   434
Freedom to Farm Act   See 1999-2001 Blue Book
Frelich, Phyllis   102
French, Davina   See 2009-11 Blue Book
Froseth, Glen   54   See also 2015-17 Blue Book

G

Gall   *See* 2003-05 Blue Book
Gallion, Joshua C.   218, 237
Gamble, Bertin C.   95
Game and Fish Department, North Dakota   255-256, 285-286
Gannon, Clell   *See* 2003-05 Blue Book
Garrison Dam   128, 149, 535   *See also* 2001-03 Blue Book
Garrison Diversion Conservancy District   315-316
Gas   *See* 2001-03 and 2007-09 Blue Books
Gates Manufacturing Inc.   *See* 2009-11 Blue Book
Gattuso, Philip   *See* 2011-13 Blue Book
Geiger, M. Richard   *See* 2017-19 Blue Book
Gender Fairness Implementation Committee   *See* 2017-19 Blue Book
General Allotment Act 1887   *See* 2001-03 Blue Book
General Aviation, Center of Excellence   *See* 2007-09 Blue Book
Geographic Center of North America   128
Geography, North Dakota   128
Geological Survey of North Dakota   76, 269, 543   *See also* 1995-97 and 2011-13 Blue Books
Geology   *See* 1997-99 and 1999-2001 Blue Books
Germans from Russia Heritage Collection   *See* 2007-09 and 2009-11 Blue Books
Germany   *See* 2009-11 Blue Book
Get Out the Vote Poster and Slogan Contest   *See* 2001-03 Blue Book
Ghana   *See* 2009-11 Blue Book
Gierke, Herman F.   211   *See also* 2003-05 Blue Book
Gillette, Rusty   *See* 2005-07 Blue Book
Gion, James D.   200
Gipp, David   429, 558-559, 562, 565, 568
GIS (Geographic Information System)   *See* 2007-09 Blue Book
Glacial Lake Agassiz   *See* 1999-2001 Blue Book
Glaciated Plains   *See* 1999-2001 Blue Book
Glaciers   *See* 1999-2001 and 2001-03 Blue Books
Glassheim, Eliot   58   *See also* 2015-17 Blue Book
Glen Ullin Airport   513
Global Trade in North Dakota   *See* 2009-11 Blue Book
Global War on Terrorism   *See* 2009-11 Blue Book
Godfread, Jon   221, 241
Goehring, Doug   222, 243, 468
Goetz, William   *See* 2011-13 Blue Book
Gold   *See* 1999-2001 Blue Book
Gold Seal Company   97   *See also* 2009-11 Blue Book
Golden Valley County   *See* 2001-03, 2005-07, 2013-15 and 2015-17 Blue Books
Golden Valley Formation   *See* 2011-13 Blue Book
Golfing   *See* 2005-07 and 2013-15 Blue Books
Goodhouse, Lois   *See* 2003-05 Blue Book
Goodiron, Nathan   424
Gordon Aamoth Indian Development Fund   *See* 2001-03 Blue Book
Goss, Evan B.   209   *See also* 2003-05 Blue Book
Gourneau, Kaishpau   *See* 2003-05 Blue Book
Gourneau, Patrick   435   *See also* 2003-05 Blue Book
Government Affairs, Bureau of   *See* 2007-09 Blue Book
Government Agencies, U.S.   *See* 2001-03 Blue Book
Governor   215, 228, 232-233, 416-417   *See also* 2001-03 and 2011-13 Blue Books
Governor's Residence   73   *See also* 2011-13 Blue Book
Grabinger, John   334, 349
Grace, Richard H.   209   *See also* 2003-05 Blue Book
Grand Forks Air Force Base   20-23, 33   *See also* 2011-13 and 2017-19 Blue Books
Grand Forks County   *See* 2001-03, 2005-07, 2009-11, 2013-15 and 2015-17 Blue Books
Grand Forks International Airport   10
Grand Sky Business Park   37
Grande, Bette   *See* 2013-15 Blue Book
Grant County   *See* 2001-03, 2005-07, 2009-11, 2013-15 and 2015-17 Blue Books

Grass, John   *See* 2003-05 and 2011-13 Blue Books
Grasslands, National   *See* 1997-99 Blue Book
Great Depression   *See* 1999-2001 and 2013-15 Blue Books
Great Plains Energy Corridor   547
Great Plains Institute of Food Safety   *See* 2007-09 Blue Book
Great Plains Synfuels Plant   *See* 1997-99 Blue Book
Great River Energy   *See* 2011-13 Blue Book
Great Seal of North Dakota   46-47, 79
Green, Sheldon   *See* 2003-05 Blue Book
Greenwood, Dann E.   200
Greenwood, John E.   *See* 2011-13 Blue Book
Gress, Betty   436
Griggs County   *See* 2001-03, 2005-07, 2011-13 and 2013-15 Blue Books
Griggs County Museum, Cooperstown   *See* 2011-13 Blue Book
Grimson, Gudmunder   210   *See also* 2003-05 Blue Book
Grindberg, Tony   *See* 2013-15 Blue Book
Grinsteiner, John W.   199
Gronna, Asle J.   166, 168
Group Decision Center   *See* 2007-09 Blue Book
Gruchalla, Edmund   *See* 2013-15 Blue Book
Grueneich, Jim   336, 349
Guggisberg, Ron   336, 348
Gussiaas Farm Inc.   *See* 2009-11 Blue Book
Gustin, Al   *See* 2003-05 Blue Book
Guy, William L.   82, 233   *See also* 2001-03 Blue Book

H

Haak, Jessica   *See* 2015-17 Blue Book
Hagar, Richard L.   201   *See also* 2011-13 Blue Book
Hager, Donald   195
Hager, LaurieBeth   336, 358
Hagerott, Mark R.   486
Hagerty, Gail   198   *See also* 2011-13 Blue Book
Hagerty, Marilyn   *See* 2003-05 Blue Book
Hall, James (Iron Bear-Nagh Bitsi Usahas)   *See* 2003-05 Blue Book
Hall, Tex G.   *See* 2003-05 and 2013-15 Blue Books
Halverson, Rev. Richard C.   108
Hamm, Adam   241   *See also* 2011-13 Blue Book
Hanna, Louis B.   52, 168, 232, 255, 402   *See also* 2001-03 and 2011-13 Blue Books
Hanson, Ben   *See* 2015-17 Blue Book
Hanson, Karla Rose   336, 381
Harrison, President Benjamin   44
Hartleib, Fred   *See* 2009-11 Blue Book
Haskell, Bruce B.   *See* 2011-13 Blue Book
Hastings, Shon Kaelberer   174
Hatch Act of 1887   *See* 2003-05 Blue Book
Hatlestad, Patrick   54-55, 336, 338
Haugland, Brynhild   109   *See also* 1989 Blue Book
Hawken, Kathy   *See* 2015-17 Blue Book
Headland, Craig   336, 366
Health, State Department of   260-261, 286-288, 412   *See also* 2011-13 Blue Book
Heckaman, Joan   334, 360
Heilman, Joe   *See* 2013-15 Blue Book
Heinert, Pat D.   336, 369
Heitkamp, Heidi   167, 240, 246, 468
Helgesen, Henry T.   168, 242
Hell Creek Delta   *See* 2011-13 Blue Book
Heller, Brenda   *See* 2013-15 Blue Book
Help America Vote Act   *See* 2007-09 Blue Book
Hemp Pilot Program, Industrial   *See* 2017-19 Blue Book
Henderson, John   *See* 2009-11 Blue Book
Herauf, William A.   200   *See also* 2011-13 Blue Book
Heritage Center, North Dakota   75-77, 142   *See also* 1997-99, 2011-13 and 2015-17 Blue Books
Heritage Renewal, Center for   *See* 2007-09 Blue Book
Herman, Douglas R.   *See* 2011-13 Blue Book
Hesperornis   *See* 2011-13 Blue Book
Hettinger County   *See* 2001-03, 2005-07, 2009-11, 2013-15 and 2015-17 Blue Books
Hidatsa Indians   *See* Three Affiliated Tribes and 1999-2001 Blue Book

Hidatsa Indians - Chieftainship   *See* 2003-05 Blue Book
Hidatsa Indians - Leadership   *See* 2003-05 Blue Book
High Line Railroad Bridge   *See* 2007-09 Blue Book
High Performance Computing, Center for   *See* 2007-09 Blue Book
Higher Education Name Changes   *See* 2015-17 Blue Book
Higher Education, North Dakota 478-512
Higher Education, State Board of 316, 418, 485   *See also* 2011-13 Blue Book
Highway Patrol, State 263, 290-291   *See also* 2011-13 Blue Book
Hill, Clint 127
Hill, James S. 199
Hill, William A. 175   *See also* 2011-13 Blue Book
Historical Society of North Dakota, State 47, 75-78, 140, 142, 317-318   *See also* 1997-99, 2011-13 and 2015-17 Blue Books
HIT Inc.   *See* 2017-19 Blue Book
Hochhalter, Clare R. 176-177
Hockey Flag, Official High School 62
Hodge, Ann Linton   *See* 1999-2001 Blue Book
Hoeven, John H. 75, 161, 163, 167, 233   *See also* 2001-03 and 2011-13 Blue Books
Hofstad, Curt   *See* 2015-17 Blue Book
Hogan, Kathy 334, 358
Hogue, David 334, 375
Holidays in North Dakota 137
Holman, Richard G. 336, 357
Holmberg, Ray 58, 334, 354
Home Education   *See* 2001-03 Blue Book
Home on the Range   *See* 2003-05 Blue Book
Home Rule Counties   *See* 2001-03 and 2009-11 Blue Books
Homecoming (Poem)   *See* 2003-05 Blue Book
Homeland Security, North Dakota   *See* 2005-07 Blue Book
Homestead Act   *See* 2007-09 Blue Book
Honey 526-530   *See also* 2001-03, 2009-11 and 2011-13 Blue Books
Honor Flights, North Dakota   *See* 2011-13 Blue Book
Hooking a Chinook an Unforgettable Experience   *See* 2005-07 Blue Book
Hops 514-523   *See also* 2015-17 Blue Book
Horses   *See* 2001-03 and 2011-13 Blue Books
Housing Finance Agency, North Dakota 268
Hoverson, Jeff A. 336, 340
Hovey, James D. 198   *See also* 2011-13 Blue Book
Hovland, Daniel L. 172-173   *See also* 2011-13 Blue Book
Howard, J. Dan   *See* 2003-05 Blue Book
Howe, Michael 336, 359
Hudson, Marilyn   *See* 2003-05 Blue Book
Human Services, North Dakota Department of 258, 291-292, 412, 415   *See also* 2007-09 and 2011-13 Blue Books
Humanities, North Dakota 329   *See also* 2007-09 and 2011-13 Blue Books
Hunskor, Bob   *See* 2015-17 Blue Book
Hunting 541-542   *See also* 2005-07 Blue Book
Hurly, Michael P. 194
Hydraulic Fracturing   *See* 2017-19 Blue Book
Hydrogen Technology, National Center for   *See* 2007-09 Blue Book
Hymn, North Dakota 55-57

I

Ice Fishing   *See* 2005-07 and 2011-13 Blue Books
Icelandic State Park Pioneer Heritage Center, Cavalier   *See* 2009-11 and 2011-13 Blue Books
Ideal Aerosmith Inc.   *See* 2009-11 Blue Book
IHS Markit 389
Income   *See* 2001-03 and 2011-13 Blue Books
Independent Study, Division of   *See* 2001-03 and 2011-13 Blue Book
Indian Affairs Commission, North Dakota 259, 292-293, 319, 420-421   *See also* 2011-13 Blue Book
Indian Affairs, Commissioner of   *See* 2001-03 Blue Book
Indian Business Alliance, North Dakota   *See* 2017-19 Blue Book

Indian Business Development
   Fund   *See* 2001-03 Blue Book
Indian Child Welfare Act   *See* 2001-03 Blue
   Book
Indian Claims Commission Act
   See 2001-03 Blue Book
Indian Education Act   *See* 2001-03 Blue
   Book
Indian Financing Act   *See* 2001-03 Blue
   Book
Indian Gaming   *See* 2005-07 Blue Book
Indian Gaming Law and Policy
   Institute   *See* 2009-11 Blue Book
Indian Gaming Regulatory Act of
   1988   *See* 2005-07 Blue Book
Indian Genealogy   *See* 2001-03 Blue Book
Indian Health Care Improvement Act
   See 2001-03 Blue Book
Indian Health Facilities Act   *See* 2001-03
   Blue Book
Indian Mineral Development Act
   See 2001-03 Blue Book
Indian Policies, Federal   *See* 2001-03 Blue
   Book
Indian Religious Freedom Act   *See* 2001-03
   Blue Book
Indian Removal Act of 1830/Cherokee Trail
   of Tears   *See* 2001-03 Blue Book
Indian Reorganization Act of 1934
   See 2001-03 and 2003-05 Blue Books
Indian Reservations   446-451
Indian Sanitation Facilities and Services Act
   See 2001-03 Blue Book
Indian Scholarships, State Board for North
   Dakota   319
Indian Self-Determination and Education
   Assistance   *See* 2001-03 Blue Book
Indian Tribal Enrollment   446-447, 449, 451
Indian Tribal Government Tax Status Act of
   1982   *See* 2001-03 Blue Book
Indian Youth Leadership Academy   457
Indians - Statistics   *See* 2001-03 Blue Book
Indians - U.S. Citizenship   *See* 2001-03 Blue
   Book
Industrial Commission, North Dakota   228,
   266-271, 464
Industry   *See* 2003-05 and 2011-13 Blue
   Books

Influenza Epidemic 1918   *See* 2017-19 Blue
   Book
Informal Complaint Panel   205
Information Technology Department, North
   Dakota   256, 293-294, 415   *See also*
   2001-03 Blue Book
Initiative   462-463, 466
Innovation, Center for   *See* Center for
   Innovation
Institute for Pharmaceutical Care, North
   Dakota   *See* 2007-09 Blue Book
Institute for Regional Studies, North Dakota
   See 2007-09 Blue Book
Institute of Barley and Malt Sciences
   See 2009-11 Blue Book
Instructional and Learning Technologies,
   Center for   *See* 2007-09 Blue Book
Insurance Commissioner   221, 230, 240-241,
   411
Insurance   *See* 2001-03 Blue Book
International Border Crossings   154-158
International Peace Garden   45, 143-144, 329
   See also 1997-99 and 2009-11 Blue Books
Interstate Compacts and Agreements
   See 1989 Blue Book
Investment Board, State   319-320
Irby, John C.   196
Iron Bear   *See* 2003-05 Blue Book
Iron Heart   *See* 2003-05 Blue Book
Irrigation   315, 538

J

J & J Corporation Inc.   *See* 2009-11 Blue
   Book
Jackson, Lydia O.   136   *See also* 2003-05
   Blue Book
Jackson, Phil   105
Jacobson, Dr. Leon Orris   99
Jacobson, Paul W.   202
Jaeger, Alvin (Al) A.   217, 236, 468
Jahnke, Lawrence E.   *See* 2011-13 Blue
   Book
Jamerson, Theodore   558   *See also* 2003-05
   Blue Book
James River   535
James River Basin   535-536
   See also 2003-05 Blue Book
Jamestown College   *See* University of
   Jamestown

Jamestown Regional Airport 10, 179
Jeanotte, Leigh 430
Jefferson, President Thomas *See* 2011-13 Blue Book
Jensen, Jon J. 187, 212
Jerome, Dan 431
JM Grain *See* 2009-11 Blue Book
Job Service North Dakota 256, 294-296
Job Training Partnership Act *See* 2001-03 Blue Book
Johnson, Benjamen J. 202
Johnson, Craig 336, 343
Johnson, Dennis 336, 352
Johnson, General Harold K. 90
Johnson, J. Philip 211 *See also* 2003-05 Blue Book
Johnson, Mary 336, 382
Johnson, Nancy *See* 2013-15 Blue Book
Johnson, Nels 210 *See also* 2003-05 Blue Book
Johnson O'Malley Act *See* 2001-03 Blue Book
Johnson, Roger 243
Johnson, Sveinbjorn 209, 239 *See also* 2003-05 Blue Book
Johnsrud Paleontology Laboratory, North Dakota Geological Survey 76 *See also* 2009-11 Blue Book
Johnston, Daniel 336, 361
Joint Committee on Attorney Standards 205
Joint Procedure Committee 205
Jollie, Edward *See* 2003-05 Blue Book
Jones, General David C. 103
Jones, H. Kent 243
Jones, Terry B. 336, 341
Judicial Branch Education Commission 205
Judicial Conduct Commission 206, 329
Judicial Conference, North Dakota 207
Judicial Districts, North Dakota 192
Judicial Nominating Committee 320
Judicial Planning Committee 206
Judicial System, North Dakota 181, 203-207
Judicial System, U.S. 171-178
Judicial Wing, State Capitol 72
Judiciary Standards Committee 206
Jury Standards Committee 206
Juvenile Policy Board 206

K

K-T Boundary Extinction *See* 2011-13 Blue Book
Kading, Tom 336, 382
Kakenowash *See* 2003-05 Blue Book
Kaldor, Lee *See* 2011-13 Blue Book
Kalk, Dr. Brian P. *See* 2015-17 Blue Book
Kallberg, Bob *See* 2005-07 Blue Book
Kannianen, Jordan 334, 341
Kapsner, Carol Ronning 212 *See also* 2015-17 Blue Book
Karls, Karen 336, 372
Kasper, Jim 336, 383
Kazakhstan *See* 2009-11 Blue Book
Keeble, Master Sgt. Woodrow W. 119, 159, 457 *See also* 2015-17 Blue Book
Keiser, George 336, 384
Kekabah, Twila Martin *See* 2003-05 Blue Book
Kelly, Josephine Gates *See* 2003-05 Blue Book
Kelsch, RaeAnn G. *See* 2011-13 Blue Book
Kelsh, Jerry *See* 2015-17 Blue Book
Kelsh, Scot *See* 2011-13 Blue Book
Kempenich, Keith 336, 376
Keplin, Wayne *See* 2003-05 Blue Book
Kidder County *See* 2001-03, 2005-07, 2013-15 and 2015-17 Blue Books
KIDS COUNT, North Dakota 129
Kiefert, Dwight 336, 361
Kildeer Mountains *See* 2001-03 Blue Book
Kilzer, Ralph *See* 2017-19 Blue Book
Kirkpatrick, Gene *See* 2013-15 Blue Book
Klapprodt, Lee *See* 2005-07 Blue Book
Klein, Jerry 334, 351
Klein, Karen K. 176 *See also* 2013-15 Blue Book
Klein, Matthew M. *See* 2015-17 Blue Book
Klemin, Lawrence R. 335-336, 384
Knauf, John 208 *See also* 2003-05 Blue Book
Knife River *See* 1999-2001 Blue Book
Knife River Indian Villages National Historic Sites *See* 1997-99 and 1999-2001 Blue Books
Knudson, Harvey B. 210 *See also* 2003-05 Blue Book
Knudson, Jay D. 195

Koeck, Dan   *See* 2003-05 Blue Book
Kolden, Angela   *See* 2003-05 Blue Book
Koppelman, Ben   336, 353
Koppelman, Kim   336, 350
Korea, Republic of   *See* 2009-11 Blue Book
Korean War   *See* 2009-11 Blue Book
Krebsbach, Karen K.   54, 334, 377
Kreidt, Gary   54, 336, 370
Kretschmar, William E.   *See* 2015-17 Blue Book
Kreun, Curt   334, 379
Kroshus, Brian   225, 250, 468
Kurz, Rudolph   *See* 2007-09 Blue Book

L

La Borge   *See* Le Borgne and 1999-2001 Blue Book
L'Amour, Louis   94
Labor and Human Rights, Department of   258, 296-297
Labor Commissioner   243
Labor Force   *See* 2001-03 Blue Book
Laducer, Jim   *See* 2013-15 Blue Book
LaDue, Henry   *See* 2013-15 Blue Book
Lady Beetle, Convergent   54
Laffen, Lonnie J.   *See* 2017-19 Blue Book
Lake Agassiz   *See* 2011-13 Blue Book
Lake Ashtabula   536
Lake Audubon   536
Lake Oahe   536
Lake Region State College   480-482, 494-495
Lake Sakakawea   128, 535-536   *See also* 2003-05 Blue Book
Lakoduk, Craig   *See* 2009-11 Blue Book
Lakota   *See* 2003-05 Blue Book
Lamb and Wool Growers Association, North Dakota   *See* 2001-03 Blue Book
Lamb, William G.   *See* 2009-11 Blue Book
LaMoure County   *See* 2001-03, 2013-15 and 2015-17 Blue Books
Land Department   *See* Trust Lands, Department of
Langer, William   68, 166, 232-233, 239   *See also* 2001-03 Blue Book
Laning, Vernon   336, 345
Larsen, Oley   334, 340
Larson, Diane   334, 367
Laughing Sun Brewing Company   516, 520-522

Law Examiners, State Board of   207
Lawrence, Frank   *See* 2003-05 Blue Book
Le Borgne (Mau-pah-pir-re-co-sa-too)   *See* La Borge and 2003-05 Blue Book
Leafy Spurge   *See* 2005-07 Blue Book
League of Cities, North Dakota - Centennial   *See* 2011-13 Blue Book
Lee, Gary A.   334, 359
Lee, Gary H.   200-201
Lee, Judy   334, 350
Lee, Peggy   88
LeFevre, Troy J.   198
Lefor, Mike   336, 374
Legacy Fund, North Dakota   319, 410, 418
Legal Counsel for Indigents, Commission on   329   *See also* 2005-07 Blue Book
Legislative Assembly, 66th   404-418
Legislative Compensation   398-400
Legislative Council   397
Legislative Leadership, Women   *See* 2017-19 Blue Book
Legislative Management   396
Legislative Redistricting   *See* 2011-13 Blue Book
Legislative Wing of the Capitol   70
Legislators, 2019 Session   334-384
Legislators, Longest-Serving   *See* 2015-17 Blue Book
Legislators Who Served During WWI   *See* 2017-19 Blue Book
Leingang, Gordon   *See* 2007-09 Blue Book
Lemm, Randy D.   334, 357
Lenoir, Melvin L.   *See* 2003-05 Blue Book
Lentils   526, 529   *See also* 2001-03, 2009-11 and 2011-13 Blue Books
Lessons from the Land   *See* 2003-05 Blue Book
Lessons in Life and Nature   *See* 2003-05 Blue Book
Levine, Beryl J.   211   *See also* 2003-05 Blue Book
Levings, Martin (Ah-pa-hi-si-pi-sas "Black Cloud")   *See* 2003-05 Blue Book
Lewis and Clark Bicentennial Events   *See* 2003-05, 2005-07 and 2007-09 Blue Books
Lewis and Clark Expedition   50, 55
Lewis and Clark Interpretive Center   64, 142   *See also* 1999-2001 Blue Book

Lewis, Meriwether 50   See also 1999-2001 Blue Book
Liberty Memorial Bridge   See 2007-09 and 2011-13 Blue Books
Liberty Memorial Building 74-75
Libraries 74   See also 1995-97 and 1999-2001 Blue Books
License Plate, North Dakota   See 2015-17 Blue Book
Lieutenant Governor 35, 216, 228, 233-235
Life on the Road Less Traveled   See 2003-05 Blue Book
Lighthouse Soy Candles   See 2017-19 Blue Book
Lignite 544-545, 549   See also 2001-03, 2007-09 and 2011-13 Blue Books
Lignite Research Council 269, 329
Like-A-Fishhook Village   See 2007-09 Blue Book
Lincoln, Abraham - Bicentennial Events   See 2009-11 Blue Book
Link, Arthur A. 170, 233   See also 2001-03 and 2011-13 Blue Books
Literature, North Dakota   See 2005-07, 2007-09, 2009-11, 2011-13, 2013-15, 2015-17 and 2017-19 Blue Books
Literature, North Dakota - Published Authors 135
Little Hoop Community College   See Cankdeska Cikana Community College
Little Missouri Badlands   See 2001-03 and 2011-13 Blue Books
Little Raven (Ka-goh-ha-mi)   See 2003-05 Blue Book
Little Shell I   See 2003-05 Blue Book
Little Shell II   See 2003-05 Blue Book
Little Shell III 439   See also 2003-05 Blue Book
Little Soldier, August   See 2003-05 Blue Book
Little Soldier, Nathan   See 2003-05 Blue Book
Little, Paul   See 2003-05 Blue Book
Livestock   See 2001-03 and 2007-09 Blue Books
Living Life Well in North Dakota   See 2003-05 Blue Book
Logan County   See 2001-03, 2005-07 and 2013-15 Blue Books
Lone Fight, Edward   See 2003-05 Blue Book
Long Bear (Wah-pi-tsi-ha-tski)   See 2003-05 Blue Book
Long X Visitor Center, Watford City   See 2011-13 Blue Book
Longie Red Hail, Claude   See 2003-05 Blue Book
Longie, Philip "Skip"   See 2003-05 Blue Book
Longmuir, Donald W. 336, 339
Looysen, Alex   See 2015-17 Blue Book
Lost Bridge   See 2007-09 Blue Book
Lottery, North Dakota   See 2011-13 Blue Book
Louisiana Purchase 50
Louser, Scott 336, 342
Louser, Stacy J. 201
Luber, Patrick Alan   See 2003-05 Blue Book
Luick, Larry 334, 362
Lyson, Stanley W.   See 2013-15 Blue Book
Lyson, Tyler   See 2009-11 Blue Book

M

Mad Bear   See 2003-05 Blue Book
Maddock, Walter J. 232, 234, 253   See also 2001-03 Blue Book
Magrum, Jeffery J. 336, 365
Main Avenue Bridge, Fargo   See 2007-09 Blue Book
Management and Budget, Office of 259, 297-299, 388-393
Mandan Indian Leadership   See 2003-05 Blue Book
Mandan Indians   See 1999-2001 Blue Book
Mandan Railroad Museum 65   See also 2007-09, 2009-11 and 2011-13 Blue Books
Mandan, Arthur   See 2003-05 Blue Book
Mandan, Hidatsa, and Arikara Nation 449-450   See also Three Affiliated Tribes and 2001-03 Blue Book
Mandaree Enterprise Corporation   See 2007-09 Blue Book
Manufacturing   See 2001-03 Blue Book
Maple River Winery   See 2017-19 Blue Book
Maps 11-12, 17, 44, 140-141, 385, 446, 528, 532-533, 536, 546, 551
Maragos, Andrew   See 2017-19 Blue Book

Marcellais, Richard 334, 346, 425
Marcil, William C. 118
Marijuana, Medical 413 *See also* 2017-19 Blue Book
Maring, Mary Meuhlen 211
Maris, Roger 87
Marmarth *See* 2011-13 Blue Book
Marmarth Research Foundation *See* 2009-11 and 2011-13 Blue Books
Marmarth Triceratops Dinosaur Dig *See* 2005-07 Blue Book
Marmot School *See* Youth Correctional Center, North Dakota
Marquart, Steven L. 196
Marschall, Andrew 336, 353
Martin Kekabah, Twila *See* 2003-05 Blue Book
Martinson, Bob 64, 264, 336, 372
Martinson, Henry R. 136 *See also* 2003-05 Blue Book
Mason, Russell "Buddy" *See* 2003-05 and 2013-15 Blue Books
Mass Spectrometry Center *See* 2007-09 Blue Book
Masters, Janelle *See* 2003-05 Blue Book
Mastodon 76
Math and English Standards, New *See* 2017-19 Blue Book
Mathern, Tim 334, 348
Mattson, Douglas L. 201
Matz, Robert *See* 2003-05 Blue Book
Maximilian of Wied-Neuweid, Prince *See* 1999-2001 and 2009-11 Blue Books
Mayville State University 478-482, 488
Mayville State University - Research Institutes *See* 2011-13 Blue Book
McCanna Site *See* 2011-13 Blue Book
McCarthy, Jason 195
McCullen, Catherine *See* 2003-05 Blue Book
McCullough, Steven E. 196
McCumber, Porter J. 166
McDonald, Anthony 426
McDonald, Leander "Russ" 568-569
McEvers, Lisa K. Fair 185, 212, 258, 468
McHenry County *See* 2001-03, 2005-07, 2009-11, 2013-15 and 2015-17 Blue Books
McIntosh County *See* 2001-03, 2005-07, 2009-11, 2013-15 and 2015-17 Blue Books
McKenzie County *See* 2001-03, 2005-07, 2009-11, 2013-15 and 2015-17 Blue Books
McKenzie Ranger District Office, Dakota Prairie Grasslands *See* 2011-13 Blue Book
McLaughlin, Pat *See* 2003-05 Blue Book
McLean County *See* 2001-03, 2005-07, 2009-11, 2013-15 and 2015-17 Blue Books
McLean County Museum, Washburn *See* 2011-13 Blue Book
McLean River *See* 1999-2001 Blue Book
McLean, James *See* 2003-05 Blue Book
McWilliams, Aaron 336, 357
Means, Warren W. 557
Measures Before the Voters 467
Medal of Honor Memorial 159 *See also* 2007-09 Blue Book
Medal of Honor Recipients *See* 2007-09 and 2015-17 Blue Books
Medd, Joel D. *See* 2013-15 Blue Book
Medora Crocodile Dig *See* 2005-07 Blue Book
Medora Ranger District, Dakota Prairie Grasslands *See* 2011-13 Blue Book
Megalonyx *See* 2011-13 Blue Book
Meier, Lisa 336, 369
Melroe Company *See* 2009-11 Blue Book
Mercer County *See* 2001-03, 2005-07, 2009-11, 2013-15 and 2015-17 Blue Books
Meriam Report *See* 2001-03 Blue Book
Meschke, Herbert L. 211 *See also* 2003-05 Blue Book
Mesohippus *See* 2011-13 Blue Book
Mesozoic Era *See* 2011-13 Blue Book
Metcalf, Ralph *See* 2011-13 Blue Book
Mexico *See* 2009-11 Blue Book
Meyer, Dean *See* 2003-05 Blue Book
Meyer, Scott 335, 355
Mielke, Jon *See* 2005-07 Blue Book
Mikey's Country Candy *See* 2017-19 Blue Book
Military Bases, North Dakota 17-24 *See also* 2017-19 Blue Book
Military in North Dakota 130-131, 410
Milk 62
Milk Marketing Board 320
Milken Awards 476-477
Mill and Elevator Association 267 *See also* 2007-09 and 2011-13 Blue Books

Miller, Charles S. Jr. 176 *See also* 2011-13 Blue Book
Miller, Joe *See* 2015-17 Blue Book
Miller, John 232 *See also* 2001-03 Blue Book
Milnor Normal School *See* 2007-09 Blue Book
Milton R. Young Station 544-545
Mineral Resources, Department of 269-270
Mining *See* 2001-03 Blue Book
Minority Justice Implementation Committee 206
Minot Air Force Base 17-20 *See also* 2017-19 Blue Book
Minot International Airport 10
Minot State University 478-482, 489, 500, 504
Minot State University - Bottineau *See* Dakota College at Bottineau
Minot State University - Research Institutes *See* 2007-09 Blue Book
Miss North Dakota 132
Miss Rodeo North Dakota 134
Missiles *See* 2001-03 Blue Book
Missouri Coteau *See* 1999-2001 Blue Book
Missouri Plateau *See* 1999-2001 Blue Book
Missouri River 128, 535
Missouri River Basin 536 *See also* 2003-05 Blue Book
Missouri River (Person) *See* 2003-05 Blue Book
Missouri-Yellowstone Confluence Center *See* 2011-13 Blue Book
Mitskog, Alisa 336, 362
Mitzel, Bill *See* 2005-07 Blue Book
Mock, Corey 336, 355
Moellring, George H. 209 *See also* 2003-05 Blue Book
Moldova *See* 2009-11 Blue Book
Monette, Richard *See* 2003-05 Blue Book
Monger, Pvt. Richard *See* 2009-11 Blue Book
Monson, David 336, 347
Moodie, Thomas H. 233 *See also* 2001-03 Blue Book
Moody's Analytics 389
Mooney, Gail *See* 2015-17 Blue Book
Mooring Stones *See* 2001-03 Blue Book
Mores, Marquis de *See* 2007-09 Blue Book

Morgan, David E. 208-209 *See also* 2003-05 Blue Book
Morgan, Emmett *See* 1999-2001 Blue Book
Morrill Land Grant College Act of 1862 *See* 2007-09 Blue Book
Morris, James 210, 240 *See also* 2003-05 Blue Book
Morton County *See* 2001-03, 2005-07, 2013-15 and 2015-17 Blue Books
Mosasaur *See* 2011-13 Blue Book
Moses, John 166, 233 *See also* 2001-03 Blue Book
Mountrail County *See* 2001-03, 2005-07, 2009-11, 2013-15 and 2015-17 Blue Books
Mouse River Basin 535-536
Mueller, Philip *See* 2011-13 Blue Book
Mund, Cara 133
Municipal Courts 180, 203
Murphy, Charles 440 *See also* 2003-05 Blue Book
Murphy, Philip M. *See* 2015-17 Blue Book
Murray, William S. 211 *See also* 2003-05 Blue Book
Muscha, Naomi *See* 2015-17 Blue Book
Museums *See* 1997-99 Blue Book
Musk Thistle *See* 2005-07 Blue Book
My Dakota Home (Poem) *See* 2003-05 Blue Book
My Life on the Plains *See* 2003-05 Blue Book
Myrdal, Janne 335, 347

N

Nanoscale Science and Engineering, Center for *See* 2007-09 Blue Book
Narum, Daniel D. 197
Nasset, Erling 3-4
Nathe, Mike 336, 367
National Alternative Fuels Laboratory *See* 2007-09 Blue Book
National Athletic Championships 500-512
National Buffalo Museum, Jamestown *See* 2011-13 Blue Book
National Center of Excellence in Women's Health *See* 2007-09 Blue Book
National Energy Center of Excellence 547 *See also* 2009-11 Blue Book
National Farmers Organization *See* 2001-03 Blue Book

National Geographic   *See* 2009-11 Blue Book
National Guard, North Dakota   25-29, 50, 130, 274-275, 411, 459, 555   *See also* 1999-2001 and 2009-11 Blue Books
National Plan of Integrated Airport Systems   11
National Resources Conservation Service   *See* 2001-03 Blue Book
National Suborbital Education and Research Center   *See* 2007-09 and 2009-11 Blue Books
Native American Aging, National Resource Center on   *See* 2007-09 and 2009-11 Blue Books
Native American Development Center   *See* 2017-19 Blue Book
Native American Hall of Honor   420-445
Native American Languages Act   *See* 2001-03 Blue Book
Native American Programs Act   *See* 2001-03 Blue Book
Native American Youth Leadership Summit   457
Native Media Center   *See* 2007-09 Blue Book
Native Tourism Alliance, North Dakota   455-456
NativeWays   *See* 2017-19 Blue Book
Natural Disasters   *See* 1997-99 Blue Book
Natural Gas   550
Natural Resources and Economic Development, Institute for   *See* 2007-09 Blue Book
Natural Resources Trust, Inc., North Dakota   321   *See also* 2005-07 Blue Book
ND VOICES   *See* 2011-13 Blue Book
NDSU Nursing at Sanford Health   *See* 2011-13 Blue Book
Nelson, Carolyn C.   *See* 2017-19 Blue Book
Nelson County   *See* 2001-03, 2005-07, 2009-11, 2011-13, 2013-15 and 2015-17 Blue Books
Nelson, Dan   *See* 2005-07 Blue Book
Nelson, Jon O.   336, 351
Nelson, Marvin E.   337, 346
Nelson, Scott   *See* 2009-11 and 2011-13 Blue Books
Ness, Gary   5, 41

Nestos, Ragnvold A.   232, 254   *See also* 2001-03 Blue Book
Nething, Dave   *See* 2011-13 Blue Book
Neumann, William A.   211   *See also* 2003-05 Blue Book
Neuroscience, Center of Excellence in   *See* 2007-09 Blue Book
New Bohemia, North Dakota   *See* 2007-09 Blue Book
New Economy Initiative   *See* 2003-05 Blue Book
News Chronology since Prehistoric Days   *See* 1989 to 2015-17 Blue Books
Newspapers   *See* 1995-97 Blue Book
Nez Perce Indians   *See* 1999-2001 Blue Book
No Child Left Behind Act of 2001   *See* 2005-07 Blue Book
Nodland, George L.   *See* 2011-13 Blue Book
Nokota Horse   66
Nolan, John   *See* 2005-07 Blue Book
North Dakota - Origin of the Name   44
North Dakota State College of Science   3, 478-482, 495-496, 504
North Dakota State University   31, 38-39, 478-482, 489-490, 500, 504-506
Northarvest Bean Growers Association   *See* 2009-11 Blue Book
Northern Crops Institute   *See* 2001-03, 2007-09 and 2009-11 Blue Books
Northern Great Plains Center for People and the Environment   *See* 2007-09 and 2009-11 Blue Books
Northern Pacific Railroad   *See* 2007-09 and 2013-15 Blue Books
Northern Pike   60
Northern Plains Center for Behavioral Research   *See* 2007-09 Blue Book
Northern Plains Commerce Center   *See* 2007-09 Blue Book
Northern Plains Indian Law Center   *See* 2007-09 Blue Book
Northern Plains UAS Test Site   35-36, 38, 40
Northern Pulse Growers Association   *See* 2009-11 Blue Book
Northwest Ordinance of 1787   *See* 2001-03 Blue Book
Nourished by Nature   *See* 2017-19 Blue Book

November 33 Ronald Reagan Minuteman Missile State Historic Site *See* 2009-11 Blue Book
Noxious Weeds *See* 2005-07 Blue Book
Nuessle, William L. 209 *See also* 2003-05 Blue Book
Nueta Hidatsa Sahnish College 453, 480-482
Nursing Center *See* 2007-09 Blue Book
Nutrition and Pregnancy, Center for *See* 2007-09 Blue Book

O

O'Brien, Emily 337, 379
O'Connell, David 65 *See also* 2015-17 Blue Book
Oak, Clarence Lewis *See* 2009-11 Blue Book
Oats 526
Obama, President Barack 154 *See also* 2015-17 Blue Book
Oban, Erin 335, 372
Ode to the Legislature (Poem) *See* 2003-05 Blue Book
Odegard, John D. 41, 125
Oehlke, Dave 335, 352
Offutt, Ronald 121
Ogden, Eloise *See* 2003-05 Blue Book
Oil 550 *See also* 2001-03, 2007-09, 2009-11 and 2011-13 Blue Books
Oil and Gas Division, Department of Mineral Resources 269-270
Oilseed Council, North Dakota 330 *See also* 2001-03 Blue Book
Oilseeds 527 *See also* 2009-11 and 2011-13 Blue Books
Oimoen, Casper 96
Olafson, Curtis *See* 2013-15 Blue Book
Old Crossing Treaty with Pembina Chippewa *See* 2001-03 Blue Book
Oliver, Bill *See* 2017-19 Blue Book
Oliver County *See* 2001-03, 2009-11, 2013-15 and 2015-17 Blue Books
Olson, Allen I. 233, 240 *See also* 2001-03 Blue Book
Olson, Christopher D. *See* 2017-19 Blue Book
Olson, Linda *See* 2003-05 Blue Book
Olson, Lonnie 194

Olson, Ole H. 233, 234 *See also* 2001-03 Blue Book
Olson, Robert *See* 2009-11 Blue Book
Olson, Thomas R. 196
Olympians *See* 2003-05 Blue Book
Omdahl, Lloyd B. 235, 246, 259
On-A-Slant Indian Villages *See* 1999-2001 and 2007-09 Blue Books
One Eye *See* La Borge
Onstad, Kenton *See* 2015-17 Blue Book
Operation Iraqi Freedom *See* 2009-11 Blue Book
Organic Act of Dakota Territory *See* 1989 Blue Book
Organic Production, North Dakota 527
Oscar Zero Ronald Reagan Minuteman Missile State Historic Site *See* 2009-11 Blue Book
Osland, Arne 335, 357
Ostlie's Sunnyside Acres 515-516
Ostriches *See* 2001-03 Blue Book
Outdoor Heritage Fund 270
Oversen, Kylie 468 *See also* 2015-17 Blue Book
Owens, Admiral William A. 110
Owens, Mark S. 337, 354

P

Pachycephalosaurus *See* 2011-13 Blue Book
Paleocene Epoch *See* 2011-13 Blue Book
Paleoenvironmental Interpretations *See* 1999-2001 Blue Book
Paleontology 76 *See also* 2001-03 and 2011-13 Blue Books
Papa's Granola *See* 2017-19 Blue Book
Parenting Investigator Review Board 207
Parks and Recreation Department 47, 141-142, 260, 299-300 *See also* 1997-99 and 2011-13 Blue Books
Parole Board, State 321
Parshall, Rose *See* Crow Flies High, Rose
Patten, Dale 335, 376
Pattern Jury Instruction Commission 207
Paul Broste Rock Museum, Parshall *See* 2011-13 Blue Book
Paulson Premium Seed *See* 2009-11 Blue Book

Paulson, Bob 337, 340
Paulson, William L. 211 *See also* 2003-05 Blue Book
Paur, Gary 337, 356
Peace Garden Conflict Resolution Center *See* 2007-09 Blue Book
Peace Garden State 45
Peace Officers Memorial 79-81
Peace Studies, Center for *See* 2007-09 Blue Book
PEAR'D *See* 2017-19 Blue Book
Pearce, Harry J. 117, 175
Pearl Harbor *See* 2009-11 Blue Book
Peas 526, 529 *See also* 2001-03 and 2009-11 Blue Books
Pederson, Vernon R. 211 *See also* 2003-05 Blue Book
Pembina County 128 *See also* 2001-03, 2005-07, 2009-11, 2013-15 and 2015-17 Blue Books
Pembina Gorge *See* 2011-13 Blue Book
Pembina Gorge Digs *See* 2005-07 Blue Book
Pembina Gorge Trails *See* 2007-09 Blue Book
Pembina State Museum *See* 2011-13 Blue Book
People and the Environment, Northern Great Plains Center for *See* 2007-09 Blue Book
Perkerewicz, Kathleen *See* 2009-11 Blue Book
Persian Gulf War *See* 2009-11 Blue Book
Personnel Board, State 321
Personnel Policy Board 207
Persons with Disabilities, North Dakota Center for *See* 2007-09 Blue Book
Peru *See* 2009-11 Blue Book
Peterson, John *See* 2009-11 Blue Book
Peterson, Robert R. 237 *See also* 2015-17 Blue Book
Peterson, Robert W. 237
Petrified Wood 59 *See also* 2001-03 Blue Book
Petroleum Marketing 551
Petroleum Safety and Technology Center *See* 2007-09 Blue Book
Phillipine Insurrection *See* 2009-11 Blue Book
Physiography *See* 1999-2001 Blue Book
Picture North Dakota! *See* 1999-2001 Blue Book
Piehl, Walter *See* 2003-05 Blue Book
Piepkorn, Merrill 335, 381
Pierce County *See* 2001-03, 2005-07, 2009-11, 2013-15 and 2015-17 Blue Books
Pietsch, Vonnie *See* 2011-13 Blue Book
Pigs 524 *See also* 2001-03 Blue Book
Pioneer Trails Regional Museum *See* 2011-13 Blue Book
Pipeline Authority, North Dakota 270-271
Pirkl, Toni *See* 2003-05 Blue Book
Pizi *See* Gall
Place to Be for Duck Hunting *See* 2005-07 Blue Book
Plant Diagnostic Lab *See* 2007-09 Blue Book
Plesiadapis *See* 2011-13 Blue Book
Ployhar, James D. 61
Poets, North Dakota Official 135-136
Political History, North Dakota *See* 2005-07 Blue Book
Politician (Poem) *See* 2003-05 Blue Book
Pollert, Chet 335, 337, 366
Pomeroy, Earl 170, 241
Poolman, Nicole 335, 344
Population Trends, County *See* 1997-99 and 2015-17 Blue Books
Pork Producers, North Dakota *See* 2001-03 Blue Book
Porter, Todd 337, 371
Posecopseha *See* 1999-2001 Blue Book
Potato Council, North Dakota *See* 2001-03 Blue Book
Potatoes 526, 529 *See also* 2001-03 Blue Book
Poultry *See* 2001-03 Blue Book
Pow Wows *See* 2005-07 Blue Book
Power Plants *See* Coal-Fired Power Plants
Prairie Knights Casino and Resort *See* 2011-13 Blue Book
Prairie Learning Center *See* 2003-05 Blue Book
Prairie Road Organic Seed *See* 2017-19 Blue Book
Prairie Rose Meadery *See* 2017-19 Blue Book

Prairie Trail, Capitol Grounds 75
Presidential Visits 150-154   *See also* 2005-07 and 2015-17 Blue Books
Pride of Dakota   *See* 2009-11, 2013-15 and 2017-19 Blue Books
Proclamation of Admission   *See* 1989 Blue Book
Project Safe Send   *See* 1999-2001 Blue Book
Project Tundra 544-545
Protease Research, Center for   *See* 2007-09 Blue Book
Protection and Advocacy, Committee on 322
Psychological Services Center   *See* 2007-09 Blue Book
Public Employees Retirement System Board 322-323
Public Finance Authority, North Dakota 268
Public Instruction, Department of 74, 473, 475-477   *See also* 2001-03 Blue Book
Public Law No. 83-280   *See* 2001-03 Blue Book
Public School Education, State Board of 323   *See also* 2007-09 Blue Book
Public School Open Enrollment   *See* 2005-07 and 2007-09 Blue Books
Public Service Commissioner 223-225, 230, 247-250
Pulitzer Prize   *See* 2017-19 Blue Book
Pulse Crops   *See* 2009-11 Blue Book
Purple Loosestrife   *See* 2005-07 Blue Book
Purpur, Cliff 101
Pyle, Brandy 337, 359

Q

Quain, Eric P.   *See* 2017-19 Blue Book
Quentin Burdick Center for Cooperatives   *See* 2007-09 Blue Book
Quinn, Mike   *See* 2005-07 Blue Book

R

Racek, Frank L. 195-196
Racing Commission, North Dakota 330   *See also* 2001-03 Blue Book
Radio Stations   *See* 1995-97 Blue Book
Railroad Museum, State 65
Railroads   *See* 1999-2001 Blue Book
Rainbow Arch Bridge   *See* 2007-09 Blue Book
Ramsey County   *See* 2001-03, 2005-07, 2009-11, 2013-15 and 2015-17 Blue Books
Rankings, North Dakota 129
Ransom County   *See* 2001-03, 2005-07, 2013-15 and 2015-17 Blue Books
Rath, Lloyd   *See* 2009-11 Blue Book
Rauschenberger, Ryan 226, 246, 468
Raven Man Chief (Car-gar-no-mok-she)   *See* 2003-05 Blue Book
Read North Dakota   *See* 2013-15 Blue Book
Real Estate   *See* 2001-03 Blue Book
Receipt of Federal Funds, 2009   *See* 2011-13 Blue Book
Recreation   *See* 2005-07 and 2013-15 Blue Books
Red River 128, 535-536
Red River Basin 535-536   *See also* 2003-05 Blue Book
Red River Formation   *See* 2009-11 Blue Book
Red River Valley 534   *See also* 2001-03, 2007-09 and 2013-15 Blue Books
Red River Valley Potato Growers Association   *See* 2001-03 Blue Book
Red River Valley Research Corridor   *See* 2007-09 Blue Book
Red River Valley University 479   *See also* 2007-09 Blue Book
Red River Valley Water Supply   *See* 2003-05 Blue Book
Red River Zoo   *See* 2017-19 Blue Book
Red Thunder   *See* 2003-05 Blue Book
Red Tomahawk, Marcellus 423   *See also* 2017-19 Blue Book
Red Wing Creek Field   *See* 2009-11 Blue Book
Referendum 462-463, 466
Referred Bills   *See* 2009-11 Blue Book
Refining 552
Regents, State Board of   *See* Higher Education, State Board of
Regional Weather Information System   *See* 2007-09 Blue Book
Reich, David E. 199
Reiten, Chester "Chet" 114
Renewable Energy   *See* 2009-11 Blue Book
Renewable Energy Council 271
Renewable Energy, Center for   *See* 2007-09 Blue Book

Renville County   *See* 2001-03, 2005-07, 2009-11, 2013-15 and 2015-17 Blue Books
Representatives, U.S. - North Dakota 160, 164-165, 167-170, 468
Research Institutes   *See* 2007-09 Blue Book
Retail Trade   *See* 2001-03 Blue Book
Retirement and Investment Office 323
Revenue Forecasting Process, North Dakota's 388-390
Rhodes Scholars   *See* 1999-2001 Blue Book
Richardson Ground Squirrel 45
Richardson, Mattie   *See* 2017-19 Blue Book
Richland County   *See* 2001-03, 2005-07, 2009-11, 2013-15 and 2015-17 Blue Books
Richter, David 337, 338
Riel, Louis   *See* 2003-05 Blue Book
Rigler, Sam   *See* 2009-11 Blue Book
Rilos + MiMi   *See* 2017-19 Blue Book
Riverboats   *See* 1999-2001 and 2013-15 Blue Books
Rivers and Water Bodies   *See* 2001-03 and 2005-07 Blue Books
Road Maker (Adi-ahu')   *See* 2003-05 Blue Book
Robinson, James E. 209   *See also* 2003-05 Blue Book
Robinson, Larry J. 63, 335, 361
Rodeos   *See* 2005-07 Blue Book
Roers, Jim P. 335, 383
Roers Jones, Shannon 337, 383
Roers, Kristin 335, 364
Rogers, Ken   *See* 2003-05 Blue Book
Rogers, Thomas Everett   *See* 2017-19 Blue Book
Rohr, Karen M. 337, 368
Rolette County   *See* 2001-03, 2005-07, 2013-15 and 2015-17 Blue Books
Rolla University 479   *See also* 2007-09 Blue Book
Romanick, Bruce A. 199
Romanick, Lolita G. 195
Roosevelt Park Zoo   *See* 2017-19 Blue Book
Roosevelt, Theodore 45, 82-83, 150-152, 159, 415
Roosevelt, Theodore Cabin   *See* 2001-03 Blue Book
Rough Rider Award   *See* Theodore Roosevelt Rough Rider Award

Rough Rider Gallery Artists   *See* 1999-2001 Blue Book
Roughrider State 45
RSVP Dakota Store   *See* 2017-19 Blue Book
Ruby, Dan 337, 375
Ruby, Matthew 337, 377
Runestones, Ancient   *See* 2001-03 Blue Book
Rural Assistance Center   *See* 2007-09 Blue Book
Rural Crime and Justice Center   *See* 2007-09 Blue Book
Rural Development, U.S. Department of Agriculture   *See* 2001-03 Blue Book
Rural Health, Center for   *See* 2007-09 Blue Book
Rural Service Delivery, Center for   *See* 2007-09 Blue Book
Rural Studies, Center for   *See* 2007-09 Blue Book
Rural Technology Incubator   *See* 2007-09 Blue Book
Rural Water Systems   *See* 2003-05 Blue Book
Russia   *See* 2009-11 Blue Book
Russian Knapweed   *See* 2005-07 Blue Book
Rust, David S. 335, 339
Rustad, Joshua B. 202

S

S&B Foods Inc.   *See* 2009-11 Blue Book
Sacred Pipe Resource Center   *See* 2017-19 Blue Book
Sahnish   *See* Three Affiliated Tribes
Sailing   *See* 2005-07 Blue Book
Sakakawea 79   *See also* 1999-2001 Blue Book
Salmon Derby, Official 61
Saltcedar   *See* 2005-07 Blue Book
Sand, Paul M. 211   *See also* 2003-05 Blue Book
Sandstrom, Dale V. 211, 249, 263   *See also* 2015-17 Blue Book
Sanford, Brent 26, 216, 235, 334
Sanford College of Nursing   *See* NDSU Nursing at Sanford Health
Sanford Health and MeritCare   *See* 2011-13 Blue Book

Sanford, Mark 337, 354
Sanstead, Dr. Wayne G. 235, 244 *See also* 2011-13 Blue Book
Sargent County *See* 2001-03, 2005-07, 2009-11, 2013-15 and 2015-17 Blue Books
Sarles, Elmore Y. 232 *See also* 2001-03 Blue Book
Sathre, Peter O. 210, 240 *See also* 2003-05 Blue Book
Satrom, Bernie 337, 349
Schafer, Edward T. 233 *See also* 2001-03 Blue Book
Schafer, Harold 97
Schaible, Donald 335, 368
Schatz, Mike 337, 373
Schauer, Austen 337, 350
Schmidt, Jim 337, 368
Schmidt, Kelly L. 220, 239
Schmidt, Robin A. 201
Schmitz, Jay A. 198
Schneider, Mac 468 *See also* 2015-17 Blue Book
Schneider, Mary 337, 358
Schneider, Thomas J. 199
Schobinger, Randy A. 337, 377
School Data, North Dakota 474-475
School District Boundary-Restructuring Program *See* 2005-07 Blue Book
School District Consolidation Bonus Program *See* 2005-07 Blue Book
School Districts *See* 2001-03 and 2005-07 Blue Books
School for the Blind *See* Vision Services/School for the Blind
School for the Deaf *See* Deaf, North Dakota School for the
School of Forestry, North Dakota *See* Dakota College at Bottineau and 2007-09 Blue Book
School Reorganization *See* 2005-07 Blue Book
School Safety 477
Schools - Contract Negotiations *See* 2005-07 Blue Book
Schools - Joint Powers Agreements *See* 2005-07 Blue Book
Schools, New in North Dakota *See* 2015-17 Blue Book
Schreiber-Beck, Cynthia 337, 362
Schulter, Rod "Reel" *See* 2003-05 Blue Book
Science and Mathematics Education, Center for *See* 2007-09 Blue Book
Scientific Computing Center *See* 2007-09 Blue Book
Scoria *See* Clinker
Seal of Biliteracy 476
Secretary of State 46, 217, 231, 235-236, 311, 460
Securities Department, North Dakota 263-264, 300
Seed Department, North Dakota State 323-324
Seibel, Jay *See* 2017-19 Blue Book
Senators, U.S. - North Dakota 160-163, 166-167
Senechal, Alice R. 176, 178
Sentinel Butte Formation *See* 1999-2001 Blue Book
Sevareid, Eric 89
Seven Vietnam War Marines and Soldiers 442
Shafer, George F. 232, 239 *See also* 2001-03 Blue Book
Sheep *See* 2001-03 Blue Book
Sheheke (White Coyote) *See* 1999-2001 and 2003-05 Blue Books
Shepherd, Robert *See* 2013-15 Blue Book
Sheridan County *See* 2001-03, 2005-07, 2013-15 and 2015-17 Blue Books
Sherman, William C. *See* 2003-05 Blue Book
Sheyenne River 535 *See also* 2013-15 Blue Book
Shirvani, Dr. Hamid A. *See* 2013-15 Blue Book
Shortridge, Eli C. D. 232 *See also* 2001-03 Blue Book
Silbernagel, Peter *See* 2015-17 Blue Book
Simons, Luke 337, 373
Sinner, George *See* 2015-17 Blue Book
Sinner, George A. 233 *See also* 2001-03 Blue Book
Sioux County *See* 2001-03, 2005-07, 2013-15 and 2015-17 Blue Books
Sioux Indians *See* 1999-2001 Blue Book
Sioux Manufacturing Corporation *See* 2007-09 Blue Book

Sisseton-Wahpeton Oyate   See 2013-15 Blue Book
Sitte, Margaret   See 2013-15 Blue Book
Sitting Bear (Ku-Nuh-Ti-Wit)   See 2003-05 Blue Book
Sitting Bull   See Tatantanka Iyotake
Sitting Bull College   453, 480-482
Sitting Crow, Henry (Peditska Amakish)   See 2003-05 Blue Book
Sjue, Kirsten M.   202
Skarpohl, Robert J.   See 2015-17 Blue Book
Skaug, Vern   See 1999-2001 Blue Book
Skiing   See 2005-07 Blue Book
Skogen, Dr. Larry C.   482, 485
Skroch, Kathy   337, 363
Skye, Douglas   See 2003-05 Blue Book
Skye, Harriett   422
Slagg, Kevin   See 2009-11 Blue Book
Slope County   128   See also 2001-03, 2005-07, 2013-15 and 2015-17 Blue Books
Small Business Institute   See 2007-09 Blue Book
Smith, Ernest H.   See 2003-05 Blue Book
Smith, John   441
Snowmobiling   See 2005-07 Blue Book
Snyder Act   See 2001-03 Blue Book
Soil   128   See also 1997-99 Blue Book
Soil Conservation Committee, State   324
Soil Conservation Districts, North Dakota Association of   See 2001-03 Blue Book
Solar, Geothermal, Hydrogen, and Hydro Power   552
SolarBee   See 2009-11 Blue Book
Solheim, David   136
Son-of-the-Star   See 2003-05 Blue Book
Song of Souris Valley (Poem)   See 2003-05 Blue Book
Song Sparrow   See 2003-05 Blue Book
Sorlie, Arthur Gustav   232, 254   See also 2001-03 Blue Book
Sorlie Bridge   See 2007-09 Blue Book
Sorvaag, Ronald   335, 382
Souris River   See Mouse River and 2013-15 Blue Book
South Korea   See 2009-11 Blue Book
Sovereign Lands   539
Soybean Council, North Dakota   See 2001-03 Blue Book
Soybean Growers Association, North Dakota   See 2001-03 Blue Book
Soybeans   526-529   See also 2001-03 and 2009-11 Blue Books
Spain   See 2009-11 Blue Book
Spalding, Burleigh F.   168, 208   See also 2003-05 Blue Book
Spanish American War   See 2009-11 and 2013-15 Blue Books
Special Elections   464-465
Spectrum Aeromed   See 2009-11 Blue Book
Spirit Lake Casino and Resort   See 2011-13 Blue Book
Spirit Lake Nation   446-447, 556   See also 2001-03 and 2003-05 Blue Books
Sports Hall of Fame   61
Spotted Bear, Alyce   See 2003-05 Blue Book
Spotted Knapweed   See 2005-07 Blue Book
Sprynczynatyk, Major General David   250, 252
STAGEnet   See 2003-05 and 2007-09 Blue Books
Standing Rock Community College   See Sitting Bull College
Standing Rock Sioux   451, 556   See also 2001-03 and 2003-05 Blue Books
Stanley, John Mix   See 2007-09 Blue Book
Stark County   See 2001-03, 2005-07, 2013-15 and 2015-17 Blue Books
State Art Museum   58
State Beverage   62
State Bird   53
State Capitol and Grounds   67-81, 128
State Coat of Arms   50-51
State Creed   48
State Dance   64
State Fish   60
State Flag   49
State Flower   52
State Fossil   59
State Fruit   55
State Government Construction Projects   See 2011-13 Blue Book
State Grass   63
State Insect   54
State Language   65
State Latin Motto   48
State March   61
State Motto   48

State Office Building 73
State Officers, Chronology of Elective 232-250
State Railroad Museum 65
State Song 55-57
State Tree 54
Statuary Hall, U.S. Capitol See 2011-13 Blue Book
Statues, Monuments and Markers, Capitol Grounds 79
Steele County See 2001-03, 2005-07, 2009-11, 2013-15 and 2015-17 Blue Books
Steiner, Vicky 337, 374
Stenehjem, Bob See 2011-13 and 2013-15 Blue Books
Stenehjem, Wayne 219, 240, 468
Stern, Herman 123
Stickney, Dorothy 85
Stiel, Stephannie N. 196
Stockdill, Patricia See 2005-07 Blue Book
Stockmen's Association, North Dakota See 2001-03 Blue Book
Streyle, Roscoe See 2017-19 Blue Book
Strinden, Marie See 2015-17 Blue Book
Strinden, Michelle 337, 378
Strom Center for Entrepreneurship and Innovation See 2009-11 Blue Book
Strutz, Alvin C. 210, 240 See also 2003-05 Blue Book
Stutsman County See 2001-03, 2005-07, 2013-15 and 2015-17 Blue Books
Stygimoloch See 2011-13 Blue Book
Sugarbeets 526, 528-529 See also 2001-03 and 2011-13 Blue Books
Sukut, Gary R. 55 See also 2017-19 Blue Book
Sun Opta See 2009-11 Blue Book
Sund Manufacturing See 2009-11 Blue Book
Sunflowers 526-529 See also 2001-03 and 2009-11 Blue Books
Supercritical and Subcritical Extraction Technologies Center See 2007-09 Blue Book
Superintendent of Public Instruction 227, 230, 243-244, 317, 417 See also 2001-03 Blue Book
Supreme Court Justices 183-187, 208-212 See also 2003-05 Blue Book
Supreme Court, North Dakota 180-182, 188-191
Surface Protection, Center for See 2007-09 Blue Book
Surface Transportation Weather Research Center See 2007-09 Blue Book
Sweet Especial Rural Scene (Poem) See 2003-05 Blue Book

T

Taborsky, Larry 7
Taken Alive, Jesse "Jay" See 2003-05 Blue Book
Tatantanka Iyotake (Sitting Bull) See 2003-05 Blue Book
Tax Commissioner 226, 231, 245-246, 416-417
Tax Department 389
Taylor, Ryan See 2011-13 Blue Book
Teacher Compensation See 2003-05 Blue Book
Teacher of the Year Program 473-474 See also 2011-13 Blue Book
Teachers' Fund for Retirement 325
Technology See 2007-09 Blue Book
Teigen, Obert C. 210 See also 2003-05 Blue Book
Television Stations See 1995-97 Blue Book
Territorial Legislators See 1989 Blue Book
Territorial Officers See 1989 Blue Book
Theatre, North Dakota 145
Thelen, John A. 195
Theodore Roosevelt National Park 142 See also 1995-97 and 2011-13 Blue Books
Theodore Roosevelt Rough Rider Award 82-127, 325
Thompson, David Clark 468
Thompson, Edward K. 92
Thompson, Era Bell 98
Thoreson, Blair See 2015-17 Blue Book
Three Affiliated Tribes 449-450, 556 See also 2001-03 and 2003-05 Blue Books
Three Affiliated Tribes Museum See 1999-2001 and 2011-13 Blue Books
Three Forks Formation See 2009-11 Blue Book
Three Forks - Sanish See 2011-13 Blue Book
Thunder Hawk, Wallace 444, 561, 567

Thunderhawk   *See* 2003-05 Blue Book
Time Zones, North Dakota History of
    See 2007-09, 2009-11 and 2011-13 Blue
    Books
Tiowaste   *See* 2003-05 Blue Book
Titan Machinery   *See* 2009-11 Blue Book
To a Pansy (Poem)   *See* 2003-05 Blue Book
Tobacco Cessation Resource Center, North
    Dakota   *See* 2007-09 Blue Book
Toman, Nathan 337, 371
Tormaschy, Gary   *See* 2009-11 Blue Book
Torosaurus   *See* 2011-13 Blue Book
Tourism 138-142   *See also* 2005-07 and
    2007-09 Blue Books
Tourism Division, North Dakota 138-139,
    264, 275, 278-279, 455
Tower University 479   *See also* 2007-09
    Blue Book
Towner County   *See* 2001-03, 2005-07,
    2009-11, 2013-15 and 2015-17 Blue Books
Towner State Nursery   *See* 2007-09 Blue
    Book
Townships   *See* 1989 Blue Book
Traffic Fatalities, North Dakota 129
Traill County   *See* 2001-03, 2005-07,
    2009-11, 2013-15 and 2015-17 Blue Books
Traill County Technology Center
    See 2007-09 Blue Book
Transfer Act   *See* 2001-03 Blue Book
Transmission 553
Transmission Authority, North Dakota 270
Transportation   *See* 1999-2001, 2007-09 and
    2013-15 Blue Books
Transportation, Department of 40, 74,
    154-155, 252-255, 301-304
Transportation Technology Transfer Center,
    North Dakota   *See* 2007-09 Blue Book
Treasurer, State 220, 231, 237-239
Treaty   *See* 2001-03 Blue Book
Trenton Indian Service Area   *See* 2001-03
    Blue Book
Trial Court Operations, Committee on
    See 2005-07 Blue Book
Triassic Period   *See* 2011-13 Blue Book
Tribal Colleges, North Dakota 452-454,
    480-482
Tribal Sovereignty   *See* 2001-03 Blue Book
Tribally Controlled Community College
    Act   *See* 2001-03 Blue Book

Triceratops   *See* 2011-13 Blue Book
Trinity Bible College and Graduate
    School 480-482, 497-498, 500
Triplett, Connie   *See* 2015-17 Blue Book
Trobriand, Philippe Regis de   *See* 2007-09
    Blue Book
Troodon   *See* 2011-13 Blue Book
Trottier, David "White Thunder"
    See 2007-09 Blue Book
Trottier, Wayne A. 337, 356
Trucking Industry   *See* 1999-2001 Blue
    Book
Truemann, Lieutenant Colonel W. E.
    See 2009-11 Blue Book
Trust Lands, Department of 271-273
Tufte, Jerod E. 186, 212
Turcotte, Andy   *See* 2003-05 Blue Book
Turkey (Country)   *See* 2009-11 Blue Book
Turkey Federation, North Dakota
    See 2001-03 Blue Book
Turtle Mountain Band of Chippewa
    Indians 447-448, 556   *See also* 2001-03
    Blue Book
Turtle Mountain Band of Chippewa - Leaders
    See 2003-05 Blue Book
Turtle Mountain Community College 454,
    480-482
Turtle Mountain High School Wrestling Team
    445
Turtle Mountain Manufacturing
    Company   *See* 2007-09 Blue Book
Turtle Mountain Reservation 447-448
    See also 2001-03 Blue Book
Turtle Mountains   *See* 2001-03 Blue Book
Tuttle, Charles 468
Tveit, Bill 337, 370
Two Bears (Mato Nopa)   *See* 2003-05 Blue
    Book
Two Crows (Pehriska-Ruhpa)   *See* 2003-05
    Blue Book
Two Track Malting Company 519-523

U

UAS Integration Pilot Program 39-40
Uglem, Gerald   *See* 2011-13 Blue Book
Ukraine   *See* 2009-11 Blue Book
United Seed   *See* 2009-11 Blue Book
United Tribes International Pow Wow
    See 2013-15 Blue Book

United Tribes Technical College 454, 480-482, 555-570
Unity Seed   *See* 2009-11 Blue Book
University Children's Center   *See* 2007-09 Blue Book
University Learning Center   *See* 2007-09 Blue Book
University of Jamestown 479-482, 498-499, 506-507
University of Mary 480-482, 499-501, 507-509
University of North Dakota 29-31, 33-34, 478-482, 490-491, 501, 509-511
University of North Dakota Art Galleries   *See* Art Museum, State
University of North Dakota - Center for Aerospace Sciences   *See* 2007-09 Blue Book
University of North Dakota - Research Institutes   *See* 2007-09 Blue Book
University of North Dakota - School of Medicine and Health Sciences   *See* 2007-09 Blue Book
University System, North Dakota 483-487
University Writing Center   *See* 2007-09 Blue Book
Unmanned Aerial Systems in Education and Research, Center for Excellence for 33   *See also* 2007-09 Blue Book
Unmanned Aircraft Systems 33-40, 409   *See also* 2017-19 Blue Book
Unruh, Jessica 335, 370
Upper Great Plains Transportation Institute 7, 325-326
U.S. Army Corps of Engineers Headquarters, Riverdale   *See* 2011-13 Blue Book
U.S. Customs and Border Protection 34-35, 154
USDA Forest Service - Dakota Prairie Grasslands Headquarters   *See* 2011-13 Blue Book
USNS City of Bismarck   *See* 2017-19 Blue Book
USS North Dakota 79   *See also* 2015-17 Blue Book
U.S. Senate Youth Winners   *See* 1999-2001 Blue Book

V

Valley City Normal School   *See* Valley City State University
Valley City State University 478-482, 491-492, 512   *See also* 2007-09 Blue Book
Valley City State University - Research Institutes   *See* 2007-09 Blue Book
Value-Added Processing Center   *See* 2007-09 Blue Book
Van De Streek, Tristan J. 197
Van Hook Arm   *See* 1999-2001 Blue Book
VandeWalle, Gerald W. 124, 183, 211
Vavra, Harold 4-5, 41
Vedaa, Shawn 335, 343
Vee, Bobby 113
Vegetable Variety Testing   *See* 2015-17 Blue Book
Vegetation   *See* 1997-99 Blue Book
Veitch, Edith Jane   *See* 2009-11 Blue Book
Venne, Joseph Z.   *See* 2009-11 Blue Book
Veterans Affairs, Administrative Committee on 326
Veterans Affairs, Department of 327
Veterans History Project   *See* 2007-09 and 2009-11 Blue Books
Veterans Home, North Dakota 327
Veterans in North Dakota 131
Veterans Service Officers 327
Veterinary Diagnostic Laboratory, North Dakota   *See* 2007-09 Blue book
Vetter, Steve 337, 355
Vietnam War   *See* 2009-11 Blue Book
Vigesaa, Don 337, 360
Vision Services/School for the Blind   *See* 2001-03 and 2007-09 Blue Books
Visitation at North Dakota Sites 142
Visual Neuroscience, Center for   *See* 2007-09 Blue Book
Vital Statistics, North Dakota 129
Vocational and Technical Education   *See* Career and Technical Education
Vocational Association, North Dakota   *See* 2007-09 Blue Book
Vogel, Robert L. 211   *See also* 2003-05 Blue Book
Vogel, Sarah 243

Voter Fraud   *See* 2001-03 Blue Book
Voter Identification   *See* 2015-17 Blue Book
Voter Qualifications   *See* 2001-03 Blue Book
Voter Registration   *See* 2001-03 Blue Book

W

Waldron, Corbin A.   136   *See also* 2003-05 Blue Book
Wall, John   *See* 2013-15 Blue Book
Wallin, Alfred M.   208   *See also* 2003-05 Blue Book
Wallman, Kris   *See* 2015-17 Blue Book
Walsh County   *See* 2001-03, 2005-07, 2013-15 and 2015-17 Blue Books
Wannagan Creek   *See* 2011-13 Blue Book
Wanner, Kyle   7
Wanzek, Terry M.   61, 63-64, 335, 366
Ward County   *See* 2001-03, 2005-07, 2013-15 and 2015-17 Blue Books
Wardner, Rich   334-335, 374
Warner, John   *See* 2015-17 Blue Book
Water Bank Program, North Dakota   *See* 2001-03 Blue Book
Water Commission, State   213, 305-306
Water Development Trust Fund   *See* 2001-03 Blue Book
Water Law and Legislation   *See* 2003-05 Blue Book
Water Management Plan, State   *See* 2003-05 Blue Book
Water Resources, North Dakota   536-539   *See also* 1997-99 and 2003-05 Blue Books
Water Resources Research Institute, North Dakota   *See* 2007-09 Blue Book
Waters, Navigable   *See* 2017-19 Blue Book
WCCO Belting   *See* 2009-11 Blue Book
Weather Modification   *See* 2007-09 Blue Book
Weather Modification Board, North Dakota   *See* Atmospheric Resource Board
Weather, North Dakota   532-535
Webb, Wade L.   197
Weed Control Association, North Dakota   *See* 2005-07 Blue Book
Wefald, Robert O.   240
Wehrman, Cecile   *See* 2003-05 Blue Book
Weigleitner, Larry   *See* 2009-11 Blue Book
Weiler, Dave   *See* 2011-13 Blue Book
Weir, H. Patrick   *See* 2011-13 Blue Book
Weisz, Robin   337, 351
Welder, Sister Thomas   116
Welford, Walter   233, 234   *See also* 2001-03 Blue Book
Welk, Lawrence   84
Wells County   *See* 2001-03, 2005-07, 2013-15 and 2015-17 Blue Books
Wells, Curt   *See* 2005-07 Blue Book
Wells, Ralph Jr. (Nahaa Nae-Good Dish)   *See* 2003-05 Blue Book
Wentz, Carson   *See* 2017-19 Blue Book
Wesley College   *See* 2007-09 Blue Book
West Park Bridge   *See* 2007-09 Blue Book
West River Anthem, The   *See* 2003-05 Blue Book
West River Teacher Center   *See* 2007-09 Blue Book
Western Area Water Supply   271   *See also* 2013-15 Blue Book
Western Meadowlark   53
Western Wheatgrass   63
Westlind, Greg   337, 352
Wetlands Trust Board of Directors   *See* 2003-05 Blue Book
Wetlands, North Dakota   *See* 2005-07 Blue Book
Wheat   524, 526-529   *See also* 2001-03 and 2009-11 Blue Books
Wheat Commission, North Dakota State   330   *See also* 2001-03 Blue Book
Wheeler-Howard Act   *See* Indian Reorganization Act of 1934
Wheeler, John   *See* 2011-13 Blue Book
Wheeling, Walter   *See* 2009-11 Blue Book
Whelan, Barbara L.   194
White Butte   128   *See also* 1999-2001 Blue Book
White Coyote   *See* Sheheke
White Eagle, Melvin   *See* 2003-05 Blue Book
White, Elmer   *See* 2003-05 Blue Book
White, Frank   232   *See also* 2001-03 Blue Book
White Shield   *See* 2003-05 Blue Book
White Shield I (Naht Asuu'taaka)   *See* 2003-05 Blue Book
Whitney, Linda   *See* 2003-05 Blue Book

Wholesale Trade and Distribution   *See* 2001-03 Blue Book
Wieland, Alon   *See* 2013-15 Blue Book
Wild Geese (Poem)   *See* 2003-05 Blue Book
Wild Prairie Rose 52
Wildlife   *See* 1997-99 and 1999-2001 Blue Books
Wildlife Refuges   *See* 2007-09 Blue Book
Wilkinson, Wilbur   *See* 2003-05 Blue Book
Will, Oscar H.   *See* 2009-11 and 2011-13 Blue Books
Williams, Clark   *See* 2013-15 Blue Book
Williams County   *See* 2001-03, 2005-07, 2009-11, 2013-15 and 2015-17 Blue Books
Williston Basin International Airport 10
Williston Research Extension Center 514-517
Williston State College 480-482, 496-497, 501   *See also* 2007-09 Blue Book
Williston State College - Research Institutes   *See* 2007-09 Blue Book
Wilson, Mary Louise Defender 432
Wilson, President Woodrow 150, 152   *See also* 2017-19 Blue Book
Wilson, Ron   *See* 2005-07 Blue Book
Wind Power 553   *See also* 2007-09 and 2009-11 Blue Books
Winistorfer, Jo Ann   *See* 2003-05 Blue Book
Winrich, Lonny B.   *See* 2011-13 Blue Book
Winter, Deena   *See* 2003-05 Blue Book
Woiwode, Larry 106, 135-136   *See also* 2003-05 Blue Book
Women's Center   *See* 2007-09 Blue Book
Women's Health CORE, North Dakota   *See* 2009-11 Blue Book
Women's Suffrage 401-403
Woodrow Keeble Award 457
Workers Compensation Bureau   *See* Workforce Safety and Insurance
Workers Development Center   *See* 2007-09 Blue Book
Workforce Safety and Insurance 146-147, 306-308   *See also* 2001-03 Blue Book
World War I   *See* 2009-11 and 2017-19 Blue Books
World War II   *See* 2009-11 Blue Book
Wrangham, Dwight   *See* 2011-13 Blue Book
Wrigley, Drew H. 235   *See also* 2015-17 Blue Book

Y

Yankton, Roger Sr.   *See* 2013-15 Blue Book
Yellow Starthistle   *See* 2001-03 and 2005-07 Blue Books
Yellowstone-Missouri Rivers Confluence Commission   *See* 2013-15 Blue Book
Young, C. H.   *See* 2009-11 Blue Book
Young, Newton C. 208   *See also* 2003-05 Blue Book

Z

Zaiser, Steven L.   *See* 2013-15 Blue Book
Zoos, North Dakota   *See* 2017-19 Blue Book
Zubke, Denton 337, 376